D1133585

SEVENTH EDITION

Rules for Writers

Diana Hacker

Nancy Sommers
Harvard University

Contributing ESL Specialist
Marcy Carbajal Van Horn
St. Edward's University

Bedford/St. Martin's
Boston ◆ New York

For Bedford/St. Martin's

Executive Editor: Michelle M. Clark
Senior Development Editor: Barbara G. Flanagan
Senior Development Editor: Mara Weible
Senior Production Editor: Rosemary R. Jaffe
Assistant Production Manager: Joe Ford
Senior Marketing Manager: Marjorie Adler
Editorial Assistant: Kylie Paul
Copyeditor: Linda McLatchie
Indexer: Ellen Kuhl Repetto
Permissions Manager: Kalina K. Ingham
Senior Art Director: Anna Palchik
Text Design: Claire Seng-Niemoeller
Cover Design: Marine Miller
Composition: Nesbitt Graphics, Inc.
Printing and Binding: RR Donnelley and Sons

President: Joan E. Feinberg
Editorial Director: Denise B. Wydra
Editor in Chief: Karen S. Henry
Director of Marketing: Karen R. Soeltz
Director of Production: Susan W. Brown
Associate Director, Editorial Production: Elise S. Kaiser
Managing Editor: Elizabeth M. Schaaf

Library of Congress Control Number: 2010941561

Manufactured in the United States of America.

6   5
m   l   k

Distributed outside North America by PALGRAVE MACMILLAN, Houndmills, Basingstoke, Hampshire RG21 6XS

For information, write: Bedford/St. Martin's, 75 Arlington Street, Boston, MA 02116   (617-399-4000)

ISBN: 978-0-312-64736-0 (Student Edition)
ISBN: 978-0-312-67735-0 (Instructor's Edition)

Acknowledgments

Preface for instructors

Hacker handbooks have long been recognized as the most innovative and practical college references — the handbooks that respond most directly to student writers' questions and challenges. Over the past six editions, students and instructors have relied on *Rules for Writers* for its comprehensive instruction and affordable price. As a classroom teacher, I know how important a trusted handbook is in helping students make the most of their writing experiences in college and beyond. The more students rely on their handbook and learn from its lessons, the more powerful and effective they become as writers. And more than a million college students have become confident writers with the practical and straightforward guidance of *Rules for Writers.*

My goal in revising the seventh edition was to create an even more useful handbook for today's college writers. With this goal in mind, I traveled to more than forty-five colleges and universities to observe how students use their handbooks and how instructors teach from them. I listened, everywhere, for clues about how to make *Rules for Writers* an even more valuable companion for students throughout their academic careers and an even stronger resource for the teachers guiding their writing development. Throughout my travels, I heard students talk about the challenges of applying the handbook's lessons to their own writing. All of the seventh edition's new features are designed to make this task easier for students. For instance, you'll find a series of writing prompts — *As you write* — to help your students connect key lessons of the handbook to their ongoing drafts. These prompts ensure that *Rules for Writers* will be even more useful — and of greater value — for students as they compose their way through college and into the wider world.

As you look through the seventh edition, you'll discover practical innovations inspired by conversations with teachers and students — content crafted to increase the handbook's ease of use in and out of the classroom. An innovative feature I'm particularly excited about is *Revising with comments.* During my travels, I asked students about the comments they receive most frequently and asked instructors to show me the comments they write most frequently on their students' drafts. The answers to these questions, combined with my own research on responding to student writers, shaped this feature, which helps students and instructors make the most of revising and commenting. In keeping with the Hacker tradition, this new feature teaches one lesson at a time — how to revise an unclear thesis, for instance — and directs students to specific sections of the handbook to guide and inform their revision strategies.

In *Rules for Writers*, Diana Hacker created a handbook that looked squarely at the writing problems students face and offered students practical solutions. Diana took everything she knew from her thirty-five years of teaching and put it to work on every page of *Rules for Writers*. It has been one of the great pleasures of my teaching career to build on that foundation and carry on this tradition. And I'm happy to extend the tradition of offering practical solutions by including new material for instructors in this edition. I hope that you and your colleagues find this edition more useful for your classroom teaching than ever before.

As coauthor, I am eager to share this handbook with you, knowing that in the seventh edition you'll find everything that you and your students trust and value about *Rules for Writers*.

Features of the seventh edition

What's new?

More choices add flexibility.   For your students, choose between two great options, both affordably priced:

- a **Classic** edition of *Rules for Writers*, spiral-bound with coverage of writing, research, and grammar
- a **tabbed** spiral-bound edition of *Rules for Writers*, with all of the Classic content *plus* coverage of writing about literature and easy navigation with eight tabbed sections

A more practical Instructor's Edition.   For your own teaching, the **IE** will come in handy; it features classroom activities, help for integrating the handbook into your course and promoting student use of the handbook, and answers to exercises.

New help that prompts students to use their handbook

- *New writing activities* — called *As you write* — help students apply handbook content to their own writing. (See p. 17.)

- *New* **Making the most of your handbook** *boxes* help students pull together the advice they need from different parts of the book to complete writing assignments. (See p. 4.)

- *New student-friendly terms (main idea, flow, representing the other side)* help students find advice using language they recognize. (See p. 93.)

Concrete strategies that help students revise

- *New* **Revising with comments** *pages, based on Nancy Sommers's research* with students at two- and four-year schools, help students understand feedback and give them strategies for revising in response to comments on their drafts — comments like "narrow your introduction" and "be specific." (See p. 30 for an example.)

- *A new stepped-out process for revising thesis statements* helps students identify a problem in a draft thesis, ask relevant questions, and then revise. (See pp. 28–29.)

More emphasis on key academic writing and research skills

- *New coverage of synthesis* — with illustrated examples — helps writers understand sources, put sources in a conversation, and then figure out what new angle they bring to that conversation. (See 58c and 63c.)

- *New advice for writing an annotated bibliography*, a common assignment in composition and other courses, features a sample entry in the handbook (see p. 449) along with two full annotated bibliography models on the companion Web site.

- *More than eighty-five new documentation models*, many annotated, help students cite sources in MLA and APA style — with special attention to new types of sources like podcasts, online videos, and blogs.

- *A new student argument essay* on the shift from print news to online news models effective reasoning, use of evidence (including visual evidence), use of counterargument, and proper MLA-style formatting.

New examples, more accessible grammar coverage

- *Grammar basics content is more straightforward than ever.* Grammar Basics, the handbook's reference within a reference, now teaches with everyday example sentences and exercise items. (See p. 369 for an example.)

- *More academic examples* reflect the types of sentences students are expected to write in college.

What's the same?

Comprehensive coverage of grammar, academic writing, and research.   A classroom tool and a reference, the handbook is designed to help students write well in any college course. This edition includes nearly one hundred exercise sets, many with answers in the back of the book, for plenty of practice.

A brief menu and a user-friendly index.   Students will find help fast by consulting either the brief list of contents on the inside front cover or the user-friendly index, which works even for writers who are unsure of grammar terminology.

Citation at a glance.   Annotated visuals show students where to find the publication information they need to cite common types of sources in MLA and APA styles.

Quick-access charts and an uncluttered design.   The seventh edition has what instructors and students have come to expect of a Hacker handbook: a clear and navigable presentation of information, with charts that summarize key content.

What's on the companion Web site?
hackerhandbooks.com/rules

Grammar, writing, and research exercises with feedback for every item.   More than 1,800 items offer students plenty of extra practice, and our gradebook gives instructors flexibility in viewing students' results.

Annotated model papers in MLA, APA, *Chicago*, CSE, and USGS styles.   Student writers can see formatting conventions and effective writing in traditional college essays and in other common genres: annotated bibliographies, literature reviews, lab reports, business proposals, and clinical documents.

Research and Documentation Online. This award-winning resource, written by a college librarian, gives students a jump start with research in over thirty academic disciplines.

Resources for writers and tutors. Checklists, hints, tips, and helpsheets are available in downloadable format.

Resources for ESL and multilingual writers. Writers will find advice and strategies for understanding college expectations and completing writing assignments. Also included are charts, exercises, activities, and an annotated student essay in draft and final form.

Language Debates. Twenty-two brief essays provide opportunities for critical thinking about grammar and usage issues.

Access to premium content. The print handbook can be packaged with premium content: The *Rules for Writers e-Book*, a series of online video tutorials, and a collection of resources that includes games, activities, readings, guides, and more. The activation code for premium content is free when packaged with a new copy of *Rules for Writers*.

Supplements for instructors

Practical

Teaching with Hacker Handbooks: Topics, Strategies, and Lesson Plans

Rules for Writers instructor resources (at hackerhandbooks.com/rules)

Professional

Teaching Composition: Background Readings

The Bedford Guide for Writing Tutors, Fifth Edition

The Bedford Bibliography for Teachers of Writing, Sixth Edition

Supplements for students

Print

Developmental Exercises for Rules for Writers

Working with Sources: Research Exercises for Rules for Writers

Research and Documentation in the Electronic Age, Fifth Edition

Resources for Multilingual Writers and ESL
Writing in the Disciplines: Advice and Models
Strategies for Online Learners
Writing about Literature

Online

Rules for Writers e-Book
CompClass for Rules for Writers

Acknowledgments

I am grateful for the expertise, enthusiasm, and classroom experience that so many individuals brought to the seventh edition.

Reviewers

Martha R. Bachman, Camden County College; Thomas P. Barrett, Ocean County College; Suzanne Biedenbach, University of Memphis; Sally Ann Boccippio, Ocean County College; Jennifer Costello Brezina, College of the Canyons; Mary Carney, Gainesville State College; Jia-Yi Cheng-Levine, College of the Canyons; Malkiel Choseed, Onondaga Community College; Amy Cruickshank, Cuyahoga Community College; Catherine P. Dice, University of Memphis; Marylynne Diggs, Clark College; Shawn M. Dowiak, Ramapo College of New Jersey; Crystal Edmonds, Robeson Community College; Don Erskine, Clark College; Rima S. Gulshan, Northern Virginia Community College; Eunice Hargett, Broward College; Anne Helms, Alamance Community College; David Hennessy, Broward College; Paula Hester, Indian Hills Community College; Matthew Horton, Gainesville State College; Kristen Iversen, University of Memphis; Laura Jeffries, Florida State College at Jacksonville; Robert Johnson, Midwestern State University; Joseph Jones, University of Memphis; Grace Kessler, California State University–San Marcos; Monique Kluczykowski, Gainesville State College; Michael Kula, Carroll University; M. Douglas Lamborne, Lord Fairfax Community College; Lisa Lopez Levers, Duquesne University; Ben Levy, Ramapo College of New Jersey; Michael Levy, University of Wisconsin–Stout; Susan P. Livermore, Millersville University (and Harrisburg Area Community College York); Dolores Mac-Naughton, Umpqua Community College; Heidi Marshall, Florida

State College at Jacksonville; Christopher Minnix, University of Arizona; Miriam P. Moore, Lord Fairfax Community College; Andrea Muldoon, University of Wisconsin–Stout; Meena Nayak, Northern Virginia Community College; D. Erik Nielson, Northern Virginia Community College; Wendy Perkins, Prince George's Community College; Linda Y. Peters, Onondaga Community College; Lynn M. Peterson, Carroll University; James P. Purdy, Duquesne University; Richard W. Rawnsley, College of the Desert; Stacy Rice, Northern Virginia Community College; Susan Roberts, United States Coast Guard Academy; Aline Carole Rogalski, Ocean County College; Marsha A. Rutter, Southwestern College; Tristan Saldaña, College of Marin; Jennifer P. Schaefer, Lord Fairfax Community College; Arthur L. Schuhart, Northern Virginia Community College–Annandale; Frances Shapiro-Skrobe, Ramapo College of New Jersey; Tracey Sherard, College of the Canyons; Katherine P. Simpson, Lord Fairfax Community College; Charles Smires, Florida State College at Jacksonville; Cheri Spiegel, Northern Virginia Community College; Jack R. Tapleshay, College of the Desert; Debra Thomas, Harrisburg Area Community College; Anita Turlington, Gainesville State College; and Michelle Wagner, Broward College.

Contributors

I am grateful to the following individuals, fellow teachers of writing, for their smart contributions to key content: Joe Bizup, Boston University, updated the coverage of writing about literature with fresh selections and relevant advice; and Marcy Carbajal Van Horn, ESL specialist, experienced composition instructor, and former online writing lab director, served as lead author for *Teaching with Hacker Handbooks* and improved our coverage for multilingual writers both in the handbook and on the companion Web site.

Student contributors

A number of bright and willing students helped identify which instructor comments provide the best guidance for revision. From Green River Community College: Kyle Baskin, Josué Cardona, Emily Dore, Anthony Hines, Stephanie Humphries, Joshua Kin, Jessica Llapitan, James Mitchell, Derek Pegram, Charlie Piehler, Lindsay Allison Rae Richards, Kristen Saladis, Jacob Simpson, Christina Starkey, Ariana Stone, and Joseph Vreeburg. From

Northern Kentucky University: Sarah Freidhoff, Marisa Hempel, Sarah Laughlin, Sean Moran, Laren Reis, and Carissa Spencer. From Palm Beach Community College: Alexis Day, Shawn Gibbons, Zachary Jennison, Jean Lacz, Neshia Neal, Sarah Reich, Jude Rene, and Sam Smith. And from the University of Maine at Farmington: Nicole Carr, Hannah Courtright, Timothy Doyle, Janelle Gallant, Amy Hobson, Shawn Menard, Jada Molton, Jordan Nicholas, Nicole Phillips, Tessa Rockwood, Emily Rose, Nicholas Tranten, and Ashley Wyman. I also thank the students who have let us use and adapt their papers as models in the handbook and on its companion Web site: Ned Bishop, Lucy Bonilla, Jamal Hammond, Sam Jacobs, Albert Lee, Luisa Mirano, Anna Orlov, Emilia Sanchez, and Matt Watson.

Bedford/St. Martin's

A handbook is truly a collaborative writing project, and it is a pleasure to acknowledge and thank the enormously talented Bedford/St. Martin's editorial team, whose deep commitment to students informs each new feature of *Rules for Writers*. Joan Feinberg, Bedford's president and Diana Hacker's first editor, offers her superb judgment on every aspect of the book. Joan's graceful and generous leadership, both within Bedford and in the national composition community, is a never-ending source of inspiration for those who work closely with her. Michelle Clark, executive editor, is the kind of editor every author dreams of having — a treasured friend and colleague — and an endless source of creativity and joy. Michelle combines wisdom with patience, imagination with practicality, and hard work with good cheer. Mara Weible, senior editor, brings to the seventh edition her teacher's sensibility and editor's unerring eye, shaping the innovative research coverage and new synthesis section and contributing wonderful ideas to strengthen the seventh edition's new features on academic writing and research. Barbara Flanagan, senior editor, who has worked on Diana Hacker's handbooks for more than twenty-five years, brings her unrelenting insistence on clarity and precision as well as her expertise in documentation. Thanks to Kylie Paul, editorial assistant, for expertly managing the review process, preparing documents, and managing many small details related to both our Web and print projects.

The passionate commitment to *Rules for Writers* of many Bedford colleagues — Denise Wydra, editorial director; Karen Henry, editor in chief; and Marjorie Adler, marketing manager — ensures that the seventh edition remains the most innovative and practical handbook on the market. Special thanks go to Jimmy Fleming, senior English specialist, for his abundant contributions, always wise and judicious, and for his enthusiasm and support as we traveled to colleges near and far. Many thanks to Rosemary Jaffe, senior production editor, who kept us on schedule and efficiently and gracefully turned a manuscript into a handbook. And thanks to Linda McLatchie, copyeditor, for her thoroughness and attention to detail; to Claire Seng-Niemoeller, text designer, who always has clarity and ease of use in mind as she designs *Rules for Writers*; to Marine Miller, cover designer, who has given the book a strikingly beautiful cover; and to Sarah Ferguson, new media editor, who developed the book's companion Web site and e-book.

Most important, I want to thank Diana Hacker. She cared enough to study her own students at Prince George's Community College, puzzling out their challenges and their needs and observing their practices. I'm honored to acknowledge her work, her legacy, and her innovative spirit — and pleased to continue in the tradition of this brilliant teacher and writer.

Last, but never least, I offer thanks to Maxine Rodburg, Laura Saltz, and Kerry Walk, friends and colleagues, for sustaining conversations about teaching writing. And I thank my family: Joshua, an attentive reader of life and literature, for his steadfastness across the drafts; Sam and Kate, for lively conversations about writing; Louise, Walter, Ron, and Charles Mary, for their wit and wisdom; and Rachel and Alexandra, whose good-natured and humorous observations about their real lives as college writers are a constant source of instruction and inspiration.

Nancy Sommers

How to use this book and its companion Web site

Though it is small enough to hold in your hand, *Rules for Writers* will answer most of the questions you are likely to ask as you plan, draft, and revise a piece of writing:

How do I choose and narrow a topic?

How do I know when to begin a new paragraph?

Should I write *each was* or *each were*?

When should I place a comma before *and*?

What is counterargument?

What is the difference between *accept* and *except*?

How do I cite a source from the Web?

The book's companion Web site extends the book beyond its covers. See page xviii for details.

How to find information with an instructor's help

When you are revising an essay that your instructor has marked, tracking down information is simple. If your instructor indicates problems with a number such as *16* or a number and letter such as *12e,* you can turn directly to the appropriate section of the handbook. Just flip through the tabs at the top of the pages until you find the number in question.

If your instructor uses an abbreviation such as *w* or *dm* instead of a number, consult the list of abbreviations and revision symbols on the next-to-last page of the book. There you will find the name of the problem (*wordy; dangling modifier*) and the number of the section to consult.

Revision Symbols

Boldface numbers refer to sections of the handbook.

Lund 3

the other snowmobiles" (Johnson 7). Whether such noise adversely affects the park's wildlife remains a debated question, but the possibility exists.   *Smart use of counterargument*

Some who favor keeping the park open to snowmobiles argue that newer, four-stroke machines cause less air and noise pollution than older models. While this is true, the new machines still pollute more than cars, and their decibel level is reduced only slightly ("Snowmobile" B25). Also, because the newer snowmobiles cost at least $3,000 more than the older ones, it is unlikely that individuals would choose to buy them or that rental companies could afford to upgrade. At present there are no strict guarantees that only the newer models would be allowed into the park.   *dm*

Like most federal agencies, budget constraints face the National Park Service. Funds that should be used to preserve Yellowstone National Park and its wildlife have been diverted to deal with the snowmobile issue. A single environmental impact study of the problem cost taxpayers nearly $250,000

abbr	faulty abbreviation **40**	
adj/adv	misuse of adjective or adverb **26**	
add	add needed word **10**	
agr	faulty agreement **21, 22**	
appr	inappropriate language **17**	
art	article (*a, an, the*) **29**	
awk	awkward	
cap	capital letter **45**	
case	error in case **24, 25**	
cliché	cliché **18e**	
coh	coherence **4d**	
coord	faulty coordination **14a**	
cs	comma splice **20**	
dev	inadequate development **4b, 6e**	
dm	dangling modifier **12e**	
-ed	error in *-ed* ending **27d**	
emph	emphasis **14**	
ESL	English as a second language **28–31**	

p	error in punctua…	
^	comma **32**	
no ,	no comma **33**…	
;	semicolon **34**	
:	colon **35**	
^v	apostrophe **3**…	
" "	quotation mar…	
. ?	period, questi…	
!	exclamation	
— ( )	dash, parenthe…	
[ ] …	brackets, elli…	
/	slash **39**	
¶	new paragraph –	
pass	ineffective passiv…	
pn agr	pronoun agreeme…	
proof	proofreading pr…	
ref	error in pronoun reference **23**	
run-on	run-on sentence…	
-s	error in *-s* endin…	
sexist	sexist language	
shift	distracting shift	
sl	slang **17c**	
sp	misspelled word…	
sub	faulty subordina…	

12e Repair dangling modifiers.

A dangling modifier fails to refer logically to any word in the sentence. Dangling modifiers are easy to repair, but they can be hard to recognize, especially in your own writing.

How to find information on your own

This handbook is designed to allow you to find information without an instructor's help — usually by consulting the brief menu inside the front cover. At times, you may consult the detailed menu inside the back cover, the index, the glossary of usage, the list of revision symbols, or one of the directories to documentation models.

The brief menu.   The brief menu inside the front cover displays the book's contents. Let's say that you want to find out how you can write with more active verbs. Your first step is to scan the menu for the appropriate numbered topic — in this case "8 Active Verbs." Then you can use the blue tabs at the top of the pages to find section 8.

active

112   **8**   Active verbs

8   Prefer active verbs.

As a rule, choose an active verb and pair it wit
names the person or thing doing the action. Acti
meaning more emphatically and vigorously tha
counterparts — forms of the verb *be* or verbs in tl

PASSIVE	The pumps *were destroyed* by a surge
BE VERB	A surge of power *was* responsible for the pumps.
ACTIVE	A surge of power *destroyed* the pumps

The detailed menu.   The detailed menu appears inside the back
cover. When the numbered section you're looking for is broken
up into quite a few lettered subsections, try consulting this menu.
For instance, if you have a question
about the proper use of commas after
introductory elements, this menu will
quickly lead you to section 32b.

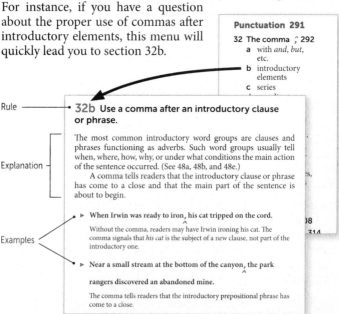

Rule ——

32b Use a comma after an introductory clause or phrase.

Explanation —

The most common introductory word groups are clauses and
phrases functioning as adverbs. Such word groups usually tell
when, where, how, why, or under what conditions the main action
of the sentence occurred. (See 48a, 48b, and 48e.)

A comma tells readers that the introductory clause or phrase
has come to a close and that the main part of the sentence is
about to begin.

Examples —

▶ When Irwin was ready to iron, his cat tripped on the cord.

Without the comma, readers may have Irwin ironing his cat. The
comma signals that *his cat* is the subject of a new clause, not part of the
introductory one.

▶ Near a small stream at the bottom of the canyon, the park

rangers discovered an abandoned mine.

The comma tells readers that the introductory prepositional phrase has
come to a close.

Once you find the right lettered subsection, you will see three kinds of advice to help you edit your writing — a rule, an explanation, and one or more hand-edited examples.

The index.   If you aren't sure which topic to choose from one of the menus, consult the index at the back of the book. For example, you may not realize that the issue of whether to use *have* or *has* is a matter of subject-verb agreement (section 21). In that case, simply look up "*has* vs. *have*" in the index. You will be directed to specific pages in two sections covering subject-verb agreement.

Making the most of your handbook.   You will find your way to helpful advice by using the index, the menus, or the contents. Once you get to where you need to be, you may also find references to additional related advice and models. These boxes help you pull together what you need from the handbook for each assignment.

> **Making the most of your handbook**
> Integrating visuals can strengthen your writing.
> ▸ Choosing appropriate visuals: page 407
> ▸ Placing and labeling visuals: page 407
> ▸ Using visuals responsibly: page 408

The glossary of usage.   When in doubt about the correct use of a particular word (such as *affect* and *effect*), consult the glossary of usage at the back of the book. This glossary explains the difference between commonly confused words; it also includes words that are inappropriate in formal written English.

Directories to documentation models.   When you are documenting a research paper with MLA or APA style, you can find documentation models by consulting the appropriate color-coded directories.

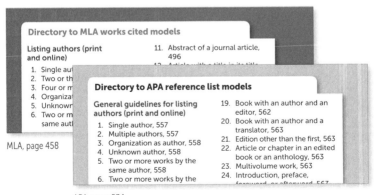

Directory to MLA works cited models

Listing authors (print and online)

1. Single au[...]
2. Two or th[...]
3. Four or m[...]
4. Organiza[...]
5. Unknow[...]
6. Two or m[...]
   same aut[...]

11. Abstract of a journal article, 496

MLA, page 458

Directory to APA reference list models

General guidelines for listing authors (print and online)

1. Single author, 557
2. Multiple authors, 557
3. Organization as author, 558
4. Unknown author, 558
5. Two or more works by the same author, 558
6. Two or more works by the

19. Book with an author and an editor, 562
20. Book with an author and a translator, 563
21. Edition other than the first, 563
22. Article or chapter in an edited book or an anthology, 563
23. Multivolume work, 563
24. Introduction, preface, foreword, or afterword, 567

APA, page 534

Answers to exercises.   *Rules for Writers* is designed to help you learn from it on your own. By providing answers to some exercise sentences, it allows you to test your understanding of the material. Most exercise sets begin with five sentences lettered *a* through *e* and conclude with five or ten numbered sentences. Answers to lettered sentences appear at the back of the book.

Using the book's companion Web site: hackerhandbooks.com/rules

Throughout *Rules for Writers*, Seventh Edition, you will see references to exercises and model papers on the book's companion Web site. Here is a complete list of resources on the site. Your instructor may use some of this material in class; each area of the site, however, has been developed for you to use on your own whenever you need it.

- *Writing exercises* Interactive exercises, including feedback for every answer, on topics such as choosing a thesis statement and conducting peer review
- *Grammar exercises* Interactive exercises on grammar, style, and punctuation, including feedback for every answer
- *Research exercises* Interactive exercises, including feedback for every answer, on topics such as integrating quotations and documenting sources in MLA and APA styles
- *Model papers* Annotated sample papers in MLA, APA, *Chicago*, CSE, and USGS styles
- *Multilingual/ESL help* Resources, strategies, model papers, and exercises to help multilingual speakers improve their college writing skills
- *Research and Documentation Online* Advice on finding sources in a variety of academic disciplines and up-to-date guidelines for documenting print and online sources in MLA, APA, *Chicago*, and CSE styles
- *Resources for writers and tutors* Revision checklists and helpsheets for common writing problems
- *Language Debates* Mini-essays exploring controversial issues of grammar and usage, such as split infinitives

- ***Additional resources*** Print-format versions of the book's exercises and links to additional online resources for every part of the book
- ***Re:Writing*** A free collection of resources for composition and other college classes: help with preparing presentation slides, avoiding plagiarism, evaluating online sources, and more
- ***Tutorials*** Interactive resources that teach essential college skills such as integrating sources in a research paper and revising with peer comments (This area of the Web site requires an activation code.)

Contents

Academic Writing 69

Clarity 111

Document Design 401

Research 419

Writing Papers in MLA Style   457

Writing Papers in APA Style   533

The Writing Process

Writing is a process of figuring out what you think, not a matter of recording already developed thoughts. Since it's not possible to think about everything all at once, most experienced writers handle a piece of writing in stages. You will generally move from planning to drafting to revising, but be prepared to return to earlier stages as your ideas develop.

Explore ideas; then sketch a plan.

Before attempting a first draft, spend some time generating ideas. Mull over your subject while listening to music or driving to work, jot down inspirations, and explore your insights with a willing listener. Ask yourself questions: What do you find puzzling, striking, or interesting about your subject? What would you like to know more about? At this stage, you should be collecting information and experimenting with ways of focusing and organizing it to reach your readers.

1a Assess the writing situation.

Begin by taking a look at your writing situation. The key elements of a writing situation include the following:

- your subject
- your purpose
- your audience
- the sources of information available to you
- any constraints (length, document design, deadlines)

It is likely that you will make final decisions about all of these matters later in the writing process — after a first draft, for example — but you can save yourself time by thinking about as many of them as possible in advance. For a quick checklist, see the chart on pages 3–4.

Academic English What counts as good writing varies from culture to culture and even among groups within cultures. In some situations, you will need to become familiar with the writing styles — such as direct or indirect, personal or impersonal, plain or embellished — that are valued by the culture or discipline for which you are writing.

Checklist for assessing the writing situation

Subject

- Has the subject (or a range of possible subjects) been given to you, or are you free to choose your own?
- What interests you about your subject? What questions would you like to explore?
- Why is your subject worth writing about? How might readers benefit from reading about it?
- Do you need to narrow your subject to a more specific topic (because of length restrictions, for instance)?

Purpose and audience

- Why are you writing: To inform readers? To persuade them? To call them to action? To entertain them? Some combination of these?
- Who are your readers? How well informed are they about the subject? What do you want them to learn?
- How interested and attentive are they likely to be? Will they resist any of your ideas?
- What is your relationship to your readers: Student to instructor? Employee to supervisor? Citizen to citizen? Expert to novice?

Sources of information

- Where will your information come from: Reading? Personal experience? Research? Direct observation? Interviews? Questionnaires?
- What documentation style is required: MLA? APA?

Checklist for assessing the writing situation (continued)

Length and document design

- Do you have any length specifications? If not, what length seems appropriate, given your subject, purpose, and audience?
- Does the assignment call for a particular kind of paper: A report? A proposal? An essay? An analysis of data? A reflection?
- Is a particular format required? If so, do you have guidelines to follow or examples to consult?
- How might visuals — charts, graphs, tables, images — help you convey information?

Reviewers and deadlines

- Who will be reviewing your draft in progress: Your instructor? A writing center tutor? Your classmates? A family member?
- What are your deadlines? How much time will you need to allow for the various stages of writing, including proofreading and printing the final draft?

Subject

Frequently your subject will be given to you. In a psychology class, for example, you might be asked to explain Bruno Bettelheim's Freudian analysis of fairy tales. In a composition course, assignments often ask you to respond to readings. In the business world, your assignment might be to draft a marketing plan.

When you are free to choose your own subject, it's a good idea to focus on something you are genuinely curious about. If you are studying television, radio, and the Internet in a communication course, for example, you might ask yourself which of these subjects interests you most. Perhaps you want to learn more about the role streaming video can play in activism and social change. Look through your readings and class notes to see if you can identify questions you'd like to explore further in an essay.

> **Making the most of your handbook**
> Effective research writers often start by asking a question.
> ▶ Posing questions for research: 53a

Ways to narrow a subject to a topic

Subdividing your subject by asking questions

One way to subdivide a subject is to ask questions sparked by reading or by talking to your classmates.

SUBJECT	teen pregnancy
QUESTION	Why do Waterford and Troy, neighboring cities, have different rates of teen pregnancy?

This question would give you a manageable topic for a short paper.

Restricting your purpose

Often you can restrict your purpose. You might realize on reflection that your initial goal — your draft purpose — is more than you could hope to accomplish in a brief paper.

SUBJECT	teen pregnancy
DRAFT PURPOSE	preventing teen pregnancy
MORE LIMITED PURPOSE	showing how changing the health curriculum for sixth graders results in lower rates of teen pregnancy

Rethinking your purpose in this way would give you a manageable topic.

Restricting your audience

Consider writing for a particular audience.

SUBJECT	teen pregnancy
AUDIENCE	general public
MORE LIMITED AUDIENCE	educators; school administrators

Addressing a specific group with a special interest is a way to make your topic more manageable.

Considering the information available to you

Look at the information you have collected. If you have gathered a great deal of information on one aspect of your subject (birth control education) and less information on other aspects (counseling for expectant teen parents), you may have found your topic.

Make sure that you can reasonably investigate your subject in the space you have. If you are limited to a few pages, for example, you could not do justice to a subject as broad as "videos as agents of social change." You could, however, focus on one aspect of the subject — perhaps experts' contradictory claims about the effectiveness of "narrowcasting," or creating video content for small, specific audiences. The chart on page 5 suggests ways to narrow a subject to a manageable topic for a paper.

Whether or not you choose your own subject, it's important to be aware of the expectations of each writing situation.

Purpose

Your purpose will often be dictated by your writing situation. Perhaps you have been asked to draft a proposal requesting funding for a student organization, to report the results of a psychology experiment, or to write about the growing controversy surrounding genetically modified (GM) foods for the school newspaper. Even though your overall purpose is fairly obvious in such situations, a closer look at the assignment can help you make a variety of necessary decisions. How detailed should the proposal be? How technical does your psychology professor expect your report to be? Do you want to inform students about the GM food controversy or change their attitudes toward it?

In many writing situations, part of your challenge will be discovering a purpose. Asking yourself why readers should care about what you are saying can help you decide what your purpose might be. Perhaps your subject is magnet schools — schools that draw students from different neighborhoods because of features such as advanced science classes or a concentration on the arts. If you have discussed magnet schools in class, a description of how these schools work probably will not interest you or your readers. But maybe you have discovered that your county's magnet schools are not promoting diversity as had been planned and you want to call your readers to action. Or maybe you are interested in comparing student performance at magnet schools and traditional schools.

Although no precise guidelines will lead you to a purpose, you can begin by asking yourself which one or more of the following aims you hope to accomplish.

PURPOSES FOR WRITING

to inform	to evaluate
to persuade	to recommend
to entertain	to request
to call readers to action	to propose
to change attitudes	to provoke thought
to analyze	to express feelings
to argue	to summarize

Writers often misjudge their own purposes, summarizing when they should be analyzing, or expressing feelings about problems instead of proposing solutions. Before beginning any writing task, pause to ask, "Why am I communicating with my readers?" This question will lead you to another important question: "Just who are my readers?"

Audience

Audience analysis can often lead you to an effective strategy for reaching your readers. A writer whose purpose was to encourage college students to recycle more by broadening their ideas about recycling began by making some observations about her audience (see p. 8).

This analysis led the writer to appeal to her reader's competitive nature — inviting college students to think about trying different kinds of recycling as achieving different levels in a video game. Her audience analysis also warned against adopting a preachy tone that her readers might find offensive. Instead of lecturing, she decided to draw examples from her own journey through the "levels" of being green — recycling paper products and plastic water bottles, carrying a refillable water bottle, biking to campus, buying used clothing, taking notes on a laptop, and so on. The result was an essay that reached its readers rather than alienating them.

Of course, in some writing situations the audience will not be neatly defined for you. Nevertheless, the choices you make as you write will tell readers who you think they are (novices or experts, for example), so it is best to be consistent.

For help with audience analysis, see the chart on pages 3–4.

AUDIENCE ANALYSIS

Academic audiences   In college writing, considerations of audience can be more complex than they seem at first. Your instructor will read your essay, of course, but most instructors play multiple roles while reading. Their first and most obvious roles are as coach and evaluator; but they are also intelligent and objective readers, the kind of people who might reasonably be informed, convinced, entertained, or called to action by what you have to say.

Some instructors specify an audience, such as a hypothetical supervisor, readers of a local newspaper, or peers in a particular field. Other instructors expect you to imagine an audience appropriate to your purpose and your subject. Still others prefer that you write for a general audience of educated readers — nonspecialists who can be expected to read with an intelligent, critical eye.

Business audiences   Writers in the business world often find themselves writing for multiple audiences. A letter to a client, for instance, might be distributed to sales representatives as well. Readers of a report might include persons with and without technical expertise or readers who want details and those who prefer a quick overview.

To satisfy the demands of multiple audiences, business writers have developed a variety of strategies: attaching cover letters to detailed reports, adding boldface headings, placing summaries of key ideas in the margin, and so on.

Public audiences   Writers in communities often write for a specific audience — the local school superintendent, a legislative representative, fellow members of a social group, readers of a local paper. With public writing, it is more likely that you are familiar with the views your readers hold and the assumptions they make, so you may be better able to judge how to engage those readers. If you are writing to a group of other parents to share ideas for lowering school bus transportation costs, for instance, you may have a good sense of whether to lead with a logical analysis of other school-related fees or with a fiery criticism of key decision makers.

Considering audience when writing e-mail messages

In academic, business, and civic contexts, you will want to show readers that you value their time. Your e-mail message may be just one of many that your readers have to wade through. Here are some strategies for writing effective e-mails:

- Use a meaningful, concise subject line to help readers sort messages and set priorities.
- Put the most important part of your message at the beginning so that your reader sees it without scrolling.
- Write concisely; keep paragraphs short.
- For long, detailed messages, provide a summary at the beginning.
- Avoid writing in all capital letters or all lowercase letters.
- Proofread for typos and obvious errors that are likely to slow down readers.

You will also want to follow conventions of good etiquette and avoid violating standards of academic integrity. Here are some strategies for writing responsible e-mails:

- E-mail messages can easily be forwarded to others and reproduced. Do not write anything that you would not want attributed to you.
- Do not forward another person's message without asking his or her permission.
- If you write an e-mail message that includes someone else's words — opinions, statistics, song lyrics, and so forth — it's best to let your reader know the source for that material and where any borrowed material begins and ends.

Considering audience when writing e-mail messages (continued)

- Choose your words carefully because e-mail messages can easily be misread. Without your voice, facial gestures, or body language, a message can be misunderstood.
- Pay careful attention to tone; avoid writing anything that you wouldn't be comfortable saying directly to a reader.

Sources of information

Where will your facts, details, and examples come from? Can you develop your topic from personal experience alone, or will you need to search for relevant information through reading, observation, interviews, or questionnaires?

Reading   Reading is an important way to deepen your understanding of a topic and expand your perspective. Reading will be your primary source of information for many college assignments, which will generally be of two kinds: (1) analytical essays that call for a close reading of one book, essay, literary work, or visual and (2) research assignments that ask you to find and consult a variety of sources on a topic.

For an analytical essay, you will select details from the work to support an interpretation. You can often assume that your readers are familiar with the work and have a copy of it on hand, but be sure to provide enough context so that someone who doesn't know the work well can still follow your interpretation. When you quote from the work, page references are usually sufficient. When in doubt about the need for documentation, ask your instructor.

For a research paper, you cannot assume that your readers are familiar with your sources. Therefore, you must document all quoted, summarized, or paraphrased material.

> **Making the most of your handbook**
> Academic writing often requires that you read critically and cite your sources.
> ▶ Guidelines for active reading: page 71
> ▶ Analyzing an essay: 5d
> ▶ Quoting, paraphrasing, and summarizing sources: 55c

Personal experience   If your interest in a subject stems from your personal experience, you will want to ask what it is about your experience that would interest your audience and why. For example, if you volunteered at a homeless shelter, you might have spent some time talking to homeless children and learning about their needs. Perhaps you can use your experience to broaden your readers' understanding of the issues, to persuade an organization to fund an after-school program for homeless children, or to propose changes in legislation.

Observation   Observation is an excellent means of collecting information about a wide range of subjects, such as gender relationships on a popular television program, the clichéd language of sports announcers, or the appeal of a local art museum. For such subjects, do not rely on your memory alone; your information will be fresher and more detailed if you actively collect it, with a notebook, laptop, or voice recorder in hand.

Interviews and questionnaires   Interviews and questionnaires can supply detailed and interesting information on many subjects. A nursing student interested in the care of terminally ill patients might interview hospice nurses; a criminal justice major might speak with a local judge about alternative sentencing for first offenders; a future teacher might conduct a survey on the use of smart board technology in local elementary schools.

It is a good idea to record interviews to preserve any lively quotations that you might want to weave into your essay. Circulating questionnaires by e-mail or on a Web site will facilitate responses. Keep questions simple and specify a deadline to ensure that you get a reasonable number of replies. (See also 53g.)

Length and document design

Writers seldom have complete control over length. Journalists usually write within strict word limits set by their editors, businesspeople routinely aim for conciseness, and most college assignments specify an approximate length.

Your writing situation may also require a certain document design. Specific formats are used in business for letters, memos, and reports. In the academic world, you may need to learn precise conventions for lab reports, critiques, research papers, and so on. For most undergraduate essays, a standard format is acceptable (see 51).

In some writing situations, you will be free to create your own design, complete with headings, displayed lists, and perhaps visuals such as charts and graphs. For a discussion of document design, see 50.

Reviewers and deadlines

Professional and business writers rarely work alone. They work with reviewers, often called *editors*, who offer advice throughout the writing process. In college classes, too, the use of reviewers is common. Some instructors play the role of reviewer for you; others may ask you to visit the writing center. Still others schedule peer review sessions in class or online. Such sessions give you a chance to hear what other students think about your draft in progress — and to play the role of reviewer yourself.

Deadlines are a key element of any writing situation. They help you plan your time and map out what you can accomplish in that time. For complex writing projects, such as research papers, you'll need to plan your time carefully. By working backward from the final deadline, you can create a schedule of target dates for completing parts of the project. (See p. 420 for an example.)

EXERCISE 1–1 Narrow three of the following subjects into topics that would be manageable for an essay of two to five pages.

1. Treatments for mental illness
2. An experience with racism or sexism
3. Handheld electronic devices in the classroom
4. Images of women in video games
5. Mandatory drug testing in the workplace

EXERCISE 1–2 Suggest a purpose and an audience for three of the following subjects.

1. Genetic modification of cash crop foods
2. Government housing for military veterans
3. The future of online advertising
4. Working with special needs children
5. Hybrid cars

1b Experiment with ways to explore your subject.

Instead of just plunging into a first draft, experiment with one or more techniques for exploring your subject, perhaps one of these:

- talking and listening
- reading and annotating texts
- listing
- clustering
- freewriting
- asking questions
- keeping a journal
- blogging

Whatever technique you turn to, the goal is the same: to generate ideas that will lead you to a question, a problem, or a topic that you want to explore. At this early stage of the writing process, don't censor yourself. Sometimes an idea that initially seems trivial or far-fetched will turn out to be worthwhile.

Talking and listening

Because writing is a process of figuring out what you think about a subject, it can be useful to try out your ideas on other people. Conversation can deepen and refine your ideas before you even begin to set them down on paper. By talking and listening to others, you can also discover what they find interesting, what they are curious about, and where they disagree with you. If you are planning to advance an argument, you can try it out on listeners with other points of view.

Many writers begin a writing project by brainstorming ideas in a group, debating a point with friends, or chatting with an instructor. Others prefer to record themselves talking through their thoughts. Some writers exchange ideas by sending e-mail or instant messages or by posting to discussion boards or blogs. You may be encouraged to share ideas with your classmates and instructor in an online workshop where you can begin to refine your thoughts before starting a draft.

Reading and annotating texts

Reading is an important way to deepen your understanding of a topic and expand your perspective. Annotating a text, written or visual, encourages you to read actively — to highlight key concepts, to note possible contradictions in an argument, or to raise questions for further research and investigation. Here, for example, is a paragraph from an essay on medical ethics, Michael Sandel's "The Case against Perfection," as one student annotated it:

> **Making the most of your handbook**
> Read critically and take notes before you write.
> ▶ Guidelines for active reading: page 71
> ▶ Taking notes: 55c
> ▶ Analyzing texts: 5

SAMPLE ANNOTATED ARTICLE

What breakthroughs?
Do all breakthroughs have the same consequences?

Stem cell research?

Is everyone really uneasy?
Is something a breakthrough if it creates a predicament?

Breakthroughs in genetics present us with a promise and a predicament. The promise is that we may soon be able to treat and prevent a host of debilitating diseases. The predicament is that our newfound genetic knowledge may also enable us to manipulate our own nature — to enhance our muscles, memories, and moods; to choose the sex, height, and other genetic traits of our children; to make ourselves "better than well." When science moves faster than moral understanding, as it does today, men and women struggle to articulate their unease. In liberal societies they reach first for the language of autonomy, fairness, and individual rights. But this part of our moral vocabulary is ill equipped to address the hardest questions posed by genetic engineering. The genomic revolution has induced a kind of moral vertigo.

Sandel's key dilemma

What does he mean by "moral understanding"?

Which questions? He doesn't seem to be taking sides.

After reading and annotating the entire article, the student noticed that several of his annotations pointed to the question of whether a scientific breakthrough should be viewed in terms of its moral consequences. He decided to reread the article, taking detailed notes with this question in mind.

Listing

Listing ideas — a technique sometimes known as *brainstorming* — is a good way to figure out what you know and what questions you have. Here is a list one student writer jotted down for an essay about community service requirements for college students:

- Volunteered in high school.
- Teaching adults to read motivated me to study education.
- "The best way to find yourself is to lose yourself in the service of others." — Gandhi
- Volunteering helps students find interests and career paths.
- Volunteering as requirement? Contradiction?
- Many students need to work to pay college tuition.
- Enough time to study, work, and volunteer?
- Can't students volunteer for their own reasons?
- What schools have community service requirements?
- What do students say about community service requirements?

Listing questions and ideas helped the writer narrow her subject and identify her position. In other words, she treated her early list as a record of her thoughts and a springboard to new ideas, not as an outline.

Clustering

Unlike listing, clustering highlights relationships among ideas. To cluster ideas, write your subject in the center of a sheet of paper, draw a circle around it, and surround the circle with related ideas connected to it with lines. If some of the satellite ideas lead to more specific clusters, write them down as well. The writer of the diagram on page 16 was exploring ideas for an essay on obesity in children.

Freewriting

In its purest form, freewriting is simply nonstop writing. You set aside ten minutes or so and write whatever comes to mind, without pausing to think about word choice, spelling, or even meaning. If you get stuck, you can write about being stuck, but you should keep your fingers moving. If nothing much happens, you have lost only ten minutes. It's more likely, though, that something interesting will emerge — perhaps an eloquent sentence, a genuine expression of curiosity, or an idea worth further investigation.

CLUSTER DIAGRAM

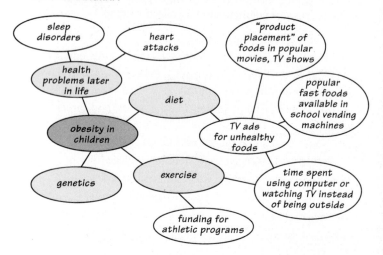

To explore ideas on a particular topic, consider using a technique known as *focused freewriting*. Again, you write quickly and freely, but this time you focus on a subject and pay attention to the connections among your ideas.

Asking questions

When gathering material for a story, journalists routinely ask themselves Who? What? When? Where? Why? and How? In addition to helping journalists get started, these questions ensure that they will not overlook an important fact.

Whenever you are writing about events, whether current or historical, asking questions is one way to get started. One student, whose topic was the negative reaction in 1915 to D. W. Griffith's silent film *The Birth of a Nation*, began exploring her topic with this set of questions:

- *Who* objected to the film?
- *What* were the objections?
- *When* were protests first voiced?
- *Where* were protests most strongly expressed?
- *Why* did protesters object to the film?
- *How* did protesters make their views known?

As often happens, the answers to these questions led to another question the writer wanted to explore. After she discovered that protesters objected to the film's racist portrayal of African Americans, she wondered whether their protests had changed attitudes. This question prompted an interesting topic for a paper: Did the film's stereotypes lead to positive, if unintended, consequences?

In academic writing, scholars often generate ideas by posing questions related to a specific discipline: one set of questions for analyzing literature, another for evaluating experiments in social psychology, still another for reporting field experiences in criminal justice. If you are writing in a particular discipline, try to find out which questions its scholars typically explore.

Keeping a journal

A journal is a collection of informal, exploratory, sometimes experimental writing. In a journal, often meant for your eyes only, you can take risks. You might freewrite, pose questions, comment on an interesting idea from one of your classes, or keep a list of questions that occur to you while reading. You might imagine a conversation between yourself and your readers or stage a debate to understand opposing positions. A journal can also serve as a sourcebook of ideas to draw on in future essays.

Blogging

Although a blog (Weblog) is a type of journal, it is a public writing space rather than a private one. In a blog, you might express opinions, make observations, recap events, have fun with language, or interpret an image. Since most blogs have a commenting feature, you can create a conversation by inviting readers to give you feedback — ask questions, pose counterarguments, or suggest other readings on a topic.

As you write

American author Annie Dillard has written: "There is something you find interesting, for a reason hard to explain. It is hard to explain because you have never read it on any page; there you begin." What subject interests you? What questions do you have about that subject? Choose a question you *don't have an answer to,* and use three different ways to explore your subject. (Eight are described in this section.) Which of these methods seems most productive for you? Why?

1c Draft a working thesis.

As you explore your topic and identify questions to investigate, you will begin to see possible ways to focus your material. At this point, try to settle on a tentative central idea. The more complex your topic, the more your focus will change as your drafts evolve. For many types of writing, you will be able to assert your central idea in a sentence or two. Such a statement, which ordinarily appears in the opening paragraph of your finished essay, is called a *thesis statement* (see also 2a).

A thesis is often one or more of the following:

- the answer to a question you have posed
- the resolution of a problem you have identified
- a statement that takes a position on a debatable topic

A tentative or working thesis will help you organize your draft. Don't worry about the exact wording because your main point may change as you refine your efforts. Here, for example, are one student's efforts to pose a question and draft a thesis statement for an essay in his film course.

QUESTION

In *Rebel without a Cause*, how does the filmmaker show that Jim Stark becomes alienated from his family and friends?

WORKING THESIS

In *Rebel without a Cause*, Jim Stark, the main character, is often seen literally on the edge of physical danger, suggesting that he is becoming more and more agitated by his family and by society.

The working thesis will need to be revised as the student thinks through and revises his paper, but it provides a useful place to start writing.

Here, another student identifies and responds to a problem to focus an argument paper.

PROBLEM

Americans who earn average incomes cannot run effective national political campaigns.

WORKING THESIS

Congress should pass legislation that would make it possible for Americans who are not wealthy to be viable candidates in national political campaigns.

The student has roughed out language for how to solve the problem — enacting federal legislation. As she reads more and learns more about her topic, she will be able to refine her thesis and suggest a specific solution, such as federal restriction of campaign spending.

Testing a working thesis

Once you have come up with a working thesis, you can use the following questions to evaluate it.

- Does your thesis answer a question, propose a solution to a problem, or take a position in a debate?
- Does the thesis require an essay's worth of development? Or will you run out of points too quickly?
- Is the thesis too obvious? If you cannot come up with interpretations that oppose your own, consider revising your thesis.
- Can you support your thesis with the evidence available?
- Can you explain why readers will want to read an essay with this thesis? Can you respond when a reader asks "So what?" or "Why does it matter?"

Keep in mind as you draft your working thesis that an effective thesis is a promise to the reader; it points both the writer and the reader in a definite direction. For a more detailed discussion of the thesis, see 2a.

1d Sketch a plan.

Once you have drafted a working thesis, listing and organizing your supporting ideas is a good next step. Creating outlines, whether formal or informal, can help you make sure your writing is credible and logical and can help you identify any gaps in your support.

When to use an informal outline

You might want to sketch an informal outline to see how you will support your thesis and to figure out a tentative structure for your ideas. Informal outlines can take many forms. Perhaps the most common is simply the thesis followed by a list of major ideas.

Working thesis: Television advertising should be regulated to help prevent childhood obesity.

- Children watch more television than ever.
- Snacks marketed to children are often unhealthy and fattening.
- Childhood obesity can cause sleep disorders and other problems.
- Addressing these health problems costs taxpayers billions of dollars.
- Therefore, these ads are actually costing the public money.
- If advertising is free speech, do we have the right to regulate it?
- We regulate alcohol and cigarette ads on television, so why not advertisements for soda and junk food?

If you began by jotting down a list of ideas (see p. 15), you can turn the list into a rough outline by crossing out some ideas, adding others, and putting the ideas in a logical order.

When to use a formal outline

Early in the writing process, rough outlines have certain advantages: They can be produced quickly, they are obviously tentative, and they can be revised easily. However, a formal outline may be useful later in the writing process, after you have written a rough draft, especially if your topic is complex. It can help you see whether the parts of your essay work together and whether your essay's structure is logical.

The following formal outline brought order to the research paper in 60c, on Internet surveillance in the workplace. The student's thesis is an important part of the outline. Everything else in the outline supports it, either directly or indirectly.

Thesis: Although companies often have legitimate concerns that lead them to monitor employees' Internet usage—from expensive security breaches to reduced productivity—the benefits of electronic surveillance are outweighed by its costs to employees' privacy and autonomy.

I. Although employers have always monitored employees, electronic surveillance is more efficient than other methods.

    A. Employers can gather data in large quantities.

    B. Electronic surveillance can be continuous.

    C.   Electronic surveillance can be conducted secretly, with keystroke logging programs.

II. Some experts argue that employers have legitimate reasons to monitor employees' Internet usage.

    A.   Unmonitored employees could accidentally breach security.

    B.   Companies are legally accountable for the online actions of employees.

III. Despite valid concerns, employers should value employee morale and autonomy and avoid creating an atmosphere of distrust.

    A.   Setting the boundaries for employee autonomy is difficult in the wired workplace.

        1.   Using the Internet is the most popular way of wasting time at work.

        2.   Employers can't easily determine if employees are working or surfing the Web.

    B.   Surveillance can create resentment among employees.

        1.   Web surfing can relieve stress, and restricting it can generate tension between managers and workers.

        2.   Enforcing Internet usage can seem arbitrary.

IV. Surveillance may not increase employee productivity, and trust may benefit productivity.

    A.   A company shouldn't care how many hours salaried employees work as long as they get the job done.

    B.   Casual Internet use can actually benefit companies.

        1.   The Internet may spark business ideas.

        2.   The Internet may suggest ideas about how to operate more efficiently.

V. Employees' rights to privacy are not well defined by the law.

    A.   Few federal guidelines on electronic surveillance exist.

    B.   Employers and employees are negotiating the boundaries without legal guidance.

    C.   As technological capabilities increase, the need to define boundaries will also increase.

Guidelines for constructing an outline

1. Put the thesis at the top.
2. Make items at the same level parallel grammatically (see section 9).
3. Use sentences unless phrases are clear.
4. Use the conventional system of numbers, letters, and indents:
   I.
      A.
      B.
         1.
         2.
            a.
            b.
   II.
      A.
      B.
         1.
         2.
            a.
            b.
5. Always include at least two items at each level.
6. Limit the number of major sections in the outline; if the list of roman numerals (at the first level) gets too long, try clustering the items into fewer major categories with more subcategories.

When to consider using visuals

You may decide that some of the support for your thesis could be one or more visuals. Visuals can convey information concisely and powerfully. Charts, graphs, and tables, for example, can simplify complex numerical information. Images — including photographs and diagrams — often express an idea more vividly than words can. With access to the Internet, digital photography, and word processing or desktop publishing software, you can download or create your own visuals to enhance your document. Keep in mind that if you download a visual — or use published information to create your own visual — you must credit your source (see p. 409).

Always consider how a visual supports your purpose and how your audience might respond to it. A student writing about electronic surveillance in the workplace, for example, used a cartoon to illustrate her point about employees' personal use of the Internet at work (see 60c). Another student, writing about treatments for childhood obesity, created a table to display data she had found in two different sources and discussed in her paper (see 65b).

As you plan your essay, carefully choose visuals that will support your point, and avoid overloading a draft with too many images. Use visuals to supplement your writing, not to substitute for it. The chart on pages 24–25 describes eight types of visuals and their purposes.

2 Draft the paper.

As you rough out a first draft, focus your attention on ideas and organization. You can deal with sentence structure and word choice later.

Before you begin to write, gather any prewriting materials — lists, diagrams, outlines, and so on — as well as sources that you plan to use. Having these close by will help you get started and keep you moving because you won't need to search for ideas. Writing tends to flow better when it is drafted relatively quickly, without many stops and starts.

2a For most types of writing, draft an introduction that includes a thesis.

Drafting an introduction

Your introduction will usually be a paragraph of 50 to 150 words (in a longer paper, it may be more than one paragraph). Perhaps the most common strategy is to open the paragraph with a few sentences that engage the reader and establish your purpose for writing and then to state your main point. (See the example on p. 26.) The statement of your main point is called the *thesis*. (See also 1c.)

Choosing visuals to suit your purpose

Pie chart

Pie charts compare a part or parts to the whole. Segments of the pie represent percentages of the whole (and always total 100 percent).

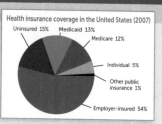

Health insurance coverage in the United States (2007)
Uninsured 15% Medicaid 13%
Medicare 12%
Individual 5%
Other public insurance 1%
Employer-insured 54%

Line graph

Line graphs highlight trends over a period of time or compare numerical data.

THE PURSUIT OF PROPERTY
Home ownership rates in the United States
1930 1940 1950 1960 1970 1980 1990 2000

Bar graph

Bar graphs can be used for the same purpose as line graphs. This bar graph displays the same data as in the line graph above.

THE PURSUIT OF PROPERTY
Home ownership rates in the United States
1930 1940 1950 1960 1970 1980 1990 2000

Table

Tables organize complicated numerical information into a digestible format.

Sources [top to bottom]: Kaiser Foundation; US Census Bureau; US Census Bureau; UNAIDS.

Prices of daily doses of AIDS drugs ($US)				
Drug	Brazil	Uganda	Côte d'Ivoire	US
3TC (Lamuvidine)	1.66	3.29	2.95	8.70
ddC (Zalcitabine)	0.24	4.17	3.75	8.80
Didanosine	2.04	5.26	3.48	7.25
Efavirenz	8.96	n/a	6.41	13.13
Indinavir	10.32	12.79	9.07	14.93
Nelfinavir	4.14	4.45	4.39	6.47
Nevirapine	5.04	n/a	n/a	8.48
Saquinavir	6.24	7.37	5.52	6.50
Stavudine	0.56	6.19	4.10	9.07
ZDV/3TC	1.44	7.34	n/a	18.78
Zidovudine	1.08	4.34	2.43	10.12

Source: UNAIDS, 2000

Photograph

Photographs vividly depict
people, scenes, or objects
discussed in a text.

Diagram

Diagrams, useful in scientific
and technical writing, concisely
illustrate processes, structures,
or interactions.

Flowchart

Flowcharts show structures or
steps in a process. (See also p. 133
for another example of a
flowchart.)

Map

Maps indicate distances,
historical information, or
demographics.

Sources [top to bottom]: Fred Zwicky;
NIAMS; Arizona Board of Regents;
Lynn Hunt et al.

In the following introduction, the thesis is highlighted.

> As the United States industrialized in the nineteenth century, using immigrant labor, social concerns took a backseat to the task of building a prosperous nation. The government did not regulate industries and did not provide an effective safety net for the poor or for those who became sick or injured on the job. Immigrants and the poor did have a few advocates, however. Settlement houses such as Hull-House in Chicago provided information, services, and a place for reform-minded individuals to gather and work to improve the conditions of the urban poor. Alice Hamilton was one of these reformers. Hamilton's efforts helped to improve the lives of immigrants and drew attention and respect to the problems and people that until then had been ignored.
>
> —Laurie McDonough, student

Ideally, the sentences leading to the thesis should hook the reader, perhaps with one of the following:

a startling statistic or an unusual fact

a vivid example

a description or an image

a paradoxical statement

a quotation or a bit of dialogue

a question

an analogy

an anecdote

Whether you are writing for a scholarly audience, a professional audience, a public audience, or a general audience, you cannot assume your readers' interest in the topic. The hook should spark curiosity and offer readers a reason to continue.

Although the thesis frequently appears at the end of the introduction, it can just as easily appear at the beginning. Much work-related writing, for example, requires a straightforward approach and commonly begins with the thesis.

> Flextime scheduling, which has proved its effectiveness at the Library of Congress, should be introduced on a trial basis at the main branch of the Montgomery County Public Library. By offering flexible work hours, the library can boost employee morale, cut down on absenteeism, and expand its hours of operation.
>
> —David Warren, student

For some types of writing, it may be difficult or impossible to express the central idea in a thesis statement; or it may be unwise or unnecessary to put a thesis statement in the essay. A personal narrative, for example, may have a focus too subtle to be distilled in a single statement. Strictly informative writing, like that found in many business memos, may be difficult to summarize in a thesis. In some academic fields, such as nursing, writers may produce reports that do not require a thesis. In such instances, do not try to force the central idea into a thesis statement. Instead, think in terms of an overriding purpose, which may or may not be stated directly.

> **Making the most of your handbook**
> The thesis statement is central to many types of writing.
> ▶ Writing about texts: 5
> ▶ Writing arguments: 6
> ▶ Writing research papers: 56 (MLA), 61 (APA)

As you write
Review the advice given on pages 23 and 26–27 for writing effective introductions. Exchange drafts with a classmate and evaluate each other's introductions. What hook have you used to focus your draft and spark readers' curiosity? Based on feedback from a classmate, what other hooks might be appropriate for your purpose and audience?

Writing effective thesis statements

An effective thesis statement is a central idea that requires supporting evidence; its scope is appropriate for the required length of the essay; and it is sharply focused. It should answer a question you have posed, resolve a problem you have identified, or take a position in a debate.

When constructing a thesis statement, ask yourself whether you can successfully develop it with the sources available to you and for the purposes you've identified. Also ask if you can explain why readers should be interested in reading an essay that explores this thesis.

> **Academic English** If you come from a culture that prefers an indirect approach in writing, you may feel that asserting a thesis early in an essay sounds unrefined or even rude. In the United States, however, readers appreciate a direct approach; when you state your point as directly as possible, you show that you understand your topic and value your readers' time.

A thesis must require proof or further development through facts and details; it cannot itself be a fact or a description.

DRAFT THESIS The first polygraph was developed by Dr. John A. Larson in 1921.

PROBLEM The thesis is *too factual.* A reader could not disagree with it or debate it; no further development of this idea is required.

STRATEGY *Enter a debate* by posing a question about your topic that has more than one possible answer. For example: Should the polygraph be used by private employers? Your thesis should be your answer to the question.

REVISED THESIS Because the polygraph has not been proved reliable, even under controlled conditions, its use by employers should be banned.

A thesis should be an answer to a question, not a question itself.

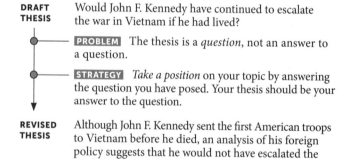

DRAFT THESIS Would John F. Kennedy have continued to escalate the war in Vietnam if he had lived?

PROBLEM The thesis is a *question,* not an answer to a question.

STRATEGY *Take a position* on your topic by answering the question you have posed. Your thesis should be your answer to the question.

REVISED THESIS Although John F. Kennedy sent the first American troops to Vietnam before he died, an analysis of his foreign policy suggests that he would not have escalated the war had he lived.

A thesis should be of sufficient scope for your assignment; it should not be too broad.

DRAFT THESIS Mapping the human genome has many implications for health and science.

PROBLEM The thesis is *too broad.* Even in a very long research paper, you would not be able to discuss all the implications of mapping the human genome.

STRATEGY *Consider subtopics of your original topic.* Once you have chosen a subtopic, take a position in an ongoing debate and pose a question that has more than one answer. For example: Should people be tested for genetic diseases? Your thesis should be your answer to the question.

REVISED THESIS   Although scientists can now detect genetic predisposition for specific diseases, policymakers should establish guidelines about whom to test and under what circumstances.

A thesis also should not be too narrow.

DRAFT THESIS   A person who carries a genetic mutation linked to a particular disease might or might not develop that disease.

> **PROBLEM**   The thesis is *too narrow*. It does not suggest any argument or debate about the topic.

> **STRATEGY**   *Identify challenging questions* that readers might have about your topic. Then pose a question that has more than one answer. For example: Do the risks of genetic testing outweigh its usefulness? Your thesis should be your answer to this question.

REVISED THESIS   Though positive results in a genetic test do not guarantee that the disease will develop, such results can cause psychological trauma; genetic testing should therefore be avoided in most cases.

A thesis should be sharply focused, not too vague. Avoid fuzzy, hard-to-define words such as *interesting, good,* or *disgusting.*

DRAFT THESIS   The Vietnam Veterans Memorial is an interesting structure.

> **PROBLEM**   This thesis is *too fuzzy and unfocused*. It's difficult to define *interesting*, and the sentence doesn't give the reader any cues about where the essay is going.

> **STRATEGY**   *Focus your thesis with concrete language and a clear plan.* Pose a question about the topic that has more than one answer. For example: How does the physical structure of the Vietnam Veterans Memorial shape the experience of visitors? Your thesis — your answer to the question — should use specific language that engages readers to follow your argument.

REVISED THESIS   By inviting visitors to see their own reflections in the wall, the Vietnam Veterans Memorial creates a link between the present and the past.

Revising with comments
Unclear thesis

UNDERSTANDING THE COMMENT

When readers point out that your thesis is unclear, the comment often signals that they have a hard time identifying your essay's main point.

> Fathers are more involved in the lives of their children today than they used to be. In the past, the father's primary role was as the provider; child care was most often left to the mother or other relatives. However, today's father drives to dance lessons, coaches his child's baseball team, hosts birthday parties, and provides homework help. <u>Do more involved fathers help or hinder the development of their children?</u>   *Unclear thesis*

One student wrote this introductory paragraph in response to an assignment that asked her to analyze the changing roles of mothers or fathers.

A writer's thesis, or main point, should be phrased as a statement, not a question. To revise, the student could answer the question she has posed, or she could pose a new question and answer it. After considering her evidence, she needs to decide what position she wants to take, state this position clearly, and show readers *why* this position — her thesis — matters.

SIMILAR COMMENTS: *vague thesis* • *state your position* • *your main point?*

REVISING WHEN *YOUR* THESIS IS UNCLEAR

1. *Ask questions.* What is the thesis, position, or main point of the draft? Can you support it with the available evidence?

2. *Reread your entire draft.* Because ideas develop as you write, you may find that your conclusion contains a clearer statement of your main point than your current thesis does. Or you may find your thesis elsewhere in your draft.

3. *Try revising your thesis* by framing it as an answer to a question you pose, the resolution of a problem you identify, or a position you take in a debate. And put your thesis to the "So what?" test: Why would a reader be interested in this thesis?

More help with writing a clear thesis: 1c and 2a

As you write

Review the advice and examples on pages 27–29 for writing effective thesis statements. Exchange drafts with a classmate, use the problem/strategy approach to evaluate each other's thesis, and then talk through how each of you might go about revising. What do you learn about your draft thesis from this discussion? What single piece of advice might help you strengthen your thesis?

EXERCISE 2–1   In each of the following pairs, which sentence might work well as a thesis for a short paper? What is the problem with the other one? Is it too factual? Too broad? Too vague?

1a. By networking with friends, a single parent can manage to strike a balance among work, school, a social life, and family.

  b. Single parents face many challenges as they try to juggle all of their responsibilities.

2a. At the Special Olympics, athletes with disabilities show that, with hard work and support from others, they can accomplish anything—that they can indeed be winners.

  b. Working with the Special Olympics program is rewarding.

3a. History 201, taught by Professor Brown, is offered at 10:00 a.m. on Tuesdays and Thursdays.

  b. Whoever said that history is nothing but polishing tombstones must have missed History 201, because in Professor Brown's class history is very much alive.

4a. So far, research suggests that zero-emissions vehicles are not a sensible solution to the problem of steadily increasing air pollution.

  b. Because air pollution is of serious concern to many people today, several US government agencies have implemented plans to begin solving the problem.

5a. Anorexia nervosa is a dangerous and sometimes deadly eating disorder occurring mainly in young, upper-middle-class teens.

  b. The eating disorder anorexia nervosa is rarely cured by one treatment alone; only by combining drug therapy with psychotherapy and family therapy can the patient begin the long journey to wellness.

PRACTICE   hackerhandbooks.com/rules
> The writing process > 2–2 to 2–4

2b Draft the body.

The body of your essay develops support for your thesis, so it's important to have at least a working thesis before you start writing. What does your thesis promise readers? Try to keep your response to that question in mind as you draft the body.

You may have already written an introduction that includes your working thesis. If not, as long as you have a draft thesis, you can begin developing the body and return later to the introduction. If your thesis suggests a plan or if you have sketched a preliminary outline, try to block out your paragraphs accordingly. Draft the body of your essay by writing at least a paragraph about each supporting point you listed in the planning stage. If you do not have a plan, pause for a few moments and sketch one (see 1d).

Keep in mind that often you might not know what you want to say until you have written a draft. It is possible to begin without a plan — assuming you are prepared to treat your first attempt as a "discovery draft" that will be radically rewritten once you discover what you really want to say. Whether or not you have a plan when you begin drafting, you can often figure out a workable order for your ideas by stopping each time you start a new paragraph to think about what your readers will need to know to follow your train of thought.

For more detailed advice about paragraphs in the body of an essay, see 4. For specific help with drafting paragraphs, see 4a. For more on developing paragraphs, see 4b.

TIP: As you draft, keep careful notes and records of any sources you read and consult. (See 55b.) If you quote, paraphrase, or summarize a source, include a citation, even in your draft. You will save time and avoid plagiarism if you follow the rules of citation and documentation while drafting.

2c Draft a conclusion.

A conclusion should remind readers of the essay's main idea without repeating it. Often the concluding paragraph can be relatively short. By the end of the essay, readers should already understand your main point; your conclusion drives it home and, perhaps, gives readers some larger idea to consider.

Revising with comments
Be specific

UNDERSTANDING THE COMMENT

When readers say that you need to "be specific," the comment often signals that you could strengthen your writing with additional details.

> There are many cultural differences between the United States and Italy. Italian citizens do not share many of the same (attitudes) or (values) as American citizens. Such (differences) make it hard for some Italian students to feel comfortable coming to the United States for extended periods of time, even for an academic year.

Be specific!

In this body paragraph, a student responds to an assignment that asked him to interview a group of international students and describe the challenges of studying in the United States.

The student presents a claim but doesn't include specific examples or evidence to support the claim. To revise, the student might focus on *one* specific example of cultural differences between the United States and Italy. The student might then ask: What vivid details illustrate this cultural difference? The answer to that question will provide specific evidence to inform and persuade readers.

SIMILAR COMMENTS: need examples • too general • evidence?

STRATEGIES FOR REVISING WHEN *YOUR* WRITING NEEDS TO BE MORE SPECIFIC

1. *Reread your topic sentence* to understand the focus of the paragraph.
2. *Ask questions.* Does the paragraph contain claims that need support? What does the paragraph promise? Have you provided evidence — specific examples, vivid details and illustrations, statistics and facts — to help readers understand your ideas and find them persuasive?
3. *Interpret your evidence.* Remember that details and examples don't speak for themselves. You'll need to show readers how your evidence supports your claims.

More help with using specific evidence: 6e

Revising with comments

Narrow your introduction

UNDERSTANDING THE COMMENT

When readers point out that your introduction needs to be "narrowed," the comment often signals that the beginning sentences of your essay are not specific or focused.

> Sports fans are an interesting breed. They have many ways of showing support for the team they love. Many fans perform elaborate rituals before, during, or after a sporting event. These rituals are performed both privately in homes with family or friends and at the stadiums and arenas where the games take place. Experiencing a sports competition where the fans are participating in rituals to support the team makes the game exciting. Some fans even believe that rituals are necessary and that their actions influence the outcome of a game. However, some fans go beyond cheering, and their actions, verbal harassment, and chanted slurs reveal a darker side of sports.   *Narrow your introduction*

One student wrote this introductory paragraph in response to an assignment that asked her to analyze a ritual.

This opening begins with such general statements that the purpose of the essay is unclear. To revise, the student might delete her first few sentences — generalizations about sports fans and rituals — and focus on one specific sports ritual. She might describe how fans who wear lucky clothes, eat certain foods, or chant a particular expression think they can influence the outcome of a game. Using a quotation, a vivid example, or a startling statistic, the student might show how a particular ritual not only unites fans but also reveals a dark side of sports. Whatever "hook" she chooses should lead readers to her thesis.

SIMILAR COMMENTS: focus your intro • too general •
engage your readers

REVISING WHEN YOU NEED TO NARROW *YOUR* INTRODUCTION

1. *Reread your introduction and ask questions.* Are the sentences leading to your thesis specific enough to engage readers and communicate your purpose? Do these sentences lead logically to your thesis? Do they spark your readers' curiosity and offer them a reason to continue reading?

2. *Try revising your introduction with a "hook"* that will engage readers — a question, quotation, paradoxical statement, or vivid example.

More advice on writing introductions: 2a

In addition to echoing your main idea, a conclusion might

- briefly summarize your essay's key points
- propose a course of action
- offer a recommendation
- discuss the topic's wider significance or implications
- pose a question for future study

To conclude an essay analyzing the shifting roles of women in the military services, one student discusses her topic's implications for society as a whole:

> As the military continues to train women in jobs formerly reserved for men, our understanding of women's roles in society will no doubt continue to change. As news reports of women training for and taking part in combat operations become commonplace, reports of women becoming CEOs, police chiefs, and even president of the United States will cease to surprise us. Or perhaps we have already reached this point.
>
> — Rosa Broderick, student

To make the conclusion memorable, you might include a detail, an example, or an image from the introduction to bring readers full circle; a quotation or a bit of dialogue; an anecdote; or a witty or ironic comment. Whatever concluding strategy you choose, keep in mind that an effective conclusion is decisive and unapologetic. Avoid introducing wholly new ideas at the end of an essay. And because the conclusion is so closely tied to the rest of the essay in both content and tone, be prepared to rework it (or even replace it) when you revise.

 ## 3 Make global revisions; then revise sentences.

Revising is rarely a one-step process. Global matters — focus, purpose, organization, content, and overall strategy — generally receive attention first. Improvements in sentence structure, word choice, grammar, punctuation, and mechanics come later.

PRACTICE AND MODELS hackerhandbooks.com/rules
> The writing process > 3–1 and 3–2
> Revising > Sample global revision
> > Sample sentence-level revision

3a Make global revisions: Think big.

Writers often resist global revisions because they find it difficult to view their work from their audience's perspective. What is clear to them, because they know what they mean to say after all, is not always clear to their audience. To distance yourself from a draft, put it aside for a while, preferably overnight or even longer. When you return to it, try to play the role of your audience as you read. If possible, enlist friends or family to be the audience for your draft. Or visit your school's writing center to go over your draft with a writing tutor. Ask your reviewers to focus on the larger issues of writing, such as purpose and organization, not on word- or sentence-level issues. You might begin with a basic question: *Do you see my main point?* The checklist for global revision below may help you and your reviewers get started.

> **Making the most of your handbook**
> Seeking and using feedback are critical steps in revising a college paper.
> ▶ Guidelines for peer reviewers: page 38

Checklist for global revision

Purpose and audience

- Does the draft address a question, a problem, or an issue that readers care about?
- Is the draft appropriate for its audience? Does it account for the audience's knowledge of and possible attitudes toward the subject?

Focus

- Is the thesis clear? Is it prominently placed?
- If there is no thesis, is there a good reason for omitting one?
- Scan the supporting paragraphs: Are any ideas obviously off the point?

Organization and paragraphing

- Are there enough organizational cues for readers (such as topic sentences or headings)?
- Are ideas presented in a logical order?
- Are any paragraphs too long or too short for easy reading?

Content

- Is the supporting material relevant and persuasive?
- Which ideas need further development? Have you left your reader with any unanswered questions?
- Are the parts proportioned sensibly? Do major ideas receive enough attention?
- Where might material be deleted? Look for redundant or irrelevant information.

Point of view

- Is the dominant point of view — first person (*I* or *we*), second person (*you*), or third person (*he, she, it, one,* or *they*) — appropriate for your purpose and audience? (See 13a.)

As you write

Use the Checklist for global revision (pp. 36–37) to gain perspective on your draft. Does your draft accomplish its purpose? Does it reach its audience? Share your draft with a writing center tutor or with a peer. What did you learn from the feedback you received? Take a moment to identify three or four revision goals.

3b Revise and edit sentences.

Much of this book offers advice on revising sentences for clarity and on editing them for grammar, punctuation, and mechanics. Some writers handle sentence-level revisions directly at the computer, experimenting with a variety of possible improvements. Other writers prefer to print out a hard copy of the draft and mark it up before making changes in the file. Page 38 shows a rough-draft paragraph as one student edited it on-screen for a variety of sentence-level problems.

Guidelines for peer reviewers

- View yourself as a coach, not a judge. Work with the writer to identify the draft's strengths and areas for improvement.
- Restate the writer's main ideas to check that they are clearly expressed.
- Where possible, give specific compliments. Let the writer know which of his or her strategies are successful.
- Ask to hear more about passages you find confusing or interesting.
- Express interest in reading the next draft.

Although some cities have found creative ways to improve access to public transportation for passengers with physical disabilities, ~~and to fund other programs, there have been problems in~~ our city has struggled with ~~due to the need to address~~ budget constraints and competing ~~needs~~ priorities. ~~This~~ The budget crunch has led citizens to question how funds are distributed.~~?~~ For example, last year ~~when~~ city officials voted to use available funds to support ~~had to choose between allocating funds for accessible transportation or allocating funds to~~ after-school programs rather than transportation upgrades. ~~, they voted for the after school programs.~~ It is not clear to some citizens why ~~these~~ after-school programs are more important.

The original paragraph was flawed by wordiness, a problem that can be addressed through any number of revisions. The following revision would also be acceptable:

> Some cities have funded improved access to public transportation for passengers with physical disabilities. Because of budget constraints, our city chose to fund after-school programs rather than transportation programs. As a result, citizens have begun to question how funds are distributed and why certain programs are more important than others.

Some of the paragraph's improvements do not involve choice and must be fixed in any revision. The hyphen in *after-school programs* is necessary; a noun must be substituted for the pronoun *these* in the last sentence; and the question mark in the second sentence must be changed to a period.

3c Proofread the final manuscript.

After revising and editing, you are ready to prepare your final copy. (See 51 for guidelines.) Make sure to allow yourself enough time for proofreading — the final step in manuscript preparation.

Proofreading is a special kind of reading: a slow and methodical search for misspellings, typographical mistakes, and omitted words or word endings. Such errors can be difficult to spot in your own work because you may read what you intended to write, not what is actually on the page. To fight this tendency, try proofreading out loud, articulating each word as it is actually written. You might also try proofreading your sentences in reverse order, a strategy that takes your attention away from the meanings you intended and forces you to focus on one word at a time.

Although proofreading may be slow, it is crucial. Errors strewn throughout an essay are distracting and annoying. If the writer doesn't care about this piece of writing, the reader might wonder, why should I? A carefully proofread essay, however, sends a positive message that you value your writing and respect your readers.

3d Use software tools wisely.

Grammar checkers, spell checkers, and autoformatting are software tools designed to help you avoid errors and save time. These tools can alert you to possible errors in words, sentence structures, or formatting. But they're not always right. If a program suggests or makes a change, be sure the change is one you really want to make. Familiarizing yourself with your software's settings can help you use these tools effectively.

Grammar checkers

Grammar checkers can help with some of the sentence-level problems in a typical draft. But they will often misdiagnose errors, especially because they cannot account for your intended meaning. When the grammar checker makes a suggestion for revision, you must decide whether the change is more effective than your original.

It's just as important to be aware of what your grammar checker isn't picking up on. If you count on your grammar checker to identify trouble spots, you might overlook problems with coordination and subordination (see 14), sentence variety (see 15), sexist language (see 17e), and passive verbs (see 28a), for example.

Spell checkers

Spell checkers flag words not found in their dictionaries; they will suggest a replacement for any word they don't recognize. They can help you spot many errors, but don't let them be your only proofreader. If you're writing about the health benefits of a Mediterranean diet, for example, don't let your software change *briam* (a vegetable dish) to *Brian*. Even if your spell checker identifies a real misspelling, the replacement word it suggests might carry a different connotation or even be nonsensical. After misspelling *probably*, you might end up with *portly*. Consider changes carefully before accepting them. If you're not sure what word or spelling you need, consult a dictionary.

Because spell checkers flag only unrecognized words, they won't catch misused words, such as *accept* when you mean *except*. For help with commonly confused or misused words and with avoiding informal speech and jargon, consult the glossary of usage at the back of the book.

Autoformatting

As you write, your software may attempt to save you effort with autoformatting. It might recognize that you've typed a URL and turn it into a link. Or if you're building a list, it might add numbering for you. Be aware of such changes and make sure they are appropriate for your paper and applied to the right text.

3e Manage your files.

Your instructor may ask you to complete assignments in stages, including notes, outlines, annotated bibliographies, rough drafts, and a final draft. Keeping track of all of these documents can be challenging. Be sure to give your files distinct names that reflect the appropriate stage of your writing process, and store them in a logical place.

Writing online or in a word processing program can make writing and revising easier. You can undo changes or return to an earlier draft if a revision misfires. Applying the following steps can help you explore revision possibilities with little risk.

- Create folders and subfolders for each assignment. Save notes, outlines, and drafts together.
- Label revised drafts with different file names and dates.

MANAGING FILES

- Print hard copies, make backup copies, and press the Save button early and often (every five to ten minutes).
- Always record complete bibliographic information about sources, including images.
- Use a comment function to make notes to yourself or to respond to the drafts of peers.

3f Student essay

Matt Watson wrote the essay "Hooked on Credit Cards" (pp. 46–49) in response to the following assignment.

> In an essay of 500–1,000 words, discuss a significant problem facing today's college students. Assume that your audience consists of general readers, not simply college students.
>
> If you use any sources, document them with in-text citations and a list of works cited in MLA style (see section 59b).

When he received the assignment, Watson considered several possibilities before settling on the topic of credit cards. He already knew something about the topic because his older sister had run up large credit card bills while in college and was working hard to pay them off. Because the assignment required him to *discuss* a problem, he decided that a good strategy would be to identify a *how* or *why* question to answer.

SAMPLE NOTES

Ideas for college problem essay 3.3.01.doc - Microsoft Word

File   Edit   View   Insert   Format   Tools   Table   Window   Help   Adobe PDF

L . . | . . **1** . . | . . **2** . . | . . **3** . . | . . **4** . , | . .

Ideas for college problem essay

Phone call with Rebecca Watson, 3.3.01

- Easy to get hooked on credit cards and run up huge debts
- Why do credit card companies try to sign up students? Aren't we a bad risk? But they must be profiting, or they'd stop.
- High interest rates
- Ads for credit cards appear on campus and on the Web
- Using plastic doesn't seem like spending money
- Tactics used by the companies—offering low interest rates at first, setting high credit limits, allowing a revolving balance
- What happens to students who get in debt but don't have parents who can bail them out?

To get started on his paper, Watson talked with his sister about her experience with credit card debt and typed some ideas on his laptop (see above).

After he listed these ideas, Watson identified the question that would drive his essay:

> Why do credit card companies put so many resources into soliciting students, who often have poor credit profiles?

Watson decided that his purpose would be to answer this question for himself and his audience. He would do so by taking a position and making an argument. He wrote his first draft quickly, focusing more on ideas and evidence than on grammar, style, and mechanics. Here is the draft he submitted, together with the most helpful comments he received from classmates. The peer reviewers were asked to comment on global issues — audience appeal, focus, organization, content, and point of view — and to ignore any problems with grammar and punctuation.

ROUGH DRAFT WITH PEER COMMENTS

Hooked on Credit Cards

Credit card companies love to extend credit to college students. You see ads for these cards on campus bulletin boards and also on the Web. Why do companies market their product to a population that has no job and lacks a substantial credit history? They seem to be trying to hook us on their cards; unfortunately many of us do get hooked on a cycle of spending that leads to financial ruin.

> Good question. Is there more to the answer than you've written here? That is, why are these companies trying to hook us? (Mark)

> Some students do have jobs. (Sara)

> The assignment asks for a general audience; your thesis shouldn't be about "us." (Sara)

> Shouldn't your thesis also explain *how* the companies hook students? (Tim)

Banks require applicants for a loan to demonstrate a good credit history and some evidence of a source of income, but credit card companies don't. On campus, students are bombarded with offers of preapproved credit cards. Then there are the Web sites. Sites with lots of student traffic are plastered with banner ads like this one: "To get a credit card, you need to establish credit. To establish credit, you need a credit card. Stop the vicious cycle! Apply for our student MasterCard."

> Good point. I never thought of it that way. (Sara)

> Mention the solicitors who show up during orientation? (Mark)

> This sentence sounds less formal than the rest of your essay. (Tim)

> I like this example. (Mark)

Credit card companies often entice students with low interest rates, then they jack up the rates later. A student may not think about the cost of interest. That new stereo or back-to-school wardrobe can get pretty expensive at 17.9% interest if it's compounded over several months. Would you have bought that $600 item if you knew it would end up costing you $900?

> Why not give us some numbers here? Just how low and how high? (Sara)

> The shift to "you" seems odd. (Sara)

Most cards allow the holder to keep a revolving balance, which means that they don't have to pay the whole bill, they just pay a minimum amount.

The minimum is usually not too much, but a young person may be tempted to keep running up debt. The companies also give students an unrealistically high credit limit. I've heard of undergraduates who had a limit as high as $4,000.

Card companies make money not just from high interest rates. Often they charge fees for late payments. I've heard of penalties for going over the credit limit too.

Often students discover too late that they are thoroughly trapped. Some drop out of school, others graduate and then can't find a good job because they have a poor credit rating. There are psychological problems too. Your parents may bail you out of debt, but you'll probably feel guilty. On a Web site, I read that two students felt so bad they committed suicide.

Credit cards are a part of life these days, and everyone is probably wise to have a charge account for emergencies. But college students must take a hard look at their financial picture. The very things that make those cards so convenient and easy to use can lead to a mountain of debt that will take years to pay off.

Maybe you could search *LexisNexis* for some statistical information. (Mark)

This paragraph seems sort of skimpy. (Tim)

This would be more convincing if you provided some evidence to back up your claim. (Mark)

You shift from "you" to "I" here. (Sara)

Cite this? (Sara)

Your paper focuses on the tactics that the companies use, but your conclusion doesn't mention them. (Tim)

After rereading his draft and considering the feedback from his classmates, Watson realized that he needed to develop his thesis further. He set out some goals for revising his essay.

MATT WATSON'S REVISION GOALS

Answer Mark's question about what credit card companies gain by hooking students.

Expand explanation of both why and how credit card companies market cards to students.

Include evidence to back up claims about how credit card companies hook students. Look at reputable Web sites: student loan provider Nellie Mae and the Consumer Federation of America.

Rework introduction to explain why credit card companies profit from students who have no steady source of income.

Adjust point of view so that essay is appropriate for a general audience, not just for other students.

When he was more or less satisfied with the paper as a whole, Watson worked to polish his sentences. His final draft begins on the next page.

Watson 1

Matt Watson

Professor Mills

English 101

12 March 2001

Hooked on Credit Cards

Introduction
hooks readers
with interesting
details.

Credit card companies love to extend credit to
college students, especially those just out of high school.
Ads for credit cards line campus bulletin boards, flash
across commercial Web sites for students, and get
stuffed into shopping bags at college bookstores. Why

Introduction
poses a question
that leads
readers to the
thesis.

do the companies market their product so vigorously to
a population that lacks a substantial credit history and
often has no steady source of income? The answer is that
significant profits can be earned through high interest
rates and assorted penalties and fees. By granting college

Thesis
announces
Watson's main
point.

students liberal lending arrangements, credit card companies
often hook them on a cycle of spending that can ultimately
lead to financial ruin.

Clear topic
sentences guide
readers through
the body of the
paper.

Whereas banks require applicants for a loan to
demonstrate a good credit history and some evidence
of income, credit card companies make no such demands
on students. On campus, students find themselves
bombarded with offers of preapproved cards—and not just
on flyers pinned to bulletin boards. Many campuses allow
credit card vendors to solicit applications during orientation
week. In addition to offering preapproved cards, these

Essay is
double-spaced
throughout.

vendors often give away T-shirts or CDs to entice students
to apply. Some companies even offer rewards program
bonuses based on a student's GPA. Students are bombarded
on the Web as well. Sites with heavy student traffic are
emblazoned with banner ads like this one: "To get a credit

Marginal annotations indicate MLA-style formatting and effective writing.

Watson 2

card, you need to establish credit. To establish credit, you need a credit card. Stop the vicious cycle! Apply for our student MasterCard."

Credit card companies often entice students with low "teaser" interest rates of 13% and later raise those rates to 18% or even higher. Others charge high rates up front, trusting that students won't read the fine print. Some young people don't think about the cost of interest, let alone the cost of interest compounding month after month. That back-to-school wardrobe can get pretty expensive at 17.9% interest compounded over several months. A $600 trip to Fort Lauderdale is not such a bargain when in the long run it costs $900 or more.

In addition to charging high interest rates, credit card companies try to maximize the amount of interest generated. One tactic is to extend an unreasonably high credit limit to students. According to Nellie Mae statistics, in 1998 undergraduates were granted an average credit limit of $3,683; for graduate students, the figure jumped to $15,721. Nearly 10% of the students in the Nellie Mae study carried balances near or exceeding these credit limits (Blair).

Another tactic is to allow students to maintain a revolving balance. A revolving balance permits the debtor to pay only part of a current bill, often an amount just a little larger than the accumulated interest. The indebted student is tempted to keep on charging, paying a minimum amount every month, because there aren't any immediate consequences to doing so.

Once a student is hooked on a cycle of debt, the companies profit even further by assessing a variety of

Body paragraphs are developed with details and examples.

Transition serves as a bridge between paragraphs.

Summary of the source is in Watson's own words.

Source is documented with an MLA in-text citation.

Watson 3

Watson cites a Web article from a reputable source.

fees and penalties. According to a press release issued by Consumer Action and the Consumer Federation of America, many credit card companies charge late fees and "over the limit" penalties as high as $29 per month. In addition, grace periods are often shortened to ensure that late fees kick in earlier. Many companies also raise interest rates for those who fail to pay on time or who exceed the credit limit. Those "penalty" rates can climb as high as 25% (1–2).

Often students discover too late that they are thoroughly hooked. The results can be catastrophic. Some students are forced to drop out of school and take low-paying full-time jobs. Others, once they graduate, have difficulty landing good jobs because of their poor credit rating. Many students suffer psychologically as well. Even those who have parents willing to bail them out of debt often experience a great deal of anxiety and guilt. Two students grew so stressed by their accumulating debt that they committed suicide (Consumer Federation of Amer. 3).

Conclusion echoes Watson's main idea.

Credit cards are a convenient part of life, and there is nothing wrong with having one or two of them. Before signing up for a particular card, however, college students should take time to read the fine print and do some comparison shopping. Students also need to learn to resist the many seductive offers that credit card companies extend to them after they have signed up. Students who can't "just say no" to temptations such as high credit limits and revolving balances could well become hooked on a cycle of debt from which there is no easy escape.

Works Cited

Blair, Alan D. "A High Wire Act: Balancing Student Loan and
    Credit Card Debt." *Credit World* 86.2 (1997): 15-17.
    Business Source Premier. Web. 4 Mar. 2001.

Consumer Action and Consumer Federation of America.
    "Card Issuers Hike Fees and Rates to Bolster Profits."
    Consumer Federation of America. Consumer Federation
    of Amer., 5 Nov. 1998. Web. 4 Mar. 2001.

Consumer Federation of America. "Credit Card Debt Imposes
    Huge Costs on Many College Students." *Consumer
    Federation of America*. Consumer Federation of Amer.,
    8 June 1999. Web. 4 Mar. 2001.

Works cited page
follows MLA
format.

As you write

What do you learn about composing and revising from
studying Matt Watson's process (pages 41–49)? How has Matt's
revised essay benefited from the advice of his peers and from
his focused revision goals? How is your writing process similar
to or different from Matt's?

4 Build effective paragraphs.

Except for special-purpose paragraphs, such as introductions and conclusions (see 2a and 2c), paragraphs are clusters of information supporting an essay's main point (or advancing a story's action). Aim for paragraphs that are clearly focused, well developed, organized, coherent, and neither too long nor too short for easy reading.

4a Focus on a main point.

A paragraph should be unified around a main point. The point should be clear to readers, and every sentence in the paragraph should relate to it.

Stating the main point in a topic sentence

As readers move into a paragraph, they need to know where they are — in relation to the whole essay — and what to expect in the sentences to come. A good topic sentence, a one-sentence summary of the paragraph's main point, acts as a signpost pointing in two directions: backward toward the thesis of the essay and forward toward the body of the paragraph.

Like a thesis sentence (see 1c and 2a), a topic sentence is more general than the material supporting it. Usually the topic sentence (highlighted in the following example) comes first in the paragraph.

> All living creatures manage some form of communication. The dance patterns of bees in their hive help to point the way to distant flower fields or announce successful foraging. Male stickleback fish regularly swim upside-down to indicate outrage in a courtship contest. Male deer and lemurs mark territorial ownership by rubbing their own body secretions on boundary stones or trees. Everyone has seen a frightened dog put his tail between his legs and run in panic. We, too, use gestures, expressions, postures, and movement to give our words point.
>
> — Olivia Vlahos, *Human Beginnings*

Sometimes the topic sentence is introduced by a transitional sentence linking it to earlier material. In the following paragraph, the topic sentence has been delayed to allow for a transition.

But flowers are not the only source of spectacle in the wilderness. An opportunity for late color is provided by the berries of wildflowers, shrubs, and trees. Baneberry presents its tiny white flowers in spring but in late summer bursts forth with clusters of red berries. Bunchberry, a ground-cover plant, puts out red berries in the fall, and the red berries of wintergreen last from autumn well into the winter. In California, the bright red, fist-sized clusters of Christmas berries can be seen growing beside highways for up to six months of the year.

— James Crockett et al., *Wildflower Gardening*

To hook readers, writers are sometimes tempted to begin paragraphs with vivid quotations or compelling statistics from a source. A topic sentence in the writer's own words, however, can remind readers of the claim of the paper, advance the argument, and introduce the evidence from a source. In the following paragraph on the effects of the 2010 oil spill in the Gulf of Mexico, the writer uses a topic sentence to state that the extent of the threat is unknown before quoting three sources that illustrate her point.

To date, the full ramifications [of the oil spill] remain a question mark. An August report from the National Oceanic and Atmospheric Administration estimated that 75 percent of the oil had "either evaporated or been burned, skimmed, recovered from the wellhead, or dispersed." However, Woods Hole Oceanographic Institution researchers reported that a 1.2-mile-wide, 650-foot-high plume caused by the spill "will persist for some time." And University of Georgia scientists conclude that almost 80 percent of the released oil hadn't been recovered and "remains a threat to the ecosystem."

— Michele Wilson, "Volunteer Army"

Some professional writers, such as informal essayists, may not always use clear topic sentences. In college writing, however, topic sentences are often necessary for clarifying the lines of an argument or for reporting the research in a field. In business writing, topic sentences (along with headings) are essential because readers often scan for information.

Sticking to the point

Sentences that do not support the topic sentence destroy the unity of a paragraph. If the paragraph is otherwise focused, such sentences can simply be deleted or perhaps moved elsewhere. In the following paragraph describing the inadequate facilities in a high school, the information about the chemistry instructor (highlighted) is clearly off the point.

> As the result of tax cuts, the educational facilities of Lincoln High School have reached an all-time low. Some of the books date back to 1990 and have long since shed their covers. The few computers in working order must share one printer. The lack of lab equipment makes it necessary for four or five students to work at one table, with most watching rather than performing experiments. Also, the chemistry instructor left to have a baby at the beginning of the semester, and most of the students don't like the substitute. As for the furniture, many of the upright chairs have become recliners, and the desk legs are so unbalanced that they play seesaw on the floor.

Sometimes the solution for a disunified paragraph is not as simple as deleting or moving material. Writers often wander into uncharted territory because they cannot think of enough evidence to support a topic sentence. Feeling that it is too soon to break into a new paragraph, they move on to new ideas for which they have not prepared the reader. When this happens, the writer is faced with a choice: Either find more evidence to support the topic sentence or adjust the topic sentence to mesh with the evidence that is available.

EXERCISE 4–1 Underline the topic sentence in the following paragraph and cross out any material that does not clarify or develop the central idea.

> Quilt making has served as an important means of social, political, and artistic expression for women. In the nineteenth century, quilting circles provided one of the few opportunities for women to forge social bonds outside of their families. Once a week or more, they came together to sew as well as trade small talk, advice, and news. They used dyed cotton fabrics much like the fabrics quilters use today; surprisingly, quilters' basic materials haven't changed that much over the years. Sometimes the women joined their efforts in support of a political cause, making quilts that would be raffled to raise money for temperance societies, hospitals for sick and wounded soldiers, and the fight against slavery. Quilt making also afforded women a means of artistic expression at a time when they had few other creative outlets. Within their socially acceptable roles as homemakers, many quilters subtly pushed back at the restrictions placed on them by experimenting with color, design, and technique.

Revising with comments

More than one point in this paragraph

UNDERSTANDING THE COMMENT

When readers tell you that you have "more than one point in this paragraph," the comment often signals that not all sentences in your paragraph support the topic sentence.

> Bringing casino gaming to Massachusetts would benefit the state in a number of ways. First, it would provide needed property tax relief for many of the state's towns and cities. Casino gaming would also bring in revenue needed to fix the state's roads and bridges. The speaker of the House of Representatives is blocking the governor's proposal because he believes the social costs are greater than the economic benefits. Many people agree with the speaker. Most important, casino gaming would provide jobs in areas of the state that have suffered economically in recent years.

More than one point in this paragraph

One student wrote this body paragraph in response to an assignment that asked him to take a position on a current issue.

The topic sentence promises a discussion of benefits, but the detour into risks strays from the point. To revise, the student should focus on the key word in his topic sentence — *benefit* — because that signals to readers that the paragraph will examine the advantages of casino gaming. He might focus his paragraph by providing specific examples of benefits and deleting references to risks, perhaps using risks as counterpoints in a separate paragraph.

SIMILAR COMMENTS: *unfocused* • *lacks unity* • *hard to follow*

STRATEGIES FOR REVISING WHEN *YOU* HAVE MORE THAN ONE POINT IN A PARAGRAPH

1. *Reread your paragraph and ask questions.* What is the main point of the paragraph? Is there a topic sentence that signals to readers what to expect in the rest of the paragraph? Does each sentence support the topic sentence and logically follow from the one before? Have you included sentences that perhaps belong elsewhere in your paper?

2. *Remember the purpose of topic sentences*; they serve as important signposts for readers. Make sure that the wording of your topic sentence is precise and that you have enough evidence to support it in the paragraph.

More advice on unifying paragraphs: 4d

4b Develop the main point.

Though an occasional short paragraph is fine, particularly if it functions as a transition or emphasizes a point, a series of brief paragraphs suggests inadequate development. How much development is enough? That varies, depending on the writer's purpose and audience.

For example, when health columnist Jane Brody wrote a paragraph attempting to convince readers that it is impossible to lose fat quickly, she knew that she would have to present a great deal of evidence because many dieters want to believe the opposite. She did *not* write only the following:

> When you think about it, it's impossible to lose — as many diets suggest — 10 pounds of *fat* in ten days, even on a total fast. Even a moderately active person cannot lose so much weight so fast. A less active person hasn't a prayer.

This three-sentence paragraph is too skimpy to be convincing. But the paragraph that Brody did write contains enough evidence to convince even skeptical readers.

> When you think about it, it's impossible to lose — as many . . . diets suggest — 10 pounds of *fat* in ten days, even on a total fast. A pound of body fat represents 3,500 calories. To lose 1 pound of fat, you must expend 3,500 more calories than you consume. Let's say you weigh 170 pounds and, as a moderately active person, you burn 2,500 calories a day. If your diet contains only 1,500 calories, you'd have an energy deficit of 1,000 calories a day. In a week's time that would add up to a 7,000-calorie deficit, or 2 pounds of real fat. In ten days, the accumulated deficit would represent nearly 3 pounds of lost body fat. Even if you ate nothing at all for ten days and maintained your usual level of activity, your caloric deficit would add up to 25,000 calories. . . . At 3,500 calories per pound of fat, that's still only 7 pounds of lost fat.
>
> — Jane Brody, *Jane Brody's Nutrition Book*

4c Choose a suitable pattern of organization.

Although paragraphs (and indeed whole essays) may be patterned in any number of ways, certain patterns of organization occur frequently, either alone or in combination: examples and illustrations, narration, description, process, comparison and contrast, analogy, cause and effect, classification and division, and definition. These patterns (sometimes called *methods of development*) have different uses, depending on the writer's subject and purpose.

Examples and illustrations

Providing examples, perhaps the most common method of development, is appropriate whenever the reader might be tempted to ask, "For example?" Though examples are just selected instances, not a complete catalog, they are enough to suggest the truth of many topic sentences, as in the following paragraph.

> Normally my parents abided scrupulously by "The Budget," but several times a year Dad would dip into his battered black strongbox and splurge on some irrational, totally satisfying luxury. Once he bought over a hundred comic books at a flea market, doled out to us thereafter at the tantalizing rate of two a week. He always got a whole flat of pansies, Mom's favorite flower, for us to give her on Mother's Day. One day a boy stopped at our house selling fifty-cent raffle tickets on a sailboat and Dad bought every ticket the boy had left — three books' worth.
>
> — Connie Hailey, student

Illustrations are extended examples, frequently presented in story form. Because they require several sentences, they are used more sparingly than examples. When well selected, however, they can be a vivid and effective means of developing a point. The writer of the following paragraph uses illustrations to demonstrate that Harriet Tubman, the underground railroad's most famous conductor, was a genius at eluding her pursuers.

> Part of [Harriet Tubman's] strategy of conducting was, as in all battle-field operations, the knowledge of how and when to retreat. Numerous allusions have been made to her moves when she suspected that she was in danger. When she feared the party was closely pursued, she would take it for a time on a train southward bound. No one seeing Negroes going in this direction would for an instant suppose them to be fugitives. Once on her return she was at a railroad station. She saw some men reading a poster and she heard one of them reading it aloud. It was a description of her, offering a reward for her capture. She took a southbound train to avert suspicion. At another time when Harriet heard men talking about her, she pretended to read a book which

she carried. One man remarked, "This can't be the woman. The one we want can't read or write." Harriet devoutly hoped the book was right side up.

— Earl Conrad, *Harriet Tubman*

Narration

A paragraph of narration tells a story or part of a story. Narrative paragraphs are usually arranged in chronological order, but they may also contain flashbacks, interruptions that take the story back to an earlier time. The following paragraph, from Jane Goodall's *In the Shadow of Man*, recounts one of the author's experiences in the African wild.

> One evening when I was wading in the shallows of the lake to pass a rocky outcrop, I suddenly stopped dead as I saw the sinuous black body of a snake in the water. It was all of six feet long, and from the slight hood and the dark stripes at the back of the neck I knew it to be a Storm's water cobra — a deadly reptile for the bite of which there was, at that time, no serum. As I stared at it an incoming wave gently deposited part of its body on one of my feet. I remained motionless, not even breathing, until the wave rolled back into the lake, drawing the snake with it. Then I leaped out of the water as fast as I could, my heart hammering.

— Jane Goodall, *In the Shadow of Man*

Description

A descriptive paragraph sketches a portrait of a person, place, or thing by using concrete and specific details that appeal to one or more of our senses — sight, sound, smell, taste, and touch. Consider, for example, the following description of the grasshopper invasions that devastated the midwestern landscape in the late 1860s.

> They came like dive bombers out of the west. They came by the millions with the rustle of their wings roaring overhead. They came in waves, like the rolls of the sea, descending with a terrifying speed, breaking now and again like a mighty surf. They came with the force of a williwaw and they formed a huge, ominous, dark brown cloud that eclipsed the sun. They dipped and touched earth, hitting objects and people like hailstones. But they were not hail. These were *live* demons. They popped, snapped, crackled, and roared. They were dark brown, an inch or longer in length, plump in the middle and

tapered at the ends. They had transparent wings, slender legs, and two black eyes that flashed with a fierce intelligence.

— Eugene Boe, "Pioneers to Eternity"

Process

A process paragraph is structured in chronological order. A writer may choose this pattern either to describe how something is made or done or to explain to readers, step by step, how to do something. The following paragraph describes what happens when water freezes.

In school we learned that with few exceptions the solid phase of matter is more dense than the liquid phase. Water, alone among common substances, violates this rule. As water begins to cool, it contracts and becomes more dense, in a perfectly typical way. But about four degrees above the freezing point, something remarkable happens. It ceases to contract and begins expanding, becoming less dense. At the freezing point the expansion is abrupt and drastic. As water turns to ice, it adds about one-eleventh to its liquid volume.

— Chet Raymo, "Curious Stuff, Water and Ice"

Here is a paragraph explaining how to perform a "roll cast," a popular fly-fishing technique.

Begin by taking up a suitable stance, with one foot slightly in front of the other and the rod pointing down the line. Then begin a smooth, steady draw, raising your rod hand to just above shoulder height and lifting the rod to the 10:30 or 11:00 position. This steady draw allows a loop of line to form between the rod top and the water. While the line is still moving, raise the rod slightly, then punch it rapidly forward and down. The rod is now flexed and under maximum compression, and the line follows its path, bellying out slightly behind you and coming off the water close to your feet. As you power the rod down through the 3:00 position, the belly of line will roll forward. Follow through smoothly so that the line unfolds and straightens above the water.

— *The Dorling Kindersley Encyclopedia of Fishing*

Comparison and contrast

To compare two subjects is to draw attention to their similarities, although the word *compare* also has a broader meaning that includes a consideration of differences. To contrast is to focus only on differences.

Whether a paragraph stresses similarities or differences, it may be patterned in one of two ways. The two subjects may be presented one at a time, as in the following paragraph of contrast.

> So Grant and Lee were in complete contrast, representing two diametrically opposed elements in American life. Grant was the modern man emerging; beyond him, ready to come on the stage, was the great age of steel and machinery, of crowded cities and a restless, burgeoning vitality. Lee might have ridden down from the old age of chivalry, lance in hand, silken banner fluttering over his head. Each man was the perfect champion of his cause, drawing both his strengths and his weaknesses from the people he led.
>
> — Bruce Catton, "Grant and Lee: A Study in Contrasts"

Or a paragraph may proceed point by point, treating the two subjects together, one aspect at a time. The following paragraph uses the point-by-point method to contrast speeches given by Abraham Lincoln in 1860 and Barack Obama in 2008.

> Two men, two speeches. The men, both lawyers, both from Illinois, were seeking the presidency, despite what seemed their crippling connection with extremists. Each was young by modern standards for a president. Abraham Lincoln had turned fifty-one just five days before delivering his speech. Barack Obama was forty-six when he gave his. Their political experience was mainly provincial, in the Illinois legislature for both of them, and they had received little exposure at the national level — two years in the House of Representatives for Lincoln, four years in the Senate for Obama. Yet each was seeking his party's nomination against a New York senator of longer standing and greater prior reputation — Lincoln against Senator William Seward, Obama against Senator Hillary Clinton. They were both known for having opposed an initially popular war — Lincoln against President Polk's Mexican War, raised on the basis of a fictitious provocation; Obama against President Bush's Iraq War, launched on false claims that Saddam Hussein possessed WMDs [weapons of mass destruction] and had made an alliance with Osama bin Laden.
>
> — Garry Wills, "Two Speeches on Race"

Analogy

Analogies draw comparisons between items that appear to have little in common. Writers turn to analogies for a variety of reasons: to make the unfamiliar seem familiar, to provide a concrete understanding of an abstract topic, to argue a point, or to provoke fresh thoughts or changed feelings about a subject. In the following paragraph, physician Lewis Thomas draws an analogy between the behavior of ants and that of humans.

> Ants are so much like human beings as to be an embarrassment. They farm fungi, raise aphids as livestock, launch armies into wars, use chemical sprays to alarm and confuse enemies, capture slaves. The families of weaver ants engage in child labor, holding their larvae like shuttles to spin out the thread that sews the leaves together for their fungus gardens. They exchange information ceaselessly. They do everything but watch television.
>
> — Lewis Thomas, "On Societies as Organisms"

Although analogies can be a powerful tool for illuminating a subject, they should be used with caution in arguments. Just because two things may be alike in one respect, we cannot conclude that they are alike in all respects. (See p. 103.)

Cause and effect

When causes and effects are a matter of argument, they are too complex to be reduced to a simple pattern (see p. 105). However, if a writer wishes merely to describe a cause-and-effect relationship that is generally accepted, then the effect may be stated in the topic sentence, with the causes listed in the body of the paragraph.

> The fantastic water clarity of the Mount Gambier sinkholes results from several factors. The holes are fed from aquifers holding rainwater that fell decades — even centuries — ago, and that has been filtered through miles of limestone. The high level of calcium that limestone adds causes the silty detritus from dead plants and animals to cling together and settle quickly to the bottom. Abundant bottom vegetation in the shallow sinkholes also helps bind the silt. And the rapid turnover of water prohibits stagnation.
>
> — Hillary Hauser, "Exploring a Sunken Realm in Australia"

Or the paragraph may move from cause to effects, as in this paragraph from a student paper on the effects of the industrial revolution on American farms.

> The rise of rail transport in the nineteenth century forever changed American farming — for better and for worse. Farmers

who once raised crops and livestock to sustain just their own families could now make a profit by selling their goods in towns and cities miles away. These new markets improved the living standard of struggling farm families and encouraged them to seek out innovations that would increase their profits. On the downside, the competition fostered by the new markets sometimes created hostility among neighboring farm families where there had once been a spirit of cooperation. Those farmers who couldn't compete with their neighbors left farming forever, facing poverty worse than they had ever known.

— Chris Mileski, student

Classification and division

Classification is the grouping of items into categories according to some consistent principle. For example, an elementary school teacher might classify children's books according to their level of difficulty, but a librarian might group them by subject matter. The principle of classification that a writer chooses ultimately depends on the purpose of the classification. The following paragraph classifies species of electric fish.

Scientists sort electric fishes into three categories. The first comprises the strongly electric species like the marine electric rays or the freshwater African electric catfish and South American electric eel. Known since the dawn of history, these deliver a punch strong enough to stun a human. In recent years, biologists have focused on a second category: weakly electric fish in the South American and African rivers that use tiny voltages for communication and navigation. The third group contains sharks, nonelectric rays, and catfish, which do not emit a field but possess sensors that enable them to detect the minute amounts of electricity that leak out of other organisms.

— Anne and Jack Rudloe, "Electric Warfare:
The Fish That Kill with Thunderbolts"

Division takes one item and divides it into parts. As with classification, division should be made according to some consistent principle. The following passage describes the components that make up a baseball.

Like the game itself, a baseball is composed of many layers. One of the delicious joys of childhood is to take apart a baseball and examine the wonders within. You begin by removing the red cotton thread and peeling off the leather cover — which comes from the hide of a Holstein cow and has been tanned, cut, printed, and punched with holes. Beneath the cover is a thin layer of cotton string, followed by several hundred yards of woolen yarn, which makes up the bulk of the ball. Finally, in the middle is a rubber ball, or "pill," which is a little smaller than a golf ball. Slice into the rubber and you'll find the ball's heart — a cork core. The cork is from Portugal, the rubber from southeast Asia, the covers are American, and the balls are assembled in Costa Rica.

— Dan Gutman, *The Way Baseball Works*

Definition

A definition puts a word or concept into a general class and then provides enough details to distinguish it from others in the same class. In the following paragraph, the writer defines *envy* as a particular kind of desire.

> Envy is so integral and so painful a part of what animates behavior in market societies that many people have forgotten the full meaning of the word, simplifying it into one of the synonyms of desire. It is that, which may be why it flourishes in market societies: democracies of desire, they might be called, with money for ballots, stuffing permitted. But envy is more or less than desire. It begins with an almost frantic sense of emptiness inside oneself, as if the pump of one's heart were sucking on air. One has to be blind to perceive the emptiness, of course, but that's just what envy is, a selective blindness. *Invidia*, Latin for envy, translates as "non-sight," and Dante has the envious plodding along under cloaks of lead, their eyes sewn shut with leaden wire. What they are blind to is what they have, God-given and humanly nurtured, in themselves.

— Nelson W. Aldrich Jr., *Old Money*

4d Make paragraphs coherent.

When sentences and paragraphs flow from one to another without discernible bumps, gaps, or shifts, they are said to be coherent. Coherence can be improved by strengthening the ties between old information and new. A number of techniques for strengthening those ties are detailed in this section.

Linking ideas clearly

Readers expect to learn a paragraph's main point in a topic sentence early in the paragraph. Then, as they move into the body of the paragraph, they expect to encounter specific details, facts, or examples that support the topic sentence — either directly or indirectly. In the following paragraph, all of the sentences following the topic sentence directly support it.

> A passenger list of the early years [of the Orient Express] would read like a *Who's Who of the World*, from art to politics. Sarah Bernhardt and her Italian counterpart Eleonora Duse used the train to thrill the stages of Europe. For musicians there were Toscanini and Mahler. Dancers Nijinsky and Pavlova were there, while lesser performers like Harry Houdini and the girls of the Ziegfeld Follies also rode the rails. Violinists were allowed to practice on the train, and occasionally one might see trapeze artists hanging like bats from the baggage racks.
>
> — Barnaby Conrad III, "Train of Kings"

If a sentence does not support the topic sentence directly, readers expect it to support another sentence in the paragraph and therefore to support the topic sentence indirectly. The following paragraph begins with a topic sentence. The highlighted sentences are direct supports, and the rest of the sentences are indirect supports.

> Though the open-space classroom works for many children, it is not practical for my son, David. First, David is hyperactive. When he was placed in an open-space classroom, he became distracted and confused. He was tempted to watch the movement going on around him instead of concentrating on his own work. Second, David has a tendency to transpose letters and numbers, a tendency that can be overcome only by individual attention from the instructor. In the open classroom he was moved from teacher to teacher, with each one responsible for a different subject. No single teacher worked with David long enough to diagnose the problem, let alone help him with it. Finally, David is not a highly motivated learner. In the open classroom, he was graded "at his own level," not by criteria for a certain grade. He could receive a B in reading and still be a grade level behind, because he was doing satisfactory work "at his own level."
>
> — Margaret Smith, student

Repeating key words

Repetition of key words is an important technique for gaining coherence. To prevent repetitions from becoming dull, you can

use variations of a key word (*hike, hiker, hiking*), pronouns referring to the word (*gamblers . . . they*), and synonyms (*run, spring,
race, dash*). In the following paragraph describing plots among
indentured servants in the seventeenth century, historian Richard Hofstadter binds sentences together by repeating the key
word *plots* and echoing it with a variety of synonyms (which are
highlighted).

> Plots hatched by several servants to run away together
> occurred mostly in the plantation colonies, and the few recorded
> servant uprisings were entirely limited to those colonies. Virginia
> had been forced from its very earliest years to take stringent steps
> against mutinous plots, and severe punishments for such behavior
> were recorded. Most servant plots occurred in the seventeenth
> century: a contemplated uprising was nipped in the bud in York
> County in 1661; apparently led by some left-wing offshoots of the
> Great Rebellion, servants plotted an insurrection in Gloucester
> County in 1663, and four leaders were condemned and executed;
> some discontented servants apparently joined Bacon's Rebellion in
> the 1670's. In the 1680's the planters became newly apprehensive
> of discontent among the servants "owing to their great necessities
> and want of clothes," and it was feared they would rise up
> and plunder the storehouses and ships; in 1682 there were
> plant-cutting riots in which servants and laborers, as well as some
> planters, took part.
>
> — Richard Hofstadter, *America at 1750*

Using parallel structures

Parallel structures are frequently used within sentences to underscore the similarity of ideas (see 9). They may also be used
to bind together a series of sentences expressing similar information. In the following passage describing folk beliefs, anthro-
pologist Margaret Mead presents similar information in parallel
grammatical form.

> Actually, almost every day, even in the most sophisticated
> home, something is likely to happen that evokes the memory of
> some old folk belief. The salt spills. A knife falls to the floor. Your
> nose tickles. Then perhaps, with a slightly embarrassed smile, the
> person who spilled the salt tosses a pinch over his left shoulder. Or
> someone recites the old rhyme, "Knife falls, gentleman calls." Or as
> you rub your nose you think, That means a letter. I wonder who's
> writing?
>
> — Margaret Mead, "New Superstitions for Old"

Maintaining consistency

Coherence suffers whenever a draft shifts confusingly from one point of view to another or from one verb tense to another. (See 13.) In addition, coherence can suffer when new information is introduced with the subject of each sentence. For advice on avoiding shifts, see 13.

Providing transitions

Transitions are bridges between what has been read and what is about to be read. Transitions help readers move from sentence to sentence; they also alert readers to more global connections of ideas — those between paragraphs or even larger blocks of text.

Sentence-level transitions   Certain words and phrases signal connections between (or within) sentences. Frequently used transitions are included in the chart below.

Skilled writers use transitional expressions with care, making sure, for example, not to use *consequently* when *also* would be more precise. They are also careful to select transitions with an appropriate tone, perhaps preferring *so* to *thus* in an informal piece, *in summary* to *in short* for a scholarly essay.

In the following paragraph, taken from an argument that dinosaurs had the "'right-sized' brains for reptiles of their body size," biologist Stephen Jay Gould uses transitions (highlighted) with skill.

> I don't wish to deny that the flattened, minuscule head of large bodied Stegosaurus houses little brain from our subjective, top-heavy perspective, but I do wish to assert that we should not expect more of the beast. First of all, large animals have relatively smaller brains than related, small animals. The correlation of brain size with body size among kindred animals (all reptiles, all mammals, for example) is remarkably regular. As we move from small to large animals, from mice to elephants or small lizards to Komodo dragons, brain size increases, but not so fast as body size. In other words, bodies grow faster than brains, and large animals have low ratios of brain weight to body weight. In fact, brains grow only about two-thirds as fast as bodies. Since we have no reason to believe that large animals are consistently stupider than their smaller relatives, we must conclude that large animals require relatively less brain to do as well as smaller animals. If we do not recognize this relationship, we are likely to underestimate the mental power of very large animals, dinosaurs in particular.
>
> — Stephen Jay Gould, "Were Dinosaurs Dumb?"

Common transitions

To show addition: and, also, besides, further, furthermore, in addition, moreover, next, too, first, second

To give examples: for example, for instance, to illustrate, in fact

To compare: also, in the same manner, similarly, likewise

To contrast: but, however, on the other hand, in contrast, nevertheless, still, even though, on the contrary, yet, although

To summarize or conclude: in short, in summary, in conclusion, to sum up, therefore

To show time: after, as, before, next, during, later, finally, meanwhile, then, when, while, immediately

To show place or direction: above, below, beyond, nearby, opposite, close, to the left

To indicate logical relationship: if, so, therefore, consequently, thus, as a result, for this reason, because, since

Paragraph-level transitions Paragraph-level transitions usually link the *first* sentence of a new paragraph with the *first* sentence of the previous paragraph. In other words, the topic sentences signal global connections.

Look for opportunities to allude to the subject of a previous paragraph (as summed up in its topic sentence) in the topic sentence of the next one. In his essay "Little Green Lies," Jonathan H. Alder uses this strategy in the following topic sentences, which appear in a passage describing the benefits of plastic packaging.

> Consider aseptic packaging, the synthetic packaging for the "juice boxes" so many children bring to school with their lunch. One criticism of aseptic packaging is that it is nearly impossible to recycle, yet on almost every other count, aseptic packaging is environmentally preferable to the packaging alternatives. Not only do aseptic containers not require refrigeration to keep their contents from spoiling, but their manufacture requires less than one-10th the energy of making glass bottles.
> What is true for juice boxes is also true for other forms of synthetic packaging. The use of polystyrene, which is commonly (and mistakenly) referred to as "Styrofoam," can reduce food waste dramatically due to its insulating properties. (Thanks to these properties, polystyrene cups are much preferred over paper for that morning cup of coffee.) Polystyrene also requires significantly fewer resources to produce than its paper counterpart.

PRACTICE hackerhandbooks.com/rules
> The writing process > 4–3

Transitions between blocks of text In long essays, you will need to alert readers to connections between blocks of text that are more than one paragraph long. You can do this by inserting transitional sentences or short paragraphs at key points in the essay. Here, for example, is a transitional paragraph from a student research paper. It announces that the first part of the paper has come to a close and the second part is about to begin.

> Although the great apes have demonstrated significant language skills, one central question remains: Can they be taught to use that uniquely human language tool we call grammar, to learn the difference, for instance, between "ape bite human" and "human bite ape"? In other words, can an ape create a sentence?

Another strategy to help readers move from one block of text to another is to insert headings in your essay. Headings, which usually sit above blocks of text, allow you to announce a new topic boldly, without the need for subtle transitions. (See 50b.)

4e If necessary, adjust paragraph length.

Most readers feel comfortable reading paragraphs that range between one hundred and two hundred words. Shorter paragraphs require too much starting and stopping, and longer ones strain readers' attention span. There are exceptions to this guideline, however. Paragraphs longer than two hundred words frequently appear in scholarly writing, where scholars explore complex ideas. Paragraphs shorter than one hundred words occur in newspapers because of narrow columns; in informal essays to quicken the pace; and in business writing and Web sites, where readers routinely skim for main ideas.

In an essay, the first and last paragraphs will ordinarily be the introduction and the conclusion. These special-purpose paragraphs are likely to be shorter than the paragraphs in the body of the essay. Typically, the body paragraphs will follow the essay's outline: one paragraph per point in short essays, several paragraphs per point in longer ones. Some ideas require more development than others, however, so it is best to be flexible. If an idea stretches to a length unreasonable for a paragraph, you should

Revising with comments

Need a transition

UNDERSTANDING THE COMMENT

When readers point out that you "need a transition," the comment often signals that they need bridges — transitional words — to follow the progression from one idea to the next.

> The United States of America is one of many countries in the world that were created by immigration. This essential characteristic is perhaps America's greatest weakness and its greatest strength. Our country has the potential to be swallowed up by the diverse beliefs, values, and social practices of its immigrants so that nothing is common to anyone. America can benefit from embracing the amazing cultural diversity within itself.   *Need a transition*

In this body paragraph, a student responded to an assignment that asked him to analyze a central feature of American identity.

Transitional words or phrases help readers follow the connections between sentences and ideas. To revise, the student might begin by asking: What idea is expressed in each sentence? Does each sentence point clearly back to the previous one? If not, what words or phrases might be added to help readers see how one idea moves to the next? The answers to these questions will help the student recognize that his last two sentences contrast with each other (one about weaknesses, one about strengths) but that he needs to provide a transitional word or phrase, such as *however*, before the last sentence to make the contrast clear.

SIMILAR COMMENTS: *something missing?* • *missing connection* • *transition?*

REVISING WHEN *YOU* NEED A TRANSITION BETWEEN SENTENCES

1. *Read your paragraph aloud* to a peer or a tutor. Ask your listeners what is missing between sentences that would help them follow the progression from one idea to the next.

2. *Ask questions.* What words or phrases might be added to help readers move from sentence to sentence? For instance, do you need transitions to show addition (*furthermore*), to give examples (*specifically*), to compare (*similarly*), to contrast (*however*), or to summarize (*in summary*)?

3. *Revise with an appropriate transition* to show connections between ideas.

More help with transitions: pages 64–66

divide the paragraph, even if you have presented comparable points in the essay in single paragraphs.

Paragraph breaks are not always made for strictly logical reasons. Writers use them for the following reasons as well.

REASONS FOR BEGINNING A NEW PARAGRAPH

- to mark off the introduction and the conclusion
- to signal a shift to a new idea
- to indicate an important shift in time or place
- to emphasize a point (by placing it at the beginning or the end, not in the middle, of a paragraph)
- to highlight a contrast
- to signal a change of speakers (in dialogue)
- to provide readers with a needed pause
- to break up text that looks too dense

Beware of using too many short, choppy paragraphs, however. Readers want to see how your ideas connect, and they become irritated when you break their momentum by forcing them to pause every few sentences. Here are some reasons you might have for combining some of the paragraphs in a rough draft.

REASONS FOR COMBINING PARAGRAPHS

- to clarify the essay's organization
- to connect closely related ideas
- to bind together text that looks too choppy

Academic Writing

5 Writing about texts

The word *texts* can refer to a variety of works, including essays, articles, government reports, books, Web sites, advertisements, and photographs. Most assignments that ask you to respond to a text call for a summary or an analysis or both.

A summary is neutral in tone and demonstrates that you have understood the author's key ideas. Assignments calling for an analysis of a text vary widely, but they usually ask you to look at how the text's parts contribute to its central argument or purpose, often with the aim of judging its evidence or overall effect.

When you write about a text, you will need to read it — or, in the case of a visual text, view it — several times to discover meaning. Two techniques will help you move beyond a superficial first reading: (1) annotating the text with your observations and questions and (2) outlining the text's key points. These techniques will help you analyze both written and visual texts.

5a Read actively: Annotate the text.

Read actively by jotting down your questions and thoughts in a notebook or in the margins of the text or visual. Use a pencil instead of a highlighter; with a pencil you can underline key concepts, mark points, or circle elements that intrigue you. If you change your mind, you can erase your early annotations and replace them with new ones. To annotate an electronic document, take notes in a separate file or use software features to highlight, underline, or insert comments.

As you write

Using the guidelines for active reading on page 71, annotate an assigned text. Pay particular attention to what surprises or intrigues you about the text and what you notice on a second reading. How do your annotations help you understand the text? If you could talk with the author of the text, what one or two questions would you pose?

THE WRITING CENTER hackerhandbooks.com/rules
> Resources for writers and tutors > Tips from writing tutors:
Benefits of reading

Guidelines for active reading

Identify the basic features and structure of a text.

- What kind of text are you reading: An essay? An editorial? A scholarly article? An advertisement? A photograph? A Web site?
- What is the author's purpose: To inform? To persuade? To call to action?
- Who is the audience? How does the author appeal to the audience?
- What is the author's thesis? What question does the text attempt to answer?
- What evidence does the author provide to support the thesis?
- What key terms does the author define?

Note details that surprise, puzzle, or intrigue you.

- Has the author revealed a fact or made a point that counters your assumptions? Is anything surprising?
- Has the author made a generalization you disagree with? Can you think of evidence that would challenge the generalization?
- Do you see any contradictions or inconsistencies in the text?
- Does the text contain words, statements, or phrases that you don't understand? If so, what reference materials do you need to consult?

Read and reread to discover meaning.

- What do you notice on a second or third reading that you didn't notice earlier?
- Does the text raise questions that it does not resolve?
- If you could address the author directly, what questions would you pose? Where do you agree and disagree with the author? Why?

Apply additional critical thinking strategies to visual texts.

- What first strikes you about the visual text? What elements do you notice immediately?
- Who or what is the main subject of the visual text?
- What colors and textures dominate?
- What is in the background? In the foreground?
- What role, if any, do words or numbers play in the text?
- When was the visual created or the information collected?

On this page and on page 73 are an article from *CQ Researcher*, a newsletter about social and political issues, and an advertisement, both annotated by students. The students, Emilia Sanchez and Ren Yoshida, were assigned to analyze these texts. They began by reading actively.

ANNOTATED ARTICLE

Big Box Stores Are Bad for Main Street

BETSY TAYLOR

There is plenty of reason to be concerned about the proliferation of Wal-Marts and other so-called "big box" stores. The question, however, is not whether or not these types of stores create jobs (although several studies claim they produce a net job loss in local communities) or whether they ultimately save consumers money. The real concern about having a 25-acre slab of concrete with a 100,000 square foot box of stuff land on a town is whether it's good for a community's soul.

Opening strategy— the problem is not x, it's y.

Sentimental— what is a community's soul?

The worst thing about "big boxes" is that they have a tendency to produce Ross Perot's famous "big sucking sound"—sucking the life out of cities and small towns across the country. On the other hand, small businesses are great for a community. They offer more personal service; they won't threaten to pack up and leave town if they don't get tax breaks, free roads and other blandishments; and small-business owners are much more responsive to a customer's needs. (Ever try to complain about bad service or poor quality products to the president of Home Depot?)

Lumps all big boxes together.

Assumes all small businesses are attentive.

Logic problem? Why couldn't customer complain to store manager?

Yet, if big boxes are so bad, why are they so successful? One glaring reason is that we've become a nation of hyperconsumers, and the big-box boys know this. Downtown shopping districts comprised of small businesses take some of the efficiency out of overconsumption. There's all that hassle of having to travel from store to store, and having to pull out your credit card so many times. Occasionally, we even find ourselves chatting with the shopkeeper, wandering into a coffee shop to visit with a friend or otherwise wasting precious time that could be spent on acquiring more stuff.

True?

Taylor wishes for a time that is long gone or never was.

But let's face it—bustling, thriving city centers are fun. They breathe life into a community. They allow cities and towns to stand out from each other. They provide an atmosphere for people to interact with each other that just cannot be found at Target, or Wal-Mart or Home Depot.

Community vs. economy. What about prices?

Is it anti-American to be against having a retail giant set up shop in one's community? Some people would say so. On the other hand, if you board up Main Street, what's left of America?

Ends with emotional appeal.

ANNOTATED ADVERTISEMENT

What is being exchanged?

"Empowering" — why in an elegant font? Who is empowering farmers?

"Farmers" in all capital letters — shows strength?

Straightforward design and not much text.

Outstretched hands. Is she giving a gift? Inviting a partnership?

Raw coffee is earthy, natural.

Positive verbs: consumers choose, join, empower; farmers stay, care, farm, support, plan.

When you choose Equal Exchange fairly traded coffee, tea or chocolate, you join a network that empowers farmers in Latin America, Africa, and Asia to:

- Stay on their land
- Care for the environment
- Farm organically
- Support their family
- Plan for the future

www.equalexchange.coop

Photo: Jesus Choqueheranca de Quevero,
Coffee farmer & CEPICAFE Cooperative member, Peru

Source: Equal Exchange.

5b Sketch a brief outline of the text.

After reading, rereading, and annotating a text, try to outline it. Seeing how the author has constructed a text can help you understand it. As you sketch an outline, pay special attention to the text's thesis (central idea) and its topic sentences. The thesis of a written text usually appears in the introduction, often in the first or second paragraph. Topic sentences can be found at the beginnings of most body paragraphs, where they announce a shift to a new topic. (See 2a and 4a.)

In your outline, put the author's thesis and key points in your own words. Here, for example, is the outline that Emilia Sanchez developed as she prepared to write her summary and analysis of the text on page 72. Notice that Sanchez's informal outline does not trace the author's ideas paragraph by paragraph; instead, it sums up the article's key points.

OUTLINE OF "BIG BOX STORES ARE BAD FOR MAIN STREET"

Thesis: Whether or not they take jobs away from a community or offer low prices to consumers, we should be worried about "big-box" stores like Wal-Mart, Target, and Home Depot because they harm communities by taking the life out of downtown shopping districts.

I. Small businesses are better for cities and towns than big-box stores are.

   A. Small businesses offer personal service, but big-box stores do not.

   B. Small businesses don't make demands on community resources as big-box stores do.

   C. Small businesses respond to customer concerns, but big-box stores do not.

II. Big-box stores are successful because they cater to consumption at the expense of benefits to the community.

   A. Buying everything in one place is convenient.

   B. Shopping at small businesses may be inefficient, but it provides opportunities for socializing.

   C. Downtown shopping districts give each city or town a special identity.

Conclusion: Although some people say that it's anti-American to oppose big-box stores, actually these stores threaten the communities that make up America by encouraging buying at the expense of the traditional interactions of Main Street.

A visual often doesn't state an explicit thesis or an explicit line of reasoning. Instead, you must sometimes infer the meaning beneath the image's surface and interpret its central point and supporting ideas from the elements of its design. One way to outline a visual text is to try to define its purpose and sketch a list of its key elements. Here, for example, are the key features that Ren Yoshida identified for the advertisement printed on page 73. Note that the student is able to draw a preliminary conclusion about the advertisement.

OUTLINE OF EQUAL EXCHANGE ADVERTISEMENT

Purpose: To persuade readers that they can improve the lives of organic farmers and their families by purchasing Equal Exchange coffee.

Key features:

- The farmer's heart-shaped hands are outstretched, offering the viewer partnership and the product of her hard work.
- The raw coffee is surprisingly fruitlike and fresh—natural and healthy looking.
- Words above and below the photograph describe the equal exchange between farmers and consumers.
- Consumer support leads to a higher quality of life for the farmers and for all people, since these farmers care for the environment and plan for the future.
- The simplicity of the design echoes the simplicity of the exchange. The consumer only has to buy a cup of coffee to make a difference.

Conclusion: Equal Exchange is selling more than a product—coffee. It is selling the idea that together farmers and consumers hold the future of land, environment, farms, and family in their hands.

5c Summarize to demonstrate your understanding.

Your goal in summarizing a text is to state the work's main ideas and key points simply, briefly, and accurately in your own words. Writing a summary does not require you to judge the author's ideas; it requires you to *understand* the author's ideas. If you have sketched a brief outline of the text (see 5b), refer to it as you draft your summary.

> **Making the most of your handbook**
> Summarizing is a key research skill.
> ▸ Summarizing without plagiarizing: 55c
> ▸ Putting summaries and paraphrases in your own words: 57c, 62c

To summarize a written text, first find the author's central idea — the thesis. Then divide the whole piece into a few major and perhaps minor ideas. Since a summary must be fairly short, you must make judgments about what is most important.

Guidelines for writing a summary

- In the first sentence, mention the title of the text, the name of the author, and the author's thesis or the visual's central point.
- Maintain a neutral tone; be objective.
- As you present the author's ideas, use the third-person point of view and the present tense: *Taylor argues. . . .* (If you are writing in APA style, see 62c.)
- Keep your focus on the text. Don't state the author's ideas as if they were your own.
- Put all or most of your summary in your own words; if you borrow a phrase or a sentence from the text, put it in quotation marks and give the page number in parentheses.
- Limit yourself to presenting the text's key points.
- Be concise; make every word count.

To summarize a visual text, begin with essential information such as who created the visual, who the intended audience is, where the visual appeared, and when it was created. Briefly explain the visual's main point or purpose and identify its key features (see p. 75).

Following is Emilia Sanchez's summary of the article that is printed on page 72.

summarizing • using your own words •
analyzing • interpreting • including your ideas
texts
5d
77

In her essay "Big Box Stores Are Bad for Main Street," Betsy Taylor argues that chain stores harm communities by taking the life out of downtown shopping districts. Explaining that a community's "soul" is more important than low prices or consumer convenience, she argues that small businesses are better than stores like Home Depot and Target because they emphasize personal interactions and don't place demands on a community's resources. Taylor asserts that big-box stores are successful because "we've become a nation of hyper-consumers" (1011), although the convenience of shopping in these stores comes at the expense of benefits to the community. She concludes by suggesting that it's not "anti-American" to oppose big-box stores because the damage they inflict on downtown shopping districts extends to America itself.

— Emilia Sanchez, student

5d Analyze to demonstrate your critical thinking.

Whereas a summary most often answers the question of *what* a text says, an analysis looks at *how* a text makes its point.

Typically, an analysis takes the form of an essay that makes its own argument about a text. Include an introduction that briefly summarizes the text, a thesis that states your own judgment about the text, and body paragraphs that support your thesis with evidence. If you are analyzing a visual, examine it as a whole and then reflect on how the individual elements contribute to its overall meaning. If you have written a summary of the text or visual, you may find it useful to refer to the main points of the summary as you write your analysis.

> **Making the most of your handbook**
> When you analyze a text, you weave words and ideas from the source into your own writing.
> ► Guidelines for using quotation marks: 55c
> ► Quoting or paraphrasing: 57, 62
> ► Using signal phrases: 58b, 63b

Using interpretation in an analysis

Student writer Emilia Sanchez begins her essay about Betsy Taylor's article (see p. 72) by summarizing Taylor's argument. She

Revising with comments
Summarize less, analyze more

UNDERSTANDING THE COMMENT

When readers point out that you need to "summarize less, analyze more," the comment often signals that they want to hear your interpretation of a text, not a summary of the text itself.

> Growing up as a borderlander, I have always considered myself bilingual. Reading "How to Tame a Wild Tongue" by Gloria Anzaldúa made me rethink that label. In the *"El lenguaje de la frontera"* section of the essay, Anzaldúa explains the origins of Chicano Spanish, a "border tongue" (326). Then she says that most Chicanos actually speak as many as eight languages. Anzaldúa lists these languages and then tells which languages she speaks with which people in her life. *Summarize less, analyze more* For example, she speaks Tex-Mex with friends, Chicano Texas Spanish with her mother, and working-class English at school (327). Finally, she talks about her experience with speaking made-up languages.

One student wrote this body paragraph in response to an assignment that asked students to analyze Gloria Anzaldúa's essay "How to Tame a Wild Tongue."

The student writer needs to go beyond summary to offer his insights about Anzaldúa's text. To revise this paragraph, the student might begin by underlining the verbs in his own sentences: *explains*, *says*, *lists*, *tells*, and *talks*. These sentences simply restate what Anzaldúa has written. Although the student may need to summarize briefly, he should move quickly to exploring the meaning of the text. In his analysis, the student might ask questions about Anzaldúa's strategies. For instance, why does she combine Spanish with English? Or why does she list the eight separate languages that most Chicanos speak?

SIMILAR COMMENTS: *too much summary* • *show, don't tell* • *go deeper*

REVISING WHEN *YOU* NEED TO SUMMARIZE LESS AND ANALYZE MORE

1. *Reread your paragraph* and highlight the sentences that summarize. Then, in a different color, highlight the sentences that contain your analysis. (Think about the differences between summary and analysis: Summary answers the question of *what* a text says; analysis offers a judgment or an interpretation of the text.)

2. *Reread the text* (or passages of the text) that you are analyzing, paying attention to the language and structure of the text.

3. *Ask questions.* What strategies does the author use? How do these strategies convey the meaning of the text? What insights can you convey to your readers about the text? How can you deepen your readers' understanding of the text?

More advice on analyzing a text: 5d and 66b

---

then states her own thesis, or claim, which offers her judgment of Taylor's article, and begins her analysis. In her first body paragraph, Sanchez interprets Taylor's use of language.

Topic sentence includes Sanchez's claim.

Quoted material shows Taylor's language and is placed in quotation marks.

Taylor's use of colorful language reveals that she has a sentimental view of American society and does not understand economic realities. In her first paragraph, Taylor refers to a big-box store as a "25-acre slab of concrete with a 100,000 square foot box of stuff" that "land[s] on a town," evoking images of a powerful monster crushing the American way of life (1011). But she oversimplifies a complex issue. Taylor does not consider. . . .

Signal phrase introduces a quotation from the text.

Quotation is followed by Sanchez's interpretation of Taylor's language.

Transition to Sanchez's next point.

5e Sample student essay: Analysis of an article

Beginning on page 80 is Emilia Sanchez's analysis of the article by Betsy Taylor (see p. 72). Sanchez used Modern Language Association (MLA) style to format her paper and cite the source.

Sanchez 1

Emilia Sanchez

Professor Goodwin

English 10

23 October 2009

Rethinking Big-Box Stores

Opening briefly summarizes the article's purpose and thesis.

In her essay "Big Box Stores Are Bad for Main Street," Betsy Taylor focuses not on the economic effects of large chain stores but on the effects these stores have on the "soul" of America. She argues that stores like Home Depot, Target, and Wal-Mart are bad for America because they draw people out of downtown shopping districts and cause them to focus on consumption. In contrast, she believes that small businesses are good for America because they provide personal attention, encourage community interaction, and make each city

Sanchez begins to analyze Taylor's argument.

and town unique. But Taylor's argument is unconvincing because it is based on sentimentality—on idealized images of a quaint Main Street—rather than on the roles that businesses play in consumers' lives and communities.

Thesis expresses Sanchez's judgment of Taylor's article.

By ignoring the complex economic relationship between large chain stores and their communities, Taylor incorrectly assumes that simply getting rid of big-box stores would have a positive effect on America's communities.

Signal phrase introduces quotations from the source; Sanchez uses an MLA in-text citation.

Taylor's use of colorful language reveals that she has a sentimental view of American society and does not understand economic realities. In her first paragraph, Taylor refers to a big-box store as a "25-acre slab of concrete with a 100,000 square foot box of stuff" that "land[s] on a town," evoking images of a powerful monster crushing the American way of life (1011). But she oversimplifies

Sanchez 2

a complex issue. Taylor does not consider that many
downtown business districts failed long before chain stores
moved in, when factories and mills closed and workers lost
their jobs. In cities with struggling economies, big-box
stores can actually provide much-needed jobs. Similarly,
while Taylor blames big-box stores for harming local
economies by asking for tax breaks, free roads, and other
perks, she doesn't acknowledge that these stores also
enter into economic partnerships with the surrounding
communities by offering financial benefits to schools and
hospitals.

 Taylor's assumption that shopping in small
businesses is always better for the customer also seems
driven by nostalgia for an old-fashioned Main Street
rather than by the facts. While she may be right that
many small businesses offer personal service and are
responsive to customer complaints, she does not consider
that many customers appreciate the service at big-box
stores. Just as customer service is better at some small
businesses than at others, it is impossible to generalize
about service at all big-box stores. For example,
customers depend on the lenient return policies and the
wide variety of products at stores like Target and Home
Depot.

 Taylor blames big-box stores for encouraging American
"hyper-consumerism," but she oversimplifies by equating
big-box stores with bad values and small businesses with
good values. Like her other points, this claim ignores the
economic and social realities of American society today.
Big-box stores do not force Americans to buy more. By
offering lower prices in a convenient setting, however,

Sanchez begins
to identify and
challenge Taylor's
assumptions.

Transition to
another point in
Sanchez's analysis.

Clear topic
sentence
announces a shift
to a new topic.

Sanchez refutes
Taylor's claim.

they allow consumers to save time and purchase goods they might not be able to afford from small businesses. The existence of more small businesses would not change what most Americans can afford, nor would it reduce their desire to buy affordable merchandise.

> Sanchez treats the author fairly.

Taylor may be right that some big-box stores have a negative impact on communities and that small businesses offer certain advantages. But she ignores the economic conditions that support big-box stores as well as the fact that Main Street was in decline before the big-box store arrived. Getting rid of big-box stores will not bring back a simpler America populated by thriving, unique Main Streets; in reality, Main Street will not survive if consumers cannot afford to shop there.

> Conclusion returns to the thesis and shows the wider significance of Sanchez's analysis.

Work Cited

> Work cited page is in MLA style.

Taylor, Betsy. "Big Box Stores Are Bad for Main Street." *CQ Researcher* 9.44 (1999): 1011. Print.

Guidelines for analyzing a text

Written texts

Instructors who ask you to analyze an essay or an article often expect you to address some of the following questions.

- What is the author's thesis or central idea? Who is the audience?
- What questions (stated or unstated) does the author address?
- How does the author structure the text? What are the key parts, and how do they relate to one another and to the thesis?
- What strategies has the author used to generate interest in the argument and to persuade readers of its merit?
- What evidence does the author use to support the thesis? How persuasive is the evidence? (See 6d and 6e.)
- Does the author anticipate objections and counter opposing views? (See 6f.)
- Does the author use any faulty reasoning? (See 7a.)

Visual texts

If you are analyzing a visual text, the following additional questions will help you evaluate an image's purpose and meaning.

- What confuses, surprises, or intrigues you about the image?
- What is the source of the visual, and who created it? What is its purpose?
- What clues suggest the visual text's intended audience? How does the image appeal to its audience?
- If the text is an advertisement, what product is it selling? Does it attempt to sell an idea or a message as well?
- If the visual text includes words, how do the words contribute to the meaning?
- How do design elements — colors, shapes, perspective, background, foreground — help convey the visual text's meaning or serve its purpose?

As you write

Using the guidelines for analyzing visual texts on this page, study a visual of your choice—for example, a photograph, a cartoon, or an advertisement. Use the guidelines to help you determine the visual's purpose and meaning. Discuss your observations with a classmate.

6   Constructing reasonable arguments

In writing an argument, you take a stand on a debatable issue. The question being debated might be a matter of public policy:

> Should companies be allowed to advertise on public school property?
>
> What is the least dangerous way to dispose of hazardous waste?
>
> Should motorists be banned from texting while driving?
>
> Should a state limit the number of charter schools?

On such questions, reasonable people may disagree.

Reasonable men and women also disagree about many scholarly issues. Psychologists debate the role of genes and environment in determining behavior; historians interpret the causes of the Civil War quite differently; biologists challenge one another's predictions about the effects of global warming.

When you construct a *reasonable* argument, your goal is not simply to win or to have the last word. Your aim is to explain your understanding of the truth about a subject or to propose the best

---

Academic English Some cultures value writers who argue with force; other cultures value writers who argue subtly or indirectly. Academic audiences in the United States will expect your writing to be assertive and confident — neither aggressive nor passive. You can create an assertive tone by acknowledging different positions and supporting your ideas with specific evidence.

TOO AGGRESSIVE	Of course only registered organ donors should be eligible for organ transplants. It's selfish and shortsighted to think otherwise.
TOO PASSIVE	I might be wrong, but I think that maybe people should have to register as organ donors if they want to be considered for a transplant.
ASSERTIVE	If only registered organ donors are eligible for transplants, more people will register as donors.

If you are uncertain about the tone of your work, ask for help at your school's writing center.

solution to a problem—without being needlessly combative. In constructing your argument, you join a conversation with other writers and readers. Your aim is to convince readers to reconsider their positions by offering new reasons to question existing viewpoints.

6a Examine your issue's social and intellectual contexts.

Arguments appear in social and intellectual contexts. Public policy debates arise in social contexts and are conducted among groups with competing values and interests. For example, the debate over offshore oil drilling has been renewed in the United States in light of skyrocketing energy costs and terrorism concerns—with environmentalists, policymakers, oil company executives, and consumers all weighing in on the argument. Most public policy debates also have intellectual dimensions that address scientific or theoretical questions. In the case of the drilling issue, geologists, oceanographers, and economists all contribute their expertise.

Scholarly debates play out in intellectual contexts, but they have a social dimension as well. For example, scholars respond to the contributions of other specialists in the field, often building on others' views and refining them, but at times challenging them.

Because many of your readers will be aware of the social and intellectual contexts in which your issue is grounded, you will be at a disadvantage if you are not informed. That's why it is a good idea to conduct some

> **Making the most of your handbook**
> Supporting your claims with evidence from sources strengthens your argument.
> ▶ Conducting research: 53

research before preparing your argument; consulting even a few sources can deepen your understanding of the debates surrounding your topic. For example, the student whose paper appears on pages 96–101 became more knowledgeable about his issue—the shift from print to online news—after reading and annotating a few sources.

As you write

Select a public policy debate and locate two documents arguing different sides of the debate. Briefly summarize the opposing positions. Which position seems more reasonable to you? Which author seems more credible? Why? Join the conversation by writing a letter to one of the authors to explain your position in the debate.

6b View your audience as a panel of jurors.

Do not assume that your audience already agrees with you; instead, envision skeptical readers who, like a panel of jurors, will make up their minds after listening to all sides of the argument. If you are arguing a public policy issue, aim your paper at readers who represent a variety of positions. In the case of the debate over offshore drilling, for example, imagine a jury that represents those who have a stake in the matter: environmentalists, policymakers, oil company executives, and consumers.

At times, you can deliberately narrow your audience. If you are working within a word limit, for example, you might not have the space in which to address all the concerns surrounding the offshore drilling debate. Or you might be primarily interested in reaching one segment of a general audience, such as consumers. In such instances, you can still view your audience as a panel of jurors; the jury will simply be a less diverse group.

In the case of scholarly debates, you will be addressing readers who share your interest in a discipline, such as literature or psychology. Such readers belong to a group with an agreed-upon way of investigating and talking about issues. Though they generally agree about disciplinary methods of asking questions and share specialized vocabulary, scholars in an academic discipline often disagree about particular issues. Once you see how they disagree about your issue, you should be able to imagine a jury that reflects the variety of positions they hold.

6c In your introduction, establish credibility and state your position.

When you are constructing an argument, make sure your introduction contains a thesis that states your position on the issue you have chosen to debate. In the sentences leading up to the thesis, establish your credibility with readers by showing that you are knowledgeable about the issue and fair-minded. If possible, build common ground with readers who may not at first agree with your views, and show them why they should consider your thesis.

> **Making the most of your handbook**
> When you write an argument, you state your position in a thesis.
> ▶ Writing effective thesis statements: 1c, 2a

In the following introduction, student Kevin Smith presents himself as someone worth listening to. Because Smith introduces both sides of the debate, readers are likely to approach his essay with an open mind.

Smith shows that he is familiar with the legal issues surrounding school prayer.

Although the Supreme Court has ruled against prayer in public schools on First Amendment grounds, many people still feel that prayer should be allowed. Such people value prayer as a practice central to their faith and believe that prayer is a way for schools to reinforce moral principles. They also compellingly point out a paradox in the First Amendment itself: at what point does the separation of church and state restrict the freedom of those who wish to practice their religion? What proponents of school prayer fail to realize, however, is that the Supreme Court's decision, although it was made on legal grounds, makes sense on religious grounds as well. Prayer is too important to be trusted to our public schools. — Kevin Smith, student

Smith is fair-minded, presenting the views of both sides.

Smith's thesis builds common ground.

TIP: A good way to test a thesis while drafting and revising is to imagine a counterargument to your argument (see 6f). If you can't think of an opposing point of view, rethink your thesis and ask a classmate or writing center tutor to respond to your argument.

6d Back up your thesis with persuasive lines of argument.

Arguments of any complexity contain lines of argument that, when taken together, might reasonably persuade readers that the thesis has merit. The following, for example, are the main lines of argument that Sam Jacobs used in his paper about the shift from print to online news (see pp. 96–101).

CENTRAL CLAIM   Thesis: The shift from print to online news provides unprecedented opportunities for readers to become more engaged with the news, to hold journalists accountable, and to participate as producers, not simply as consumers.

(continued)

THE WRITING CENTER   hackerhandbooks.com/rules

> Resources for writers and tutors > Tips from writing tutors:
         Writing assignments;
         Writing essays in English

SUPPORTING CLAIMS

- Print news has traditionally had a one-sided relationship with its readers, delivering information for passive consumption.
- Online news invites readers to participate in a collaborative process—to question and even contribute to the content.
- Links within news stories provide transparency, allowing readers to move easily from the main story to original sources, related articles, or background materials.
- Technology has made it possible for readers to become news producers—posting text, audio, images, and video of news events.
- Citizen journalists can provide valuable information, sometimes more quickly than traditional journalists can.

If you sum up your main lines of argument, as Jacobs did, you will have a rough outline of your essay. In your paper, you will provide evidence for each of your claims.

As you write

Study Sam Jacobs's line of argument above. Draft an outline of your central claim and supporting claims, as he did. Ask a classmate to comment on the effectiveness of your thesis and claims. Do you have enough support for your thesis? Are your claims persuasive?

6e Support your claims with specific evidence.

You will need to support your central claim and any subordinate claims with evidence: facts, statistics, examples and illustrations, visuals, expert opinion, and so on. Most debatable topics require that you consult some written sources. As you read through the sources, you will learn more about the arguments and counter-arguments at the center of your debate.

Making the most of your handbook
Sources, when used responsibly, can provide supporting evidence.
- Paraphrasing, summarizing, and quoting sources: 55c
- Punctuating direct quotations: 37a
- Citing sources: 57a, 62a

Remember that you must document your sources. Documentation gives credit to the authors and shows readers how to locate a source in case they want to assess its credibility or explore the issues further.

Using facts and statistics

A fact is something that is known with certainty because it has been objectively verified: The capital of Wyoming is Cheyenne. Carbon has an atomic weight of 12. John F. Kennedy was assassinated on November 22, 1963. Statistics are collections of numerical facts: Alcohol abuse is a factor in nearly 40 percent of traffic fatalities. More than four in ten businesses in the United States are owned by women.

Most arguments are supported at least to some extent by facts and statistics. For example, in the following passage the writer uses statistics to show that college students are granted unreasonably high credit limits.

> A 2009 study by Sallie Mae revealed that undergraduates are carrying record-high credit card balances and are relying on credit cards more than ever, especially in the economic downturn. The average credit card debt per college undergraduate is $3,173, and 82 percent of undergraduates carry balances and incur finance charges each month (Sallie Mae).

Writers often use statistics in selective ways to bolster their own positions. If you suspect that a writer's handling of statistics is not quite fair, track down the original sources for those statistics or read authors with opposing views, who may give you a fuller understanding of the numbers.

Using examples and illustrations

Examples and illustrations (extended examples, often in story form) rarely prove a point by themselves, but when used in combination with other forms of evidence they flesh out an argument with details and specific instances and bring it to life. Because examples are often concrete and sometimes vivid, they can reach readers in ways that statistics and abstract ideas cannot.

In a paper arguing that online news provides opportunities for readers that print news does not, Sam Jacobs describes how regular citizens armed with only cell phones and laptops helped save lives during Hurricane Katrina by relaying critical news updates.

Using visuals

Visuals — charts, graphs, diagrams, photographs — can support your argument by providing vivid and detailed evidence and by capturing your readers' attention. Bar or line graphs, for instance, describe and organize complex statistical data; photographs can immediately and evocatively convey abstract ideas. Writers in almost every academic field use visual evidence to support their arguments or to counter opposing arguments. For example, to explain a conflict among Southeast Asian countries, a historian might choose a map to illustrate the geography and highlight particular issues. Or to refute another scholar's hypothesis about the dangers of a vegetarian diet, a nutritionist might support her claims by using a table to organize and highlight detailed numerical information. (See pp. 24–25.)

As you consider using visual evidence, ask yourself the following questions:

- Is the visual accurate, credible, and relevant?

- How will the visual appeal to readers? Logically? Ethically? Emotionally?

- How will the visual evidence function? Will it provide background information? Present complex numerical information or an abstract idea? Lend authority? Anticipate or refute counterarguments?

> **Making the most of your handbook**
> Integrating visuals can strengthen your writing.
> ▶ Choosing appropriate visuals: page 407
> ▶ Placing and labeling visuals: page 407
> ▶ Using visuals responsibly: page 408

Like all forms of evidence, visuals don't speak for themselves; you'll need to analyze and interpret the evidence to show readers how the visuals inform and support your argument.

As you write

Review an argument you are drafting. Analyze the types of evidence you selected. Have you varied the type of evidence? Could you strengthen your argument with more vivid or more detailed evidence? How might visual evidence, for example, lend authority to your argument and appeal to readers? Note what changes you might make to your evidence.

Citing expert opinion

Although they are no substitute for careful reasoning of your own, the views of an expert can contribute to the force of your argument. For example, to help him make the case that print journalism has a one-sided relationship with its readers, Sam Jacobs integrates an expert's key description:

> With the rise of the Internet, however, this one-sided relationship
> has been criticized by journalists such as Dan Gillmor, founder
> of the Center for Citizen Media, who argues that traditional print
> journalism treats "news as a lecture," whereas online news is "more
> of a conversation" (xxiv).

When you rely on expert opinion, make sure that your source is an expert in the field you are writing about. In some cases, you may need to provide credentials showing why your source is worth listening to. When including expert testimony in your paper, you can summarize or paraphrase the expert's opinion or you can quote the expert's exact words. You will of course need to document the source, as Jacobs did in the example just given.

Anticipating and countering opposing arguments

To anticipate a possible objection (see 6f) to your argument, consider the following questions:

- Could a reasonable person draw a different conclusion from your facts or examples?
- Might a reader question any of your assumptions?
- Could a reader offer an alternative explanation of this issue?
- Is there any evidence that might weaken your position?

The following questions may help you respond to a reader's potential objection:

- Can you concede the point to the opposition but challenge the point's importance or usefulness?
- Can you explain why readers should consider a new perspective or question a piece of evidence?
- Should you explain how your position responds to contradictory evidence?
- Can you suggest a different interpretation of the evidence?

When you write, use phrasing to signal to readers that you're about to present an objection. Often the signal phrase can go in the lead sentence of a paragraph:

Critics of this view argue that. . . .

Some readers might point out that. . . .

Researchers challenge these claims by. . . .

Revising with comments
Develop more

UNDERSTANDING THE COMMENT

When readers suggest that you "develop more," the comment often signals that you stopped short of providing a full and detailed discussion of your idea.

> Distancing ourselves from our family is a natural part of growing up. There are many ways in which we try doing so. For essayist Richard Rodriguez, it was his drive for academic success that separated him from his parents and his past (195). In his desire to become educated, he removed himself from his family and distanced himself from his culture. In his essay "The Achievement of Desire," he admits regretting the separation from his family and acknowledges the particular challenges of growing up between two cultures.

Develop more

In this body paragraph, a student responded to an assignment that asked her to explore one theme in Richard Rodriguez's essay "The Achievement of Desire."

The student has not included enough evidence or developed a thorough analysis of that evidence. To revise, she might look for specific examples and details from Rodriguez's essay to support her claim that Rodriguez "removed . . . and distanced himself" from his family. Then she might develop the claim by analyzing *how* and *why* Rodriguez's "desire to become educated" removed him from his family.

SIMILAR COMMENTS: undeveloped • give examples • explain

REVISING WHEN *YOU* NEED TO DEVELOP MORE

1. *Read your paragraph to a peer or a tutor* and ask specific questions: What's missing? Do readers need more background information or examples to understand your point? Do they need more evidence to be convinced? Is it clear what point you are making with your details?

2. *Keep your purpose in mind.* You aren't being asked to restate what you've already written or what the author has written.

3. *Think about why your main point matters to your readers.* Take another look at your points and support, and answer the question "So what?"

More advice on using specific evidence: 6e

6f Anticipate objections; counter opposing arguments.

Readers who already agree with you need no convincing, but indifferent or skeptical readers may resist your arguments. To be willing to give up positions that seem reasonable to them, readers need to see that another position is even more reasonable. In addition to presenting your own case, therefore, you should consider the opposing arguments and attempt to counter them. (See the box on p. 91.)

It might seem at first that drawing attention to an opposing point of view or contradictory evidence would weaken your argument. But by anticipating and countering objections, you show yourself as a reasonable and well-informed writer. You also establish your purpose, demonstrate the significance of the issue you are debating, and ultimately strengthen your argument.

There is no best place in an essay to deal with opposing views. Often it is useful to summarize the opposing position early in your essay. After stating your thesis but before developing your own arguments, you might have a paragraph that addresses the most important counterargument. Or you can anticipate objections paragraph by paragraph as you develop your case. Wherever you decide to address opposing arguments, you will enhance your credibility if you explain the arguments of others accurately and fairly.

As you write

Exchange drafts with your classmates. Pose objections to their arguments, and invite them to pose objections to yours. Practice using the language of counterargument: "Some readers might point out . . . " or "But isn't it possible that . . . ?" What do you learn about the persuasiveness of your argument from hearing objections? Do you need to revise your thesis? Modify your position? Consider new evidence? Which counterarguments would you need to address to convince readers that you are a reasonable and informed writer?

6g Build common ground.

As you counter opposing arguments, try to seek out one or two assumptions you might share with readers who do not initially agree with your views. If you can show that you share their concerns, your readers may be more likely to acknowledge the

Revising with comments
Consider opposing viewpoints

UNDERSTANDING THE COMMENT

When readers suggest that you "consider opposing viewpoints," the comment often signals that you need to recognize and respond to possible objections to your argument.

> For many American workers, drug testing is a routine part of their working life. In her book *Nickel and Dimed*, Barbara Ehrenreich observes how random drug testing leads to a hostile work environment (128). In addition, researchers Shepard and Clifton have found that companies using drug-testing programs are likelier to have lower productivity levels than those that have not adopted such practices (1). *Consider* Drug testing in the workplace has shown *opposing* no benefits for employers or employees. *viewpoints*

In response to an assignment about changes in the workplace, one student wrote this body paragraph.

The student jumps to a conclusion too quickly without recognizing any opposing points of view. To revise, the student might begin by reading two or more sources to gain a different perspective and to learn more about the debate surrounding her topic. As she reads more sources, she might ask: What evidence do those in favor of drug testing provide to support their point of view? How would they respond to my conclusion against drug testing? By anticipating and countering opposing views, she will show herself as a fair and reasonable writer.

SIMILAR COMMENTS: *what about the other side?* • *counterargument?*

REVISING WHEN *YOU* NEED TO CONSIDER OTHER POINTS OF VIEW

1. *Read more* to learn about the debates surrounding the topic. Ask questions: Are there other sides to the issue? Would a reasonable person offer an alternative explanation for the evidence?

2. *Be open-minded.* Although it might seem counterintuitive to introduce opposing arguments, you'll show your knowledge of the topic by recognizing that not everyone draws the same conclusion.

3. *Introduce and counter objections* with phrases like these: "Some readers might point out that . . ." or "Critics of this view argue that. . . ."

4. *Revise your thesis*, if necessary, to account for multiple points of view.

More advice on considering opposing viewpoints: 6f and 7c

validity of your argument. For example, to persuade people opposed to controlling the deer population with a regulated hunting season, a state wildlife commission would have to show that
it too cares about preserving deer and does not want them to die
needlessly. Having established these values in common, the commission might be able to persuade critics that reducing the total
number of deer prevents starvation caused by overpopulation.

People believe that intelligence and decency support their side
of an argument. To be persuaded, they must see these qualities in
your argument. Otherwise they will persist in their opposition.

6h Sample argument paper

In the paper that begins on the next page, student Sam Jacobs
argues that the shift from print to online news benefits readers
by providing them with new opportunities to produce news and
to think more critically as consumers of news. Notice that he
is careful to present opposing views fairly before providing his
counterarguments.

In writing the paper, Jacobs consulted both print and online
sources. When he quotes or uses information from a source, he
cites the source with an MLA (Modern Language Association)
in-text citation. Citations in the paper refer readers to the list of
works cited at the end of the paper. (For more details about citing
sources, see 59.)

MODELS hackerhandbooks.com/rules
> Model papers > MLA argument papers: Jacobs; Hammond; Lund;
Sanghvi
> MLA research papers: Orlov; Daly; Levi

Jacobs 1

Sam Jacobs

Professor Alperini

English 101

19 March 2010

From Lecture to Conversation: Redefining What's "Fit to Print"

"All the news that's fit to print," the motto of the *New York Times* since 1896, plays with the word *fit*, asserting that a news story must be newsworthy and must not exceed the limits of the printed page. The increase in online news consumption, however, challenges both meanings of the word *fit*, allowing producers and consumers alike to rethink who decides which topics are worth covering and how extensive that coverage should be. Any cultural shift usually means that something is lost, but in this case there are clear gains. The shift from print to online news provides unprecedented opportunities for readers to become more engaged with the news, to hold journalists accountable, and to participate as producers, not simply as consumers.

Guided by journalism's code of ethics—accuracy, objectivity, and fairness—print news reporters have gathered and delivered stories according to what editors decide is fit for their readers. Except for op-ed pages and letters to the editor, print news has traditionally had a one-sided relationship with its readers. The print news media's reputation for objective reporting has been held up as "a stop sign" for readers, sending a clear message that no further inquiry is necessary (Weinberger). With the rise of the Internet, however, this model has been criticized by journalists such as Dan Gillmor, founder of the Center for Citizen Media, who argues that traditional print journalism

Marginal annotations:

In his opening sentences, Jacobs provides background for his thesis.

Thesis states the main point.

Jacobs does not need a citation for common knowledge.

Jacobs 2

treats "news as a lecture," whereas online news is "more of a conversation" (xxiv). Print news arrives on the doorstep every morning as a fully formed lecture, a product created without participation from its readership. By contrast, online news invites readers to participate in a collaborative process—to question and even help produce the content.

One of the most important advantages online news offers over print news is the presence of built-in hyperlinks, which carry readers from one electronic document to another. If readers are curious about the definition of a term, the roots of a story, or other perspectives on a topic, links provide a path. Links help readers become more critical consumers of information by engaging them in a totally new way. For instance, the link embedded in the story "Window into Fed Debate over a Crucial Program" (Healy) allows readers to find out more about the trends in consumer spending and to check the journalist's handling of an original source (see Fig. 1). This kind of link gives readers the opportunity to conduct their own evaluation of the evidence and verify the journalist's claims.

Transition moves from Jacobs's main argument to specific examples.

Links provide a kind of transparency impossible in print because they allow readers to see through online news to the "sources, disagreements, and the personal assumptions and values" that may have influenced a news story (Weinberger). The International Center for Media and the Public Agenda underscores the importance of news organizations letting "customers in on the often tightly held little secrets of journalism." To do so, they suggest, will lead to "accountability and accountability leads to credibility" ("Openness"). These tools alone don't guarantee

*Jacobs clarifies key terms (*transparency* and *accountability*).*

Source is cited in MLA style.

Jacobs 3

that news producers will be responsible and trustworthy, but they encourage an open and transparent environment that benefits news consumers.

But economists greeted the news with a small cheer because sales excluding automobiles actually grew in September, suggesting that consumer spending was stabilizing.

Over all, retail sales fell 1.5 percent in September from a month earlier, the Commerce Department reported, better than an anticipated decline of 2.1 percent.

Retail sales excluding automobiles and parts grew 0.5 percent, largely because of higher sales at gas stations and grocery stores.

Auto dealers bore the brunt of the month's declines.

Consumers swamped dealerships in late July and August to take advantage of the government's $3 billion cash-for-clunkers program, which offered rebates of up to $4,500 to entice people to swap their older cars for more fuel-efficient models.

Sales at auto dealers surged in August, but fell 11 percent in September.

Sign in to Recommend

A version of this article appeared in print on October 15, 2009, on page B3 of the New York edition.

More Articles in Business »

Timothy Winters / Ian Thomas
CB09-154
Service Sector Statistics Division
(301) 763-2713

U.S. Census Bureau News
U.S. Department of Commerce - Washington, D.C. 20233

INSIDE NYT

FOR IMMEDIATE RELEASE

WEDNESDAY, OCTOBER 14, 2009 AT 8:30 A.M. EDT

ADVANCE MONTHLY SALES FOR RETAIL TRADE AND FOOD SERVICES

SEPTEMBER 2009

The U.S. Census Bureau announced today that advance estimates of U.S. retail and food services sales for September, adjusted for seasonal variation and holiday and trading-day differences, but not for price changes, were $344.7 billion, a decrease of 1.5 percent (±0.5%) from the previous month and 5.7 percent (±0.7%) below September 2008. Total sales for the July through September 2009 period were down 6.6 percent (±0.3%) from the same period a year ago. The July to

Fig. 1. Links embedded in online news articles allow readers to move from the main story to original sources, related articles, or background materials. The link in this online article (Healy) points to a government report, the original source of the author's data on consumer spending.

Jacobs 4

Not only has technology allowed readers to become more critical news consumers, but it also has helped some to become news producers. The Web gives ordinary people the power to report on the day's events. Anyone with an Internet connection can publish on blogs and Web sites, engage in online discussion forums, and contribute video and audio recordings. Citizen journalists with laptops, cell phones, and digital camcorders have become news producers alongside large news organizations.

Not everyone embraces the spread of unregulated news reporting online. Critics point out that citizen journalists are not necessarily trained to be fair or ethical, for example, nor are they subject to editorial oversight. Acknowledging that citizen reporting is more immediate and experimental, critics also question its accuracy and accountability: "While it has its place . . . it really isn't journalism at all, and it opens up information flow to the strong probability of fraud and abuse. . . . Information without journalistic standards is called gossip," writes David Hazinski in the *Atlanta Journal-Constitution* (23A). In his book *Losing the News*, media specialist Alex S. Jones argues that what passes for news today is in fact "pseudo news" and is "far less reliable" than traditional print news (27). Even a supporter like Gillmor is willing to agree that citizen journalists are "nonexperts," but he argues that they are "using technology to make a profound contribution, and a real difference" (140).

Citizen reporting made a difference in the wake of Hurricane Katrina in 2005. Armed with cell phones and laptops, regular citizens relayed critical news updates in a rapidly developing crisis, often before traditional journalists were even on the scene. In 2006, the enormous

Jacobs develops the thesis.

Opposing views are presented fairly.

Jacobs counters opposing arguments.

A vivid example helps Jacobs make his point.

Jacobs 5

contributions of citizen journalists were recognized when
the New Orleans *Times-Picayune* received the Pulitzer
Prize in public service for its online coverage—largely
citizen-generated—of Hurricane Katrina. In recognizing
the paper's "meritorious public service," the Pulitzer Prize
board credited the newspaper's blog for "heroic, multi-
faceted coverage of [the storm] and its aftermath" ("2006
Pulitzer"). Writing for the *Online Journalism Review*, Mark
Glaser emphasizes the role that blog updates played in
saving storm victims' lives. Further, he calls the *Times-
Picayune*'s partnership with citizen journalists a "watershed
for online journalism."

Jacobs uses specific evidence for support.

The Internet has enabled consumers to participate
in a new way in reading, questioning, interpreting, and
reporting the news. Decisions about appropriate content
and coverage are no longer exclusively in the hands of news
editors. Ordinary citizens now have a meaningful voice in
the conversation—a hand in deciding what's "fit to print."
Some skeptics worry about the apparent free-for-all and loss
of tradition. But the expanding definition of news provides
opportunities for consumers to be more engaged with events
in their communities, their nations, and the world.

Conclusion echoes the thesis without dully repeating it.

Jacobs 6

Works Cited

Gillmor, Dan. *We the Media: Grassroots Journalism by the People, for the People*. Sebastopol: O'Reilly, 2006. Print.

Glaser, Mark. "NOLA.com Blogs and Forums Help Save Lives after Katrina." *OJR: The Online Journalism Review*. Knight Digital Media Center, 13 Sept. 2005. Web. 2 Mar. 2010.

Hazinski, David. "Unfettered 'Citizen Journalism' Too Risky." *Atlanta Journal-Constitution* 13 Dec. 2007: 23A. *General OneFile*. Web. 2 Mar. 2010.

Healy, Jack. "Window into Fed Debate over a Crucial Program." *New York Times*. New York Times, 14 Oct. 2009. Web. 4 Mar. 2010.

Jones, Alex S. *Losing the News: The Future of the News That Feeds Democracy*. New York: Oxford UP, 2009. Print.

"Openness and Accountability: A Study of Transparency in Global Media Outlets." *ICMPA: International Center for Media and the Public Agenda*. Intl. Center for Media and the Public Agenda, 2006. Web. 26 Feb. 2010.

"The 2006 Pulitzer Prize Winners: Public Service." *The Pulitzer Prizes*. Columbia U, n.d. Web. 2 Mar. 2010.

Weinberger, David. "Transparency Is the New Objectivity." *Joho the Blog*. David Weinberger, 19 July 2009. Web. 26 Feb. 2010.

Works cited page uses MLA style.

List is alphabetized by authors' last names (or by title when a work has no author).

Abbreviation "n.d." indicates that the online source has no update date.

7 Evaluating arguments

In your reading and in your own writing, evaluate all arguments for logic and fairness. Many arguments can stand up to critical scrutiny. Sometimes, however, a line of argument that at first seems reasonable turns out to be illogical, unfair, or both. Recognizing flawed arguments as you read can help you avoid such problems in your own writing.

7a Distinguish between reasonable and fallacious argumentative tactics.

A number of unreasonable argumentative tactics are known as *logical fallacies.* Most of the fallacies — such as hasty generalizations and false analogies — are misguided or dishonest uses of legitimate argumentative strategies. The examples in this section suggest when such strategies are reasonable and when they are not.

Generalizing (inductive reasoning)

Writers and thinkers generalize all the time. We look at a sample of data and conclude that data we have not observed will most likely conform to what we have seen. From a spoonful of soup, we conclude just how salty the whole bowl will be. After numerous unpleasant experiences with an airline, we decide to book future flights with a competitor.

When we draw a conclusion from an array of facts, we are engaged in inductive reasoning. Such reasoning deals in probability, not certainty. For a conclusion to be highly probable, it must be based on evidence that is sufficient, representative, and relevant. (See the chart on p. 104.)

The fallacy known as *hasty generalization* is a conclusion based on insufficient or unrepresentative evidence.

HASTY GENERALIZATION

In a single year, scores on standardized tests in California's public schools rose by ten points. Therefore, more children than ever are succeeding in America's public school systems.

Data from one state do not justify a conclusion about the whole United States.

A *stereotype* is a hasty generalization about a group. Here are a few examples.

STEREOTYPES

Women are bad bosses.

All politicians are corrupt.

Athletes are never strong students.

Stereotyping is common because of our tendency to perceive selectively. We tend to see what we want to see; we notice evidence confirming our already formed opinions and fail to notice evidence to the contrary. For example, if you have concluded that all politicians are corrupt, this stereotype will be confirmed by news reports of legislators being indicted — even though every day the media describe conscientious officials serving the public honestly and well.

> **Academic English** Many hasty generalizations contain words such as *all*, *ever*, *always*, and *never*, when qualifiers such as *most*, *many*, *usually*, and *seldom* would be more accurate.

Drawing analogies

An analogy points out a similarity between two things that are otherwise different. Analogies can be an effective means of arguing a point. Our system of judicial decision making, or case law, which relies heavily on previous decisions, makes extensive use of reasoning by analogy. One lawyer may point out, for example, that specific facts or circumstances resemble those from a previous case and will thus argue for a similar result or decision. In response, the opposing lawyer may maintain that such facts or circumstances bear only a superficial resemblance to those in the previous case and that in legally relevant respects they are quite different and thus require a different result or decision.

It is not always easy to draw the line between a reasonable and an unreasonable analogy. At times, however, an analogy is clearly off base, in which case it is called a *false analogy*.

FALSE ANALOGY

If we can send a spacecraft to Pluto, we should be able to find a cure for the common cold.

The writer has falsely assumed that because two things are alike in one respect, they must be alike in others. Exploring the outer reaches of the solar system and finding a cure for the common cold are both scientific challenges, but the problems confronting medical researchers are quite different from those solved by space scientists.

Testing inductive reasoning

Though inductive reasoning leads to probable and not absolute truth, you can assess a conclusion's likely probability by asking three questions. This chart shows how to apply those questions to a sample conclusion based on a survey.

CONCLUSION The majority of students on our campus would volunteer at least five hours a week in a community organization if the school provided a placement service for volunteers.

EVIDENCE In a recent survey, 723 of 1,215 students questioned said they would volunteer at least five hours a week in a community organization if the school provided a placement service for volunteers.

1. Is the evidence sufficient?

   That depends. On a small campus (say, 3,000 students), the pool of students surveyed would be sufficient for market research, but on a large campus (say, 30,000), 1,215 students are only 4 percent of the population. If that 4 percent were known to be truly representative of the other 96 percent, however, even such a small sample would be sufficient (see question 2).

2. Is the evidence representative?

   The evidence is representative if those responding to the survey reflect the characteristics of the entire student population: age, sex, race, field of study, overall number of extracurricular commitments, and so on. If most of those surveyed are majors in a field like social work, however, the researchers would be wise to question the survey's conclusion.

3. Is the evidence relevant?

   Yes. The results of the survey are directly linked to the conclusion. Evidence based on a survey about the number of hours students work for pay, by contrast, would not be relevant because it would not be about *choosing to volunteer*.

Tracing causes and effects

Demonstrating a connection between causes and effects is rarely simple. For example, to explain why a chemistry course has a high failure rate, you would begin by listing possible causes: inadequate preparation of students, poor teaching, lack of qualified tutors, and so on. Next you would investigate each possible cause. Only after investigating the possible causes would you be able to weigh the relative impact of each cause and suggest appropriate remedies.

Because cause-and-effect reasoning is so complex, it is not surprising that writers frequently oversimplify it. In particular, writers sometimes assume that because one event follows another, the first is the cause of the second. This common fallacy is known as *post hoc*, from the Latin *post hoc, ergo propter hoc*, meaning "after this, therefore because of this."

POST HOC FALLACY

Since Governor Cho took office, unemployment of minorities in the state has decreased by 7 percent. Governor Cho should be applauded for reducing unemployment among minorities.

The writer must show that Governor Cho's policies are responsible for the decrease in unemployment; it is not enough to show that the decrease followed the governor's taking office.

Weighing options

Especially when reasoning about problems and solutions, writers must weigh options. To be fair, a writer should mention the full range of options, showing why one is superior to the others or might work well in combination with others.

It is unfair to suggest that there are only two alternatives when in fact there are more. When writers set up a false choice between their preferred option and one that is clearly unsatisfactory, they create an *either . . . or* fallacy.

***EITHER . . . OR* FALLACY**

Our current war against drugs has not worked. Either we should legalize drugs or we should turn the drug war over to our armed forces and let them fight it.

Clearly there are other options, such as increased funding for drug abuse prevention and treatment.

Making assumptions

An assumption is a claim that is taken to be true — without the need of proof. Most arguments are based to some extent on assumptions, since writers rarely have the time and space to prove all the conceivable claims on which an argument is based. For example, someone arguing about the best means of limiting population growth in developing countries might well assume that the goal of limiting population growth is worthwhile. For most audiences, there would be no need to articulate this assumption or to defend it.

There is a danger, however, in failing to spell out and prove a claim that is clearly controversial. Consider the following short argument, in which a key claim is missing.

ARGUMENT WITH MISSING CLAIM

Violent crime is increasing. Therefore, we should vigorously enforce the death penalty.

The writer seems to be assuming that the death penalty deters violent criminals — and that most audiences will agree. The writer also assumes that the death penalty is a fair punishment for violent crimes. These are not safe assumptions; the writer will need to state and support both claims.

When a missing claim is an assertion that few would agree with, we say that a writer is guilty of a *non sequitur* (Latin for "it does not follow").

NON SEQUITUR

Christopher gets plenty of sleep; therefore he will be a successful student in the university's pre-med program.

Few people would agree with the missing claim — that people with good sleep habits always make successful students.

Deducing conclusions (deductive reasoning)

When we deduce a conclusion, we — like Sherlock Holmes — put things together. We establish that a general principle is true, that a specific case is an example of that principle, and that therefore a particular conclusion about that case is a certainty. In real life, such absolute reasoning rarely happens. Approximations of it, however, sometimes occur.

Deductive reasoning can often be structured in a three-step argument called a *syllogism*. The three steps are the major premise, the minor premise, and the conclusion.

1. Anything that increases radiation in the environment is dangerous to public health. (Major premise)
2. Nuclear reactors increase radiation in the environment. (Minor premise)
3. Therefore, nuclear reactors are dangerous to public health. (Conclusion)

The major premise is a generalization. The minor premise is a specific case. The conclusion follows from applying the generalization to the specific case.

Deductive arguments break down if one of the premises is not true or if the conclusion does not logically follow from the premises. In the following argument, the major premise is very likely untrue.

UNTRUE PREMISE

The police do not give speeding tickets to people driving less than five miles per hour over the limit. Dominic is driving fifty-nine miles per hour in a fifty-five-mile-per-hour zone. Therefore, the police will not give Dominic a speeding ticket.

The conclusion is true only if the premises are true. If the police sometimes give speeding tickets for driving less than five miles per hour over the limit, Dominic cannot safely conclude that he will avoid a ticket.

In the following argument, both premises might be true, but the conclusion does not follow logically from them.

CONCLUSION DOES NOT FOLLOW

All members of our club ran in this year's Boston Marathon. Jay ran in this year's Boston Marathon. Therefore, Jay is a member of our club.

The fact that Jay ran the marathon is no guarantee that he is a member of the club. Presumably, many marathon runners are nonmembers.

Assuming that both premises are true, the following argument holds up.

CONCLUSION FOLLOWS

All members of our club ran in this year's Boston Marathon. Jay is a member of our club. Therefore, Jay ran in this year's Boston Marathon.

7b Distinguish between legitimate and unfair emotional appeals.

There is nothing wrong with appealing to readers' emotions. After all, many issues worth arguing about have an emotional as well as a logical dimension. Even the Greek logician Aristotle lists *pathos* (emotion) as a legitimate argumentative tactic. For example, in an essay criticizing big-box stores, writer Betsy Taylor has a good reason for tugging at readers' emotions: Her subject is the decline of city and town life. In her conclusion, Taylor appeals to readers' emotions by invoking their national pride.

LEGITIMATE EMOTIONAL APPEAL

Is it anti-American to be against having a retail giant set up shop in one's community? Some people would say so. On the other hand, if you board up Main Street, what's left of America?

As we all know, however, emotional appeals are frequently misused. Many of the arguments we see in the media, for instance, strive to win our sympathy rather than our intelligent agreement. A TV commercial suggesting that you will be thin and sexy if you drink a certain diet beverage is making a pitch to emotions. So is a political speech that recommends electing a candidate because he is a devoted husband and father who serves as a volunteer firefighter.

The following passage illustrates several types of unfair emotional appeals.

UNFAIR EMOTIONAL APPEALS

This progressive proposal to build a ski resort in the state park has been carefully researched by Western Trust, the largest bank in the state; furthermore, it is favored by a majority of the local merchants. The only opposition comes from narrow-minded, hippie environmentalists who care more about trees than they do about people; one of their leaders was actually arrested for disturbing the peace several years ago.

Words with strong positive or negative connotations, such as *progressive* and *hippie*, are examples of *biased language*. Attacking the people who hold a belief (environmentalists) rather than refuting their argument is called *ad hominem*, a Latin term meaning "to the man." Associating a prestigious name (Western Trust) with the writer's side is called *transfer*. Claiming that an idea should be accepted because a large number of people (the majority of merchants) are in favor is called the *bandwagon appeal*. Bringing in irrelevant issues (the arrest) is a *red herring*, named after a trick used in fox hunts to mislead the dogs by dragging a smelly fish across the trail.

7c Judge how fairly a writer handles opposing views.

The way in which a writer deals with opposing views is revealing. Some writers address the arguments of the opposition fairly, conceding points when necessary and countering others, all in a civil spirit. Other writers will do almost anything to win an argument: either ignoring opposing views altogether or misrepresenting such views and attacking their proponents.

In your own writing, you build credibility by addressing opposing arguments fairly. (See also 6f.) In your reading, you can assess the credibility of your sources by looking at how they deal with views not in agreement with their own.

Describing the views of others

Writers and politicians often deliberately misrepresent the views of others. One way they do this is by setting up a "straw man," a character so weak that he is easily knocked down. The *straw man* fallacy consists of an oversimplification or outright distortion of opposing views. For example, in a California debate over attempts to control the mountain lion population, pro-lion groups characterized their opponents as trophy hunters bent on shooting harmless lions and sticking them on the walls of their dens. In truth, such hunters were only one faction of those who saw a need to control the lion population.

During the District of Columbia's struggle for voting representation, some politicians set up a straw man, as shown in the following example.

STRAW MAN FALLACY

Washington, DC, residents are lobbying for statehood. Giving a city such as the District of Columbia the status of a state would be unfair.

The straw man wanted statehood. In fact, most District citizens lobbied for voting representation in any form, not necessarily through statehood.

Quoting opposing views

Writers often quote the words of writers who hold opposing views. In general, this is a good idea, for it assures some level of fairness and accuracy. At times, though, both the fairness and the accuracy are an illusion.

A source may be misrepresented when it is quoted out of context. All quotations are to some extent taken out of context, but a fair writer will explain the context to readers. To select a provocative sentence from a source and to ignore the more moderate sentences surrounding it is both unfair and misleading. Sometimes a writer deliberately distorts a source by using ellipsis dots. Ellipsis dots tell readers that words have been omitted from the original source. When those words are crucial to an author's meaning, omitting them is unfair. (See 39d.)

ORIGINAL SOURCE

Johnson's *History of the American West* is riddled with inaccuracies and astonishing in its blatantly racist description of the Indian wars.

— B. R., reviewer

MISLEADING QUOTATION

According to B. R., Johnson's *History of the American West* is "astonishing in its . . . description of the Indian wars."

EXERCISE 7–1 Explain what is illogical in the following brief arguments. It may be helpful to identify the logical fallacy or fallacies by name. Answers to lettered sentences appear in the back of the book.

a. My roommate, who is an engineering major, is taking a course called Structures of Tall Buildings. All engineers have to know how to design tall buildings.

b. If you're old enough to vote, you're old enough to drink. Therefore, the drinking age should be lowered to eighteen.

c. If you're not part of the solution, you're part of the problem.

d. Whenever I wash my car, it rains. I have discovered a way to end all droughts — get all the people to wash their cars.

e. Ninety percent of the students oppose a tuition increase; therefore, the board of trustees should not pass the proposed increase.

Clarity

8 Prefer active verbs.

As a rule, choose an active verb and pair it with a subject that names the person or thing doing the action. Active verbs express meaning more emphatically and vigorously than their weaker counterparts — forms of the verb *be* or verbs in the passive voice.

PASSIVE The pumps *were destroyed* by a surge of power.

***BE* VERB** A surge of power *was* responsible for the destruction of the pumps.

ACTIVE A surge of power *destroyed* the pumps.

Verbs in the passive voice lack strength because their subjects receive the action instead of doing it. Forms of the verb *be* (*be, am, is, are, was, were, being, been*) lack vigor because they convey no action.

Although passive verbs and the forms of *be* have legitimate uses, choose an active verb if it can carry your meaning. Even among active verbs, some are more active — and therefore more vigorous and colorful — than others. Carefully selected verbs can energize a piece of writing.

▶ The goalie crouched low, ~~reached~~ out his stick, and ~~sent~~ the

              swept   *hooked*

rebound away from the mouth of the net.

> **Academic English** Although you may be tempted to avoid the passive voice completely, keep in mind that some writing situations call for it, especially scientific writing. For appropriate uses of the passive voice, see page 113; for advice about forming the passive voice, see 28b and 47c.

8a Use the active voice unless you have a good reason for choosing the passive.

In the active voice, the subject does the action; in the passive voice, the subject receives the action (see also 47c). Although both voices are grammatically correct, the active voice is usually more effective because it is clearer and more direct.

ACTIVE   Hernando *caught* the fly ball.

PASSIVE   The fly ball *was caught* by Hernando.

Passive sentences often identify the actor in a *by* phrase, as in the preceding example. Sometimes, however, that phrase is omitted, and who or what is responsible for the action becomes unclear: *The fly ball was caught.*

Most of the time, you will want to emphasize the actor, so you should use the active voice. To replace a passive verb with an active one, make the actor the subject of the sentence.

> The settlers stripped the land of timber before realizing
> ▶ ~~The land was stripped of timber before the settlers realized~~ the
>   ^
>
> consequences of their actions.

The revision emphasizes the actors (*settlers*) by naming them in the subject.

> The contractor removed the
> ▶ ~~The~~ debris ~~was removed~~ from the construction site.
>   ^

Sometimes the actor does not appear in a passive-voice sentence. To turn such a sentence into the active voice, the writer must determine an appropriate subject, in this case *contractor.*

Appropriate uses of the passive

The passive voice is appropriate if you wish to emphasize the receiver of the action or to minimize the importance of the actor.

APPROPRIATE PASSIVE   Many Hawaiians *were forced* to leave their homes after the earthquake.

APPROPRIATE PASSIVE   As the time for harvest approaches, the tobacco plants *are sprayed* with a chemical to retard the growth of suckers.

The writer of the first sentence wished to emphasize the receiver of the action, *Hawaiians.* The writer of the second sentence wished to focus on the tobacco plants, not on the people spraying them.

In much scientific writing, the passive voice properly emphasizes the experiment or process being described, not the researcher. Check with your instructor for the preference in your discipline.

APPROPRIATE PASSIVE   The solution *was heated* to the boiling point, and then it was reduced in volume by 50%.

8b Replace *be* verbs that result in dull or wordy sentences.

Not every *be* verb needs replacing. The forms of *be* (*be, am, is, are, was, were, being, been*) work well when you want to link a subject to a noun that clearly renames it or to an adjective that describes it: *Orchard House was the home of Louisa May Alcott. The harvest will be bountiful after the summer rains.* And *be* verbs are essential as helping verbs before present participles (*is flying, are disappearing*) to express ongoing action: *Derrick was fighting the fire when his wife went into labor.* (See 27f.)

If using a *be* verb makes a sentence needlessly dull and wordy, however, consider replacing it. Often a phrase following the verb will contain a noun or an adjective (such as *violation, resistant*) that suggests a more vigorous, active verb (*violate, resist*).

▶ Burying nuclear waste in Antarctica would ~~be in violation of~~ *violate* an

international treaty.

Violate is less wordy and more vigorous than be in violation of.

▶ When Rosa Parks ~~was resistant to~~ *resisted* giving up her seat on the bus,

she became a civil rights hero.

Resisted is stronger than was resistant to.

8c As a rule, choose a subject that names the person or thing doing the action.

In weak, unemphatic prose, both the actor and the action may be buried in sentence elements other than the subject and the verb. In the following sentence, for example, both the actor and the action appear in prepositional phrases, word groups that do not receive much attention from readers.

WEAK   The institution of the New Deal had the effect of reversing some of the economic inequalities of the Great Depression.

EMPHATIC The New Deal reversed some of the economic inequalities of the Great Depression.

Consider the subjects and verbs of the two versions — *institution had* versus *New Deal reversed*. The latter expresses the writer's point more emphatically.

▶ ~~The use of~~ pure oxygen can ~~cause~~ healing ~~in~~ wounds that are
     P   ^
otherwise untreatable.

In the original sentence, the subject and verb — *use can cause* — express the point blandly. *Pure oxygen can heal* makes the point more emphatically and directly.

EXERCISE 8–1   Revise any weak, unemphatic sentences by replacing *be* verbs or passive verbs with active alternatives and, if necessary, by naming in the subject the person or thing doing the action. Some sentences are emphatic; do not change them. Revisions of lettered sentences appear in the back of the book. Example:

> *The ranger doused the campfire before giving us*
> ~~The campfire was doused by the ranger before we were given~~
>   ^
> a ticket for unauthorized use of a campsite.

a. The Prussians were victorious over the Saxons in 1745.

b. The entire operation is managed by Ahmed, the producer.

c. The sea kayaks were expertly paddled by the tour guides.

d. At the crack of rocket and mortar blasts, I jumped from the top bunk and landed on my buddy below, who was crawling on the floor looking for his boots.

e. There were shouting protesters on the courthouse steps.

1. A strange sound was made in the willow tree by the monkey that had escaped from the zoo.

2. Her letter was in acknowledgment of the student's participation in the literacy program.

3. The bomb bay doors rumbled open, and freezing air whipped through the plane.

4. The work of Paul Oakenfold and Sandra Collins was influential in my choice of music for my audition.

5. The only responsibility I was given by my parents was putting my little brother to bed when they had to work late.

PRACTICE   hackerhandbooks.com/rules
   > Clarity > 8-2 to 8-5

9   Balance parallel ideas.

If two or more ideas are parallel, they are easier to grasp when expressed in parallel grammatical form. Single words should be balanced with single words, phrases with phrases, clauses with clauses.

A kiss can be a comma, a question mark, or an exclamation point.

— Mistinguett

This novel is not to be tossed lightly aside, but to be hurled with great force.

— Dorothy Parker

In matters of principle, stand like a rock; in matters of taste, swim with the current.

— Thomas Jefferson

Writers often use parallelism to create emphasis. (See p. 151.)

9a Balance parallel ideas in a series.

Readers expect items in a series to appear in parallel grammatical form. When one or more of the items violate readers' expectations, a sentence will be needlessly awkward.

▶ Children who study music also learn confidence, discipline,
  creativity.
  and ~~they are creative.~~
       ^

The revision presents all the items in the series as nouns: *confidence, discipline,* and *creativity.*

▶ Impressionist painters believed in focusing on ordinary subjects,
                                                  using
  capturing the effects of light on those subjects, and ~~to use~~
                                                          ^
  short brushstrokes.

The revision uses *-ing* forms for all the items in the series: *focusing, capturing,* and *using.*

► Racing to get to work on time, Sam drove down the middle
          ignored
of the road, ran one red light, and two stop signs.
             ^

The revision adds a verb to make the three items parallel: *drove, ran,*
and *ignored.*

In headings and lists, aim for as much parallelism as the content allows. (See 50b and 50c.)

9b Balance parallel ideas presented as pairs.

When pairing ideas, underscore their connection by expressing them in similar grammatical form. Paired ideas are usually connected in one of these ways:

- with a coordinating conjunction such as *and, but,* or *or*
- with a pair of correlative conjunctions such as *either . . . or* or *not only . . . but also*
- with a word introducing a comparison, usually *than* or *as*

Parallel ideas linked with coordinating conjunctions

Coordinating conjunctions (*and, but, or, nor, for, so,* and *yet*) link ideas of equal importance. When those ideas are closely parallel in content, they should be expressed in parallel grammatical form.

► Emily Dickinson's poetry features the use of dashes and
   the capitalization of
~~capitalizing~~ common words.
  ^

The revision balances the nouns *use* and *capitalization.*

► Many states are reducing property taxes for home owners
    extending
and ~~extend~~ financial aid in the form of tax credits to renters.
  ^

The revision balances the verb *reducing* with the verb *extending.*

Parallel ideas linked with correlative conjunctions

Correlative conjunctions come in pairs: *either . . . or, neither . . . nor, not only . . . but also, both . . . and, whether . . . or.* Make sure that the grammatical structure following the second half of the pair is the same as that following the first half.

▶ Thomas Edison was not only a prolific inventor but also ~~was~~ a successful entrepreneur.

> The words *a prolific inventor* follow *not only*, so *a successful entrepreneur* should follow *but also*. Repeating *was* creates an unbalanced effect.

▶ The clerk told me either to change my flight or ^*to*^ take the train.

> *To change my flight*, which follows *either*, should be balanced with *to take the train*, which follows *or*.

Comparisons linked with *than* or *as*

In comparisons linked with *than* or *as*, the elements being compared should be expressed in parallel grammatical structure.

▶ It is easier to speak in abstractions than ~~grounding~~ ^*to ground*^ one's thoughts in reality.

> *To speak* is balanced with *to ground*.

Comparisons should also be logical and complete. (See 10c.)

9c Repeat function words to clarify parallels.

Function words such as prepositions (*by, to*) and subordinating conjunctions (*that, because*) signal the grammatical nature of the word groups to follow. Although you can sometimes omit them, be sure to include them whenever they signal parallel structures that readers might otherwise miss.

▶ Our study revealed that left-handed students were more likely to have trouble with classroom desks and ^*that*^ rearranging desks for exam periods was useful.

> A second subordinating conjunction helps readers sort out the two parallel ideas: *that* left-handed students have trouble with classroom desks and *that* rearranging desks was useful.

EXERCISE 9–1 Edit the following sentences to correct faulty parallelism. Revisions of lettered sentences appear in the back of the book. Example:

> Rowena began her workday by pouring a cup of coffee and
> *checking*
> ~~checked~~ her e-mail.
> ^

a. Police dogs are used for finding lost children, tracking criminals, and the detection of bombs and illegal drugs.

b. Hannah told her rock-climbing partner that she bought a new harness and of her desire to climb Otter Cliffs.

c. It is more difficult to sustain an exercise program than starting one.

d. During basic training, I was not only told what to do but also what to think.

e. Jan wanted to drive to the wine country or at least Sausalito.

1. Camp activities include fishing trips, dance lessons, and computers.

2. Arriving at Lake Powell in a thunderstorm, the campers found it safer to remain in their cars than setting up their tents.

3. The streets were not only too steep but also were too narrow for anything other than pedestrian traffic.

4. More digital artists in the show are from the South Shore than the North Shore.

5. To load her toolbox, Anika the Clown gathered hats of different sizes, put in two tubes of face paint, arranged a bundle of extra-long straws, added a bag of colored balloons, and a battery-powered hair dryer.

10   Add needed words.

Sometimes writers leave out words intentionally, and the meaning of the sentence is not affected. But leaving out words can occasionally cause confusion for readers or make the sentence ungrammatical. Readers need to see at a glance how the parts of a sentence are connected.

> **MULTILINGUAL** Languages sometimes differ in the need for certain words. In particular, be alert for missing articles, verbs, subjects, or expletives. See 29, 30a, and 30b.

10a Add words needed to complete compound structures.

In compound structures, words are often left out for economy: *Tom is a man who means what he says and [who] says what he means.* Such omissions are acceptable as long as the omitted words are common to both parts of the compound structure.

If a sentence defies grammar or idiom because an omitted word is not common to both parts of the compound structure, the simplest solution is to put the word back in.

▶ Successful advertisers target customers whom they identify

who

through demographic research or have purchased their product
ʌ
in the past.

The word *who* must be included because *whom . . . have purchased* is not grammatically correct.

accepted
▶ Mayor Davis never has and never will accept a bribe.
ʌ

Has . . . accept is not grammatically correct.

in
▶ Many South Pacific islanders still believe and live by ancient laws.
ʌ

Believe . . . by is not idiomatic in English. (For a list of common idioms, see 18d.)

NOTE: Even when the omitted word is common to both parts of the compound structure, occasionally it must be inserted to avoid ambiguity.

My favorite *professor* and *mentor* influenced my choice of a career. [Professor and mentor are the same person.]

My favorite *professor* and *my mentor* influenced my choice of a career. [Professor and mentor are two different people; *my* must be repeated.]

10b Add the word *that* if there is any danger of misreading without it.

If there is no danger of misreading, the word *that* may be omitted when it introduces a subordinate clause. *The value of a principle is the number of things [that] it will explain.* Occasionally, however, a sentence might be misread without *that*.

▶ In his famous obedience experiments, psychologist Stanley
        that
   Milgram discovered ⌃ordinary people were willing to inflict

   physical pain on strangers.

   Milgram didn't discover ordinary people; he discovered that
   ordinary people were willing to inflict pain on strangers. The word
   that tells readers to expect a clause, not just *ordinary people*, as the
   direct object of *discovered*.

10c Add words needed to make comparisons logical and complete.

Comparisons should be made between items that are alike. To compare unlike items is illogical and distracting.

▶ The forests of North America are much more extensive than
   those of
   ⌃Europe.

   Forests must be compared with forests, not with all of Europe.

                      | *died*
▶ ~~The death rate of~~ ⌐nfantry soldiers in the Vietnam War ~~was~~ ⌃
   at a   *rate*
   much higher than the other combat troops.
   ⌃   ⌃

   The death rate cannot logically be compared to troops. The writer could
   revise the sentence by inserting *that of* after *than*, but the preceding
   revision is more concise.

▶ Some say that Ella Fitzgerald's renditions of Cole Porter's
                              singer's.
   songs are better than any other ~~singer.~~

   Ella Fitzgerald's renditions cannot logically be compared with a singer.
   The revision uses the possessive form *singer's*, with the word *renditions*
   being implied.

Sometimes the word *other* must be inserted to make a comparison logical.

▶ Jupiter is larger than any ^{*other*} planet in our solar system.

Jupiter is a planet, and it cannot be larger than itself.

Sometimes the word *as* must be inserted to make a comparison grammatically complete.

▶ The city of Lowell is as old, ^{*as*} if not older than, the neighboring

city of Lawrence.

The construction *as old* is not complete without a second *as: as old as . . . the neighboring city of Lawrence.*

Comparisons should be complete enough to ensure clarity. The reader should understand what is being compared.

INCOMPLETE Brand X is less salty.

COMPLETE Brand X is less salty than Brand Y.

Finally, comparisons should leave no ambiguity for readers. If more than one interpretation is possible, revise the sentence to state clearly which interpretation you intend. In the following ambiguous sentence, two interpretations are possible.

AMBIGUOUS Ken helped me more than my roommate.

CLEAR Ken helped me more than *he helped* my roommate.

CLEAR Ken helped me more than my roommate *did.*

10d Add the articles *a*, *an*, and *the* where necessary for grammatical completeness.

It is not always necessary to repeat articles with paired items: *We bought a computer and printer.* However, if one of the items requires *a* and the other requires *an*, both articles must be included.

▶ We bought a computer and ^{*an*} antivirus program.

Articles are sometimes omitted in recipes and other instructions that are meant to be followed while they are being read. In nearly all other forms of writing, whether formal or informal, such omissions are inappropriate.

 MULTILINGUAL Choosing and using articles can be challenging for multilingual writers. See 29.

EXERCISE 10–1 Add any words needed for grammatical or logical completeness in the following sentences. Revisions of lettered sentences appear in the back of the book. Example:

that
The officer feared the prisoner would escape.
^

a. A grapefruit or orange is a good source of vitamin C.
b. The women entering VMI can expect haircuts as short as the male cadets.
c. Looking out the family room window, Sarah saw her favorite tree, which she had climbed as a child, was gone.
d. The graphic designers are interested and knowledgeable about producing posters for the balloon race.
e. The Great Barrier Reef is larger than any coral reef in the world.

1. Very few black doctors were allowed to serve in the Civil War, and their qualifications had to be higher than white doctors.
2. Rachel is interested and committed to working at a school in Ecuador next semester.
3. Vassily likes mathematics more than his teacher.
4. The inspection team saw many historic buildings had been damaged by the earthquake.
5. Lila knows seven languages, but she found English harder to learn than any language.

 11 **Untangle mixed constructions.**

A mixed construction contains sentence parts that do not sensibly fit together. The mismatch may be a matter of grammar or of logic.

PRACTICE hackerhandbooks.com/rules
> Clarity > 10–2 to 10–4

11a Untangle the grammatical structure.

Once you begin a sentence, your choices are limited by the range of grammatical patterns in English. (See 47 and 48.) You cannot begin with one grammatical plan and switch without warning to another. Often you must rethink the purpose of the sentence and revise.

> **MIXED**   For most drivers who have a blood alcohol content of .05 percent double their risk of causing an accident.

The writer begins the sentence with a long prepositional phrase and makes it the subject of the verb *double*. But a prepositional phrase can serve only as a modifier; it cannot be the subject of a sentence.

> **REVISED**   For most drivers who have a blood alcohol content of .05 percent, the risk of causing an accident is doubled.

> **REVISED**   Most drivers who have a blood alcohol content of .05 percent double their risk of causing an accident.

In the first revision, the writer begins with the prepositional phrase and finishes the sentence with a proper subject and verb (*risk . . . is doubled*). In the second revision, the writer stays with the original verb (*double*) and heads into the sentence another way, making *drivers* the subject of *double*.

> *Electing*
> ► ~~When the country elects~~ a president is the most important
>   ^
>
>   responsibility in a democracy.

The adverb clause *When the country elects a president* cannot serve as the subject of the verb *is*. The revision replaces the adverb clause with a gerund phrase, a word group that can function as a subject. (See 48e and 48b.)

> ► Although the United States is one of the wealthiest nations in
>
>   the world, ~~but~~ more than twelve million of our children live
>
>   in poverty.

The coordinating conjunction *but* cannot link a subordinate clause (*Although the United States . . .*) with an independent clause (*more than twelve million of our children live in poverty*).

avoiding mixed grammar • logic •
revising awkward sentences
mix
11b
125

Occasionally a mixed construction is so tangled that it defies grammatical analysis. When this happens, back away from the sentence, rethink what you want to say, and then rewrite the sentence.

MIXED   In the whole-word method, children learn to recognize entire words rather than by the phonics method in which they learn to sound out letters and groups of letters.

REVISED   The whole-word method teaches children to recognize entire words; the phonics method teaches them to sound out letters and groups of letters.

MULTILINGUAL English does not allow double subjects, nor does it allow an object or an adverb to be repeated in an adjective clause. Unlike some other languages, English does not allow a noun and a pronoun to be repeated in a sentence if they have the same grammatical function. See 30c and 30d.

▶ My father ~~he~~ moved to Peru before he met my mother.

                                                                    the final exam
▶ ~~The final exam~~ I should really study for ~~it~~ to pass the

  course.

11b Straighten out the logical connections.

The subject and the predicate (the verb and its modifiers) should make sense together; when they don't, the error is known as *faulty predication*.

                    Tiffany
▶ We decided that ~~Tiffany's welfare~~ would not be safe living with

  her mother.

Tiffany, not her welfare, may not be safe.

                                        double personal exemption for the
▶ Under the revised plan, the elderly, ~~who now receive a double~~

  ~~personal exemption,~~ will be abolished.

The exemption, not the elderly, will be abolished.

An appositive is a noun that renames a nearby noun. When an appositive and the noun it renames are not logically equivalent, the error is known as *faulty apposition.* (See 48c.)

▶ ~~The tax accountant,~~ *Tax accounting,* a very lucrative profession, requires

intelligence, patience, and attention to mathematical detail.

The tax accountant is a person, not a profession.

11c Avoid *is when, is where,* and *reason . . . is because* constructions.

In formal English, readers sometimes object to *is when, is where,* and *reason . . . is because* constructions on grammatical or logical grounds.

▶ The ~~reason the~~ experiment failed ~~is~~ because conditions in the lab

were not sterile.

Grammatically, the verb *is* should not be followed by an adverb clause beginning with *because.* (See 62b and 62e.) The writer might have changed *because* to *that* (*The reason the experiment failed is that conditions in the lab were not sterile*), but the preceding revision is more concise.

▶ Anorexia nervosa is ~~where people~~ *a disorder suffered by people who* think they are too fat and diet

to the point of starvation.

Where refers to places. Anorexia nervosa is a disorder, not a place.

EXERCISE 11–1   Edit the following sentences to untangle mixed constructions. Revisions of lettered sentences appear in the back of the book. Example:

▶ ~~By taking~~ *Taking* the oath of allegiance made Ling a US citizen.

a. Using surgical gloves is a precaution now worn by dentists to prevent contact with patients' blood and saliva.

b. A physician, the career my brother is pursuing, requires at least ten years of challenging work.

c. The reason the pharaohs had bad teeth was because tiny particles of sand found their way into Egyptian bread.

d. Recurring bouts of flu among team members set a record for number of games forfeited.

e. In this box contains the key to your future.

1. Early diagnosis of prostate cancer is often curable.

2. Depending on our method of travel and our destination determines how many suitcases we are allowed to pack.

3. Dyslexia is where people have a learning disorder that impairs reading ability.

4. Even though Ellen had heard French spoken all her life, yet she could not speak it.

5. In understanding artificial intelligence code is a critical skill for computer game designers.

12 Repair misplaced and dangling modifiers.

Modifiers, whether they are single words, phrases, or clauses, should point clearly to the words they modify. As a rule, related words should be kept together.

12a Put limiting modifiers in front of the words they modify.

Limiting modifiers such as *only*, *even*, *almost*, *nearly*, and *just* should appear in front of a verb only if they modify the verb: *At first, I couldn't even touch my toes, much less grasp them.* If they limit the meaning of some other word in the sentence, they should be placed in front of that word.

▶ St. Vitus Cathedral, commissioned by Charles IV in the mid-

almost

fourteenth century, ~~almost~~ took six centuries to complete.
    ^

Almost limits the meaning of *six centuries*, not *took*.

▶ If you ~~just~~ interview *just* chemistry majors, your picture of the

student body's response to the new grading policies will

be incomplete.

The adverb *just* limits the meaning of *chemistry majors*, not *interview*.

When the limiting modifier *not* is misplaced, the sentence usually suggests a meaning the writer did not intend.

▶ In the United States in 1860, all black southerners were ~~not~~ *not*

slaves.

The original sentence says that no black southerners were slaves. The revision makes the writer's real meaning clear: Some (but not all) black southerners were slaves.

12b Place phrases and clauses so that readers can see at a glance what they modify.

Although phrases and clauses can appear at some distance from the words they modify, you will want to make sure your meaning is clear. When phrases or clauses are oddly placed, absurd misreadings can result.

MISPLACED	The soccer player returned to the clinic where he had undergone emergency surgery in 2004 in a limousine sent by Adidas.
REVISED	Traveling in a limousine sent by Adidas, the soccer player returned to the clinic where he had undergone emergency surgery in 2004.

The revision corrects the false impression that the soccer player underwent emergency surgery in a limousine.

▶ ~~There~~ *On the walls* are many pictures of comedians who have performed

at Gavin's. ~~on the walls.~~

The comedians weren't performing on the walls; the pictures were on the walls.

> *170-pound,*
> The robber was described as a six-foot-tall man with a heavy
>   ^
> mustache. ~~weighing 170 pounds.~~
>   ^
> The robber, not the mustache, weighed 170 pounds.

Occasionally the placement of a modifier leads to an ambiguity — a squinting modifier. In such a case, two revisions will be possible, depending on the writer's intended meaning.

AMBIGUOUS	The exchange students we met for coffee occasionally questioned us about our latest slang.
CLEAR	The exchange students we occasionally met for coffee questioned us about our latest slang.
CLEAR	The exchange students we met for coffee questioned us occasionally about our latest slang.

In the original version, it was not clear whether the meeting or the questioning happened occasionally. Both revisions eliminate the ambiguity.

12c Move awkwardly placed modifiers.

As a rule, a sentence should flow from subject to verb to object, without lengthy detours along the way. When a long adverbial word group separates a subject from its verb, a verb from its object, or a helping verb from its main verb, the result is often awkward.

>   *A*   *Hong Kong*
> ~~Hong Kong,~~ After more than 150 years of British rule, was
>   ^   ^
> transferred back to Chinese control in 1997.
>
> There is no reason to separate the subject, *Hong Kong*, from the verb,
> *was transferred*, with a long phrase.

MULTILINGUAL English does not allow an adverb to appear between a verb and its object. See 30f.

>   *easily*
> Yolanda lifted ~~easily~~ the fifty-pound weight.
>   ^

12d Avoid split infinitives when they are awkward.

An infinitive consists of *to* plus the base form of a verb: *to think, to breathe, to dance*. When a modifier appears between *to* and the verb, an infinitive is said to be "split": *to carefully balance, to completely understand*.

When a long word or a phrase appears between the parts of the infinitive, the result is usually awkward.

▶ ~~The~~ *If possible, the* patient should try to ~~if possible~~ avoid going up and

down stairs.

Attempts to avoid split infinitives can result in equally awkward sentences. When alternative phrasing sounds unnatural, most experts allow — and even encourage — splitting the infinitive.

AWKWARD   We decided actually to enforce the law.

BETTER   We decided to actually enforce the law.

At times, neither the split infinitive nor its alternative sounds particularly awkward. In such situations, it is usually better not to split the infinitive, especially in formal writing.

▶ Nursing students learn to ~~accurately~~ record a patient's vital
signs/ *accurately.*

EXERCISE 12–1   Edit the following sentences to correct misplaced or awkwardly placed modifiers. Revisions of lettered sentences appear in the back of the book. Example:

Answering questions can be annoying. *in a telephone survey* ~~in a telephone survey.~~

a. More research is needed to effectively evaluate the risks posed by volcanoes in the Pacific Northwest.

b. Many students graduate with debt from college totaling more than fifty thousand dollars.

c. It is a myth that humans only use 10 percent of their brains.

d. A coolhunter is a person who can find in the unnoticed corners of modern society the next wave of fashion.

e. All geese do not fly beyond Narragansett for the winter.

1. The flood nearly displaced half of the city's residents, who packed into several overcrowded shelters.

2. Most lions at night hunt for medium-size prey, such as zebra.

3. Several recent studies have encouraged heart patients to more carefully watch their cholesterol levels.

4. The garden's centerpiece is a huge sculpture that was carved by three women called *Walking in Place*.

5. The old Marlboro ads depicted a man on a horse smoking a cigarette.

12e Repair dangling modifiers.

A dangling modifier fails to refer logically to any word in the sentence. Dangling modifiers are easy to repair, but they can be hard to recognize, especially in your own writing.

Recognizing dangling modifiers

Dangling modifiers are usually word groups (such as verbal phrases) that suggest but do not name an actor. When a sentence opens with such a modifier, readers expect the subject of the next clause to name the actor. If it doesn't, the modifier dangles.

▶ **Understanding the need to create checks and balances on power,**
the framers of
the Constitution divided the government into three branches.
^

The framers of the Constitution (not the document itself) understood the need for checks and balances.

▶ **After completing seminary training,** *women have often been denied*
~~**women's**~~ **access to the**
^

priesthood. ~~has often been denied.~~
^

Women (not their access to the priesthood) complete the training.

The following sentences illustrate four common kinds of dangling modifiers.

DANGLING *Deciding to join the navy*, the recruiter enthusiastically pumped Joe's hand. [Participial phrase]

DANGLING *Upon entering the doctor's office*, a skeleton caught my attention. [Preposition followed by a gerund phrase]

DANGLING *To satisfy her mother*, the piano had to be practiced every day. [Infinitive phrase]

DANGLING *Though not eligible for the clinical trial*, the doctor was willing to prescribe the drug for Ethan on compassionate grounds. [Elliptical clause with an understood subject and verb]

These dangling modifiers falsely suggest that the recruiter decided to join the navy, that the skeleton entered the doctor's office, that the piano intended to satisfy the mother, and that the doctor was not eligible for the clinical trial.

Although most readers will understand the writer's intended meaning in such sentences, the inadvertent humor can be distracting.

Repairing dangling modifiers

To repair a dangling modifier, you can revise the sentence in one of two ways:

- Name the actor in the subject of the sentence.
- Name the actor in the modifier.

Depending on your sentence, one of these revision strategies may be more appropriate than the other.

ACTOR NAMED IN SUBJECT

▶ Upon entering the doctor's office, a skeleton. ~~caught my~~ *I noticed*
   ^   ^

~~attention.~~

▶ To satisfy her mother, the piano ~~had to be practiced~~ every day. *Jing-mei had to practice*
   ^

Checking for dangling modifiers

ACTOR NAMED IN MODIFIER

► *When Joe decided*
~~Deciding~~ to join the navy, the recruiter enthusiastically
his
pumped ~~Joe's~~ hand.

► *Ethan was*
Though not eligible for the clinical trial, the doctor was
him
willing to prescribe the drug for ~~Ethan~~ on compassionate
grounds.

NOTE: You cannot repair a dangling modifier just by moving it. Consider, for example, the sentence about the skeleton. If you put the modifier at the end of the sentence (*A skeleton caught my attention upon entering the doctor's office*), you are still suggesting — absurdly, of course — that the skeleton entered the office. The only way to avoid the problem is to put the word *I* in the sentence, either as the subject or in the modifier.

▶ Upon entering the doctor's office, *I noticed* a skeleton. ~~caught my attention.~~

▶ ~~Upon entering~~ *As I entered* the doctor's office, a skeleton caught my attention.

EXERCISE 12–2 Edit the following sentences to correct dangling modifiers. Most sentences can be revised in more than one way. Revisions of lettered sentences appear in the back of the book. Example:

To acquire a degree in almost any field, *a student must complete* two science courses. ~~must be completed.~~

a. Though only sixteen, UCLA accepted Martha's application.
b. To replace the gear mechanism, attached is a form to order the part by mail.
c. Settled in the cockpit, the pounding of the engine was muffled only slightly by my helmet.
d. After studying polymer chemistry, computer games seemed less complex to Phuong.
e. When a young man, my mother enrolled me in tap dance classes.

1. While working as a ranger in Everglades National Park, a Florida panther crossed the road in front of my truck one night.
2. By following the new recycling procedure, the city's landfill costs will be reduced significantly.
3. Serving as president of the missionary circle, one of Sophia's duties is to raise money for the church.
4. After buying an album by Ali Farka Toure, the rich and rolling rhythms of Malian music made more sense to Silas.
5. Opening the window to let out a huge bumblebee, the car swerved into an oncoming truck.

Eliminate distracting shifts.

The following sections can help you avoid unnecessary shifts that might distract or confuse your readers: shifts in point of view, in verb tense, in mood or voice, or from indirect to direct questions or quotations.

13a Make the point of view consistent in person and number.

The point of view of a piece of writing is the perspective from which it is written: first person (*I* or *we*), second person (*you*), or third person (*he, she, it, one, they,* or any noun).

The *I* (or *we*) point of view, which emphasizes the writer, is a good choice for informal letters and writing based primarily on personal experience. The *you* point of view, which emphasizes the reader, works well for giving advice or explaining how to do something. The third-person point of view, which emphasizes the subject, is appropriate in formal academic and professional writing.

Writers who are having difficulty settling on an appropriate point of view sometimes shift confusingly from one to another. The solution is to choose a suitable perspective and then stay with it.

▶ Our class practiced rescuing a victim trapped in a wrecked car.
                                                              We
We learned to dismantle the car with the essential tools. ~~You~~
        our   *our*
were graded on ~~your~~ speed and ~~your~~ skill in freeing the victim.

The writer should have stayed with the *we* point of view. *You* is inappropriate because the writer is not addressing readers directly. *You* should not be used in a vague sense meaning "anyone." (See 23d.)

          You need
▶ ~~One needs~~ a password and a credit card number to access the

database. You will be billed at an hourly rate.

You is an appropriate choice because the writer is giving advice directly to readers.

EXERCISE 13–1 Edit the following paragraph to eliminate distracting shifts in point of view (person and number).

When online dating first became available, many people thought that it would simplify romance. We believed that you could type in a list of criteria — sense of humor, college education, green eyes, good job — and a database would select the perfect mate. Thousands of people signed up for services and filled out their profiles, confident that true love was only a few mouse clicks away. As it turns out, however, virtual dating is no easier than traditional dating. I still have to contact the people I find, exchange e-mails and phone calls, and meet him in the real world. Although a database might produce a list of possibilities and screen out obviously undesirable people, you can't predict chemistry. More often than not, people who seem perfect online just don't click in person. Electronic services do help a single person expand their pool of potential dates, but it's no substitute for the hard work of romance.

13b Maintain consistent verb tenses.

Consistent verb tenses clearly establish the time of the actions being described. When a passage begins in one tense and then shifts without warning and for no reason to another, readers are distracted and confused.

▶ There was no way I could fight the current and win. Just as I

was losing hope, a stranger ~~jumps~~ ^{jumped} off a passing boat and

~~swims~~ ^{swam} toward me.

The writer thought that the present tense (*jumps, swims*) would convey immediacy and drama. But having begun in the past tense (*could fight, was losing*), the writer should follow through in the past tense.

Writers often encounter difficulty with verb tenses when writing about literature. Because fictional events occur outside the time frames of real life, the past tense and the present tense may seem equally appropriate. The literary convention, however,

is to describe fictional events consistently in the present tense.
(See 69b.)

> The scarlet letter is a punishment sternly placed on Hester's
>
>   *is*
> breast by the community, and yet it ~~was~~ a fanciful and
>
> imaginative product of Hester's own needlework.

EXERCISE 13–2   Edit the following paragraphs to eliminate distracting shifts in tense.

The English colonists who settled in Massachusetts received
assistance at first from the local Indian tribes, but by 1675 there
had been friction between the English and the Indians for many
years. On June 20 of that year, Metacomet, whom the colonists
called Philip, leads the Wampanoag tribe in the first of a series
of attacks on the colonial settlements. The war, known today as
King Philip's War, rages on for more than a year and leaves three
thousand Indians and six hundred colonists dead. Metacomet's
attempt to retain power in his native land failed. Finally he too is
killed, and the victorious colonists sell his wife and children into
slavery.

The Indians did not leave records of their encounters with the
English settlers, but the settlers recorded some of their experiences
at the hands of the Indians. One of the few accounts to survive
was written by a captured colonist, Mrs. Mary Rowlandson. She
is a minister's wife who is kidnapped by an Indian war party and
held captive for eleven weeks in 1676. Her history, *A Narrative of
the Captivity and Restoration of Mrs. Mary Rowlandson*, tells the
story of her experiences with the Wampanoags. Although it did not
paint a completely balanced picture of the Indians, Rowlandson's
narrative, which is considered a classic early American text, showed
its author to be a keen observer of life in an Indian camp.

13c Make verbs consistent in mood and voice.

Unnecessary shifts in the mood of a verb can be distracting
and confusing to readers. There are three moods in English: the

indicative, used for facts, opinions, and questions; the *imperative*, used for orders or advice; and the *subjunctive*, used in certain contexts to express wishes or conditions contrary to fact (see 27g).

The following passage shifts confusingly from the indicative to the imperative mood.

▶ The counselor advised us to spread out our core requirements

She also suggested that we
over two or three semesters. ~~Also,~~ pay attention to pre-
        ^

requisites for elective courses.

The writer began by reporting the counselor's advice in the indicative mood (*counselor advised*) and switched to the imperative mood (*pay attention*); the revision puts both sentences in the indicative.

A verb may be in either the active voice (with the subject doing the action) or the passive voice (with the subject receiving the action). (See 8a.) If a writer shifts without warning from one to the other, readers may be left wondering why.

                                                gives it
▶ Each student completes a self-assessment ∕, ~~The self-assessment~~
                                          ^

                              exchanges
~~is then given~~ to the teacher, and a copy ~~is exchanged~~ with
              ^   ^

a classmate.

Because the passage began in the active voice (*student completes*) and then switched to the passive (*self-assessment is given, copy is exchanged*), readers are left wondering who gives the self-assessment to the teacher and the classmate. The active voice, which is clearer and more direct, leaves no ambiguity.

13d Avoid sudden shifts from indirect to direct questions or quotations.

An indirect question reports a question without asking it: *We asked whether we could visit Miriam.* A direct question asks directly: *Can we visit Miriam?* Sudden shifts from indirect to direct questions are awkward. In addition, sentences containing such shifts are impossible to punctuate because indirect questions must end with a period and direct questions must end with a question mark. (See 38b.)

▶ I wonder whether Karla knew of the theft and, if so, ~~did~~

   whether she reported
   ~~she report~~ it to the police~~?~~.
      ^   ^

The revision poses both questions indirectly. The writer could also ask both questions directly: *Did Karla know of the theft, and, if so, did she report it to the police?*

An indirect quotation reports someone's words without quoting word for word: *Annabelle said that she is a Virgo.* A direct quotation presents the exact words of a speaker or writer, set off with quotation marks: *Annabelle said, "I am a Virgo."* Unannounced shifts from indirect to direct quotations are distracting and confusing, especially when the writer fails to insert the necessary quotation marks, as in the following example.

▶ The patient said she had been experiencing heart palpitations

   asked me to   *was*
and ~~please~~ run as many tests as possible to find out what~~'s~~
  ^   ^

wrong.

The revision reports the patient's words indirectly. The writer also could quote the words directly: *The patient said, "I have been experiencing heart palpitations. Please run as many tests as possible to find out what's wrong."*

EXERCISE 13–3   Edit the following sentences to make the verbs consistent in mood and voice and to eliminate distracting shifts from indirect to direct questions or quotations. Revisions of lettered sentences appear in the back of the book. Example:

   As a public relations intern, I wrote press releases, managed
                    fielded all phone calls.
   the Web site, and ~~all phone calls were fielded by me.~~
                 ^

a. An incredibly talented musician, Ray Charles mastered R&B, soul, and gospel styles. Even country music was performed well by him.

b. Environmentalists point out that shrimp farming in Southeast Asia is polluting water and making farmlands useless. They warn that action must be taken by governments before it is too late.

c. The samples were observed for five days before we detected any growth.

d. In his famous soliloquy, Hamlet contemplates whether death would be preferable to his difficult life and, if so, is he capable of committing suicide?

e. The lawyer told the judge that Miranda Hale was innocent and allow her to prove the allegations false.

1. When the photographs were taken on the beach at sunset, I intentionally left the foreground out of focus.

2. If the warning sirens sound, evacuate at once. It is not advised that you return to the building until the alarm has stopped.

3. Most baby products warn parents to follow all directions carefully. Also, supervise children closely during use.

4. The advertisement promised that results would be seen in five days or consumers could return the product for a full refund.

5. Investigators need to determine first whether there was a forcible entry and then what was the motive?

EXERCISE 13–4 Edit the following sentences to eliminate distracting shifts. Revisions of lettered sentences appear in the back of the book. Example:

> For many first-year engineering students, adjusting to a
>
> rigorous course load can be so challenging that ~~you~~ *they*
>
> sometimes feel overwhelmed.

a. A courtroom lawyer has more than a touch of theater in their blood.

b. The interviewer asked if we had brought our proof of citizenship and did we bring our passports?

c. The reconnaissance scout often has to make fast decisions and use sophisticated equipment to keep their team from being detected.

d. After the animators finish their scenes, the production designer arranges the clips according to the storyboard. Synchronization notes must also be made for the sound editor and the composer.

e. Madame Defarge is a sinister figure in Dickens's *A Tale of Two Cities.* On a symbolic level, she represents fate; like the Greek Fates, she knitted the fabric of individual destiny.

1. Everyone should protect yourself from the sun, especially on the first day of extensive exposure.

2. Our neighbors told us that the island was being evacuated because of the coming storm. Also, take the northern route to the mainland.

3. Rescue workers put water on her face and lifted her head gently onto a pillow. Finally, she opens her eyes.

4. In my first tai chi class, the instructor asked if I had ever done yoga stretches and did I have good balance?

5. The artist has often been seen as a threat to society, especially when they refuse to conform to conventional standards of taste.

14 Emphasize key ideas.

Within each sentence, emphasize your point by expressing it in the subject and verb of an independent clause, the words that receive the most attention from readers (see 14a–14e).

Within longer stretches of prose, you can draw attention to ideas deserving special emphasis by using a variety of techniques, often involving an unusual twist or some element of surprise (see 14f).

14a Coordinate equal ideas; subordinate minor ideas.

When combining two or more ideas in one sentence, you have two choices: coordination or subordination. Choose coordination to indicate that the ideas are equal or nearly equal in importance. Choose subordination to indicate that one idea is less important than another.

Coordination

Coordination draws attention equally to two or more ideas. To coordinate single words or phrases, join them with a coordinating conjunction or with a pair of correlative conjunctions: *bananas and strawberries; not only a lackluster plot but also inferior acting* (see 46g).

To coordinate independent clauses — word groups that express a complete thought and that can stand alone as a sentence — join them with a comma and a coordinating conjunction or with a semicolon:

| , and | , but | , or | , nor |
| , for | , so | , yet | ; |

The semicolon is often accompanied by a conjunctive adverb such as *moreover*, *furthermore*, *therefore*, or *however* or by a transitional phrase such as *for example*, *in other words*, or *as a matter of fact*. (For a longer list, see p. 143.)

Assume, for example, that your intention is to draw equal attention to the following two ideas.

> Social networking Web sites offer ways for people to connect in the virtual world. They do not replace face-to-face forms of social interaction.

To coordinate these ideas, you can join them with a comma and the coordinating conjunction *but* or with a semicolon and the conjunctive adverb *however*.

> Social networking Web sites offer ways for people to connect in the virtual world, but they do not replace face-to-face forms of social interaction.

> Social networking Web sites offer ways for people to connect in the virtual world; however, they do not replace face-to-face forms of social interaction.

It is important to choose a coordinating conjunction or conjunctive adverb appropriate to your meaning. In the preceding example, the two ideas contrast with each other, calling for *but* or *however*. (For specific coordination strategies, see the chart on p. 143.)

Subordination

To give unequal emphasis to two or more ideas, express the major idea in an independent clause and place any minor ideas in subordinate clauses or phrases. (For specific subordination strategies, see the chart on p. 144.)

Let your intended meaning determine which idea you emphasize. Consider the two ideas about social networking Web sites.

> Social networking Web sites offer ways for people to connect in the virtual world. They do not replace face-to-face forms of social interaction.

If your purpose is to stress the ways that people can connect in the virtual world rather than the limitations of these connections, subordinate the idea about the limitations.

> Although they do not replace face-to-face forms of social interaction, social networking Web sites offer ways for people to connect in the virtual world.

To focus on the limitations of the virtual world, subordinate the idea about the Web sites.

> Although social networking Web sites offer ways for people to connect in the virtual world, they do not replace face-to-face forms of social interaction.

Using coordination to combine sentences of equal importance

1. Consider using a comma and a coordinating conjunction. (See 32a.)

, and	, but	, or	, nor
, for	, so	, yet	

▶ In Orthodox Jewish funeral ceremonies, the shroud is a simple linen
and the
vestment/, ~~The~~ coffin is plain wood.

2. Consider using a semicolon with a conjunctive adverb or transitional phrase. (See 34b.)

also	however	next
as a result	in addition	now
besides	in fact	of course
consequently	in other words	otherwise
finally	in the first place	still
for example	meanwhile	then
for instance	moreover	therefore
furthermore	nevertheless	thus

moreover, she
▶ Alicia scored well on the SAT/; ~~She also~~ had excellent grades and a

record of community service.

3. Consider using a semicolon alone. (See 34a.)

in
▶ In youth we learn/; ~~In~~ age we understand.

Using subordination to combine sentences of unequal importance

1. Consider putting the less important idea in a subordinate clause beginning with one of the following words. (See 48e.)

after	before	that	which
although	even though	unless	while
as	if	until	who
as if	since	when	whom
because	so that	where	whose

When
▶ ~~Elizabeth~~ Cady Stanton proposed a convention to discuss the
  ^

status of women in America ~~.~~/, Lucretia Mott agreed.
                                    ^

2. Consider putting the less important idea in an appositive phrase. (See 48c.)

▶ Karate ~~,~~ ~~is~~ a discipline based on the philosophy of nonviolence ~~.~~/,
        ^   ^

~~It~~ teaches the art of self-defense.

3. Consider putting the less important idea in a participial phrase. (See 48b.)

Noticing
▶ ~~I noticed~~ the EpiPen in her tote bag ~~.~~/, I asked her if she has
  ^   ^

food allergies.

EXERCISE 14–1 Use the coordination or subordination technique in brackets to combine each pair of independent clauses. Revisions of lettered sentences appear in the back of the book. Example:

Ted Williams was one of the best hitters in the history of
baseball, but he
~~baseball. He~~ never won a World Series ring. [*Use a comma*
^

and a coordinating conjunction.]

a. Williams played for the Boston Red Sox from 1939 to 1960. He managed the Washington Senators and the Texas Rangers for several years after retiring as a player. [*Use a comma and a coordinating conjunction.*]

b. In 1941, Williams finished the season with a batting average of .406. No player has hit over .400 for a season since then. [*Use a semicolon.*]

c. Williams acknowledged that Joe DiMaggio was a better all-around player. Williams felt that he was a better hitter than DiMaggio. [*Use the subordinating conjunction* although.]

d. Williams was a stubborn man. He always refused to tip his cap to the crowd after a home run because he claimed that fans were fickle. [*Use a semicolon and the transitional phrase* for example.]

e. Williams's relationship with the media was unfriendly at best. He sarcastically called baseball writers the "knights of the keyboard" in his memoir. [*Use a semicolon.*]

1. Williams took time out from his baseball career to serve in the Marines during World War II. He went on active duty a second time during the Korean War. [*Use a semicolon and the transitional phrase* in addition.]

2. Williams was named most valuable player twice in his career. He was listed as the eighth-best baseball player of all time by the *Sporting News* in 1999. [*Use the relative pronoun* who.]

3. Williams hit a home run in his final at bat in September 1960. Then he retired as a player. [*Use a comma and a coordinating conjunction.*]

4. Williams surprised many people with his 1966 Hall of Fame induction speech. It called for recognition of Negro League players and their inclusion in the Hall of Fame. [*Use the relative pronoun* which.]

5. At the 1999 All-Star game, Ted Williams returned to Fenway Park in Boston to throw out the ceremonial first pitch. For the first time he waved his hat to the cheering fans. [*Use a comma and a coordinating conjunction.*]

14b Combine choppy sentences.

Short sentences demand attention, so you should use them primarily for emphasis. Too many short sentences, one after the other, make for a choppy style.

If an idea is not important enough to deserve its own sentence, try combining it with a sentence close by. Put any minor ideas in subordinate structures such as phrases or subordinate clauses. (See 48.)

▶ The Parks Department keeps the use of insecticides to a

because the

minimum/ ~~The~~ city is concerned about the environment.

The writer wanted to emphasize that the Parks Department minimizes its use of chemicals, so she put the reason in a subordinate clause beginning with *because*.

▶ The Chesapeake and Ohio Canal, ~~is~~ a 184-mile waterway

constructed in the 1800s/, ~~It~~ was a major source of

transportation for goods during the Civil War.

A minor idea is now expressed in an appositive phrase (*a 184-mile waterway constructed in the 1800s*).

E

▶ ~~Sister Consilio was~~ Enveloped in a black robe with only her

Sister Consilio

face and hands visible/, ~~She~~ was an imposing figure.

Because Sister Consilio's overall impression was more important to the writer's purpose, the writer put the description of the clothing in a participial phrase beginning with *Enveloped*.

Although subordination is ordinarily the most effective technique for combining short, choppy sentences, coordination is appropriate when the ideas are equal in importance.

and

▶ At 3:30 p.m., Forrest displayed a flag of truce/~~Forrest~~ sent

in a demand for unconditional surrender.

Combining two short sentences by joining their predicates (*displayed . . . sent*) is an effective coordination technique.

MULTILINGUAL Unlike some other languages, English does not repeat objects or adverbs in adjective clauses. The relative pronoun (*that, which, whom*) or relative adverb (*where*) in the adjective clause represents the object or adverb. See 30d.

▶ The apartment that we rented ~~it~~ needed repairs.

The pronoun *it* cannot repeat the relative pronoun *that*.

▶ The small town where my grandfather was born ~~there~~ is

now a big city.

The adverb *there* cannot repeat the relative adverb *where*.

EXERCISE 14–2   Combine the following sentences by subordinating minor ideas or by coordinating ideas of equal importance. You must decide which ideas are minor because the sentences are given out of context. Revisions of lettered sentences appear in the back of the book. Example:

> Agnes, ~~was~~ another girl I worked with~~,~~ ~~She~~ was a hyperactive
>
> child.

a. The X-Men comic books and Japanese woodcuts of kabuki dancers were part of Marlena's research project on popular culture. They covered the tabletop and the chairs.

b. Our waitress was costumed in a kimono. She had painted her face white. She had arranged her hair in a lacquered beehive.

c. Students can apply for a spot in the leadership program. The program teaches thinking and communication skills.

d. Shore houses were flooded up to the first floor. Beaches were washed away. Brant's Lighthouse was swallowed by the sea.

e. Laura Thackray is an engineer at Volvo Car Corporation. She addressed women's safety needs. She designed a pregnant crash-test dummy.

1. I noticed that the sky was glowing orange and red. I bent down to crawl into the bunker.

2. The Market Inn is located on North Wharf. It doesn't look very impressive from the outside. The food, however, is excellent.

3. He walked up to the pitcher's mound. He dug his toe into the ground. He swung his arm around backward and forward. Then he threw the ball and struck the batter out.

4. Eryn and Maeve have decided to start a business. They have known each other since kindergarten. They will renovate homes for people with disabilities.

5. The first football card set was released by the Goudey Gum Company in 1933. The set featured only three football players. They were Red Grange, Bronko Nagurski, and Knute Rockne.

14c Avoid ineffective or excessive coordination.

Coordinate structures are appropriate only when you intend to draw readers' attention equally to two or more ideas: *Professor Sakellarios praises loudly, and she criticizes softly.* If one idea is more important than another — or if a coordinating conjunction does not clearly signal the relationship between the ideas — you should subordinate the less important idea.

INEFFECTIVE COORDINATION Closets were taxed as rooms, and most colonists stored their clothes in chests or clothespresses.

IMPROVED WITH SUBORDINATION Because closets were taxed as rooms, most colonists stored their clothes in chests or clothespresses.

Because it is so easy to string ideas together with *and*, writers often rely too heavily on coordination in their rough drafts. The cure for excessive coordination is simple: Look for opportunities to tuck minor ideas into subordinate clauses or phrases.

> *After four hours,*
> ~~Four hours went by, and~~ a rescue truck finally arrived, but
>
> by that time we had been evacuated in a helicopter.

Three independent clauses were excessive. The least important idea has become a prepositional phrase.

EXERCISE 14–3 The following sentences show coordinated ideas (ideas joined with a coordinating conjunction or a semicolon). Restructure the sentences by subordinating minor ideas. You must decide which ideas are minor because the sentences are given out of context. Revisions of lettered sentences appear in the back of the book. Example:

> *where they*
> The rowers returned to shore, ~~and~~ had a party on the beach
> *to celebrate*
> ~~and celebrated~~ the start of the season.

a. These particles are known as "stealth liposomes," and they can hide in the body for a long time without detection.

b. Jan is a competitive gymnast and majors in biology; her goal is to apply her athletic experience and her science degree to a career in sports medicine.

c. Students, textile workers, and labor unions have loudly protested sweatshop abuses, so apparel makers have been forced to examine their labor practices.

d. IRC (Internet relay chat) was developed in a European university; it was created as a way for a group of graduate students to talk about projects from their dorm rooms.

e. The cafeteria's new menu has an international flavor, and it includes everything from enchiladas and pizza to pad thai and sauerbraten.

1. Victor switched on his remote-control lawn mower, and it began to shudder and emit clouds of smoke.

2. Iguanas are dependent on ultraviolet rays from the sun, so in the winter months they must be put under ultraviolet-coated lights that can be purchased at most pet stores.

3. The Civil War Trust was founded in 1991; it spearheads a nation-wide campaign to protect America's Civil War battlefields.

4. We did not expect to receive so many large orders so quickly, and we are short on inventory.

5. Mother spread her love equally among us all, but she made each of us feel special in our own way.

14d Do not subordinate major ideas.

If a sentence buries its major idea in a subordinate construction, readers may not give the idea enough attention. Make sure to express your major idea in an independent clause and to subordinate any minor ideas.

▶ Harry S. Truman, who was the unexpected winner of the *defeated Thomas E. Dewey,*

1948 presidential election, . ~~defeated Thomas E. Dewey.~~

The writer wanted to focus on Truman's unexpected victory, but the original sentence buried this information in an adjective clause. The revision puts the more important idea in an independent clause and tucks the less important idea into an adjective clause (*who defeated Thomas E. Dewey*).

▶ *As*
I was driving home from my new job, heading down

Ranchitos Road, ~~when~~ my car suddenly overheated.

The writer wanted to emphasize that the car overheated, not the fact of driving home. The revision expresses the major idea in an independent clause and places the less important idea in an adverb clause (*As I was driving home from my new job*).

14e Do not subordinate excessively.

In attempting to avoid short, choppy sentences, writers some-times go to the opposite extreme, putting more subordinate ideas into a sentence than its structure can bear. If a sentence collapses of its own weight, occasionally it can be restructured. More often, however, such sentences must be divided.

▶ In *Animal Liberation*, Peter Singer argues that animals possess
                                                            H
nervous systems and can feel pain. ~~and that~~ ⱨe therefore
                                   ^   ^
believes that "the ethical principle on which human equality

rests requires us to extend equal consideration to animals" (1).

Excessive subordination makes it difficult for the reader to focus on the quoted passage. By splitting the original sentence into two separate sentences, the writer draws attention to Peter Singer's main claim, that humans should give "equal consideration to animals."

EXERCISE 14–4 In each of the following sentences, the idea that the writer wished to emphasize is buried in a subordinate construction. Restructure each sentence so that the independent clause expresses the major idea, as indicated in brackets, and lesser ideas are subordinated. Revisions of lettered sentences appear in the back of the book. Example:

> *Although*
> Catherine has weathered many hardships, ~~although~~ she has
> ^
> rarely become discouraged. [*Emphasize that Catherine has*
>
> *rarely become discouraged.*]

a. Gina worked as an aide for the relief agency, distributing food and medical supplies. [*Emphasize distributing food and medical supplies.*]

b. Janbir spent every Saturday learning tabla drumming, noticing with each hour of practice that his memory for complex patterns was improving. [*Emphasize Janbir's memory.*]

c. The rotor hit, gouging a hole about an eighth of an inch deep in my helmet. [*Emphasize that the rotor gouged a hole in the helmet.*]

d. My grandfather, who raised his daughters the old-fashioned way, was born eighty years ago in Puerto Rico. [*Emphasize how the grandfather raised his daughters.*]

e. The Narcan reversed the depressive effect of the drug, saving the patient's life. [*Emphasize that the patient's life was saved.*]

1. Fatima, who studied Persian miniature painting after college, majored in early childhood education. [*Emphasize Fatima's studies after college.*]

2. I was losing consciousness when my will to live kicked in. [*Emphasize the will to live.*]

3. Using a sliding compound miter saw, the carpenter made intricate edges on the cabinets. [*Emphasize the carpenter's use of the saw.*]

4. Ernie was using origami to solve some tricky manufacturing problems when he decided to leave engineering and become an artist. [*Emphasize Ernie's decision.*]

5. As the undulating waves glinted in the sun, the paddlers synchronized their strokes. [*Emphasize the brightness of the waves.*]

14f Experiment with techniques for gaining special emphasis.

By experimenting with certain techniques, usually involving some element of surprise, you can draw attention to ideas that deserve special emphasis. Use such techniques sparingly, however, or they will lose their punch. The writer who tries to emphasize everything ends up emphasizing nothing.

Using sentence endings for emphasis

You can highlight an idea simply by withholding it until the end of a sentence. The technique works something like a punch line. In the following example, the sentence's meaning is not revealed until its very last word.

> The only completely consistent people are the dead.
>
> — Aldous Huxley

Using parallel structure for emphasis

Parallel grammatical structure draws special attention to paired ideas or to items in a series. (See 9.) When parallel ideas are paired, the emphasis falls on words that underscore comparisons or contrasts, especially when they occur at the end of a phrase or clause.

> We must *stop talking* about the *American dream* and *start listening* to the *dreams of Americans.* — Reubin Askew

In a parallel series, the emphasis falls at the end, so it is generally best to end with the most dramatic or climactic item in the series.

> Sister Charity enjoyed passing out writing punishments: translate the Ten Commandments into Latin, type a thousand-word essay on good manners, copy the New Testament with a quill pen.
>
> — Marie Visosky, student

Using an occasional short sentence for emphasis

Too many short sentences in a row will fast become monotonous (see 14b), but an occasional short sentence, when played off against longer sentences in the same passage, will draw attention to an idea.

> The great secret, known to internists and learned early in marriage by internists' wives [or husbands], but still hidden from the general public, is that most things get better by themselves. Most things, in fact, are better by morning. — Lewis Thomas

15 Provide some variety.

When a rough draft is filled with too many sentences that begin the same way or have the same structure, try injecting some variety — as long as you can do so without sacrificing clarity or ease of reading.

15a Vary your sentence openings.

Most sentences in English begin with the subject, move to the verb, and continue to the object, with modifiers tucked in along the way or put at the end. For the most part, such sentences are fine. Put too many of them in a row, however, and they become monotonous.

Adverbial modifiers are easily movable when they modify verbs; they can often be inserted ahead of the subject. Such modifiers might be single words, phrases, or clauses.

> *Eventually a*
> ▸ A few drops of sap ~~eventually~~ began to trickle into the
>
> bucket.

Like most adverbs, *eventually* does not need to appear close to the verb it modifies (*began*).

> *Just as the sun was coming up, a*
> ▸ A pair of black ducks flew over the pond. ~~just as the sun was~~
>
> ~~coming up.~~

The adverb clause, which modifies the verb *flew*, is as clear at the beginning of the sentence as it is at the end.

Adjectives and participial phrases can frequently be moved to the beginning of a sentence without loss of clarity.

> *Dejected and withdrawn,*
> ▸ Edward, ~~dejected and withdrawn,~~ nearly gave up his search
>
> for a job.

>   *A*   *John and I*
> ▸ ~~John and I,~~ anticipating a peaceful evening, sat down at the
>
> campfire to brew a cup of coffee.

TIP: When beginning a sentence with an adjective or a participial phrase, make sure that the subject of the sentence names the person or thing described in the introductory phrase. If it doesn't, the phrase will dangle. (See 12e.)

15b Use a variety of sentence structures.

A writer should not rely too heavily on simple sentences and compound sentences, for the effect tends to be both monotonous and choppy. (See 14b and 14c.) Too many complex or compound-complex sentences, however, can be equally monotonous. If your style tends to one or the other extreme, try to achieve a better mix of sentence types.

The major sentence types are illustrated in the following sentences, all taken from Flannery O'Connor's "The King of the Birds," an essay describing the author's pet peafowl.

SIMPLE	Frequently the cock combines the lifting of his tail with the raising of his voice.
COMPOUND	Any chicken's dusting hole is out of place in a flower bed, but the peafowl's hole, being the size of a small crater, is more so.
COMPLEX	The peacock does most of his serious strutting in the spring and summer when he has a full tail to do it with.
COMPOUND-COMPLEX	The cock's plumage requires two years to attain its pattern, and for the rest of his life, this chicken will act as though he designed it himself.

For a fuller discussion of sentence types, see 49a.

15c Try inverting sentences occasionally.

A sentence is inverted if it does not follow the normal subject-verb-object pattern (see 47c). Many inversions sound artificial and should be avoided except in the most formal contexts. But if an inversion sounds natural, it can provide a welcome touch of variety.

> *Opposite the produce section is a*
> ▶ A refrigerated case of mouthwatering cheeses; is opposite
>   ^   ^
>
> the produce section; a friendly attendant will cut off just
>
> the amount you want.

The revision inverts the normal subject-verb order by moving the verb, *is*, ahead of its subject, *case*.

> *Set at the top two corners of the stage were huge*
> ▶ Huge lavender hearts outlined in bright white lights. were
>   ^   ^
>
> set at the top two corners of the stage.

In the revision, the subject, *hearts*, appears after the verb, *were set*. Notice that the two parts of the verb are also inverted — and separated from each other (*Set . . . were*) — without any awkwardness or loss of meaning.

Inverted sentences are used for emphasis as well as for variety (see 14f).

EXERCISE 15–1 Improve sentence variety in each of the following sentences by using the technique suggested in brackets. Revisions of lettered sentences appear in the back of the book. Example:

> *To protect endangered marine turtles, fishing*
> ~~Fishing~~ crews place turtle excluder devices in fishing nets.
> ^
> ~~to protect endangered marine turtles.~~ [*Begin the sentence*
>
> *with the adverbial infinitive phrase.*]

a. The exhibits for insects and spiders are across the hall from the fossils exhibit. [*Invert the sentence.*]

b. Sayuri becomes a successful geisha after growing up desperately poor in Japan. [*Move the adverb clause to the beginning of the sentence.*]

c. The 1980 eruption of Mount St. Helens was the deadliest, most destructive volcanic eruption in US history. Researchers believe that a series of nearby earthquakes contributed to the eruption. [*Combine the two sentences into a complex sentence.*]

d. Ice cream typically contains 10 percent milk fat. Premium ice cream may contain up to 16 percent milk fat and has considerably less air in the product. [*Combine the two sentences as a compound sentence.*]

e. The economy may recover more quickly than expected if home values climb. [*Move the adverb clause to the beginning of the sentence.*]

1. The Dust Bowl farmers, looking wearily into the cameras of US government photographers, represented the harshest effects of the Great Depression. [*Move the participial phrase to the beginning of the sentence.*]

2. The Trans Alaska Pipeline was completed in 1977. It has moved more than fifteen billion barrels of oil since 1977. [*Combine the two sentences into a complex sentence.*]

3. Mr. Guo habitually dresses in loose clothing and canvas shoes for his wushu workout. [*Move the adverb to the beginning of the sentence.*]

4. A number of obstacles are strategically placed throughout a firefighter training maze. [*Invert the sentence.*]

5. Ian McKellen is a British actor who made his debut in 1961 and was knighted in 1991, and he played Gandalf in the movie trilogy *The Lord of the Rings*. [*Make a simple sentence. See also 49a.*]

EXERCISE 15–2   Edit the following paragraph to increase sentence variety.

Making architectural models is a skill that requires patience and precision. It is an art that illuminates a design. Architects come up with a grand and intricate vision. Draftspersons convert that vision into blueprints. The model maker follows the blueprints. The model maker builds a miniature version of the structure. Modelers can work in traditional materials like wood and clay and paint. Modelers can work in newer materials like Styrofoam and liquid polymers. Some modelers still use cardboard, paper, and glue. Other modelers prefer glue guns, deformable plastic, and thin aluminum and brass wire. The modeler may seem to be making a small mess in the early stages of model building. In the end the modeler has completed a small-scale structure. Architect Rem Koolhaas has insisted that plans reveal the logic of a design. He has argued that models expose the architect's vision. The model maker's art makes this vision real.

16   Tighten wordy sentences.

Long sentences are not necessarily wordy, nor are short sentences always concise. A sentence is wordy if it can be tightened without loss of meaning.

16a Eliminate redundancies.

Writers often repeat themselves unnecessarily, thinking that expressions such as *cooperate together*, *yellow in color*, or *basic essentials* add emphasis to their writing. In reality, such redundancies do just the opposite. There is no need to say the same thing twice.

▶ Daniel ~~is now employed~~ ^{works} at a private rehabilitation center ~~working~~ as a registered physical therapist.

Though modifiers ordinarily add meaning to the words they modify, occasionally they are redundant.

▶ Sylvia ~~very hurriedly~~ scribbled her name, address, and phone number on a greasy napkin.

The word *scribbled* already suggests that Sylvia wrote *very hurriedly*.

▶ Gabriele Muccino's film *The Pursuit of Happyness* tells the

story of a single father determined ~~in his mind~~ to pull

himself and his son out of homelessness.

The word *determined* contains the idea that his resolution formed
in his mind.

16b Avoid unnecessary repetition of words.

Though words may be repeated deliberately for effect, repetitions
will seem awkward if they are clearly unnecessary. When a more
concise version is possible, choose it.

▶ Our fifth patient, in room six, is a̶ mentally ill. ~~patient.~~

▶ The best teachers help each student ~~become a better student~~ (grow)

both academically and emotionally.

16c Cut empty or inflated phrases.

An empty phrase can be cut with little or no loss of meaning.
Common examples are introductory word groups that weaken
the writer's authority by apologizing or hedging: *in my opinion, I
think that, it seems that, one must admit that,* and so on.

▶ ~~In my opinion,~~ O̶ur current immigration policy is misguided.

Readers understand without being told that they are hearing the
writer's opinion.

Inflated phrases can be reduced to a word or two without
loss of meaning.

INFLATED	CONCISE
along the lines of	like
as a matter of fact	in fact
at all times	always
at the present time	now, currently
at this point in time	now, currently
because of the fact that	because

INFLATED	CONCISE
by means of	by
by virtue of the fact that	because
due to the fact that	because
for the purpose of	for
for the reason that	because
have the ability to	be able to, can
in light of the fact that	because
in order to	to
in spite of the fact that	although, though
in the event that	if
in the final analysis	finally
in the nature of	like
in the neighborhood of	about
until such time as	until

▶ ~~At this point in time~~ M̂y skills and experience are a perfect

match for the position of assistant manager.

16d Simplify the structure.

If the structure of a sentence is needlessly indirect, try simplifying it. Look for opportunities to strengthen the verb.

▶ The financial analyst claimed that because of volatile market

conditions she could not ~~make an~~ estimate ~~of~~ the company's

future profits.

The verb *estimate* is more vigorous and concise than *make an estimate of.*

The colorless verbs *is, are, was,* and *were* frequently generate excess words.

▶ Investigators ~~were involved in~~ *studied* ~~studying~~ the effect of classical

music on unborn babies.

The revision is more direct and concise. The action (*studying*), originally appearing in a subordinate structure, has become a strong verb, *studied*.

The expletive constructions *there is* and *there are* (or *there was* and *there were*) can also generate excess words. The same is true of expletive constructions beginning with *it*. (See 47c.)

▶ ~~There is~~ ^A^ nother module ~~that~~ tells the story of Charles Darwin

and introduces the theory of evolution.

▶ ~~It is imperative that~~ ^A^ ll night managers ^must^ follow strict procedures

when locking the safe.

Finally, verbs in the passive voice may be needlessly indirect. When the active voice expresses your meaning as effectively, use it. (See 8a.)

▶ All too often, athletes with marginal academic skills ^*our coaches have recruited*^ ~~have~~

~~been recruited by our coaches.~~

16e Reduce clauses to phrases, phrases to single words.

Word groups functioning as modifiers can often be made more compact. Look for any opportunities to reduce clauses to phrases or phrases to single words.

▶ We took a side trip to Monticello, ~~which was~~ the home of

Thomas Jefferson.

▶ In ~~the~~ ^*this*^ essay, ~~that follows,~~ I argue against Immanuel Kant's

^*problematic*^ claim that we should not lie under any circumstances ~~,~~ .

~~which is a problematic claim.~~

EXERCISE 16–1 Edit the following sentences to reduce wordiness. Revisions of lettered sentences appear in the back of the book. Example:

> *even though*
> The Wilsons moved into the house ~~in spite of the fact that~~
> ^
>
> the back door was only ten yards from the train tracks.

a. Martin Luther King Jr. was a man who set a high standard for future leaders to meet.

b. Alice has been deeply in love with cooking since she was little and could first peek over the edge of a big kitchen tabletop.

c. In my opinion, Bloom's race for the governorship is a futile exercise.

d. It is pretty important in being a successful graphic designer to have technical knowledge and at the same time an eye for color and balance.

e. Your task will be the delivery of correspondence to all employees in the company.

1. Seeing the barrels, the driver immediately slammed on his brakes.

2. A really well-stocked bookshelf should have classical literature on it as well as important modern works of the current day.

3. China's enormously huge workforce has an effect on the global world of high-tech manufacturing of things.

4. A typical autocross course consists of at least two straightaways, and the rest of the course is made up of numerous slaloms and several sharp turns.

5. At breakfast time, Mehrdad always started his day with cantaloupe, lemon yogurt, and black coffee.

EXERCISE 16–2 Edit the following business memo to reduce wordiness.

To:	District managers
From:	Margaret Davenport, Vice President
Subject:	Customer database

It has recently been brought to my attention that a percentage of our sales representatives have been failing to log reports of their client calls in our customer database each and every day. I have also learned that some representatives are not checking the database on a routine basis.

Our clients sometimes receive a multiple number of sales calls from us when a sales representative is not cognizant of the fact that the client has been contacted at a previous time. Repeated telephone calls from our representatives annoy our customers. These repeated telephone calls also portray our company as one that is lacking in organization.

Effective as of immediately, direct your representatives to do the following:

- Record each and every customer contact in the customer database at the end of each day, without fail.

- Check the database at the very beginning of each day to ensure that telephone communications will not be initiated with clients who have already been called.

Let me extend my appreciation to you for cooperating in this important matter.

17 Choose appropriate language.

Language is appropriate when it suits your subject, engages your audience, and blends naturally with your own voice.

To some extent, your choice of language will be governed by the conventions of the genre in which you are writing. When in doubt about the conventions of a particular genre — lab reports, informal essays, business memos, and so on — consult your instructor or look at models written by experts in the field.

17a Stay away from jargon.

Jargon is specialized language used among members of a trade, profession, or group. Use jargon only when readers will be familiar with it; even then, use it only when plain English will not do as well.

JARGON   We outsourced the work to an outfit in Ohio because we didn't have the bandwidth to tackle it in-house.

REVISED   We hired a company in Ohio because we had too few employees to do the work.

Broadly defined, jargon includes puffed-up language designed more to impress readers than to inform them. The following are common examples from business, government, higher education, and the military, with plain English alternatives in parentheses.

ameliorate (improve)	indicator (sign)
commence (begin)	optimal (best, most favorable)
components (parts)	parameters (boundaries, limits)
endeavor (try)	peruse (read, look over)
facilitate (help)	prior to (before)
impact (v.) (affect)	utilize (use)

Sentences filled with jargon are hard to read, and they are often wordy as well.

▶ All ~~employees functioning in the capacity of~~ work-study students ~~are required to give evidence of current enrollment.~~
    must prove that they are currently enrolled.

▶ The CEO should ~~dialogue~~ *talk* with investors about ~~partnering~~ *working* with clients to ~~purchase~~ *buy* land in ~~economically deprived zones.~~ *poor neighborhoods.*

17b Avoid pretentious language, most euphemisms, and "doublespeak."

Hoping to sound profound or poetic, some writers embroider their thoughts with large words and flowery phrases. Such pretentious language is so ornate and wordy that it obscures the writer's meaning.

▶ Taylor's ~~employment of multihued means of expression draws~~ *use of colorful language reveals that she has a* ~~back the curtains and lets slip the~~ nostalgic ~~vantage point~~ *view of* ~~from which she observes~~ American society ~~as well as her lack~~ *and does not* ~~of comprehension of~~ *understand* economic realities.

Euphemisms — nice-sounding words or phrases substituted for words thought to sound harsh or ugly — are sometimes appropriate.

Many cultures, for example, accept euphemisms when speaking or writing about excretion (*I have to go to the bathroom*), sexual intercourse (*They did not sleep together*), and the like. Most euphemisms, however, are needlessly evasive or even deceitful. Like pretentious language, they obscure the intended meaning.

EUPHEMISM	PLAIN ENGLISH
adult entertainment	pornography
preowned automobile	used car
economically deprived	poor
negative savings	debts
strategic withdrawal	retreat or defeat
revenue enhancers	taxes
chemical dependency	drug addiction
downsize	lay off, fire
correctional facility	prison

The term *doublespeak* applies to any deliberately evasive or deceptive language, including euphemisms. Doublespeak is especially common in politics and business. A military retreat is described as *tactical redeployment*; *enhanced interrogation* is a euphemism for "torture"; and *downsizing* really means "firing employees."

EXERCISE 17–1 Edit the following sentences to eliminate jargon, pretentious or flowery language, euphemisms, and doublespeak. You may need to make substantial changes in some sentences. Revisions of lettered sentences appear in the back of the book. Example:

> After two weeks in the legal department, Sue has ~~worked~~ *mastered*
> ~~into~~ the routine, ~~of the office,~~ and her ~~functional and self-~~
> ~~management skills have~~ exceeded all expectations.
> *office*   *performance has*

a. In my youth, my family was under the constraints of difficult financial circumstances.
b. In order that I may increase my expertise in the area of delivery of services to clients, I feel that participation in this conference will be beneficial.

c. The prophetic meteorologist cautioned the general populace regarding the possible deleterious effects of the impending tempest.

d. Government-sanctioned investigations into the continued value of after-school programs indicate a perceived need in the public realm at large.

e. Passengers should endeavor to finalize the customs declaration form prior to exiting the aircraft.

1. We learned that the mayor had been engaging in a creative transfer of city employees' pension funds.

2. After a cursory examination of brand-new research findings on textiles, Patricia and the members of her team made the decision to engage in a series of visits to fashion manufacturers in the local vicinity.

3. The nurse announced that there had been a negative patient-care outcome due to a therapeutic misadventure on the part of the surgeon.

4. A generally leisurely pace at the onset of tai chi exercises can yield a variety of beneficial points within a short period of time.

5. The bottom line is that the company is experiencing a negative cash flow.

EXERCISE 17–2   Edit the following e-mail message to eliminate jargon.

Dear Ms. Jackson:

We members of the Nakamura Reyes team value our external partnering arrangements with Creative Software, and I look forward to seeing you next week at the trade show in Fresno. Per Mr. Reyes, please let me know when you'll have some downtime there so that he and I can conduct a strategizing session with you concerning our production schedule. It's crucial that we all be on the same page re our 2011–2012 product release dates.

Before we have some face time, however, I have some findings to share. Our customer-centric approach to the new products will necessitate that user testing periods trend upward. The enclosed data should help you effectuate any adjustments to your timeline; let me know ASAP if you require any additional information to facilitate the above.

Before we convene in Fresno, Mr. Reyes and I will agendize any further talking points. Thanks for your help.

Sincerely,

Sylvia Nakamura

17c In most contexts, avoid slang, regional expressions, and nonstandard English.

Slang is an informal and sometimes private vocabulary that expresses the solidarity of a group such as teenagers, rock musicians, or football fans; it is subject to more rapid change than standard English. For example, the slang teenagers use to express approval changes every few years; *cool, groovy, neat, awesome, phat*, and *sick* have replaced one another within the last three decades. Sometimes slang becomes so widespread that it is accepted as standard vocabulary. *Jazz*, for example, started out as slang but is now a standard term for a style of music.

Although slang has a certain vitality, it is a code that not everyone understands, and it is very informal. Therefore, it is inappropriate in most written work.

▶ When the server crashed unexpectedly, three hours of *we lost*

unsaved data. ~~went down the tubes.~~

▶ The government's "filth" guidelines for food will ~~make you~~ *disgust you.*

~~yack.~~

Regional expressions are common to a group in a geographic area. *Let's talk with the bark off* (for *Let's speak frankly*) is an expression in the southern United States, for example. Regional expressions have the same limitations as slang and are therefore inappropriate in most writing.

▶ John was four blocks from the house before he remembered

to ~~cut~~ *turn on* the headlights. ~~on.~~

▶ Seamus wasn't ~~for~~ sure, but he thought the whales might

be migrating during his visit to Oregon.

Standard English is the language used in all academic, business, and professional fields. Nonstandard English is spoken by people with a common regional or social heritage. Although nonstandard

English may be appropriate when spoken within a close group, it is out of place in most formal and informal writing.

▶ The governor said he ~~don't~~ *doesn't* know if he will approve the budget

without the clean air provision.

If you speak a nonstandard dialect, try to identify the ways in which your dialect differs from standard English. Look especially for the following features of nonstandard English, which commonly cause problems in writing.

Misusing verb forms such as *began* and *begun* (See 27a.)

Leaving *-s* endings off verbs (See 27c.)

Leaving *-ed* endings off verbs (See 27d.)

Leaving out necessary verbs (See 27e.)

Using double negatives (See 26e.)

17d Choose an appropriate level of formality.

In deciding on a level of formality, consider both your subject and your audience. Does the subject demand a dignified treatment, or is a relaxed tone more suitable? Will readers be put off if you assume too close a relationship with them, or might you alienate them by seeming too distant?

For most college and professional writing, some degree of formality is appropriate. In a job application letter, for example, it is a mistake to sound too breezy and informal.

TOO INFORMAL	I'd like to get that sales job you've got in the paper.
MORE FORMAL	I would like to apply for the position of sales associate advertised in the *Peoria Journal Star*.

Informal writing is appropriate for private letters, personal e-mail and text messages, and business correspondence between close associates. Like spoken conversation, informal writing allows contractions (*don't*, *I'll*) and colloquial words (*kids*, *kinda*). Vocabulary and sentence structure are rarely complex.

In choosing a level of formality, above all be consistent. When a writer's voice shifts from one level of formality to another, readers receive mixed messages.

▶ Once a pitcher for the Blue Jays, Jorge shared with me
  began
  the secrets of his trade. His lesson ~~commenced~~ with his
      thrown
          ^
  famous curveball, ~~implemented~~ by tucking the little finger
          ^   *revealed*
  behind the ball. Next he ~~elucidated~~ the mysteries of the
          ^
  sucker pitch, a slow ball coming behind a fast windup.

Words such as *commenced* and *elucidated* are inappropriate for the
subject matter, and they clash with informal terms such as *sucker pitch*
and *fast windup*.

EXERCISE 17–3   Revise the following passage so that the level of formality is appropriate for a letter to the editor of a major newspaper.

> In pop culture, college grads who return home to live with
> the folks are seen as good-for-nothing losers who mooch off their
> families. And many older adults seem to feel that the trend of
> moving back home after school, which was rare in their day, is
> becoming too commonplace today. But society must realize that
> times have changed. Most young adults want to live on their own
> ASAP, but they graduate with heaps of debt and need some time to
> get back on their feet. College tuition and the cost of housing have
> increased way more than salary increases in the past fifty years. Also,
> the job market is tighter and more jobs require advanced degrees
> than in the past. So before people go off on college graduates who
> move back into their parents' house for a spell, they'd better consider
> all the facts.

17e Avoid sexist language.

Sexist language is language that stereotypes or demeans women
or men. Using nonsexist language is a matter of courtesy — of
respect for and sensitivity to the feelings of others.

Recognizing sexist language

Some sexist language is easy to recognize because it reflects genuine contempt for women: referring to a woman as a "chick," for
example, or calling a lawyer a "lady lawyer."

Other forms of sexist language are less blatant. The following
practices, while they may not result from conscious sexism, reflect

stereotypical thinking: referring to members of one profession as exclusively male or exclusively female (teachers as women or computer engineers as men, for instance), using different conventions when naming or identifying women and men, or assuming that all of one's readers are men.

STEREOTYPICAL LANGUAGE

After a nursing student graduates, *she* must face a difficult state board examination. [Not all nursing students are women.]

Running for city council are Boris Stotsky, an attorney, and *Mrs.* Cynthia Jones, a professor of English and *mother of three*. [The title *Mrs.* and the phrase *mother of three* are irrelevant.]

Still other forms of sexist language result from outdated traditions. The pronouns *he, him,* and *his,* for instance, were traditionally used to refer generically to persons of either sex. Nowadays, to avoid that sexist usage, some writers use *she, her,* and *hers* generically or substitute the female pronouns alternately with the male pronouns.

GENERIC PRONOUNS

A journalist is motivated by *his* deadline.

A good interior designer treats *her* clients' ideas respectfully.

But both forms are sexist — for excluding one sex entirely and for making assumptions about the members of particular professions.

Similarly, the nouns *man* and *men* were once used to refer generically to persons of either sex. Current usage demands gender-neutral terms for references to both men and women.

INAPPROPRIATE	APPROPRIATE
chairman	chairperson, moderator, chair, head
congressman	member of Congress, representative, legislator
fireman	firefighter
foreman	supervisor
mailman	mail carrier, postal worker, letter carrier
to man	to operate, to staff
mankind	people, humans
manpower	personnel, staff
policeman	police officer
weatherman	forecaster, meteorologist

Revising sexist language

When revising sexist language, you may be tempted to substitute *he or she* and *his or her*. These terms are inclusive but wordy; fine in small doses, they can become awkward when repeated throughout an essay. A better revision strategy is to write in the plural; yet another strategy is to recast the sentence so that the problem does not arise.

SEXIST

A journalist is motivated by *his* deadline.

A good interior designer treats *her* clients' ideas respectfully.

ACCEPTABLE BUT WORDY

A journalist is motivated by *his or her* deadline.

A good interior designer treats *his or her* clients' ideas respectfully.

BETTER: USING THE PLURAL

Journalists are motivated by *their* deadlines.

Good interior designers treat *their* clients' ideas respectfully.

BETTER: RECASTING THE SENTENCE

A journalist is motivated by *a* deadline.

A good interior designer treats clients' ideas respectfully.

For more examples of these revision strategies, see 22.

EXERCISE 17–4   Edit the following sentences to eliminate sexist language or sexist assumptions. Revisions of lettered sentences appear in the back of the book. Example:

Scholarship athletes   their
~~A scholarship athlete~~ must be as concerned about ~~his~~
^
                                they are   their   ^
academic performance as ~~he is~~ about ~~his~~ athletic performance.
                          ^   ^

a. Mrs. Geralyn Farmer, who is the mayor's wife, is the chief surgeon at University Hospital. Dr. Paul Green is her assistant.

b. Every applicant wants to know how much he will earn.

c. An elementary school teacher should understand the concept of nurturing if she intends to be effective.

d. An obstetrician needs to be available to his patients at all hours.

e. If man does not stop polluting his environment, mankind will perish.

1. A fireman must always be on call even when he is off duty.

2. The chairman for the new program in digital art is Ariana Tamlin, an accomplished portrait painter, computer programmer, and cookie baker.

3. In the governor's race, Lena Weiss, a defense lawyer and mother of two, easily defeated Harvey Tower, an architect.

4. Recent military history has shown that lady combat helicopter pilots are as skilled, reliable, and resourceful as men.

5. An emergency room head nurse must know how to use sophisticated digital equipment if she is to keep track of all her patients' data and guide her medical team.

EXERCISE 17–5 Eliminate sexist language or sexist assumptions in the following job posting for an elementary school teacher.

We are looking for qualified women for the position of elementary school teacher. The ideal candidate should have a bachelor's degree, a state teaching certificate, and one year of student teaching. She should be knowledgeable in all elementary subject areas, including science and math. While we want our new teacher to have a commanding presence in the classroom, we are also looking for motherly characteristics such as patience and trustworthiness. She must be able to both motivate an entire classroom and work with each student one-on-one to assess his individual needs. She must also be comfortable communicating with the parents of her students. For salary and benefits information, including maternity leave policy, please contact the Martin County School Board. Any qualified applicant should submit her résumé by March 15.

17f Revise language that may offend groups of people.

Obviously it is impolite to use offensive terms such as *Polack* and *redneck*, but biased language can take more subtle forms. Because language evolves over time, names once thought acceptable may become offensive. When describing groups of people, choose names that the groups currently use to describe themselves.

▶ North Dakota takes its name from the ~~Indian~~ word meaning
                           Lakota

"friend" or "ally."

      Asian
▶ Many ~~Oriental~~ immigrants have recently settled in our town.

Negative stereotypes (such as "drives like a teenager" or "sour as a spinster") are of course offensive. But you should avoid stereotyping a person or a group even if you believe your generalization to be positive.

                     an excellent math and science student,
▶ It was no surprise that Greer, ~~a Chinese American,~~ was

selected for the honors chemistry program.

18 Find the exact words.

Two reference works (or their online equivalents) will help you find words to express your meaning exactly: a good dictionary, such as *The American Heritage Dictionary* or *Merriam-Webster's Online Dictionary*, and a collection of synonyms and antonyms, such as *Roget's International Thesaurus*.

TIP: Do not turn to a thesaurus in search of flowery or impressive words. Look instead for words that exactly express your meaning.

18a Select words with appropriate connotations.

In addition to their strict dictionary meanings (or *denotations*), words have *connotations*, emotional colorings that affect how readers respond to them. The word *steel* denotes "commercial iron that contains carbon," but it also calls up a cluster of images associated with steel. These associations give the word its connotations — cold, hard, smooth, unbending.

    If the connotation of a word does not seem appropriate for your purpose, your audience, or your subject matter, you should change the word. When a more appropriate synonym does not come quickly to mind, consult a dictionary or a thesaurus.

▶ **When American soldiers returned home after World War II,**
left
many women ~~abandoned~~ their jobs in favor of marriage.
     ^

The word *abandoned* is too negative for the context.

EXERCISE 18–1 Use a dictionary and a thesaurus to find at least four synonyms for each of the following words. Be prepared to explain any slight differences in meaning.

1. decay (verb)   3. hurry (verb)   5. secret (adjective)
2. difficult (adjective)   4. pleasure (noun)   6. talent (noun)

18b Prefer specific, concrete nouns.

Unlike general nouns, which refer to broad classes of things, specific nouns point to particular items. *Film*, for example, names a general class, *fantasy film* names a narrower class, and *The Golden Compass* is more specific still. Other examples: *team, football team, Denver Broncos; music, symphony, Beethoven's Ninth.*

Unlike abstract nouns, which refer to qualities and ideas (*justice, beauty, realism, dignity*), concrete nouns point to immediate, often sensory experience and to physical objects (*steeple, asphalt, lilac, stone, garlic*).

Specific, concrete nouns express meaning more vividly than general or abstract ones. Although general and abstract language is sometimes necessary to convey your meaning, use specific, concrete words whenever possible.

▶ **The senator spoke about the challenges of the future:**
pollution, dwindling resources, and terrorism.
~~the environment and world peace.~~
   ^

Nouns such as *thing, area, aspect, factor,* and *individual* are especially dull and imprecise.

                                    motherhood, and memory.
▶ **Toni Morrison's *Beloved* is about slavery, ~~among other things.~~**
                                             ^
                              experienced technician.
▶ **Try pairing a trainee with an ~~individual with technical experience.~~**
                                  ^

18c Do not misuse words.

If a word is not in your active vocabulary, you may find yourself misusing it, sometimes with embarrassing consequences. When in doubt, check the dictionary.

▶ The fans were ~~migrating~~ *climbing* up the bleachers in search of seats.

▶ The Internet has so ~~diffused~~ *permeated* our culture that it touches all

segments of society.

Be especially alert for misused word forms — using a noun such as *absence*, *significance*, or *persistence*, for example, when your meaning requires the adjective *absent*, *significant*, or *persistent*.

▶ Most dieters are not ~~persistence~~ *persistent* enough to make a permanent

change in their eating habits.

EXERCISE 18–2   Edit the following sentences to correct misused words. Revisions of lettered sentences appear in the back of the book. Example:

These days the training required for a ballet dancer

is ~~all-absorbent.~~ *all-absorbing.*

a. We regret this delay; thank you for your patients.
b. Ada's plan is to require education and experience to prepare herself for a position as property manager.
c. Peyton Manning, the penultimate competitor, has earned millions of dollars just in endorsements.
d. Many people take for granite that public libraries have up-to-date computer systems.
e. The affect of Gao Xinjian's novels on Chinese exiles is hard to gauge.
1. Because Anne Tyler often writes about family loyalties, her illusions to *King Lear* are not surprising.
2. Designers of handheld devices understand that changes in ambience temperatures can damage the tiny circuit boards.

3. The Keweenaw Peninsula is surrounded on three sides by Lake Superior.

4. At the cooking school in Tuscany, I learned that rosemary is a perfect compliment to lamb.

5. The person who complained to the human resources manager wishes to remain unanimous.

18d Use standard idioms.

Idioms are speech forms that follow no easily specified rules. The English say "Bernice went *to hospital,*" an idiom strange to American ears, which are accustomed to hearing *the* in front of *hospital*. Native speakers of a language seldom have problems with idioms, but prepositions (such as *with*, *to*, *at*, and *of*) sometimes cause trouble, especially when they follow certain verbs and adjectives. When in doubt, consult a dictionary.

UNIDIOMATIC	IDIOMATIC
abide with (a decision)	abide by (a decision)
according with	according to
agree to (an idea)	agree with (an idea)
angry at (a person)	angry with (a person)
capable to	capable of
comply to	comply with
desirous to	desirous of
different than (a person or thing)	different from (a person or thing)
intend on doing	intend to do
off of	off
plan on doing	plan to do
preferable than	preferable to
prior than	prior to
similar than	similar to
superior than	superior to
sure and	sure to
think on	think of, about
try and	try to
type of a	type of

MULTILINGUAL Because idioms follow no particular rules, you must learn them individually. You may find it helpful to keep a list of idioms that you frequently encounter in conversation and in reading.

EXERCISE 18–3 Edit the following sentences to eliminate errors in the use of idiomatic expressions. If a sentence is correct, write "correct" after it. Answers to lettered sentences appear in the back of the book. Example:

> We agreed to abide ~~with~~ *by* the decision of the judge.

a. Queen Anne was so angry at Sarah Churchill that she refused to see her again.

b. Jean-Pierre's ambitious travel plans made it impossible for him to comply with the residency requirement for in-state tuition.

c. The parade moved off of the street and onto the beach.

d. The frightened refugees intend on making the dangerous trek across the mountains.

e. What type of a wedding are you planning?

1. Be sure and report on the danger of releasing genetically engineered bacteria into the atmosphere.

2. Why do you assume that embezzling bank assets is so different than robbing the bank?

3. The wilderness guide seemed capable to show us where the trail of petroglyphs was located.

4. In Evan's cautious mind, packing his own parachute seemed preferable to letting an indifferent teenager fold all that silk and cord into a small pack.

5. Andrea plans on joining the Peace Corps after graduation.

18e Do not rely heavily on clichés.

The pioneer who first announced that he had "slept like a log" no doubt amused his companions with a fresh and unlikely comparison. Today, however, that comparison is a cliché, a saying that has lost its dazzle from overuse. No longer can it surprise.

To see just how dully predictable clichés are, put your hand over the right-hand column in the following list and then finish the phrases on the left.

cool as a	cucumber
beat around	the bush
blind as a	bat
busy as a	bee, beaver
crystal	clear
dead as a	doornail
out of the frying pan and	into the fire
light as a	feather
like a bull	in a china shop
playing with	fire
nutty as a	fruitcake
selling like	hotcakes
starting out at the bottom	of the ladder
water under the	bridge
white as a	sheet, ghost
avoid clichés like the	plague

The solution for clichés is simple: Just delete them or rewrite them.

▶ When I received a full scholarship from my second-choice
        felt squeezed to settle for second best.
  school, I ~~found myself between a rock and a hard place.~~
      ^

Sometimes you can write around a cliché by adding an element of surprise. One student, for example, who had written that she had butterflies in her stomach, revised her cliché like this:

> If all of the action in my stomach is caused by butterflies, there must be a horde of them, with horseshoes on.

The image of butterflies wearing horseshoes is fresh and unlikely, not predictable like the original cliché.

18f Use figures of speech with care.

A figure of speech is an expression that uses words imaginatively (rather than literally) to make abstract ideas concrete. Most often, figures of speech compare two seemingly unlike things to reveal surprising similarities.

In a *simile*, the writer makes the comparison explicitly, usually by introducing it with *like* or *as*: *By the time cotton had to be picked, Grandfather's neck was as red as the clay he plowed*. In a *metaphor*, the *like* or *as* is omitted, and the comparison is implied. For example, in the Old Testament Song of Solomon, a young woman compares the man she loves to a fruit tree: *With great delight I sat in his shadow, and his fruit was sweet to my taste*.

Although figures of speech are useful devices, writers sometimes use them without thinking through the images they evoke. The result is sometimes a *mixed metaphor*, the combination of two or more images that don't make sense together.

> Our manager decided to put all controversial issues
>
> ~~in a holding pattern~~ on a back burner until after the
>
> annual meeting.

Here the writer is mixing airplanes and stoves. Simply deleting one of the images corrects the problem.

EXERCISE 18–4 Edit the following sentences to replace worn-out expressions and clarify mixed figures of speech. Revisions of lettered sentences appear in the back of the book. Example:

the color drained from his face.
When he heard about the accident, he ~~turned white as a sheet.~~

a. John stormed into the room like a bull in a china shop.

b. Some people insist that they'll always be there for you, even when they haven't been before.

c. The Cubs easily beat the Mets, who were in the soup early in the game today at Wrigley Field.

d. We ironed out the sticky spots in our relationship.

e. My mother accused me of beating around the bush when in fact I was just talking off the top of my head.

1. Priscilla was used to burning the candle at both ends to get her assignments done.

2. No matter how many books he reads, André can never seem to quench his thirst for knowledge.

3. In an era of cutbacks and outsourcing, the best tech-savvy workers discover that being a jack of all trades is a solid gold key to continued success.

4. Too many cooks are spoiling the broth at corporate headquarters.

5. Juanita told Kyle that keeping skeletons in the closet would be playing with fire.

Grammar

19   Repair sentence fragments.

A sentence fragment is a word group that pretends to be a sentence. Sentence fragments are easy to recognize when they appear out of context, like these:

> When the cat leaped onto the table.

> Running for the bus.

> And immediately popped their flares and life vests.

When fragments appear next to related sentences, however, they are harder to spot.

> We had just sat down to dinner. When the cat leaped onto the table.

> I tripped and twisted my ankle. Running for the bus.

> The pilots ejected from the burning plane, landing in the water not far from the ship. And immediately popped their flares and life vests.

Recognizing sentence fragments

To be a sentence, a word group must consist of at least one full independent clause. An independent clause includes a subject and a verb, and it either stands alone or could stand alone.

To test whether a word group is a complete sentence or a fragment, use the flowchart on page 181. By using the flowchart, you can see exactly why *When the cat leaped onto the table* is a fragment: It has a subject (*cat*) and a verb (*leaped*), but it begins with a subordinating word (*When*), which makes the word group a dependent clause. *Running for the bus* is a fragment because it lacks a subject and a verb (*Running* is a verbal, not a verb). *And immediately popped their flares and life vests* is a fragment because it lacks a subject. (See also 48b and 48e.)

Test for fragments

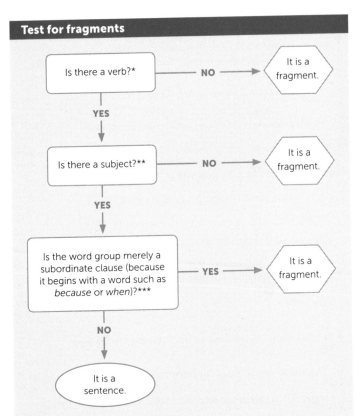

*Do not mistake verbals for verbs. A verbal is a verb form (such as *walking, to act*) that does not function as a verb of a clause. (See 48b.)

**The subject of a sentence may be *you*, understood but not present in the sentence. (See 47a.)

***A sentence may open with a subordinate clause, but the sentence must also include an independent clause. (See 19a and 49a.)

If you find any fragments, try one of these methods of revision (see 19a–19c):

1. Attach the fragment to a nearby sentence.
2. Rewrite the fragment as a complete sentence.

MULTILINGUAL Unlike some other languages, English requires a subject and a verb in every sentence (except in commands, where the subject *you* is understood but not present: *Sit down*). See 30a and 30b.

▶ *It is*
~~Is~~ often hot and humid during the summer.
^

▶ *are*
Students usually very busy at the end of the semester.
^

Repairing sentence fragments

You can repair most fragments in one of two ways:

- Pull the fragment into a nearby sentence.
- Rewrite the fragment as a complete sentence.

▶ *when*
We had just sat down to dinner./ ~~When~~ the cat leaped onto
^
the table.

▶ *Running for the bus,*
I tripped and twisted my ankle. ~~Running for the bus.~~
^

▶ The pilots ejected from the burning plane, landing in the
water not far from the ship. *They*
~~And~~ immediately popped their
^
flares and life vests.

19a Attach fragmented subordinate clauses or turn them into sentences.

A subordinate clause is patterned like a sentence, with both a subject and a verb, but it begins with a word that marks it as subordinate. The following words commonly introduce subordinate clauses.

after	before	so that	until	while
although	even though	than	when	who
as	how	that	where	whom
as if	if	though	whether	whose
because	since	unless	which	why

Subordinate clauses function within sentences as adjectives, as adverbs, or as nouns. They cannot stand alone. (See 48e.)

Most fragmented clauses beg to be pulled into a sentence nearby.

▶ Americans have come to fear the West Nile virus./~~Because~~ *because*

it is transmitted by the common mosquito.

Because introduces a subordinate clause, so it cannot stand alone. (For punctuation of subordinate clauses appearing at the end of a sentence, see 33f.)

▶ Although psychiatrist Peter Kramer expresses concerns

about Prozac./, ~~Many~~ *many* other doctors believe that the

benefits of antidepressants outweigh the risks.

Although introduces a subordinate clause, so it cannot stand alone. (For punctuation of subordinate clauses at the beginning of a sentence, see 32b.)

If a fragmented clause cannot be attached to a nearby sentence or if you feel that attaching it would be awkward, try turning the clause into a sentence. The simplest way to do this is to delete the opening word or words that mark it as subordinate.

▶ Population increases and uncontrolled development are

taking a deadly toll on the environment. ~~So that across~~ *Across* the

globe, fragile ecosystems are collapsing.

19b Attach fragmented phrases or turn them into sentences.

Like subordinate clauses, phrases function within sentences as adjectives, as adverbs, or as nouns. They cannot stand alone. Fragmented phrases are often prepositional or verbal phrases; sometimes they are appositives, words or word groups that rename nouns or pronouns. (See 48a, 48b, and 48c.)

Often a fragmented phrase may simply be pulled into a nearby sentence.

▶ The archaeologists worked slowly/, ~~Examining~~ *examining* and labeling

every pottery shard they uncovered.

The word group beginning with *Examining* is a verbal phrase.

▶ The patient displayed symptoms of ALS/, ~~A~~ *a* neuro-

degenerative disease.

A neurodegenerative disease is an appositive renaming the noun *ALS*. (For punctuation of appositives, see 32e.)

If a fragmented phrase cannot be pulled into a nearby sentence effectively, turn the phrase into a sentence. You may need to add a subject, a verb, or both.

▶ In the training session, Jamie explained how to access our new

database. ~~Also~~ *She also taught us* how to submit expense reports and request

vendor payments.

The revision turns the fragmented phrase into a sentence by adding a subject and a verb.

19c Attach other fragmented word groups or turn them into sentences.

Other word groups that are commonly fragmented include parts of compound predicates, lists, and examples introduced by *for example*, *in addition*, or similar expressions.

Parts of compound predicates

A predicate consists of a verb and its objects, complements, and modifiers (see 47b). A compound predicate includes two or more predicates joined with a coordinating conjunction such as *and*, *but*,

incomplete sentences • implied vs. dictionary meaning •
lists as fragments • fragments with *for example, such as*, etc.

frag
19c   185

or *or*. Because the parts of a compound predicate have the same subject, they should appear in the same sentence.

▶ The woodpecker finch of the Galápagos Islands carefully

                                   and

selects a twig of a certain size and shape/. ~~And~~ then uses this

tool to pry out grubs from trees.

> The subject is *finch*, and the compound predicate is *selects . . . and . . . uses*. (For punctuation of compound predicates, see 33a.)

Lists

To correct a fragmented list, often you can attach it to a nearby sentence with a colon or a dash. (See 35a and 39a.)

▶ It has been said that there are only three indigenous American

                  musical

art forms/: ~~Musical~~ comedy, jazz, and soap opera.

Sometimes terms like *especially, namely, like,* and *such as* introduce fragmented lists. Such fragments can usually be attached to the preceding sentence.

▶ In the twentieth century, the South produced some great

                such

American writers/, ~~Such~~ as Flannery O'Connor, William

Faulkner, Alice Walker, and Tennessee Williams.

Examples introduced by *for example, in addition,* or similar expressions

Other expressions that introduce examples or explanations can lead to unintentional fragments. Although you may begin a sentence with some of the following words or phrases, make sure that what follows has a subject and a verb.

also	for example	mainly
and	for instance	or
but	in addition	that is

Often the easiest solution is to turn the fragment into a sentence.

▶ In his memoir, Primo Levi describes the horrors of living

in a concentration camp. For example, ~~working~~ _he worked_ without

food and ~~suffering~~ _suffered_ emotional abuse.

The writer corrected this fragment by adding a subject — _he_ — and substituting verbs for the verbals _working_ and _suffering_.

▶ Deborah Tannen's research reveals that men and women

have different ideas about communication. For example,

Tannen explains
that a woman "expects her husband to be a new and

improved version of her best friend" (441).

A quotation must be part of a complete sentence. _That a woman "expects her husband to be a new and improved version of her best friend"_ is a fragment — a subordinate clause. In this case, adding a signal phrase that includes a subject and a verb (_Tannen explains_) corrects the fragment and clarifies that the quotation is from Tannen.

19d Exception: A fragment may be used for effect.

Writers occasionally use sentence fragments for special purposes.

FOR EMPHASIS	Following the dramatic Americanization of their children, even my parents grew more publicly confident. _Especially my mother._
	— Richard Rodriguez
TO ANSWER A QUESTION	Are these new drug tests 100 percent reliable? _Not in the opinion of most experts._
TRANSITIONS	_And now the opposing arguments._
EXCLAMATIONS	_Not again!_
IN ADVERTISING	_Fewer carbs. Improved taste._

Although fragments are sometimes appropriate, writers and readers do not always agree on when they are appropriate. That's why you will find it safer to write in complete sentences.

EXERCISE 19–1   Repair any fragment by attaching it to a nearby sentence or by rewriting it as a complete sentence. If a word group is correct, write "correct" after it. Revisions of lettered sentences appear in the back of the book. Example:

One Greek island that should not be missed is Mykonos. A
vacation spot for Europeans and a playground for the rich
and famous.

a. Listening to the CD her sister had sent, Mia was overcome with a mix of emotions. Happiness, homesickness, and nostalgia.

b. Cortés and his soldiers were astonished when they looked down from the mountains and saw Tenochtitlán. The magnificent capital of the Aztecs.

c. Although my spoken Spanish is not very good. I can read the language with ease.

d. There are several reasons for not eating meat. One reason being that dangerous chemicals are used throughout the various stages of meat production.

e. To learn how to sculpt beauty from everyday life. This is my intention in studying art and archaeology.

1. The panther lay motionless behind the rock. Waiting for its prey.

2. Aunt Mina loved to play all my favorite games. Cat's cradle, Uno, mancala, and even hopscotch.

3. With machetes, the explorers cut their way through the tall grasses to the edge of the canyon. Then they began to lay out the tapes for the survey.

4. The owners of the online grocery store rented a warehouse in the Market district. An area catering to small businesses.

5. If a woman from the desert tribe showed anger toward her husband, she was whipped in front of the whole village. And shunned by the rest of the women.

EXERCISE 19–2   Repair each fragment in the following passage by attaching it to a sentence nearby or by rewriting it as a complete sentence.

Digital technology has revolutionized information delivery. Forever blurring the lines between information and entertainment. Yesterday's readers of books and newspapers are today's readers of e-books and news blogs. Countless readers have moved on from print information entirely. Choosing instead to point, click, and scroll their way through a text on their Amazon Kindle or in an online forum. Once a nation of people spoon-fed television commercials and the six o'clock evening news. We are now seemingly addicted to *YouTube*. Remember the family trip when Dad or Mom wrestled with a road map? On the way to St. Louis or Seattle? No wrestling is required with a slick GPS navigator by the driver's side. Unless it's Mom and Dad wrestling over who gets to program the address. Accessing information now seems to be America's favorite pastime. John Horrigan, associate director for research at the Pew Internet and American Life Project, reports that 31 percent of American adults are "elite" users of technology. Who are "highly engaged" with digital content. As a country, we embrace information and communication technologies. Which include iPods, cell phones, laptops, and handheld devices. Among children and adolescents, Internet and other personal technology use is on the rise. For activities like socializing, gaming, and information gathering.

Revise run-on sentences.

Run-on sentences are independent clauses that have not been joined correctly. An independent clause is a word group that can stand alone as a sentence. (See 49a.) When two independent clauses appear in one sentence, they must be joined in one of these ways:

- with a comma and a coordinating conjunction (*and, but, or, nor, for, so, yet*)
- with a semicolon (or occasionally with a colon or a dash)

Recognizing run-on sentences

There are two types of run-on sentences. When a writer puts no mark of punctuation and no coordinating conjunction between independent clauses, the result is called a *fused sentence*.

	┌——— INDEPENDENT CLAUSE ———┐ ┌———
FUSED	Air pollution poses risks to all humans it can be
	┌— INDEPENDENT CLAUSE —┐
	deadly for asthma sufferers.

A far more common type of run-on sentence is the *comma splice* — two or more independent clauses joined with a comma but without a coordinating conjunction. In some comma splices, the comma appears alone.

COMMA SPLICE   Air pollution poses risks to all humans, it can be deadly for asthma sufferers.

In other comma splices, the comma is accompanied by a joining word that is *not* a coordinating conjunction. There are only seven co-ordinating conjunctions in English: *and, but, or, nor, for, so,* and *yet*.

COMMA SPLICE   Air pollution poses risks to all humans, however, it can be deadly for asthma sufferers.

However is a transitional expression and cannot be used with only a comma to join two independent clauses (see 20b).

Recognizing run-on sentences

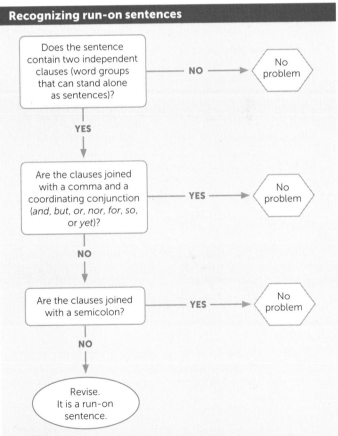

If you find an error, choose an effective method of revision. See 20a–20d for revision strategies.

Revising run-on sentences

To revise a run-on sentence, you have four choices.

1. Use a comma and a coordinating conjunction (*and, but, or, nor, for, so, yet*).

   ▶ Air pollution poses risks to all humans, *but* it can be deadly for

   asthma sufferers.

2. Use a semicolon (or, if appropriate, a colon or a dash). A semicolon may be used alone or with a transitional expression.

   ▶ Air pollution poses risks to all humans/; it can be deadly

   for asthma sufferers.

   ▶ Air pollution poses risks to all humans/; *however,* it can be deadly for

   asthma sufferers.

3. Make the clauses into separate sentences.

   ▶ Air pollution poses risks to all humans/. *It* ~~it~~ can be deadly for

   asthma sufferers.

4. Restructure the sentence, perhaps by subordinating one of the clauses.

   ▶ *Although air* ~~Air~~ pollution poses risks to all humans, it can be deadly for

   asthma sufferers.

One of these revision techniques usually works better than the others for a particular sentence. The fourth technique, the one requiring the most extensive revision, is often the most effective.

20a Consider separating the clauses with a comma and a coordinating conjunction.

There are seven coordinating conjunctions in English: *and, but, or, nor, for, so,* and *yet.* When a coordinating conjunction joins independent clauses, it is usually preceded by a comma. (See 32a.)

▶ Some lesson plans include exercises, *but* completing them should not be the focus of all class periods.

20b Consider separating the clauses with a semicolon (or, if appropriate, with a colon or a dash).

When the independent clauses are closely related and their relation is clear without a coordinating conjunction, a semicolon is an acceptable method of revision. (See 34a.)

▶ Tragedy depicts the individual confronted with the fact of death*;* comedy depicts the adaptability of human society.

A semicolon is required between independent clauses that have been linked with a transitional expression (such as *however, therefore, moreover, in fact,* or *for example*). For a longer list, see 34b.

▶ In his film adaptation of the short story "Killings," director Todd Field changed key details of the plot*;* in fact, he added whole scenes that do not appear in the story.

A colon or a dash may be more appropriate if the first independent clause introduces the second or if the second clause summarizes or explains the first. (See 35b and 39a.) In formal writing, the colon is usually preferred to the dash.

▶ Nuclear waste is hazardous: ~~this~~ *This* is an indisputable fact.

▶ The female black widow spider is often a widow of her own

making/she has been known to eat her partner after mating.

A colon is an appropriate method of revision if the first independent clause introduces a quoted sentence.

▶ Nobel Peace Prize winner Al Gore had this to say about

climate change/: "The truth is that our circumstances are

not only new; they are completely different than they

have ever been in all of human history."

20c Consider making the clauses into separate sentences.

▶ Why should we spend money on expensive space

exploration/? ~~we~~ *We* have enough underfunded programs here

on Earth.

Since one independent clause is a question and the other is a statement, they should be separate sentences.

▶ Some studies have suggested that the sexual relationships

of bonobos set them apart from common chimpanzees/.

According
~~according~~ to Stanford (1998), these differences have been

exaggerated.

Using a comma to join two independent clauses creates a comma splice. In this example, an effective revision is to separate the first independent clause (*Some studies . . .*) from the second independent clause (*these differences . . .*) and to keep the signal phrase with the second clause. (See also 63.)

NOTE: When two quoted independent clauses are divided by explanatory words, make each clause its own sentence.

▶ "It's always smart to learn from your mistakes," quipped my

"It's

supervisor/. "~~it's~~ even smarter to learn from the mistakes of

others."

20d Consider restructuring the sentence, perhaps by subordinating one of the clauses.

If one of the independent clauses is less important than the other, turn it into a subordinate clause or phrase. (For more about subordination, see 14, especially the chart on p. 144.)

▶ One of the most famous advertising slogans is Wheaties

which

cereal's "Breakfast of Champions," ~~it~~ was penned in 1933.

▶ Mary McLeod Bethune**,** ~~was~~ the seventeenth child of former

slaves, ~~she~~ founded the National Council of Negro Women

in 1935.

Minor ideas in these sentences are now expressed in subordinate clauses or phrases.

EXERCISE 20–1 Revise the following run-on sentences using the method of revision suggested in brackets. Revisions of lettered sentences appear in the back of the book. Example:

Because

Daniel had been obsessed with his weight as a teenager, he

rarely ate anything sweet. [*Restructure the sentence.*]

a. The city had one public swimming pool, it stayed packed with children all summer long. [*Restructure the sentence.*]
b. The building is being renovated, therefore at times we have no heat, water, or electricity. [*Use a comma and a coordinating conjunction.*]

PRACTICE hackerhandbooks.com/rules
 > Grammar > 20–4 to 20–7

c. The view was not what the travel agent had described, where were the rolling hills and the shimmering rivers? [*Make two sentences.*]

d. All those gnarled equations looked like toxic insects, maybe I was going to have to rethink my major. [*Use a semicolon.*]

e. City officials had good reason to fear a major earthquake, most of the business district was built on landfill. [*Use a colon.*]

1. The car was hardly worth trading, the frame was twisted and the block was warped. [*Restructure the sentence.*]

2. The next time an event is canceled because of bad weather, don't blame the meteorologist, blame nature. [*Make two sentences.*]

3. Ray was fluent in American Sign Language he could sign as easily as he could speak. [*Restructure the sentence.*]

4. Susanna arrived with a stack of her latest hats she hoped the gift shop would place a big winter order. [*Restructure the sentence.*]

5. There was one major reason for John's wealth, his grandfather had been a multimillionaire. [*Use a colon.*]

EXERCISE 20–2 Revise any run-on sentences using a technique that you find effective. If a sentence is correct, write "correct" after it. Revisions of lettered sentences appear in the back of the book. Example:

> Crossing so many time zones on an eight-hour flight, I knew
>
>   *but*
>
> I would be tired when I arrived, ~~however,~~ I was too excited
>   ^
>
> to sleep on the plane.

a. Wind power for the home is a supplementary source of energy, it can be combined with electricity, gas, or solar energy.

b. Aidan viewed Sofia Coppola's *Lost in Translation* three times and then wrote a paper describing the film as the work of a mysterious modern painter.

c. In the Middle Ages, the streets of London were dangerous places, it was safer to travel by boat along the Thames.

d. "He's not drunk," I said, "he's in a state of diabetic shock."

e. Are you able to endure extreme angle turns, high speeds, frequent jumps, and occasional crashes, then supermoto racing may be a sport for you.

1. Death Valley National Monument, located in southern California and Nevada, is one of the hottest places on Earth, temperatures there have soared as high as 134° Fahrenheit.

2. Anamaria opened the boxes crammed with toys, out sprang griffins, dragons, and phoenixes.

3. Subatomic physics is filled with strange and marvelous particles, tiny bodies of matter that shiver, wobble, pulse, and flatten to no thickness at all.

4. As his first major project, Frederick Law Olmsted designed New York City's Central Park, one of the most beautiful urban spaces in the United States.

5. The neurosurgeon explained that the medication could have one side effect, it might cause me to experience temporary memory loss.

EXERCISE 20–3   In the rough draft that follows, revise any run-on sentences.

   Some parents and educators argue that requiring uniforms in public schools would improve student behavior and performance. They think that uniforms give students a more professional attitude toward school, moreover, they believe that uniforms help create a sense of community among students from diverse backgrounds. But parents and educators should consider the drawbacks to requiring uniforms in public schools.

   Uniforms do create a sense of community, they do this, however, by stamping out individuality. Youth is a time to express originality, it is a time to develop a sense of self. One important way young people express their identities is through the clothes they wear. The self-patrolled dress code of high school students may be stricter than any school-imposed code, nevertheless, trying to control dress habits from above will only lead to resentment or to mindless conformity.

   If children are going to act like adults, they need to be treated like adults, they need to be allowed to make their own choices. Telling young people what to wear to school merely prolongs their childhood. Requiring uniforms undermines the educational purpose of public schools, which is not just to teach facts and figures but to help young people grow into adults who are responsible for making their own choices.

21   Make subjects and verbs agree.

In the present tense, verbs agree with their subjects in number (singular or plural) and in person (first, second, third): *I sing, you sing, he sings, she sings, we sing, they sing.* Even if your ear recognizes the standard subject-verb combinations presented in 21a, you will no doubt encounter tricky situations such as those described in 21b–21k.

21a   Consult this section for standard subject-verb combinations.

This section describes the basic guidelines for making present-tense verbs agree with their subjects. The present-tense ending *-s* (or *-es*) is used on a verb if its subject is third-person singular (*he, she, it,* and singular nouns); otherwise, the verb takes no ending. Consider, for example, the present-tense forms of the verbs *love* and *try,* given at the beginning of the chart on the following page.

The verb *be* varies from this pattern; unlike any other verb, it has special forms in *both* the present and the past tense. These forms appear at the end of the chart.

If you aren't confident that you know the standard forms, use the charts on pages 198 and 199 as you proofread for subject-verb agreement. You may also want to look at 27c on *-s* endings of regular and irregular verbs.

21b   Make the verb agree with its subject, not with a word that comes between.

Word groups often come between the subject and the verb. Such word groups, usually modifying the subject, may contain a noun that at first appears to be the subject. By mentally stripping away such modifiers, you can isolate the noun that is in fact the subject.

The *samples* on the tray in the lab *need* testing.

▶ High levels of air pollution causes damage to the respiratory

tract.

The subject is *levels*, not *pollution*. Strip away the phrase *of air pollution* to hear the correct verb: *levels cause.*

has
▶ The slaughter of pandas for their pelts ~~have~~ caused the
^

panda population to decline drastically.

The subject is *slaughter*, not *pandas* or *pelts.*

NOTE: Phrases beginning with the prepositions *as well as, in addition to, accompanied by, together with,* and *along with* do not make a singular subject plural.

was
▶ The governor as well as his press secretary ~~were~~ on the plane.
^

To emphasize that two people were on the plane, the writer could use *and* instead: *The governor and his press secretary were on the plane.*

21c Treat most subjects joined with *and* as plural.

A subject with two or more parts is said to be compound. If the parts are connected with *and,* the subject is almost always plural.

Leon and Jan often *jog* together.

▶ The Supreme Court's willingness to hear the case and its
have
affirmation of the original decision ~~has~~ set a new precedent.
^

EXCEPTIONS: When the parts of the subject form a single unit or when they refer to the same person or thing, treat the subject as singular.

Fish and chips was a last-minute addition to the menu.

Sue's friend and adviser was surprised by her decision.

Subject-verb agreement at a glance

Present-tense forms of *love* and *try* (typical verbs)

	SINGULAR		PLURAL	
FIRST PERSON	I	love	we	love
SECOND PERSON	you	love	you	love
THIRD PERSON	he/she/it*	loves	they**	love

	SINGULAR		PLURAL	
FIRST PERSON	I	try	we	try
SECOND PERSON	you	try	you	try
THIRD PERSON	he/she/it*	tries	they**	try

Present-tense forms of *have*

	SINGULAR		PLURAL	
FIRST PERSON	I	have	we	have
SECOND PERSON	you	have	you	have
THIRD PERSON	he/she/it*	has	they**	have

Present-tense forms of *do* (including negative forms)

	SINGULAR		PLURAL	
FIRST PERSON	I	do/don't	we	do/don't
SECOND PERSON	you	do/don't	you	do/don't
THIRD PERSON	he/she/it*	does/doesn't	they**	do/don't

Present-tense and past-tense forms of *be*

	SINGULAR		PLURAL	
FIRST PERSON	I	am/was	we	are/were
SECOND PERSON	you	are/were	you	are/were
THIRD PERSON	he/she/it*	is/was	they**	are/were

*And singular nouns (*child*, *Roger*)
**And plural nouns (*children*, *the Mannings*)

When to use the -s (or -es) form of a present-tense verb

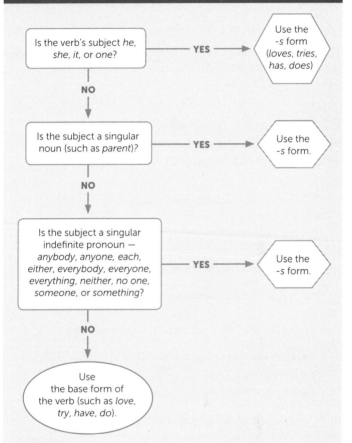

Is the verb's subject *he, she, it,* or *one*? — **YES** → Use the -s form (*loves, tries, has, does*)

NO ↓

Is the subject a singular noun (such as *parent*)? — **YES** → Use the -s form.

NO ↓

Is the subject a singular indefinite pronoun — *anybody, anyone, each, either, everybody, everyone, everything, neither, no one, someone,* or *something*? — **YES** → Use the -s form.

NO ↓

Use the base form of the verb (such as *love, try, have, do*).

EXCEPTION: Choosing the correct present-tense form of *be* (*am, is,* or *are*) is not quite so simple. See the chart on the previous page for both present- and past-tense forms of *be*.

TIP: Do not use the -s form of a verb if it follows a modal verb such as *can, must,* or *should* or another helping verb. (See 28c.)

When a compound subject is preceded by *each* or *every*, treat it as singular.

> Every car, truck, and van is required to pass inspection.

This exception does not apply when a compound subject is followed by *each*: *Alan and Marcia each have different ideas.*

21d With subjects joined with *or* or *nor* (or with *either . . . or* or *neither . . . nor*), make the verb agree with the part of the subject nearer to the verb.

> A driver's *license* or credit *card is* required.

> A driver's *license* or two credit *cards are* required.

> ▶ If an infant or a child ~~are~~ *is* having difficulty breathing, seek
>
> medical attention immediately.

> ▶ Neither the chief financial officer nor the marketing
>
> managers ~~was~~ *were* able to convince the client to reconsider.
>
> The verb must be matched with the part of the subject closer to it: *child is* in the first sentence, *managers were* in the second.

NOTE: If one part of the subject is singular and the other is plural, put the plural one last to avoid awkwardness.

21e Treat most indefinite pronouns as singular.

Indefinite pronouns are pronouns that do not refer to specific persons or things. The following commonly used indefinite pronouns are singular.

anybody	each	everyone	nobody	somebody
anyone	either	everything	no one	someone
anything	everybody	neither	nothing	something

Many of these words appear to have plural meanings, and they are often treated as such in casual speech. In formal written English, however, they are nearly always treated as singular.

Everyone on the team *supports* the coach.

> has
> **Each of the essays ~~have~~ been graded.**
>   ^

>   was
> **Nobody who participated in the clinical trials ~~were~~ given a**
>   ^
> **placebo.**

The subjects of these sentences are *Each* and *Nobody.* These indefinite pronouns are third-person singular, so the verbs must be *has* and *was.*

A few indefinite pronouns (*all, any, none, some*) may be singular or plural depending on the noun or pronoun they refer to.

SINGULAR   *Some* of our *luggage was* lost.

None of his *advice makes* sense.

PLURAL   *Some* of the *rocks are* slippery.

None of the *eggs were* broken.

NOTE: When the meaning of *none* is emphatically "not one," *none* may be treated as singular: *None* [meaning "Not one"] *of the eggs was broken.* Using *not one* instead is sometimes clearer: *Not one of the eggs was broken.*

21f Treat collective nouns as singular unless the meaning is clearly plural.

Collective nouns such as *jury, committee, audience, crowd, troop, family,* and *couple* name a class or a group. In American English, collective nouns are nearly always treated as singular: They emphasize the group as a unit. Occasionally, when there is some reason to draw attention to the individual members of the group, a collective noun may be treated as plural. (See also 22b.)

SINGULAR The *class respects* the teacher.

PLURAL The *class are* debating among themselves.

To underscore the notion of individuality in the second sentence, many writers would add a clearly plural noun.

PLURAL The class *members are* debating among themselves.

> *meets*
> The board of trustees ~~meet~~ in Denver twice a year.

The board as a whole meets; there is no reason to draw attention to its individual members.

> *were*
> A young couple ~~was~~ arguing about politics while holding

hands.

The meaning is clearly plural. Only separate individuals can argue and hold hands.

NOTE: The phrase *the number* is treated as singular, *a number* as plural.

SINGULAR *The number* of school-age children *is* declining.

PLURAL *A number* of children *are* attending the wedding.

NOTE: In general, when fractions or units of measurement are used with a singular noun, treat them as singular; when they are used with a plural noun, treat them as plural.

SINGULAR *Three-fourths* of the salad *has* been eaten.

Twenty *inches* of wallboard *was* covered with mud.

PLURAL *One-fourth* of the drivers *were* texting.

Two *pounds* of blueberries *were* used to make the pie.

21g Make the verb agree with its subject even when the subject follows the verb.

Verbs ordinarily follow subjects. When this normal order is reversed, it is easy to become confused. Sentences beginning with *there is* or *there are* (or *there was* or *there were*) are inverted; the subject follows the verb.

There *are* surprisingly few *honeybees* left in southern China.

▶ There ~~was~~ a social worker and a neighbor at the meeting.
were

The subject, *worker and neighbor*, is plural, so the verb must be *were*.

Occasionally you may decide to invert a sentence for variety or effect. When you do so, check to make sure that your subject and verb agree.

▶ Of particular concern ~~is~~ penicillin and tetracycline, antibiotics
are

used to make animals more resistant to disease.

The subject, *penicillin and tetracycline*, is plural, so the verb must be *are*.

21h Make the verb agree with its subject, not with a subject complement.

One basic sentence pattern in English consists of a subject, a linking verb, and a subject complement: *Jack is a lawyer.* Because the subject complement (*lawyer*) names or describes the subject (*Jack*), it is sometimes mistaken for the subject. (See 47b on subject complements.)

These *exercises* are a way to test your ability to perform under pressure.

▶ A major force in today's economy ~~are~~ children — as consumers,
is

decision makers, and trend spotters.

Force is the subject, not *children*. If the corrected version seems too awkward, make *children* the subject: *Children are a major force in today's economy — as consumers, decision makers, and trend spotters.*

▶ A tent and a sleeping bag *are*~~is~~ the required equipment for all

campers.

Tent and bag is the subject, not *equipment.*

21i *Who, which,* and *that* take verbs that agree with their antecedents.

Like most pronouns, the relative pronouns *who, which,* and *that* have antecedents, nouns or pronouns to which they refer. Relative pronouns used as subjects of subordinate clauses take verbs that agree with their antecedents.

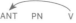

ANT   PN   V

Take a *course that prepares* you for classroom management.

One of the

Constructions such as *one of the students who* [or *one of the things that*] cause problems for writers. Do not assume that the antecedent must be *one.* Instead, consider the logic of the sentence.

▶ Our ability to use language is one of the things that sets us

apart from animals.

The antecedent of *that* is *things,* not *one.* Several things set us apart from animals.

Only one of the

When the phrase *the only* comes before *one,* you are safe in assuming that *one* is the antecedent of the relative pronoun.

▶ Veronica was the only one of the first-year Spanish students

who *was*~~were~~ fluent enough to apply for the exchange program.

The antecedent of *who* is *one,* not *students.* Only one student was fluent enough.

21j Words such as *athletics, economics, mathematics, physics, politics, statistics, measles,* and *news* are usually singular, despite their plural form.

>   *is*
> ▶ Politics ~~are~~ among my mother's favorite pastimes.
>   ^

EXCEPTION: Occasionally some of these words, especially *economics, mathematics, politics,* and *statistics,* have plural meanings.

> ▶ Office politics often sway decisions about hiring and
>
> promotion.

> ▶ The economics of the building plan are prohibitive.

21k Titles of works, company names, words mentioned as words, and gerund phrases are singular.

>   *describes*
> ▶ *Lost Cities* ~~describe~~ the discoveries of fifty ancient civilizations.
>   ^

>   *specializes*
> ▶ Delmonico Brothers ~~specialize~~ in organic produce and
>   ^
>
> additive-free meats.

>   *is*
> ▶ *Controlled substances* ~~are~~ a euphemism for illegal drugs.
>   ^

A gerund phrase consists of an *-ing* verb form followed by any objects, complements, or modifiers (see 48b). Treat gerund phrases as singular.

>   *makes*
> ▶ Encountering long hold times ~~make~~ customers impatient with
>   ^
>
> telephone tech support.

EXERCISE 21–1 For each sentence in the following passage, underline the subject (or compound subject) and then select the verb that agrees with it. (If you have trouble identifying the subject, consult 47a.)

Loggerhead sea turtles (migrate / migrates) thousands of miles before returning to their nesting location every two to three years. The nesting season for loggerhead turtles (span / spans) the hottest months of the summer. Although the habitat of Atlantic loggerheads (range / ranges) from Newfoundland to Argentina, nesting for these turtles (take / takes) place primarily along the southeastern coast of the United States. Female turtles that have reached sexual maturity (crawl / crawls) ashore at night to lay their eggs. The cavity that serves as a nest for the eggs (is / are) dug out with the female's strong flippers. Deposited into each nest (is / are) anywhere from fifty to two hundred spherical eggs, also known as a *clutch*. After a two-month incubation period, all eggs in the clutch (begin / begins) to hatch, and within a few days the young turtles attempt to make their way into the ocean. A major cause of the loggerhead's decreasing numbers (is / are) natural predators such as raccoons, birds, and crabs. Beach erosion and coastal development also (threaten / threatens) the turtles' survival. For example, a crowd of curious humans or lights from beachfront residences (is / are) enough to make the female abandon her nesting plans and return to the ocean. Since only one in one thousand loggerheads survives to adulthood, special care should be taken to protect this threatened species.

EXERCISE 21–2 Edit the following sentences to eliminate problems with subject-verb agreement. If a sentence is correct, write "correct" after it. Answers to lettered sentences appear in the back of the book. Example:

Jack's first days in the infantry ~~was~~ *were* grueling.

a. One of the main reasons for elephant poaching are the profits received from selling the ivory tusks.

b. Not until my interview with Dr. Hwang were other possibilities opened to me.

c. A number of students in the seminar was aware of the importance of joining the discussion.

d. Batik cloth from Bali, blue and white ceramics from Delft, and a bocce ball from Turin has made Angelie's room the talk of the dorm.

e. The board of directors, ignoring the wishes of the neighborhood, has voted to allow further development.

1. Measles is a contagious childhood disease.

2. Adorning a shelf in the lab is a Vietnamese figurine, a set of Korean clay gods, and an American plastic village.

3. The presence of certain bacteria in our bodies is one of the factors that determines our overall health.

4. Sheila is the only one of the many applicants who has the ability to step into this job.

5. Neither the explorer nor his companions was ever seen again.

22 Make pronouns and antecedents agree.

A pronoun is a word that substitutes for a noun. (See 46b.) Many pronouns have antecedents, nouns or pronouns to which they refer. A pronoun and its antecedent agree when they are both singular or both plural.

SINGULAR *Dr. Ava Berto* finished *her* rounds.

PLURAL The hospital *interns* finished *their* rounds.

MULTILINGUAL The pronouns *he, his, she, her, it,* and *its* must agree in gender (masculine, feminine, or neuter) with their antecedents, not with the words they modify.

Steve visited *his* [not *her*] sister in Seattle.

22a Do not use plural pronouns to refer to singular antecedents.

Writers are frequently tempted to use plural pronouns to refer to two kinds of singular antecedents: indefinite pronouns and generic nouns.

Indefinite pronouns

Indefinite pronouns refer to nonspecific persons or things. Even though some of the following indefinite pronouns may seem to have plural meanings, treat them as singular in formal English.

anybody	each	everyone	nobody	somebody
anyone	either	everything	no one	someone
anything	everybody	neither	nothing	something

Everyone performs at *his or her* [not *their*] own fitness level.

When a plural pronoun refers mistakenly to a singular indefinite pronoun, you can usually choose one of three options for revision:

1. Replace the plural pronoun with *he or she* (or *his or her*).
2. Make the antecedent plural.
3. Rewrite the sentence so that no problem of agreement exists.

▶ When someone travels outside the United States for the
    he or she needs
  first time, ~~they need~~ to apply for a passport.

    people travel
▶ When ~~someone travels~~ outside the United States for the

  first time, they need to apply for a passport.

    Anyone who
▶ ~~When someone~~ travels outside the United States for the
            needs
  first time,/~~they need~~ to apply for a passport.

Because the *he or she* construction is wordy, often the second or third revision strategy is more effective. Using *he* (or *his*) to refer to persons of either sex, while less wordy, is considered sexist, as is using *she* (or *her*) for all persons. Some writers alternate male and female pronouns throughout a text, but the result is often awkward. See 17e and the chart on page 210 for strategies that avoid sexist usage.

NOTE: If you change a pronoun from singular to plural (or vice versa), check to be sure that the verb agrees with the new pronoun (see 21e).

Generic nouns

A generic noun represents a typical member of a group, such as a *typical student*, or any member of a group, such as *any lawyer*. Although generic nouns may seem to have plural meanings, they are singular.

> Every *runner* must train rigorously if *he or she wants* [not *they want*] to excel.

When a plural pronoun refers mistakenly to a generic noun, you will usually have the same three revision options as mentioned on page 208 for indefinite pronouns.

▶ A medical student must study hard if ~~they want~~ *he or she wants* to succeed.

▶ ~~A medical student~~ *Medical students* must study hard if they want to succeed.

▶ A medical student must study hard ~~if they want~~ to succeed.

22b Treat collective nouns as singular unless the meaning is clearly plural.

Collective nouns such as *jury, committee, audience, crowd, class, troop, family, team,* and *couple* name a group. Ordinarily the group functions as a unit, so the noun should be treated as singular; if the members of the group function as individuals, however, the noun should be treated as plural. (See also 21f.)

AS A UNIT   The *committee* granted *its* permission to build.

AS INDIVIDUALS   The *committee* put *their* signatures on the document.

When treating a collective noun as plural, many writers prefer to add a clearly plural antecedent such as *members* to the

Choosing a revision strategy that avoids sexist language

Because many readers object to sexist language, avoid using *he, him,* and *his* (or *she, her,* and *hers*) to refer to both men and women. Also try to avoid the wordy expressions *he or she* and *his or her*. More graceful alternatives are usually possible.

Use an occasional *he or she* (or *his or her*).

▶ In our office, everyone works at ~~their~~ *his or her* own pace.

Make the antecedent plural.

▶ ~~An employee~~ *Employees* on extended disability leave may continue their

life insurance.

Recast the sentence.

▶ The amount of vacation time a federal worker may accrue depends

on ~~their~~ length of service.

▶ ~~If a~~ *A* child ~~is~~ born to parents who are both bipolar~~,~~ ~~they have~~ *has* a high

chance of being bipolar.

▶ In his autobiography, Benjamin Franklin suggests that anyone can

achieve success ~~as long as they live~~ *by living* a virtuous life and ~~work~~ *working* hard.

sentence: *The members of the committee put their signatures on the document.*

▶ Defense attorney Clarence Darrow surprisingly urged the

jury to find his client, John Scopes, guilty so that he could

appeal the case to a higher court. The jury complied,

returning ~~their~~ *its* verdict in only nine minutes.

There is no reason to draw attention to the individual members of the jury, so *jury* should be treated as singular.

22c Treat most compound antecedents joined with *and* as plural.

In 1987, *Reagan and Gorbachev* held a summit where *they* signed the Intermediate-Range Nuclear Forces Treaty.

22d With compound antecedents joined with *or* or *nor* (or with *either . . . or* or *neither . . . nor*), make the pronoun agree with the nearer antecedent.

Either *Bruce* or *Tom* should receive first prize for *his* poem.

Neither the *mouse* nor the *rats* could find *their* way through the maze.

NOTE: If one of the antecedents is singular and the other plural, as in the second example, put the plural one last to avoid awkwardness.

EXCEPTION: If one antecedent is male and the other female, do not follow the traditional rule. The sentence *Either Bruce or Elizabeth should receive first prize for her short story* makes no sense. The best solution is to recast the sentence: *The prize for best short story should go to either Bruce or Elizabeth.*

EXERCISE 22–1 Edit the following sentences to eliminate problems with pronoun-antecedent agreement. Most of the sentences can be revised in more than one way, so experiment before choosing a solution. If a sentence is correct, write "correct" after it. Revisions of lettered sentences appear in the back of the book. Example:

> Recruiters
> ~~The recruiter~~ may tell the truth, but there is much that they
>   ^
>
> choose not to tell.

a. Every presidential candidate must appeal to a wide variety of ethnic and social groups if they want to win the election.

b. David lent his motorcycle to someone who allowed their friend to use it.

c. The aerobics teacher motioned for everyone to move their arms in wide, slow circles.

d. The parade committee was unanimous in its decision to allow all groups and organizations to join the festivities.

e. The applicant should be bilingual if they want to qualify for this position.

1. If a driver refuses to take a blood or breath test, he or she will have their licenses suspended for six months.

2. Why should anyone learn a second language? One reason is to sharpen their minds.

3. The Department of Education issued guidelines for school security. They were trying to anticipate problems and avert disaster.

4. The logger in the Northwest relies on the old forest growth for their living.

5. If anyone notices any suspicious activity, they should report it to the police.

EXERCISE 22–2 Edit the following paragraph to eliminate problems with pronoun-antecedent agreement or sexist language.

A common practice in businesses is to put each employee in their own cubicle. A typical cubicle resembles an office, but their walls don't reach the ceiling. Many office managers feel that a cubicle floor plan has its advantages. Cubicles make a large area feel spacious. In addition, they can be moved around so that each new employee can be accommodated in his own work area. Of course, the cubicle model also has problems. The typical employee is not as happy with a cubicle as they would be with a traditional office. Also, productivity can suffer. Neither a manager nor a frontline worker can ordinarily do their best work in a cubicle because of noise and lack of privacy. Each worker can hear his neighbors tapping on computer keyboards, making telephone calls, and muttering under their breath.

23   Make pronoun references clear.

Pronouns substitute for nouns; they are a kind of shorthand. In a sentence like *After Andrew intercepted the ball, he kicked it as hard as he could,* the pronouns *he* and *it* substitute for the nouns *Andrew* and *ball.* The word a pronoun refers to is called its *antecedent.*

23a Avoid ambiguous or remote pronoun reference.

Ambiguous pronoun reference occurs when a pronoun could refer to two possible antecedents.

> *The pitcher broke when Gloria set it*
> ► ~~When Gloria set the pitcher~~ on the glass-topped table~~,~~
>   ~~it broke.~~

> "*You have*
> ► Tom told James, ~~that he had~~ won the lottery."
>
> What broke — the pitcher or the table? Who won the lottery — Tom or James? The revisions eliminate the ambiguity.

Remote pronoun reference occurs when a pronoun is too far away from its antecedent for easy reading.

> ► After the court ordered my ex-husband to pay child support, he refused. Approximately eight months later, we were back in court. This time the judge ordered him to make payments directly to the Support and Collections Unit, which would in turn pay me. For the first six months, I received regular payments, but then they stopped. Again ~~he~~ *my ex-husband* was summoned to appear in court; he did not respond.
>
> The pronoun *he* was too distant from its antecedent, *ex-husband*, which appeared several sentences earlier.

23b Generally, avoid broad reference of *this, that, which,* and *it.*

For clarity, the pronouns *this, that, which,* and *it* should ordinarily refer to specific antecedents rather than to whole ideas or sentences. When a pronoun's reference is needlessly broad, either replace the pronoun with a noun or supply an antecedent to which the pronoun clearly refers.

► By advertising on television, pharmaceutical companies gain

exposure for their prescription drugs. Patients respond to
the ads
~~this~~ by requesting drugs they might not need.
  ^

For clarity, the writer substituted the noun *ads* for the pronoun *this*,
which referred broadly to the idea expressed in the preceding sentence.

► Romeo and Juliet were both too young to have acquired
                                    a fact
much wisdom, ~~and~~ that accounts for their rash actions.
             ^

The writer added an antecedent (*fact*) that the pronoun *that* clearly
refers to.

23c Do not use a pronoun to refer to an implied antecedent.

A pronoun should refer to a specific antecedent, not to a word
that is implied but not present in the sentence.

                                          the braids
► After braiding Ann's hair, Sue decorated ~~them~~ with ribbons.
                                            ^

The pronoun *them* referred to Ann's braids (implied by the term
braiding), but the word *braids* did not appear in the sentence.

Modifiers, such as possessives, cannot serve as antecedents.
A modifier may strongly imply the noun that a pronoun might
logically refer to, but it is not itself that noun.

                      Jamaica Kincaid
► In ~~Jamaica Kincaid's~~ "Girl," ~~she~~ describes the advice a
                                    ^

mother gives her daughter, including the mysterious

warning not to be "the kind of woman who the baker won't

let near the bread" (454).

Using the possessive form of an author's name to introduce a source
leads to a problem later in this sentence: The pronoun *she* cannot refer
logically to a possessive modifier (*Jamaica Kincaid's*). The revision
substitutes the noun *Jamaica Kincaid* for the pronoun *she*, thereby
eliminating the problem.

23d Avoid the indefinite use of *they, it,* and *you*.

Do not use the pronoun *they* to refer indefinitely to persons who have not been specifically mentioned. *They* should always refer to a specific antecedent.

▶ In June, ~~they~~ announced that parents would have to pay a fee

     the board

for their children to participate in sports and music programs

starting in September.

The word *it* should not be used indefinitely in constructions such as *It is said on television . . .* or *In the article, it says that. . . .*

     The

▶ ~~In the~~ encyclopedia ~~it~~ states that male moths can smell

female moths from several miles away.

The pronoun *you* is appropriate only when the writer is addressing the reader directly: *Once you have kneaded the dough, let it rise in a warm place.* Except in informal contexts, however, *you* should not be used to mean "anyone in general." Use a noun instead.

     a guest

▶ Ms. Pickersgill's *Guide to Etiquette* stipulates that ~~you~~ should

not arrive at a party too early or leave too late.

23e To refer to persons, use *who, whom,* or *whose,* not *which* or *that*.

In most contexts, use *who, whom,* or *whose* to refer to persons, *which* or *that* to refer to animals or things. *Which* is reserved only for animals or things, so it is impolite to use it to refer to persons.

     whom

▶ All thirty-two women in the study, half of ~~which~~ were

unemployed for more than six months, reported higher

self-esteem after job training.

Although *that* is sometimes used to refer to persons, many readers will find such references dehumanizing. It is more polite to use a form of *who* — a word reserved only for people.

▶ During the two-day festival El Día de los Muertos (Day of the

  Dead), Mexican families celebrate loved ones ~~that~~ have died.
  ^{who}

EXERCISE 23–1 Edit the following sentences to correct errors in pronoun reference. In some cases, you will need to decide on an antecedent that the pronoun might logically refer to. Revisions of lettered sentences appear in the back of the book. Example:

  Although Apple makes the most widely recognized MP3

  player, other companies have gained a share of the market.

  The competition
  ~~This~~ has kept prices from skyrocketing.

a. They say that engineering students should have hands-on experience with dismantling and reassembling machines.

b. She had decorated her living room with posters from chamber music festivals. This led her date to believe that she was interested in classical music. Actually she preferred rock.

c. In my high school, you didn't need to get all A's to be considered a success; you just needed to work to your ability.

d. Marianne told Jenny that she was worried about her mother's illness.

e. Though Lewis cried for several minutes after scraping his knee, eventually it subsided.

1. Our German conversation group is made up of six people, three of which I had never met before.

2. Many people believe that the polygraph test is highly reliable if you employ a licensed examiner.

3. Parent involvement is high at Mission San Jose High School. They participate in many committees and activities that affect all aspects of school life.

4. Because of Paul Robeson's outspoken attitude toward fascism, he was labeled a Communist.

5. In the report, it points out that the bald eagle, after several decades of protection, was removed from the endangered species list in 1997.

EXERCISE 23–2 Edit the following passage to correct errors in pronoun reference. In some cases, you will need to decide on an antecedent that the pronoun might logically refer to.

Since the Internet's inception in the 1980s, it has grown to be one of the largest communications forums in the world. The Internet was created by a team of academics who were building on a platform that government scientists had started developing in the 1950s. They initially viewed it as a noncommercial enterprise that would serve only the needs of the academic and technical communities. But with the introduction of user-friendly browser technology in the 1990s, it expanded tremendously. By the late 1990s, many businesses were connecting to the Internet with high-speed broadband and fiber-optic connections, which is also true of many home users today. Accessing information, shopping, and communicating are easier than ever before. This, however, can lead to some possible drawbacks. You can be bombarded with spam and pop-up ads or attacked by harmful viruses and worms. They say that the best way to protect home computers from harm is to keep antivirus protection programs up-to-date and to shut them down when not in use.

24

Distinguish between pronouns such as *I* and *me*.

The personal pronouns in the following chart change what is known as *case form* according to their grammatical function in a sentence. Pronouns functioning as subjects or subject complements appear in the *subjective* case; those functioning as objects appear in the *objective* case; and those showing ownership appear in the *possessive* case.

	SUBJECTIVE CASE	OBJECTIVE CASE	POSSESSIVE CASE
SINGULAR	I	me	my
	you	you	your
	he/she/it	him/her/it	his/her/its
PLURAL	we	us	our
	you	you	your
	they	them	their

Pronouns in the subjective and objective cases are frequently confused. Most of the rules in this section specify when to use one or the other of these cases (*I* or *me*, *he* or *him*, and so on). Section 24g explains a special use of pronouns and nouns in the possessive case.

24a Use the subjective case (*I, you, he, she, it, we, they*) for subjects and subject complements.

When personal pronouns are used as subjects, ordinarily your ear will tell you the correct pronoun. Problems sometimes arise, however, with compound word groups containing a pronoun, so it is not always safe to trust your ear.

> Joel ran away from home because his stepfather and ~~him~~ *he* had quarreled.

His stepfather and he is the subject of the verb *had quarreled*. If we strip away the words *his stepfather and*, the correct pronoun becomes clear: *he had quarreled* (not *him had quarreled*).

When a pronoun is used as a subject complement (a word following a linking verb), your ear may mislead you, since the incorrect form is frequently heard in casual speech. (See "subject complement," 47b.)

> During the Lindbergh trial, Bruno Hauptmann repeatedly denied that the kidnapper was ~~him.~~ *he.*

If *kidnapper was he* seems too stilted, rewrite the sentence: *During the Lindbergh trial, Bruno Hauptmann repeatedly denied that he was the kidnapper.*

24b Use the objective case (*me, you, him, her, it, us, them*) for all objects.

When a personal pronoun is used as a direct object, an indirect object, or the object of a preposition, ordinarily your ear will lead you to the correct pronoun. When an object is compound, however, you may occasionally become confused.

▶ Janice was indignant when she realized that the salesclerk

her.
was insulting her mother and ~~she.~~
⌃

Her mother and her is the direct object of the verb *was insulting*. Strip
away the words *her mother and* to hear the correct pronoun: *was
insulting her* (not *was insulting she*).

me
▶ The most traumatic experience for her father and ~~I~~ occurred
⌃

long after her operation.

Her father and me is the object of the preposition *for*. Strip away the words
her father and to test for the correct pronoun: *for me* (not *for I*).

When in doubt about the correct pronoun, some writers try
to avoid making the choice by using a reflexive pronoun
such as *myself*. Using a reflexive pronoun in such situations is
nonstandard.

me
▶ The Indian cab driver gave my cousin and ~~myself~~ some good
⌃

tips on traveling in New Delhi.

My cousin and me is the indirect object of the verb *gave*. For correct uses
of *myself*, see the glossary of usage.

24c Put an appositive and the word to which it refers in the same case.

Appositives are noun phrases that rename nouns or pronouns.
A pronoun used as an appositive has the same function (usually
subject or object) as the word(s) it renames.

I,
▶ The chief strategists, Dr. Bell and ~~me,~~ could not agree on a plan.
⌃

The appositive *Dr. Bell and I* renames the subject, *strategists*. Test: *I could
not agree* (not *me could not agree*).

▶ The reporter interviewed only two witnesses, the bicyclist

me.
and ~~I.~~
⌃

The appositive *the bicyclist and me* renames the direct object, *witnesses*.
Test: *interviewed me* (not *interviewed I*).

24d Following *than* or *as*, choose the pronoun that expresses your meaning.

When a comparison begins with *than* or *as*, your choice of a pronoun will depend on your meaning. To test for the correct pronoun, mentally complete the sentence: *My roommate likes football more than I [do].*

▶ In our position paper supporting nationalized health care

in the United States, we argued that Canadians are much

we.
better off than ~~us.~~
    ^

We is the subject of the verb *are*, which is understood: *Canadians are much better off than we [are].* If the correct English seems too formal, you can always add the verb.

▶ We respected no other candidate for the city council as much

her.
as ~~she.~~
  ^

This sentence means that we respected no other candidate as much as *we respected her. Her* is the direct object of the understood verb *respected*.

24e For *we* or *us* before a noun, choose the pronoun that would be appropriate if the noun were omitted.

We
▶ ~~Us~~ tenants would rather fight than move.
  ^

                               us
▶ Management is shortchanging ~~we~~ tenants.
                       ^

No one would say *Us would rather fight than move* or *Management is shortchanging we.*

24f Use the objective case for subjects and objects of infinitives.

An infinitive is the word *to* followed by the base form of a verb. (See 48b.) Subjects of infinitives are an exception to the rule that subjects must be in the subjective case. Whenever an infinitive has

pronouns following *than* or *as* • *we* vs. *us* • object pronouns
with infinitives (*to see*) • pronouns with *-ing* noun form

case
24g

221

a subject, it must be in the objective case. Objects of infinitives also are in the objective case.

▶ Sue asked John and ~~I~~ *me* to drive the senator and ~~she~~ *her* to the airport.

John and me is the subject of the infinitive *to drive; senator and her* is the direct object of the infinitive.

24g Use the possessive case to modify a gerund.

A pronoun that modifies a gerund or a gerund phrase should be in the possessive case (*my, our, your, his, her, its, their*). A gerund is a verb form ending in *-ing* that functions as a noun. Gerunds frequently appear in phrases; when they do, the whole gerund phrase functions as a noun. (See 48b.)

▶ The chances of ~~you~~ *your* being hit by lightning are about two million

to one.

Your modifies the gerund phrase *being hit by lightning.*

Nouns as well as pronouns may modify gerunds. To form the possessive case of a noun, use an apostrophe and an *-s* (*victim's*) or just an apostrophe (*victims'*). (See 36a.)

▶ The old order in France paid a high price for the ~~aristocracy~~ *aristocracy's*

exploiting the lower classes.

The possessive noun *aristocracy's* modifies the gerund phrase *exploiting the lower classes.*

EXERCISE 24–1 Edit the following sentences to eliminate errors in pronoun case. If a sentence is correct, write "correct" after it. Answers to lettered sentences appear in the back of the book. Example:

Papa chops wood for neighbors much younger than ~~him.~~ *he.*

a. Rick applied for the job even though he heard that other candidates were more experienced than he.

PRACTICE hackerhandbooks.com/rules
> Grammar > 24–3 and 24–4
> 25–3 and 25–4 (pronoun review)

b. The volleyball team could not believe that the coach was she.

c. She appreciated him telling the truth in such a difficult situation.

d. The director has asked you and I to draft a proposal for a new recycling plan.

e. Five close friends and myself rented a station wagon, packed it with food, and drove two hundred miles to Mardi Gras.

1. The squawk of the brass horns nearly overwhelmed us oboe and bassoon players.

2. Ushio, the last rock climber up the wall, tossed Teri and she the remaining pitons and carabiners.

3. The programmer realized that her and the interface designers were creating an entirely new Web application.

4. My desire to understand classical music was aided by me working as an usher at Symphony Hall.

5. The shower of sinking bricks caused he and his diving partner to race away from the collapsing seawall.

EXERCISE 24–2 In the following paragraph, choose the correct pronoun in each set of parentheses.

We may blame television for the number of products based on characters in children's TV shows — from Big Bird to SpongeBob — but in fact merchandising that capitalizes on a character's popularity started long before television. Raggedy Ann began as a child's rag doll, and a few years later books about (she / her) and her brother, Raggedy Andy, were published. A cartoonist named Johnny Gruelle painted a cloth face on a family doll and applied for a patent in 1915. Later Gruelle began writing and illustrating stories about Raggedy Ann, and in 1918 (he / him) and a publisher teamed up to publish the books and sell the dolls. He was not the only one to try to sell products linked to children's stories. Beatrix Potter published the first of many Peter Rabbit picture books in 1902, and no one was better than (she / her) at making a living from spin-offs. After Peter Rabbit and Benjamin Bunny became popular, Potter began putting pictures of (they / them) and their little animal friends on merchandise. Potter had fans all over the world, and she understood (them / their) wanting to see Peter Rabbit not only in books but also on teapots and plates and lamps and other furnishings for the nursery. Potter and Gruelle, like countless others before and since, knew that entertaining children could be a profitable business.

Distinguish between *who* and *whom*.

The choice between *who* and *whom* (or *whoever* and *whomever*) occurs primarily in subordinate clauses and in questions. *Who* and *whoever*, subjective-case pronouns, are used for subjects and subject complements. *Whom* and *whomever*, objective-case pronouns, are used for objects. (See 25a and 25b.)

An exception to this general rule occurs when the pronoun functions as the subject of an infinitive (see 25c). See also 24f.

25a In subordinate clauses, use *who* and *whoever* for subjects and subject complements, *whom* and *whomever* for all objects.

When *who* and *whom* (or *whoever* and *whomever*) introduce subordinate clauses, their case is determined by their function *within the clause they introduce*.

In the following two examples, the pronouns *who* and *whoever* function as the subjects of the clauses they introduce.

▶ First prize goes to the runner ~~whom~~ *who* earns the most points.

The subordinate clause is *who earns the most points*. The verb of the clause is *earns*, and its subject is *who*.

▶ Maya Angelou's *I Know Why the Caged Bird Sings* should be
read by ~~whomever~~ *whoever* is interested in the effects of racial prejudice
on children.

The writer selected the pronoun *whomever*, thinking that it was the object of the preposition *by*. However, the object of the preposition is the entire subordinate clause *whoever is interested in the effects of racial prejudice on children*. The verb of the clause is *is*, and the subject of the verb is *whoever*.

When functioning as an object in a subordinate clause, *whom* (or *whomever*) also appears out of order, before the subject and verb. To choose the correct pronoun, you can mentally restructure the clause.

> *whom*
> ► You will work with our senior traders, ~~who~~ you will meet later.
>   ^

The subordinate clause is *whom you will meet later*. The subject of the clause is *you*, and the verb is *will meet*. *Whom* is the direct object of the verb. The correct choice becomes clear if you mentally restructure the clause: *you will meet whom*.

When functioning as the object of a preposition in a subordinate clause, *whom* is often separated from its preposition.

> *whom*
> ► The tutor ~~who~~ I was assigned to was very supportive.
>   ^

Whom is the object of the preposition *to*. In this sentence, the writer might choose to drop *whom*: *The tutor I was assigned to was very supportive*.

NOTE: Inserted expressions such as *they know*, *I think*, and *she says* should be ignored in determining whether to use *who* or *whom*.

> ► The speech pathologist reported a particularly difficult
>
>   *who*
>   session with a stroke patient ~~whom~~ she knew was suffering
>   ^
>   from aphasia.

Who is the subject of *was suffering*, not the object of *knew*.

25b In questions, use *who* and *whoever* for subjects, *whom* and *whomever* for all objects.

When *who* and *whom* (or *whoever* and *whomever*) are used to open questions, their case is determined by their function within the question. In the following example, *who* functions as the subject of the question.

> *Who*
> ► ~~Whom~~ was responsible for creating that computer virus?
>   ^

Who is the subject of the verb *was*.

When *whom* functions as the object of a verb or the object of a preposition in a question, it appears out of normal order. To choose the correct pronoun, you can mentally restructure the question.

> *Whom*
> ~~Who~~ did the Democratic Party nominate in 2008?
>   ^
>
> *Whom* is the direct object of the verb *did nominate*. This becomes clear if you restructure the question: *The Democratic Party did nominate whom in 2008?*

25c Use *whom* for subjects or objects of infinitives.

An infinitive is the word *to* followed by the base form of a verb. (See 48b.) Subjects of infinitives are an exception to the rule that subjects must be in the subjective case. The subject of an infinitive must be in the objective case. Objects of infinitives also are in the objective case.

> *whom*
> When it comes to money, I know ~~who~~ to believe.
>   ^
>
> The infinitive phrase *whom to believe* is the direct object of the verb *know*, and *whom* is the subject of the infinitive *to believe*.

NOTE: In spoken English, *who* is frequently used when the correct *whom* sounds too stuffy. Even educated speakers are likely to say *Who* [not *Whom*] *did Senator Boxer replace?* Although some readers will accept such constructions in informal written English, it is safer to use *whom* in formal English.

EXERCISE 25–1   Edit the following sentences to eliminate errors in the use of *who* and *whom* (or *whoever* and *whomever*). If a sentence is correct, write "correct" after it. Answers to lettered sentences appear in the back of the book. Example:

> *whom*
> What is the address of the artist ~~who~~ Antonio hired?
>   ^

a. The roundtable featured scholars who I had never heard of.

b. Arriving late for rehearsal, we had no idea who was supposed to dance with whom.

c. Whom did you support for student government president?

d. Daniel always gives a holiday donation to whomever needs it.

e. So many singers came to the audition that Natalia had trouble deciding who to select for the choir.

PRACTICE   hackerhandbooks.com/rules
   > Grammar > 25–2
          > 25–3 and 25–4 (pronoun review)

1. My cousin Sylvie, who I am teaching to fly a kite, watches us every time we compete.
2. Who decided to research the history of Hungarians in New Brunswick?
3. According to Greek myth, the Sphinx devoured those who could not answer her riddles.
4. The people who ordered their medications from Canada were retirees whom don't have health insurance.
5. Who did the committee select?

26 Choose adjectives and adverbs with care.

Adjectives modify nouns or pronouns. They usually come before the word they modify; occasionally they function as complements following the word they modify. Adverbs modify verbs, adjectives, or other adverbs. (See 46d and 46e.)

Many adverbs are formed by adding -*ly* to adjectives (*normal, normally; smooth, smoothly*). But don't assume that all words ending in -*ly* are adverbs or that all adverbs end in -*ly*. Some adjectives end in -*ly* (*lovely, friendly*), and some adverbs don't (*always, here, there*). When in doubt, consult a dictionary.

MULTILINGUAL Placement of adjectives and adverbs can be a tricky matter for multilingual writers. See 30f and 30h.

26a Use adjectives to modify nouns.

Adjectives ordinarily precede the nouns they modify. But they can also function as subject complements or object complements, following the nouns they modify.

MULTILINGUAL In English, adjectives are not pluralized to agree with the words they modify: *The red* [not *reds*] *roses were a surprise.*

Subject complements

A subject complement follows a linking verb and completes the meaning of the subject. (See 47b.) When an adjective functions as a subject complement, it describes the subject.

Justice is blind.

Problems can arise with verbs such as *smell, taste, look*, and *feel*, which sometimes, but not always, function as linking verbs. If the word following one of these verbs describes the subject, use an adjective; if the word following the verb modifies the verb, use an adverb.

ADJECTIVE   The detective looked *cautious*.

ADVERB   The detective looked *cautiously* for fingerprints.

The adjective *cautious* describes the detective; the adverb *cautiously* modifies the verb *looked*.

Linking verbs suggest states of being, not actions. Notice, for example, the different meanings of *looked* in the preceding examples. To look cautious suggests the state of being cautious; to look cautiously is to perform an action in a cautious way.

▶ The lilacs in our backyard smell especially ~~sweetly~~ *sweet* this year.

The verb *smell* suggests a state of being, not an action. Therefore, it should be followed by an adjective, not an adverb.

▶ The drawings looked ~~well~~ *good* after the architect made a few

changes.

The verb *looked* is a linking verb suggesting a state of being, not an action. The adjective *good* is appropriate following the linking verb to describe *drawings*. (See also 26c.)

Object complements

An object complement follows a direct object and completes its meaning. (See 47b.) When an adjective functions as an object complement, it describes the direct object.

Sorrow makes *us wise.*

Object complements occur with verbs such as *call, consider, create, find, keep,* and *make.* When a modifier follows the direct object of one of these verbs, use an adjective to describe the direct object; use an adverb to modify the verb.

ADJECTIVE The referee called the plays *perfect.*

ADVERB The referee called the plays *perfectly.*

The first sentence means that the referee considered the plays to be perfect; the second means that the referee did an excellent job of calling the plays.

26b Use adverbs to modify verbs, adjectives, and other adverbs.

When adverbs modify verbs (or verbals), they nearly always answer the question When? Where? How? Why? Under what conditions? How often? or To what degree? When adverbs modify adjectives or other adverbs, they usually qualify or intensify the meaning of the word they modify. (See 46e.)

Adjectives are often used incorrectly in place of adverbs in casual or nonstandard speech.

▶ The travel arrangement worked out ~~perfect~~ *perfectly* for everyone.

▶ The manager must see that the office runs ~~smooth~~ *smoothly* and ~~efficient.~~ *efficiently.*

The adverb *perfectly* modifies the verb *worked out*; the adverbs *smoothly* and *efficiently* modify the verb *runs.*

▶ The chance of recovering any property lost in the fire looks ~~real~~ *really* slim.

Only adverbs can modify adjectives or other adverbs. *Really* intensifies the meaning of the adjective *slim.*

26c Distinguish between *good* and *well, bad* and *badly.*

Good is an adjective (*good performance*). *Well* is an adverb when it modifies a verb (*speak well*). The use of the adjective *good* in place of the adverb *well* to modify a verb is nonstandard and especially common in casual speech.

adverbs with verb, adjective, adverb • *good* vs. *well* •
bad vs. *badly* • *more* vs. *most* • *-er* vs. *-est* forms

adj/adv
26d   229

well
▶ We were glad that Sanya had done ~~good~~ on the CPA exam.
                                          ^

The adverb *well* modifies the verb *had done*.

Confusion can arise because *well* is an adjective when it modifies a noun or pronoun and means "healthy" or "satisfactory" (*The babies were well and warm*).

well,
▶ Adrienne did not feel ~~good,~~ but she made her presentation
                         ^

anyway.

As an adjective following the linking verb *did feel*, *well* describes Adrienne's health.

Bad is always an adjective and should be used to describe a noun; *badly* is always an adverb and should be used to modify a verb. The adverb *badly* is often used inappropriately to describe a noun, especially following a linking verb.

bad
▶ The sisters felt ~~badly~~ when they realized they had left their
                     ^

brother out of the planning.

The adjective *bad* is used after the linking verb *felt* to describe the noun *sisters*.

26d Use comparatives and superlatives with care.

Most adjectives and adverbs have three forms: the positive, the comparative, and the superlative.

POSITIVE	COMPARATIVE	SUPERLATIVE
soft	softer	softest
fast	faster	fastest
careful	more careful	most careful
bad	worse	worst
good	better	best

Comparative versus superlative

Use the comparative to compare two things, the superlative to compare three or more.

▶ Which of these two low-carb drinks is ~~best?~~ *better?*

▶ Though Shaw and Jackson are impressive, Zhao is the ~~more~~ *most*

qualified of the three candidates running for mayor.

Forming comparatives and superlatives

To form comparatives and superlatives of most one- and two-syllable adjectives, use the endings *-er* and *-est*: *smooth, smoother, smoothest*; *easy, easier, easiest*. With longer adjectives, use *more* and *most* (or *less* and *least* for downward comparisons): *exciting, more exciting, most exciting*; *helpful, less helpful, least helpful*.

Some one-syllable adverbs take the endings *-er* and *-est* (*fast, faster, fastest*), but longer adverbs and all of those ending in *-ly* form the comparative and superlative with *more* and *most* (or *less* and *least*).

The comparative and superlative forms of some adjectives and adverbs are irregular: *good, better, best*; *well, better, best*; *bad, worse, worst*; *badly, worse, worst*.

▶ The Kirov is the ~~talentedest~~ *most talented* ballet company we have seen.

▶ According to our projections, sales at local businesses will

be ~~worser~~ *worse* than those at the chain stores this winter.

Double comparatives or superlatives

Do not use double comparatives or superlatives. When you have added *-er* or *-est* to an adjective or adverb, do not also use *more* or *most* (or *less* or *least*).

▶ Of all her family, Julia is the ~~most~~ happiest about the move.

▶ All the polls indicated that Gore was more ~~likelier~~ *likely* to win

than Bush.

Absolute concepts

Avoid expressions such as *more straight, less perfect, very round,* and *most unique*. Either something is unique or it isn't. It is illogical to suggest that absolute concepts come in degrees.

> *unusual*
> That is the most ~~unique~~ wedding gown I have ever seen.
>   ^

> *valuable*
> The painting would have been even more ~~priceless~~ had it
>   ^
>
> been signed.

26e Avoid double negatives.

Standard English allows two negatives only if a positive meaning
is intended: *The orchestra was not unhappy with its performance*
(meaning that the orchestra was happy). Using a double negative
to emphasize a negative meaning is nonstandard.

Negative modifiers such as *never, no,* and *not* should not be
paired with other negative modifiers or with negative words such
as *neither, none, no one, nobody,* and *nothing.*

> *anything*
> The county is not doing ~~nothing~~ to see that the trash is
>   ^
>
> picked up.

> The double negative *not . . . nothing* is nonstandard.

The modifiers *hardly, barely,* and *scarcely* are considered
negatives in standard English, so they should not be used with
negatives such as *not, no one,* or *never.*

> *can*
> Maxine is so weak that she ~~can't~~ hardly climb stairs.
>   ^

EXERCISE 26–1   Edit the following sentences to eliminate errors in the
use of adjectives and adverbs. If a sentence is correct, write "correct" after
it. Answers to lettered sentences appear in the back of the book. Example:

> *well*
> We weren't surprised by how ~~good~~ the sidecar racing team
>   ^
>
> flowed through the tricky course.

a. Did you do good on last week's chemistry exam?
b. With the budget deadline approaching, our office hasn't hardly
   had time to handle routine correspondence.
c. Some flowers smell surprisingly bad.

d. The customer complained that he hadn't been treated nice.

e. Of all my relatives, Uncle Roberto is the most cleverest.

1. When you answer the phone, speak clear and courteous.

2. Who was more upset about the loss? Was it the coach or the quarterback or the owner of the team?

3. To a novice skateboarder, even the basic ollie seems real challenging.

4. After checking how bad I had been hurt, my sister dialed 911.

5. If the college's Web page had been updated more regular, students would have learned about the new course offerings.

EXERCISE 26–2   Edit the following passage to eliminate errors in the use of adjectives and adverbs.

Doctors recommend that to give skin the most fullest protection from ultraviolet rays, people should use plenty of sunscreen, limit sun exposure, and wear protective clothing. The commonest sunscreens today are known as "broad spectrum" because they block out both UVA and UVB rays. These lotions don't feel any differently on the skin from the old UVA-only types, but they work best at preventing premature aging and skin cancer. Many sunscreens claim to be waterproof, but they won't hardly provide adequate coverage after extended periods of swimming or perspiring. To protect good, even waterproof sunscreens should be reapplied liberal and often. All areas of exposed skin, including ears, backs of hands, and tops of feet, need to be coated good to avoid burning or damage. Some people's skin reacts bad to PABA, or para-aminobenzoic acid, so PABA-free (hypoallergenic) sunscreens are widely available. In addition to recommending sunscreen, doctors almost unanimously agree that people should stay out of the sun when rays are the most strongest — between 10:00 a.m. and 3:00 p.m. — and should limit time in the sun. They also suggest that people wear long-sleeved shirts, broad-brimmed hats, and long pants whenever possible.

27   Choose appropriate verb forms, tenses, and moods in standard English.

In speech, some people use verb forms and tenses that match a home dialect or variety of English. In writing, use standard English verb forms unless you are quoting nonstandard speech or using alternative forms for literary effect. (See 17c.)

standard verb forms • verbs with irregular
endings (*go, went, gone; see, saw, seen,* etc.)

vb
27a

233

Except for the verb *be*, all verbs in English have five forms. The following list shows the five forms and provides a sample sentence in which each might appear.

BASE FORM	Usually I (*walk, ride*).
PAST TENSE	Yesterday I (*walked, rode*).
PAST PARTICIPLE	I have (*walked, ridden*) many times before.
PRESENT PARTICIPLE	I am (*walking, riding*) right now.
-S FORM	He/she/it (*walks, rides*) regularly.

The verb *be* has eight forms instead of the usual five: *be, am, is, are, was, were, being, been.*

27a Choose standard English forms of irregular verbs.

For all regular verbs, the past-tense and past-participle forms are the same (ending in *-ed* or *-d*), so there is no danger of confusion. This is not true, however, for irregular verbs, such as the following.

BASE FORM	PAST TENSE	PAST PARTICIPLE
go	went	gone
break	broke	broken
fly	flew	flown
sing	sang	sung

The past-tense form always occurs alone, without a helping verb. It expresses action that occurred entirely in the past: *I rode to work yesterday. I walked to work last Tuesday.* The past participle is used with a helping verb. It forms the perfect tenses with *has, have,* or *had*; it forms the passive voice with *be, am, is, are, was, were, being,* or *been.* (See 46c for a complete list of helping verbs and 27f for a survey of tenses.)

PAST TENSE	Last July, we *went* to Paris.
HELPING VERB + PAST PARTICIPLE	We *have gone* to Paris twice.

The list of common irregular verbs beginning on the next page will help you distinguish between the past tense and the past participle. Choose the past-participle form if the verb in your sentence requires a helping verb; choose the past-tense form if the verb does not require a helping verb. (See verb tenses in 27f.)

▶ Yesterday we ~~seen~~ *saw* a documentary about Isabel Allende.

The past-tense *saw* is required because there is no helping verb.

▶ The truck was apparently ~~stole~~ *stolen* while the driver ate lunch.

▶ By Friday, the stock market had ~~fell~~ *fallen* two hundred points.

Because of the helping verbs *was* and *had*, the past-participle forms are required: *was stolen, had fallen*.

Common irregular verbs

BASE FORM	PAST TENSE	PAST PARTICIPLE
arise	arose	arisen
awake	awoke, awaked	awaked, awoke, awoken
be	was, were	been
beat	beat	beaten, beat
become	became	become
begin	began	begun
bend	bent	bent
bite	bit	bitten, bit
blow	blew	blown
break	broke	broken
bring	brought	brought
build	built	built
burst	burst	burst
buy	bought	bought
catch	caught	caught
choose	chose	chosen
cling	clung	clung
come	came	come
cost	cost	cost
deal	dealt	dealt
dig	dug	dug
dive	dived, dove	dived
do	did	done

BASE FORM	PAST TENSE	PAST PARTICIPLE
drag	dragged	dragged
draw	drew	drawn
dream	dreamed, dreamt	dreamed, dreamt
drink	drank	drunk
drive	drove	driven
eat	ate	eaten
fall	fell	fallen
fight	fought	fought
find	found	found
fly	flew	flown
forget	forgot	forgotten, forgot
freeze	froze	frozen
get	got	gotten, got
give	gave	given
go	went	gone
grow	grew	grown
hang (execute)	hanged	hanged
hang (suspend)	hung	hung
have	had	had
hear	heard	heard
hide	hid	hidden
hurt	hurt	hurt
keep	kept	kept
know	knew	known
lay (put)	laid	laid
lead	led	led
lend	lent	lent
let (allow)	let	let
lie (recline)	lay	lain
lose	lost	lost
make	made	made
prove	proved	proved, proven
read	read	read
ride	rode	ridden
ring	rang	rung
rise (get up)	rose	risen

(continued)

BASE FORM	PAST TENSE	PAST PARTICIPLE
run	ran	run
say	said	said
see	saw	seen
send	sent	sent
set (place)	set	set
shake	shook	shaken
shoot	shot	shot
shrink	shrank	shrunk
sing	sang	sung
sink	sank	sunk
sit (be seated)	sat	sat
slay	slew	slain
sleep	slept	slept
speak	spoke	spoken
spin	spun	spun
spring	sprang	sprung
stand	stood	stood
steal	stole	stolen
sting	stung	stung
strike	struck	struck, stricken
swear	swore	sworn
swim	swam	swum
swing	swung	swung
take	took	taken
teach	taught	taught
throw	threw	thrown
wake	woke, waked	waked, woken
wear	wore	worn
wring	wrung	wrung
write	wrote	written

27b Distinguish among the forms of *lie* and *lay*.

Writers and speakers frequently confuse the various forms of *lie* (meaning "to recline or rest on a surface") and *lay* (meaning "to put or place something"). *Lie* is an intransitive verb; it does not take a direct object: *The tax forms lie on the table.* The verb *lay* is transitive; it takes a direct object: *Please lay the tax forms on the table.* (See 47b.)

In addition to confusing the meaning of *lie* and *lay,* writers and speakers are often unfamiliar with the standard English forms of these verbs.

BASE FORM	PAST TENSE	PAST PARTICIPLE	PRESENT PARTICIPLE
lie ("recline")	lay	lain	lying
lay ("put")	laid	laid	laying

▶ Sue was so exhausted that she ~~laid~~ _lay_ down for a nap.

The past-tense form of *lie* ("to recline") is *lay.*

▶ The patient had ~~laid~~ _lain_ in an uncomfortable position all night.

The past-participle form of *lie* ("to recline") is *lain.* If the correct English seems too stilted, recast the sentence: *The patient had been lying in an uncomfortable position all night.*

▶ The prosecutor ~~lay~~ _laid_ the pistol on a table close to the jurors.

The past-tense form of *lay* ("to place") is *laid.*

▶ Letters dating from the Civil War were ~~laying~~ _lying_ in the corner of

the chest.

The present participle of *lie* ("to rest on a surface") is *lying.*

EXERCISE 27–1 Edit the following sentences to eliminate problems with irregular verbs. If a sentence is correct, write "correct" after it. Answers to lettered sentences appear in the back of the book. Example:

The ranger ~~seen~~ _saw_ the forest fire ten miles away.

a. When I get the urge to exercise, I lay down until it passes.
b. Grandmother had drove our new hybrid to the sunrise church service on Savage Mountain, so we were left with the station wagon.
c. A pile of dirty rags was laying at the bottom of the stairs.

PRACTICE hackerhandbooks.com/rules
> Grammar > 27–4 and 27–5

d. How did the game know that the player had went from the room with the blue ogre to the hall where the gold was heaped?

e. Abraham Lincoln took good care of his legal clients; the contracts he drew for the Illinois Central Railroad could never be broke.

1. The burglar must have gone immediately upstairs, grabbed what looked good, and took off.

2. Have you ever dreamed that you were falling from a cliff or flying through the air?

3. Tomás reached for the pen, signed the title page of his novel, and then laid the book on the table for the first customer in line.

4. In her junior year, Cindy run the 400-meter dash in 58.1 seconds.

5. Larry claimed that he had drank too much soda, but Esther suspected the truth.

27c Use -s (or -es) endings on present-tense verbs that have third-person singular subjects.

All singular nouns (*child*, *tree*) and the pronouns *he*, *she*, and *it* are third-person singular; indefinite pronouns such as *everyone* and *neither* are also third-person singular. When the subject of a sentence is third-person singular, its verb takes an *-s* or *-es* ending in the present tense. (See also 21.)

	SINGULAR		PLURAL	
FIRST PERSON	I	know	we	know
SECOND PERSON	you	know	you	know
THIRD PERSON	he/she/it	knows	they	know
	child	knows	parents	know
	everyone	knows		

▶ My neighbor ~~drive~~ *drives* to Marco Island every weekend.

▶ Sulfur dioxide ~~turn~~ *turns* leaves yellow, ~~dissolve~~ *dissolves* marble, and ~~eat~~ *eats* away iron and steel.

The subjects *neighbor* and *sulfur dioxide* are third-person singular, so the verbs must end in *-s*.

TIP: Do not add the *-s* ending to the verb if the subject is not third-person singular. The writers of the following sentences, knowing they sometimes dropped *-s* endings from verbs, over-corrected by adding the endings where they don't belong.

▶ I prepares program specifications and logic diagrams for

every installation.

The writer mistakenly concluded that the *-s* ending belongs on present-tense verbs used with *all* singular subjects, not just *third-person* singular subjects. The pronoun *I* is first-person singular, so its verb does not require the *-s*.

▶ The dirt floors requires continual sweeping.

The writer mistakenly thought that the verb needed an *-s* ending because of the plural subject. But the *-s* ending is used only on present-tense verbs with third-person *singular* subjects.

Has versus *have*

In the present tense, use *has* with third-person singular subjects; all other subjects require *have*.

	SINGULAR		PLURAL	
FIRST PERSON	I	have	we	have
SECOND PERSON	you	have	you	have
THIRD PERSON	he/she/it	has	they	have

▶ This respected musician almost always ~~have~~ *has* a message to

convey in his work.

The subject *musician* is third-person singular, so the verb should be *has*.

▶ My law classes ~~has~~ *have* helped me understand contracts.

The subject of this sentence — *classes* — is third-person plural, so standard English requires *have*. *Has* is used only with third-person singular subjects.

Does versus *do* and *doesn't* versus *don't*

In the present tense, use *does* and *doesn't* with third-person singular subjects; all other subjects require *do* and *don't*.

	SINGULAR		PLURAL	
FIRST PERSON	I	do/don't	we	do/don't
SECOND PERSON	you	do/don't	you	do/don't
THIRD PERSON	he/she/it	does/doesn't	they	do/don't

           doesn't
▶ **Grandfather really ~~don't~~ have a place to call home.**
                  ^

Grandfather is third-person singular, so the verb should be *doesn't*.

Am, is, and *are; was* and *were*

The verb *be* has three forms in the present tense (*am, is, are*) and two in the past tense (*was, were*).

	SINGULAR		PLURAL	
FIRST PERSON	I	am/was	we	are/were
SECOND PERSON	you	are/were	you	are/were
THIRD PERSON	he/she/it	is/was	they	are/were

           were
▶ **Did you think you ~~was~~ going to drown?**
                  ^

The subject *you* is second-person singular, so the verb should be *were*.

27d Do not omit -*ed* endings on verbs.

Speakers who do not fully pronounce -*ed* endings sometimes omit them unintentionally in writing. Leaving off -*ed* endings is common in many dialects and in informal speech even in standard English. In the following frequently used words and phrases, for example, the -*ed* ending is not always fully pronounced.

advised	developed	prejudiced	supposed to
asked	fixed	pronounced	used to
concerned	frightened	stereotyped	

When a verb is regular, both the past tense and the past participle are formed by adding *-ed* (or *-d*) to the base form of the verb.

Past tense

Use the ending *-ed* or *-d* to express the past tense of regular verbs. The past tense is used when the action occurred entirely in the past.

>   *fixed*
> ► Over the weekend, Ed ~~fix~~ his brother's skateboard and tuned
>
>   up his mother's 1991 Fiat.

>   *advised*
> ► Last summer, my counselor ~~advise~~ me to ask my chemistry
>
>   instructor for help.

Past participles

Past participles are used in three ways: (1) following *have, has,* or *had* to form one of the perfect tenses; (2) following *be, am, is, are, was, were, being,* or *been* to form the passive voice; and (3) as adjectives modifying nouns or pronouns. The perfect tenses are listed on page 244, and the passive voice is discussed in 8a. For a discussion of participles as adjectives, see 48b.

>   *asked*
> ► Robin has ~~ask~~ for more housing staff for next year.
>
> *Has asked* is present perfect tense (*have* or *has* followed by a past participle).

> ► Though it is not a new phenomenon, domestic violence is
>   *publicized*
> now ~~publicize~~ more than ever.
>
> *Is publicized* is a verb in the passive voice (a form of *be* followed by a past participle).

> ► All kickboxing classes end in a cool-down period to stretch
> *tightened*
> ~~tighten~~ muscles.
>
> The past participle *tightened* functions as an adjective modifying the noun *muscles*.

27e Do not omit needed verbs.

Although standard English allows some linking verbs and helping verbs to be contracted in informal contexts, it does not allow
them to be omitted.

Linking verbs, used to link subjects to subject complements,
are frequently a form of *be: be, am, is, are, was, were, being, been.*
(See 47b.) Some of these forms may be contracted (*I'm, she's, we're,
you're, they're*), but they should not be omitted altogether.

> When we ^*are* quiet in the evening, we can hear crickets in the woods.

Helping verbs, used with main verbs, include forms of *be,
do,* and *have* and the modal verbs *can, will, shall, could, would,
should, may, might,* and *must.* (See 46c.) Some helping verbs may
be contracted (*he's leaving, we'll celebrate, they've been told*), but
they should not be omitted altogether.

> We ^*have* been in Chicago since last Thursday.

> Do you know someone who ^*would* be good for the job?

MULTILINGUAL Some languages do not require a linking verb
between a subject and its complement. English, however, requires a
verb in every sentence. See 30a.

> Every night, I read a short book to my daughter. When I ^*am* too busy,
>
> my husband reads to her.

EXERCISE 27–2 Edit the following sentences to eliminate problems
with *-s* and *-ed* verb forms and with omitted verbs. If a sentence is correct, write "correct" after it. Answers to lettered sentences appear in the
back of the book. Example:

The Pell Grant sometimes ~~cover~~ ^*covers* the student's full tuition.

missing verbs • linking verbs (*is, were*) • tenses •
simple (*walk*) • perfect (*had walked*) • progressive (*am walking*)

vb
27f 243

a. The glass sculptures of the Swan Boats was prominent in the brightly lit lobby.

b. Visitors to the glass museum were not suppose to touch the exhibits.

c. Our church has all the latest technology, even a close-circuit television.

d. Christos didn't know about Marlo's promotion because he never listens. He always talking.

e. Most psychologists agree that no one performs well under stress.

1. Have there ever been a time in your life when you were too depressed to get out of bed?

2. My days in this department have taught me to do what I'm told without asking questions.

3. We have change our plan and are waiting out the storm before leaving.

4. Winter training for search-and-rescue divers consist of building up a tolerance to icy water temperatures.

5. How would you feel if a love one had been a victim of a crime like this?

27f Choose the appropriate verb tense.

Tenses indicate the time of an action in relation to the time of the speaking or writing about that action.

The most common problem with tenses—shifting confusingly from one tense to another—is discussed in section 13. Other problems with tenses are detailed in this section, after the following survey of tenses.

Survey of tenses

Tenses are classified as present, past, and future, with simple, perfect, and progressive forms for each.

Simple tenses   The simple tenses indicate relatively simple time relations. The *simple present* tense is used primarily for actions occurring at the same time they are being discussed or for actions occurring regularly. The *simple past* tense is used for actions completed in the past. The *simple future* tense is used for actions that will occur in the future. In the following table, the simple tenses are given for the regular verb *walk*, the irregular verb *ride*, and the highly irregular verb *be*.

SIMPLE PRESENT

SINGULAR		PLURAL	
I	walk, ride, am	we	walk, ride, are
you	walk, ride, are	you	walk, ride, are
he/she/it	walks, rides, is	they	walk, ride, are

SIMPLE PAST

SINGULAR		PLURAL	
I	walked, rode, was	we	walked, rode, were
you	walked, rode, were	you	walked, rode, were
he/she/it	walked, rode, was	they	walked, rode, were

SIMPLE FUTURE

I, you, he/she/it, we, they	will walk, ride, be

Perfect tenses   More complex time relations are indicated by the perfect tenses. A verb in one of the perfect tenses (a form of *have* plus the past participle) expresses an action that was or will be completed at the time of another action.

PRESENT PERFECT

I, you, we, they	have walked, ridden, been
he/she/it	has walked, ridden, been

PAST PERFECT

I, you, he/she/it, we, they	had walked, ridden, been

FUTURE PERFECT

I, you, he/she/it, we, they	will have walked, ridden, been

Progressive forms   The simple and perfect tenses have progressive forms that describe actions in progress. A progressive verb consists of a form of *be* followed by a present participle. The progressive forms are not normally used with certain verbs, such as *believe*, *know*, *hear*, *seem*, and *think*.

PRESENT PROGRESSIVE

I	am walking, riding, being
he/she/it	is walking, riding, being
you, we, they	are walking, riding, being

PAST PROGRESSIVE

I, he/she/it	was walking, riding, being
you, we, they	were walking, riding, being

FUTURE PROGRESSIVE

I, you, he/she/it, we, they	will be walking, riding, being

PRESENT PERFECT PROGRESSIVE

I, you, we, they	have been walking, riding, being
he/she/it	has been walking, riding, being

PAST PERFECT PROGRESSIVE

I, you, he/she/it, we, they	had been walking, riding, being

FUTURE PERFECT PROGRESSIVE

I, you, he/she/it, we, they	will have been walking, riding, being

MULTILINGUAL See 28a for more specific examples of verb tenses that can be challenging for multilingual writers.

Special uses of the present tense

Use the present tense when expressing general truths, when writing about literature, and when quoting, summarizing, or paraphrasing an author's views.

General truths or scientific principles should appear in the present tense unless such principles have been disproved.

▶ Galileo taught that the earth ~~revolved~~ around the sun.
  _{revolves}

Because Galileo's teaching has not been discredited, the verb should be in the present tense. The following sentence, however, is acceptable: *Ptolemy taught that the sun revolved around the earth.*

When writing about a work of literature, you may be tempted to use the past tense. The convention, however, is to describe fictional events in the present tense.

> In Masuji Ibuse's *Black Rain*, a child ~~reached~~ *reaches* for a

pomegranate in his mother's garden, and a moment later

he ~~was~~ *is* dead, killed by the blast of the atomic bomb.

When you are quoting, summarizing, or paraphrasing the author of a nonliterary work, use present-tense verbs such as *writes*, *reports*, *asserts*, and so on to introduce the source. This convention is usually followed even when the author is dead (unless a date or the context specifies the time of writing).

> Dr. Jerome Groopman ~~argued~~ *argues* that doctors are "susceptible

to the subtle and not so subtle efforts of the pharmaceutical

industry to sculpt our thinking" (9).

In MLA style, signal phrases are written in the present tense, not the past tense. (See also 59a.)

APA NOTE: When you are documenting a paper with the APA (American Psychological Association) style of in-text citations, use past tense verbs such as *reported* or *demonstrated* or present perfect verbs such as *has reported* or *has demonstrated* to introduce the source.

E. Wilson (1994) reported that positive reinforcement alone was a less effective teaching technique than a mixture of positive reinforcement and constructive criticism.

The past perfect tense

The past perfect tense consists of a past participle preceded by *had* (*had worked*, *had gone*). This tense is used for an action already completed by the time of another past action or for an action already completed at some specific past time.

Everyone *had spoken* by the time I arrived.

I pleaded my case, but Paula *had made up* her mind.

Writers sometimes use the simple past tense when they should use the past perfect.

▶ We built our cabin high on a pine knoll, forty feet above an

had been
abandoned quarry that ~~was~~ flooded in 1920 to create a lake.

The building of the cabin and the flooding of the quarry both
occurred in the past, but the flooding was completed before the time
of building.

had
▶ By the time dinner was served, the guest of honor left.

The past perfect tense is needed because the action of leaving was
already completed at a specific past time (when dinner was served).

Some writers tend to overuse the past perfect tense. Do not use
the past perfect if two past actions occurred at the same time.

wrote
▶ When Ernest Hemingway lived in Cuba, he ~~had written~~

For Whom the Bell Tolls.

Sequence of tenses with infinitives and participles

An infinitive is the base form of a verb preceded by *to*. (See 48b.)
Use the present infinitive to show action at the same time as or
later than the action of the verb in the sentence.

raise
▶ The club had hoped to ~~have raised~~ a thousand dollars by

April 1.

The action expressed in the infinitive (*to raise*) occurred later than the
action of the sentence's verb (*had hoped*).

Use the perfect form of an infinitive (*to have* followed by the
past participle) for an action occurring earlier than that of the
verb in the sentence.

have joined
▶ Dan would like to ~~join~~ the navy, but he did not pass the

physical.

The liking occurs in the present; the joining would have occurred in
the past.

Like the tense of an infinitive, the tense of a participle is
governed by the tense of the sentence's verb. Use the present

participle (ending in -*ing*) for an action occurring at the same time as that of the sentence's verb.

> *Hiking* the Appalachian Trail in early spring, we spotted many wildflowers.

Use the past participle (such as *given* or *helped*) or the present perfect participle (*having* plus the past participle) for an action occurring before that of the verb.

> *Discovered* off the coast of Florida, the Spanish galleon yielded many treasures.

> *Having worked* her way through college, Lee graduated debt-free.

27g Use the subjunctive mood in the few contexts that require it.

There are three moods in English: the *indicative*, used for facts, opinions, and questions; the *imperative*, used for orders or advice; and the *subjunctive*, used in certain contexts to express wishes, requests, or conditions contrary to fact. For many writers, the subjunctive causes the most problems.

Forms of the subjunctive

In the subjunctive mood, present-tense verbs do not change form to indicate the number and person of the subject (see 21). Instead, the subjunctive uses the base form of the verb (*be, drive, employ*) with all subjects.

> It is important that you *be* [not *are*] prepared for the interview.

> We asked that she *drive* [not *drives*] more slowly.

Also, in the subjunctive mood, there is only one past-tense form of *be*: *were* (never *was*).

> If I *were* [not *was*] you, I'd try a new strategy.

Uses of the subjunctive

The subjunctive mood appears only in a few contexts: in contrary-to-fact clauses beginning with *if* or expressing a wish; in *that* clauses following verbs such as *ask, insist, recommend, request,* and *suggest*; and in certain set expressions.

In contrary-to-fact clauses beginning with *if*   When a subordinate clause beginning with *if* expresses a condition contrary to fact, use the subjunctive *were* in place of *was.*

> If I ~~was~~ a member of Congress, I would vote for the new
>
> health care bill.

were

> The astronomers would be able to see the moons of Jupiter
>
> tonight if the weather ~~was~~ clearer.

were

The verbs in these sentences express conditions that do not exist: The writer is not a member of Congress, and the weather is not clear.

Do not use the subjunctive mood in *if* clauses expressing conditions that exist or may exist.

If Dana *wins* the contest, she will leave for Barcelona in June.

In contrary-to-fact clauses expressing a wish   In formal English, use the subjunctive *were* in clauses expressing a wish or desire. While use of the indicative is common in informal speech, it is not appropriate in academic writing.

INFORMAL   I wish that Dr. Vaughn *was* my professor.

FORMAL   I wish that Dr. Vaughn *were* my professor.

In *that* clauses following verbs such as *ask, insist, request,* and *suggest*   Because requests have not yet become reality, they are expressed in the subjunctive mood.

> Professor Moore insists that her students ~~are~~ on time.

be

> We recommend that Lambert ~~files~~ form 1050 soon.

file

In certain set expressions   The subjunctive mood, once more widely used, remains in certain set expressions: *Be that as it may, as it were, far be it from me,* and so on.

EXERCISE 27–3 Edit the following sentences to eliminate errors in verb tense or mood. If a sentence is correct, write "correct" after it. Answers to lettered sentences appear in the back of the book. Example:

> *had been*
> After the path ~~was~~ plowed, we were able to walk through
>   ^
>
> the park.

a. The palace of Knossos in Crete is believed to have been destroyed by fire around 1375 BCE.

b. Watson and Crick discovered the mechanism that controlled inheritance in all life: the workings of the DNA molecule.

c. When city planners proposed rezoning the waterfront, did they know that the mayor promised to curb development in that neighborhood?

d. Tonight's concert begins at 9:30. If it were earlier, I'd consider going.

e. As soon as my aunt applied for the position of pastor, the post was filled by an inexperienced seminary graduate who had been so hastily snatched that his mortarboard was still in midair.

1. Don Quixote, in Cervantes's novel, was an idealist ill suited for life in the real world.

2. Visiting the technology museum inspired the high school seniors and had reminded them that science could be fun.

3. I would like to have been on the *Mayflower* but not to have experienced the first winter.

4. When the director yelled "Action!" I forgot my lines, even though I practiced my part every waking hour for three days.

5. If midday naps were a regular practice in American workplaces, employees would be far more productive.

Multilingual Writers and ESL Challenges

This section of *Rules for Writers* is primarily for multilingual writers. You may find this section helpful if you learned English as a second language (ESL) or if you speak a language other than English with your friends and family.

28 Verbs

Both native and nonnative speakers of English encounter challenges with verbs. Section 28 focuses on specific challenges that multilingual writers sometimes face. You can find more help with verbs in other sections in the book:

making subjects and verbs agree (21)

using irregular verb forms (27a, 27b)

leaving off verb endings (27c, 27d)

choosing the correct verb tense (27f)

avoiding inappropriate uses of the passive voice (8a)

28a Use the appropriate verb form and tense.

This section offers a brief review of English verb forms and tenses. For additional help, see 27 and 46c.

Basic verb forms

Every main verb in English has five forms, which are used to create all of the verb tenses in standard English. The chart at the top of page 253 shows these forms for the regular verb *help* and the irregular verbs *give* and *be*. See 27a for the forms of other common irregular verbs.

PRACTICE AND MODELS hackerhandbooks.com/rules

> Multilingual/ESL > Charts and study help
> Sample student paper (draft and final)
> Exercises
> Links to online resources

Basic verb forms

	REGULAR VERB *HELP*	IRREGULAR VERB *GIVE*	IRREGULAR VERB *BE**
BASE FORM	help	give	be
PAST TENSE	helped	gave	was, were
PAST PARTICIPLE	helped	given	been
PRESENT PARTICIPLE	helping	giving	being
-S FORM	helps	gives	is

*Be also has the forms *am* and *are*, which are used in the present tense.

Verb tenses

Section 27f describes all the verb tenses in English, showing the forms of a regular verb, an irregular verb, and the verb *be* in each tense. The chart on this page provides more details about the tenses commonly used in the active voice in writing; the chart on page 256 gives details about tenses commonly used in the passive voice.

Verb tenses commonly used in the active voice

For descriptions and examples of all verb tenses, see 27f. For verb tenses commonly used in the passive voice, see the chart on page 256.

Simple tenses
For general facts, states of being, habitual actions

Simple present	**Base form or -s form**
• general facts	College students often *study* late at night.
• states of being	Water *becomes* steam at 100° centigrade.
• habitual, repetitive actions	We *donate* to a different charity each year.
• scheduled future events	The train *arrives* tomorrow at 6:30 p.m.

NOTE: For uses of the present tense in writing about literature, see page 245.

Verb tenses commonly used in the active voice (continued)

Simple past	**Base form + -ed or -d or irregular form**
• completed actions at a specific time in the past	The storm *destroyed* their property. She *drove* to Montana three years ago.
• facts or states of being in the past	When I *was* young, I usually *walked* to school with my sister.

Simple future	**will + base form**
• future actions, promises, or predictions	I *will exercise* tomorrow. The snowfall *will begin* around midnight.

Simple progressive forms
For continuing actions

Present progressive	**am, is, are + present participle**
• actions in progress at the present time, not continuing indefinitely	The students *are taking* an exam in Room 105. The valet *is parking* the car.
• future actions (with *leave*, *go*, *come*, *move*, etc.)	I *am leaving* tomorrow morning.

Past progressive	**was, were + present participle**
• actions in progress at a specific time in the past	They *were swimming* when the storm struck.
• *was going to*, *were going to* for past plans that did not happen	We *were going to* drive to Florida for spring break, but the car broke down.

NOTE: Some verbs are not normally used in the progressive: *appear*, *believe*, *belong*, *contain*, *have*, *hear*, *know*, *like*, *need*, *see*, *seem*, *taste*, *understand*, and *want*.

>   *want*
> ▶ I ~~am wanting~~ to see August Wilson's *Radio Golf*.
>   ^

Perfect tenses
For actions that happened or will happen before another time

Present perfect	**has, have + past participle**
• repetitive or constant actions that began in the past and continue to the present	I *have loved* cats since I was a child. Alicia *has worked* in Kenya for ten years.

Present perfect	**has, have + past participle**
• actions that happened at an unknown or unspecific past time	Stephen *has visited* Wales three times.

Past perfect	**had + past participle**
• actions that began or occurred before another time in the past	She *had* just *crossed* the street when the runaway car crashed into the building.

NOTE: For more discussion of uses of the past perfect, see 27f. For uses of the past perfect in conditional sentences, see 28e.

Perfect progressive forms
For continuous past actions before another time

Present perfect progressive	**has, have + been + present participle**
• continuous actions that began in the past and continue to the present	Yolanda *has been trying* to get a job in Boston for five years.

Past perfect progressive	**had + been + present participle**
• actions that began and continued in the past until another past action	By the time I moved to Georgia, I *had been supporting* myself for five years.

28b To write a verb in the passive voice, use a form of *be* with the past participle.

When a sentence is written in the passive voice, the subject receives the action instead of doing it. (See 47c.)

> The solution *was measured* by the lab assistant.

To form the passive voice, use a form of *be* — *am, is, are, was, were, being, be,* or *been* — followed by the past participle of the main verb: *was sent, are served.* (Sometimes a form of *be* follows another helping verb: *will be cut, could have been done.*)

>   *written*
> ▶ *Dreaming in Cuban* was ~~writing~~ by Cristina García.

In the passive voice, the past participle *written*, not the present participle *writing*, must follow *was* (the past tense of *be*).

Verb tenses commonly used in the passive voice

For details about verb tenses in the active voice, see pages 253–55.

Simple tenses (passive voice)

Simple present   *am, is, are* + past participle
- general facts   Breakfast *is served* daily.
- habitual, repetitive actions   The receipts *are counted* every night.

Simple past   *was, were* + past participle
- completed past actions   He *was punished* for being late.

Simple future   *will be* + past participle
- future actions, promises, or predictions   The decision *will be made* by the committee next week.

Simple progressive forms (passive voice)

Present progressive   *am, is, are* + *being* + past participle
- actions in progress at the present time   The new stadium *is being built* with private money.
- future actions (with *leave, go, come, move,* etc.)   Jo *is being moved* to a new class next month.

Past progressive   *was, were* + *being* + past participle
- actions in progress at a specific time in the past   We thought we *were being followed.*

Perfect tenses (passive voice)

Present perfect   *has, have* + *been* + past participle
- actions that began in the past and continue to the present   The flight *has been delayed* because of storms in the Midwest.
- actions that happened at an unknown or un-specific time in the past   Wars *have been fought* throughout history.

Past perfect   *had* + *been* + past participle
- actions that began or occurred before another time in the past   He *had been given* all the hints he needed to complete the puzzle.

NOTE: Future progressive, future perfect, and perfect progressive forms are not used in the passive voice.

> *be*
► Senator Dixon will ∧ defeated.

The passive voice requires a form of *be* before the past participle.

> *teased.*
► The child was being ~~tease.~~
> ∧

The past participle *teased*, not the base form *tease*, must be used with
was being to form the passive voice.

For details on forming the passive in various tenses, consult
the chart on page 256. (For appropriate uses of the passive voice,
see 8a.)

NOTE: Only transitive verbs, those that take direct objects, may be
used in the passive voice. Intransitive verbs such as *occur, happen,
sleep, die, become,* and *fall* are not used in the passive. (See 47b.)

► The accident ~~was~~ happened suddenly.

EXERCISE 28–1 Revise the following sentences to correct errors in
verb forms and tenses in the active and the passive voice. You may need
to look at 27a for the correct form of some irregular verbs and at 27f for
help with tenses. Answers to lettered sentences appear in the back of the
book. Example:

> *begins*
> The meeting ~~begin~~ tonight at 7:30.
> ∧

a. In the past, tobacco companies deny any connection between
   smoking and health problems.
b. There is nothing in the world that TV has not touch on.
c. I am wanting to register for a summer tutoring session.
d. By the end of the year, the state will have test 139 birds for avian flu.
e. The benefits of eating fruits and vegetables have been promoting
   by health care providers.
1. By the time he was twelve years old, Mozart had compose an
   entire opera.
2. The sound was occurred whenever someone stepped on the loose
   board.
3. My family has been gone to Sam's restaurant ever since we moved
   to this neighborhood.

4. I have ate Thai food only once before.

5. The bear is appearing to be sedated.

28c Use the base form of the verb after a modal.

The modal verbs are *can, could, may, might, must, shall, should, will,* and *would.* (*Ought to* is also considered a modal verb.) The modals are used with the base form of a verb to show certainty, necessity, or possibility.

Modals and the verbs that follow them do not change form to indicate tense. For a summary of modals and their meanings, see the chart on pages 259–60. (See also 27e.)

▶ The art museum will ~~launches~~ its fundraising campaign
launch
^

next month.

> The modal *will* must be followed by the base form *launch*, not the present tense *launches*.

▶ The translator could ~~spoke~~ many languages, so the ambas-
speak
^

sador hired her for the European tour.

> The modal *could* must be followed by the base form *speak*, not the past tense *spoke*.

TIP: Do not use *to* in front of a main verb that follows a modal.

▶ Gina can ~~to~~ drive us home if we miss the last train.

For the use of modals in conditional sentences, see 28e.

EXERCISE 28–2 Edit the following sentences to correct errors in the use of verb forms with modals. You may find it helpful to consult the chart on pages 259–60. If a sentence is correct, write "correct" after it. Answers to lettered sentences appear in the back of the book. Example:

We should ~~to~~ order pizza for dinner.

a. A major league pitcher can to throw a baseball more than ninety-five miles per hour.

b. The writing center tutor will helps you revise your essay.

c. A reptile must adjusted its body temperature to its environment.

d. In some states, individuals may renew a driver's license online or in person.

e. My uncle, a cartoonist, could sketched a face in less than two minutes.

1. Working more than twelve hours a day might to contribute to insomnia, according to researchers.

2. A wasp will carry its immobilized prey back to the nest.

3. Hikers should not wandered too far from the trail.

4. Should we continued to submit hard copies of our essays?

5. Physical therapy may to help people after heart surgery.

Modals and their meanings

can

• general ability (present)	Ants *can survive* anywhere, even in space. Jorge *can run* a marathon faster than his brother.
• informal requests or permission	*Can* you *tell* me where the light is? Sandy *can borrow* my calculator.

could

• general ability (past)	Lea *could read* when she was only three years old.
• polite, informal requests or permission	*Could* you *give* me that pen?

may

• formal requests or permission	*May* I *see* the report? Students *may park* only in the yellow zone.
• possibility	I *may try* to finish my homework tonight, or I *may wake up* early and *finish* it tomorrow.

Modals and their meanings (continued)

might

- possibility | Funding for the language lab *might double* by 2017.

NOTE: *Might* usually expresses a stronger possibility than *may*.

must

- necessity (present or future) | To be effective, welfare-to-work programs *must provide* access to job training.

- strong probability | Amy *must be* nervous. [She is probably nervous.]

- near certainty (present or past) | I *must have left* my wallet at home. [I almost certainly left my wallet at home.]

should

- suggestions or advice | Diabetics *should drink* plenty of water every day.

- obligations or duties | The government *should protect* citizens' rights.

- expectations | The books *should arrive* soon. [We expect the books to arrive soon.]

will

- certainty | If you don't leave now, you *will be* late for your rehearsal.

- requests | *Will* you *help* me study for my psychology exam?

- promises and offers | Jonah *will arrange* the carpool.

would

- polite requests | *Would* you *help* me carry these books? I *would like* some coffee. [*Would like* is more polite than *want*.]

- habitual or repeated actions (past) | Whenever Elena needed help with sewing, she *would call* her aunt.

28d To make negative verb forms, add *not* in the appropriate place.

If the verb is the simple present or past tense of *be* (*am, is, are, was, were*), add *not* after the verb.

> Gianna *is not* a member of the club.

For simple present-tense verbs other than *be*, use *do* or *does* plus *not* before the base form of the verb. (For the correct forms of *do* and *does*, see the chart on p. 198.)

> *does not*
> ► Mariko ~~no~~ want more dessert.

> ► Mariko does not wants̸ more dessert.

For simple past-tense verbs other than *be*, use *did* plus *not* before the base form of the verb.

> *plant*
> ► They did not ~~planted~~ corn this year.

In a verb phrase consisting of one or more helping verbs and a present or past participle (*is watching, were living, has played, could have been driven*), use the word *not* after the first helping verb.

> *not*
> ► Inna should have ~~not~~ gone dancing last night.

> *not*
> ► Bonnie is ~~no~~ singing this weekend.

NOTE: English allows only one negative in an independent clause to express a negative idea; using more than one is an error known as a *double negative* (see 26e).

> *any*
> ► We could not find ~~no~~ books about the history of our school.

28e In a conditional sentence, choose verb tenses according to the type of condition expressed in the sentence.

Conditional sentences contain two clauses: a subordinate clause (usually starting with *if, when,* or *unless*) and an independent clause. The subordinate clause (sometimes called the *if* or *unless* clause) states the condition or cause; the independent clause states the result or effect. In each example in this section, the subordinate clause (*if* clause) is marked SUB, and the independent clause is marked IND. (See 48e on clauses.)

Factual

Factual conditional sentences express factual relationships. If the relationship is a scientific truth, use the present tense in both clauses.

> ┌─────── SUB ───────┐ ┌─IND─┐
> If water *cools* to 32° Fahrenheit, it *freezes.*

If the sentence describes a condition that is (or was) habitually true, use the same tense in both clauses.

> ┌─────────SUB─────────┐ ┌─────────IND─────────┐
> When Sue *jogs* along the canal, her dog *runs* ahead of her.

> ┌─────────SUB─────────┐ ┌─IND─┐
> Whenever the coach *asked* for help, I *volunteered.*

Predictive

Predictive conditional sentences are used to predict the future or to express future plans or possibilities. To form a predictive sentence, use a present-tense verb in the subordinate clause; in the independent clause, use the modal *will, can, may, should,* or *might* plus the base form of the verb.

> ┌─────────SUB─────────┐ ┌─────────IND─────────┐
> If you *practice* regularly, your tennis game *should improve.*

> ┌─────────IND─────────┐ ┌─────SUB─────┐
> We *will lose* our remaining wetlands unless we *act* now.

TIP: In all types of conditional sentences (factual, predictive, and speculative), *if* or *unless* clauses do not use the modal verb *will.*

> *passes*
> ▶ If Jenna ~~will pass~~ her history test, she will graduate this year.
>   ^

Speculative

Speculative conditional sentences express unlikely, contrary-to-fact, or impossible conditions. English uses the past or past perfect tense in the *if* clause, even for conditions in the present or the future.

Unlikely possibilities   If the condition is possible but unlikely in the present or the future, use the past tense in the subordinate clause; in the independent clause, use *would*, *could*, or *might* plus the base form of the verb.

> ┌──────SUB──────┐ ┌────────IND────────┐
> If I *won* the lottery, I *would travel* to Egypt.

The writer does not expect to win the lottery. Because this is a possible but unlikely present or future situation, the subordinate clause uses the past tense.

Conditions contrary to fact   In conditions that are currently unreal or contrary to fact, use the past-tense verb *were* (not *was*) in the *if* clause for all subjects. (See also 27g, on the subjunctive mood.)

>
> ▶ **If I ~~was~~ president, I would make children's issues a priority.**
>   ^
> The writer is not president, so *were* is correct in the *if* clause.

Events that did not happen   In a conditional sentence that speculates about an event that did not happen or was impossible in the past, use the past perfect tense in the *if* clause; in the independent clause, use *would have*, *could have*, or *might have* with the past participle. (See also past perfect tense, p. 255.)

> ┌──────────SUB──────────┐ ┌────────────IND────────────┐
> If I *had saved* more money, I *would have visited* Laos last year.

The writer did not save more money and did not travel to Laos. This sentence shows a possibility that did not happen.

>
> ┌───────────────SUB───────────────┐ ┌──IND──┐
> If Aunt Grace *had been* alive for your graduation, she *would*
> ┌──────────────┐
> *have been* very proud.

Aunt Grace was not alive at the time of the graduation. This sentence shows an impossible situation in the past.

EXERCISE 28–3 Edit the following sentences to correct problems with verbs. In some cases, more than one revision is possible. Suggested revisions of lettered sentences appear in the back of the book. Example:

> had
> If I ~~have~~ time, I would study both French and Russian next
>   ^
> semester.

a. The electrician might have discovered the broken circuit if she went through the modules one at a time.

b. If Verena wins a scholarship, she would go to graduate school.

c. Whenever there is a fire in our neighborhood, everybody came out to watch.

d. Sarah did not understood the terms of her internship.

e. If I live in Budapest with my cousin Szusza, she would teach me Hungarian cooking.

1. If the science fiction festival starts Monday, we wouldn't need to plan entertainment for our visitors.

2. If everyone has voted in the last election, the results would have been very different.

3. The tenants will not pay the rent unless the landlord fixed the furnace.

4. When dark gray clouds appeared on a hot summer afternoon, a thunderstorm often follows.

5. Rosalie should no offer to volunteer at the shelter on school nights.

28f Become familiar with verbs that may be followed by gerunds or infinitives.

A gerund is a verb form that ends in -*ing* and is used as a noun: *sleeping, dreaming.* (See 48b.) An infinitive is the word *to* plus the base form of the verb: *to sleep, to dream.* (The word *to* is an infinitive marker, not a preposition, in this use.)

A few verbs may be followed by either a gerund or an infinitive; others may be followed by a gerund but not by an infinitive; still others may be followed by an infinitive but not by a gerund.

Verb + gerund or infinitive (no change in meaning)

The following commonly used verbs may be followed by a gerund or an infinitive, with little or no difference in meaning:

begin	hate	love
continue	like	start

I love *skiing*. I love *to ski*.

Verb + gerund or infinitive (change in meaning)

With a few verbs, the choice of a gerund or an infinitive changes the meaning dramatically:

forget	remember	stop	try

She stopped *speaking* to Lucia. [She no longer spoke to Lucia.]

She stopped *to speak* to Lucia. [She paused so that she could speak to Lucia.]

Verb + gerund

These verbs may be followed by a gerund but not by an infinitive:

admit	discuss	imagine	put off	risk
appreciate	enjoy	miss	quit	suggest
avoid	escape	postpone	recall	tolerate
deny	finish	practice	resist	

Bill enjoys *playing* [not *to play*] the piano.

Jamie quit *smoking*.

Verb + infinitive

These verbs may be followed by an infinitive but not by a gerund:

agree	decide	manage	plan	wait
ask	expect	mean	pretend	want
beg	help	need	promise	wish
claim	hope	offer	refuse	would like

Jill has offered *to water* [not *watering*] the plants while we are away.

Joe finally managed *to find* a parking space.

The man refused *to join* the rebellion.

A few of these verbs may be followed either by an infinitive directly or by a noun or pronoun plus an infinitive:

ask	help	promise	would like
expect	need	want	

We asked *to speak* to the congregation.

We asked *Rabbi Abrams to speak* to our congregation.

Alex expected *to get* the lead in the play.

Ira expected *Alex to get* the lead in the play.

Verb + noun or pronoun + infinitive

With certain verbs in the active voice, a noun or pronoun must come between the verb and the infinitive that follows it. The noun or pronoun usually names a person who is affected by the action of the verb.

advise	convince	order	tell
allow	encourage	persuade	urge
cause	have ("own")	remind	warn
command	instruct	require	

The class encouraged Luis to tell the story of his escape.

The counselor *advised Haley to take* four courses instead of five.

Professor Howlett *instructed us to write* our names on the left side of the paper.

Verb + noun or pronoun + unmarked infinitive

An unmarked infinitive is an infinitive without *to*. A few verbs (often called *causative verbs*) may be followed by a noun or pronoun and an unmarked infinitive.

have ("cause")	let ("allow")
help	make ("force")

Jorge *had the valet park* his car.

▶ Please let me ~~to~~ pay for the tickets.

▶ Frank made me ~~to~~ carry his book for him.

verb + gerund (*running*) • verb + infinitive (*to run*) • articles
(*a, an, the*) • other noun markers (*my, their, this, any, most*)

ESL

29a 267

NOTE: *Help* can be followed by a noun or pronoun and either an unmarked or a marked infinitive.

> Emma *helped Brian wash* the dishes.

> Emma *helped Brian to wash* the dishes.

EXERCISE 28–4 Form sentences by adding gerund or infinitive constructions to the following sentence openings. In some cases, more than one kind of construction is possible. Possible answers to lettered items appear in the back of the book. Example:

> **Please remind** *your sister to call me.*
> ^

a. I enjoy
b. The tutor told Samantha
c. The team hopes
d. Ricardo and his brothers miss
e. The babysitter let

1. Pollen makes
2. The club president asked
3. Next summer we plan
4. My supervisor intends
5. Please stop

Articles

Articles (*a, an, the*) are part of a category of words known as *noun markers* or *determiners*.

29a Be familiar with articles and other noun markers.

Standard English uses noun markers to help identify the nouns that follow. In addition to articles (*a, an,* and *the*), noun markers include

- possessive nouns, such as *Elena's* (See 36a.)

- possessive pronoun/adjectives: *my, your, his, her, its, our, their* (See 46b.)
- demonstrative pronoun/adjectives: *this, that, these, those* (See 46b.)
- quantifiers: *all, any, each, either, every, few, many, more, most, much, neither, several, some,* and so on (See 29d.)
- numbers: *one, twenty-three,* and so on

Using articles and other noun markers

Articles and other noun markers always appear before nouns; sometimes other modifiers, such as adjectives, come between a noun marker and a noun.

> ART N
> Felix is reading a book about mythology.

> ART ADJ N
> We took an exciting trip to Alaska last summer.

> NOUN
> MARKER ADV ADJ N
> That very delicious meal was expensive.

In most cases, do not use an article with another noun marker.

▶ ~~The~~ Natalie's older brother lives in Wisconsin.

Expressions like *a few, the most,* and *all the* are exceptions: *a few potatoes, all the rain.* See also 29d.

Types of articles and types of nouns

To choose an appropriate article for a noun, you must first determine whether the noun is *common* or *proper, count* or *noncount, singular* or *plural,* and *specific* or *general.* The chart on pages 270–71 describes the types of nouns.

Articles are classified as *indefinite* and *definite.* The indefinite articles, *a* and *an,* are used with general nouns. The definite article, *the,* is used with specific nouns. (The last section of the chart on p. 271 explains general and specific nouns.)

A and *an* both mean "one" or "one among many." Use *a* before a consonant sound: *a banana, a tree, a picture, a happy child, a united family.* Use *an* before a vowel sound: *an eggplant, an occasion, an uncle, an honorable person.* (See also *a, an* in the glossary of usage.)

other noun markers (*this, any, etc.*) • indefinite article (*a, an*) •
definite article (*the*) • *the* with specific nouns

ESL
29b   269

The shows that a noun is specific; use *the* with one or more than one specific thing: *the newspaper, the soldiers.*

29b   Use *the* with most specific common nouns.

The definite article, *the*, is used with most nouns — both count and noncount — that the reader can identify specifically. Usually the identity will be clear to the reader for one of the following reasons. (See also the chart on pages 272–73.)

1. The noun has been previously mentioned.

   the
   ▶ A truck cut in front of our van. When truck skidded a few
   ^

   seconds later, we almost crashed into it.

   The article *A* is used before *truck* when the noun is first mentioned. When the noun is mentioned again, it needs the article *the* because readers can now identify which truck skidded — the one that cut in front of the van.

2. A phrase or clause following the noun restricts its identity.

   the
   ▶ Bryce warned me that GPS in his car was not working.
   ^

   The phrase *in his car* identifies the specific GPS.

NOTE: Descriptive adjectives do not necessarily make a noun specific. A specific noun is one that readers can identify within a group of nouns of the same type.

   a
   ▶ If I win the lottery, I will buy ~~the~~ brand-new bright red
   ^

   sports car.

   The reader cannot identify which specific brand-new bright red sports car the writer will buy. Even though *car* has many adjectives in front of it, it is a general noun in this sentence.

3. A superlative adjective such as *best* or *most intelligent* makes the noun's identity specific. (See also 26d on comparatives and superlatives.)

   the
   ▶ Our petite daughter dated tallest boy in her class.
   ^

   The superlative *tallest* makes the noun *boy* specific. Although there might be several tall boys, only one boy can be the tallest.

Types of nouns

Common or proper

Common nouns

- name general persons, places, things, or ideas
- begin with lowercase

Examples

religion	beauty
knowledge	student
rain	country

Proper nouns

- name specific persons, places, things, or ideas
- begin with capital letter

Examples

Hinduism	President Adams
Philip	Washington Monument
Vietnam	Renaissance

Count or noncount (common nouns only)

Count nouns

- name persons, places, things, or ideas that can be counted
- have plural forms

Examples

girl, girls
city, cities
goose, geese
philosophy, philosophies

Noncount nouns

- name things or abstract ideas that cannot be counted
- cannot be made plural

Examples

water	patience
silver	knowledge
furniture	air

NOTE: See the chart on page 273 for commonly used noncount nouns.

Singular or plural (both common and proper)

Singular nouns (count and noncount)

- represent one person, place, thing, or idea

Examples

backpack	rain
country	beauty
woman	Nile River
achievement	Block Island

Plural nouns (count only)

- represent more than one person, place, thing, or idea
- must be count nouns

Examples

backpacks	Ural Mountains
countries	Falkland Islands
women	achievements

Specific (definite) or general (indefinite) (count and noncount)

Specific nouns	**Examples**
• name persons, places, things, or ideas that can be identified within a group of the same type	*The students* in Professor Martin's *class* should study. *The airplane* carrying *the senator* was late. *The furniture* in *the truck* was damaged.

General nouns	**Examples**
• name categories of persons, places, things, or ideas (often plural)	*Students* should study. *Books* bridge *gaps* between *cultures.* *The airplane* has made commuting between *cities* easy.

---

4. The noun describes a unique person, place, or thing.

   the
► During an eclipse, one should not look directly at sun.
                                                        ^

   There is only one sun in our solar system, so its identity is clear.

5. The context or situation makes the noun's identity clear.

   the
► Please don't slam door when you leave.
                    ^

   Both the speaker and the listener know which door is meant.

6. The noun is singular and refers to a scientific class or category of items (most often animals, musical instruments, and inventions).

   The tin
► ~~Tin~~ whistle is common in traditional Irish music.
   ^

   The writer is referring to the tin whistle as a class of musical instruments.

29c Use *a* (or *an*) with common singular count nouns that refer to "one" or "any."

If a count noun refers to one unspecific item (not a whole category), use the indefinite article, *a* or *an*. *A* and *an* usually mean "one among many" but can also mean "any one." (See the chart below.)

>   *a*
► My English professor asked me to bring ^dictionary to class.

The noun *dictionary* refers to "one unspecific dictionary" or "any dictionary."

>   *an*
► We want to rent ^apartment close to the lake.

The noun *apartment* refers to "any apartment close to the lake," not a specific apartment.

Choosing articles for common nouns

Use *the*

• if the reader has enough information to identify the noun specifically	**COUNT:** Please turn on *the lights*. We're going to *the lake* tomorrow. **NONCOUNT:** *The food* throughout Italy is excellent.

Use *a* or *an*

• if the noun refers to one item *and* • if the item is singular but not specific	**COUNT:** Bring *a pencil* to class. Charles wrote *an essay* about his first job.

NOTE: Do not use *a* or *an* with plural or noncount nouns.

Use a quantifier (*enough, many, some*, etc.)

• if the noun represents an unspecified amount of something • if the amount is more than one but not all items in a category	**COUNT (plural):** Amir showed us *some photos* of India. *Many turtles* return to the same nesting site each year. **NONCOUNT:** We didn't get *enough rain* this summer.

NOTE: Sometimes no article conveys an unspecified amount: *Amir showed us photos of India.*

Use no article

• if the noun represents all items in a category	**COUNT (plural):** *Students* can attend the show for free.

- if the noun represents a   **NONCOUNT:** *Coal is a natural resource.*
  category in general

NOTE: *The* is occasionally used when a singular count noun refers to all items in a class or a specific category: *The bald eagle is no longer endangered in the United States.*

Commonly used noncount nouns

Food and drink

beef, bread, butter, candy, cereal, cheese, cream, meat, milk, pasta, rice, salt, sugar, water, wine

Nonfood substances

air, cement, coal, dirt, gasoline, gold, paper, petroleum, plastic, rain, silver, snow, soap, steel, wood, wool

Abstract nouns

advice, anger, beauty, confidence, courage, employment, fun, happiness, health, honesty, information, intelligence, knowledge, love, poverty, satisfaction, wealth

Other

biology (and other areas of study), clothing, equipment, furniture, homework, jewelry, luggage, machinery, mail, money, news, poetry, pollution, research, scenery, traffic, transportation, violence, weather, work

NOTE: A few noncount nouns (such as *love*) can also be used as count nouns: *He had two loves: music and archery.*

29d Use a quantifier such as *some* or *more*, not *a* or *an*, with a noncount noun to express an approximate amount.

Do not use *a* or *an* with noncount nouns. Also do not use numbers or words such as *several* or *many* because they must be used with plural nouns, and noncount nouns do not have plural forms. (See the chart on p. 273 for a list of commonly used noncount nouns.)

▶ Dr. Snyder gave us ~~an~~ information about the Peace Corps.

▶ Do you have ~~many~~ money with you?

You can use quantifiers such as *enough*, *less*, and *some* to suggest approximate amounts or nonspecific quantities of noncount nouns: *a little salt, any homework, enough wood, less information, much pollution.*

▶ Vincent's mother told him that she had ~~a~~ *some* news that would

surprise him.

29e Do not use articles with nouns that refer to all of something or something in general.

When a noncount noun refers to all of its type or to a concept in general, it is not marked with an article.

▶ ~~The kindness~~ *Kindness* is a virtue.

The noun represents kindness in general; it does not represent a specific type of kindness.

▶ In some parts of the world, ~~the~~ rice is preferred to all other

grains.

The noun *rice* represents rice in general, not a specific type or serving of rice.

In most cases, when you use a count noun to represent a general category, make the noun plural. Do not use unmarked singular count nouns to represent whole categories.

▶ ~~Fountain is~~ *Fountains are* an expensive element of landscape design.

Fountains is a count noun that represents fountains in general.

EXCEPTION: In some cases, *the* can be used with singular count nouns to represent a class or specific category: *The Chinese alligator is smaller than the American alligator.* See also number 6 in 29b.

29f Do not use articles with most singular proper nouns. Use *the* with most plural proper nouns.

Since singular proper nouns are already specific, they typically do not need an article: *Prime Minister Cameron, Jamaica, Lake Huron, Mount Etna*.

There are, however, many exceptions. In most cases, if the proper noun consists of a common noun with modifiers (adjectives or an *of* phrase), use *the* with the proper noun.

▶ We visited ^*the*^ Great Wall of China last year.

▶ Rob wants to be a translator for ^*the*^ Central Intelligence Agency.

The is used with most plural proper nouns: *the McGregors, the Bahamas, the Finger Lakes, the United States*.

Geographic names create problems because there are so many exceptions to the rules. When in doubt, consult the chart on page 276, check a dictionary, or ask a native speaker.

EXERCISE 29–1 Edit the following sentences for proper use of articles and nouns. If a sentence is correct, write "correct" after it. Answers to lettered sentences appear in the back of the book. Example:

~~The~~ Josefina's dance routine was flawless.

a. Doing volunteer work often brings a satisfaction.

b. As I looked out the window of the plane, I could see the Cape Cod.

c. Melina likes to drink her coffees with lots of cream.

d. Recovering from abdominal surgery requires patience.

e. I completed the my homework assignment quickly.

1. The attorney argued that her client should receive a money for emotional suffering.

2. Please check to see if there is a mail in the mailbox.

3. The Times Square in New York City is known for its billboards and theaters.

4. A cement is one of the components of concrete.

5. I took all the boys on the roller coaster after lunch.

Using *the* with geographic nouns

When to omit *the*

streets, squares, parks	Ivy Street, Union Square, Denali National Park
cities, states, counties	Miami, New Mexico, Bee County
most countries, continents	Italy, Nigeria, China, South America, Africa
bays, single lakes	Tampa Bay, Lake Geneva
single mountains, islands	Mount Everest, Crete

When to use *the*

country names with *of* phrase	the United States (of America), the People's Republic of China
large regions, deserts	the East Coast, the Sahara
peninsulas	the Baja Peninsula, the Sinai Peninsula
oceans, seas, gulfs	the Pacific Ocean, the Dead Sea, the Persian Gulf
canals and rivers	the Panama Canal, the Amazon
mountain ranges	the Rocky Mountains, the Alps
groups of islands	the Solomon Islands

EXERCISE 29–2 Articles have been omitted from the following description of winter weather. Insert the articles *a*, *an*, and *the* where English requires them and be prepared to explain the reasons for your choices.

Many people confuse terms *hail*, *sleet*, and *freezing rain*. Hail normally occurs in thunderstorm and is caused by strong updrafts that lift growing chunks of ice into clouds. When chunks of ice, called hailstones, become too heavy to be carried by updrafts, they fall to ground. Hailstones can cause damage to crops, windshields, and people. Sleet occurs during winter storms and is caused by snowflakes falling from layer of cold air into warm layer, where they become raindrops, and then into another cold layer. As they fall through last layer of cold air, raindrops freeze and become small ice pellets, forming sleet. When it hits car windshield or windows of house, sleet can make annoying racket. Driving and walking can be hazardous when sleet accumulates on roads and sidewalks. Freezing rain is basically rain that falls onto ground and then freezes after it hits ground. It causes icy glaze on trees and any surface that is below freezing.

30 Sentence structure

Although their structure can vary widely, sentences in English generally flow from subject to verb to object or complement: *Bears eat fish.* This section focuses on the major challenges that multilingual students face when writing sentences in English. For more details on the parts of speech and the elements of sentences, consult sections 46–49.

30a Use a linking verb between a subject and its complement.

Some languages, such as Russian and Turkish, do not use linking verbs (*is, are, was, were*) between subjects and complements (nouns or adjectives that rename or describe the subject). Every English sentence, however, must include a verb. For more on linking verbs, see 27e.

▶ Jim *is* intelligent.

▶ Many streets in San Francisco *are* very steep.

30b Include a subject in every sentence.

Some languages, such as Spanish and Japanese, do not require a subject in every sentence. Every English sentence, however, needs a subject. Commands are an exception: The subject *you* is understood but not present in the sentence ([*You*] *Give me the book*).

▶ Your aunt is very energetic. ~~Seems~~ *She seems* young for her age.

The word *it* is used as the subject of a sentence describing the weather or temperature, stating the time, indicating distance, or suggesting an environmental fact.

▶ *It is* ~~Is~~ raining in the valley and snowing in the mountains.

▶ In July, *it* is very hot in Arizona.

▶ ~~Is~~ *It is* 9:15 a.m.

In most English sentences, the subject appears before the verb. Some sentences, however, are inverted: The subject comes after the verb. In these sentences, a placeholder called an *expletive* (*there* or *it*) often comes before the verb.

EXP V ⌐—— S ——⌐   ⌐—— S ——⌐ V
There are many people here today. (Many people are here today.)

▶ ~~Is~~ *There is* an apple pie in the refrigerator.

▶ As you know, *there are* many religious sects in India.

Notice that the verb agrees with the subject that follows it: *apple pie is, sects are.* (See 21g.)

Sometimes an inverted sentence has an infinitive (*to work*) or a noun clause (*that she is intelligent*) as the subject. In such sentences, the placeholder *it* is needed before the verb. (Also see 48b and 48e.)

EXP V   ⌐— S —⌐   ⌐— S —⌐   V
It is important to study daily. (To study daily is important.)

▶ Because the road is flooded, *it* is necessary to change our route.

TIP: The words *here* and *there* are not used as subjects. When they mean "in this place" (*here*) or "in that place" (*there*), they are adverbs, not nouns.

▶ I just returned from a vacation in Japan. ~~There~~ *It* is very beautiful/ *there.*

▶ ~~Here~~ *This school* offers a master's degree in physical therapy; ~~there~~ *that school* has only a bachelor's program.

30c Do not use both a noun and a pronoun to perform the same grammatical function in a sentence.

English does not allow a subject to be repeated in its own clause.

▶ The doctor ~~she~~ advised me to cut down on salt.

The pronoun *she* cannot repeat the subject, *doctor.*

Do not add a pronoun even when a word group comes between the subject and the verb.

▶ The watch that I lost on vacation ~~it~~ was in my backpack.

The pronoun *it* cannot repeat the subject, *watch.*

Some languages allow "topic fronting," placing a word or phrase (a "topic") at the beginning of a sentence and following it with an independent clause that explains something about the topic. This form is not allowed in English because the sentence seems to start with one subject but then introduces a new subject in an independent clause.

$$\overset{\ulcorner\text{TOPIC}\urcorner}{}\overset{\ulcorner\text{IND CLAUSE}\urcorner}{}$$
INCORRECT   The seeds I planted them last fall.

The sentence can be corrected by bringing the topic (*seeds*) into the independent clause.

　　　　　　　the seeds
▶ ~~The seeds~~ I planted ~~them~~ last fall.
　　　　　　　　　^

30d Do not repeat an object or an adverb in an adjective clause.

Adjective clauses begin with relative pronouns (*who, whom, whose, which, that*) or relative adverbs (*when, where*). Relative pronouns usually serve as subjects or objects in the clauses they introduce; another word in the clause cannot serve the same function. Relative adverbs should not be repeated by other adverbs later in the clause.

┌──────────ADJ CLAUSE──────────┐
The cat ran under the car that was parked on the street.

▶ The cat ran under the car that ~~it~~ was parked on the street.

The relative pronoun *that* is the subject of the adjective clause, so the pronoun *it* cannot be added as a subject.

▶ Myrna enjoyed the investment seminars that she attended

~~them~~ last week.

The relative pronoun *that* is the object of the verb *attended*. The pronoun *them* cannot also serve as an object.

Sometimes the relative pronoun is understood but not present in the sentence. In such cases, do not add another word with the same function as the omitted pronoun.

▶ Myrna enjoyed the investment seminars she attended ~~them~~

last week.

The relative pronoun *that* is understood after *seminars* even though it is not present in the sentence.

If the clause begins with a relative adverb, do not use another adverb with the same meaning later in the clause.

▶ The office where I work ~~there~~ is one hour from the city.

The adverb *there* cannot repeat the relative adverb *where*.

EXERCISE 30–1 In the following sentences, add needed subjects or expletives and delete any repeated subjects, objects, or adverbs. Answers to lettered sentences appear in the back of the book. Example:

The new geology professor is the one whom we saw ~~him~~ on TV

this morning.

a. Are some cartons of ice cream in the freezer.
b. I don't use the subway because am afraid.
c. The prime minister she is the most popular leader in my country.
d. We tried to get in touch with the same manager whom we spoke to him earlier.
e. Recently have been a number of earthquakes in Turkey.

1. We visited an island where several ancient ruins are being excavated there.
2. In this city is difficult to find a high-paying job.
3. Beginning knitters they are often surprised that their fingers are sore at first.
4. Is a banyan tree in our backyard.
5. The CD that teaches Italian for opera lovers it was stolen from my backpack.

30e Avoid mixed constructions beginning with *although* or *because*.

A word group that begins with *although* cannot be linked to a word group that begins with *but* or *however*. The result is an error called a *mixed construction* (see also 11a). Similarly, a word group that begins with *because* cannot be linked to a word group that begins with *so* or *therefore*.

If you want to keep *although* or *because*, drop the other linking word.

▶ Although Nikki Giovanni is best known for her poetry for

adults, ~~but~~ she has written several books for children.

▶ Because German and Dutch are related languages, ~~therefore~~

tourists from Berlin can usually read a few signs in Amsterdam.

If you want to keep the other linking word, omit *although* or *because*.

▶ ~~Although~~ Nikki Giovanni is best known for her poetry for

adults, but she has written several books for children.

▶ ~~Because~~ German and Dutch are related languages/; therefore,
^   ^

tourists from Berlin can usually read a few signs in

Amsterdam.

For advice about using commas and semicolons with linking words, see 32a and 34b.

30f Do not place an adverb between a verb and its direct object.

Adverbs modifying verbs can appear in various positions: at the beginning or end of a sentence, before or after a verb, or between a helping verb and its main verb.

Slowly, we drove along the rain-slick road.

Mia handled the teapot *very carefully*.

Martin *always* wins our tennis matches.

Christina is *rarely* late for our lunch dates.

My daughter has *often* spoken of you.

The election results were being *closely* followed by analysts.

However, an adverb cannot appear between a verb and its direct object.

       carefully
▶ Mother wrapped ~~carefully~~ the gift.
         ^

The adverb *carefully* cannot appear between the verb, *wrapped*, and its direct object, *the gift*.

EXERCISE 30–2 Edit the following sentences for proper sentence structure. If a sentence is correct, write "correct" after it. Answers to lettered sentences appear in the back of the book. Example:

                    slowly.
She peeled ~~slowly~~ the banana/
                 ^

a. Although freshwater freezes at 32° Fahrenheit, however ocean water freezes at 28° Fahrenheit.

b. Because we switched cable packages, so our channel lineup has changed.

c. The competitor mounted confidently his skateboard.

d. My sister performs well the *legong*, a Balinese dance.

e. Because product development is behind schedule, we will have to launch the product next spring.

1. The bank teller counted methodically the stack of twenty-dollar bills.

2. I gasped when I saw lightning strike repeatedly the barn.

3. Although hockey is traditionally a winter sport, but many towns offer skills programs all year long.

4. Because salmon can survive in both freshwater and salt water, so they are classified as anadromous fish.

5. A surveyor determines precisely the boundaries of a piece of property.

30g Distinguish between present participles and past participles used as adjectives.

Both present and past participles may be used as adjectives. The present participle always ends in *-ing*. Past participles usually end in *-ed*, *-d*, *-en*, *-n*, or *-t*. (See 27a.)

PRESENT PARTICIPLES   confusing, speaking, boring

PAST PARTICIPLES   confused, spoken, bored

Like all other adjectives, participles can come before nouns; they also can follow linking verbs, in which case they describe the subject of the sentence. (See 47b.)

Use a present participle to describe a person or thing *causing or stimulating an experience.*

The *boring lecture* put us to sleep. [The lecture caused boredom.]

Use a past participle to describe a person or thing *undergoing an experience.*

The *audience* was *bored* by the lecture. [The audience experienced boredom.]

Participles that describe emotions or mental states often cause the most confusion.

annoying/annoyed
boring/bored
confusing/confused
depressing/depressed
exciting/excited

exhausting/exhausted
fascinating/fascinated
frightening/frightened
satisfying/satisfied
surprising/surprised

▶ Our hike was ~~exhausted.~~ *exhausting.*

Exhausting suggests that the hike caused exhaustion.

▶ The ~~exhausting~~ *exhausted* hikers reached the campground at sunset.

Exhausted describes how the hikers felt.

EXERCISE 30–3 Edit the following sentences for proper use of present and past participles. If a sentence is correct, write "correct" after it. Answers to lettered sentences appear in the back of the book. Example:

> Danielle and Monica were very ~~exciting~~ *excited* to be going to a Broadway show for the first time.

a. Listening to everyone's complaints all day was irritated.

b. The long flight to Singapore was exhausted.

c. His skill at chess is amazing.

d. After a great deal of research, the scientist made a fascinated discovery.

e. Surviving that tornado was one of the most frightened experiences I've ever had.

1. I couldn't concentrate on my homework because I was distracted.

2. The directions to the new board game seem extremely complicating.

3. How interested are you in visiting Civil War battlefields?

4. The aerial view of the devastated villages was depressing.

5. Even after the lecturer went over the main points again, the students were still confusing.

30h Place cumulative adjectives in an appropriate order.

Adjectives usually come before the nouns they modify and may also come after linking verbs. (See 46d and 47b.)

> ADJ   N   V   ADJ
> Janine wore a new necklace. Janine's necklace was new.

Cumulative adjectives, which cannot be joined by the word *and* or separated by commas, must come in a particular order. If you use cumulative adjectives before a noun, see the chart on page 286. The chart is only a guide; don't be surprised if you encounter exceptions. (See also 33d.)

> ▶ My dorm room has only a desk and a ~~plastic red stained~~ chair.
>   *stained red plastic*

> ▶ Nice weather, ~~blue clear~~ water, and ancient monuments
>   *clear blue*
>
> attract many people to Italy.

EXERCISE 30–4 Using the chart on page 286 as necessary, arrange the following modifiers and nouns in their proper order. Answers to lettered items appear in the back of the book. Example:

> *two new French racing bicycles*
> **new, French, two, bicycles, racing**

a. sculptor, young, an, Vietnamese, intelligent
b. dedicated, a, priest, Catholic
c. old, her, sweater, blue, wool
d. delicious, Joe's, Scandinavian, bread
e. many, boxes, jewelry, antique, beautiful

1. oval, nine, brass, lamps, miniature
2. several, yellow, tulips, tiny
3. the, tree, gingko, yellow, ancient, Mongolian
4. courtyard, a, square, small, brick
5. charming, restaurants, Latvian, several

Order of cumulative adjectives

FIRST

ARTICLE OR OTHER NOUN MARKER   a, an, the, her, Joe's, two, many, some

EVALUATIVE WORD   attractive, dedicated, delicious, ugly, disgusting

SIZE   large, enormous, small, little

LENGTH OR SHAPE   long, short, round, square

AGE   new, old, young, antique

COLOR   yellow, blue, crimson

NATIONALITY   French, Peruvian, Vietnamese

RELIGION   Catholic, Protestant, Jewish, Muslim

MATERIAL   silver, walnut, wool, marble

LAST   **NOUN/ADJECTIVE**   tree (as in *tree* house), kitchen (as in *kitchen* table)

THE NOUN MODIFIED   house, coat, bicycle, bread, woman, coin

> My *large blue wool* coat is in the attic.
>
> Joe's collection includes *two small antique silver* coins.

31   Prepositions and idiomatic expressions

31a Become familiar with prepositions that show time and place.

The most frequently used prepositions in English are *at*, *by*, *for*, *from*, *in*, *of*, *on*, *to*, and *with*. Prepositions can be difficult to master because the differences among them are subtle and idiomatic. The chart on page 288 is limited to three troublesome prepositions that show time and place: *at*, *on*, and *in*.

Not every possible use is listed in the chart, so don't be surprised when you encounter exceptions and idiomatic uses that you must learn one at a time. For example, in English a person rides *in* a car but *on* a bus, plane, train, or subway.

> My first class starts ~~on~~ *at* 8:00 a.m.

> The farmers go to market ~~in~~ *on* Wednesday.

> I want to work at one of the biggest companies ~~on~~ *in* the world.

EXERCISE 31–1 In the following sentences, replace prepositions that are not used correctly. You may need to refer to the chart on page 288. If a sentence is correct, write "correct" after it. Answers to lettered sentences appear in the back of the book. Example:

The play begins ~~on~~ *at* 7:20 p.m.

a. Whenever we eat at the Centerville Café, we sit at a small table on the corner of the room.

b. In the 1990s, entrepreneurs created new online businesses in record numbers.

c. In Thursday, Nancy will attend her first home repair class at the community center.

d. Alex began looking for her lost mitten in another location.

e. We decided to go to a restaurant because there was no fresh food on the refrigerator.

1. I like walking at my neighborhood in night.

2. If the train is on time, it will arrive on six o'clock at the morning.

3. In the corner of the room is a large bookcase with a pair of small Russian dolls standing at the top shelf.

4. She licked the stamp, stuck it in the envelope, put the envelope on her pocket, and walked to the nearest mailbox.

5. The mailbox was in the intersection of Laidlaw Avenue and Williams Street.

31b Use nouns (including *-ing* forms) after prepositions.

In a prepositional phrase, use a noun (not a verb) after the preposition. Sometimes the noun will be a gerund, the *-ing* verb form that functions as a noun (see 48b).

> Our student government is good at ~~save~~ *saving* money.

PRACTICE hackerhandbooks.com/rules
> Multilingual/ESL > 31–2

At, on, and *in* to show time and place

Showing time

AT	*at* a specific time: *at* 7:20, *at* dawn, *at* dinner
ON	*on* a specific day or date: *on* Tuesday, *on* June 4
IN	*in* a part of a 24-hour period: *in* the afternoon, *in* the daytime
	[but *at* night]
	in a year or month: *in* 2008, *in* July
	in a period of time: finished *in* three hours

Showing place

AT	*at* a meeting place or location: *at* home, *at* the club
	at the edge of something: sitting *at* the desk
	at the corner of something: turning *at* the intersection
	at a target: throwing the snowball *at* Lucy
ON	*on* a surface: placed *on* the table, hanging *on* the wall
	on a street: the house *on* Spring Street
	on an electronic medium: *on* television, *on* the Internet
IN	*in* an enclosed space: *in* the garage, *in* an envelope
	in a geographic location: *in* San Diego, *in* Texas
	in a print medium: *in* a book, *in* a magazine

Distinguish between the preposition *to* and the infinitive marker *to*. If *to* is a preposition, it should be followed by a noun or a gerund.

>   *helping*
> ▶ We are dedicated to ~~help~~ the poor.
>   ^

If *to* is an infinitive marker, it should be followed by the base form of the verb.

>   *help*
> ▶ We want to ~~helping~~ the poor.
>   ^

To test whether *to* is a preposition or an infinitive marker, insert a word that you know is a noun after the word *to*. If the noun makes sense in that position, *to* is a preposition. If the noun does not make sense after *to*, then *to* is an infinitive marker.

> Zoe is addicted *to* _____.

> They are planning *to* _____.

In the first sentence, a noun (such as *magazines*) makes sense after *to*, so *to* is a preposition and should be followed by a noun or a gerund: Zoe is addicted *to magazines*. Zoe is addicted *to running*.

In the second sentence, a noun (such as *magazines*) does not make sense after *to*, so *to* is an infinitive marker and must be followed by the base form of the verb: They are planning *to build* a new school.

31c Become familiar with common adjective + preposition combinations.

Some adjectives appear only with certain prepositions. These expressions are idiomatic and may be different from the combinations used in your native language.

> *to*
> ► Paula is married ~~with~~ Jon.
>   ^

Check an ESL dictionary for combinations that are not listed in the chart on page 290.

31d Become familiar with common verb + preposition combinations.

Many verbs and prepositions appear together in idiomatic phrases. Pay special attention to the combinations that are different from the combinations used in your native language.

> *on*
> ► Your success depends ~~of~~ your effort.
>   ^

Check an ESL dictionary for combinations that are not listed in the chart on page 290.

Adjective + preposition combinations

accustomed to
addicted to
afraid of
angry with
ashamed of
aware of
committed to
concerned
    about
concerned with

connected to
covered with
dedicated to
devoted to
different from
engaged in
engaged to
excited about
familiar with
full of

guilty of
interested in
involved in
involved with
known as
known for
made of (*or*
    made from)
married to
opposed to

preferable to
proud of
responsible
    for
satisfied with
scared of
similar to
tired of
worried
    about

Verb + preposition combinations

agree with
apply to
approve of
arrive at
arrive in
ask for
believe in
belong to
care about
care for
compare to

compare with
concentrate on
consist of
count on
decide on
depend on
differ from
disagree with
dream about
dream of
feel like

forget about
happen to
hope for
insist on
listen to
participate in
rely on
reply to
respond to
result in
search for

speak to (*or*
    speak with)
stare at
succeed at
succeed in
take advantage of
take care of
think about
think of
wait for
wait on

Punctuation

32   The comma

The comma was invented to help readers. Without it, sentence parts can collide into one another unexpectedly, causing misreadings.

| **CONFUSING** | If you cook Elmer will do the dishes. |
| **CONFUSING** | While we were eating a rattlesnake approached our campsite. |

Add commas in the logical places (after *cook* and *eating*), and suddenly all is clear. No longer is Elmer being cooked, the rattlesnake being eaten.

Various rules have evolved to prevent such misreadings and to speed readers along through complex grammatical structures. Those rules are detailed in this section. (Section 33 explains when not to use commas.)

32a Use a comma before a coordinating conjunction joining independent clauses.

When a coordinating conjunction connects two or more in-dependent clauses — word groups that could stand alone as separate sentences — a comma must precede it. There are seven coordinating conjunctions in English: *and, but, or, nor, for, so,* and *yet.*

A comma tells readers that one independent clause has come to a close and that another is about to begin.

▶ The department sponsored a seminar on college survival

skills, and it also hosted a barbecue for new students.
  ^

EXCEPTION: If the two independent clauses are short and there is no danger of misreading, the comma may be omitted.

The plane took off and we were on our way.

TIP: As a rule, do *not* use a comma to separate coordinate word groups that are not independent clauses. (See 33a.)

▶ A good money manager controls expenses⁄and invests surplus

dollars to meet future needs.

The word group following *and* is not an independent clause; it is the
second half of a compound predicate (*controls . . . and invests*).

32b Use a comma after an introductory clause or phrase.

The most common introductory word groups are clauses and
phrases functioning as adverbs. Such word groups usually tell
when, where, how, why, or under what conditions the main action
of the sentence occurred. (See 48a, 48b, and 48e.)

A comma tells readers that the introductory clause or phrase
has come to a close and that the main part of the sentence is
about to begin.

▶ When Irwin was ready to iron, his cat tripped on the cord.

Without the comma, readers may have Irwin ironing his cat. The
comma signals that *his cat* is the subject of a new clause, not part of the
introductory one.

▶ Near a small stream at the bottom of the canyon, the park

rangers discovered an abandoned mine.

The comma tells readers that the introductory prepositional phrase has
come to a close.

EXCEPTION: The comma may be omitted after a short adverb
clause or phrase if there is no danger of misreading.

In no time we were at 2,800 feet.

Sentences also frequently begin with participial phrases describing the noun or pronoun immediately following them. The
comma tells readers that they are about to learn the identity of
the person or thing described; therefore, the comma is usually
required even when the phrase is short. (See 48b.)

▶ Thinking his motorcade drive through Dallas was routine,

President Kennedy smiled and waved at the crowds.

▶ **Buried under layers of younger rocks, the earth's oldest rocks**

contain no fossils.

NOTE: Other introductory word groups include transitional expressions and absolute phrases (see 32f).

EXERCISE 32–1   Add or delete commas where necessary in the following sentences. If a sentence is correct, write "correct" after it. Answers to lettered sentences appear in the back of the book. Example:

Because we had been saving molding for a few weeks, we had

enough wood to frame all thirty paintings.

a. Alisa brought the injured bird home, and fashioned a splint out of Popsicle sticks for its wing.
b. Considered a classic of early animation *The Adventures of Prince Achmed* used hand-cut silhouettes against colored backgrounds.
c. If you complete the evaluation form and return it within two weeks you will receive a free breakfast during your next stay.
d. After retiring from the New York City Ballet in 1965, legendary dancer Maria Tallchief went on to found the Chicago City Ballet.
e. Roger had always wanted a handmade violin but he couldn't afford one.
1. While I was driving a huge delivery truck ran through a red light.
2. He pushed the car beyond the tollgate, and poured a bucket of water on the smoking hood.
3. Lit by bright halogen lamps hundreds of origami birds sparkled like diamonds in sunlight.
4. As the first chord sounded, Aileen knew that her spirits were about to rise.
5. Many musicians of Bach's time played several instruments but few mastered them as early or played with as much expression as Bach.

EXERCISE 32–2   Add or delete commas where necessary in the following sentences. If a sentence is correct, write "correct" after it. Answers to lettered sentences appear in the back of the book. Example:

The car had been sitting idle for a month, so the battery was

completely dead.

a. J. R. R. Tolkien finished writing his draft of *The Lord of the Rings* trilogy in 1949 but the first book in the series wasn't published until 1954.

b. In the first two minutes of its ascent the space shuttle had broken the sound barrier and reached a height of over twenty-five miles.

c. German shepherds can be gentle guide dogs or they can be fierce attack dogs.

d. Some former professional cyclists claim that the use of performance-enhancing drugs is widespread in cycling and they argue that no rider can be competitive without doping.

e. As an intern, I learned most aspects of the broadcasting industry but I never learned about fundraising.

1. To be considered for the position candidates must demonstrate initiative and strong communication skills.

2. The cinematic lighting effect known as *chiaroscuro* was first used in German Expressionist filmmaking, and was later seen in American film noir.

3. Reptiles are cold-blooded and they are covered with scales.

4. Using a variety of techniques, advertisers grab the audience's attention and imprint their messages onto consumers' minds.

5. By the end of the first quarter the operating budget will be available online.

32c Use a comma between all items in a series.

When three or more items are presented in a series, those items should be separated from one another with commas. Items in a series may be single words, phrases, or clauses.

▶ Langston Hughes's poetry is concerned with racial pride,

social justice, and the diversity of the African American

experience.

▶ Bubbles of air, leaves, ferns, bits of wood, and insects are

often found trapped in amber.

Although some writers view the comma between the last two items as optional, most experts advise using the comma because its omission can result in ambiguity or misreading.

▶ **My uncle willed me all of his property, houses, and boats.**

Did the uncle will his property *and* houses *and* boats — or simply his property, consisting of houses and boats? If the former meaning is intended, a comma is necessary to prevent ambiguity.

▶ **The activities include touring the White House, visiting**

the Air and Space Museum, attending a lecture about the

Founding Fathers, and kayaking on the Potomac River.

Without the comma, the activities might seem to include a lecture about kayaking, not participating in kayaking. The comma makes it clear that *kayaking on the Potomac River* is a separate item in the series.

32d Use a comma between coordinate adjectives not joined with *and*. Do not use a comma between cumulative adjectives.

When two or more adjectives each modify a noun separately, they are coordinate.

Roberto is a *warm, gentle, affectionate* father.

If the adjectives can be joined with *and*, the adjectives are coordinate, so you should use commas: *warm* and *gentle* and *affectionate* (*warm, gentle, affectionate*).

Adjectives that do not modify the noun separately are cumulative.

Three large gray shapes moved slowly toward us.

Beginning with the adjective closest to the noun *shapes*, these modifiers lean on one another, piggyback style, with each modifying a larger word group. *Gray* modifies *shapes*, *large* modifies *gray shapes*, and *three* modifies *large gray shapes*. Cumulative adjectives cannot be joined with *and* (not *three* and *large* and *gray shapes*).

COORDINATE ADJECTIVES

▶ **Should patients with severe, irreversible brain damage be put**

on life support systems?

Adjectives are coordinate if they can be connected with *and*: *severe and irreversible.*

CUMULATIVE ADJECTIVES

▶ Ira ordered a rich/chocolate/layer cake.

Ira didn't order a cake that was rich and chocolate and layer: He ordered a *layer cake* that was *chocolate*, a *chocolate layer cake* that was *rich*.

EXERCISE 32–3   Add or delete commas where necessary in the following sentences. If a sentence is correct, write "correct" after it. Answers to lettered sentences appear in the back of the book. Example:

We gathered our essentials, took off for the great outdoors,

and ignored the fact that it was Friday the 13th.

a. The cold impersonal atmosphere of the university was unbearable.
b. An ambulance threaded its way through police cars, fire trucks and irate citizens.
c. The *1812 Overture* is a stirring, magnificent piece of music.
d. After two broken arms, three cracked ribs and one concussion, Ken quit the varsity football team.
e. My cat's pupils had constricted to small black shining slits.
1. We prefer our staff to be orderly, prompt and efficient.
2. For breakfast the children ordered cornflakes, English muffins with peanut butter and cherry Cokes.
3. It was a small, unimportant part, but I was happy to have it.
4. Cyril was clad in a luminous orange rain suit and a brilliant white helmet.
5. Animation master Hironobu Sakaguchi makes computer-generated scenes look realistic, vivid and seductive.

EXERCISE 32–4   Add or delete commas where necessary in the following sentences. If a sentence is correct, write "correct" after it. Answers to lettered sentences appear in the back of the book. Example:

Good social workers excel in patience, diplomacy, and

positive thinking.

a. NASA's rovers on Mars are equipped with special cameras that can take close-up high-resolution pictures of the terrain.

b. A baseball player achieves the triple crown by having the highest batting average, the most home runs, and the most runs batted in during the regular season.

c. If it does not get enough sunlight, a healthy green lawn can turn into a shriveled brown mess within a matter of days.

d. Love, vengeance, greed and betrayal are common themes in Western literature.

e. Many experts believe that shark attacks on surfers are a result of the sharks' mistaking surfboards for small, injured seals.

1. In Sherman's march to the sea, the Union army set fire to all crops, killed all livestock and destroyed all roads and bridges in its path.

2. Milk that comes from grass-fed steroid-free cows has been gaining market share.

3. The film makes three main points about global warming: It is real, it is the result of human activity, and it should not be ignored.

4. The three, handmade, turquoise bracelets brought in the most money at the charity auction.

5. Matisse is well known for vibrant colorful prints that have been reproduced extensively on greeting cards and posters.

32e Use commas to set off nonrestrictive (nonessential) elements. Do not use commas to set off restrictive (essential) elements.

Certain word groups that modify nouns or pronouns can be restrictive or nonrestrictive — that is, essential or not essential to the meaning of a sentence. These word groups are usually adjective clauses, adjective phrases, or appositives.

Restrictive elements

A restrictive element defines or limits the meaning of the word it modifies; it is therefore essential to the meaning of the sentence and is not set off with commas. If you remove a restrictive modifier from a sentence, the meaning changes significantly, becoming more general than you intended.

RESTRICTIVE (NO COMMAS)

The campers need clothes *that are durable.*

Scientists *who study the earth's structure* are called geologists.

The first sentence does not mean that the campers need clothes in general. The intended meaning is more limited: The campers need durable clothes. The second sentence does not mean that scientists in general are called geologists; only those scientists who specifically study the earth's structure are called geologists. The italicized word groups are essential and are therefore not set off with commas.

Nonrestrictive elements

A nonrestrictive modifier describes a noun or pronoun whose meaning has already been clearly defined or limited. Because the modifier contains nonessential or parenthetical information, it is set off with commas. If you remove a nonrestrictive element from a sentence, the meaning does not change dramatically. Some meaning may be lost, but the defining characteristics of the person or thing described remain the same.

NONRESTRICTIVE (WITH COMMAS)

The campers need sturdy shoes, *which are expensive.*

The scientists, *who represented eight different universities*, met to review applications for the prestigious O'Hara Award.

In the first sentence, the campers need sturdy shoes, and the shoes happen to be expensive. In the second sentence, the scientists met to review applications for the O'Hara Award; that they represented eight different universities is informative but not critical to the meaning of the sentence. The nonessential information in both sentences is set off with commas.

NOTE: Often it is difficult to tell whether a word group is restrictive or nonrestrictive without seeing it in context and considering the writer's meaning. Both of the following sentences are grammatically correct, but their meaning is slightly different.

The dessert made with fresh raspberries was delicious.

The dessert, made with fresh raspberries, was delicious.

In the first example, the phrase *made with fresh raspberries* tells readers which of two or more desserts the writer is referring to. In the example with commas, the phrase merely adds information about the dessert.

Adjective clauses

Adjective clauses are patterned like sentences, containing subjects and verbs, but they function within sentences as modifiers of nouns or pronouns. They always follow the word they modify, usually immediately. Adjective clauses begin with a relative pronoun (*who, whom, whose, which, that*) or with a relative adverb (*where, when*).

Nonrestrictive adjective clauses are set off with commas; restrictive adjective clauses are not.

NONRESTRICTIVE CLAUSE (WITH COMMAS)

▶ Ed's house, which is located on thirteen acres, was completely

furnished with bats in the rafters and mice in the kitchen.

The adjective clause *which is located on thirteen acres* does not restrict the meaning of *Ed's house*; the information is nonessential and is therefore enclosed in commas.

RESTRICTIVE CLAUSE (NO COMMAS)

▶ The giant panda/that was born at the San Diego Zoo in

2003/was sent to China in 2007.

Because the adjective clause *that was born at the San Diego Zoo in 2003* identifies one particular panda out of many, the information is essential and is therefore not enclosed in commas.

NOTE: Use *that* only with restrictive (essential) clauses. Many writers prefer to use *which* only with nonrestrictive (nonessential) clauses, but usage varies.

Adjective phrases

Prepositional or verbal phrases functioning as adjectives may be restrictive or nonrestrictive. Nonrestrictive phrases are set off with commas; restrictive phrases are not.

NONRESTRICTIVE PHRASE (WITH COMMAS)

▶ The helicopter, with its million-candlepower spotlight

illuminating the area, circled above.

The *with* phrase is nonessential because its purpose is not to specify which of two or more helicopters is being discussed. The phrase is not required for readers to understand the meaning of the sentence.

RESTRICTIVE PHRASE (NO COMMAS)

▶ One corner of the attic was filled with newspapers⁄dating

from the early 1900s.

Dating from the early 1900s restricts the meaning of *newspapers*, so the comma should be omitted.

▶ The bill⁄proposed by the Illinois representative⁄would

lower taxes and provide services for middle-income

families.

Proposed by the Illinois representative identifies exactly which bill is meant.

Appositives

An appositive is a noun or noun phrase that renames a nearby noun. Nonrestrictive appositives are set off with commas; restrictive appositives are not.

NONRESTRICTIVE APPOSITIVE (WITH COMMAS)

▶ Darwin's most important book‸ *On the Origin of Species*‸

was the result of many years of research.

Most important restricts the meaning to one book, so the appositive *On the Origin of Species* is nonrestrictive and should be set off with commas.

RESTRICTIVE APPOSITIVE (NO COMMAS)

▶ The song⁄ "Viva la Vida⁄" was blasted out of huge amplifiers

at the concert.

Once they've read *song*, readers still don't know precisely which song the writer means. The appositive following *song* restricts its meaning, so the appositive should not be enclosed in commas.

EXERCISE 32–5 Add or delete commas where necessary in the following sentences. If a sentence is correct, write "correct" after it. Answers to lettered sentences appear in the back of the book. Example:

My sister, who plays center on the Sparks, now lives at

The Sands, a beach house near Los Angeles.

a. Choreographer Alvin Ailey's best-known work *Revelations* is more than just a crowd-pleaser.

b. Twyla Tharp's contemporary ballet *Push Comes to Shove* was made famous by the Russian dancer Baryshnikov. [*Tharp has written more than one contemporary ballet.*]

c. The glass sculptor sifting through hot red sand explained her technique to the other glassmakers. [*There is more than one glass sculptor.*]

d. A member of an organization, that provides job training for teens, was also appointed to the education commission.

e. Brian Eno who began his career as a rock musician turned to meditative compositions in the late 1970s.

1. I had the pleasure of talking to a woman who had just returned from India where she had lived for ten years.

2. Patrick's oldest sister Fiona graduated from MIT with a degree in aerospace engineering.

3. The artist painting a portrait of Aung San Suu Kyi, the Burmese civil rights leader, was once a political prisoner himself.

4. *Jumanji*, the 1982 Caldecott Medal winner, is my nephew's favorite book.

5. The flame crawled up a few blades of grass to reach a low-hanging palmetto branch which quickly ignited.

32f Use commas to set off transitional and parenthetical expressions, absolute phrases, and word groups expressing contrast.

Transitional expressions

Transitional expressions serve as bridges between sentences or parts of sentences. They include conjunctive adverbs such as *however*, *therefore*, and *moreover* and transitional phrases such as *for example, as a matter of fact,* and *in other words.* (For complete lists of these expressions, see 34b.)

When a transitional expression appears between independent clauses in a compound sentence, it is preceded by a semicolon and is usually followed by a comma. (See 34b.)

▶ Minh did not understand our language; moreover, he was

unfamiliar with our customs.

When a transitional expression appears at the beginning of a sentence or in the middle of an independent clause, it is usually set off with commas.

▶ As a matter of fact, American football was established in the

mid-nineteenth century by fans who wanted to play a more

organized game of rugby.

▶ Natural foods are not always salt free; celery, for example,

contains more sodium than most people would imagine.

EXCEPTION: If a transitional expression blends smoothly with the rest of the sentence, calling for little or no pause in reading, it does not need to be set off with a comma. Expressions such as *also, at least, certainly, consequently, indeed, of course, moreover, no doubt, perhaps, then,* and *therefore* do not always call for a pause.

Alice's bicycle is broken; *therefore* you will need to borrow Sue's.

Parenthetical expressions

Expressions that are distinctly parenthetical, providing only supplemental information, should be set off with commas. They interrupt the flow of a sentence or appear at the end as afterthoughts.

▶ Evolution, as far as we know, doesn't work this way.

▶ The bass weighed about twelve pounds, give or take a few

ounces.

Absolute phrases

An absolute phrase, which modifies the whole sentence, usually consists of a noun followed by a participle or participial phrase. (See 48d.) Absolute phrases may appear at the beginning or at the end of a sentence. Wherever they appear, they should be set off with commas.

> ──────── ABSOLUTE PHRASE ────────
> N PARTICIPLE
> The sun appearing for the first time in a week, we were at last able to begin the archaeological dig.

▶ Elvis Presley made music industry history in the 1950s, his records having sold more than ten million copies.

NOTE: Do not insert a comma between the noun and the participle in an absolute construction.

▶ The next contestant/being five years old, the host adjusted the height of the microphone.

Word groups expressing contrast

Sharp contrasts beginning with words such as *not*, *never*, and *unlike* are set off with commas.

▶ The Epicurean philosophers sought mental, not bodily, pleasures.

▶ Unlike Robert, Celia loved dance contests.

32g Use commas to set off nouns of direct address, the words *yes* and *no*, interrogative tags, and mild interjections.

▶ Forgive me, Angela, for forgetting your birthday.

▶ Yes, the loan will probably be approved.

▸ The film was faithful to the book, wasn't it?

▸ Well, cases like these are difficult to decide.

32h Use commas with expressions such as *he said* to set off direct quotations. (See also 37e.)

▸ In his "Letter from Birmingham Jail," Martin Luther King
Jr. wrote, "We know through painful experience that freedom
is never voluntarily given by the oppressor; it must be
demanded by the oppressed" (225).

▸ "Happiness in marriage is entirely a matter of chance," says
Charlotte Lucas in *Pride and Prejudice*, a novel that ends with
two happy marriages (ch. 6; 69).

See 37 on the use of quotation marks and pages 489–90 on citing literary sources in MLA style.

32i Use commas with dates, addresses, titles, and numbers.

Dates

In dates, the year is set off from the rest of the sentence with a pair of commas.

▸ On December 12, 1890, orders were sent out for the arrest of
Sitting Bull.

EXCEPTIONS: Commas are not needed if the date is inverted or if only the month and year are given.

The security alert system went into effect on 15 April 2009.

January 2008 was an extremely cold month.

Addresses

The elements of an address or a place name are separated with commas. A zip code, however, is not preceded by a comma.

▶ John Lennon was born in Liverpool, England, in 1940.

▶ Please send the package to Greg Tarvin at 708 Spring Street,

Washington, IL 61571.

Titles

If a title follows a name, separate the title from the rest of the sentence with a pair of commas.

▶ Ann Hall, MD, has been appointed to the board of trustees.

Numbers

In numbers more than four digits long, use commas to separate the numbers into groups of three, starting from the right. In numbers four digits long, a comma is optional.

> 3,500 [*or* 3500]
>
> 100,000
>
> 5,000,000

EXCEPTIONS: Do not use commas in street numbers, zip codes, telephone numbers, or years with four or fewer digits.

32j Use a comma to prevent confusion.

In certain situations, a comma is necessary to prevent confusion. If the writer has intentionally left out a word or phrase, for example, a comma may be needed to signal the omission.

▶ To err is human; to forgive, divine.

If two words in a row echo each other, a comma may be needed for ease of reading.

▶ The catastrophe that we had feared might happen, happened.

Sometimes a comma is needed to prevent readers from grouping words in ways that do not match the writer's intention.

▶ Patients who can‚ walk up and down the halls every day.

EXERCISE 32–6   This exercise covers the major uses of the comma described in 32a–32e. Add or delete commas where necessary. If a sentence is correct, write "correct" after it. Answers to lettered sentences appear in the back of the book. Example:

> Even though our brains actually can't focus on two tasks
>
> at a time‚ many people believe they can multitask.

a. Cricket which originated in England is also popular in Australia, South Africa and India.
b. At the sound of the starting pistol the horses surged forward toward the first obstacle, a sharp incline three feet high.
c. After seeing an exhibition of Western art Gerhard Richter escaped from East Berlin, and smuggled out many of his notebooks.
d. Corrie's new wet suit has an intricate, blue pattern.
e. The cookies will keep for two weeks in sturdy airtight containers.

1. Research on Andean condors has shown that high levels of the pesticide chlorinated hydrocarbon can cause the thinning of eggshells.
2. Founded in 1868 Hampton University was one of the first colleges for African Americans.
3. Aunt Emilia was an impossible demanding guest.
4. The Mirage, a high-tech fighter, is an astonishing machine to fly.
5. At the bottom of the ship's rusty hold sat several, well-preserved trunks, reminders of a bygone era of sea travel.

EXERCISE 32–7   This exercise covers all uses of the comma. Add or delete commas where necessary in the following sentences. If a sentence is correct, write "correct" after it. Answers to lettered sentences appear in the back of the book. Example:

> "Yes‚ dear, you can have dessert," my mother said.

a. On January 15, 2008 our office moved to 29 Commonwealth Avenue, Mechanicsville VA 23111.

b. The coach having bawled us out thoroughly, we left the locker room with his harsh words ringing in our ears.

c. Ms. Carlson you are a valued customer whose satisfaction is very important to us.

d. Mr. Mundy was born on July 22, 1939 in Arkansas, where his family had lived for four generations.

e. Her board poised at the edge of the half-pipe, Nina waited her turn to drop in.

1. President Lincoln's original intention was to save the Union, not to destroy slavery.

2. For centuries people believed that Greek culture had developed in isolation from the world. Today however scholars are acknowledging the contributions made by Egypt and the Middle East.

3. Putting together a successful fundraiser, Patricia discovered, requires creativity and good timing.

4. Fortunately science is creating many alternatives to research performed on animals.

5. While the machine was printing the oversize paper jammed the input tray.

33   Unnecessary commas

Many common misuses of the comma result from a misunderstanding of the major comma rules presented in 32.

33a Do not use a comma between compound elements that are not independent clauses.

Though a comma should be used before a coordinating conjunction joining independent clauses (see 32a), this rule should not be extended to other compound word groups.

▶ Marie Curie discovered radium/and later applied her work on

radioactivity to medicine.

And links two verbs in a compound predicate: *discovered* and *applied*.

▶ Jake told us that his illness is serious⁄ but that changes in

his lifestyle can improve his chances for survival.

The coordinating conjunction *but* links two subordinate clauses, each
beginning with *that*: *that his illness is serious* and *that changes in his
lifestyle....*

33b Do not use a comma to separate a verb from its subject or object.

A sentence should flow from subject to verb to object without
unnecessary pauses. Commas may appear between these major
sentence elements only when a specific rule calls for them.

▶ Zoos large enough to give the animals freedom to roam⁄are

becoming more popular.

The comma should not separate the subject, *Zoos*, from the verb, *are
becoming*.

▶ Maxine Hong Kingston writes⁄that many Chinese American

families struggle "to figure out how the invisible world the

emigrants built around our childhoods fits in solid America" (107).

The comma should not separate the verb, *writes*, from its object, the
subordinate clause beginning with *that*. A signal phrase ending in a
word like *writes* or *says* is followed by a comma only when a direct
quotation immediately follows: *Kingston writes, "Those of us in the first
American generations have had to figure out how the invisible world ..."*
(107). (See also 37e.)

33c Do not use a comma before the first or after the last item in a series.

Though commas are required between items in a series (32c), do
not place them either before or after the whole series.

▶ Other causes of asthmatic attacks are⁄stress, change in

temperature, and cold air.

▶ Ironically, even novels that focus on horror, evil, and alienation/

often have themes of spiritual renewal and redemption as well.

33d Do not use a comma between cumulative adjectives, between an adjective and a noun, or between an adverb and an adjective.

Commas are required between coordinate adjectives (those that can be joined with *and*), but they do not belong between cumulative adjectives (those that cannot be joined with *and*). (For a full discussion, see 32d.)

▶ In the corner of the closet, we found an old/maroon hatbox.

A comma should never be used between an adjective and the noun that follows it.

▶ It was a senseless, dangerous/mission.

Nor should a comma be used between an adverb and an adjective that follows it.

▶ The Hillside is a good home for severely/disturbed youths.

33e Do not use commas to set off restrictive or mildly parenthetical elements.

Restrictive elements are modifiers or appositives that restrict the meaning of the nouns they follow. Because they are essential to the meaning of the sentence, they are not set off with commas. (For a full discussion of restrictive and nonrestrictive elements, see 32e.)

▶ Drivers/who think they own the road/make cycling a

dangerous sport.

The modifier *who think they own the road* restricts the meaning of *Drivers* and is essential to the meaning of the sentence. Putting

commas around the *who* clause falsely suggests that all drivers think
they own the road.

▶ Margaret Mead's book/*Coming of Age in Samoa*/stirred up

considerable controversy when it was published in 1928.

Since Mead wrote more than one book, the appositive contains
information essential to the meaning of the sentence.

Although commas should be used with distinctly parenthetical expressions (see 32f), do not use them to set off elements
that are only mildly parenthetical.

▶ Texting has/essentially/replaced e-mail for casual

communication.

33f Do not use a comma to set off a concluding adverb clause that is essential to the meaning of the sentence.

When adverb clauses introduce a sentence, they are nearly always
followed by a comma (see 32b). When they conclude a sentence,
however, they are not set off by commas if their content is essential to the meaning of the earlier part of the sentence. Adverb
clauses beginning with *after, as soon as, because, before, if, since,
unless, until,* and *when* are usually essential.

▶ Don't visit Paris at the height of the tourist season/unless

you have booked hotel reservations.

Without the *unless* clause, the meaning of the sentence might at first
seem broader than the writer intended.

When a concluding adverb clause is nonessential, it should
be preceded by a comma. Clauses beginning with *although, even
though, though,* and *whereas* are usually nonessential.

▶ The lecture seemed to last only a short time‸ although the

clock said it had gone on for more than an hour.

33g Do not use a comma after a phrase that begins an inverted sentence.

Though a comma belongs after most introductory phrases (see 32b), it does not belong after phrases that begin an inverted sentence. In an inverted sentence, the subject follows the verb, and a phrase that ordinarily would follow the verb is moved to the beginning (see 47c).

▶ At the bottom of the hill⁄sat the stubborn mule.

33h Avoid other common misuses of the comma.

Do not use a comma in the following situations.

AFTER A COORDINATING CONJUNCTION (*AND, BUT, OR, NOR, FOR, SO, YET*)

▶ Occasionally TV talk shows are performed live, but⁄more often they are taped.

AFTER *SUCH AS* OR *LIKE*

▶ Shade-loving plants such as⁄begonias, impatiens, and coleus can add color to a shady garden.

BEFORE *THAN*

▶ Touring Crete was more thrilling for us⁄than visiting the Greek islands frequented by the rich.

AFTER *ALTHOUGH*

▶ Although⁄the air was balmy, the water was too cold for swimming.

BEFORE A PARENTHESIS

▶ At InterComm, Sylvia began at the bottom⁄(with only three and a half walls and a swivel chair), but within three years she had been promoted to supervisor.

TO SET OFF AN INDIRECT (REPORTED) QUOTATION

▶ Samuel Goldwyn once said⁄that a verbal contract isn't worth

the paper it's written on.

WITH A QUESTION MARK OR AN EXCLAMATION POINT

▶ "Why don't you try it?⁄" she coaxed. "You can't do any worse

than the rest of us."

EXERCISE 33–1 Delete any unnecessary commas in the following sentences. If a sentence is correct, write "correct" after it. Answers to lettered sentences appear in the back of the book. Example:

In his Silk Road Project, Yo-Yo Ma incorporates work by

musicians such as⁄Kayhan Kahlor and Richard Danielpour.

a. After the morning rains cease, the swimmers emerge from their cottages.

b. Tricia's first artwork was a bright, blue, clay dolphin.

c. Some modern musicians, (trumpeter John Hassell is an example) blend several cultural traditions into a unique sound.

d. Myra liked hot, spicy foods such as, chili, kung pao chicken, and buffalo wings.

e. On the display screen, was a soothing pattern of light and shadow.

1. Mesquite, the hardest of the softwoods, grows primarily in the Southwest.

2. Jolie's parents encouraged independent thinking, but required respect for others' opinions.

3. The border guards told their sergeant, that their heat-sensing equipment was malfunctioning.

4. The streets that three hours later would be bumper to bumper with commuters, were quiet and empty except for a few prowling cats.

5. Some first-year architecture students, expect to design intricate structures immediately.

EXERCISE 33–2 Delete unnecessary commas in the following passage.

Each spring since 1970, New Orleans has hosted the Jazz and Heritage Festival, an event that celebrates the music, food, and culture, of the region. Although, it is often referred to as "Jazz Fest," the festival typically includes a wide variety of musical styles such as, gospel, Cajun, blues, zydeco, and, rock and roll. Famous musicians who have appeared regularly at Jazz Fest, include Dr. John, B. B. King, and Aretha Franklin. Large stages are set up throughout the fairgrounds in a way, that allows up to ten bands to play simultaneously without any sound overlap. Food tents are located throughout the festival, and offer popular, local dishes like crawfish Monica, jambalaya, and fried, green tomatoes. In 2009, New Orleans held its fortieth annual Jazz Fest. Fans, who could not attend the festival, still enjoyed the music by downloading MP3 files, and watching performances online.

34 The semicolon

The semicolon is used to connect major sentence elements of equal grammatical rank.

34a Use a semicolon between closely related independent clauses not joined with a coordinating conjunction.

When two independent clauses appear in one sentence, they are usually linked with a comma and a coordinating conjunction (*and, but, or, nor, for, so, yet*). The coordinating conjunction signals the relation between the clauses. If the clauses are closely related and the relation is clear without a conjunction, they may be linked with a semicolon instead.

> In film, a low-angle shot makes the subject look powerful; a high-angle shot does just the opposite.

A semicolon must be used whenever a coordinating conjunction has been omitted between independent clauses. To use merely a comma creates a type of run-on sentence known as a *comma splice.* (See 20.)

> ▶ In 1800, a traveler needed six weeks to get from New York City
>
> to Chicago **;** in 1860, the trip by railroad took only two days.

34b Use a semicolon between independent clauses linked with a transitional expression.

Transitional expressions include conjunctive adverbs and transitional phrases.

CONJUNCTIVE ADVERBS

accordingly	furthermore	moreover	still
also	hence	nevertheless	subsequently
anyway	however	next	then
besides	incidentally	nonetheless	therefore
certainly	indeed	now	thus
consequently	instead	otherwise	
conversely	likewise	similarly	
finally	meanwhile	specifically	

TRANSITIONAL PHRASES

after all	even so	in fact
as a matter of fact	for example	in other words
as a result	for instance	in the first place
at any rate	in addition	on the contrary
at the same time	in conclusion	on the other hand

When a transitional expression appears between independent clauses, it is preceded by a semicolon and usually followed by a comma.

▶ Many corals grow very gradually⌃**; in fact,** the creation of a

 coral reef can take centuries.

When a transitional expression appears in the middle or at the end of the second independent clause, the semicolon goes *between the clauses.*

▶ Biologists have observed laughter in primates other than

 humans⌃**;** chimpanzees, however, sound more like they are

 panting than laughing.

Transitional expressions should not be confused with the coordinating conjunctions *and, but, or, nor, for, so,* and *yet,* which are preceded by a comma when they link independent clauses. (See 32a.)

34c Use a semicolon between items in a series containing internal punctuation.

▶ Classic science fiction sagas are *Star Trek*, with Mr. Spock/;

Battlestar Galactica, with its Cylons/; and *Star Wars*, with

Han Solo, Luke Skywalker, and Darth Vader.

Without the semicolons, the reader would have to sort out the major groupings, distinguishing between important and less important pauses according to the logic of the sentence. By inserting semicolons at the major breaks, the writer does this work for the reader.

34d Avoid common misuses of the semicolon.

Do not use a semicolon in the following situations.

BETWEEN A SUBORDINATE CLAUSE AND THE REST OF THE SENTENCE

▶ Although children's literature was added to the National

Book Awards in 1969/, it has had its own award, the Newbery

Medal, since 1922.

BETWEEN AN APPOSITIVE AND THE WORD IT REFERS TO

▶ The scientists were fascinated by the species *Argyroneta*

aquatica/, a spider that lives underwater.

TO INTRODUCE A LIST

▶ Some of my favorite celebrities have their own blogs/:

Ashton Kutcher, Rosie O'Donnell, and Zach Braff.

BETWEEN INDEPENDENT CLAUSES JOINED BY *AND*, *BUT*, *OR*, *NOR*, *FOR*, *SO*, OR *YET*

▶ Five of the applicants had worked with spreadsheets⁁, but

only one was familiar with database management.

EXCEPTIONS: If at least one of the independent clauses contains internal punctuation, you may use a semicolon even though the clauses are joined with a coordinating conjunction.

> As a vehicle [the model T] was hard-working, commonplace, and heroic; and it often seemed to transmit those qualities to the person who rode in it. — E. B. White

Although a comma would also be correct in this sentence, the semicolon is more effective, for it indicates the relative weights of the pauses.

Occasionally, a semicolon may be used to emphasize a sharp contrast or a firm distinction between clauses joined with a coordinating conjunction.

> We hate some persons because we do not know them; and we will not know them because we hate them. — Charles Caleb Colton

EXERCISE 34–1 Add commas or semicolons where needed in the following well-known quotations. If a sentence is correct, write "correct" after it. Answers to lettered sentences appear in the back of the book. Example:

> If an animal does something⁁ we call it instinct⁏ if we do
>
> the same thing⁁ we call it intelligence. — Will Cuppy

a. Do not ask me to be kind just ask me to act as though I were.
   — Jules Renard

b. When men talk about defense they always claim to be protecting women and children but they never ask the women and children what they think. — Pat Schroeder

c. When I get a little money I buy books if any is left I buy food and clothes. — Desiderius Erasmus

d. America is a country that doesn't know where it is going but is determined to set a speed record getting there.
   — Lawrence J. Peter

e. Wit has truth in it wisecracking is simply calisthenics with words.
— Dorothy Parker

1. Standing in the middle of the road is very dangerous you get knocked down by the traffic from both sides.
— Margaret Thatcher

2. I do not believe in an afterlife, although I am bringing a change of underwear. — Woody Allen

3. Once the children were in the house the air became more vivid and more heated every object in the house grew more alive.
— Mary Gordon

4. We don't know what we want but we are ready to bite someone to get it. — Will Rogers

5. I've been rich and I've been poor rich is better. — Sophie Tucker

EXERCISE 34–2 Edit the following sentences to correct errors in the use of the comma and the semicolon. If a sentence is correct, write "correct" after it. Answers to lettered sentences appear in the back of the book. Example:

> Love is blind; envy has its eyes wide open.

a. Strong black coffee will not sober you up, the truth is that time is the only way to get alcohol out of your system.

b. Margaret was not surprised to see hail and vivid lightning, conditions had been right for violent weather all day.

c. There is often a fine line between right and wrong; good and bad; truth and deception.

d. My mother always says that you can't learn common sense; either you're born with it or you're not.

e. Severe, unremitting pain is a ravaging force; especially when the patient tries to hide it from others.

1. Another delicious dish is the chef's special; a roasted duck rubbed with spices and stuffed with wild rice.

2. Martin Luther King Jr. had not always intended to be a preacher, initially, he had planned to become a lawyer.

3. We all assumed that the thief had been Jean's boyfriend; even though we had seen him only from the back.

4. The Victorians avoided the subject of sex but were obsessed with death, a hundred years later, people were obsessed with sex but avoided thinking about death.

5. Some educators believe that African American history should be taught in separate courses, others prefer to see it integrated into survey courses.

The colon

The colon is used primarily to call attention to the words that follow it. In addition, the colon has some conventional uses.

35a Use a colon after an independent clause to direct attention to a list, an appositive, a quotation, or a summary or an explanation.

A LIST

The daily routine should include at least the following: twenty knee bends, fifty sit-ups, and five minutes of running in place.

AN APPOSITIVE

My roommate is guilty of two of the seven deadly sins: gluttony and sloth.

A QUOTATION

Consider the words of Benjamin Franklin: "There never was a good war or a bad peace."

A SUMMARY OR AN EXPLANATION

Faith is like love: It cannot be forced.

The novel is clearly autobiographical: The author even gives his own name to the main character.

NOTE: For other ways of introducing quotations, see "Introducing quoted material" on pages 329–31. When an independent clause follows a colon, begin with a capital letter. Some disciplines use a lowercase letter instead. See 45f for variations.

35b Use a colon according to convention.

SALUTATION IN A LETTER   Dear Sir or Madam:

HOURS AND MINUTES   5:30 p.m.

PROPORTIONS   The ratio of women to men was 2:1.

TITLE AND SUBTITLE   *The Glory of Hera: Greek Mythology and the Greek Family*

BIBLIOGRAPHIC ENTRIES   Boston: Bedford, 2009

NOTE: In biblical references, a colon is ordinarily used between chapter and verse (Luke 2:14). The Modern Language Association (MLA) recommends a period instead (Luke 2.14).

35c Avoid common misuses of the colon.

A colon must be preceded by a full independent clause. Therefore, avoid using it in the following situations.

BETWEEN A VERB AND ITS OBJECT OR COMPLEMENT

▶ Some important vitamins found in vegetables are: vitamin A,

thiamine, niacin, and vitamin C.

BETWEEN A PREPOSITION AND ITS OBJECT

▶ The heart's two pumps each consist of: an upper chamber,

or atrium, and a lower chamber, or ventricle.

AFTER *SUCH AS, INCLUDING,* **OR** *FOR EXAMPLE*

▶ The NCAA regulates college athletic teams, including:

basketball, baseball, softball, and football.

EXERCISE 35–1   Edit the following sentences to correct errors in the use of the comma, the semicolon, or the colon. If a sentence is correct, write "correct" after it. Answers to lettered sentences appear in the back of the book. Example:

Lifting the cover gently, Luca found the source of the odd

sound: a marble in the gears.

a. We always looked forward to Thanksgiving in Vermont: It was our only chance to see our Grady cousins.
b. If we have come to fight, we are far too few, if we have come to die, we are far too many.
c. The travel package includes: a round-trip ticket to Athens, a cruise through the Cyclades, and all hotel accommodations.

d. The news article portrays the land use proposal as reckless; although 62 percent of the town's residents support it.

e. Psychologists Kindlon and Thompson (2000) offer parents a simple starting point for raising male children, "Teach boys that there are many ways to be a man" (p. 256).

1. Harry Potter prevails against pain and evil for one reason, his heart is pure.

2. While traveling through France, Rose visited: the Loire Valley, Chartres, the Louvre, and the McDonald's stand at the foot of the Eiffel Tower.

3. There are three types of leave; annual leave, used for vacations, sick leave, used for medical appointments and illness, and personal leave, used for a variety of personal reasons.

4. American poet Carl Sandburg once asked these three questions, "Who paid for my freedom? What was the price? And am I somehow beholden?"

5. Amelie had four goals: to be encouraging, to be effective, to be efficient, and to be elegant.

36 The apostrophe

36a Use an apostrophe to indicate that a noun is possessive.

Possessive nouns usually indicate ownership, as in *Tim's hat, the lawyer's desk,* or *someone's glove.* Frequently, however, ownership is only loosely implied: *the tree's roots, a day's work.* If you are not sure whether a noun is possessive, try turning it into an *of* phrase: *the roots of the tree, the work of a day.*

When to add -'s

1. If the noun does not end in *-s*, add *-'s*.

   Luck often propels a rock musician's career.

   The Children's Defense Fund is a nonprofit organization that supports programs for poor and minority children.

2. If the noun is singular and ends in *-s* or an *s* sound, add *-'s* to indicate possession.

> Lois's sister spent last year in India.

> Her article presents an overview of Marx's teachings.

NOTE: To avoid potentially awkward pronunciation, some writers use only the apostrophe with a singular noun ending in *-s*: *Sophocles'*.

When to add only an apostrophe

If the noun is plural and ends in *-s*, add only an apostrophe.

> Both diplomats' briefcases were searched by guards.

Joint possession

To show joint possession, use *-'s* or (*-s'*) with the last noun only; to show individual possession, make all nouns possessive.

> Have you seen Joyce and Greg's new camper?

> John's and Marie's expectations of marriage couldn't have been more different.

Joyce and Greg jointly own one camper. John and Marie individually have different expectations.

Compound nouns

If a noun is compound, use *-'s* (or *-s'*) with the last element.

> My father-in-law's memoir about his childhood in Sri Lanka was published in October.

36b Use an apostrophe and -s to indicate that an indefinite pronoun is possessive.

Indefinite pronouns refer to no specific person or thing: *everyone, someone, no one, something*. (See 46b.)

> Someone's raincoat has been left behind.

36c Use an apostrophe to mark omissions in contractions and numbers.

In a contraction, the apostrophe takes the place of one or more missing letters.

> It's a shame that Frank can't go on the tour.

It's stands for *it is*, *can't* for *cannot*.

The apostrophe is also used to mark the omission of the first two digits of a year (*the class of '08*) or years (*the '60s generation*).

36d Do not use an apostrophe to form the plural of numbers, letters, abbreviations, and words mentioned as words.

An apostrophe typically is not used to pluralize numbers, letters, abbreviations, and words mentioned as words. Note the few exceptions and be consistent throughout your paper.

Plural of numbers

Do not use an apostrophe in the plural of any numbers, including decades.

> Oksana skated nearly perfect figure 8s.

> The 1920s are known as the Jazz Age.

Plural of letters

Italicize the letter and use roman (regular) font style for the *-s* ending. Do not italicize academic grades.

> Two large *J*s were painted on the door.

> He received two Ds for the first time in his life.

EXCEPTIONS: To avoid misreading, use an apostrophe to form the plural of lowercase letters and the capital letters *A* and *I*.

> Beginning readers often confuse *b*'s and *d*'s.

> Students with straight A's earn high honors.

MLA NOTE: The Modern Language Association recommends using an apostrophe for the plural of both capital and lowercase letters: *J*'s, *p*'s.

Plural of abbreviations

Do not use an apostrophe to pluralize an abbreviation.

> Harriet has thirty DVDs on her desk.

> Marco earned two PhDs before his thirtieth birthday.

Plural of words mentioned as words

Generally, omit the apostrophe to form the plural of words mentioned as words. If the word is italicized, the *-s* ending appears in roman (regular) type.

> We've heard enough *maybe*s.

Words mentioned as words may also appear in quotation marks. When you choose this option, use the apostrophe.

> We've heard enough "maybe's."

36e Avoid common misuses of the apostrophe.

Do not use an apostrophe in the following situations.

WITH NOUNS THAT ARE NOT POSSESSIVE

>   *outpatients*
> ▶ Some ~~outpatient's~~ have special parking permits.

IN THE POSSESSIVE PRONOUNS *ITS, WHOSE, HIS, HERS, OURS, YOURS,* AND *THEIRS*

>   *its*
> ▶ Each area has ~~it's~~ own conference room.

> *It's* means "it is." The possessive pronoun *its* contains no apostrophe despite the fact that it is possessive.

> ▶ *The House on Mango Street* was written by Sandra Cisneros,
>   *whose*
> ~~who's~~ work focuses on the Latino community in the
> United States.

> *Who's* means "who is." The possessive pronoun is *whose*.

EXERCISE 36–1   Edit the following sentences to correct errors in the use of the apostrophe. If a sentence is correct, write "correct" after it. Answers to lettered sentences appear in the back of the book. Example:

> _Richard's_
> **Our favorite barbecue restaurant is Poor ~~Richards~~ Ribs.**
> ^

a. This diet will improve almost anyone's health.

b. The innovative shoe fastener was inspired by the designers young son.

c. Each days menu features a different European country's dish.

d. Sue worked overtime to increase her families earnings.

e. Ms. Jacobs is unwilling to listen to students complaints about computer failures.

1. Siddhartha sat by the river and listened to its many voices.

2. Three teenage son's can devour about as much food as four full-grown field hands. The only difference is that they dont do half as much work.

3. The small biotech company has contracts with NASA and other government agency's.

4. Patience and humor are key tools in a travelers survival kit.

5. My sister-in-law's quilts are being shown at the Fendrick Gallery.

EXERCISE 36–2   Edit the following passage to correct errors in the use of the apostrophe.

> Its never too soon to start holiday shopping. In fact, some people choose to start shopping as early as January, when last seasons leftover's are priced at their lowest. Many stores try to lure customers in with promise's of savings up to 90 percent. Their main objective, of course, is to make way for next years inventory. The big problem with postholiday shopping, though, is that there isn't much left to choose from. Store's shelves have been picked over by last-minute shoppers desperately searching for gifts. The other problem is that its hard to know what to buy so far in advance. Next year's hot items are anyones guess. But proper timing, mixed with lot's of luck and determination, can lead to good purchases at great price's.

37 Quotation marks

Writers use quotation marks primarily to enclose direct quotations of another person's spoken or written words. You will also find these other uses and exceptions:

- for quotations within quotations (single quotation marks: 37b)
- for titles of short works (37c)
- for words used as words (37d)
- with other marks of punctuation (37e)
- with brackets and ellipsis marks (39c–39d)
- no quotation marks for long quotations (p. 327)
- no quotation marks for indirect quotations, summaries, and paraphrases (p. 327)

37a Use quotation marks to enclose direct quotations.

Direct quotations of a person's words, whether spoken or written, must be in quotation marks.

> "The contract negotiations are stalled," the airline executive told reporters, "but I am prepared to work night and day to bring both sides together."

In dialogue, begin a new paragraph to mark a change in speaker.

> "Mom, his name is Willie, not William. A thousand times I've told you, it's *Willie.*"
> "Willie is a derivative of William, Lester. Surely his birth certificate doesn't have Willie on it, and I like calling people by their proper names."
> "Yes, it does, ma'am. My mother named me Willie K. Mason."
> — Gloria Naylor

If a single speaker utters more than one paragraph, introduce each paragraph with a quotation mark, but do not use a closing quotation mark until the end of the speech.

with direct quotations • not with indirect or
indented quotations • for quotation within a quotation
" "
37b 327

Exception: indirect quotations

Do not use quotation marks around indirect quotations. An indirect quotation reports someone's ideas without using that person's exact words. In academic writing, indirect quotation is called *paraphrase* or *summary*. (See p. 452.)

> The airline executive told reporters that although contract negotiations were at a standstill, she was prepared to work hard with both labor and management to bring about a settlement.

Exception: long quotations

Long quotations of prose or poetry are generally set off from the text by indenting. Quotation marks are not used because the indented format tells readers that the quotation is taken word-for-word from the source.

> After making an exhaustive study of the historical record, James Horan evaluates Billy the Kid like this:
>
>> The portrait that emerges of [the Kid] from the thousands of pages of affidavits, reports, trial transcripts, his letters, and his testimony is neither the mythical Robin Hood nor the stereotyped adenoidal moron and pathological killer. Rather Billy appears as a disturbed, lonely young man, honest, loyal to his friends, dedicated to his beliefs, and betrayed by our institutions and the corrupt, ambitious, and compromising politicians in his time. (158)

The number in parentheses is a citation handled according to MLA style. (See p. 465.)

MLA and APA have specific guidelines for what constitutes a long quotation and how it should be indented (see pp. 471 and 545, respectively).

37b Use single quotation marks to enclose a quotation within a quotation.

> Megan Marshall notes that what Elizabeth Peabody "hoped to accomplish in her school was not merely 'teaching' but 'educating children morally and spiritually as well as intellectually from the first'" (107).

37c Use quotation marks around the titles of short works.

Short works include newspaper and magazine articles, poems, short stories, songs, episodes of television and radio programs, and chapters or subdivisions of books.

> James Baldwin's story "Sonny's Blues" tells the story of two brothers who come to understand each other's suffering.

NOTE: Titles of books, plays, Web sites, television and radio programs, films, magazines, and newspapers are put in italics. (See 42a.)

37d Quotation marks may be used to set off words used as words.

Although words used as words are ordinarily italicized (see 42d), quotation marks are also acceptable. Be consistent throughout your paper.

> The words "accept" and "except" are frequently confused.

> The words *accept* and *except* are frequently confused.

37e Use punctuation with quotation marks according to convention.

This section describes the conventions American publishers use in placing various marks of punctuation inside or outside quotation marks. It also explains how to punctuate when introducing quoted material.

Periods and commas

Place periods and commas inside quotation marks.

> "I'm here as part of my service-learning project," I told the classroom teacher. "I'm hoping to become a reading specialist."

This rule applies to single quotation marks as well as double quotation marks. (See 37b.) It also applies to all uses of quotation marks: for quoted material, for titles of works, and for words used as words.

EXCEPTION: In the Modern Language Association's style of parenthetical in-text citations (see p. 465), the period follows the citation in parentheses.

> James M. McPherson comments, approvingly, that the Whigs "were not averse to extending the blessings of American liberty, even to Mexicans and Indians" (48).

Colons and semicolons

Put colons and semicolons outside quotation marks.

> Harold wrote, "I regret that I am unable to attend the fundraiser for AIDS research"; his letter, however, came with a substantial contribution.

Question marks and exclamation points

Put question marks and exclamation points inside quotation marks unless they apply to the whole sentence.

> Contrary to tradition, bedtime at my house is marked by "Mommy, can I tell you a story now?"

> Have you heard the old proverb "Do not climb the hill until you reach it"?

In the first sentence, the question mark applies only to the quoted question. In the second sentence, the question mark applies to the whole sentence.

NOTE: In MLA style for a quotation that ends with a question mark or an exclamation point, the parenthetical citation and a period should follow the entire quotation.

> Rosie Thomas asks, "Is nothing in life ever straight and clear, the way children see it?" (77).

Introducing quoted material

After a word group introducing a quotation, choose a colon, a comma, or no punctuation at all, whichever is appropriate in context. See page 330.

Formal introduction   If a quotation is formally introduced, a colon is appropriate. A formal introduction is a full independent clause, not just an expression such as *he said* or *she remarked*.

> Thomas Friedman provides a challenging yet optimistic view of the future: "We need to get back to work on our country and on our planet. The hour is late, the stakes couldn't be higher, the project couldn't be harder, the payoff couldn't be greater" (25).

Expression such as *he said*   If a quotation is introduced with an expression such as *he said* or *she remarked* — or if it is followed by such an expression — a comma is needed.

> About New England's weather, Mark Twain once declared, "In the spring I have counted one hundred and thirty-six different kinds of weather within four and twenty hours" (55).

> "Unless another war is prevented it is likely to bring destruction on a scale never before held possible and even now hardly conceived," Albert Einstein wrote in the aftermath of the atomic bomb (29).

Blended quotation   When a quotation is blended into the writer's own sentence, either a comma or no punctuation is appropriate, depending on the way in which the quotation fits into the sentence structure.

> The future champion could, as he put it, "float like a butterfly and sting like a bee."

> Virginia Woolf wrote in 1928 that "a woman must have money and a room of her own if she is to write fiction; and that, as you will see, leaves the great problem of the true nature of woman and the true nature of fiction unsolved" (4).

Beginning of sentence   If a quotation appears at the beginning of a sentence, use a comma after it unless the quotation ends with a question mark or an exclamation point.

> "I've always thought of myself as a reporter," claimed American poet Gwendolyn Brooks (162).

> "What is it?" she asked, bracing herself.

Interrupted quotation   If a quoted sentence is interrupted by explanatory words, use commas to set off the explanatory words.

> "With regard to air travel," Stephen Ambrose notes, "Jefferson was a full century ahead of the curve" (53).

If two successive quoted sentences from the same source are interrupted by explanatory words, use a comma before the explanatory words and a period after them.

> "Everyone agrees journalists must tell the truth," Bill Kovach and Tom Rosenstiel write. "Yet people are befuddled about what 'the truth' means" (37).

37f Avoid common misuses of quotation marks.

Do not use quotation marks to draw attention to familiar slang, to disown trite expressions, or to justify an attempt at humor.

▶ The economist estimated that single-family home prices would decline another 5 percent by the end of the year, emphasizing that this was only a ~~"~~ballpark figure.~~"~~

Do not use quotation marks around the title of your own essay.

EXERCISE 37–1   Add or delete quotation marks as needed and make any other changes in punctuation in the following sentences. If a sentence is correct, write "correct" after it. Answers to lettered sentences appear in the back of the book. Example:

Gandhi once said, ^"An eye for an eye only ends up making the whole world blind.^"

a. As for the advertisement "Sailors have more fun", if you consider chipping paint and swabbing decks fun, then you will have plenty of it.

b. Even after forty minutes of discussion, our class could not agree on an interpretation of Robert Frost's poem "The Road Not Taken."

c. After winning the lottery, Juanita said that "she would give half the money to charity."

d. After the movie, Vicki said, "The reviewer called this flick "trash of the first order." I guess you can't believe everything you read."

e. "Cleaning your house while your kids are still growing," said Phyllis Diller, "is like shoveling the walk before it stops snowing."

1. "That's the most beautiful seashell I've ever seen!", shouted Alexa.

2. "Get your head in the game, and the rest will come" advised the coach just before the whistle.

3. Gloria Steinem once twisted an old proverb like this, "A woman without a man is like a fish without a bicycle."

4. "Even when freshly washed and relieved of all obvious confections," says Fran Lebowitz, "children tend to be sticky."

5. Have you heard the Cowboy Junkies' cover of Hank Williams's "I'm So Lonesome I Could Cry?"

EXERCISE 37–2   Add or delete quotation marks as needed and make any other necessary changes in punctuation in the following passage. Citations should conform to MLA style (see 57a).

In his article The Moment of Truth, former vice president Al Gore argues that global warming is a genuine threat to life on Earth and that we must act now to avoid catastrophe. Gore calls our situation a "true *planetary emergency*" and cites scientific evidence of the greenhouse effect and its consequences (170-71). "What is at stake, Gore insists, is the survival of our civilization and the habitability of the Earth (197)." With such a grim predicament at hand, Gore questions why so many political and economic leaders are reluctant to act. "Is it simply more convenient to ignore the warnings," he asks (171)?

The crisis, of course, will not go away if we just pretend it isn't there. Gore points out that in Chinese two symbols form the character for the word crisis. The first of those symbols means "danger", and the second means "opportunity." The danger we face, he claims, is accompanied by "unprecedented opportunity." (172) Gore contends that throughout history we have won battles against seemingly unbeatable evils such as slavery and fascism and that we did so by facing the truth and choosing the moral high ground. Gore's final appeal is to our humanity:

> "Ultimately, [the fight to end global warming] is not about any scientific discussion or political dialogue; it is about who we are as human beings. It is about our capacity to transcend our limitations, to rise to this new occasion. To see with our hearts, as well as our heads, the response that is now called for." (244)

Gore feels that the fate of our world rests in our own hands, and his hope is that we will make the choice to save the planet. Source of quotations: Al Gore; "The Moment of Truth"; *Vanity Fair* May 2006: 170+; print.

38 End punctuation

38a The period

Use a period to end all sentences except direct questions or genuine exclamations. Also use periods in abbreviations according to convention.

To end sentences

Most sentences should end with a period. Problems sometimes arise when a writer must choose between a period and a question mark or between a period and an exclamation point.

If a sentence reports a question instead of asking it directly, it should end with a period, not a question mark.

▶ The professor asked whether talk therapy was more beneficial

than antidepressants~~?~~.
      ∧

If a sentence is not a genuine exclamation, it should end with a period, not an exclamation point. (See also 38c.)

▶ After years of working her way through school, Geeta finally

graduated with high honors~~!~~.
      ∧

In abbreviations

A period is conventionally used in abbreviations of titles and Latin words or phrases, including the time designations for morning and afternoon.

Mr.	i.e.	a.m. (or AM)
Ms.	e.g.	p.m. (or PM)
Dr.	etc.	

NOTE: If a sentence ends with a period marking an abbreviation, do not add a second period.

Do not use a period with US Postal Service abbreviations for states: MD, TX, CA.

Current usage is to omit the period in abbreviations of organization names, academic degrees, and designations for eras.

NATO	UNESCO	UCLA	BS	BC
IRS	AFL-CIO	NIH	PhD	BCE

38b The question mark

A direct question should be followed by a question mark.

> What is the horsepower of a 777 engine?

If a polite request is written in the form of a question, it may be followed by a period.

> Would you please send me your catalog of lilies.

TIP: Do not use a question mark after an indirect question, one that is reported rather than asked directly. Use a period instead.

▶ He asked me who was teaching the mythology course this year?.

NOTE: Questions in a series may be followed by question marks even when they are not complete sentences.

> We wondered where Calamity had hidden this time. Under the sink? Behind the furnace? On top of the bookcase?

38c The exclamation point

Use an exclamation point after a word group or sentence to express exceptional feeling or to provide special emphasis. The exclamation point is rarely appropriate in academic writing.

> When Gloria entered the room, I switched on the lights, and we all yelled, "Surprise!"

TIP: Do not overuse the exclamation point.

▶ In the fisherman's memory, the fish lives on, increasing in

length and weight with each passing year, until at last it is

big enough to shade a fishing boat!.

This sentence doesn't need to be pumped up with an exclamation point. It is emphatic enough without it.

▶ Whenever I see my favorite hitter, Derek Lee, up at bat,

I dream of making it to the big leagues! My team would

win every time!

The first exclamation point should be deleted so that the second one will have more force.

EXERCISE 38–1   Add appropriate end punctuation in the following paragraph.

Although I am generally rational, I am superstitious I never walk under ladders or put shoes on the table If I spill the salt, I go into frenzied calisthenics picking up the grains and tossing them over my left shoulder As a result of these curious activities, I've always wondered whether knowing the roots of superstitions would quell my irrational responses Superstition has it, for example, that one should never place a hat on the bed This superstition arises from a time when head lice were common and placing a guest's hat on the bed stood a good chance of spreading lice through the host's bed Doesn't this make good sense And doesn't it stand to reason that, if I know that my guests don't have lice, I shouldn't care where their hats go Of course it does It is fair to ask, then, whether I have changed my ways and place hats on beds Are you kidding I wouldn't put a hat on a bed if my life depended on it

39 Other punctuation marks: the dash, parentheses, brackets, the ellipsis mark, the slash

39a The dash

When typing, use two hyphens to form a dash (--). Do not put spaces before or after the dash. If your word processing program has what is known as an "em-dash" (—), you may use it instead, with no space before or after it. Dashes are used for the following purposes.

To set off parenthetical material that deserves emphasis

Everything that went wrong—from the peeping Tom at her window last night to my head-on collision today—we blamed on our move.

To set off appositives that contain commas

An appositive is a noun or noun phrase that renames a nearby noun. Ordinarily most appositives are set off with commas (32e), but when the appositive itself contains commas, a pair of dashes helps readers see the relative importance of all the pauses.

> In my hometown, people's basic needs — food, clothing, and shelter — are less costly than in a big city like Los Angeles.

To introduce a list, a restatement, an amplification, or a dramatic shift in tone or thought

> Along the wall are the bulk liquids — sesame seed oil, honey, safflower oil, and that half-liquid "peanuts only" peanut butter.

> In his last semester, Peter tried to pay more attention to his priorities — applying to graduate school and getting financial aid.

> Everywhere we looked there were little kids — a bag of Skittles in one hand and their mommy or daddy's sleeve in the other.

> Kiere took a few steps back, came running full speed, kicked a mighty kick — and missed the ball.

In the first two examples, the writer could also use a colon. (See 35a.) The colon is more formal than the dash and not quite as dramatic.

TIP: Unless there is a specific reason for using the dash, avoid it. Unnecessary dashes create a choppy effect.

> ▶ Insisting that students use computers as instructional
>
> tools ⟋ for information retrieval ⟋ makes good sense. Herding
>
> them ⟋ sheeplike ⟋ into computer technology does not.

39b Parentheses

Use parentheses to enclose supplemental material, minor digressions, and afterthoughts.

> Nurses record patients' vital signs (temperature, pulse, and blood pressure) several times a day.

Use parentheses to enclose letters or numbers labeling items in a series.

> Regulations stipulated that only the following equipment could be used on the survival mission: (1) a knife, (2) thirty feet of parachute line, (3) a book of matches, (4) two ponchos, (5) an E tool, and (6) a signal flare.

TIP: Do not overuse parentheses. Rough drafts are likely to contain more afterthoughts than necessary. As writers head into a sentence, they often think of additional details, occasionally working them in as best they can with parentheses. Usually such sentences should be revised so that the additional details no longer seem to be afterthoughts.

> ► Researchers have said that seventeen million ~~(estimates run~~ *from*
>
> ~~as high as~~ twenty-three million) Americans have diabetes. *to*

39c Brackets

Use brackets to enclose any words or phrases that you have inserted into an otherwise word-for-word quotation.

> *Audubon* reports that "if there are not enough young to balance deaths, the end of the species [California condor] is inevitable" (4).

The sentence quoted from the *Audubon* article did not contain the words *California condor* (since the context of the full article made clear what species was meant), so the writer needed to add the name in brackets.

The Latin word "sic" in brackets indicates that an error in a quoted sentence appears in the original source.

> According to the review, Nelly Furtado's performance was brilliant, "exceding [sic] the expectations of even her most loyal fans."

Do not overuse "sic," however, since calling attention to others' mistakes can appear snobbish. The preceding quotation, for example, might have been paraphrased instead: *According to the review, even Nelly Furtado's most loyal fans were surprised by the brilliance of her performance.*

39d The ellipsis mark

The ellipsis mark consists of three spaced periods. Use an ellipsis mark to indicate that you have deleted words from an otherwise word-for-word quotation.

> Shute (2010) acknowledges that treatment for autism can be expensive: "Sensory integration therapy . . . can cost up to $200 an hour" (82).

If you delete a full sentence or more in the middle of a quoted passage, use a period before the three ellipsis dots.

> "If we don't properly train, teach, or treat our growing prison population," says long-time reform advocate Luis Rodríguez, "somebody else will. . . . This may well be the safety issue of the new century" (16).

TIP: Ordinarily, do not use the ellipsis mark at the beginning or at the end of a quotation. Readers will understand that the quoted material is taken from a longer passage. If you have cut some words from the end of the final quoted sentence, however, MLA requires an ellipsis mark.

In quoted poetry, use a full line of ellipsis dots to indicate that you have dropped a line or more from the poem, as in this example from "To His Coy Mistress" by Andrew Marvell:

> Had we but world enough, and time,
> This coyness, lady, were no crime.
> . . . .
> But at my back I always hear
> Time's wingèd chariot hurrying near; (1-2, 21-22)

The ellipsis mark may also be used for other purposes — to indicate a hesitation or an interruption in speech or to suggest unfinished thoughts.

> "The apartment building next door . . . it's going up in flames!" yelled Marcia.

> Before falling into a coma, the victim whispered, "It was a man with a tattoo on his . . . "

39e The slash

Use the slash to separate two or three lines of poetry that have been run into your text. Add a space both before and after the slash.

> In the opening lines of "Jordan," George Herbert pokes gentle fun at popular poems of his time: "Who says that fictions only and false hair / Become a verse? Is there in truth no beauty?" (1-2).

More than three lines of poetry should be handled as an indented quotation. (See p. 327.)

The slash may occasionally be used to separate paired terms such as *pass/fail* and *producer/director*. Do not use a space before or after the slash. Be sparing in this use of the slash. In particular, avoid the use of *and/or*, *he/she*, and *his/her*. Instead of using *he/she* and *his/her* to solve sexist language problems, you can usually find more graceful alternatives. (See 17e and 22a.)

EXERCISE 39–1 Edit the following sentences to correct errors in punctuation, focusing especially on appropriate use of the dash, parentheses, brackets, the ellipsis mark, and the slash. If a sentence is correct, write "correct" after it. Answers to lettered sentences appear in the back of the book. Example:

> Social insects/——bees, for example,/——are able to
> communicate complicated messages to one another.

a. A client left his/her cell phone in our conference room after the meeting.

b. The films we made of Kilauea — on our trip to Hawaii Volcanoes National Park — illustrate a typical spatter cone eruption.

c. Although he was confident in his course selections, Greg chose the pass/fail option for Chemistry 101.

d. Masahiro poked through his backpack — laptop, digital camera, guidebook — to make sure he was ready for a day's study at the Ryoanji Temple garden.

e. Of three engineering fields, chemical, mechanical, and materials, Keegan chose materials engineering for its application to toy manufacturing.

1. The old Valentine verse we used to chant says it all: "Sugar is sweet, / And so are you."

2. In studies in which mothers gazed down at their infants in their cribs but remained facially unresponsive, for example, not smiling, laughing, or showing any change of expression, the infants responded with intense weariness and eventual withdrawal.

3. There are three points of etiquette in poker: 1. always allow someone else to cut the cards, 2. don't forget to ante up, and 3. never stack your chips.

4. In *Lifeboat*, Alfred Hitchcock appears [some say without his knowledge] in a newspaper advertisement for weight loss.

5. The writer Chitra Divakaruni explained her work with other Indian American immigrants: "Many women who came to Maitri [a women's support group in San Francisco] needed to know simple things like opening a bank account or getting citizenship. . . . Many women in Maitri spoke English, but their English was functional rather than emotional. They needed someone who understands their problems and speaks their language."

Mechanics

40 Abbreviations

40a Use standard abbreviations for titles immediately before and after proper names.

TITLES BEFORE PROPER NAMES	TITLES AFTER PROPER NAMES
Mr. Rafael Zabala	William Albert Sr.
Ms. Nancy Linehan	Thomas Hines Jr.
Mrs. Edward Horn	Anita Lor, PhD
Dr. Margaret Simmons	Robert Simkowski, MD
Rev. John Stone	Margaret Chin, LLD
Prof. James Russo	Polly Stein, DDS

Do not abbreviate a title if it is not used with a proper name.

▶ My history ~~prof.~~ *professor* is an expert on race relations in South Africa.

Avoid redundant titles such as *Dr. Amy Day, MD*. Choose one title or the other: *Dr. Amy Day* or *Amy Day, MD*.

40b Use abbreviations only when you are sure your readers will understand them.

Familiar abbreviations, written without periods, are acceptable.

CIA	FBI	MD	NAACP
NBA	CEO	PhD	CD-ROM
YMCA	CBS	USA	ESL

Talk show host Conan O'Brien is a Harvard graduate with a BA in history.

The YMCA has opened a new gym close to my office.

NOTE: When using an unfamiliar abbreviation (such as NASW for National Association of Social Workers) throughout a paper, write the full name followed by the abbreviation in parentheses at the first mention of the name. Then use just the abbreviation throughout the rest of the paper.

for titles with names (*Dr., Prof.*) • for familiar terms (*YMCA, FBI*) • dates • times of day • money • Latin (*e.g., et al.*)

abbr

40d   343

40c Use *BC*, *AD*, *a.m.*, *p.m.*, *No.*, and *$* only with specific dates, times, numbers, and amounts.

The abbreviation *BC* ("before Christ") follows a date, and *AD* ("*anno Domini*") precedes a date. Acceptable alternatives are *BCE* ("before the common era") and *CE* ("common era"), both of which follow a date.

40 BC (or 40 BCE)	4:00 a.m. (or AM)	No. 12 (or no. 12)
AD 44 (or 44 CE)	6:00 p.m. (or PM)	$150

Avoid using *a.m.*, *p.m.*, *No.*, or *$* when not accompanied by a specific figure.

▶ The governor argued that the new sales tax would raise
  money
  much-needed $ for the state.
              ^

40d Be sparing in your use of Latin abbreviations.

Latin abbreviations are acceptable in footnotes and bibliographies and in informal writing for comments in parentheses.

cf. (Latin *confer*, "compare")

e.g. (Latin *exempli gratia*, "for example")

et al. (Latin *et alia*, "and others")

etc. (Latin *et cetera*, "and so forth")

i.e. (Latin *id est*, "that is")

N.B. (Latin *nota bene*, "note well")

Harold Simms et al., *The Race for Space*

Alfred Hitchcock directed many classic thrillers (e.g., *Psycho*, *Rear Window*, and *Vertigo*).

In formal writing, use the appropriate English phrases.

▶ Many obsolete laws remain on the books. A law in
       for example,
  Vermont, ~~e.g.,~~ forbids an unmarried man and woman to
          ^
  sit closer than six inches apart on a park bench.

40e Avoid inappropriate abbreviations.

In formal writing, abbreviations for the following are not commonly accepted: personal names, units of measurement, days of the week, holidays, months, courses of study, divisions of written works, states, and countries (except in complete addresses and except Washington, DC). Do not abbreviate *Company* and *Incorporated* unless their abbreviated forms are part of an official name.

PERSONAL NAMES   Charles (not Chas.)

UNITS OF MEASUREMENT   feet (not ft.)

DAYS OF THE WEEK   Monday (not Mon.)

HOLIDAYS   Christmas (not Xmas)

MONTHS   January, February, March (not Jan., Feb., Mar.)

COURSES OF STUDY   political science (not poli. sci.)

DIVISIONS OF WRITTEN WORKS   chapter, page (not ch., p.)

STATES AND COUNTRIES   Massachusetts (not MA or Mass.)

PARTS OF A BUSINESS NAME   Adams Lighting Company (not Adams Lighting Co.); Kim and Brothers (not Kim and Bros.)

▶ The American Red Cross requires that blood donors be at

least seventeen ~~yrs.~~ *years* old, weigh at least 110 ~~lb.,~~ *pounds,* and not

have given blood in the past eight ~~wks.~~ *weeks.*

EXCEPTION: Abbreviate states and provinces in complete addresses, and always abbreviate *DC* when used with *Washington*.

EXERCISE 40–1   Edit the following sentences to correct errors in abbreviations. If a sentence is correct, write "correct" after it. Answers to lettered sentences appear in the back of the book. Example:

This year ~~Xmas~~ *Christmas* will fall on a ~~Tues.~~ *Tuesday.*

a. Since its inception, the BBC has maintained a consistently high standard of radio and television broadcasting.

b. Some combat soldiers are trained by govt. diplomats to be sensitive to issues of culture, history, and religion.

c. Mahatma Gandhi has inspired many modern leaders, including Martin Luther King Jr.

d. How many lb. have you lost since you began running four miles a day?

e. Denzil spent all night studying for his psych. exam.

1. My favorite prof., Dr. Barker, is on sabbatical this semester.

2. When we visited NYU in early September, we were charmed by the lull of summer crickets in Washington Square Park.

3. Some historians think that the New Testament was completed by AD 100.

4. My mother's birthday was on Fri. the 13th this year.

5. Some first-time Flash users panic before the complex menus — i.e., they develop a blank stare and the tingling of a migraine.

41 Numbers

41a Follow the conventions in your discipline for spelling out or using numerals to express numbers.

In the humanities, which generally follow Modern Language Association (MLA) style, use numerals only for specific numbers above one hundred: *353, 1,020*. Spell out numbers one hundred and below and large round numbers: *eleven, thirty-five, sixty, fifteen million*.

The social sciences, which follow American Psychological Association (APA) style, use numerals for all but the numbers one through nine.

In all fields, treat related numbers in a passage consistently: *The survey found that 89 of 157 respondents had not taken any courses related to alcohol use.*

When one number immediately follows another, spelling out one number and using numerals for the other is usually effective: *three 100-meter events, 25 four-poster beds.*

▶ It's been ~~8~~ *eight* years since I visited Peru.

▶ Enrollment in the charter school in its first year will be limited to ~~three hundred forty~~ *340* students.

If a sentence begins with a number, spell out the number or rewrite the sentence.

> *One hundred fifty*
> ~~150~~ children in our program need expensive dental treatment.
>   ^

Rewriting the sentence will also correct the error and may be less awkward if the number is long: *In our program, 150 children need expensive dental treatment.*

41b Use numerals according to convention in dates, addresses, and so on.

DATES   July 4, 1776; 56 BC; AD 30

ADDRESSES   77 Latches Lane, 519 West 42nd Street

PERCENTAGES   55 percent (or 55%)

FRACTIONS, DECIMALS   ½, 0.047

SCORES   7 to 3, 21–18

STATISTICS   average age 37, average weight 180

SURVEYS   4 out of 5

EXACT AMOUNTS OF MONEY $105.37, $106,000

DIVISIONS OF BOOKS   volume 3, chapter 4, page 189

DIVISIONS OF PLAYS   act 3, scene 3 (or act III, scene iii)

IDENTIFICATION NUMBERS   serial number 10988675

TIME OF DAY   4:00 p.m., 1:30 a.m.

>   *$430,000*
> The foundation raised ~~four hundred thirty thousand dollars~~
>   ^
> for cancer research.

NOTE: When not using *a.m.* or *p.m.*, write out the time in words (*two o'clock in the afternoon, twelve noon, seven in the morning*).

EXERCISE 41–1   Edit the following sentences to correct errors in the use of numbers. If a sentence is correct, write "correct" after it. Answers to lettered sentences appear in the back of the book. Example:

>   *$3.06*
> By the end of the evening, Ashanti had only ~~three dollars~~
>   ^
> ~~and six cents~~ left.

a. The carpenters located 3 maple timbers, 21 sheets of cherry, and 10 oblongs of polished ebony for the theater set.

b. The program's cost is well over one billion dollars.

c. The score was tied at 5–5 when the momentum shifted and carried the Standards to a decisive 12–5 win.

d. 8 students in the class had been labeled "learning disabled."

e. The Vietnam Veterans Memorial in Washington, DC, had fifty-eight thousand one hundred thirty-two names inscribed on it when it was dedicated in 1982.

1. One of my favorite scenes in Shakespeare is the property division scene in act 1 of *King Lear*.

2. The botany lecture will begin at precisely 3:30 p.m.

3. 40 percent of all gamers in the United States are women.

4. In two thousand twelve, the world population may reach 7 billion.

5. On a normal day, I spend at least 4 to 5 hours surfing the Internet.

42 Italics

This section describes conventional uses for italics. While italics is accepted by both style guides covered in this handbook (MLA and APA), some instructors may prefer underlining in student papers. If that is the case in your course, simply substitute underlining for italics in the examples in this section.

Some computer and online applications do not allow for italics. To indicate words that should be italicized, you can use underscore marks or asterisks before and after the italic words.

I am planning to write my senior thesis on _The Kite Runner_.

NOTE: Excessive use of italics to emphasize words or ideas, especially in academic writing, is distracting and should be avoided.

42a Italicize the titles of works according to convention.

Titles of the following types of works, including electronic works, should be italicized.

TITLES OF BOOKS *The Color Purple, Middlesex, Encarta*

MAGAZINES *Time, Scientific American, Salon.com*

NEWSPAPERS the *Baltimore Sun,* the *Orlando Sentinel Online*

PAMPHLETS *Common Sense, Facts about Marijuana*

LONG POEMS *The Waste Land, Paradise Lost*

PLAYS *'Night Mother, Wicked*

FILMS *Casablanca, Do the Right Thing*

TELEVISION PROGRAMS *American Idol, Frontline*

RADIO PROGRAMS *All Things Considered*

MUSICAL COMPOSITIONS *Porgy and Bess*

CHOREOGRAPHIC WORKS *Brief Fling*

WORKS OF VISUAL ART *American Gothic*

ELECTRONIC DATABASES *ProQuest*

WEB SITES *ZDNet, Google*

ELECTRONIC GAMES *Everquest, Call of Duty*

The titles of other works, such as short stories, essays, episodes of radio and television programs, songs, and short poems, are enclosed in quotation marks. (See 37c.)

NOTE: Do not use italics when referring to the Bible, titles of books in the Bible (Genesis, not *Genesis*), or titles of legal documents (the Constitution, not the *Constitution*). Do not italicize the titles of computer software (Keynote, Photoshop). Do not italicize the title of your own paper.

42b Italicize the names of specific ships, spacecraft, and aircraft.

Queen Mary 2, Challenger, Spirit of St. Louis

The success of the Soviets' *Sputnik* energized the US space program.

42c Italicize foreign words used in an English sentence.

Shakespeare's Falstaff is a comic character known for both his excessive drinking and his general *joie de vivre*.

EXCEPTION: Do not italicize foreign words that have become a standard part of the English language — "laissez-faire," "fait accompli," "modus operandi," and "per diem," for example.

42d Italicize words mentioned as words, letters mentioned as letters, and numbers mentioned as numbers.

Tomás assured us that the chemicals could probably be safely mixed, but his *probably* stuck in our minds.

Some toddlers have trouble pronouncing the letters *f* and *s*.

A big *3* was painted on the stage door.

NOTE: Quotation marks may be used instead of italics to set off words mentioned as words. (See 37d.)

EXERCISE 42–1 Edit the following sentences to correct errors in the use of italics. If a sentence is correct, write "correct" after it. Answers to lettered sentences appear in the back of the book. Example:

We had a lively discussion about Gini Alhadeff's memoir

The Sun at Midday. Correct

a. Howard Hughes commissioned the Spruce Goose, a beautifully built but thoroughly impractical wooden aircraft.

b. The old man *screamed* his anger, *shouting* to all of us, "I will not leave my money to you worthless layabouts!"

c. I learned the Latin term ad infinitum from an old nursery rhyme about fleas: "Great fleas have little fleas upon their back to bite 'em, / Little fleas have lesser fleas and so on ad infinitum."

d. Cinema audiences once gasped at hearing the word *damn* in *Gone with the Wind*.

e. Neve Campbell's lifelong interest in ballet inspired her involvement in the film "The Company," which portrays a season with the Joffrey Ballet.

1. Yasmina spent a year painting white flowers in imitation of Georgia O'Keeffe's Calla Lilies.

2. On the monastery walls are murals depicting scenes from the book of Kings and the book of Proverbs.

3. My per diem allowance was $200.
4. Cecily watched in amazement as the tattoo artist made angles and swooping loops into the Gothic letter G.
5. The blend of poetic lyrics and progressive instruments on Seal's "Human Being" makes it one of my favorite CDs.

43 Spelling

You learned to spell from repeated experience with words in both reading and writing, but especially writing. Words have a look, a sound, and even a feel to them as the hand moves across the page or keyboard. As you proofread, you can probably tell if a word doesn't look quite right. In such cases, the solution is simple: Look up the word in the dictionary. (See 43b.)

43a Become familiar with the major spelling rules.

i before *e* except after *c*

In general, use *i* before *e* except after *c* and except when sounded like *ay*, as in *neighbor* and *weigh*.

I BEFORE E	relieve, believe, sieve, niece, fierce, frieze
E BEFORE I	receive, deceive, sleigh, freight, eight
EXCEPTIONS	seize, either, weird, height, foreign, leisure

Suffixes

Final silent -e   Generally, drop a final silent *-e* when adding a suffix that begins with a vowel. Keep the final *-e* if the suffix begins with a consonant.

combine, combination	achieve, achievement
desire, desiring	care, careful
prude, prudish	entire, entirety
remove, removable	gentle, gentleness

Words such as *changeable, judgment, argument,* and *truly* are exceptions.

Final -y When adding *-s* or *-d* to words ending in *-y*, ordinarily change *-y* to *-ie* when the *-y* is preceded by a consonant but not when it is preceded by a vowel.

comedy, comedies	monkey, monkeys
dry, dried	play, played

With proper names ending in *-y*, however, do not change the *-y* to *-ie* even if it is preceded by a consonant: *the Dougherty family, the Doughertys.*

Final consonants If a final consonant is preceded by a single vowel *and* the consonant ends a one-syllable word or a stressed syllable, double the consonant when adding a suffix beginning with a vowel.

bet, betting	occur, occurrence
commit, committed	

Plurals

-s or -es Add *-s* to form the plural of most nouns; add *-es* to singular nouns ending in *-s*, *-sh*, *-ch*, and *-x*.

table, tables	church, churches
paper, papers	dish, dishes

Ordinarily add *-s* to nouns ending in *-o* when the *-o* is preceded by a vowel. Add *-es* when it is preceded by a consonant.

radio, radios	hero, heroes
video, videos	tomato, tomatoes

Other plurals To form the plural of a hyphenated compound word, add *-s* to the chief word even if it does not appear at the end.

mother-in-law, mothers-in-law

English words derived from other languages such as Latin, Greek, or French sometimes form the plural as they would in their original language.

medium, media	chateau, chateaux
criterion, criteria	

MULTILINGUAL Spelling varies slightly among English-speaking countries. This can be particularly confusing for multilingual students in the United States, who may have learned British English. Following is a list of some common words spelled differently in American and British English. Consult a dictionary for others.

AMERICAN	BRITISH
canceled, traveled	cancelled, travelled
color, humor	colour, humour
judgment	judgement
check	cheque
realize, apologize	realise, apologise
defense	defence
anemia, anesthetic	anaemia, anaesthetic
theater, center	theatre, centre
fetus	foetus
mold, smolder	mould, smoulder
civilization	civilisation
connection, inflection	connexion, inflexion
licorice	liquorice

43b Become familiar with your dictionary.

A good dictionary, whether print or online — such as *The American Heritage Dictionary of the English Language*, *The Random House College Dictionary*, or *Merriam-Webster's Collegiate Dictionary* — is an indispensable writer's aid.

A sample print dictionary entry, taken from *The American Heritage Dictionary*, appears on page 353. Labels show where various kinds of information about a word can be found in that dictionary.

A sample online dictionary entry, taken from *Merriam-Webster Online*, appears on page 354.

Spelling, word division, pronunciation

The main entry (*re·gard* in the sample entries) shows the correct spelling of the word. When there are two correct spellings of a word (as in *collectible, collectable*, for example), both are given, with the preferred spelling usually appearing first.

The main entry also shows how the word is divided into syllables. The dot between *re* and *gard* separates the two syllables and indicates where the word should be divided if it can't fit at the end of a line of type (see 44f). When a word is compound, the main entry shows how to write it: as one word (*crossroad*), as a hyphenated word (*cross-stitch*), or as two words (*cross section*).

The word's pronunciation is given just after the main entry. The accents indicate which syllables are stressed; the other marks are explained in the dictionary's pronunciation key. In print dictionaries, this key usually appears at the bottom of every page or every other page. Many online entries include an audio link to a person's voice pronouncing the word. And most online dictionaries have an audio pronunciation guide.

PRINT DICTIONARY ENTRY

Pronunciation

Grammatical
label

Word
division

Part of
speech label

Word endings
(inflections)

Usage label

Spelling — **re•gard** (rĭ-gärd′) *v.* **-gard•ed, -gard•ing, -gards** —*tr.* **1.** To look at attentively; observe closely. **2.** To look upon or consider in a particular way: *I regard him as a fool.* **3.** To hold in esteem or respect: *She regards her teachers highly.* **4.** To relate or refer to; concern: *This item regards their liability.* **5.** To take into account; consider. **6.** *Obsolete* To take care of. —*intr.* **1.** To look or gaze. **2.** To give heed; pay attention. ❖ *n.* **1.** A look or gaze. **2.** Careful thought or attention; heed: *She gives little regard to her sister's teasing.* **3a.** Respect, affection, or esteem: *He has high regard for your work.* **b. regards** Good wishes expressing such sentiment: *Give the family my best regards.* **4.** A particular point or aspect; respect: *She was lucky in that regard.* **5.** Basis for action; motive. **6.** *Obsolete* Appearance or aspect. **—*idioms:* as regards** Concerning. **in** (or **with**) **regard to** With respect to. [Middle English *regarden*, from Old French *regarder* : *re-*, re- + *guarder*, to guard (of Germanic origin; see GUARD).]

Meanings

Idioms

Synonyms *regard, esteem, admiration, respect* These nouns refer to a feeling based on perception of and approval for the worth of a person or thing. *Regard* is the most general: *"I once thought you had a kind of regard for her"* (George Borrow). *Esteem* connotes considered appraisal and positive regard: *"The near-unanimity of esteem he enjoyed during his lifetime has by no means been sustained since"* (Will Crutchfield). *Admiration* is a feeling of keen approbation: *"Greatness is a spiritual condition worthy to excite love, interest, and admiration"* (Matthew Arnold). *Respect* implies appreciative, often deferential regard resulting from careful assessment: *"I have a great respect for any man who makes his own way in life"* (Winston Churchill). See also synonyms at **consider.**

Synonyms

Usage Note *Regard* is traditionally used in the singular in the phrase *in regard* (not *in regards*) *to. Regarding* and *as regards* are also standard in the sense "with reference to." In the same sense *with respect to* is acceptable, but *respecting* is not. • *Respects* is sometimes considered preferable to *regards* in the sense of "particulars": *In some respects* (not *regards*) *the books are alike.*

Usage note

Word origin
(etymology)

ONLINE DICTIONARY ENTRY

Source: Merriam-Webster, www.Merriam-Webster.com (2010).

Word endings and grammatical labels

When a word takes endings to indicate grammatical functions (called *inflections*), the endings are listed in boldface, as with *-garded*, *-garding*, and *-gards* in the sample print entry (p. 353).

Labels for the parts of speech and for other grammatical terms are sometimes abbreviated, as they are in the print entry. The most commonly used abbreviations are these:

n.	noun	adj.	adjective
pl.	plural	adv.	adverb
sing.	singular	pron.	pronoun
v.	verb	prep.	preposition
tr.	transitive verb	conj.	conjunction
intr.	intransitive verb	interj.	interjection

Meanings, word origin, synonyms, and antonyms

Each meaning for the word is given a number. Occasionally a word's use is illustrated in a quoted sentence.

Sometimes a word can be used as more than one part of speech (*regard*, for instance, can be used as either a verb or a noun). In such a case, all the meanings for one part of speech are given before all the meanings for another, as in the sample entries. The entries also give idiomatic uses of the word.

The origin of the word, called its *etymology*, appears in brackets after all the meanings in the print and online versions.

Synonyms, words similar in meaning to the main entry, are frequently listed. In the sample print entry, the dictionary draws distinctions in meaning among the various synonyms. In the online entry, synonyms appear as hyperlinks. Antonyms, which do not appear in the sample entries, are words having a meaning opposite from that of the main entry.

Usage

Usage labels indicate when, where, or under what conditions a particular meaning for a word is appropriately used. Common labels are *informal* (or *colloquial*), *slang*, *archaic*, *poetic*, *nonstandard*, *dialect*, *obsolete*, and *British*. In the sample print entry (p. 353), two meanings of *regard* are labeled *obsolete* because they are no longer in use. The sample online entry (p. 354) has one meaning labeled *archaic*.

Dictionaries sometimes include usage notes as well. In the sample print entry, the dictionary offers advice on several uses of *regard* not specifically covered by the meanings. Such advice is based on the opinions of many experts and on actual usage in current magazines, newspapers, and books.

43c Discriminate between words that sound alike but have different meanings.

Words that sound alike or nearly alike but have different meanings and spellings are called *homophones*. The following sets of words are so commonly confused that a careful writer will double-check their every use.

affect (verb: to exert an influence)
effect (verb: to accomplish; noun: result)

its (possessive pronoun: of or belonging to it)
it's (contraction of *it is* or *it has*)

loose (adjective: free, not securely attached)
lose (verb: to fail to keep, to be deprived of)

principal (adjective: most important; noun: head of a school)
principle (noun: a fundamental guideline or truth)

their (possessive pronoun: belonging to them)
they're (contraction of *they are*)
there (adverb: that place or position)

who's (contraction of *who is* or *who has*)
whose (possessive form of *who*)

your (possessive pronoun: belonging to you)
you're (contraction of *you are*)

To check for the correct use of these and other commonly confused words, see the glossary of usage at the back of the book.

43d Be alert to commonly misspelled words.

absence	accommodate	acquaintance	all right
academic	achievement	acquire	amateur
accidentally	acknowledge	address	analyze

answer	desperate	irresistible	publicly
apparently	dictionary	knowledge	quiet
appearance	different	library	quite
arctic	disastrous	license	quizzes
argument	eighth	lightning	receive
arithmetic	eligible	loneliness	recognize
arrangement	embarrass	maintenance	referred
ascend	emphasize	maneuver	restaurant
athlete	entirely	marriage	rhythm
athletics	environment	mathematics	roommate
attendance	especially	mischievous	sandwich
basically	exaggerated	necessary	schedule
beautiful	exercise	noticeable	seize
beginning	exhaust	occasion	separate
believe	existence	occurred	sergeant
benefited	extraordinary	occurrence	siege
bureau	extremely	pamphlet	similar
business	familiar	parallel	sincerely
calendar	fascinate	particularly	sophomore
candidate	February	pastime	strictly
cemetery	foreign	permanent	subtly
changeable	forty	permissible	succeed
column	fourth	perseverance	surprise
commitment	friend	phenomenon	thorough
committed	government	physically	tomorrow
committee	grammar	playwright	tragedy
competitive	guard	practically	transferred
completely	harass	precede	tries
conceivable	height	preference	truly
conscience	humorous	preferred	unnecessarily
conscientious	incidentally	prejudice	usually
conscious	incredible	presence	vacuum
criticism	independence	prevalent	vengeance
criticize	indispensable	privilege	villain
decision	inevitable	proceed	weird
definitely	intelligence	professor	whether
descendant	irrelevant	pronunciation	writing

EXERCISE 43–1 The following memo has been run through a spell checker. Proofread it carefully, editing the spelling and typographical errors that remain.

November 3, 2010

To: Patricia Wise
From: Constance Mayhew
Subject: Express Tours annual report

Thank you for agreeing to draft the annual report for Express Tours. Before you begin you're work, let me outline the initial steps.

First, its essential for you to include brief profiles of top management. Early next week, I'll provide profiles for all manages accept Samuel Heath, who's biographical information is being revised. You should edit these profiles carefully and than format them according to the enclosed instructions. We may ask you to include other employee's profiles at some point.

Second, you should arrange to get complete financial information for fiscal year 2010 from our comptroller, Richard Chang. (Helen Boyes, to, can provide the necessary figures.) When you get this information, precede according tot he plans we discuss in yesterday's meeting. By the way, you will notice from the figures that the sale of our Charterhouse division did not significantly effect net profits.

Third, you should submit first draft of the report by December 15. I assume that you won a laser printer, but if you don't, you can e-mail a file and we'll print out a draft here. Of coarse, you should proofread you writing.

I am quiet pleased that you can take on this project. If I can answers questions, don't hesitate to call.

44 The hyphen

44a Consult the dictionary to determine how to treat a compound word.

The dictionary will tell you whether to treat a compound word as a hyphenated compound (*water-repellent*), one word (*waterproof*), or two words (*water table*). If the compound word is not in the dictionary, treat it as two words.

▶ The prosecutor chose not to cross-examine any witnesses.

▶ All students are expected to record their data in a small

note book.

▶ Alice walked through the looking glass into a backward world.

44b Hyphenate two or more words used together as an adjective before a noun.

▶ Mrs. Douglas gave Toshiko a seashell and some newspaper-

wrapped fish to take home to her mother.

▶ Richa Gupta is not yet a well-known candidate.

Newspaper-wrapped and *well-known* are adjectives used before the nouns *fish* and *candidate.*

Generally, do not use a hyphen when such compounds follow the noun.

▶ After our television campaign, Richa Gupta will be well known.

Do not use a hyphen to connect *-ly* adverbs to the words they modify.

▶ A slowly moving truck tied up traffic.

NOTE: When two or more hyphenated adjectives in a row modify the same noun, you can suspend the hyphens.

Do you prefer first-, second-, or third-class tickets?

44c Hyphenate fractions and certain numbers when they are spelled out.

▶ One-fourth of my income goes to pay my child care

expenses.

44d Use a hyphen with the prefixes *all-*, *ex-* (meaning "former"), and *self-* and with the suffix *-elect*.

▶ The private foundation is funneling more money into

self-help projects.
   ^

▶ The Student Senate bylaws require the president-elect to
                                                     ^
attend all senate meetings between the election and the

official transfer of office.

44e Use a hyphen in certain words to avoid ambiguity or to separate awkward double or triple letters.

Without the hyphen, there would be no way to distinguish between words such as *re-creation* and *recreation*.

Bicycling in the city is my favorite form of recreation.

The film was praised for its astonishing re-creation of nineteenth-century London.

Hyphens are sometimes used to separate awkward double or triple letters in compound words (*anti-intellectual*, *cross-stitch*). Always check a dictionary for the standard form of the word.

44f Check for correct word breaks when words must be divided at the end of a line.

Some word processing programs and other computer applications automatically generate word breaks at the ends of lines. When you're writing an academic paper, it's best to set your computer application not to hyphenate automatically. This setting will ensure that only words already containing a hyphen (such as *long-distance*, *pre-Roman*) will be hyphenated at the ends of lines.

E-mail addresses and URLs need special attention when they occur at the end of a line of text or in bibliographic citations. You can't rely on your word processor to divide these terms correctly, so you must make a decision in each case. Do not insert a hyphen to divide electronic addresses. Instead, break an e-mail address after the @ symbol or before a period. Break a URL after a slash or a double slash or before any other punctuation mark.

> I repeatedly e-mailed Janine at janine.r.rose@dunbaracademy
> .org before I gave up and called her cell phone.

> To find a zip code quickly, I always use the United States
> Postal Service Web site at http://zip4.usps.com/zip4/
> welcome.jsp.

For breaks in URLs in MLA and APA documentation styles, see pages 506 and 566.

EXERCISE 44–1   Edit the following sentences to correct errors in hyphenation. If a sentence is correct, write "correct" after it. Answers to lettered sentences appear in the back of the book. Example:

> **Zola's first readers were scandalized by his slice-of-life novels.**

a. Gold is the seventy-ninth element in the periodic table.

b. The swiftly-moving tugboat pulled alongside the barge and directed it away from the oil spill in the harbor.

c. The Moche were a pre-Columbian people who established a sophisticated culture in ancient Peru.

d. Your dog is well-known in our neighborhood.

e. Road-blocks were set up along all the major highways leading out of the city.

1. We knew we were driving too fast when our tires skidded on the rain slick surface.

2. The Black Death reduced the population of some medieval villages by two thirds.

3. Sewing forty-eight sequined tutus for the ballet recital nearly made Karyn cross-eyed.

4. Olivia had hoped to find a pay as you go plan to finance the construction of her observatory.

5. Gail Sheehy writes that at age twenty five many people assume that the choices they make are irrevocable.

45 Capitalization

In addition to the rules in this section, a good dictionary can tell you when to use capital letters.

45a Capitalize proper nouns and words derived from them; do not capitalize common nouns.

Proper nouns are the names of specific persons, places, and things. All other nouns are common nouns. The following types of words are usually capitalized: names of deities, religions, religious followers, sacred books; words of family relationship used as names; particular places; nationalities and their languages, races, tribes; educational institutions, departments, degrees, particular courses; government departments, organizations, political parties; historical movements, periods, events, documents; specific electronic sources; and trade names.

PROPER NOUNS	COMMON NOUNS
God (used as a name)	a god
Book of Common Prayer	a sacred book
Uncle Pedro	my uncle
Father (used as a name)	my father
Lake Superior	a picturesque lake
the Capital Center	a center for advanced studies
the South	a southern state
Wrigley Field	a baseball stadium
University of Wisconsin	a state university
Geology 101	geology
Environmental Protection Agency	a federal agency
Phi Kappa Psi	a fraternity
the Democratic Party	a political party
the Enlightenment	the eighteenth century
the Treaty of Versailles	a treaty
the World Wide Web, the Web	a home page
the Internet, the Net	a computer network
Advil	a painkiller

Months, holidays, and days of the week are treated as proper nouns; the seasons and numbers of the days of the month are not.

> Our academic year begins on a Tuesday in early September, right after Labor Day.

> Graduation is in late spring, on the second of June.

EXCEPTION: Capitalize Fourth of July (or July Fourth) when referring to the holiday.

Names of school subjects are capitalized only if they are names of languages. Names of particular courses are capitalized.

> This semester Austin is taking math, geography, geology, French, and English.

> Professor Obembe offers Modern American Fiction 501 to graduate students.

CAUTION: Do not capitalize common nouns to make them seem important: *Our company is currently hiring computer programmers* [not *Company, Computer Programmers*].

45b Capitalize titles of persons when used as part of a proper name but usually not when used alone.

> Professor Margaret Barnes; Dr. Sinyee Sein; John Scott Williams Jr.

> District Attorney Marshall was reprimanded for badgering the witness.

> The district attorney was elected for a two-year term.

Usage varies when the title of an important public figure is used alone: *The president* [or *President*] *vetoed the bill.*

45c Capitalize the first, last, and all major words in titles and subtitles of works such as books, articles, songs, and online documents.

In both titles and subtitles, major words such as nouns, pronouns, verbs, adjectives, and adverbs should be capitalized. Minor words such as articles, prepositions, and coordinating conjunctions are not capitalized unless they are the first or last word of a title or subtitle. Capitalize the second part of a hyphenated term in a title if it is a major word but not if it is a minor word. Capitalize chapter titles and the titles of other major divisions of a work following the same guidelines used for titles of complete works.

> *Seizing the Enigma: The Race to Break the German U-Boat Codes*
> *A River Runs through It*
> "I Want to Hold Your Hand"
> *The Canadian Green Page*

To see why some of the titles in the list are italicized and some are put in quotation marks, see 42a and 37c.

45d Capitalize the first word of a sentence.

The first word of a sentence should be capitalized. When a sentence appears within parentheses, capitalize its first word unless the parentheses appear within another sentence.

> Early detection of breast cancer significantly increases survival rates. (See table 2.)

> Early detection of breast cancer significantly increases survival rates (see table 2).

45e Capitalize the first word of a quoted sentence but not a quoted phrase.

> Robert Hughes writes, "There are only about sixty Watteau paintings on whose authenticity all experts agree" (102).

> Russell Baker has written that in this country, sports are "the opiate of the masses" (46).

If a quoted sentence is interrupted by explanatory words, do not capitalize the first word after the interruption. (See 37e.)

> "If you want to go out," he said, "tell me now."

When quoting poetry, copy the poet's capitalization exactly. Many poets capitalize the first word of every line of poetry; a few contemporary poets dismiss capitalization altogether.

> it was the week   that
> i felt the city's narrow breezes rush about
> me   — Don L. Lee

45f Capitalize the first word after a colon if it begins an independent clause.

If a group of words following a colon could stand on its own as a complete sentence, capitalize the first word.

> Clinical trials called into question the safety profile of the drug: A high percentage of participants reported hypertension and kidney problems.

> Preferences vary among academic disciplines. See 60c and 65b.

Always use lowercase for a list or an appositive that follows a colon (see 35a).

> Students were divided into two groups: residents and commuters.

45g Capitalize abbreviations according to convention.

Abbreviations for government agencies, companies, and other organizations as well as call numbers for radio and television stations are capitalized.

> EPA, FBI, DKNY, IBM, WCRB, KNBC-TV

EXERCISE 45–1   Edit the following sentences to correct errors in capitalization. If a sentence is correct, write "correct" after it. Answers to lettered sentences appear in the back of the book. Example:

> On our trip to the West, we visited the ~~g~~rand ~~c~~anyon and the *(G)* *(C)*
> ~~g~~reat ~~s~~alt ~~d~~esert. *(G)* *(S)* *(D)*

a. Assistant dean Shirin Ahmadi recommended offering more world language courses.

b. We went to the Mark Taper Forum to see a production of *Angels in America*.

c. Kalindi has an ambitious semester, studying differential calculus, classical hebrew, brochure design, and greek literature.

d. Lydia's Aunt and Uncle make modular houses as beautiful as modernist works of art.

PRACTICE   hackerhandbooks.com/rules
   > Mechanics > 45–2

e. We amused ourselves on the long flight by discussing how Spring in Kyoto stacks up against Summer in London.

1. When the truck will not start, I try a few tricks with the ignition key: Jiggling it to the left, pulling it out a quarter of an inch, and gently pulling down on it.

2. When you slowly bake a clove of garlic, the most amazing thing happens: It loses its bitter tang and becomes sweet and buttery.

3. After World War II, aunt Helena left Poland to study in Italy.

4. When we drove through the south last year, we enjoyed stopping at the peanut stands along the road.

5. Following in his sister's footsteps, Leonid is pursuing a degree in Marketing Research.

Grammar Basics

46 Parts of speech

Traditional grammar recognizes eight parts of speech: noun, pronoun, verb, adjective, adverb, preposition, conjunction, and interjection. Many words can function as more than one part of speech. For example, depending on its use in a sentence, the word *paint* can be a noun (*The paint is wet*) or a verb (*Please paint the ceiling next*).

46a Nouns

A noun is the name of a person, place, thing, or concept.

> N N N
> The *lion* in the *cage* growled at the *zookeeper*.

Nouns sometimes function as adjectives modifying other nouns. Because of their dual roles, nouns used in this manner may be called *noun/adjectives*.

> N/ADJ N/ADJ
> The *leather* notebook was tucked in the *student's* backpack.

Nouns are classified in a variety of ways. *Proper* nouns are capitalized, but *common* nouns are not (see 45a). For clarity, writers choose between *concrete* and *abstract* nouns (see 18b). The distinction between *count* nouns and *noncount* nouns can be especially helpful to multilingual writers (see 29a). Most nouns have singular and plural forms; *collective* nouns may be either singular or plural, depending on how they are used (see 21f and 22b). *Possessive* nouns require an apostrophe (see 36a).

EXERCISE 46–1 Underline the nouns (and noun/adjectives) in the following sentences. Answers to lettered sentences appear in the back of the book. Example:

> The best <u>part</u> of <u>dinner</u> was the <u>chef's</u> newest <u>dessert</u>.

a. The stage was set for a confrontation of biblical proportions.
b. The courage of the mountain climber was an inspiration to the rescuers.

PRACTICE hackerhandbooks.com/rules
> Grammar basics > 46–5 and 46–6
> 46–15 and 46–16 (all parts of speech)

c. The need to arrive before the guest of honor motivated us to navigate the thick fog.

d. The defense attorney made a final appeal to the jury.

e. A national museum dedicated to women artists opened in 1987.

1. Truthfulness is a virtue lacking in some public officials.

2. The Wright Brothers used a wind tunnel to test their airplane designs.

3. The miners' work clothes were clogged with fine black dust.

4. Virginia Woolf wrote that women needed their own income and their own space.

5. The child's language was a charming combination of her father's English and her mother's French.

46b Pronouns

A pronoun is a word used in place of a noun. Usually the pronoun substitutes for a specific noun, known as its *antecedent*.

When the *battery* wears down, we recharge *it*.

Although most pronouns function as substitutes for nouns, some can function as adjectives modifying nouns. Because they have the form of a pronoun and the function of an adjective, such pronouns may be called *pronoun/adjectives*.

PN/ADJ
This bird was at the same window yesterday morning.

Pronouns are classified as personal, possessive, intensive and reflexive, relative, interrogative, demonstrative, indefinite, and reciprocal.

Personal pronouns Personal pronouns refer to specific persons or things. They always function as noun equivalents.

Singular: I, me, you, she, her, he, him, it

Plural: we, us, you, they, them

Possessive pronouns Possessive pronouns indicate ownership.

Singular: my, mine, your, yours, her, hers, his, its

Plural: our, ours, your, yours, their, theirs

Some of these possessive pronouns function as adjectives modifying nouns: *my, your, his, her, its, our, their.*

Intensive and reflexive pronouns   Intensive pronouns emphasize a noun or another pronoun (The senator *herself* met us at the door). Reflexive pronouns, which have the same form as intensive pronouns, name a receiver of an action identical with the doer of the action (Paula cut *herself*).

> *Singular:* myself, yourself, himself, herself, itself
>
> *Plural:* ourselves, yourselves, themselves

Relative pronouns   Relative pronouns introduce subordinate clauses functioning as adjectives (The writer *who won the award* refused to accept it). In addition to introducing the clause, the relative pronoun, in this case *who*, points back to a noun or pronoun that the clause modifies (*writer*). (See 48e.)

> who, whom, whose, which, that

Some textbooks also treat *whichever, whoever, whomever, what,* and *whatever* as relative pronouns. These words introduce noun clauses; they do not point back to a noun or pronoun. (See "Noun clauses" in 48e.)

Interrogative pronouns   Interrogative pronouns introduce questions (*Who* is expected to win the election?).

> who, whom, whose, which, what

Demonstrative pronouns   Demonstrative pronouns identify or point to nouns. Frequently they function as adjectives (*This* chair is my favorite), but they may also function as noun equivalents (*This* is my favorite chair).

> this, that, these, those

Indefinite pronouns   Indefinite pronouns refer to nonspecific persons or things. Most are always singular (*everyone, each*); some are always plural (*both, many*); a few may be singular or plural (see 21e). Most indefinite pronouns function as noun equivalents (*Something* is burning), but some can also function as adjectives (*All* campers must check in at the lodge).

pronouns • substitutes for nouns (*we, their, yourself, who, anyone,* etc.)

basic

46b

371

all	anything	everyone	nobody	several
another	both	everything	none	some
any	each	few	no one	somebody
anybody	either	many	nothing	someone
anyone	everybody	neither	one	something

Reciprocal pronouns   Reciprocal pronouns refer to individual parts of a plural antecedent (By turns, the penguins fed *one another*).

each other, one another

NOTE: Using pronouns correctly can be challenging. See pronoun-antecedent agreement (22), pronoun reference (23), distinguishing between pronouns such as *I* and *me* (24), and distinguishing between *who* and *whom* (25).

EXERCISE 46–2   Underline the pronouns (and pronoun/adjectives) in the following sentences. Answers to lettered sentences appear in the back of the book. Example:

We were intrigued by the video that the fifth graders

produced as their final project.

a. The governor's loyalty was his most appealing trait.
b. In the fall, the geese that fly south for the winter pass through our town in huge numbers.
c. Carl Sandburg once said that even he himself did not understand some of his poetry.
d. I appealed my parking ticket, but you did not get one.
e. Angela did not mind gossip as long as no one gossiped about her.

1. The Tigers stood unhappily in front of their dugout while the victorious Jaguars tossed their hats in the air.
2. Nothing fascinated the toddler like something that was not his.
3. We understood that we were expected to submit our dissertations in triplicate.
4. The trick-or-treaters helped themselves to their neighbors' candy.
5. She found herself peering into the mouth of a creepy cave.

PRACTICE   hackerhandbooks.com/rules

> Grammar basics   > 46–7 and 46–8
> 46–15 and 46–16 (all parts of speech)

46c Verbs

The verb of a sentence usually expresses action (*jump*, *think*) or being (*is*, *become*). It is composed of a main verb possibly preceded by one or more helping verbs.

> MV
> The horses *exercise* every day.

> HV   MV
> The task force report *was* not *completed* on schedule.

> HV HV   MV
> No one *has been defended* with more passion than our pastor.

Notice that words, usually adverbs, can intervene between the helping verb and the main verb (was *not* completed). (See 46e.)

Helping verbs

There are twenty-three helping verbs in English: forms of *have*, *do*, and *be*, which may also function as main verbs; and nine modals, which function only as helping verbs. *Have*, *do*, and *be* change form to indicate tense; the nine modals do not.

FORMS OF *HAVE, DO,* AND *BE*

have, has, had

do, does, did

be, am, is, are, was, were, being, been

MODALS

can, could, may, might, must, shall, should, will, would

The verb phrase *ought to* is often classified as a modal as well.

Main verbs

The main verb of a sentence is always the kind of word that would change form if put into these test sentences:

BASE FORM	Usually I (*walk, ride*).
PAST TENSE	Yesterday I (*walked, rode*).
PAST PARTICIPLE	I have (*walked, ridden*) many times before.
PRESENT PARTICIPLE	I am (*walking, riding*) right now.
***-S* FORM**	Usually he/she/it (*walks, rides*).

actions • states of being (*be, seem, become,* etc.) •
helping verbs (*have, do, be*) • modals (*can, may, must,* etc.)

basic

46c

373

If a word doesn't change form when slipped into the test sentences, you can be certain that it is not a main verb. For example, the noun *revolution,* though it may seem to suggest an action, can never function as a main verb. Just try to make it behave like one (*Today I revolution . . . Yesterday I revolutioned . . .*) and you'll see why.

When both the past-tense and the past-participle forms of a verb end in *-ed,* the verb is regular (*walked, walked*). Otherwise, the verb is irregular (*rode, ridden*). (See 27a.)

The verb *be* is highly irregular, having eight forms instead of the usual five: the base form *be;* the present-tense forms *am, is,* and *are;* the past-tense forms *was* and *were;* the present participle *being;* and the past participle *been.*

Helping verbs combine with the various forms of main verbs to create tenses. For a survey of tenses, see 28a.

NOTE: Some verbs are followed by words that look like prepositions but are so closely associated with the verb that they are a part of its meaning. These words are known as *particles.* Common verb-particle combinations include *bring up, call off, drop off, give in, look up, run into,* and *take off.*

> Sharon *packed up* her broken laptop and *sent* it *off* to the repair shop.

TIP: You can find more information about using verbs in other sections of the handbook: active verbs (8), subject-verb agreement (21), standard English verb forms (27), verb tense and mood (27f and 27g), and Multilingual/ESL challenges with verbs (28).

EXERCISE 46–3 Underline the verbs in the following sentences, including helping verbs and particles. If a verb is part of a contraction (such as *is* in *isn't* or *would* in *I'd*), underline only the letters that represent the verb. Answers to lettered sentences appear in the back of the book. Example:

> The ground under the pine trees <u>was</u>n't wet from the rain.

a. My grandmother always told me a soothing story before bed.

b. There were fifty apples on the tree before the frost killed them.

c. Morton brought down the box of letters from the attic.

PRACTICE   hackerhandbooks.com/rules
> Grammar basics > 46–9 and 46–10
> 46–15 and 46–16 (all parts of speech)

d. Stay on the main road and you'll arrive at the base camp before us.

e. The fish struggled vigorously but was trapped in the net.

1. Do not bring up that issue again.

2. Galileo lived the last years of his life under house arrest because of his revolutionary theories about the universe.

3. Cynthia asked for a raise, but she didn't expect one immediately.

4. We should plant the roses early this year.

5. The documentary was engrossing. It humanized World War II.

46d Adjectives

An adjective is a word used to modify, or describe, a noun or pronoun. An adjective usually answers one of these questions: Which one? What kind of? How many?

ADJ
the *frisky* horse [Which horse?]

ADJ   ADJ
cracked old plates [What kind of plates?]

ADJ
nine months [How many months?]

Adjectives usually precede the words they modify. They may also follow linking verbs, in which case they describe the subject. (See 47b.)

ADJ
The decision was *unpopular.*

The definite article *the* and the indefinite articles *a* and *an* are also classified as adjectives.

ART   ART   ART
A defendant should be judged on *the* evidence provided to *the* jury, not on hearsay.

Some possessive, demonstrative, and indefinite pronouns can function as adjectives: *their, its, this, all* (see 46b). And nouns can function as adjectives when they modify other nouns: *apple pie* (the noun *apple* modifies the noun *pie*; see 46a).

TIP: You can find more details about using adjectives in 26. If you are a multilingual writer, you may also find help with articles and specific uses of adjectives in 29, 30g, and 30h.

46e Adverbs

An adverb is a word used to modify, or qualify, a verb (or verbal), an adjective, or another adverb. It usually answers one of these questions: When? Where? How? Why? Under what conditions? To what degree?

> Pull *firmly* on the emergency handle. [Pull how?]
>
> Read the text *first* and *then* work the exercises. [Read when? Work when?]

Adverbs modifying adjectives or other adverbs usually intensify or limit the intensity of the word they modify.

>   ADV   ADV
> Be *extremely* kind, and you will *probably* have many friends.

The words *not* and *never* are classified as adverbs.

EXERCISE 46–4   Underline the adjectives and circle the adverbs in the following sentences. If a word is a noun or pronoun functioning as an adjective, underline it and mark it as a noun/adjective or pronoun/adjective. Also treat the articles *a*, *an*, and *the* as adjectives. Answers to lettered sentences appear in the back of the book. Example:

> **Finding <u>an</u> <u>available</u> room during <u>the</u> convention**
>
> **was ⓝⓞⓣ <u>easy</u>.**

a. Generalizations lead to weak, unfocused essays.
b. The Spanish language is wonderfully flexible.
c. The wildflowers smelled especially fragrant after the steady rain.
d. I'd rather be slightly hot than bitterly cold.
e. The cat slept soundly in its wicker basket.

1. Success can be elusive to those who object to working hard.
2. After three hours, the discussion had dwindled from a lively sprint to a tedious crawl.
3. She made a fairly earnest attempt at solving the most difficult calculus problems.
4. The black bear sniffed eagerly at the broken honeycomb.
5. The bacteria in the dish grew steadily over twenty-four hours.

PRACTICE   hackerhandbooks.com/rules
> Grammar basics > 46–11 to 46–14
> > 46–15 and 46–16 (all parts of speech)

46f Prepositions

A preposition is a word placed before a noun or pronoun to form a phrase modifying another word in the sentence. The prepositional phrase nearly always functions as an adjective or as an adverb.

The road *to* the summit travels *past* craters *from* an extinct volcano.

To the summit functions as an adjective modifying the noun *road*; *past craters* functions as an adverb modifying the verb *travels*; *from an extinct volcano* functions as an adjective modifying the noun *craters*. (For more on prepositional phrases, see 48a.)

English has a limited number of prepositions. The most common are included in the following list.

about	beside	from	outside	toward
above	besides	in	over	under
across	between	inside	past	underneath
after	beyond	into	plus	unlike
against	but	like	regarding	until
along	by	near	respecting	unto
among	concerning	next	round	up
around	considering	of	since	upon
as	despite	off	than	with
at	down	on	through	within
before	during	onto	throughout	without
behind	except	opposite	till	
below	for	out	to	

Some prepositions are more than one word long. *Along with*, *as well as*, *in addition to*, *next to*, and *rather than* are common examples.

TIP: Prepositions are used in idioms such as *capable of* and *dig up* (see 18d). For a discussion of specific issues for multilingual writers, see 31.

46g Conjunctions

Conjunctions join words, phrases, or clauses, and they indicate the relation between the elements joined.

Coordinating conjunctions   A coordinating conjunction is used to connect grammatically equal elements. (See 9b and 14a.) The coordinating conjunctions are *and, but, or, nor, for, so,* and *yet.*

Correlative conjunctions   Correlative conjunctions come in pairs. Like coordinating conjunctions, they connect grammatically equal elements.

either . . . or   whether . . . or
neither . . . nor   both . . . and
not only . . . but also

Subordinating conjunctions   A subordinating conjunction introduces a subordinate clause and indicates the relation of the clause to the rest of the sentence. (See 48e.) The most common subordinating conjunctions are *after, although, as, as if, because, before, if, in order that, once, since, so that, than, that, though, unless, until, when, where, whether,* and *while.* (For a complete list, see p. 396.)

Conjunctive adverbs   Conjunctive adverbs connect independent clauses and indicate the relation between the clauses. They can be used with a semicolon to join two independent clauses in one sentence, or they can be used alone with an independent clause. The most common conjunctive adverbs are *finally, furthermore, however, moreover, nevertheless, similarly, then, therefore,* and *thus.* (For a complete list, see p. 380.)

TIP: The ability to distinguish between conjunctive adverbs and coordinating conjunctions will help you avoid run-on sentences and make punctuation decisions (see 20, 32a, and 32f). The ability to recognize subordinating conjunctions will help you avoid sentence fragments (see 19).

46h Interjections

An interjection is a word used to express surprise or emotion (*Oh! Hey! Wow!*).

Parts of speech

- A **noun** names a person, place, thing, or concept.

  N   N   N
  Repetition does not transform a *lie* into *truth*.

- A **pronoun** substitutes for a noun.

                                   PN   PN   PN
  Before the attendant let *us* board the small plane, *he* weighed *us*

      PN
  and *our* baggage.

  Personal pronouns: I, me, you, he, him, she, her, it, we, us, they, them

  Possessive pronouns: my, mine, your, yours, her, hers, his, its, our, ours, their, theirs

  Intensive and reflexive pronouns: myself, yourself, himself, herself, itself, ourselves, yourselves, themselves

  Relative pronouns: that, which, who, whom, whose

  Interrogative pronouns: who, whom, whose, which, what

  Demonstrative pronouns: this, that, these, those

  Indefinite pronouns

all	each	many	one
another	either	neither	several
any	everybody	nobody	some
anybody	everyone	none	somebody
anyone	everything	no one	someone
anything	few	nothing	something
both			

  Reciprocal pronouns: each other, one another

- A **helping verb** comes before a main verb.

  Modals: can, could, may, might, must, shall, should, will, would (*also* ought to)

  Forms of *be*: be, am, is, are, was, were, being, been

  Forms of *have*: have, has, had

  Forms of *do*: do, does, did

(The forms of *be*, *have*, and *do* may also function as main verbs.)

- A **main verb** shows action or a state of being.

  MV
  The novel *opens* with a tense description of a grim murder, but

  HV   MV
  the author *does* not *maintain* the initial level of suspense.

  A main verb will always change form when put into these positions in sentences:

Usually I _____ .	(*walk, ride*)
Yesterday I _____ .	(*walked, rode*)
I have _____ many times before.	(*walked, ridden*)
I am _____ right now.	(*walking, riding*)
Usually he _____ .	(*walks, rides*)

  The highly irregular verb *be* has eight forms: *be, am, is, are, was, were, being, been*.

- An **adjective** modifies a noun or pronoun, usually answering one of these questions: Which one? What kind of? How many? The articles *a*, *an*, and *the* are also adjectives.

  PN/ADJ N/ADJ ADJ   ADJ   PN/ADJ
  Our family's strong ties gave us *welcome* comfort in *our*

  grief.

- An **adverb** modifies a verb, an adjective, or an adverb, usually answering one of these questions: When? Where? Why? How? Under what conditions? To what degree?

  ADV   ADV
  Young people *often* approach history *skeptically*.

- A **preposition** indicates the relationship between the noun or pronoun that follows it and another word in the sentence.

  P   P
  A journey *of* a thousand miles begins *with* a single step.

Parts of speech (continued)

Common prepositions

about	besides	like	since
above	between	near	than
across	beyond	next	through
after	but	next to	throughout
against	by	of	till
along	concerning	off	to
along with	considering	on	toward
among	despite	onto	under
around	down	opposite	underneath
as	during	out	unlike
as well as	except	outside	until
at	for	over	unto
because of	from	past	up
before	in	plus	upon
behind	in addition to	rather than	with
below	inside	regarding	within
beside	into	respecting	without

- A **conjunction** connects words or word groups.

  Coordinating conjunctions: and, but, or, nor, for, so, yet

  Subordinating conjunctions: after, although, as, as if, because, before, even though, if, in order that, once, since, so that, than, that, though, unless, until, when, where, whether, while

  Correlative conjunctions: either . . . or; neither . . . nor; not only . . . but also; both . . . and; whether . . . or

  Conjunctive adverbs: accordingly, also, anyway, besides, certainly, consequently, conversely, finally, furthermore, hence, however, incidentally, indeed, instead, likewise, meanwhile, moreover, nevertheless, next, nonetheless, now, otherwise, similarly, specifically, still, subsequently, then, therefore, thus

- An **interjection** expresses surprise or emotion (*Oh! Wow! Hooray!*).

Sentence patterns

Most English sentences flow from subject to verb to any objects or complements. The vast majority of sentences conform to one of these five patterns:

> subject/verb/subject complement
>
> subject/verb/direct object
>
> subject/verb/indirect object/direct object
>
> subject/verb/direct object/object complement
>
> subject/verb

Adverbial modifiers (single words, phrases, or clauses) may be added to any of these patterns, and they may appear nearly anywhere — at the beginning, in the middle, or at the end.

Predicate is the grammatical term given to the verb plus its objects, complements, and adverbial modifiers.

For a quick-reference chart of sentence patterns, see page 386.

47a Subjects

The subject of a sentence names who or what the sentence is about. The simple subject is always a noun or pronoun; the complete subject consists of the simple subject and any words or word groups modifying the simple subject.

The complete subject

To find the complete subject, ask Who? or What?, insert the verb, and finish the question. The answer is the complete subject.

> ┌────── COMPLETE SUBJECT ──────┐
> The devastating effects of famine can last for many years.

Who or what can last for many years? *The devastating effects of famine.*

> ┌────────── COMPLETE SUBJECT ──────────┐
> Adventure novels that contain multiple subplots are often made into successful movies.

Who or what are often made into movies? *Adventure novels that contain multiple subplots.*

COMPLETE
┌─── SUBJECT ───┐
In our program, student teachers work full-time for ten months.

Who or what works full-time for ten months? *Student teachers.*
Notice that *In our program, student teachers* is not a sensible answer to the question. (It is not safe to assume that the subject
must always appear first in a sentence.)

The simple subject

To find the simple subject, strip away all modifiers in the complete subject. This includes single-word modifiers such as *the* and
devastating, phrases such as *of famine*, and subordinate clauses
such as *that contain multiple subplots.*

┌─SS─┐
The devastating effects of famine can last for many years.

┌─SS─┐
Adventure novels that contain multiple subplots are often made into
successful movies.

A sentence may have a compound subject containing two
or more simple subjects joined with a coordinating conjunction
such as *and, but,* or *or.*

┌──────SS──────┐   ┌─SS─┐
Great commitment and a little luck make a successful actor.

Understood subjects

In imperative sentences, which give advice or issue commands,
the subject is understood but not actually present in the sentence.
The subject of an imperative sentence is understood to be *you.*

[*You*] Put your hands on the steering wheel.

Subject after the verb

Although the subject ordinarily comes before the verb (*The planes
took off*), occasionally it does not. When a sentence begins with
There is or *There are* (or *There was* or *There were*), the subject follows the verb. In such inverted constructions, the word *There* is an
expletive, an empty word serving merely to get the sentence started.

┌─SS─┐
There are *eight planes waiting to take off.*

Occasionally a writer will invert a sentence for effect.

┌─SS─┐
Joyful is *the child whose school closes for snow.*

Joyful is an adjective, so it cannot be the subject. Turn this sentence around and its structure becomes obvious.

The *child* whose school closes for snow is joyful.

In questions, the subject frequently appears between the helping verb and the main verb.

HV   ┌────SS────┐   MV
Do *Kenyan marathoners* train year-round?

TIP: The ability to recognize the subject of a sentence will help you edit for a variety of problems: sentence fragments (19), subject-verb agreement (21), choice of pronouns such as *I* and *me* (24), missing subjects (30b), and repeated subjects (30c).

EXERCISE 47–1   In the following sentences, underline the complete subject and write *SS* above the simple subject(s). If the subject is an understood *you*, insert *you* in parentheses. Answers to lettered sentences appear in the back of the book. Example:

┌─*SS*─┐   ┌─*SS*─┐
Parents and their children often look alike.

a. The hills and mountains seemed endless, and the snow atop them glistened.
b. In foil fencing, points are scored by hitting an electronic target.
c. Do not stand in the aisles or sit on the stairs.
d. There were hundreds of fireflies in the open field.
e. The evidence against the defendant was staggering.

1. The size of the new building caused an uproar in the town.
2. Eat heartily. You need your strength.
3. In the opinion of the court, siblings must be kept together.
4. All of the books in the old library smelled like mothballs.
5. There were no tour buses at the customs booth.

47b Verbs, objects, and complements

Section 46c explains how to find the verb of a sentence. A sentence's verb is classified as linking, transitive, or intransitive, depending on the kinds of objects or complements the verb can (or cannot) take.

Linking verbs and subject complements

Linking verbs connect the subject to a subject complement, a word or word group that completes the meaning of the subject by renaming or describing it.

If the subject complement renames the subject, it is a noun or noun equivalent (sometimes called a *predicate noun*).

$$\overbrace{\text{An e-mail requesting personal information}}^{S} \overbrace{\text{may be}}^{V} \overbrace{\text{a scam.}}^{SC}$$

If the subject complement describes the subject, it is an adjective or adjective equivalent (sometimes called a *predicate adjective*).

$$\overbrace{\text{Last month's temperatures}}^{S} \overset{V}{\text{were}} \overset{SC}{\text{mild.}}$$

Whenever they appear as main verbs (rather than helping verbs), the forms of *be* — *be, am, is, are, was, were, being, been* — usually function as linking verbs. In the preceding examples, for instance, the main verbs are *be* and *were*.

Verbs such as *appear, become, feel, grow, look, make, seem, smell, sound,* and *taste* are linking when they are followed by a word group that renames or describes the subject.

$$\text{As it thickens, } \overbrace{\text{the sauce}}^{S} \overbrace{\text{will look}}^{V} \overset{SC}{\text{unappealing.}}$$

Transitive verbs and direct objects

A transitive verb takes a direct object, a word or word group that names a receiver of the action.

$$\overbrace{\text{The hungry cat}}^{S} \overset{V}{\text{clawed}} \overbrace{\text{the bag of dry food.}}^{DO}$$

The simple direct object is always a noun or pronoun, in this case *bag*. To find it, simply strip away all modifiers.

Transitive verbs usually appear in the active voice, with the subject doing the action and a direct object receiving the action. Active-voice sentences can be transformed into the passive voice, with the subject receiving the action instead. (See 47c.)

Transitive verbs, indirect objects, and direct objects

The direct object of a transitive verb is sometimes preceded by an indirect object, a noun or pronoun telling to whom or for whom the action of the sentence is done.

> S   V IO ┌—DO—┐   S ┌—V—┐ IO ┌—DO—┐
> You give her some yarn, and she will knit you a scarf.

Transitive verbs, direct objects, and object complements

The direct object of a transitive verb is sometimes followed by an object complement, a word or word group that renames or describes the object.

> S   V   DO ┌————OC————┐
> People often consider chivalry a thing of the past.

> ┌—S—┐ V DO ┌———OC———┐
> The kiln makes clay firm and strong.

When the object complement renames the direct object, it is a noun or pronoun (such as *thing*). When it describes the direct object, it is an adjective (such as *firm* and *strong*).

Intransitive verbs

Intransitive verbs take no objects or complements.

> ┌———S———┐ V
> The audience laughed.

> ┌——S——┐   V
> The driver accelerated in the straightaway.

Nothing receives the actions of laughing and accelerating in these sentences, so the verbs are intransitive. Notice that such verbs may or may not be followed by adverbial modifiers. In the second sentence, *in the straightaway* is an adverbial prepositional phrase modifying *accelerated*.

Sentence patterns

Subject / linking verb / subject complement

S   V SC
Acting is art. [*Art* renames *Acting*.]

S ——— V   SC
Good researchers are curious. [*Curious* describes *researchers*.]

Subject / transitive verb / direct object

——S—— ——V—— ——DO——
An antihistamine may prevent an allergic reaction.

Subject / transitive verb / indirect object / direct object

———S——— V IO ——DO——
The elevator's rapid ascent gave Irina an attack of vertigo.

Subject / transitive verb / direct object / object complement

—S— V —DO— —OC—
The reviewer called the film a masterpiece. [*Masterpiece* renames *film*.]

———S——— V —DO— OC
The new double-glazed windows made the house warmer.
[*Warmer* describes *house*.]

Subject / intransitive verb

—S— V
The kettle whistles.

NOTE: The dictionary will tell you whether a verb is transitive or intransitive. Some verbs have both transitive and intransitive functions.

TRANSITIVE   Sandra *flew* her small plane over the canyon.

INTRANSITIVE   A flock of migrating geese *flew* overhead.

In the first example, *flew* has a direct object that receives the action: *her small plane*. In the second example, the verb is followed by an adverb (*overhead*), not by a direct object.

EXERCISE 47–2 Label the subject complements and direct objects in the following sentences, using the labels *SC* and *DO*. If a subject complement or direct object consists of more than one word, bracket and label all of it. Example:

$$\overline{DO}$$
The sharp right turn confused most drivers.

a. Textbooks are expensive.
b. Samurai warriors never fear death.
c. Successful coaches always praise their players' efforts.
d. St. Petersburg was the capital of the Russian Empire for two centuries.
e. The medicine tasted bitter.

1. Solar flares emit UV radiation.
2. The friends' quarrel was damaging their relationship.
3. Feng shui is the practice of achieving harmony between the physical and the spiritual in one's environment.
4. A well-made advertisement captures viewers' attention.
5. The island's climate was neither too hot nor too rainy.

EXERCISE 47–3 Each of the following sentences has either an indirect object followed by a direct object or a direct object followed by an object complement. Label the objects and complements, using the labels *IO*, *DO*, and *OC*. If an object or a complement consists of more than one word, bracket and label all of it. Example:

$$\overline{DO}\;\overline{OC}$$
Most people consider their own experience normal.

a. Stress can make adults and children weary.
b. Zita has made community service her priority this year.
c. Consider the work finished.
d. We showed the agent our tickets, and she gave us boarding passes.
e. The dining hall offered students healthy meal choices.

1. Send the registrar your scholarship form today.
2. The independent research institute gives its scholars the freedom to work without government or military interference.
3. Computer viruses make networks vulnerable.
4. Give me a book's title, and I can tell you the author.
5. The dire forecast made us extremely cautious about riding out the storm at home.

PRACTICE hackerhandbooks.com/rules
> Grammar basics > 47–6 to 47–9

47c Pattern variations

Although most sentences follow one of the five patterns in the chart on page 386, variations of these patterns commonly occur in questions, commands, sentences with delayed subjects, and passive transformations.

Questions and commands

Questions are sometimes patterned in normal word order, with the subject preceding the verb.

> S   ⌐ V ⌐
> Who will have the most hits this season?

Just as frequently, however, the pattern of a question is inverted, with the subject appearing between the helping verb and the main verb or after the verb.

> HV S   MV
> Will he have the most hits this season?

> V ⌐   S ⌐
> Why is the number of hits an important statistic?

In commands, the subject of the sentence is an understood *you*.

> S   V
> [You] Pay attention to the road.

Sentences with delayed subjects

Writers sometimes choose to delay the subject of a sentence to achieve a special effect such as suspense or humor.

> V ⌐   S ⌐
> Behind the phony tinsel of Hollywood lies the real tinsel.

The subject of the sentence is also delayed in sentences opening with the expletive *There* or *It*. When used as expletives, the words *There* and *It* have no strict grammatical function; they serve merely to get the sentence started.

> V ⌐   S ⌐
> There are thirty thousand spectators in the stadium.

> V   ⌐   S ⌐
> It is best to avoid trans fats.

The subject in the second example is an infinitive phrase. (See 48b.)

Passive transformations

Transitive verbs, those that can take direct objects, usually appear in the active voice. In the active voice, the subject does the action, and a direct object receives the action.

ACTIVE ┌─────── S ───────┐ V ┌────── DO──────
The fireworks display dazzled the viewers on the
┌──────┐
Esplanade.

Sentences in the active voice may be transformed into the passive voice, with the subject receiving the action instead.

PASSIVE ┌─────────── S ───────────┐ HV MV
The viewers on the Esplanade were dazzled by the
fireworks display.

What was once the direct object (*the viewers on the Esplanade*) has become the subject in the passive-voice transformation, and the original subject appears in a prepositional phrase beginning with *by*. The *by* phrase is frequently omitted in passive-voice constructions.

PASSIVE The viewers on the Esplanade were dazzled.

Verbs in the passive voice can be identified by their form alone. The main verb is always a past participle, such as *dazzled* (see 46c), preceded by a form of *be* (*be, am, is, are, was, were, being, been*): *were dazzled.* Sometimes adverbs intervene (*were usually dazzled*).

TIP: Avoid using the passive voice when the active voice would be more appropriate (see 8a).

Subordinate word groups

Subordinate word groups include phrases and clauses. Phrases are subordinate because they lack a subject and a verb; they are classified as prepositional, verbal, appositive, and absolute (see 48a–48d). Subordinate clauses have a subject and a verb, but they begin with a word (such as *although, that,* or *when*) that marks them as subordinate (see 48e).

48a Prepositional phrases

A prepositional phrase begins with a preposition such as *at*, *by*, *for*, *from*, *in*, *of*, *on*, *to*, or *with* (see 46f) and usually ends with a noun or noun equivalent: *on the table*, *for him*, *by sleeping late*. The noun or noun equivalent is known as the *object of the preposition*.

Prepositional phrases function either as adjectives or as adverbs. When functioning as an adjective, a prepositional phrase nearly always appears immediately following the noun or pronoun it modifies.

The hut had *walls of mud*.

Adjective phrases usually answer one or both of the questions Which one? and What kind of? If we ask Which walls? or What kind of walls? we get a sensible answer: *walls of mud*.

Adverbial prepositional phrases usually modify the verb, but they can also modify adjectives or other adverbs. When a prepositional phrase modifies the verb, it can appear nearly anywhere in a sentence.

James *walked* his dog *on a leash*.

Sabrina *will in time adjust* to life in Ecuador.

During a mudslide, the terrain *can change* drastically.

Adverbial word groups usually answer one of these questions: When? Where? How? Why? Under what conditions? To what degree?

James walked his dog *how*? *On a leash*.

Sabrina will adjust to life in Ecuador *when*? *In time*.

The terrain can change drastically *under what conditions*? *During a mudslide*.

EXERCISE 48–1   Underline the prepositional phrases in the following sentences. Tell whether each one is an adjective phrase or an adverb phrase and what it modifies in the sentence. Answers to lettered sentences appear in the back of the book. Example:

> **Flecks of mica glittered in the new granite floor.** (*Adjective phrase modifying "Flecks"; adverb phrase modifying "glittered"*)

a. In northern Italy, some people speak German as their first language.

b. William completed the hike through the thick forest with ease.

c. To my boss's dismay, I was late for work again.

d. The traveling exhibit of Mayan artifacts gave viewers new insight into pre-Columbian culture.

e. In 2002, the euro became the official currency in twelve European countries.

1. The Silk Road was an old trade route between China and other parts of the world.

2. Dough with too much flour yields heavy baked goods.

3. On one side of the barricades were revolutionary students; on the other was a government militia.

4. You can tell with just one whiff whether the milk is fresh.

5. At first, we couldn't decide whether to take the car or the train, but in the end we decided to take the train.

48b Verbal phrases

A verbal is a verb form that does not function as the verb of a clause. Verbals include infinitives (the word *to* plus the base form of the verb), present participles (the *-ing* form of the verb), and past participles (the verb form usually ending in *-d*, *-ed*, *-n*, *-en*, or *-t*). (See 27a and 46c.)

INFINITIVE	PRESENT PARTICIPLE	PAST PARTICIPLE
to dream	dreaming	dreamed
to choose	choosing	chosen
to build	building	built
to grow	growing	grown

PRACTICE   hackerhandbooks.com/rules
  > Grammar basics > 48–4 to 48–6

Instead of functioning as the verb of a clause, a verbal functions as an adjective, a noun, or an adverb.

ADJECTIVE *Broken* promises cannot be fixed.

NOUN Constant *complaining* becomes wearisome.

ADVERB Can you wait *to celebrate*?

Verbals with objects, complements, or modifiers form verbal phrases. Like verbals, verbal phrases function as adjectives, nouns, or adverbs. Verbal phrases are ordinarily classified as participial, gerund, and infinitive.

Participial phrases

Participial phrases always function as adjectives. Their verbals are either present participles (such as *dreaming*, *asking*) or past participles (such as *stolen*, *reached*).

Participial phrases frequently appear immediately following the noun or pronoun they modify.

Congress shall make no *law abridging the freedom of speech or of the press.*

Unlike other word groups that function as adjectives (prepositional phrases, infinitive phrases, adjective clauses), which must always follow the noun or pronoun they modify, participial phrases are often movable. They can precede the word they modify.

Being a weight-bearing joint, the *knee* is among the most frequently injured.

They may also appear at some distance from the word they modify.

Last night we saw a *play* that affected us deeply, *written with profound insight into the lives of immigrants.*

participle (*stolen from the bank, waking early*) • gerund
(*following the crowd*) • *-ing* verb forms • infinitive (*to ask*)

basic

48b

393

Gerund phrases

Gerund phrases are built around present participles (verb forms that end in *-ing*), and they always function as nouns: usually as subjects, subject complements, direct objects, or objects of a preposition.

$\overline{\quad\quad S\quad\quad}$
Rationalizing a fear can eliminate it.

$\overline{\quad\quad DO\quad\quad}$
Lizards usually enjoy sunning themselves.

Infinitive phrases

Infinitive phrases, usually constructed around *to* plus the base form of the verb (*to call, to drink*), can function as nouns, as adjectives, or as adverbs. When functioning as a noun, an infinitive phrase may appear in almost any noun slot in a sentence, usually as a subject, subject complement, or direct object.

$\overline{\quad\quad S\quad\quad}$
To live without health insurance is risky.

Infinitive phrases functioning as adjectives usually appear immediately following the noun or pronoun they modify.

The Twentieth Amendment gave women the *right to vote*.

Adverbial infinitive phrases usually qualify the meaning of the verb, telling when, where, how, why, under what conditions, or to what degree an action occurred.

Volunteers *rolled up* their pants *to wade through the flood waters*.

Why did they roll up their pants? *To wade through the flood waters*.

NOTE: In some constructions, the infinitive is unmarked; in other words, the *to* does not appear. (See 28f.)

Graphs and charts can help researchers [*to*] *present complex data*.

EXERCISE 48–2 Underline the verbal phrases in the following sentences. Tell whether each phrase is participial, gerund, or infinitive and how each is used in the sentence. Answers to lettered sentences appear in the back of the book. Example:

> **Do you want <u>to watch that documentary</u>?** *(Infinitive phrase used as direct object of "Do want")*

a. Updating your software will fix the computer glitch.
b. The challenge in decreasing the town budget is identifying nonessential services.
c. Cathleen tried to help her mother by raking the lawn.
d. Understanding little, I had no hope of passing my biology final.
e. Working with animals gave Steve a sense of satisfaction.

1. Driving through South Carolina, we saw kudzu growing out of control along the roadside.
2. Some people now use a patch to repel mosquitoes.
3. We helped the schoolchildren find their way to the station.
4. Painting requires the ability to keep a steady hand.
5. My father could not see a weed without pulling it out of the ground.

48c Appositive phrases

Appositive phrases describe nouns or pronouns. Instead of modifying nouns or pronouns, however, appositive phrases rename them. In form they are nouns or noun equivalents.

> Bloggers, *conversationalists at heart*, are the online equivalent of radio talk show hosts.

48d Absolute phrases

An absolute phrase modifies a whole clause or sentence, not just one word. It consists of a noun or noun equivalent usually followed by a participial phrase.

> *Her words reverberating in the hushed arena*, the senator urged the crowd to support her former opponent.

48e Subordinate clauses

Subordinate clauses are patterned like sentences, having subjects and verbs and sometimes objects or complements. But they function within sentences as adjectives, adverbs, or nouns. They cannot stand alone as complete sentences.

Adjective clauses

Adjective clauses modify nouns or pronouns, usually answering the question Which one? or What kind of? They begin with a relative pronoun (*who, whom, whose, which,* or *that*) or occasionally with a relative adverb (usually *when, where,* or *why*). (See the box on p. 396.)

The coach chose *players who would benefit from intense drills.*

In addition to introducing the clause, the relative pronoun points back to the noun that the clause modifies.

A *book that goes unread* is a writer's worst nightmare.

Relative pronouns are sometimes "understood."

The things [*that*] *we cherish most* are the things [*that*] *we might lose.*

The parts of an adjective clause are often arranged as in sentences (subject/verb/object or complement).

$$\text{S} \quad \text{V} \quad \text{DO}$$
Sometimes it is our closest friends who disappoint us.

Frequently, however, the object or complement appears first, violating the normal order of subject/verb/object.

$$\text{DO} \quad \text{S} \quad \text{V}$$
They can be the very friends whom we disappoint.

TIP: For punctuation of adjective clauses, see 32e and 33e. For advice about avoiding repeated words in adjective clauses, see 30d.

basic

Words that introduce subordinate clauses
Words introducing adjective clauses
Relative pronouns: that, which, who, whom, whose **Relative adverbs:** when, where, why
Words introducing adverb clauses
Subordinating conjunctions: after, although, as, as if, because, before, even though, if, in order that, since, so that, than, that, though, unless, until, when, where, whether, while
Words introducing noun clauses
Relative pronouns: that, which, who, whom, whose **Other pronouns:** what, whatever, whichever, whoever, whomever **Other subordinating words:** how, if, when, whenever, where, wherever, whether, why

Adverb clauses

Adverb clauses modify verbs, adjectives, or other adverbs, usually answering one of these questions: When? Where? Why? How? Under what conditions? To what degree? They always begin with a subordinating conjunction (such as *after, although, because, that, though, unless,* or *when*). (For a complete list, see the box on this page.)

When the sun went down, the hikers *prepared* their camp.

Kate *would have made* the team *if she hadn't broken her ankle.*

Noun clauses

A noun clause functions just like a single-word noun, usually as a subject, a subject complement, a direct object, or an object of a preposition. It usually begins with one of the following words: *how, if, that, what, whatever, when, where, whether, which, who, whoever, whom, whomever, whose, why.* (For a complete list, see the box on p. 396.)

$\qquad$ S $\qquad$
Whoever leaves the house last must double-lock the door.

$\qquad$ DO $\qquad$
Copernicus argued that the sun is the center of the universe.

The subordinating word introducing the clause may or may not play a significant role in the clause. In the preceding example sentences, *Whoever* is the subject of its clause, but *that* does not perform a function in its clause.

As with adjective clauses, the parts of a noun clause may appear in normal order (subject/verb/object or complement) or out of their normal order.

S   V   ┌─ DO ─┐
Loyalty is what keeps a friendship strong.

DO   S   V
New Mexico is where we live.

EXERCISE 48–3   Underline the subordinate clauses in the following sentences. Tell whether each clause is an adjective, adverb, or noun clause and how it is used in the sentence. Answers to lettered sentences appear in the back of the book. Example:

Show the committee the latest draft before you print the

final report. *(Adverb clause modifying "Show")*

a. The city's electoral commission adjusted the voting process so that every vote would count.

b. A marketing campaign that targets baby boomers may not appeal to young professionals.

c. After the Tambora volcano erupted in the southern Pacific in 1815, no one realized that it would contribute to the "year without a summer" in Europe and North America.

d. The concept of peak oil implies that at a certain point there will be no more oil to extract from the earth.

e. Details are easily overlooked when you are rushing.

1. What her internship taught her was that she worked well with children with special needs.

PRACTICE   hackerhandbooks.com/rules
  > Grammar basics > 48–9 to 48–12

2.   Whether you like it or not, you cannot choose your family.
3.   The meteorologist who underestimated the total snowfall of the first winter storm was right on target about the second storm.
4.   If Ramon didn't have to work every afternoon, he would be willing to sign up for the yoga class with Andrea.
5.   The book that we saw in the shop in Dublin was not available when we returned home.

49 Sentence types

Sentences are classified in two ways: according to their structure (simple, compound, complex, and compound-complex) and according to their purpose (declarative, imperative, interrogative, and exclamatory).

49a Sentence structures

Depending on the number and the types of clauses they contain, sentences are classified as simple, compound, complex, or compound-complex.

Clauses come in two varieties: independent and subordinate. An independent clause contains a subject and a predicate, and it either stands alone or could stand alone as a sentence. A subordinate clause also contains a subject and a predicate, but it functions within a sentence as an adjective, an adverb, or a noun; it cannot stand alone. (See 48e.)

Simple sentences

A simple sentence is one independent clause with no subordinate clauses.

———————— INDEPENDENT CLAUSE ————————
Without a passport, Eva could not visit her grandparents in
Hungary.

A simple sentence may contain compound elements—a compound subject, verb, or object, for example—but it does not contain more than one full sentence pattern. The following

sentence is simple because its two verbs (*comes in* and *goes out*)
share a subject (*Spring*).

```
┌─────────────── INDEPENDENT CLAUSE ───────────────┐
Spring comes in like a lion and goes out like a lamb.
```

Compound sentences

A compound sentence is composed of two or more independent
clauses with no subordinate clauses. The independent clauses are
usually joined with a comma and a coordinating conjunction (*and,
but, or, nor, for, so, yet*) or with a semicolon. (See 14a.)

```
  INDEPENDENT              INDEPENDENT
┌── CLAUSE ──┐          ┌─────── CLAUSE ───────┐
The car broke down, but a rescue van arrived within minutes.
```

```
┌─── INDEPENDENT CLAUSE ───┐ ┌─INDEPENDENT CLAUSE─┐
A shark was spotted near shore; people left immediately.
```

Complex sentences

A complex sentence is composed of one independent clause with
one or more subordinate clauses. (See 48e.)

ADJECTIVE
```
                        SUBORDINATE
                     ┌── CLAUSE──┐
The pitcher who won the game is a rookie.
```

ADVERB
```
      SUBORDINATE
   ┌─ CLAUSE ─┐
If you leave late, take a cab home.
```

NOUN
```
                SUBORDINATE
             ┌─── CLAUSE ───┐
What matters most to us is a quick commute.
```

Compound-complex sentences

A compound-complex sentence contains at least two independent clauses and at least one subordinate clause. The following
sentence contains two independent clauses, each of which contains a subordinate clause.

```
┌──INDEPENDENT CLAUSE ──┐   ┌── INDEPENDENT CLAUSE
              ┌──SUB CL──┐                      ┌──
Tell the doctor how you feel, and she will decide whether

┌─────────────┐
┌── SUB CL──┐
you can go home.
```

49b Sentence purposes

Writers use declarative sentences to make statements, imperative sentences to issue requests or commands, interrogative sentences to ask questions, and exclamatory sentences to make exclamations.

DECLARATIVE	The echo sounded in our ears.
IMPERATIVE	Love your neighbor.
INTERROGATIVE	Did the better team win tonight?
EXCLAMATORY	We're here to save you!

EXERCISE 49–1 Identify the following sentences as simple, compound, complex, or compound-complex. Identify the subordinate clauses and classify them according to their function: adjective, adverb, or noun. (See 48e.) Answers to lettered sentences appear in the back of the book. Example:

The deli in Courthouse Square was crowded with lawyers

at lunchtime. (Simple)

a. Fires that are ignited in dry areas spread especially quickly.
b. The early Incas were advanced; they used a calendar and developed a decimal system.
c. Elaine's jacket was too thin to block the wintry air.
d. Before we leave for the station, we always check the Amtrak Web site.
e. Decide when you want to leave, and I will be there to pick you up.
1. The fact is that the network outage could have been avoided.
2. Those who lose a loved one in a tragic accident may find group therapy comforting.
3. The outlets in the garment district are the best places to find Halloween costumes.
4. There were six lunar Apollo missions, but people usually remember Apollo 13 best.
5. Our generator kicks in whenever we lose power.

Document Design

The term *document* is broad enough to describe anything you might write in a college class, in the business world, and in everyday life. How you design a document (format it for the printed page or for a computer screen) will affect how readers respond to it.

50 Become familiar with the principles of document design.

Good document design promotes readability, but what *readability* means depends on your purpose and audience and perhaps on other elements of your writing situation, such as your subject, length restrictions, or any other specific requirements. All of your design choices — formatting options, headings, and lists — should be made with your writing situation in mind. Likewise, different types of visuals — tables, charts, and images — can support your writing if they are used appropriately.

50a Select appropriate format options.

Similar documents share common design features. Together, these features — layout, margins and line spacing, alignment, fonts, and font styles — can help guide readers through a document.

Layout

Most readers have set ideas about how different kinds of documents should look. Advertisements, for example, have a distinctive appearance, as do newsletters and brochures. Instructors have expectations about how a college paper should look (see 51). Employers, too, expect documents such as letters, résumés, memos, and e-mail messages to be presented in standard ways (see 52).

Unless you have a compelling reason to stray from convention, it's best to choose a document layout that conforms to your readers' expectations. If you're not sure what readers expect, look at examples of the kind of document you are producing.

Margins and line spacing

Margins help control the look of a page. For most academic and business documents, leave a margin of one to one and a half inches on all sides. These margins create a visual frame for the text and provide room for annotations, such as an instructor's comments or a peer's suggestions. Tight margins generally make a page crowded and difficult to read.

Most manuscripts in progress are double-spaced to allow room for editing. Final copy is often double-spaced as well, since single-spaced text is less inviting to read. If you are unsure about margin and spacing requirements for your document, check with your instructor or consult documents similar to the one you are writing.

At times, the advantages of wide margins and double-spaced lines are offset by other considerations. For example, most business and technical documents are single-spaced, with double-spacing between paragraphs, to save paper and promote quick scanning. Keep your purpose and audience in mind as you determine appropriate margins and line spacing for your document.

SINGLE-SPACED, UNFORMATTED   **DOUBLE-SPACED, FORMATTED**

Planning a document: Design checklist for purpose and audience

- What is the purpose of your document? How can your document design help you achieve this purpose?
- Who are your readers? What are their expectations?
- What format is required? What format options — layout, margins, line spacing, and font styles — will readers expect?
- How can you use visuals — charts, graphs, tables, images — to help you convey information and achieve your purpose?

As you write

Using the checklist on page 403, evaluate the design of a paper you're working on. Exchange drafts with a classmate, and ask for specific feedback. How can your document design help you better achieve your purpose and reach your audience?

Fonts

If you have a choice, select a font that fits your writing situation in an easy-to-read size (usually 10 to 12 points). Although offbeat fonts may seem attractive, they slow readers down and can distract them from your ideas. For example, using *Comic Sans*, a font with a handwritten, childish feel, can make an essay seem too informal or unpolished, regardless of how well it's written. Fonts that are easy to read and appropriate for college and workplace documents include the following: Arial, Courier, Georgia, Times New Roman, and Verdana. Check with your instructor; he or she may expect or prefer a particular font.

Font styles

Font styles — such as **boldface**, *italics*, and <u>underlining</u> — can be useful for calling attention to parts of a document. On the whole, it is best to use restraint when selecting styles. Applying too many different styles within a document can result in busy-looking pages and may confuse readers.

TIP: Never write a document in all capital or all lowercase letters. Although some readers have become accustomed to instant messages and e-mails that omit capital letters entirely, their absence makes a piece of writing difficult to read and too informal.

50b Use headings to guide readers.

In short essays, you will have little need for headings, especially if you use paragraphing and clear topic sentences to guide readers. In more complex documents, however, such as longer essays, research papers, business reports, and Web sites, headings can be a useful visual cue for readers.

Headings help readers see at a glance the organization of a document. If more than one level of heading is used, the headings also indicate the hierarchy of ideas — as they do throughout this book.

Headings can serve a number of functions in a document, depending on the needs of different readers. When readers are looking for specific information and don't want to read the entire document, headings can guide them to the appropriate place quickly. When

> **Making the most of your handbook**
> Headings can help writers plan and readers understand a document.
> ▶ Paper organized with headings: page 580

readers are scanning, hoping to pick up a document's meaning or message, headings can provide an overview. Even when readers are committed enough to read every word, headings can help them preview a document before they begin reading or can help them easily revisit a specific section after they've read through the document once.

TIP: While headings can be useful, they cannot substitute for transitions between paragraphs (see 4d).

Phrasing headings

Headings should be as brief and as informative as possible. Certain styles of headings — the most common being *-ing* phrases, noun phrases, questions, and imperative sentences — work better for some purposes, audiences, and subjects than for others.

Whatever style you choose, use it consistently. Headings on the same level of organization should be written in parallel structure (see 9), as in the following examples from a report, a history textbook, a financial brochure, and a nursing manual, respectively.

-ING PHRASES AS HEADINGS

Safeguarding the earth's atmosphere

Charting the path to sustainable energy

Conserving global forests

NOUN PHRASES AS HEADINGS

The civil rights movement

The antiwar movement

The feminist movement

QUESTIONS AS HEADINGS

How do I buy shares?

How do I redeem shares?

How has the fund performed in the past three years?

IMPERATIVE SENTENCES AS HEADINGS

Ask the patient to describe current symptoms.

Take a detailed medical history.

Record the patient's vital signs.

Placing and formatting headings

Headings on the same level of organization should be placed and formatted in a consistent way. If you have more than one level of heading, you might center your first-level headings and make them boldface; then you might make the second-level headings left-aligned and italicized.

First-level heading

Second-level heading

A college paper with headings typically has only one level, and the headings are often centered, as in the sample paper on pages 583–94. In a report or a brochure, important headings can be highlighted by using white space above and below them. Less important headings can be downplayed by using less white space or by running them into the text.

50c Use lists to guide readers.

Lists are easy to read or scan when they are displayed, item by item, rather than run into your text. You might choose to display the following kinds of lists:

- steps in a process
- advice or recommendations
- items to be discussed
- criteria for evaluation (as in checklists)
- parts of an object

Lists are usually introduced with an independent clause followed by a colon (*All mammals share the following five characteristics:*). Periods are not used after items in a list unless the items are complete sentences. Lists are most readable when they are presented in parallel grammatical form (see 9).

Use bullets (circles or squares) or dashes to draw readers' eyes to a list and to emphasize individual items. If you are describing a sequence or a set of steps, number your list with arabic numerals (1, 2, 3) followed by periods.

Although lists can be useful visual cues, don't overdo them. Too many will clutter a document.

50d Add visuals that support your purpose.

In many business and professional contexts, readers expect visuals in a text. Visuals — charts, graphs, tables, and photos, for example — are often used to display data, show trends, illustrate ideas, or humanize a problem or issue. You may be encouraged or required to use visuals in your college assignments. Be sure to think through how visuals support your purpose and satisfy the expectations of your readers. See pages 24–25 for a chart that describes different types of visuals and their purposes. See also the research sections in this book; one student uses a cartoon to illustrate a point in her paper (p. 531), and another uses a table to display key data (p. 589).

Choosing appropriate visuals

In many cases, the same information can be presented visually in different formats. When you're deciding whether to display data in a table or a graph, for example, think about the message you want to convey and the information your readers need. Take a look at the examples on page 408.

If your discussion refers to specific numbers, a table will be more useful to readers. If, however, you want readers to grasp at a glance that sales of hybrid electric vehicles increased from 2001 to 2008 and then declined, a line graph will be more effective.

As you draft and revise a document, carefully choose or design only those visuals that support your main point.

Placing and labeling visuals

A visual may be placed in the text of a document, near a discussion to which it relates, or it can be put in an appendix, labeled, and referred to in the text.

INFORMATION DISPLAYED IN TWO TYPES OF VISUALS These visuals present the same information in two different ways. The table provides exact numbers for comparison. The line graph allows readers to see the trend in sales.

Hybrid electric vehicle sales by year in the United States

Year	Number of vehicles sold
2001	20,282
2002	36,035
2003	47,600
2004	84,199
2005	209,711
2006	252,636
2007	352,274
2008	312,386

Source: US Dept. of Energy (2009).

Hybrid electric vehicle sales by year in the United States

Placing visuals in the text of a document can be tricky. Usually you will want the visual to appear close to the sentences that relate to it, but page breaks won't always allow this placement. At times you may need to insert the visual at a later point and tell readers where it can be found; sometimes you can make the text flow, or wrap, around the visual. No matter where you place a visual, refer to it in your text. Don't expect visuals to speak for themselves.

> **Making the most of your handbook**
> Guidelines for using visuals vary by academic discipline.
> ▶ English and other humanities: 60a
> ▶ Social sciences: 65a

Most of the visuals you include in a document will require some sort of label. A label, which is typically placed above or below the visual, should be brief but descriptive. Most commonly, a visual is labeled with the word "Figure" or the abbreviation "Fig.," followed by a number: *Fig. 4.* Sometimes a title might be included to explain how the visual relates to the text: *Fig. 4. Voter turnout by age.*

Using visuals responsibly

Most word processing and spreadsheet software will allow you to produce your own visuals. If you create a chart, a table, or a graph using information from your research, you must cite the source of the information even though the visual is your own. The visual at the right credits the source of its data.

VISUAL WITH A SOURCE CREDITED

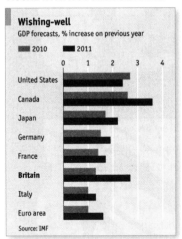

Source: International Monetary Fund (2010).

If you download a photograph from the Web or scan an image from a magazine or book, you must credit the person or organization that created it, just as you would cite any other source you use in a college paper (see 55). Make sure any cropping or other changes you make to the visual do not distort the meaning of the original. If your document is written for publication outside the classroom, you will need to request permission to use any visual you borrow.

51 Use standard academic formatting.

Instructors have certain expectations about how a college paper should look. If your instructor provides guidelines for formatting an essay, a report, a research paper, or another document, you should follow them. Otherwise, use the manuscript format that is recommended for your academic discipline.

In most English and other humanities classes, you will be asked to use the MLA (Modern Language Association) format (see 60a). In most social science classes, such as psychology and sociology, and in most business and health-related classes, you will be asked to use APA (American Psychological Association) format (see 65a).

Most composition instructors require MLA format, which is illustrated in the sample on pages 410–11. For more detailed MLA manuscript guidelines and a sample MLA-style research paper, see 60.

MLA ESSAY FORMAT

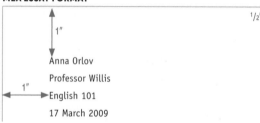

1/2"

Orlov 1

1"

Anna Orlov

Professor Willis

1"

English 101

17 March 2009

Title is centered.

Online Monitoring:

A Threat to Employee Privacy in the Wired Workplace

1/2"

As the Internet has become an integral tool of businesses,

company policies on Internet usage have become as common as

1"

policies regarding vacation days or sexual harassment. A 2005

study by the American Management Association and ePolicy

Institute found that 76% of companies monitor employees' use

of the Web, and the number of companies that block employees'

access to certain Web sites has increased 27% since 2001 (1).

Double-spacing is used throughout.

Unlike other company rules, however, Internet usage policies

often include language authorizing companies to secretly monitor

their employees, a practice that raises questions about rights

in the workplace. Although companies often have legitimate

concerns that lead them to monitor employees' Internet usage—

from expensive security breaches to reduced productivity—the

benefits of electronic surveillance are outweighed by its costs to

employees' privacy and autonomy.

While surveillance of employees is not a new phenomenon,

electronic surveillance allows employers to monitor workers

with unprecedented efficiency. In his book *The Naked*

Employee, Frederick Lane describes offline ways in which

employers have been permitted to intrude on employees'

privacy for decades, such as drug testing, background checks,

psychological exams, lie detector tests, and in-store video

surveillance. The difference, Lane argues, between these old

methods of data gathering and electronic surveillance involves

quantity:

1"

Marginal annotations indicate MLA-style formatting.

1"

½"
Orlov 6

Works Cited

Heading is centered.

Adams, Scott. *Dilbert and the Way of the Weasel*. New York: Harper, 2002. Print.

American Management Association and ePolicy Institute. "2005 Electronic Monitoring and Surveillance Survey." *American Management Association*. Amer. Management Assn., 2005. Web. 15 Feb. 2009.

½"

"Automatically Record Everything They Do Online! Spector Pro 5.0 FAQ's." *Netbus.org*. Netbus.Org, n.d. Web. 17 Feb. 2009.

1"

1"

Flynn, Nancy. "Internet Policies." *ePolicy Institute*. ePolicy Inst., n.d. Web. 15 Feb. 2009.

Frauenheim, Ed. "Stop Reading This Headline and Get Back to Work." *CNET News.com*. CNET Networks, 11 July 2005. Web. 17 Feb. 2009.

Gonsalves, Chris. "Wasting Away on the Web." *eWeek.com*. Ziff Davis Enterprise Holdings, 8 Aug. 2005. Web. 16 Feb. 2009.

Kesan, Jay P. "Cyber-Working or Cyber-Shirking? A First Principles Examination of Electronic Privacy in the Workplace." *Florida Law Review* 54.2 (2002): 289-332. Print.

Lane, Frederick S., III. *The Naked Employee: How Technology Is Compromising Workplace Privacy*. New York: Amer. Management Assn., 2003. Print.

Tam, Pui-Wing, et al. "Snooping E-mail by Software Is Now a Workplace Norm." *Wall Street Journal* 9 Mar. 2005: B1+. Print.

Tynan, Daniel. "Your Boss Is Watching." *PC World*. PC World Communications, 6 Oct. 2004. Web. 17 Feb. 2009.

Verespej, Michael A. "Inappropriate Internet Surfing." *Industry Week*. Penton Media, 7 Feb. 2000. Web. 16 Feb. 2009.

Double-spacing is used throughout; no extra space between entries.

52 Use standard business formatting.

This section provides guidelines for preparing business letters, résumés, and memos.

52a Use established conventions for business letters.

In writing a business letter, be direct, clear, and courteous, but do not hesitate to be firm if necessary. State your purpose or request at the beginning of the letter and include only relevant information in the body. By being as direct and concise as possible, you show that you value your reader's time.

For the format of the letter, use established business conventions. The sample business letter on page 413 is typed in what is known as *full block* style. Paragraphs are not indented and are typed single-spaced, with double-spacing between them. This style is usually preferred when the letter is typed on letterhead stationery, as in the example.

Below the signature, aligned at the left, you may include the abbreviation *Enc.* to indicate that something is enclosed with the letter or the abbreviation *cc* followed by a colon and the name of someone who is receiving a copy of the letter.

52b Write effective résumés and cover letters.

An effective résumé gives relevant information in a clear and concise form. You may be asked to produce a traditional résumé, a scannable résumé, or a Web résumé. The cover letter gives a prospective employer a reason to look at your résumé. The goal is to present yourself in a favorable light without including unnecessary details.

Cover letters   Always include a cover letter to introduce yourself, state the position you seek, and tell where you learned about it. The letter also should highlight past experiences that qualify you for the position and should emphasize what you can

MODELS   hackerhandbooks.com/rules
    > Model papers > Résumés and cover letters

BUSINESS LETTER IN FULL BLOCK STYLE

Latino**Voice**

March 16, 2011 — Date

Jonathan Ross
Managing Editor
Latino World Today
2971 East Oak Avenue
Baltimore, MD 21201

Inside
address

Dear Mr. Ross: — Salutation

Body

Thank you very much for taking the time yesterday to speak to the University of Maryland's Latino Club. A number of students have told me that they enjoyed your presentation and found your job search suggestions to be extremely helpful.

As I mentioned to you when we first scheduled your appearance, the club publishes a monthly newsletter, *Latino Voice*. Our purpose is to share up-to-date information and expert advice with members of the university's Latino population. Considering how much students benefited from your talk, I would like to publish excerpts from it in our newsletter.

I have taken the liberty of transcribing parts of your presentation and organizing them into a question-and-answer format for our readers. When you have a moment, would you mind looking through the enclosed article and letting me know if I may have your permission to print it? I would be happy, of course, to make any changes or corrections that you request. I'm hoping to include this article in our next newsletter, so I would need your response by April 4.

Once again, Mr. Ross, thank you for sharing your experiences with us. You gave an informative and entertaining speech, and I would love to be able to share it with the students who couldn't hear it in person.

Sincerely, — Close

Jeffrey Richardson

Signature

Jeffrey Richardson
Associate Editor

Enc.

210 Student Center University of Maryland **College Park MD 20742**

do for the employer (not what the job will do for you). End the letter with a suggestion for a meeting, and tell your prospective employer when you will be available.

Traditional résumés   Traditional résumés are produced on paper, and they are screened by people, not by computers. Because screeners often face stacks of applications, they may spend very

TRADITIONAL RÉSUMÉ

Jeffrey Richardson

121 Knox Road, #6
College Park, MD 20740
301-555-2651
jrichardson@example.net

OBJECTIVE	To obtain an editorial internship with a magazine
EDUCATION	
Fall 2007– present	University of Maryland
	• BA expected in June 2011
	• Double major: English and Latin American studies
	• GPA: 3.7 (on a 4-point scale)
EXPERIENCE	
Fall 2009– present	Associate editor, *Latino Voice*, newsletter of Latino Club
	• Assign and edit feature articles
	• Coordinate community outreach
Fall 2008– present	Photo editor, *The Diamondback*, college paper
	• Shoot and organize photos for print and online publication
	• Oversee photo staff assignments; evaluate photos
Summer 2009	Intern, *The Globe,* Fairfax, Virginia
	• Wrote stories about local issues and personalities
	• Interviewed political candidates
	• Edited and proofread copy
	• Coedited "The Landscapes of Northern Virginia: A Photoessay"
Summers 2008, 2009	Tutor, Fairfax County ESL Program
	• Tutored Latino students in English as a Second Language
	• Trained new tutors
ACTIVITIES	Photographers' Workshop, Latino Club
PORTFOLIO	Available at http://jrichardson.example.net/jrportfolio.htm
REFERENCES	Available on request

---

little time looking at each résumé. Therefore, you will need to make your résumé as reader-friendly as possible. Here are a few guidelines:

- Limit your résumé to one page if possible, two pages at the most. (If your résumé is longer than a page, repeat your name at the top of the second page.)

- Organize your information into clear categories — Education, Experience, and so on.
- Present the information in each category in reverse chronological order to highlight your most recent accomplishments.
- Use bulleted lists or some other simple, clear visual device to organize information.
- Use strong, active verbs to state your accomplishments. For current activities, use present-tense verbs (*manage*); for past activities, use past-tense verbs (*managed*).

Scannable résumés   Scannable résumés might be submitted on paper, by e-mail, or through an online employment service. The résumés are scanned and searched electronically, and a database matches keywords in the job description with keywords in the résumés. A human screener reads the résumés selected by the database.

A scannable résumé must be formatted simply so that the scanner can accurately pick up its content. In general, follow these guidelines when preparing a scannable résumé:

- Include a Keywords section that lists words likely to be searched by a scanner. Use nouns (*manager*), not verbs (*manage* or *managed*).
- Use standard résumé headings (for example, Education, Experience, References).
- Avoid special characters, graphics, or font styles.
- Avoid formatting such as tabs, indents, columns, or tables.

Web résumés   Posting your résumé on a Web site is an easy way to provide recent information about your goals and accomplishments and examples of your work. Most guidelines for traditional résumés apply to Web résumés. You may want to include a downloadable version of your résumé and link to an electronic portfolio. Always list the date that you last updated your résumé.

52c Write clear and concise memos.

Usually brief and to the point, a memo reports information, makes a request, or recommends an action. The format of a memo, which varies from company to company, is designed for easy distribution, quick reading, and efficient filing.

BUSINESS MEMO

COMMONWEALTH PRESS

MEMORANDUM

February 24, 2011

To:	Editorial assistants, Advertising Department
cc:	Stephen Chapman
From:	Helen Brown
Subject:	New database software

The new database software will be installed on your computers next week. I have scheduled a training program to help you become familiar with the software and with our new procedures for data entry and retrieval.

Training program
A member of our IT staff will teach in-house workshops on how to use the new software. If you try the software before the workshop, please be prepared to discuss any problems you encounter.

We will keep the training groups small to encourage hands-on participation and to provide individual attention. The workshops will take place in the training room on the third floor from 10:00 a.m. to 2:00 p.m.

Lunch will be provided in the cafeteria.

Sign-up
Please sign up by March 1 for one of the following dates by adding your name in the department's online calendar:

- Wednesday, March 2
- Friday, March 4
- Monday, March 7

If you will not be in the office on any of those dates, please let me know by March 1.

Most memos display the date, the name of the recipient, the name of the sender, and the subject on separate lines at the top. Many companies have preprinted forms for memos, and most word processing programs have memo templates.

The subject line of a memo should describe the topic as clearly and concisely as possible, and the introductory paragraph should get right to the point. In addition, the body of the memo should be well organized and easy to skim. To promote skimming, use headings where possible and set off any items that deserve special attention (in a list, for example, or in boldface). A sample memo appears on page 416.

52d Write effective e-mail messages.

E-mail is one of the primary means of communicating in business settings. As in all business communications, you should keep your purpose and audience in mind as you write. Effective e-mail messages are straightforward and clear and are formatted in a way that makes them easy to read. See the chart on pages 9–10 for more advice about writing e-mail.

Research

53   Conducting research

College research assignments ask you to pose a question worth exploring, to read widely in search of possible answers, to interpret what you read, to draw reasoned conclusions, and to support those conclusions with valid and well-documented evidence.

The process takes time: time for researching and time for drafting, revising, and documenting the paper in the style recommended by your instructor. Before beginning a research project,

SAMPLE CALENDAR FOR A RESEARCH ASSIGNMENT

2	3	4	5	6	7	8
	Receive and analyze the assignment.	Pose questions you might explore.	Talk with a reference librarian; plan a search strategy.	→	Settle on a topic; narrow the focus.	Revise research questions. Locate sources. →
9	**10**	**11**	**12**	**13**	**14**	**15**
Read, take notes, and compile a working bibliography. →				Draft a working thesis and an outline.	Draft the paper. →	
16	**17**	**18**	**19**	**20**	**21**	**22**
→ Draft the paper. →			Visit the writing center for feedback.	Do additional research if needed. →		
23	**24**	**25**	**26**	**27**	**28**	**29**
Ask peers for feedback. Revise the paper; if necessary, revise the thesis. →				Prepare a list of works cited. →		Proofread the final draft. →
30	**31**					
Proofread the final draft. →	**Submit the final draft.**					

set a realistic schedule of deadlines. Think about how much time you might need for each step on the way to your final draft.

One student created a calendar to map out her tasks for a research paper assigned on October 3 and due October 31, keeping in mind that some tasks might overlap or need to be repeated. Notice that she has budgeted more than a week for drafting and revising the paper.

RESEARCH TIP: Think of research as a process. As your topic evolves, you may find new questions arising that require you to create a new search strategy, find additional sources, and challenge your initial assumptions. Keep an open mind throughout the process, be curious, and enjoy the detective work.

Throughout this section, you will encounter examples related to three sample student research papers:

- A paper on Internet surveillance in the workplace, written by a student in an English composition class (see pp. 527–32). The student, Anna Orlov, uses the MLA (Modern Language Association) style of documentation.

- A paper on the limitations of medications to treat childhood obesity, written by a student in a psychology class (see pp. 583–94). The student, Luisa Mirano, uses the APA (American Psychological Association) style of documentation.

- A paper on the extent to which Civil War general Nathan Bedford Forrest can be held responsible for the Fort Pillow massacre, written by a student in a history class. The student, Ned Bishop, uses the *Chicago Manual of Style* documentation system. Bishop's paper and guidelines for *Chicago*-style documentation appear on the *Rules for Writers* Web site (hackerhandbooks.com/rules).

53a Pose questions worth exploring.

Working within the guidelines of your assignment, pose a few questions that seem worth researching — questions that you are interested in exploring, that you feel would engage your audience, and about which there is a substantial debate. On the next page, for example, are some preliminary research questions jotted down by students enrolled in a variety of courses in different disciplines.

- Should the FCC broaden its definition of indecency to include violence?
- Which geological formations are the safest repositories for nuclear waste?
- What was Marcus Garvey's contribution to the fight for racial equality?
- How can governments and zoos help preserve Asia's endangered snow leopard?

As you think about possible questions, make sure that they are appropriate lines of inquiry for a research paper. Choose questions that are narrow (not too broad), challenging (not too bland), and grounded (not too speculative).

Choosing a narrow question

If your initial question is too broad, given the length of the paper you plan to write, look for ways to restrict your focus (see the chart on p. 5). Here, for example, is how two students narrowed their initial questions.

TOO BROAD	NARROWER
What are the hazards of fad diets?	Why are low-carbohydrate diets hazardous?
What are the benefits of stricter auto emissions standards?	How will stricter auto emissions standards create new, more competitive auto industry jobs?

Choosing a challenging question

Your research paper will be more interesting to both you and your audience if you base it on an intellectually challenging line of inquiry. Draft questions that provoke thought or engage readers in a debate.

TOO BLAND	CHALLENGING
What is obsessive-compulsive disorder?	Why is obsessive-compulsive disorder so difficult to treat?
How does DNA testing work?	How reliable is DNA testing?

You may need to address a bland question in the course of answering a more challenging one. For example, if you were writing about promising treatments for obsessive-compulsive disorder, you would no doubt answer the question "What is obsessive-compulsive disorder?" at some point in your paper. It would be a mistake, however, to use the bland question as the focus for the whole paper.

Choosing a grounded question

Finally, you will want to make sure that your research question is grounded, not too speculative. Although speculative questions — such as those that address morality or beliefs — are worth asking and may receive some attention in a research paper, they are inappropriate central questions. For most college courses, the central argument of a research paper should be grounded in facts.

TOO SPECULATIVE	GROUNDED
Is it wrong to share pornographic personal photos by cell phone?	What role should the US government play in regulating mobile content?
Do medical scientists have the right to experiment on animals?	How have technical breakthroughs made medical experiments on animals increasingly unnecessary?

As you write

Take a few minutes to talk through your tentative research question with a classmate or two. Explain what question you plan to research and why this question is worth exploring. Ask your classmates to suggest revisions to your research question to make it narrower, more challenging, or grounded. See the examples on pages 422 and 423.

53b Map out a search strategy.

A search strategy is a systematic plan for tracking down sources. To create a search strategy appropriate for your research question, consult a reference librarian and take a look at your library's Web site, which will give you an overview of available resources.

Including the library in your plan

Reference librarians are information specialists who can save you time by steering you toward relevant and reliable sources. With the help of an expert, you can make the best use of electronic databases, Web search engines, your library's catalog, and other reference tools.

Before you ask a reference librarian for help, be sure you have thought through the following questions:

- What is your assignment?
- In which academic discipline are you writing?
- What is your tentative research question?
- How long will the paper be?
- How much time can you spend on the project?

It's a good idea to bring a copy of the assignment with you.

In addition to speaking with a reference librarian, take some time to explore your library's Web site. You will typically find links to the library's catalog and to a variety of databases and electronic sources. You may also find resources listed by subject, research guides, information about interlibrary loans, and links to Web sites selected by librarians for their quality. Many libraries offer online reference assistance to help you locate information and refine your search strategy.

NOTE FOR ONLINE STUDENTS: Even if you are unable to visit the library, as an enrolled student you can still use its resources. Most libraries offer chat reference services and access to online databases, though you may have to follow special procedures to use them. Check your library's Web site for information for online students.

Starting with your library's databases

You may be tempted to go straight to the Web and ignore your library's resources, but using them early and often in the research process can save you time in the end. Libraries make a wide range of quality materials readily available, and they weed out questionable sources.

While a general Internet search might seem quick and convenient, it is often more time-consuming and can be less reliable than a search in a library's databases. Initial Internet searches may generate thousands of results. Figuring out which of these are credible, relevant, and worth further investigation can require many additional steps:

- Refining search terms (See the chart on refining keyword searches on p. 429.)
- Narrowing the domain to include only .org, .gov, or .edu sites
- Weeding out any advertisements associated with results
- Scanning titles and sometimes content for relevant results
- Combing through sites to determine their currency and relevance as well as the credibility of their authors

Starting with your library's collection of databases can save you time and effort. Because you can limit library database searches to only academic databases, you can count on finding reliable sources. Not all of the results will be worth examining in detail, but many library searches automatically sort them into subject categories that allow you to view narrowed results with just one click.

Choosing an appropriate search strategy

No single search strategy works for every topic. For some topics, it may be appropriate to search for information in popular newspapers, magazines, and Web sites. For others, the best sources might be found in scholarly journals and books and specialized reference works. Still other topics might be enhanced by field research — interviews, surveys, or direct observation.

With the help of a reference librarian, each of the students mentioned on page 421 constructed a search strategy appropriate for his or her research question.

Anna Orlov   Anna Orlov's topic, Internet surveillance in the workplace, was current and influenced by technological changes, so she relied heavily on recent sources, especially those online. To find information on her topic, Orlov decided to

- search her library's general database for articles in magazines, newspapers, and journals
- check the library's catalog for recently published books
- use Web search engines, such as *Google*, to locate articles and government publications that might not show up in a database search

Luisa Mirano Luisa Mirano's topic, the limitations of medications for childhood obesity, is the subject of psychological studies as well as articles in newspapers and magazines aimed at the general public. Thinking that both scholarly and popular works would be appropriate, Mirano decided to

- locate books through the library's online catalog
- check a specialized encyclopedia, *Encyclopedia of Psychology*
- search a specialized database, *PsycINFO*, for scholarly articles
- search the library's general database for popular articles

Ned Bishop Ned Bishop's topic, Nathan Bedford Forrest's role in the Fort Pillow massacre, has been investigated and debated by professional historians. Given the nature of his historical topic, Bishop decided to

- locate books through the library's online catalog
- locate scholarly articles by searching a specialized database, *America: History and Life*
- locate newspaper articles from 1864 by searching the historical archive at the *New York Times* Web site
- search the Web for other historical primary sources

As you write

Before you begin looking for sources, write some notes about your search strategy. Write down your tentative research question. Then answer the following questions: What is the current debate about this topic? In which online or print publications is the debate taking place? Who has written about your research topic? Show your notes to a reference librarian and ask for feedback. Based on the comments you receive, revise your search strategy and clarify your search terms.

53c To locate articles, search a database or consult a print index.

Libraries subscribe to a variety of electronic databases (sometimes called *periodical* or *article databases*) that give students access to articles and other materials without charge. Because many databases are limited to relatively recent works, you may need to consult a print index as well.

What databases offer

Your library has access to databases that can lead you to articles in periodicals such as newspapers, magazines, and scholarly or technical journals. General databases cover several subject areas; subject-specific databases cover one subject area in depth.

Many databases, especially general databases, include the full text of at least some articles; others list only citations or citations with short summaries called *abstracts* (see also p. 442). In the case of full-text articles, you may have the option to print an article, save it, or e-mail it to yourself.

When the full text is not available, a citation usually will give you enough information to track down an article. Your library's Web site will help you determine which articles are available in your library, either in print or in electronic form.

> **Making the most of your handbook**
> Freewriting, listing, and clustering can help you come up with additional search terms.
> ▶ Exploring your subject: 1b

Your library might subscribe to some of the databases listed below and on page 428.

General databases   The information in general databases is not restricted to a specific discipline or subject area. You may find searching a general database helpful in the early stages of your research process.

Academic Search Premier.   An interdisciplinary database that indexes thousands of popular and scholarly journals on all subjects.

Expanded Academic ASAP.   An interdisciplinary database that indexes the contents of magazines, newspapers, and scholarly journals in all subject areas.

JSTOR.   A full-text archive of scholarly journals from many disciplines; unlike most databases, it includes articles published decades ago but does not include articles from the most recent issues of publications.

LexisNexis.   A database that is particularly strong in coverage of news, business, legal, and political topics.

ProQuest.   A database of periodical articles, many in full text. Through *ProQuest*, your library may subscribe to databases in subjects such as nursing, biology, and psychology.

Subject-specific databases Libraries have access to dozens of specialized databases, each of which covers a specific area of research. To find out what's available, consult your library's Web site or ask your reference librarian. The following are examples of subject-specific databases.

> *ERIC.* A database offering education-related documents and abstracts of articles published in education journals.

> *MLA Bibliography.* A database of literary criticism, with citations to help researchers find articles, books, and dissertations.

> *PsycINFO.* A comprehensive database of psychology research, including abstracts of articles in journals and books.

> *Public Affairs Information Service (PAIS).* A database that indexes books, journals, government documents, statistical directories, and research reports in the social sciences.

> *PubMed.* A database offering millions of abstracts of medical research studies.

How to search a database

To find articles on your topic in a database, start by searching with keywords, terms that describe the information you need. If the first keyword you try results in too few or no matches, experiment with synonyms or ask a librarian for suggestions. For example, if you're searching for sources on a topic related to education, you might also try the terms *teaching, learning,* and *curriculum.* If your keyword search generates too many matches, narrow it by using one of the strategies in the chart on the next page.

For her paper on Internet surveillance in the workplace, Anna Orlov conducted a keyword search in a general database. She typed *"internet use"* and *employee* and *surveillance* (see the database screen on p. 430). This search brought up twenty possible articles, some of which looked promising. Orlov e-mailed several full-text articles to herself and printed citations to other sources so that she could locate them in the library.

Refining keyword searches in databases and search engines

Although command terms and characters vary in electronic databases and Web search engines, some common functions are listed here.

- Use quotation marks around words that are part of a phrase: "gateway drug".

- Use AND to connect any words that must appear in a document: hyperactivity AND children. In some search engines — *Google*, for example — AND is assumed, so typing it is unnecessary. Other search engines require a plus sign instead: hyperactivity + children.

- Use NOT in front of words that must not appear in a document: Persian Gulf NOT war. Some search engines require a minus sign (hyphen) instead: Persian Gulf-war.

- Use OR if only one of the terms must appear in a document: "mountain lion" OR cougar.

- Use an asterisk as a substitute for letters that might vary: "marine biolog*" (to find *marine biology* or *marine biologist*, for example).

- Use parentheses to group a search expression and combine it with another: (standard OR student OR test*) AND reform.

NOTE: Many search engines and databases offer an advanced search option for refining your search with filters for exact phrases that must appear, specific words that should not appear, date restrictions, and so on.

When to use a print index

A print index to periodical articles is a useful tool when you are researching a historical topic, especially from the early to mid-twentieth century. The *Readers' Guide to Periodical Literature* and *Poole's Index to Periodical Literature* index magazine articles beginning around 1900, many of which are too old to appear in electronic databases. You can usually access the print articles themselves in your library's shelves or on microfilm.

DATABASE SCREEN: KEYWORD SEARCH

53d To locate books, consult the library's catalog.

The books your library owns, along with other resources, are listed in its catalog. You can search the catalog by author, title, or subject.

If your first search calls up too few results, try different keywords or search for books on broader topics. If your search gives you too many results, use the strategies in the chart on page 429 or try an advanced search tool to combine concepts and limit your results. If those strategies don't work, ask a librarian for suggestions.

When Luisa Mirano, whose topic was childhood obesity, entered the term *obesity* into the library's catalog, she was faced with an unmanageable number of hits. She narrowed her search by adding two more specific terms to *obesity*: *child** (to include the terms *child*, *children*, and *childhood*) and *treatment*. When she still got too many results, she limited the first two terms to subject searches

LIBRARY CATALOG SCREEN 1: ADVANCED SEARCH

LIBRARY CATALOG SCREEN 2: COMPLETE RECORD FOR A BOOK

to find books that had obesity in children as their primary subject (see screen 1).

Screen 2 shows the complete record for one of the books she found. The call number, listed beside *Availability*, is the book's address on the library shelf. When you're retrieving a book from the shelf, take the time to scan other books in the area since they are likely to be on the same topic.

RESEARCH TIP: The catalog record for a book lists related subject headings. These headings are a good way to locate other books on your subject. For example, the record in screen 2 (p. 431) lists the terms *obesity in children* and *obesity in adolescence* as related subject headings. By clicking on these new terms, Mirano found a few more books on her subject. Subject headings can be useful terms for a database search as well.

53e To locate other sources, use a variety of online tools.

You can find a variety of reliable sources using online tools beyond those offered by your library. For example, most government agencies post information on their Web sites, and federal and state governments use Web sites to communicate with citizens. The sites of many private organizations, such as Doctors without Borders and the Sierra Club, contain useful information about current issues. Museums and libraries often post digital versions of primary sources, such as photographs, political speeches, and classic literary texts.

Although the Web at large can be a rich source of information, some of which can't be found anywhere else, it lacks quality control. The material on many sites has not necessarily been reviewed by experts. So when you're not working with your library's tools to locate online sources, carefully evaluate what you find (see 54e).

This section describes the following Web resources: search engines, directories, digital archives, government and news sites, blogs, and wikis.

Search engines

When using a search engine, such as *Google* or *Yahoo!*, focus your search as narrowly as possible. You can refine your search by using many of the tips in the chart on page 429 or by using the search engine's advanced search form. For her paper on Internet surveillance in the workplace, Anna Orlov had difficulty restricting the number of hits. When she typed the words *internet*, *surveillance*, *workplace*, and *privacy* into a search engine, she got more than 80,000 matches. After examining the first page of

SEARCH ENGINE SCREEN: RESULTS OF AN ADVANCED SEARCH

Web Results 1 - 5 of about 9 over the past 3 months for "Internet surveillance" employee "workplace privacy" site:.org 0.44 seconds)

Web Results 1 - 5 of about 9 over the past 3 months for "Internet surveillance" employee "workplace privacy" site:.org 0.44 seconds)

Tip: Try removing quotes from your search to get more results.

EPIC/PI - Privacy & Human Rights 2000
Now the supervision of **employee**'s performance, behavior and ... [89]Information and
Privacy Commissioner/Ontario, **Workplace Privacy**: The Need for a..
www.privacyinternational.org/survey/phr2000/threats.html - 131k Cached - Similar pages

Privacy and Human Rights 2003: Threats to Privacy
Other issues that raise **workplace privacy** concerns are employer requirements that
employees complete medical tests, questionnaires, and polygraph tests..
www.privacyinternational.org/survey/phr2003/threats.htm - 279k Cached - Similar pages
[More results from www.privacyinternational.org]

[P DF] Monitoring **Employee** E-Mail And Internet Usage: Avoiding The..
File Format: PDF/Adobe Acrobat - View as HTML
Internet surveillance by employers in the American workplace. At present, US **employees**
in the private workplace have no constitutional, common law or statu
lsr.nellco.org/cgi/viewcontent.cgi?article=1006&context=suffolk/ip - Similar pages

Previous EPIC Top News
The agencies plan to use RFID to track **employees**' movements and in ID cards... For more
information on **workplace privacy**, see the EPIC **Workplace Privacy** ...
www.epic.org/news/2005.html - 163k Cached - Similar pages

results and viewing some that looked promising, Orlov grouped
her search terms into the phrases "*internet surveillance*" and
"*workplace privacy*" and added the term *employee* to narrow the
focus. The result was 422 matches. To refine her search further,
Orlov clicked on Advanced Search and restricted her search to
sites with URLs ending in *.org* and to those updated in the last
three months. (See the results screen above.)

Directories

If you want to find good resources on topics too broad for a search
engine, try a directory. Unlike search engines, directories are put
together by information specialists who choose reputable sites and
arrange them by topic: education, health, politics, and so on.
    Try the following directories for scholarly research:

Internet Scout Project: http://scout.wisc.edu/Archives

Librarian's Internet Index: http://www.lii.org

Open Directory Project: http://dmoz.org

WWW Virtual Library: http://www.vlib.org

Digital archives

Archives are a good place to find primary sources: the texts of poems, books, speeches, and historically significant documents; photographs; and political cartoons (see p. 443).

The materials in these sites are usually limited to official documents and older works because of copyright laws.

American Memory: http://memory.loc.gov

Avalon Project: http://www.yale.edu/lawweb/avalon/avalon.htm

Eurodocs: http:// eudocs.lib.byu.edu

Google Books: http:// books.google.com

Google Scholar: http://scholar.google.com

The Making of America: http://quod.lib.umich.edu/m/moagrp

The New York Public Library Digital Collections: http://www.nypl.org/digital

Online Books Page: http://digital.library.upenn.edu/books

Government and news sites

For current topics, both government and news sites can prove useful. Many government agencies at every level provide online information. Government-maintained sites include resources such as legal texts, facts and statistics, government reports, and searchable reference databases. Here are just a few government sites:

Fedstats: http://www.fedstats.gov

GPO Access: http://www.gpoaccess.gov

United Nations: http://www.un.org

University of Michigan Documents Center: http://www.lib.umich.edu/m/moagrp

US Census Bureau: http://www.census.gov

NOTE: You can access a state's Web site by putting the two-letter state abbreviation into a standard URL: http://www.state.ga.us. Substitute any state's two-letter abbreviation for the letters *ga*, which in this case stand for Georgia.

Many news organizations offer up-to-date information on the Web. Some require registration and may charge fees for some articles. (Find out if your library subscribes to news sites so that you can access them at no charge.) The following news sites offer many free resources:

BBC: http://www.bbc.co.uk

Google News: http://news.google.com

Kidon Media-Link: http://www.kidon.com/media-link

New York Times: http://nytimes.com

Reuters: http://www.reuters.com

Blogs

A blog (short for *Weblog*) is a site that contains dated text or multimedia entries usually written and maintained by one person, with comments contributed by readers. Though some blogs are personal diaries and others are devoted to partisan politics, many journalists and academics maintain blogs that cover topics of interest to researchers. Some blogs feature short essays that provide useful insights or analysis; others point to new developments in a particular area of interest. The following Web sites can lead you to a wide range of blogs:

Academic Blog Portal: http://academicblogs.org

Google Blog Search: http://www.google.com/blogsearch

Science Blogs: http://scienceblogs.com

Technorati: http://technorati.com

Wikis

A wiki is a collaborative Web site with many contributors and with content that may change frequently. *Wikipedia*, the collaborative online encyclopedia, is one of the most frequently consulted wikis.

In general, *Wikipedia* may be helpful if you're checking for something that is common knowledge (facts available in multiple sources, such as dates and well-known historical events) or if you're looking for current information about a topic in contemporary culture that isn't covered elsewhere. However, many scholars do not consider *Wikipedia* and wikis in general to be appropriate sources for college research. Authorship is open to anyone, not limited to experts; articles may be written by enthusiastic amateurs who are not well informed. And because the articles can be changed by anyone, controversial texts are often altered to reflect a particular perspective and are especially susceptible to bias. When possible, locate and cite another, more reliable source for any useful information you find in a wiki.

53f Use other search tools.

In addition to articles, books, and online sources, you may want to consult references such as encyclopedias and almanacs. Citations in scholarly works can also lead you to additional sources.

Reference works

The reference section of the library holds both general and specialized encyclopedias, dictionaries, almanacs, atlases, and biographical references, some available in electronic form through the library's Web site. Such works often provide a good overview of your subject and include references to the most significant works on a topic. Check with a reference librarian to see which works are most appropriate for your project.

General reference works General reference works are good places to check facts and get basic information. Here are a few frequently used general references:

> *American National Biography*
>
> *National Geographic Atlas of the World*
>
> *The New Encyclopaedia Britannica*
>
> *The Oxford English Dictionary*
>
> *Statistical Abstract of the United States*

Although general encyclopedias are often a good place to find background for your topic, you should rarely use them in your final paper. Most instructors expect you to rely on more specialized sources.

Specialized reference works Specialized reference works often explore a topic in depth, usually in the form of articles written by leading authorities. They offer a quick way to gain an expert's overview of a complex topic. Many specialized works are available, including these:

> *Contemporary Authors*
>
> *Encyclopedia of Bioethics*
>
> *Encyclopedia of Crime and Justice*

Encyclopedia of Psychology
Encyclopedia of World Environmental History
International Encyclopedia of Communication
New Encyclopedia of Africa

Bibliographies and scholarly citations as shortcuts

Scholarly books and articles list the works the author has cited, usually at the end. These lists are useful shortcuts to additional reliable sources on your topic. For example, most of the scholarly articles Luisa Mirano consulted contained citations to related research studies; through these citations, she quickly located other sources related to her topic, treatments for childhood obesity.

53g Conduct field research, if appropriate.

Your own field research can enhance or be the focus of a writing project. For a composition class, for example, you might want to interview a local politician about a current issue, such as the use of alternative energy sources. For a sociology class, you might decide to conduct a survey regarding campus trends in community service. At work, you might need to learn how food industry executives have responded to reports that their products are contributing to health problems.

NOTE: Colleges and universities often require researchers to submit projects to an institutional review board (IRB) if the research involves human subjects outside of a classroom setting. Before administering a survey or conducting other fieldwork, check with your instructor to see if IRB approval is required.

54 Evaluating sources

You can often locate dozens or even hundreds of potential sources for your topic — far more than you will have time to read. Your challenge will be to determine what kinds of sources you need and to zero in on a reasonable number of quality sources, those truly worth your time and attention.

Later, once you have decided on some sources worth consulting, your challenge will be to read them with an open mind and a critical eye (see 54d).

54a Think about how sources might contribute to your writing.

How you plan to use sources will affect how you evaluate them. Not every source must directly support your thesis; sources can have other functions in a paper. They can

- provide background information or context for your topic
- explain terms or concepts that your readers might not understand
- provide evidence for your argument
- lend authority to your argument
- offer alternative interpretations and counterevidence to your argument

For examples of how student writers use sources for a variety of purposes, see 56c and 61c.

As you write

Read and reread three sources you've selected for a research project. Ask yourself: How will each source function in my research paper? Consult page 438 to understand the various ways to use sources to develop your points. For each of your sources, write a brief note about what role that source will play in your essay. Will it offer background information, an explanation of a key term, a counterpoint, expert testimony, or something else?

54b Select sources worth your time and attention.

Section 53 shows how to refine your searches in databases, in the library's book catalog, and in search engines. This section explains how to scan through the results for the most promising sources and how to preview them to see whether they are likely to live up to your expectations and meet your needs.

Scanning search results

As you scan through a list of search results, watch for clues indicating whether a source might be useful for your purposes or is not worth pursuing. You will need to use somewhat different strategies when scanning search results from a database, a library catalog, and a Web search engine.

Databases Most databases list at least the following information, which can help you decide if a source is relevant, current, scholarly enough (see the chart on p. 441), and a suitable length for your purposes.

Title and brief description (How relevant?)

Date (How current?)

Name of periodical (How scholarly?)

Length (How extensive in coverage?)

On this page are just a few of the hits Ned Bishop came up with when he consulted a general database for articles on the Fort Pillow massacre, using the search term *Fort Pillow*.

Many databases allow you to sort your list of results by relevance or date; sorting may help you scan the information more efficiently. By scanning the titles in his search results, Bishop saw that only one contained the words *Fort Pillow*. The name of the periodical in which it appeared, *Journal of American History*, suggested that the source was scholarly. The 1989 publication date was not a problem, since currency is not necessarily a criterion for sources in the field of history. The article's

EVALUATING SEARCH RESULTS: LIBRARY DATABASE

☐ **Black, blue and gray: the other Civil War; African-American soldiers, sailors and spies were the**
Mark **unsung heroes.** *Ebony* Feb 1991 v46 n4 p96(6)
   View text and retrieval choices

Popular magazine. Not relevant.

☐ **The Civil War.** (movie reviews) Lewis Cole. *The Nation* Dec 3, 1990 v251 n19 p694(5)
Mark   View text and retrieval choices

Movie review. Not relevant.

☐ **The hard fight was getting into the fight at all.** (black soldiers in the Civil War) Jack Fincher.
Mark *Smithsonian* Oct 1990 v21 n7 p46(13)
   View text and retrieval choices

Subject too broad.

☑ **The Fort Pillow massacre: a statistical note.** John Cimprich, Robert C. Mainfort Jr.. *Journal of Americ*
Mark *History* Dec 1989 v76 n3 p830(8)
   View extended citation and retrieval choices

Brief scholarly article. Matches the topic. Promising.

length (eight pages) is given in parentheses at the end of the citation. While the article may seem short, the topic — a statistical note — is narrow enough to ensure adequate depth of coverage. Bishop decided that the article was worth consulting. Because the other sources were irrelevant or too broad, he decided not to consult them.

Library catalogs   A library's catalog usually lists enough basic information about books, periodicals, DVDs, and other material to give you a first impression. A book's title and date of publication, for example, will often be your first clues as to whether the book is worth consulting. If a title looks interesting, you can click on it for further information about the book's subject matter and its length. The table of contents may also be available, offering a glimpse of what's inside. (See also p. 431.)

Web search engines   Because anyone can publish a Web site, legitimate sources and unreliable sources live side-by-side online. As you scan through search results, look for the following clues about the probable relevance, currency, and reliability of a site — but be aware that the clues are by no means foolproof.

The title, keywords, and lead-in text (How relevant?)

A date (How current?)

An indication of the site's sponsor or purpose (How reliable?)

The URL, especially the domain name extension: for example, .com, .edu, .gov, or .org (How relevant? How reliable?)

On the next page are a few of the results that Luisa Mirano retrieved after typing the keywords *childhood obesity* into a search engine; she limited her search to works with those words in the title.

Mirano found the first site, sponsored by a research-based organization, promising enough to explore for her paper. The second and fourth sites held less promise because they seemed to offer popular rather than scholarly information. In addition, the second site was full of distracting commercial advertisements. Mirano rejected the third source not because she doubted its reliability — in fact, research from the National Institutes of Health was what she hoped to find — but because a skim of its contents revealed that the information was too general for her purposes.

EVALUATING SEARCH RESULTS: INTERNET SEARCH ENGINE

American **Obesity** Association - **Childhood Obesity**
Childhood Obesity. Obesity in **children** ... Note: The term "**childhood obesity**" may refer to both **children** and adolescents. In general, we ...
www.**obesity**.org/subs/**childhood**/ - 17k - Jan 8, 2005 - Cached - Similar pages

Content from a research-based organization. Promising.

Childhood Obesity
KS Logo, **Childhood Obesity**. advertisement. Source. ERIC Clearinghouse on Teaching and Teacher Education. Contents. ... Back to the Top Causes of **Childhood Obesity**. ...
www.kidsource.com/kidsource/content2/**obesity**.html - 18k - Cached - Similar pages

Popular rather than scholarly source. Not relevant.

Childhood Obesity, June 2002 Word on Health - National Institutes ...
Childhood Obesity on the Rise, an article in the June 2002 edition of The NIH Word on Health - Consumer Information Based on Research from the National ...
www.nih.gov/news/WordonHealth/ jun2002/**childhoodobesity**.htm - 22k - Cached - Similar pages

Content too general. Not relevant.

MayoClinic.com - **Childhood obesity**: Parenting advice
... **Childhood obesity**: Parenting advice By Mayo Clinic staff. ... Here are some other tips to help your **obese child** — and yourself: Be a positive role model. ...
www.mayoclinic.com/invoke.cfm?id=FL00058 - 42k - Jan 8, 2005 - Cached - Similar pages

Popular and too general. Not relevant.

Determining if a source is scholarly

For many college assignments, you will be asked to use scholarly sources. These are written by experts for a knowledgeable audience and usually go into more depth than books and articles written for a general audience. (Scholarly sources are sometimes called *refereed* or *peer-reviewed* because the work is evaluated by experts in the field before publication.) To determine if a source is scholarly, you should look for the following:

- Formal language and presentation
- Authors with academic or scientific credentials
- Footnotes or a bibliography documenting the works cited by the author in the source
- Original research and interpretation rather than a summary of other people's work
- Quotations from and analysis of primary sources (in humanities disciplines such as literature, history, and philosophy)
- A description of research methods or a review of related research (in the sciences and social sciences)

NOTE: In some databases, searches can be limited to refereed or peer-reviewed journals.

54c Select appropriate versions of online sources.

An online source may appear as an abstract, an excerpt, or a full-text article or book. It is important to distinguish among these versions of sources and to use a complete version of a source for your research.

Abstracts and excerpts are shortened versions of complete works. An abstract — a summary of a work's contents — might appear in a database record for a periodical article. An excerpt is the first few sentences or paragraphs of a newspaper or magazine article; it sometimes appears in a list of hits in an online search. Abstracts and excerpts often provide enough information for you to determine whether the complete article would be useful for your paper but generally do not contain enough information to function alone as sources in a research paper. Reading the complete article is the best way to understand the author's argument before referring to it in your own writing. A full-text work may appear online as a PDF (portable document format) file or as an HTML file (sometimes called a *text file*). If your source is available in both formats, choose the PDF file for your research because it will include page numbers for your citations.

54d Read with an open mind and a critical eye.

As you begin reading the sources you have chosen, keep an open mind. Do not let your personal beliefs prevent you from listening to new ideas and opposing viewpoints. Your research question — not a snap judgment about the question — should guide your reading.

When you read critically, you are not necessarily judging an author's work harshly; you are simply examining its assumptions, assessing its evidence, and weighing its conclusions.

NOTE: When you research on the Web, it is easy to ignore views different from your own. Web pages that appeal to you will often link to other pages that support the same viewpoint. If your sources all seem to agree with you — and with one another — try to find sources with opposing views and evaluate them with an open mind.

Distinguishing between primary and secondary sources

As you begin assessing evidence in a source, determine whether you are reading a primary or a secondary source. Primary sources are original documents such as letters, diaries, legislative bills, laboratory studies, field research reports, and eyewitness accounts. Secondary sources are commentaries on primary sources — another writer's opinions about or interpretation of a primary source. A primary source for Ned Bishop was Nathan Bedford Forrest's official report on the battle at Fort Pillow. Bishop also consulted a number of secondary sources, some of which relied heavily on primary sources such as letters.

Although a primary source is not necessarily more reliable than a secondary source, it has the advantage of being a

Evaluating all sources

Checking for signs of bias

- Does the author or publisher endorse political or religious views that could affect objectivity?
- Is the author or publisher associated with a special-interest group, such as Greenpeace or the National Rifle Association, that might present only one side of an issue?
- Are alternative views presented and addressed? How fairly does the author treat opposing views? (See 7c.)
- Does the author's language show signs of bias? (See 7b.)

Assessing an argument

- What is the author's central claim or thesis?
- How does the author support this claim — with relevant and sufficient evidence or with just a few anecdotes or emotional examples?
- Are statistics consistent with those you encounter in other sources? Have they been used fairly? (It is possible to "lie" with statistics by using them selectively or by omitting mathematical details.) Does the author explain where the statistics come from?
- Are any of the author's assumptions questionable?
- Does the author consider opposing arguments and refute them persuasively? (See 7c.)
- Does the author fall prey to any logical fallacies? (See 7a.)

firsthand account. Naturally, you can better evaluate what a secondary source says if you have first read any primary sources it discusses.

Being alert for signs of bias

Some sources are more objective than others. Even publications that are considered reputable can be editorially biased. For example, *USA Today*, *National Review*, and *The Economist* are all credible sources, but they are also likely to interpret events quite differently from one another. If you are uncertain about a periodical's special interests, consult *Magazines for Libraries*. To check for bias in a book, see what book reviewers have written about it. A reference librarian can help you locate reviews and assess the credibility of both the book and the reviewers.

Like publishers, some authors are more objective than others. If you have reason to believe that a writer is particularly biased, you will want to assess his or her arguments with special care. For questions to ask about a source's possible bias, see the chart on page 443.

Assessing the author's argument

In nearly all academic writing, there is some element of argument, so don't be surprised to encounter experts who argue opposing sides of the same issue. When you find areas of disagreement, read the arguments of each source with special care, testing them with your own critical intelligence. The questions in the chart on page 443 can help you weigh the strengths and weaknesses of each author's arguments.

> **Making the most of your handbook**
> Good college writers read critically.
> ▶ Judging whether a source is reasonable: 7a
> ▶ Judging whether a source is fair: 7c

54e Assess Web sources with special care.

Web sources can provide valuable information, but verifying their credibility may take time. Before using a Web source in your paper, make sure you know who created the material and for what purpose.

Evaluating Web sources

Authorship

- Does the Web site or document have an author? You may need to do some clicking and scrolling to find the author's name. If you have landed directly on an internal page of a site, for example, you may need to navigate to the home page or find an "about this site" link to learn the name of the author.

- If there is an author, can you tell whether he or she is knowledgeable and credible? When the author's qualifications aren't listed on the site itself, look for links to the author's home page, which may provide evidence of his or her interests and expertise.

Sponsorship

- Who, if anyone, sponsors the site? The sponsor of a site is often named and described on the home page and is sometimes listed alongside the copyright date: © 2010 Plymouth State College.

- What does the URL tell you? The domain name extension often indicates the type of group hosting the site: commercial (.com or .co), educational (.edu), nonprofit (.org), governmental (.gov), military (.mil), or network (.net). URLs may also indicate a country of origin: .uk (United Kingdom) or .jp (Japan), for instance.

Purpose and audience

- Why was the site created: To argue a position? To sell a product? To inform readers?
- Who is the site's intended audience?

Currency

- How current is the site? Check for the date of publication or the latest update, often located at the bottom of the home page or at the beginning or end of an internal page.

- How current are the site's links? If many of the links no longer work, the site may be too dated for your purposes.

EVALUATING A WEB SITE: CHECKING RELIABILITY

1 This article on Internet monitoring is on a site sponsored by the Massachusetts Nurses Association, a professional health care association and union whose staff and members advocate for nurses in the workplace. The URL ending .org marks this sponsor as a nonprofit organization.

2 Clear dates of publication show currency.

3 The author is a credible expert whose credentials can be verified.

Many sophisticated-looking sites contain questionable information. Even a well-designed hate site may at first appear unbiased and informative. Sites with reliable information, however, can stand up to careful scrutiny. For a checklist on evaluating Web sources, see the chart on page 445.

As you write

Using the guidelines for evaluating Web sources on page 445, evaluate two Web sources that you've selected for your research project. Evaluate the authorship, sponsorship, purpose, audience, and currency for each site. Based on your analysis, are these sources credible? Reliable? Right for your project?

EVALUATING A WEB SITE: CHECKING PURPOSE

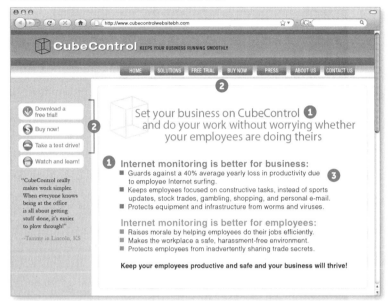

1   The site is sponsored by a company that specializes in software for monitoring employee Internet use.

2   Repeated links for trial downloads and purchase suggest the site's intended audience: consumers seeking to purchase software (probably not researchers seeking detailed information about employees' use of the Internet in the workplace).

3   The site appears to provide information and even shows statistics from studies, but ultimately the purpose of the site is to sell a product.

In researching Internet surveillance and workplace privacy, Anna Orlov encountered sites that raised her suspicions. In particular, some sites were authored by surveillance software companies, which have an obvious interest in focusing on the benefits of such software to company management.

When you know something about the creator of a site and have a sense of a site's purpose, you will be in a good position to evaluate the likely worth of its information. Consider, for example, the two sites pictured on this page and on page 446. Anna Orlov decided that the first Web site would be more useful for her project than sites like the second.

55 Managing information; avoiding plagiarism

Whether you decide to keep records on paper or on your computer — or both — you will need methods for managing information: maintaining a working bibliography (see 55a), keeping track of source materials (see 55b), and taking notes without plagiarizing your sources (see 55c). (For more on avoiding plagiarism, see 56 for MLA style and 62 for APA style.)

55a Maintain a working bibliography.

Keep a record of any sources you decide to consult. This record, called a *working bibliography*, will help you compile the list of sources that will appear at the end of your paper. The format of this list depends on the documentation style you are using (for MLA style, see 59b; for APA style, see 64b). Using the proper style in your working bibliography will ensure that you have all the information you need to correctly cite any sources you use.

Most researchers save bibliographic information from the library's online catalog, its periodical databases, and the Web. The information you need to collect is given in the chart on pages 450–51. If you download a visual, you must gather the same information as for a print source.

For Web sources, some bibliographic information may not be available, but spend time looking for it before assuming that it doesn't exist. When information isn't available on the home page, you may have to drill into the site, following links to interior pages.

Once you have created a working bibliography, you can annotate it. Writing several brief sentences summarizing key points of a source will help you identify how it relates to your argument and to your other sources. You should evaluate the source in your own words and use quotations sparingly. Clarifying the source's ideas at this stage will help you separate them from your own and avoid plagiarizing them later.

MODELS hackerhandbooks.com/rules
> Model papers
>> MLA annotated bibliography: Orlov
>> APA annotated bibliography: Haddad

keeping records of sources •
avoiding plagiarism • annotated bibliography
res
55b
449

SAMPLE ANNOTATED BIBLIOGRAPHY ENTRY (MLA STYLE)

Gonsalves, Chris. "Wasting Away on the Web." *eWeek.com.* Ziff Davis
Enterprise Holdings, 8 Aug. 2005. Web. 16 Feb. 2009.

Summarize the source. ——→ In this editorial, Gonsalves considers the
implications of several surveys, including one

Annotations should be three to seven sentences long. in which 61% of respondents said that their
companies have the right to spy on them. The
author agrees with this majority, claiming that
it's fine if his company chooses to monitor him
as long as the company discloses its monitoring
practices. He argues that "the days of Internet •——— Use quotations sparingly. Keep quotation marks around any words from the source.
freedom at work are justifiably finished," adding
that he would prefer not to know the extent of
the surveillance. Gonsalves writes for *eWeek.com*, •——— Evaluate the source for bias and relevance.
a publication focused on technology products.
He presents himself as an employee who is
comfortable with being monitored, but his job
may be a source of bias. This editorial contradicts •——— Interpret the relationship between this source and others in the bibliography.
some of my other sources, which claim that
employees want to know and should know all the
details of their company's monitoring procedures.

As you write

Develop an annotated bibliography for your research project.
In each annotation, summarize the key points of the source,
evaluate the source for bias and relevance, and comment
briefly about how each source relates to others in your
bibliography.

55b Keep track of source materials.

The best way to keep track of source materials is to save a copy of
each one. Many database subscription services will allow you to
e-mail, save, or print citations or full texts of articles, and you can
easily download, copy, or take screen shots of information from
the Web.

Information for a working bibliography

For an entire book

- All authors; any editors or translators
- Title and subtitle
- Edition (if not the first)
- Publication information: city, publisher, and date

For a periodical article

- All authors of the article
- Title and subtitle of the article
- Title of the magazine, journal, or newspaper
- Date; volume, issue, and page numbers

For a periodical article retrieved from a database (in addition to preceding information)

- Name of the database and an item number, if available
- Name of the subscription service
- URL of the subscription service (for an online database)
- Accession number or other number assigned by the database
- Digital object identifier (DOI), if there is one
- Date you retrieved the source

NOTE: Use care when printing or saving articles in PDF format. These files may not include some of the elements you need to cite the electronic source. You may need to record additional information from the database or Web site where you found the file.

For a Web source (text, visual, or audio)

- All authors, editors, or creators of the source
- Editor or compiler of the Web site, if there is one
- Title and subtitle of the source
- Title of the site
- Publication information for the source, if available
- Page or paragraph numbers, if any
- Date of online publication (or latest update)
- Sponsor of the site
- Date you accessed the source
- The site's URL

NOTE: For the exact bibliographic format to use in your working bibliography and in the final paper, see 59b (MLA) or 64b (APA).

Working with saved files or printouts — as opposed to relying on memory or hastily written notes — lets you highlight key passages and make notes in the margins of the source as you read. You also reduce the chances of unintentional plagiarism, since you will be able to compare your use of a source in your paper with the actual source, not just with your notes (see 55c).

NOTE: It's especially important to keep print or electronic copies of Web sources, which may change or even become inaccessible over time. Make sure that your copy includes the site's URL and your date of access.

TIP: Your school may provide citation software, which allows researchers to download references directly from databases, import saved searches, or type in citations. Similarly, many databases format citations with a mouse click, and Web sites offer fill-in-the-blank forms for generating formatted citations. You must proofread these results carefully, however, because the programs sometimes provide incorrect results.

55c As you take notes, avoid unintentional plagiarism.

When you take notes and jot down ideas, be very careful not to use language from your sources unless you clearly identify borrowed words and phrases as quotations. Even if you half-copy the author's sentences — either by mixing the author's phrases with your own without using quotation marks or by plugging your synonyms into the author's sentence structure — you are committing plagiarism, a serious academic offense. (For examples of this kind of plagiarism, see 57b and 62b.)

To prevent unintentional borrowing, resist the temptation to look at the source as you take notes — except when you are quoting. Keep the source close by so you can check for accuracy, but don't try to put ideas in your own words with the source's sentences in front of you. When you need to quote the exact words of a source, make sure you copy the words precisely and put quotation marks around them.

TIP: Be especially careful when using copy and paste functions in electronic files. Some researchers have unintentionally plagiarized their sources because they lost track of which words came from sources and which were their own. To prevent unintentional plagiarism, put quotation marks around any exact language you save from your sources.

Academic English Even in the early stages of note taking, it is important to keep in mind that in the United States written texts are considered an author's property. (This "property" isn't a physical object, so it is often referred to as *intellectual property*.) The author (or publisher) owns the language as well as any original ideas contained in the writing, whether the source is published in print or electronic form. When you use another author's property in your own writing, you are required to follow certain conventions for citing the material, or you risk committing *plagiarism*.

Summarizing, paraphrasing, and quoting are three ways of taking notes. Be sure to include exact page references for all three types of notes since you will need the page numbers later if you use the information in your paper.

Summarizing without plagiarizing

A summary condenses information, perhaps reducing a chapter to a short paragraph or a paragraph to a single sentence. A summary should be written in your own words; if you use phrases from the source, put them in quotation marks.

Here is a passage from a source about mountain lions. Following the passage is the student's summary. (The bibliographic information is recorded in MLA style.)

ORIGINAL SOURCE

In some respects, the increasing frequency of mountain lion encounters in California has as much to do with a growing *human* population as it does with rising mountain lion numbers. The scenic solitude of the western ranges is prime cougar habitat, and it is falling swiftly to the developer's spade. Meanwhile, with their ideal habitat already at its carrying capacity, mountain lions are forcing younger cats into less suitable terrain, including residential areas. Add that cougars have generally grown bolder under a lengthy ban on their being hunted, and an unsettling scenario begins to emerge.

— Rychnovsky, Ray. "Clawing into Controversy."
Outdoor Life Jan. 1995: 38-42. Print. [p. 40]

SUMMARY

Source: Rychnovsky, Ray. "Clawing into Controversy." *Outdoor Life*
Jan. 1995: 38-42. Print. [p. 40]

Encounters between mountain lions and humans are on the rise in California because increasing numbers of lions are competing for a shrinking habitat. As the lions' wild habitat shrinks, older lions force younger lions into residential areas. These lions have lost some of their fear of humans because of a ban on hunting (Rychnovsky 40).

Paraphrasing without plagiarizing

Like a summary, a paraphrase is written in your own words; but whereas a summary reports significant information in fewer words than the source, a paraphrase retells the information in roughly the same number of words. If you retain occasional choice phrases from the source, use quotation marks so that later you will know which phrases are not your own.

As you read the following paraphrase of the original source (see p. 452), notice that the language is significantly different from that in the original.

PARAPHRASE

Source: Rychnovsky, Ray. "Clawing into Controversy." *Outdoor Life*
Jan. 1995: 38-42. Print. [p. 40]

Californians are encountering mountain lions more frequently because increasing numbers of humans and a rising population of lions are competing for the same territory. Humans have moved into mountainous regions once dominated by the lions, and the wild habitat that is left cannot sustain the current lion population. Therefore, the older lions are forcing younger lions into residential areas. And because of a ban on hunting, these younger lions have become bolder—less fearful of encounters with humans (Rychnovsky 40).

Using quotation marks to avoid plagiarizing

A quotation consists of the exact words from a source. In your notes, put all quoted material in quotation marks; do not assume that you will remember later which words, phrases, and passages you have quoted and which are your own. When you quote, be sure to copy the words of your source exactly, including punctuation and capitalization.

QUOTATION

Source: Rychnovsky, Ray. "Clawing into Controversy." *Outdoor Life*
Jan. 1995: 38-42. Print. [p. 40]

Rychnovsky explains that as humans expand residential areas into mountain ranges, the cougar's natural habitat "is falling swiftly to the developer's spade" (40).

Avoiding Internet plagiarism

Understand what plagiarism is. When you use another author's intellectual property — language, visuals, or ideas — in your own writing without giving proper credit, you commit a kind of academic theft called *plagiarism*.

Treat Web sources the same way you treat print sources. Any language that you find on the Internet must be carefully cited, even if the material is in the public domain or is publicly accessible on free sites. When you use material from Web sites sponsored by federal, state, or municipal governments (.gov sites) or by nonprofit organizations (.org sites), you must acknowledge that material, too, as intellectual property owned by those agencies.

Keep track of which words come from sources and which are your own. To prevent unintentional plagiarism when you copy and paste passages from Web sources to an electronic file, put quotation marks around any text that you have inserted into your own work. In addition, during note taking and drafting, you might use highlighting or a different color font to draw attention to text taken from sources — so that material from articles, Web sites, and other sources stands out unmistakably as someone else's words.

Avoid Web sites that bill themselves as "research services" and sell essays. When you use Web search engines to research a topic, you will often see links to sites that appear to offer legitimate writing support but that actually sell college essays. Of course, submitting a paper that you have purchased is cheating, but even using material from such a paper is considered plagiarism.

For details on avoiding plagiarism while working with sources, see 57 (MLA style) and 62 (APA style).

Integrating and citing sources to avoid plagiarism

Source text

Our language is constantly changing. Like the Mississippi, it keeps forging new channels and abandoning old ones, picking up debris, depositing unwanted silt, and frequently bursting its banks. In every generation, there are people who deplore changes in the language and many who wish to stop the flow. But if our language stopped changing it would mean that American society had ceased to be dynamic, innovative, pulsing with life — that the river had frozen up.

— Robert MacNeil and William Cran,
Do You Speak American?, p. 1

NOTE: The examples in this chart follow MLA style (see 58). For APA style, see 63.

Avoiding plagiarism

If you are using an exact sentence from a source, with no changes . . .	→	. . . put quotation marks around the sentence. Use a signal phrase and include a page number in parentheses.
		MacNeil and Cran write, "Our language is constantly changing" (1).
If you are using a few exact words from the source but not an entire sentence . . .	→	. . . put quotation marks around the exact words that you have used from the source. Use a signal phrase and include a page number in parentheses.
		Some people, according to MacNeil and Cran, "deplore changes in the language" (1).

Integrating and citing sources to avoid plagiarism (continued)

If you are using near-exact words from the source but changing some word forms (*I* to *she*, *walk* to *walked*) or adding words to clarify and make the quotation flow with your own text . . .

→ . . . put quotation marks around the quoted words and put brackets around the changes you have introduced. Use a signal phrase and include a page number in parentheses.

MacNeil and Cran compare the English language to the Mississippi River, which "forg[es] new channels and abandon[s] old ones" (1).

MacNeil and Cran write, "In every generation, there are people who deplore changes in the [English] language and many who wish to stop the flow" (1).

If you are paraphrasing or summarizing the source, using the author's ideas but not any of the author's exact words . . .

→ . . . introduce the ideas with a signal phrase and put the page number at the end of your sentence. Do not use quotation marks. (See 57 and 62.)

MacNeil and Cran argue that changes in the English language are natural and that they represent cultural progress (1).

If you have used the source's sentence structure but substituted a few synonyms for the author's words . . .

→ STOP! This is a form of plagiarism even if you use a signal phrase and a page number. Change your sentence by using one of the techniques given in this chart or in 58 or 63.

PLAGIARIZED
MacNeil and Cran claim that, like a river, English creates new waterways and discards old ones.

INTEGRATED AND CITED CORRECTLY
MacNeil and Cran claim, "Like the Mississippi, [English] keeps forging new channels and abandoning old ones" (1).

Writing Papers in MLA Style

Directory to MLA in-text citation models

Directory to MLA works cited models

Directory to MLA works cited models (continued)

Most English instructors and some humanities instructors will ask you to document your sources with the Modern Language Association (MLA) system of citations described in section 59.

When writing an MLA paper that is based on sources, you face three main challenges: (1) supporting a thesis, (2) citing your sources and avoiding plagiarism, and (3) integrating quotations and other source material.

Examples in sections 56–58 are drawn from a student's research related to online monitoring of employees' computer use. Anna Orlov's research paper, which argues that electronic surveillance in the workplace threatens employees' privacy, appears on pages 527–32.

NOTE: For advice on finding and evaluating sources and on managing information in all your college courses, see sections 53–55.

56 Supporting a thesis

Most college research assignments ask you to form a thesis, or main idea, and to support that thesis with well-organized evidence.

56a Form a working thesis.

Once you have read a variety of sources and considered your issue from different perspectives, you are ready to form a working thesis: a one-sentence (or occasionally a two-sentence) statement of your central idea. (See also 1c.) Because it is a working, or tentative, thesis, you can remain flexible and revise it as your ideas develop.

In a research paper, your thesis will answer the central research question that you posed earlier (see 53a). Here, for example, are Anna Orlov's research question and working thesis.

RESEARCH QUESTION

Should employers monitor their employees' online activities in the workplace?

WORKING THESIS

Employers should not monitor their employees' online activities because electronic surveillance can compromise workers' privacy.

After you have written a rough draft and perhaps done more reading, you may decide to revise your thesis, as Orlov did.

REVISED THESIS

Although companies often have legitimate concerns that lead them to monitor employees' Internet usage—from expensive security breaches to reduced productivity—the benefits of electronic surveillance are outweighed by its costs to employees' privacy and autonomy.

The thesis usually appears at the end of the introductory paragraph. To read Anna Orlov's thesis in the context of her introduction, see page 527.

56b Organize ideas with a rough outline.

The body of your paper will consist of evidence in support of your thesis. Instead of getting tangled up in a formal outline early in the process, sketch an informal plan that organizes your ideas in bold strokes. Anna Orlov, for example, used this simple plan to outline the structure of her argument:

- Compared with older types of surveillance, electronic surveillance allows employers to monitor workers more efficiently.

- Some experts argue that companies have important financial and legal reasons to monitor employees' Internet usage.

- But monitoring employees' Internet usage may lower worker productivity when the threat to privacy creates distrust.

- Current laws do little to protect employees' privacy rights, so employees and employers have to negotiate the potential risks and benefits of electronic surveillance.

> **Making the most of your handbook**
> It's helpful to start off with a working thesis and a rough outline—especially when writing from sources.
> ▶ Draft a working thesis: 1c
> ▶ Sketch a plan: 1d

After you have written a rough draft, a more formal outline can be a useful way to shape the complexities of your argument. See pages 20–21 for an example.

56c Use sources to inform and support your argument.

Used thoughtfully, the source materials you have gathered will make your argument more complex and convincing for readers. Sources can play several different roles as you develop your points.

Providing background information or context

You can use facts and statistics to support generalizations or to establish the importance of your topic, as student writer Anna Orlov does in her introduction.

> As the Internet has become an integral tool of businesses, company policies on Internet usage have become as common as policies regarding vacation days or sexual harassment. A 2005 study by the American Management Association and ePolicy Institute found that 76% of companies monitor employees' use of the Web, and the number of companies that block employees' access to certain Web sites has increased 27% since 2001 (1).

Explaining terms or concepts

If readers are unlikely to be familiar with a word or an idea important to your topic, you must explain it for them. Quoting or paraphrasing a source can help you define terms and concepts in accessible language.

> One popular monitoring method is keystroke logging, which is done by means of an undetectable program on employees' computers. . . . As Lane explains, these programs record every key entered into the computer in hidden directories that can later be accessed or uploaded by supervisors; the programs can even scan for keywords tailored to individual companies (128-29).

Supporting your claims

As you draft your argument, make sure to back up your assertions with facts, examples, and other evidence from your research. (See also 6e.) Orlov, for example, uses an anecdote from one of her sources to support her claim that limiting computer access causes resentment among a company's staff.

> Monitoring online activities can have the unintended effect of making employees resentful. . . . Kesan warns that "prohibiting personal use can seem extremely arbitrary and can seriously harm morale. . . . Imagine a concerned parent who is prohibited from checking on a sick child by a draconian company policy" (315-16). As this analysis indicates, employees can become disgruntled when Internet usage policies are enforced to their full extent.

Lending authority to your argument

Expert opinion can give weight to your argument. (See also 6e.) But don't rely on experts to make your arguments for you. Construct your argument in your own words and, when appropriate, cite the judgment of an authority in the field to support your position.

> Additionally, many experts disagree with employers' assumption that online monitoring can increase productivity. Employment law attorney Joseph Schmitt argues that, particularly for employees who are paid a salary rather than an hourly wage, "a company shouldn't care whether employees spend one or 10 hours on the Internet as long as they are getting their jobs done—and provided that they are not accessing inappropriate sites" (qtd. in Verespej).

Anticipating and countering objections

Do not ignore sources that seem contrary to your position or that offer arguments different from your own. Instead, use them to give voice to opposing points of view and to state potential objections to your argument before you counter them (see 6f). Readers often have opposing points of view in mind already, whether or not they agree with you. Anna Orlov, for example, cites conflicting evidence to acknowledge that some readers may feel that unlimited Internet access in the workplace hinders productivity. In doing so, she creates an opportunity to counter that objection and persuade those readers.

> On the one hand, computers and Internet access give employees powerful tools to carry out their jobs; on the other hand, the same technology offers constant temptations to avoid work. As a 2005 study by *Salary.com* and *America Online* indicates, the Internet ranked as the top choice among employees for ways of wasting time on the job; it beat talking with co-workers—the second most popular method—by a margin of nearly two to one (Frauenheim).

57 Citing sources; avoiding plagiarism

Your research paper is a collaboration between you and your sources. To be fair and ethical, you must acknowledge your debt to the writers of those sources. When you acknowledge your sources, you avoid plagiarism, a serious academic offense.

In general, these three acts are considered plagiarism: (1) failing to cite quotations and borrowed ideas, (2) failing to enclose borrowed language in quotation marks, and (3) failing to put summaries and paraphrases in your own words. Definitions of plagiarism may vary; it's a good idea to find out how your school defines this kind of academic dishonesty.

57a Cite quotations and borrowed ideas.

Sources are cited for two reasons:

1. to tell readers where your information comes from — so that they can assess its reliability and, if interested, find and read the original source
2. to give credit to the writers from whom you have borrowed words and ideas

You must cite anything you borrow from a source, including direct quotations; statistics and other specific facts; visuals such as cartoons, graphs, and diagrams; and any ideas you present in a summary or paraphrase.

The only exception is common knowledge — information your readers could easily find in any number of general sources. For example, most encyclopedias will tell readers that Alfred Hitchcock directed *Notorious* in 1946 and that Emily Dickinson published only a handful of her many poems during her lifetime.

> **Making the most of your handbook**
> When you use exact language from a source, you need to show that it is a quotation.
> ▶ Quotation marks for direct quotations: 37a

As a rule, when you have seen information repeatedly in your reading, you don't need to cite it. However, when information has appeared in only one or two sources, when it is highly specific (as with statistics), or when it is controversial, you should cite the source. If a topic is new to you and you are not sure what is considered common knowledge or what is controversial, ask your instructor or someone else with expertise. When in doubt, cite the source.

The Modern Language Association recommends a system of in-text citations. Here, briefly, is how the MLA citation system usually works:

1. The source is introduced by a signal phrase that names its author.

2. The material being cited is followed by a page number in parentheses.

3. At the end of the paper, a list of works cited (arranged alphabetically by authors' last names) gives complete publication information about the source.

IN-TEXT CITATION

Legal scholar Jay Kesan points out that the law holds employers liable for employees' actions such as violations of copyright laws, the distribution of offensive or graphic sexual material, and illegal disclosure of confidential information (312).

ENTRY IN THE LIST OF WORKS CITED

Kesan, Jay P. "Cyber-Working or Cyber-Shirking? A First Principles Examination of Electronic Privacy in the Workplace." *Florida Law Review* 54.2 (2002): 289-332. Print.

This basic MLA format varies for different types of sources. For a detailed discussion of other models, see 59.

57b Enclose borrowed language in quotation marks.

To indicate that you are using a source's exact phrases or sentences, you must enclose them in quotation marks unless they have been set off from the text by indenting (see p. 471). To omit the quotation marks is to claim — falsely — that the language is your own. Such an omission is plagiarism even if you have cited the source.

ORIGINAL SOURCE

Without adequate discipline, the World Wide Web can be a tremendous time sink; no other medium comes close to matching the Internet's depth of materials, interactivity, and sheer distractive potential.   — Frederick Lane, *The Naked Employee*, p. 142

PLAGIARISM

Frederick Lane points out that if people do not have adequate discipline, the World Wide Web can be a tremendous time sink; no other medium comes close to matching the Internet's depth of materials, interactivity, and sheer distractive potential (142).

BORROWED LANGUAGE IN QUOTATION MARKS

Frederick Lane points out that for those not exercising self-control, "the World Wide Web can be a tremendous time sink; no other medium comes close to matching the Internet's depth of materials, interactivity, and sheer distractive potential" (142).

57c Put summaries and paraphrases in your own words.

A summary condenses information from a source; a paraphrase conveys the information using roughly the same number of words as the original source. When you summarize or paraphrase, it is not enough to name the source; you must restate the source's meaning using your own language. (See also 55c.) You commit plagiarism if you half-copy the author's sentences — either by mixing the author's phrases with your own without using quotation marks or by plugging your synonyms into the author's sentence structure.

The first paraphrase of the following source is plagiarized — even though the source is cited — because too much of its language is borrowed from the original. The highlighted strings of words have been copied exactly (without quotation marks). In addition, the writer has closely echoed the sentence structure of the source, merely substituting some synonyms (*restricted* for *limited*, *modern era* for *computer age*, *monitoring* for *surveillance*, and *inexpensive* for *cheap*).

ORIGINAL SOURCE

In earlier times, surveillance was limited to the information that a supervisor could observe and record firsthand and to primitive counting devices. In the computer age surveillance can be instantaneous, unblinking, cheap, and, maybe most importantly, easy.

— Carl Botan and Mihaela Vorvoreanu, "What Do Employees Think about Electronic Surveillance at Work?," p. 126

PLAGIARISM: UNACCEPTABLE BORROWING

Scholars Carl Botan and Mihaela Vorvoreanu argue that in earlier times monitoring of employees was restricted to the information that a supervisor could observe and record firsthand. In the modern era, monitoring can be instantaneous, inexpensive, and, most importantly, easy (126).

To avoid plagiarizing an author's language, resist the temptation to look at the source while you are summarizing or paraphrasing. After you have read the original passage, set the source aside. Ask yourself, "What is the author's meaning?" In your own words, state the author's basic point. Return to the source and check that you haven't used the author's language or sentence structure or misrepresented the author's ideas. When you fully understand another writer's meaning, you can more easily and accurately present those ideas in your own words.

ACCEPTABLE PARAPHRASE

Scholars Carl Botan and Mihaela Vorvoreanu claim that the nature of workplace surveillance has changed over time. Before the arrival of computers, managers could collect only small amounts of information about their employees based on what they saw or heard. Now, because computers are standard workplace technology, employers can monitor employees efficiently (126).

Revising with comments

Your words?

UNDERSTANDING THE COMMENT

When a teacher or tutor asks "Your words?" the comment often signals that it's unclear whether certain words you've used are your own or those of your sources.

> Internet technology has made it possible for extremist groups to recruit and train members and carry out terrorist activity. The membership of these groups reaches beyond local geographic areas because of the Web. The world has become a cacophony of parochialisms where individuals seek association with coreligionists in a mystique of participation. Combating the influences of these groups is now harder than ever.

Your words?

One student wrote this body paragraph in a research paper on the Internet's role in facilitating terrorism.

Part of this paragraph doesn't sound like the student's voice. To revise, the student must determine which words are his own and which come from sources he consulted. If he chooses to include words or ideas from a source, he'll need to decide if he wants to quote, summarize, or paraphrase the source. He'll also need to properly cite the source in his paper.

SIMILAR COMMENTS: *source?* • *quotation?* • *who's talking here?*

REVISING WHEN *YOUR* READERS WONDER WHOSE WORDS THEY'RE READING

1. *Reread your sentences* to see if you have clearly marked the boundaries between your source material and your own words. Is every word your own? Or have you borrowed words from sources without properly acknowledging them?

2. *Use signal phrases* to introduce each source and provide context. Doing so prepares readers for a source's words.

3. *Use quotation marks* to enclose language that you borrow word-for-word from a source, and follow each quotation with a parenthetical citation.

4. *Put summaries and paraphrases in your own words* and always cite your sources.

More advice on citing quotations, paraphrases, and summaries: 57, 58 (MLA) and 62, 63 (APA)

Integrating sources

Quotations, summaries, paraphrases, and facts will help you develop your argument, but they cannot speak for you. You can use several strategies to integrate information from research sources into your paper while maintaining your own voice.

58a Use quotations appropriately.

In your academic writing, keep the emphasis on your ideas and your language; use your own words to summarize and to paraphrase your sources and to explain your points. Sometimes, however, quotations can be the most effective way to integrate a source's ideas.

Limiting your use of quotations

Although it is tempting to insert many quotations in your paper and to use your own words only for connecting passages, do not quote excessively. It is almost impossible to integrate numerous quotations smoothly into your own text.

WHEN TO USE QUOTATIONS

- When language is especially vivid or expressive
- When exact wording is needed for technical accuracy
- When it is important to let the debaters of an issue explain their positions in their own words
- When the words of an authority lend weight to an argument
- When the language of a source is the topic of your discussion (as in an analysis or interpretation)

It is not always necessary to quote full sentences from a source. To reduce your reliance on the words of others, you can often integrate language from a source into your own sentence structure.

> Kizza and Ssanyu observe that technology in the workplace has been accompanied by "an array of problems that needed quick answers," such as electronic monitoring to prevent security breaches (4).

Using the ellipsis mark and brackets

Two useful marks of punctuation, the ellipsis mark and brackets, allow you to keep quoted material to a minimum and to integrate it smoothly into your text.

The ellipsis mark   To condense a quoted passage, you can use the ellipsis mark (three periods, with spaces between) to indicate that you have left words out. What remains must be grammatically complete.

> Lane acknowledges the legitimate reasons that many companies have for monitoring their employees' online activities, particularly management's concern about preventing "the theft of information that can be downloaded to a . . . disk, e-mailed to oneself . . . , or even posted to a Web page for the entire world to see" (12).

The writer has omitted from the source the words *floppy or Zip* before *disk* and *or a confederate* after *oneself.*

On the rare occasions when you want to leave out one or more full sentences, use a period before the three ellipsis dots.

> Charles Lewis, director of the Center for Public Integrity, points out that "by 1987, employers were administering nearly 2,000,000 polygraph tests a year to job applicants and employees. . . .
> Millions of workers were required to produce urine samples under observation for drug testing . . ." (22).

Ordinarily, do not use an ellipsis mark at the beginning or at the end of a quotation. Your readers will understand that the quoted material is taken from a longer passage, so such marks are not necessary. The only exception occurs when you have dropped words at the end of the final quoted sentence. In such cases, put three ellipsis dots before the closing quotation mark and parenthetical reference, as in the previous example.

Make sure omissions and ellipsis marks do not distort the meaning of your source.

Brackets   Brackets allow you to insert your own words into quoted material. You can insert words in brackets to clarify a confusing reference or to keep a sentence grammatical in your context. You also use brackets to indicate that you are changing a letter from capital to lowercase (or vice versa) to fit into your sentence.

> Legal scholar Jay Kesan notes that "[a] decade ago, losses [from
> employees' computer crimes] were already mounting to five billion
> dollars annually" (311).

This quotation began *A decade ago* . . . in the source, so the writer indicated the change to lowercase with brackets and inserted words in brackets to clarify the meaning of *losses.*

To indicate an error such as a misspelling in a quotation, insert the word "sic" in brackets right after the error.

> Johnson argues that "while online monitoring is often imagined as
> harmles [sic], the practice may well threaten employees' rights to
> privacy" (14).

Setting off long quotations

When you quote more than four typed lines of prose or more than three lines of poetry, set off the quotation by indenting it one inch from the left margin.

Long quotations should be introduced by an informative sentence, usually followed by a colon. Quotation marks are unnecessary because the indented format tells readers that the passage is taken word-for-word from the source.

> Botan and Vorvoreanu examine the role of gender in company
> practices of electronic surveillance:
>
> > There has never been accurate documentation of the extent
> > of gender differences in surveillance, but by the middle
> > 1990s, estimates of the proportion of surveilled employees
> > that were women ranged from 75% to 85%. . . . Ironically,
> > this gender imbalance in workplace surveillance may
> > be evening out today because advances in surveillance
> > technology are making surveillance of traditionally male
> > dominated fields, such as long-distance truck driving, cheap,
> > easy, and frequently unobtrusive. (127)

Notice that at the end of an indented quotation the parenthetical citation goes outside the final mark of punctuation. (When a quotation is run into your text, the opposite is true. See the sample citations on p. 470.)

Revising with comments

Cite your sources

UNDERSTANDING THE COMMENT

When a teacher or tutor responds "Cite your sources," the comment often signals that you need to acknowledge and properly credit the contributions of others.

> At the story's end, Edna Pontellier is described as a "naked . . . new-born creature" who, in the act of ending her own life, is experiencing a kind of re-birth.

Cite your sources

One student wrote this sentence in an essay interpreting Kate Chopin's novel *The Awakening*.

The student has borrowed language from both a primary source and a secondary source without proper citation. To revise, she needs to consult her notes or return to the novel to locate the exact page number for the quotation she uses. In addition, she needs to include quotation marks around the words "a kind of re-birth," which come from a secondary source, and to provide a parenthetical citation.

SIMILAR COMMENTS: *cite this • documentation • source?*

REVISING WHEN *YOU* NEED TO CITE YOUR SOURCES

1. *Reread your sentence and ask questions.* Have you properly acknowledged all the contributions — words, ideas, or facts — that you use as evidence? Have you given credit to the sources you quote, summarize, or paraphrase? Have you made it clear to readers how to locate the source if they want to consult it?

2. *Ask your instructor* which documentation style you are required to use — MLA, APA, or *Chicago*.

3. *Read your notes* or check the source itself to find the exact words. Make sure you have the author's name, the title, the date of publication, and the page number for each source you cite.

4. *Revise* by including an in-text citation for any words, ideas, or facts that you used as evidence — and by including quotation marks around any language borrowed word-for-word from a source.

More on citing sources: 59 (MLA) and 64 (APA)

58b Use signal phrases to integrate sources.

Whenever you include a paraphrase, summary, or direct quotation of another writer in your paper, prepare your readers for it with introductory words called a *signal phrase*. A signal phrase usually names the author of the source and often provides some context. It commonly appears before the source material. To vary your sentence structure, you may decide to interrupt source material with a signal phrase or place the signal phrase after your paraphrase, summary, or quotation.

When you write a signal phrase, choose a verb that is appropriate for the way you are using the source (see 56c). Are you providing background, explaining a concept, supporting a claim, lending authority, or refuting a belief? See the chart on this page for a list of verbs commonly used in signal phrases.

Using signal phrases in MLA papers

To avoid monotony, try to vary both the language and the placement of your signal phrases.

Model signal phrases

In the words of researchers Greenfield and Davis, ". . ."

As legal scholar Jay Kesan has noted, ". . ."

The ePolicy Institute, an organization that advises companies about reducing risks from technology, reports that ". . ."

". . .," writes Daniel Tynan, ". . ."

". . .," attorney Schmitt claims.

Kizza and Ssanyu offer a persuasive counterargument: ". . ."

Verbs in signal phrases

acknowledges	comments	endorses	reasons
adds	compares	grants	refutes
admits	confirms	illustrates	rejects
agrees	contends	implies	reports
argues	declares	insists	responds
asserts	denies	notes	suggests
believes	disputes	observes	thinks
claims	emphasizes	points out	writes

NOTE: MLA style calls for verbs in the present or present perfect tense (*argues, has argued*) to introduce source material unless you include a date that specifies the time of the original author's writing.

Marking boundaries

Readers need to move from your words to the words of a source without feeling a jolt. Avoid dropping quotations into the text without warning. Instead, provide clear signal phrases, including at least the author's name, to indicate the boundary between your words and the source's words. (The signal phrase is highlighted in the second example.)

DROPPED QUOTATION

Some experts have argued that a range of legitimate concerns justifies employer monitoring of employee Internet usage. "Employees could accidentally (or deliberately) spill confidential corporate information . . . or allow worms to spread throughout a corporate network" (Tynan).

QUOTATION WITH SIGNAL PHRASE

Some experts have argued that a range of legitimate concerns justifies employer monitoring of employee Internet usage. As *PC World* columnist Daniel Tynan points out, "Employees could accidentally (or deliberately) spill confidential corporate information . . . or allow worms to spread throughout a corporate network."

NOTE: Because this quotation is from an unpaginated Web source, no page number appears in parentheses after the quotation. See item 4 on page 482.

Establishing authority

Good research writing uses evidence from reliable sources. The first time you mention a source, include in the signal phrase the author's title, credentials, or experience — anything that would help your readers recognize the source's authority. (Signal phrases are highlighted in the next two examples.)

SOURCE WITH NO CREDENTIALS

Jay Kesan points out that the law holds employers liable for employees' actions such as violations of copyright laws, the distribution of offensive or graphic sexual material, and illegal disclosure of confidential information (312).

SOURCE WITH CREDENTIALS

Legal scholar Jay Kesan points out that the law holds employers liable for employees' actions such as violations of copyright laws, the distribution of offensive or graphic sexual material, and illegal disclosure of confidential information (312).

When you establish your source's authority, as with the phrase *Legal scholar* in the previous example, you also signal to readers your own credibility as a responsible researcher who has located reliable sources.

Introducing summaries and paraphrases

Introduce most summaries and paraphrases with a signal phrase that names the author and places the material in the context of your argument. (See also 58c and 60b.) Readers will then understand that everything between the signal phrase and the parenthetical citation summarizes or paraphrases the cited source.

Without the signal phrase (highlighted) in the following example, readers might think that only the quotation at the end is being cited, when in fact the whole paragraph is based on the source.

Frederick Lane believes that the personal computer has posed new challenges for employers worried about workplace productivity. Whereas early desktop computers were primitive enough to prevent employees from using them to waste time, the machines have become so sophisticated that they now make non-work-related computer activities easy and inviting. Many employees spend considerable company time customizing features and playing games on their computers. But perhaps most problematic from the employer's point of view, Lane asserts, is giving employees access to the Internet, "roughly the equivalent of installing a gazillion-channel television set for each employee" (15-16).

There are times when a summary or a paraphrase does not require a signal phrase. When the context makes clear where the cited material begins, you may omit the signal phrase and include the author's last name in parentheses.

Using signal phrases with statistics and other facts

When you are citing a statistic or another specific fact, a signal phrase is often not necessary. In most cases, readers will understand that the citation refers to the statistic or fact (not the whole paragraph).

> Roughly 60% of responding companies reported disciplining employees who had used the Internet in ways the companies deemed inappropriate; 30% had fired their employees for those transgressions (Greenfield and Davis 347).

There is nothing wrong, however, with using a signal phrase to introduce a statistic or fact.

Putting source material in context

Readers should not have to guess why source material appears in your paper. A signal phrase can help you make the connection between your own ideas and those of another writer by clarifying how the source will contribute to your paper (see 54a).

If you use another writer's words, you must explain how they relate to your point. It's a good idea to embed a quotation between sentences of your own. In addition to introducing it with a signal phrase, follow it with interpretive comments that link the quotation to your paper's argument (see also 58c).

QUOTATION WITH EFFECTIVE CONTEXT

The difference, Lane argues, between old methods of data gathering and electronic surveillance involves quantity:

> Technology makes it possible for employers to gather enormous amounts of data about employees, often far beyond what is necessary to satisfy safety or productivity

concerns. And the trends that drive technology—faster, smaller, cheaper—make it possible for larger and larger numbers of employers to gather ever-greater amounts of personal data. (3-4)

In an age when employers can collect data whenever employees use their computers—when they send e-mail, surf the Web, or even arrive at or depart from their workstations—the challenge for both employers and employees is to determine how much is too much.

58c Synthesize sources.

When you synthesize multiple sources in a research paper, you create a conversation about your research topic. You show readers how the ideas of one source relate to those of another by connecting and analyzing the ideas in the context of your argument. Keep the emphasis on your own writing. The thread of your argument should be easy to identify and to understand, with or without your sources.

SAMPLE SYNTHESIS (DRAFT)

Student writer Anna Orlov begins with a claim that needs support. → Productivity is not easily measured in the wired workplace. As a result, employers find it difficult to determine how much freedom to allow their employees. On the one hand, computers and Internet access give employees powerful tools to carry out their jobs; on the other hand, the same technology offers constant temptations to avoid work. As a 2005 study by *Salary.com* and *America Online* indicates, the Internet ranked as the top choice among employees for ways of wasting time on the job (Frauenheim). Chris Gonsalves, an editor for *eWeek.com*, argues that technology has changed the terms between employers and

Student writer

Signal phrases indicate how sources contribute to Orlov's paper and show that the ideas that follow are not her own. →

Source 1

Source 2

employees: "While bosses can easily detect and interrupt water-cooler chatter," he writes, "the employee who is shopping at Lands' End or IMing with fellow fantasy baseball managers may actually appear to be working." The gap between observable behaviors and actual online activities has motivated some employers to invest in surveillance programs.

Source 2

Student writer

Many experts, however, disagree with employers' assumption that online monitoring can increase productivity. Employment law attorney Joseph Schmitt argues that, particularly for salaried employees, "a company shouldn't care whether employees spend one or 10 hours on the Internet as long as they are getting their jobs done—and provided that they are not accessing inappropriate sites" (qtd. in Verespej). Other experts even argue that time spent on personal Internet browsing can actually be productive for companies. According to Bill Coleman, an executive at *Salary.com,* "Personal Internet use and casual office conversations often turn into new business ideas or suggestions for gaining operating efficiencies" (qtd. in Frauenheim). Employers, in other words, may benefit from showing more faith in their employees' ability to exercise their autonomy.

Orlov presents a counterposition to extend her argument.

Source 3

Orlov builds her case—each quoted passage offers a more detailed claim or example in support of her larger claim.

Student writer

Source 4

Student writer

In this draft, Orlov uses her own analyses to shape the conversation among her sources. She does not simply string quotations together or allow her sources to overwhelm her writing. The final sentence, written in her own voice, gives her an opportunity to explain to readers how the various sources support her argument.

When synthesizing sources, ask yourself the following questions:

- Which sources inform, support, or extend your argument?
- Have you varied the function of sources — to provide background, to explain concepts, to lend authority, and to anticipate counterarguments? Do you use signal phrases to indicate these functions?
- Do you explain how your sources support your argument?
- Do you connect and analyze sources in your own voice?
- Is your own argument easy to identify and to understand, with or without your sources?

59 Documenting sources in MLA style

In English and other humanities classes, you may be asked to use the MLA (Modern Language Association) system for documenting sources, which is set forth in the *MLA Handbook for Writers of Research Papers*, 7th ed. (New York: MLA, 2009).

MLA recommends in-text citations that refer readers to a list of works cited. A typical in-text citation names the author of the source, often in a signal phrase, and gives a page number in parentheses. At the end of the paper, a list of works cited provides publication information about the source; the list is alphabetized by authors' last names (or by titles for works without authors). There is a direct connection between the in-text citation and the alphabetized listing. In the following example, that connection is highlighted in blue.

IN-TEXT CITATION

Jay Kesan notes that even though many companies now routinely monitor employees through electronic means, "there may exist less intrusive safeguards for employers" (293).

ENTRY IN THE LIST OF WORKS CITED

Kesan, Jay P. "Cyber-Working or Cyber-Shirking? A First Principles Examination of Electronic Privacy in the Workplace." *Florida Law Review* 54.2 (2002): 289-332. Print.

For a list of works cited that includes this entry, see page 532.

59a MLA in-text citations

MLA in-text citations are made with a combination of signal phrases and parenthetical references. A signal phrase introduces information taken from a source (a quotation, summary, para-phrase, or fact); usually the signal phrase includes the author's name. The parenthetical reference comes after the cited material, often at the end of the sentence. It includes at least a page number (except for unpaginated sources, such as those found online). In the models in 59a, the elements of the in-text citation are high-lighted in blue.

IN-TEXT CITATION

Kwon points out that the Fourth Amendment does not give employees any protections from employers' "unreasonable searches and seizures" (6).

Readers can look up the author's last name in the alphabetized list of works cited, where they will learn the work's title and other pub-lication information. If readers decide to consult the source, the page number will take them straight to the passage that has been cited.

Basic rules for print and online sources

The MLA system of in-text citations, which depends heavily on au-thors' names and page numbers, was created with print sources in mind. Although many online sources have unclear authorship and lack page numbers, the basic rules are the same for both print and online sources.

The models in this section (items 1–5) show how the MLA system usually works and explain what to do if your source has no author or page numbers.

■ **1. Author named in a signal phrase** Ordinarily, introduce the material being cited with a signal phrase that includes the author's name. In addition to preparing readers for the source, the signal phrase allows you to keep the parenthetical citation brief.

> Frederick Lane reports that employers do not necessarily have
> to use software to monitor how their employees use the Web:
> employers can "use a hidden video camera pointed at an employee's
> monitor" and even position a camera "so that a number of monitors
> [can] be viewed at the same time" (147).

The signal phrase — *Frederick Lane reports* — names the author; the parenthetical citation gives the page number of the book in which the quoted words may be found.

Notice that the period follows the parenthetical citation. When a quotation ends with a question mark or an exclamation point, leave the end punctuation inside the quotation mark and add a period at the end of your sentence. (See also the note on p. 329.)

> O'Connor asks a critical question: "When does Internet surveillance
> cross the line between corporate responsibility and invasion of
> privacy?" (16).

2. Author named in parentheses If a signal phrase does not name the author, put the author's last name in parentheses along with the page number. Use no punctuation between the name and the page number.

> Companies can monitor employees' every keystroke without legal
> penalty, but they may have to combat low morale as a result
> (Lane 129).

3. Author unknown Either use the complete title in a signal phrase or use a short form of the title in parentheses. Titles of books are italicized; titles of articles are put in quotation marks.

> A popular keystroke logging program operates invisibly on workers'
> computers yet provides supervisors with details of the workers'
> online activities ("Automatically").

TIP: Before assuming that a Web source has no author, do some detective work. Often the author's name is available but is not easy to find. For example, it may appear at the end of the page, in tiny print. Or it may appear on another page of the site, such as the home page.

NOTE: If a source has no author and is sponsored by a corporation or government agency, name the corporation or agency as the author (see items 8 and 17 on pp. 483 and 486, respectively).

■ **4. Page number unknown** Do not include the page number if a work lacks page numbers, as is the case with many Web sources. Even if a printout from a Web site shows page numbers, treat the source as unpaginated in the in-text citation because not all printouts give the same page numbers. (When the pages of a Web source are stable, as in PDF files, supply a page number in your in-text citation.)

> As a 2005 study by *Salary.com* and *America Online* indicates, the
> Internet ranked as the top choice among employees for ways of
> wasting time on the job; it beat talking with co-workers—the
> second most popular method—by a margin of nearly two to one
> (Frauenheim).

If a source has numbered paragraphs or sections, use "par." (or "pars.") or "sec." (or "secs.") in the parentheses: (Smith, par. 4). Notice that a comma follows the author's name.

■ **5. One-page source** If the source is one page long, MLA allows (but does not require) you to omit the page number. Even so, it's a good idea to supply the page number because without it readers may not know where your citation ends or, worse, may not realize that you have provided a citation at all.

NO PAGE NUMBER IN CITATION

> Anush Yegyazarian reports that in 2000 the National Labor
> Relations Board's Office of the General Counsel helped win
> restitution for two workers who had been dismissed because
> their employers were displeased by the employees' e-mails
> about work-related issues. The case points to the ongoing
> struggle to define what constitutes protected speech in the
> workplace.

PAGE NUMBER IN CITATION

> Anush Yegyazarian reports that in 2000 the National Labor
> Relations Board's Office of the General Counsel helped win

restitution for two workers who had been dismissed because their
employers were displeased by the employees' e-mails about work-
related issues (62). The case points to the ongoing struggle to
define what constitutes protected speech in the workplace.

Variations on the basic rules

This section describes the MLA guidelines for handling a variety
of situations not covered by the basic rules in items 1–5. These
rules for in-text citations are the same for both print and online
sources.

■ **6. Two or three authors**   Name the authors in a signal phrase,
as in the following example, or include their last names in the
parenthetical reference: (Kizza and Ssanyu 2).

> Kizza and Ssanyu note that "employee monitoring is a dependable,
> capable, and very affordable process of electronically or otherwise
> recording all employee activities at work" and elsewhere (2).

When three authors are named in the parentheses, separate the
names with commas: (Alton, Davies, and Rice 56).

■ **7. Four or more authors**   Name all of the authors or include
only the first author's name followed by "et al." (Latin for "and
others"). The format you use should match the format in your
works cited entry (see item 3 on p. 492).

> The study was extended for two years, and only after results were
> reviewed by an independent panel did the researchers publish their
> findings (Blaine et al. 35).

■ **8. Organization as author**   When the author is a corporation
or an organization, name that author either in the signal phrase
or in the parentheses. (For a government agency as author, see
item 17 on p. 486.)

> According to a 2001 survey of human resources managers by the
> American Management Association, more than three-quarters of the
> responding companies reported disciplining employees for "misuse
> or personal use of office telecommunications equipment" (2).

In the list of works cited, the American Management Association is treated as the author and alphabetized under *A*. When you give the organization name in parentheses, abbreviate common words in the name: "Assn.," "Dept.," "Natl.," "Soc.," and so on.

> In a 2001 survey of human resources managers, more than three-quarters of the responding companies reported disciplining employees for "misuse or personal use of office telecommunications equipment" (Amer. Management Assn. 2).

■ **9. Authors with the same last name** If your list of works cited includes works by two or more authors with the same last name, include the author's first name in the signal phrase or first initial in the parentheses.

> Estimates of the frequency with which employers monitor employees' use of the Internet each day vary widely (A. Jones 15).

■ **10. Two or more works by the same author** Mention the title of the work in the signal phrase or include a short version of the title in the parentheses.

> The American Management Association and ePolicy Institute have tracked employers' practices in monitoring employees' e-mail use. The groups' 2003 survey found that one-third of companies had a policy of keeping and reviewing employees' e-mail messages ("2003 E-mail" 2); in 2005, more than 55% of companies engaged in e-mail monitoring ("2005 Electronic" 1).

Titles of articles and other short works are placed in quotation marks; titles of books are italicized.

In the rare case when both the author's name and a short title must be given in parentheses, separate them with a comma.

> A 2004 survey found that 20% of employers responding had employees' e-mail "subpoenaed in the course of a lawsuit or regulatory investigation," up 7% from the previous year (Amer. Management Assn. and ePolicy Inst., "2004 Workplace" 1).

◼ **11. Two or more works in one citation**   To cite more than one source in the parentheses, give the citations in alphabetical order and separate them with a semicolon.

> Several researchers have analyzed the reasons that companies
> monitor employees' use of the Internet at work (Botan and
> Vorvoreanu 128-29; Kesan 317-19; Kizza and Ssanyu 3-7).

Multiple citations can be distracting, so you should not overuse the technique. If you want to point to several sources that discuss a particular topic, consider using an information note instead (see 59c).

◼ **12. Repeated citations from the same source**   When your paper is about a single work of fiction or nonfiction (such as an essay), you do not need to include the author's name each time you quote from or paraphrase the work. After you mention the author's name at the beginning of your paper, you may include just the page numbers in your parenthetical citations.

> In Susan Glaspell's short story "A Jury of Her Peers," two
> women accompany their husbands and a county attorney to an
> isolated house where a farmer named John Wright has been choked
> to death in his bed with a rope. The chief suspect is Wright's wife,
> Minnie, who is in jail awaiting trial. The sheriff's wife, Mrs. Peters,
> has come along to gather some personal items for Minnie, and
> Mrs. Hale has joined her. Early in the story, Mrs. Hale sympathizes
> with Minnie and objects to the way the male investigators are
> "snoopin' round and criticizin'" her kitchen (191). In contrast, Mrs.
> Peters shows respect for the law, saying that the men are doing "no
> more than their duty" (191).

In a paper with multiple sources, if you are citing a source more than once in a paragraph, you may omit the author's name after the first mention in the paragraph as long as it is clear that you are still referring to the same source.

◼ **13. Encyclopedia or dictionary entry**   Unless an entry in an encyclopedia or a dictionary has an author, the source will be alphabetized in the list of works cited under the word or entry that you consulted (see item 27 on p. 501). Either in your text or in your parenthetical citation, mention the word or entry. No page number is required, since readers can easily look up the word or entry.

> The word *crocodile* has a surprisingly complex etymology
>
> ("Crocodile").

■ **14. Multivolume work** If your paper cites more than one volume of a multivolume work, indicate in the parentheses the volume you are referring to, followed by a colon and the page number.

> In his studies of gifted children, Terman describes a pattern of
>
> accelerated language acquisition (2: 279).

If you cite only one volume of a multivolume work throughout your paper, you will include the volume number in the list of works cited and will not need to include it in the parentheses. (See the second example in item 26, on p. 501.)

■ **15. Entire work** Use the author's name in a signal phrase or a parenthetical citation. There is no need to use a page number.

> Lane explores the evolution of surveillance in the workplace.

■ **16. Selection in an anthology** Put the name of the author of the selection (not the editor of the anthology) in the signal phrase or the parentheses.

> In "Love Is a Fallacy," the narrator's logical teachings disintegrate
>
> when Polly declares that she should date Petey because "[h]e's got
>
> a raccoon coat" (Shulman 379).

In the list of works cited, the work is alphabetized by the author's last name, not by the name of the editor of the anthology. (See item 24 on p. 500.)

> Shulman, Max. "Love Is a Fallacy." *Current Issues and Enduring Questions.*
>
> > Ed. Sylvan Barnet and Hugo Bedau. 8th ed. Boston: Bedford, 2008.
> >
> > 371-79. Print.

■ **17. Government document** When a government agency is the author, you will alphabetize it in the list of works cited under the name of the government, such as *United States* or *Great Britain* (see item 73 on p. 519). For this reason, you must name the government as well as the agency in your in-text citation.

> Online monitoring by the United States Department of the Interior
> over a one-week period found that employees' use of "sexually
> explicit and gambling websites . . . accounted for over 24 hours
> of Internet use" and that "computer users spent over 2,004 hours
> accessing game and auction sites" during the same period (3).

18. Historical document   For a historical document, such as the United States Constitution or the Canadian Charter of Rights and Freedoms, provide the document title, neither italicized nor in quotation marks, along with relevant article and section numbers. In parenthetical citations, use common abbreviations such as "art." and "sec." and abbreviations of well-known titles: (US Const., art. 1, sec. 2).

> While the United States Constitution provides for the formation of
> new states (art. 4, sec. 3), it does not explicitly allow or prohibit
> the secession of states.

For other historical documents, cite as you would any other work, by the first element in the works cited entry (see item 74 on pp. 519–20).

19. Legal source   For legislative acts (laws) and court cases, name the act or case either in a signal phrase or in parentheses. Italicize the names of cases but not the names of acts.

> The Jones Act of 1917 granted US citizenship to Puerto Ricans.

> In 1857, Chief Justice Roger B. Taney declared in *Dred Scott v.*
> *Sandford* that blacks, whether enslaved or free, could not be citizens
> of the United States.

20. Visual such as a photograph, map, or chart   To cite a visual that has a figure number in the source, use the abbreviation "fig." and the number in place of a page number in your parenthetical citation: (Manning, fig. 4). Spell out the word "figure" if you refer to it in your text.

To cite a visual that does not have a figure number in a print source, use the visual's title or a general description in your text and cite the author and page number as for any other source.

For a visual that is not contained in a source such as a book or periodical, identify the visual in your text and then cite it using the first element in the works cited entry: the photographer's or artist's name or the title of the work. (See items 69 and 72 on pp. 518–19.)

> Photographs such as *Woman Aircraft Worker* (Bransby) and *Women Welders* (Parks) demonstrate the US government's attempt to document the contributions of women on the home front during World War II.

■ **21. E-mail, letter, or personal interview** Cite e-mail messages, personal letters, and personal interviews by the name listed in the works cited entry, as you would for any other source. Identify the type of source in your text if you feel it is necessary. (See item 53 on p. 513 and items 83 and 84 on p. 522.)

■ **22. Web site or other electronic source** Your in-text citation for an electronic source should follow the same guidelines as for other sources. If the source lacks page numbers but has numbered paragraphs, sections, or divisions, use those numbers with the appropriate abbreviation in your in-text citation: "par.," "sec.," "ch.," "pt.," and so on. Do not add such numbers if the source itself does not use them; simply give the author or title in your in-text citation.

> Julian Hawthorne points out profound differences between his father and Ralph Waldo Emerson but concludes that, in their lives and their writing, "together they met the needs of nearly all that is worthy in human nature" (ch. 4).

■ **23. Indirect source (source quoted in another source)** When a writer's or a speaker's quoted words appear in a source written by someone else, begin the parenthetical citation with the abbreviation "qtd. in."

> According to Bill Coleman, an executive at *Salary.com*, "Personal Internet use and casual office conversations often turn into new business ideas or suggestions for gaining operating efficiencies" (qtd. in Frauenheim).

Literary works and sacred texts

Literary works and sacred texts are usually available in a variety of editions. Your list of works cited will specify which edition you are using, and your in-text citation will usually consist of a page number from the edition you consulted (see item 24). When possible, give enough information — such as book parts, play divisions, or line numbers — so that readers can locate the cited passage in any edition of the work (see items 25–27).

■ **24. Literary work without parts or line numbers** Many literary works, such as most short stories and many novels and plays, do not have parts or line numbers. In such cases, simply cite the page number.

> At the end of Kate Chopin's "The Story of an Hour," Mrs. Mallard
> drops dead upon learning that her husband is alive. In the final
> irony of the story, doctors report that she has died of a "joy that
> kills" (25).

■ **25. Verse play or poem** For verse plays, give act, scene, and line numbers that can be located in any edition of the work. Use arabic numerals and separate the numbers with periods.

> In Shakespeare's *King Lear,* Gloucester, blinded for suspected
> treason, learns a profound lesson from his tragic experience: "A
> man may see how this world goes / with no eyes" (4.2.148-49).

For a poem, cite the part, stanza, and line numbers, if it has them, separated by periods.

> The Green Knight claims to approach King Arthur's court "because
> the praise of you, prince, is puffed so high, / And your manor and
> your men are considered so magnificent" (1.12.258-59).

For poems that are not divided into numbered parts or stanzas, use line numbers. For a first reference, use the word "lines": (lines 5-8). Thereafter use just the numbers: (12-13).

■ **26. Novel with numbered divisions** When a novel has numbered divisions, put the page number first, followed by a semicolon and the book, part, or chapter in which the passage may be found. Use abbreviations such as "bk.," "pt.," and "ch."

> One of Kingsolver's narrators, teenager Rachel, pushes her
> vocabulary beyond its limits. For example, Rachel complains that
> being forced to live in the Congo with her missionary family is "a
> sheer tapestry of justice" because her chances of finding a boyfriend
> are "dull and void" (117; bk. 2, ch. 10).

■ **27. Sacred text** When citing a sacred text such as the Bible or the Qur'an, name the edition in your works cited entry (see item 28 on p. 503). In your parenthetical citation, give the book, chapter, and verse (or the equivalent), separated with periods. Abbreviations for books of the Bible are acceptable.

> Consider the words of Solomon: "If your enemy is hungry, give him
> bread to eat; and if he is thirsty, give him water to drink" (*Oxford*
> *Annotated Bible*, Prov. 25.21).

The title of a sacred work is italicized when it refers to a specific edition of the work, as in the preceding example. If you refer to the book in a general sense in your text, neither italicize it nor put it in quotation marks. (See also the note in 42a, p. 348.)

> The Bible and the Qur'an provide allegories that help readers
> understand how to lead a moral life.

59b MLA list of works cited

An alphabetized list of works cited, at the end of your paper, gives publication information for each source you have cited in the paper. Include only sources that you have quoted, summarized, or paraphrased. (For information about preparing the list, see p. 526; for a sample list of works cited, see p. 532.)

General guidelines for works cited in MLA style

In an MLA works cited entry, invert the first author's name (last name first, followed by a comma and the first name); put all other names in normal order. In titles of works, capitalize all words except articles (*a, an, the*), prepositions (*into, between*, and so on), coordinating conjunctions (*and*, *but*, *or*, *nor*, *for*, *so*, *yet*), and the *to* in infinitives — unless they are the first or last word of the title or subtitle. Use quotation marks for titles of articles and other short works, such as brief documents from Web sites; italicize titles of books and other long works, such as entire Web sites.

Give the city of publication without a state name. Shorten publishers' names, usually to the first principal word ("Wiley" for "John Wiley and Sons," for instance); abbreviate "University" and "Press" in the names of university publishers: UP of Florida. For the date of publication, use the date on the title page or the most recent date on the copyright page.

For all works cited entries, include the medium in which a work was published, produced, or delivered. Usually put the medium at the end of the entry, capitalized but neither italicized nor in quotation marks. Typical designations for the medium are "Print," "Web," "Radio," "Television," "CD," "Film," "Video-cassette," "DVD," "Photograph," "Performance," "Lecture," "MP3 file," and "PDF file." (See specific items throughout 59b.)

Listing authors (print and online)

Alphabetize entries in the list of works cited by authors' last names (or by title if a work has no author). The author's name is important because citations in the text of the paper refer to it and readers will look for it at the beginning of an entry in the alphabetized list.

NAME CITED IN TEXT

According to Nancy Flynn, . . .

BEGINNING OF WORKS CITED ENTRY

Flynn, Nancy.

1. Single author

author: last name first / title (book) / city of publication / publisher / date / medium

Wood, James. *How Fiction Works*. New York: Farrar, 2008. Print.

2. Two or three authors

first author: last name first / second author: in normal order / title (book)

Gourevitch, Philip, and Errol Morris. *Standard Operating Procedure.*

city of publication / publisher / date / medium

New York: Penguin, 2008. Print.

first author:
last name first   other authors:
in normal order   title (newspaper article)

Farmer, John, John Azzarello, and Miles Kara. "Real Heroes, Fake Stories."

       date of
newspaper title   publication   page(s) medium

New York Times 14 Sept. 2008: WK10. Print.

3. Four or more authors

first author:
last name first   other authors:
in normal order

Harris, Shon, Allen Harper, Chris Eagle, and Jonathan Ness.

           edition   city of
title (book)   number   publication   publisher   date   medium

Gray Hat Hacking. 2nd ed. New York: McGraw, 2007. Print.

Name all the authors or name the first author followed by "et al." (Latin for "and others"). In an in-text citation, use the same form for the authors' names as you use in the works cited entry. See item 7 on page 483.

4. Organization as author

author: organization name,
not abbreviated   title (book)

National Wildlife Federation. *Rain Check: Conservation Groups Monitor*

                      city of   publisher,
publication   with abbreviations

Mercury Levels in Milwaukee's Rain. Ann Arbor: Natl. Wildlife

          date   medium
Federation, 2001. Print.

For a publication by a government agency, see item 73. Your in-text citation should also treat the organization as the author (see item 8 on p. 483).

5. Unknown author

Article or other short work

                                 newspaper   date of
title (newspaper article)   label   title   publication

"Poverty, by Outdated Numbers." Editorial. *Boston Globe* 20 Sept. 2008:

page(s) medium
A16. Print.

title (TV   title (TV   city of   date of
episode)   program)   producer   network station broadcast broadcast

"Heat." *Frontline*. Prod. Martin Smith. PBS. KTWU, Topeka, 21 Oct. 2008.

        medium

Television.

For other examples of an article with no author and of a television program, see items 13 and 65, respectively.

Book, entire Web site, or other long work

                                 city of
      title (book)   publication publisher   date medium

New Concise World Atlas. New York: Oxford UP, 2007. Print.

                              title (Web site)

Women of Protest: Photographs from the Records of the National Woman's

                      no
       sponsor of site   date medium   access date

   Party. Lib. of Cong., n.d. Web. 29 Sept. 2008.

Before concluding that the author of an online source is unknown, check carefully (see the tip at the bottom of p. 481). Also remember that an organization or a government may be the author (see items 4 and 73).

▪ **6. Two or more works by the same author**   If your list of works cited includes two or more works by the same author, first alphabetize the works by title (ignoring the article *A*, *An*, or *The* at the beginning of a title). Use the author's name for the first entry only; for subsequent entries, use three hyphens followed by a period. The three hyphens must stand for exactly the same name or names as in the first entry.

Knopp, Lisa. *Field of Vision*. Iowa City: U of Iowa P, 1996. Print.

---. *The Nature of Home: A Lexicon and Essays*. Lincoln: U of Nebraska P,

   2002. Print.

Articles in periodicals (print)

This section shows how to prepare works cited entries for articles in print magazines, journals, and newspapers. See "General guidelines" and "Listing authors" on pages 490 and 491 for how to handle basic parts of the entries. See also "Online sources" beginning on page 504 for articles from Web sites and articles accessed through a library's database.

For articles appearing on consecutive pages, provide the range of pages (see items 7 and 8). When an article does not appear on consecutive pages, give the first page number followed by a plus sign: 32+. For dates requiring a month, abbreviate all but May, June, and July. For an illustrated citation of an article in a periodical, see page 495.

■ 7. Article in a journal (paginated by volume or by issue)

author: last
name first   article title

Blackburn, Robin. "Economic Democracy: Meaningful, Desirable, Feasible?"

    journal   volume,
    title   issue   year   page(s)   medium

    Daedalus   136.3   (2007):   36-45.   Print.

■ 8. Article in a monthly magazine

author: last   magazine
name first   article title   title   date: month + year

Lanting, Frans. "Life: A Journey through Time." *Audubon* Nov.-Dec. 2006:

page(s)   medium

48-52.   Print.

■ 9. Article in a weekly magazine

                                      magazine   date: day +
author: last name first   article title   title   month + year   page(s)

von Drehle, David. "The Ghosts of Memphis." *Time* 7 Apr. 2008: 34-37.

medium

Print.

■ 10. Article in a daily newspaper

Give the page range of the article. If the article does not appear on consecutive pages, use a plus sign (+) after the first page number. If the city of publication is not obvious from the title of the newspaper, include the city in brackets after the name of the newspaper.

If sections are identified by letter, include the section letter as part of the page number. If sections are numbered, include the section number between the date and the page number, using the abbreviation "sec." (See the top of p. 496 for examples.)

Citation at a glance: Article in a periodical (MLA)

To cite an article in a print periodical in MLA style, include the following elements:

1. Author of article
2. Title and subtitle of article
3. Title of periodical
4. Volume and issue numbers (for journal)
5. Date or year of publication
6. Page number(s) of article
7. Medium

TITLE PAGE

FIRST PAGE OF ARTICLE

WORKS CITED ENTRY FOR AN ARTICLE IN A PRINT PERIODICAL

Ruzich, Constance M. "For the Love of Joe: Language of Starbucks."

Journal of Popular Culture 41.3 (2008): 428-42. Print.

For more on citing print periodical articles in MLA style, see pages 493–97.

Page number with section letter

author: last
name first   article title   newspaper title   date: day +
month + year

McKenna, Phil. "It Takes Just One Village." *New York Times* 23 Sept. 2008,

       name of
edition   page medium

    New England ed.: D1. Print.

Page number with section number

author: last
name first   article title   newspaper title   city of
publication

Knox, David Blake. "Lord Archer, Storyteller." *Sunday Independent* [Dublin]

   date: day +
month + year   section page medium

   14 Sept. 2008, sec. 2: 9. Print.

11. Abstract of a journal article   Include the word "Abstract" after the title of the article.

Walker, Joyce. "Narratives in the Database: Memorializing September 11th

    Online." Abstract. *Computers and Composition* 24.2 (2007): 121. Print.

12. Article with a title in its title   Use single quotation marks around a title of a short work or a quoted term that appears in an article title. Italicize a title or term normally italicized. (See also 37c.)

Shen, Min. "'Quite a Moon!' The Archetypal Feminine in *Our Town*."

    American Drama 16.2 (2007): 1-14. Print.

13. Editorial or other unsigned article   Begin with the article title and alphabetize the entry by the title in the list of works cited.

"Getting the Message: Communicating Electronically with Doctors Can

    Spur Honesty from Young Patients." Editorial. *Columbus* [OH]

    Dispatch 19 June 2008: 10A. Print.

14. Letter to the editor

Morris, David. "Fiercely Proud." Letter. *Progressive* Feb. 2008: 6. Print.

15. Review   For a review of a book, a film, or another type of work, begin with the name of the reviewer and the title of the review, if it has one. Add the words "Rev. of " and the title of the work reviewed, followed by the author, director, or other significant contributor. Give the publication information for the periodical in which the review appears. If the review has no author and no title, begin with "Rev. of " and alphabetize the entry by the first principal word in the title of the work reviewed.

Dodge, Chris. Rev. of *The Radical Jack London: Writings on War and*

Revolution, ed. Jonah Raskni. *Utne Reader* Sept.-Oct. 2008: 35. Print.

Lane, Anthony. "Dream On." Rev. of *The Science of Sleep* and *Renaissance,*

dir. Michel Gondry. *New Yorker* 25 Sept. 2006: 155-57. Print.

Books (print)

Items 16–33 apply to print books. For online books, see items 41 and 42. For an illustrated citation of a print book, see page 499.

16. Basic format for a book

author: last
name first   book title   city of
publication

Sacks, Oliver. *Musicophilia: Tales of Music and the Brain.* New York:

publisher   date   medium

Knopf, 2007. Print.

Take the information about the book from its title page and copyright page. Use a short form of the publisher's name; omit terms such as "Press," "Inc.," and "Co." except when naming university presses ("Howard UP," for example). If the copyright page lists more than one date, use the most recent one.

17. Book with an author and an editor

author: last
name first   book title   editor:
in normal order

Plath, Sylvia. *The Unabridged Journals of Sylvia Plath.* Ed. Karen V. Kukil.

city of
publication   imprint-publisher   date   medium

New York: Anchor-Doubleday, 2000. Print.

The abbreviation "Ed." means "Edited by," so it is the same for one or multiple editors.

■ **18. Book with an author and a translator** "Trans." means "Translated by," so it is the same for one or multiple translators.

Scirocco, Alfonso. *Garibaldi: Citizen of the World*. Trans. Allan Cameron.

Princeton: Princeton UP, 2007. Print.

■ **19. Book with an editor** Begin with the editor's name. For one editor, use "ed." (for "editor") after the name; for multiple editors, use "eds." (for "editors").

Lago, Mary, Linda K. Hughes, and Elizabeth MacLeod Walls, eds. *The BBC Talks*

of E. M. Forster, 1929-1960. Columbia: U of Missouri P, 2008. Print.

■ **20. Graphic narrative or illustrated book** For a book that combines text and illustrations, begin your citation with the person you wish to emphasize (writer, illustrator, artist) and list any other contributors after the title of the book. Use the abbreviation "illus." and other common labels to identify contributors. If the writer and illustrator are the same person, cite the work as you would a book, with no labels.

Weaver, Dustin, illus. *The Tenth Circle*. By Jodi Picoult. New York:

Washington Square, 2006. Print.

Moore, Alan. *V for Vendetta*. Illus. David Lloyd. New York: Vertigo-DC

Comics, 2008. Print.

Thompson, Craig. *Blankets*. Marietta: Top Shelf, 2005.

■ **21. Book with an author using a pseudonym** Give the author's name as it appears on the title page (the pseudonym), and follow it with the author's real name in brackets.

Dinesen, Isak [Karen Blixen]. *Winter's Tales*. 1942. New York: Vintage,

1993. Print.

■ **22. Book in a language other than English** If your readers are not familiar with the language of the book, include a translation of the title, italicized and in brackets. Capitalize the title according to the conventions of the book's language, and give the original publication information.

Nemtsov, Boris, and Vladimir Milov. *Putin. Itogi. Nezavisimyi Ekspertnyi*

Doklad [*Putin. The Results: An Independent Expert Report*]. Moscow:

Novaya Gazeta, 2008. Print.

Citation at a glance: Book (MLA)

To cite a print book in MLA style, include the following elements:

1 Author
2 Title and subtitle
3 City of publication
4 Publisher
5 Date of publication
6 Medium

TITLE PAGE

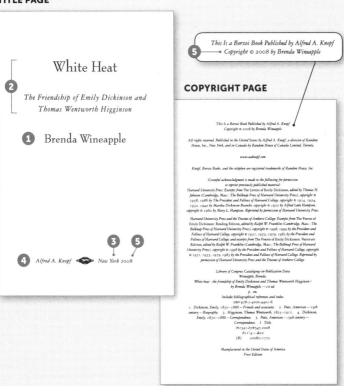

COPYRIGHT PAGE

WORKS CITED ENTRY FOR A PRINT BOOK

Wineapple, Brenda. *White Heat: The Friendship of Emily Dickinson and Thomas Wentworth Higginson*. New York: Knopf, 2008. Print.

For more on citing print books in MLA style, see pages 497–504.

■ **23. Entire anthology** An anthology is a collection of works on a common theme, often with different authors for the selections and usually with an editor for the entire volume. (For an anthology with one editor, use the abbreviation "ed." after the editor's name. For more than one editor, use "eds.")

Dumanis, Michael, and Cate Marvin, eds. *Legitimate Dangers: American*

 Poets of the New Century. Louisville: Sarabande, 2006. Print.

■ **24. One or more selections from an anthology**

One selection from anthology

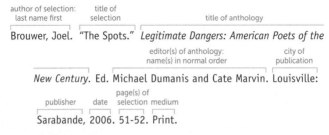

The abbreviation "Ed." means "Edited by," so it is the same for one or multiple editors. For an illustrated citation of a selection from an anthology, see pages 502–03.

Two or more selections, with separate anthology entry

If you use two or more works from the same anthology in your paper, provide an entry for the entire anthology (see item 23) and give a shortened entry for each selection. Use the medium only in the entry for the complete anthology. For an illustrated citation of a selection from an anthology, see pages 502–03.

author of selection	title of selection	editor(s) of anthology: last name(s) only	pages(s) of selection

Brouwer, Joel. "The Spots." Dumanis and Marvin 51-52.

editor(s) of anthology		title of anthology

Dumanis, Michael, and Cate Marvin, eds. *Legitimate Dangers: American*

	city of publication	publisher	date	medium

 Poets of the New Century. Louisville: Sarabande, 2006. Print.

author of selection	title of selection	editor(s) of anthology: last name(s) only	page(s) of selection

Keith, Sally. "Orphean Song." Dumanis and Marvin 195-96.

■   **25. Edition other than the first**   Include the number of the edition (1st, 2nd, 3rd, and so on). If the book has a translator or an editor in addition to the author, give the name of the translator or editor before the edition number, using the abbreviation "Trans." for "Translated by" (see item 18) or "Ed." for "Edited by" (see item 17).

Auletta, Ken. *The Underclass*. 2nd ed. Woodstock: Overlook, 2000. Print.

■   **26. Multivolume work**   Include the total number of volumes before the city and publisher, using the abbreviation "vols." If the volumes were published over several years, give the inclusive dates of publication. The abbreviation "Ed." means "Edited by," so it is the same for one or multiple editors.

| author: last name first | title | editor: in normal order | total volumes | city of publication | publisher |

Stark, Freya. *Letters*. Ed. Lucy Moorehead. 8 vols. Salisbury: Compton,

| inclusive dates | medium |

1974-82. Print.

If you cite only one of the volumes in your paper, include the volume number before the city and publisher and give the date of publication for that volume. After the date, give the medium of publication followed by the total number of volumes.

| author: last name first | title | editor: in normal order | volume cited | city of publication | publisher |

Stark, Freya. *Letters*. Ed. Lucy Moorehead. Vol. 5. Salisbury: Compton,

| date of volume | medium | total volumes |

1978. Print. 8 vols.

■   **27. Encyclopedia or dictionary entry**   List the author of the entry (if there is one), the title of the entry, the title of the reference work, the edition number (if any), the date of the edition, and the medium. Volume and page numbers are not necessary because the entries in the source are arranged alphabetically and are therefore easy to locate.

Posner, Rebecca. "Romance Languages." *The Encyclopaedia Britannica: Macropaedia*. 15th ed. 1987. Print.

"Sonata." *The American Heritage Dictionary of the English Language*. 4th ed. 2000. Print.

Citation at a glance: Selection from an anthology (MLA)

To cite a selection from a print anthology in MLA style, include the following elements:

1 Author of selection
2 Title of selection
3 Title and subtitle of anthology
4 Editor(s) of anthology
5 City of publication
6 Publisher
7 Date of publication
8 Page number(s) of selection
9 Medium

TITLE PAGE

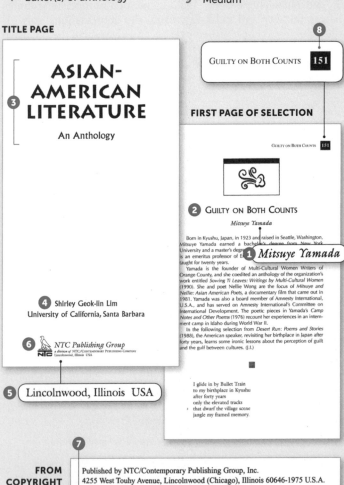

8 GUILTY ON BOTH COUNTS   151

3 ASIAN-AMERICAN LITERATURE
   An Anthology

FIRST PAGE OF SELECTION

GUILTY ON BOTH COUNTS   151

2 GUILTY ON BOTH COUNTS
   Mitsuye Yamada

Born in Kyushu, Japan, in 1923 and raised in Seattle, Washington, Mitsuye Yamada earned a bachelor's degree from New York University and a master's degree   1 *Mitsuye Yamada*
is an emeritus professor of E
taught for twenty years.

Yamada is the founder of Multi-Cultural Women Writers of Orange County, and she coedited an anthology of the organization's work entitled *Sowing Ti Leaves: Writings by Multi-Cultural Women* (1990). She and poet Nellie Wong are the focus of *Mitsuye and Nellie: Asian American Poets*, a documentary film that came out in 1981. Yamada was also a board member of Amnesty International, U.S.A., and has served on Amnesty International's Committee on International Development. The poetic pieces in Yamada's *Camp Notes and Other Poems* (1976) recount her experiences in an internment camp in Idaho during World War II.

In the following selection from *Desert Run: Poems and Stories* (1988), the American speaker, revisiting her birthplace in Japan after forty years, learns some ironic lessons about the perception of guilt and the gulf between cultures. (J.I.)

4 Shirley Geok-lin Lim
   University of California, Santa Barbara

6 NTC Publishing Group
   a division of NTC/CONTEMPORARY PUBLISHING COMPANY
   Lincolnwood, Illinois USA

I glide in by Bullet Train
to my birthplace in Kyushu
after forty years
only the elevated tracks
that dwarf the village scene
jangle my framed memory.

5 Lincolnwood, Illinois USA

7 FROM COPYRIGHT PAGE

Published by NTC/Contemporary Publishing Group, Inc.
4255 West Touhy Avenue, Lincolnwood (Chicago), Illinois 60646-1975 U.S.A.
©2000 NTC/Contemporary Publishing Group, Inc.

WORKS CITED ENTRY FOR A SELECTION FROM A PRINT ANTHOLOGY

┌───1───┐ ┌────────2────────┐ ┌──────────3──────────┐
Yamada, Mitsuye. "Guilty on Both Counts." *Asian-American Literature:*

┌─────────┐ ┌────────4────────┐ ┌───5───┐ ┌6┐ ┌7┐
An Anthology. Ed. Shirley Geok-lin Lim. Lincolnwood: NTC, 2000.

┌8┐ ┌9┐
151-54. Print.

For more on citing selections from print anthologies in MLA style, see page 500.

■ **28. Sacred text** Give the title of the sacred text (taken from the title page), italicized; the editor's or translator's name (if any); publication information; and the medium. Add the name of the version, if there is one.

The Oxford Annotated Bible with the Apocrypha. Ed. Herbert G. May and

Bruce M. Metzger. New York: Oxford UP, 1965. Print. Rev. Standard Vers.

The Qur'an: Translation. Trans. Abdullah Yusuf Ali. Elmhurst: Tahrike,

2000. Print.

■ **29. Foreword, introduction, preface, or afterword**

author of foreword:
last name first   book part   book title
┌─────────────┐   ┌──────┐   ┌──────────────────────────────────
Bennett, Hal Zina. Foreword. *Shimmering Images: A Handy Little Guide to*

                              author of book: city of
                              in normal order   publication   imprint-publisher
                              ┌──────────────┐ ┌──────────┐ ┌──────────────┐
Writing Memoir. By Lisa Dale Norton. New York: Griffin-St. Martin's,

date   page(s) of
        foreword   medium
┌──┐   ┌────────┐ ┌────┐
2008. xiii-xvi. Print.

If the book part has a title, include it in quotation marks immediately after the author's name and before the label for the book part. If the author of the book part is also the author or editor of the complete work, give only the last name of the author the second time it is used.

Ozick, Cynthia. "Portrait of the Essay as a Warm Body." Introduction.

The Best American Essays 1998. Ed. Ozick. Boston: Houghton, 1998.

xv-xxi. Print.

■ **30. Book with a title in its title** If the book title contains a title normally italicized, neither italicize the internal title nor place it in quotation marks.

Woodson, Jon. *A Study of Joseph Heller's* Catch-22: *Going Around Twice*.

New York: Lang, 2001. Print.

If the title within the title is normally put in quotation marks, retain the quotation marks and italicize the entire book title.

Millás, Juan José. *"Personality Disorders" and Other Stories*. Trans. Gregory

B. Kaplan. New York: MLA, 2007. Print. MLA Texts and Trans.

■ **31. Book in a series** After the publication information, give the medium of publication and then the series name as it appears on the title page, followed by the series number, if any.

Douglas, Dan. *Assessing Languages for Specific Purposes*. Cambridge:

Cambridge UP, 2000. Print. Cambridge Applied Linguistics Ser.

■ **32. Republished book** After the title of the book, give the original publication date, followed by the current publication information. If the republished book contains new material, such as an introduction or afterword, include information about the new material after the original date.

Trilling, Lionel. *The Liberal Imagination*. 1950. Introd. Louis Menand. New

York: New York Review of Books, 2008. Print.

■ **33. Publisher's imprint** If a book was published by a division (an imprint) of a publishing company, give the name of the imprint, a hyphen, and the name of the publisher.

Ackroyd, Peter. *The Fall of Troy*. New York: Talese-Doubleday, 2007. Print.

Online sources

MLA guidelines assume that readers can locate most online sources by entering the author, title, or other identifying information in a search engine or a database. Consequently, the *MLA Handbook* does not require a Web address (URL) in citations for online sources. If your instructor requires one, see the note at the end of item 34.

MLA style calls for a sponsor or a publisher in works cited entries for most online sources. If a source has no sponsor or publisher, use the abbreviation "N.p." (for "No publisher") in the sponsor position. If there is no date of publication or update, use "n.d." (for "no date") after the sponsor. For an article in an online journal or an article from a database, give page numbers if they are available; if they are not, use the abbreviation "n. pag." (See item 37.)

34. Entire Web site

Web site with author

author: last name first   title of Web site   sponsor of site (personal page)   update   medium

Peterson, Susan Lynn. *The Life of Martin Luther*. Susan Lynn Peterson, 2005. Web.

date of access:
day + month + year

24 Jan. 2009.

Web site with organization (group) as author

organization name: not abbreviated   title of Web site   sponsor: abbreviated   update   medium

American Library Association. *American Library Association*. ALA, 2008. Web.

date of access:
day + month + year

14 Jan. 2009.

Web site with no author

title of Web site   sponsor of site   update   medium

Margaret Sanger Papers Project. History Dept., New York U, 18 Oct. 2000. Web.

date of access:
day + month + year

6 Jan. 2009.

Web site with editor

See item 19 (p. 498) for listing the name(s) of editor(s).

Halsall, Paul, ed. *Internet Modern History Sourcebook*. Fordham U,

22 Sept. 2001. Web. 19 Jan. 2009.

Web site with no title

Use the label "Home page" or another appropriate description in place of a title.

Yoon, Mina. Home page. Oak Ridge Natl. Laboratory, 28 Dec. 2006. Web.

12 Jan. 2009.

NOTE: If your instructor requires a URL for Web sources, include the URL, enclosed in angle brackets, at the end of the entry. When a URL in a works cited entry must be divided at the end of a line, break it after a double slash or a slash. Do not insert a hyphen.

Peterson, Susan Lynn. *The Life of Martin Luther.* Susan Lynn Peterson, 2005.

  Web. 24 Jan. 2009. <http://www.susanlynnpeterson.com/index_files/

  luther.htm >.

■ **35. Short work from a Web site**   Short works include articles, poems, podcasts, songs, fact sheets, and other documents that are not book length or that appear as internal pages on a Web site. For an illustrated citation of a short work from a Web site, see pages 508–09.

Short work with author

| author: last name first | title of short work | title of Web site | sponsor | no update date |

Shiva, Vandana. "Bioethics: A Third World Issue." *NativeWeb.* NativeWeb, n.d.

| medium | date of access: day + month + year |

  Web. 22 Jan. 2010.

Short work with no author

| title of short work | title of Web site | sponsor of site | update | medium |

"Sister Aimee." *American Experience.* PBS Online, 2 Apr. 2007. Web.

| date of access: day + month + year |

  30 Oct. 2010.

■ **36. Web site with an author using a pseudonym**   Begin the entry with the pseudonym and add the author's or creator's real name, if known, in brackets. Follow with the information required for a Web site or a short work from a Web site (see item 34 or 35).

Grammar Girl [Mignon Fogarty]. "What Is the Plural of 'Mouse'?" *Grammar*

  Girl: Quick and Dirty Tips for Better Writing. Holtzbrinck, 16 Sept.

  2008. Web. 10 Nov. 2010.

■ 37. Article in an online journal

author: last name first · · · · · · · · · · · · · · · · · · · article title

Mason, John Edwin. "'Mannenberg': Notes on the Making of an Icon and

journal title | volume, issue | year | not paginated | medium

Anthem." *African Studies Quarterly* 9.4 (2007): n. pag. Web.

date of access:
day + month + year

23 Feb. 2010.

■ 38. Article in an online magazine

Give the author; the title of the article, in quotation marks; the title of the magazine, italicized; the sponsor or publisher of the site (use "N.p." if there is none); the date of publication; the medium; and your date of access.

Burton, Robert. "The Certainty Epidemic." *Salon.com*. Salon Media Group,

29 Feb. 2008. Web. 18 Jan. 2010.

■ 39. Article in an online newspaper

Give the author; the title of the article, in quotation marks; the title of the newspaper, italicized; the sponsor or publisher of the site (use "N.p." if there is none); the date of publication; the medium; and your date of access.

Smith, Andrew D. "Poll: More than 70% of US Workers Use Internet on the

Job." *Dallasnews.com*. Dallas Morning News, 25 Sept. 2008. Web.

29 Sept. 2008.

■ 40. Article from a database

For an article retrieved from a library's subscription database, first list the publication information for the article (see items 7–15) and then provide information about the database. For an illustrated citation of an article from a database, see page 510.

author of source: last name first | title of article | journal title | volume, issue | year | page(s)

Heyen, William. "Sunlight." *American Poetry Review* 36.2 (2007): 55-56.

database name | medium | date of access: day + month + year

Expanded Academic ASAP. Web. 24 Mar. 2010.

Williams, Jeffrey J. "Why Today's Publishing World Is Reprising the Past."

Chronicle of Higher Education 13 June 2008: n. pag. *LexisNexis*

Academic. Web. 29 Sept. 2009.

Citation at a glance: Short work from a Web site (MLA)

To cite a short work from a Web site in MLA style, include the following elements:

1 Author of short work (if any)
2 Title of short work
3 Title of Web site
4 Sponsor of Web site ("N.p." if none)
5 Update date ("n.d." if none)
6 Medium
7 Date you accessed the source

INTERNAL PAGE OF WEB SITE

FOOTER ON HOME PAGE

the local area. It houses the most extensive collection of art, artifacts, and manuscripts pertaining to American whaling in the age of sail - late eighteenth century to the early twentieth, when sailing ships dominated merchant trade and whaling.

18 Johnny Cake Hill | New Bedford, MA | 02740-6398 | Tel. (508) 997-0046
Fax: (508) 997-0018 | Library Fax: (508) 207-1064

©Copyright 2009 Old Dartmouth Historical Society / New Bedford Whaling Museum

WORKS CITED ENTRY FOR A SHORT WORK FROM A WEB SITE

———— 2 ———— ———— 3 ————
"Overview of American Whaling." *New Bedford Whaling Museum.*

———————————— 4 ———————————— ┌—5—┐
Old Dartmouth Hist. Soc./New Bedford Whaling Museum, 2009.

┌—6—┐ ┌——7——┐
Web. 27 Oct. 2010.

For more on citing sources from Web sites in MLA style, see pages 505–06.

■ **41. Online book-length work** Cite an online book or an online book-length work, such as a play or a long poem, as you would a short work from a Web site (see item 35), but italicize the title of the work.

author: last
name first   title of long poem   title of Web site   sponsor of site

Milton, John. *Paradise Lost: Book I. Poetryfoundation.org.* Poetry Foundation,

                    date of access:
update medium day + month + year

    2008. Web. 14 Dec. 2009.

Give the print publication information for the work, if available (see items 16–33), followed by the title of the Web site, the medium, and your date of access.

author: last
name first   book title

Jacobs, Harriet A. *Incidents in the Life of a Slave Girl: Written by Herself.*

        editor of   city of
    original book publication year   title of Web site

    Ed. L. Maria Child. Boston, 1861. *Documenting the American South.*

            date of access:
medium day + month + year

    Web. 3 Feb. 2010.

■ **42. Part of an online book** Begin as for a part of a print book (see item 29). If the online book part has no page numbers, use "N. pag." following the publication information. End with the Web site on which the work is found, the medium, and your date of access.

Adams, Henry. "Diplomacy." *The Education of Henry Adams.* Boston: Houghton,

    1918. N. pag. *Bartleby.com: Great Books Online.* Web. 8 Jan. 2010.

Citation at a glance: Article from a database (MLA)

To cite an article from a database in MLA style, include the following elements:

1 Author of article
2 Title of article
3 Title of periodical
4 Volume and issue numbers (for journal)
5 Date or year of publication

6 Page number(s) of article ("n. pag." if none)
7 Name of database
8 Medium
9 Date you accessed the source

WORKS CITED ENTRY FOR AN ARTICLE FROM A DATABASE

```
┌──1──┐ ┌─────────────────────2─────────────────────
Kranz, David L. "Tracking the Sounds of Franco Zeffirelli's The Taming of
        ┌──────────3──────────┐ ┌4┐ ┌5┐  ┌──6──┐ ┌──7──
        the Shrew." Literature-Film Quarterly 36.2 (2008): 94-112. Academic
        ┌8┐ ┌──9──┐
        OneFile. Web. 28 Oct. 2010.
```

For more on citing articles from a database in MLA style, see item 40.

■ **43. Digital archives** Digital archives are online collections of documents or records — books, letters, photographs, data — that have been converted to digital form. Cite publication information for the original document, if it is available, using the models throughout section 59b. Then give the location of the document, if any, neither italicized nor in quotation marks; the name of the archive, italicized; the medium ("Web"); and your date of access.

Fiore, Mark. *Shockwaves*. 18 Oct. 2001. *September 11 Digital Archive*. Web.

3 Apr. 2009.

Oblinger, Maggie. Letter to Charlie Thomas. 31 Mar. 1895. Nebraska State

Hist. Soc. *Prairie Settlement: Nebraska Photographs and Family*

Letters, 1862-1912. Web. 3 Nov. 2009.

WPA Household Census for 1047 W. 50th Street, Los Angeles County. 1939. USC

Lib. Spec. Collections. *USC Libraries Digital Archive*. Web. 12 Mar. 2010.

■ **44. Entry in an online reference work** Give the author of the entry, if there is one. Otherwise begin with the title of the entry, in quotation marks. Then give the title of the site; the sponsor and the update date (use "n.d." if there is none); the medium; and your date of access.

"Native American Church." *Britannica*. Encyclopaedia Britannica, 2008.

Web. 29 Jan. 2010.

■ **45. Online poem** Cite as you would a short work from a Web site (item 35) or part of an online book (item 42).

Bell, Acton [Anne Brontë]. "Mementos." *Poems by Currer, Ellis, and Acton*

Bell. London, 1846. N. pag. *A Celebration of Women Writers*. Web.

18 Sept. 2009.

■ **46. Entire blog (Weblog)** Cite a blog as you would an entire Web site (see item 34).

Gristmill. Grist Magazine, 2008. Web. 19 Jan. 2009.

■ **47. Entry or comment in a blog (Weblog)** Cite an entry or a comment (a response to an entry) in a blog as you would a short work from a Web site (see item 35). If the comment or entry has no title, use the label "Weblog entry" or "Weblog comment."

Follow with the remaining information as for an entire blog in item 46.

"Social Media: Facebook and MySpace as University Curricula." *Open*

Education. Open Education.net, n.d. Web. 19 Sept. 2008.

Cynthia. Weblog comment. *Open Education*. Open Education.net, 8 Jan.

2010. Web. 14 Feb. 2010.

48. Academic course or department home page   Cite as a short work from a Web site (see item 35). For a course home page, begin with the name of the instructor and the title of the course or title of the page (use "Course home page" if there is no other title). For a department home page, begin with the name of the department and the label "Dept. home page."

Marrone, Carole. "355:301: College Writing and Research." *Rutgers School*

of Arts and Sciences. Writing Program, Rutgers U, 2010. Web. 19 Mar.

2010.

Comparative Media Studies. Dept. home page. *Massachusetts Institute of*

Technology. MIT, 2010. Web. 6 Feb. 2010.

49. *YouTube* clip or other short online video   Cite as you would a short work from a Web site (see item 35).

author: last
name first   title of
                   video title   Web site sponsor   update

Murphy, Beth. "Tips for a Good Profile Piece." *YouTube*. YouTube, 7 Sept. 2008.

           date of access:
medium day + month + year

Web. 19 Apr. 2010.

50. Online abstract   Cite as you would an abstract of a journal article (see item 11), giving whatever print information is available, followed by the medium and your date of access. If you found the abstract in an online periodical database, include the name of the database after the print publication information (see item 40).

Turner, Fred. "Romantic Automatism: Art, Technology, and Collaborative

Labor in Cold War America." Abstract. *Journal of Visual Culture* 7.1

(2008): 5. Web. 25 Oct. 2009.

51. Online editorial or letter to the editor   Cite as you would an editorial or a letter to the editor in a print publication (see

item 13 or 14), followed by information for a short work from a
Web site (see item 35).

"Compromise Is Key with Religion at Work." Editorial. *StarTribune.com*.

Star Tribune, 18 June 2008. Web. 25 June 2008.

■   **52. Online review**   Begin the entry as you would for a review in a magazine or newspaper (see item 15). If the review is
published in print as well as online, first give publication information as for an article in a periodical (see items 7–10). Then add
the Web site on which the review appears, the medium ("Web"),
and your date of access. If the review is published only on the
Web, give the information required for a short work from a Web
site (see item 35). If you found the review in a database, cite as in
item 40.

Greer, W. R. "Who's the Fairest One of All?" Rev. of *Mirror, Mirror*, by

Gregory Maguire. *Reviewsofbooks.com*. Reviewsofbooks.com, 2003.

Web. 26 Oct. 2009.

■   **53. E-mail message**   Begin with the writer's name and the
subject line. Then write "Message to" followed by the name of
the recipient. End with the date of the message and the medium
("E-mail").

Lowe, Walter. "Review Questions." Message to the author. 15 Mar. 2010. E-mail.

■   **54. Posting to an online discussion list**   When possible, cite
archived versions of postings. If you cannot locate an archived
version, keep a copy of the posting for your records. Begin with
the author's name, followed by the title or subject line, in quotation marks (use the label "Online posting" if the posting has
no title). Then proceed as for a short work from a Web site (see
item 35).

Fainton, Peter. "Re: Backlash against New Labour." *Media Lens Message*

Board. Media Lens, 7 May 2008. Web. 2 June 2008.

■   **55. Entry in a wiki**   A wiki is an online reference that is openly
edited by its users. Treat an entry in a wiki as you would a short
work from a Web site (see item 35). Because wiki content is, by
definition, collectively edited and can be updated frequently, do
not include an author. Give the title of the entry; the name of the
wiki, italicized; the sponsor or publisher of the wiki (use "N.p." if

there is none); the date of the last update; the medium; and your date of access.

"Hip Hop Music." *Wikipedia*. Wikimedia Foundation, 2 Mar. 2010. Web.

18 Mar. 2010.

"Negation in Languages." *UniLang Wiki*. UniLang, 12 Jan. 2009. Web.

9 Mar. 2010.

Audio and visual sources (including online versions)

■ **56. Digital file**   A digital file is any document or image that exists in digital form, independent of a Web site. To cite a digital file, begin with information required for the source (such as a photograph, a report, a sound recording, or a radio program), following the guidelines throughout 59b. Then for the medium, indicate the type of file: "JPEG file," "PDF file," "MP3 file," and so on.

photographer	photograph title	date of composition	location of photograph

Hine, Lewis W. *Girl in Cherryville Mill*. 1908. Prints and Photographs Div.,

medium: file type

Lib. of Cong. JPEG file.

"Scenes from a Recession." *This American Life*. Narr. Ira Glass. Natl. Public

Radio, 30 Mar. 2009. MP3 file.

National Institute of Mental Health. *What Rescue Workers Can Do*.

Washington: US Dept. of Health and Human Services, 2006. PDF file.

■ **57. Podcast**   If you view or listen to a podcast online, cite it as you would a short work from a Web site (see item 35). If you download the podcast and view or listen to it on a computer or portable player, cite it as a digital file (see item 56).

Podcast online

"Calculating the Demand for Charter Schools." Narr. David Guenthner.

Texas PolicyCast. Texas Public Policy Foundation, 28 Aug. 2008. Web.

10 Jan. 2009.

Podcast downloaded as digital file

"Calculating the Demand for Charter Schools." Narr. David Guenthner. *Texas

PolicyCast*. Texas Public Policy Foundation, 28 Aug. 2008. MP3 file.

■ **58. Musical score**   For both print and online versions, begin with the composer's name; the title of the work, italicized (unless it is named by form, number, and key); and the date of composition. For a print source, give the place of publication; the name of the publisher and date of publication; and the medium. For an online source, give the title of the Web site; the publisher or sponsor of the site; the date of Web publication; the medium; and your date of access.

Handel, G. F. *Messiah: An Oratorio*. N.d. *CCARH Publications: Scores and*

　　Parts. Center for Computer Assisted Research in the Humanities,

　　2003. Web. 5 Jan. 2009.

■ **59. Sound recording**   Begin with the name of the person you want to emphasize: the composer, conductor ("Cond."), or performer ("Perf."). For a long work, give the title, italicized (unless it is named by form, number, and key); the names of pertinent artists (such as performers, readers, or musicians); and the orchestra and conductor, if relevant. End with the manufacturer, the date, and the medium.

Bizet, Georges. *Carmen*. Perf. Jennifer Laramore, Thomas Moser, Angela

　　Gheorghiu, and Samuel Ramey. Bavarian State Orch. and Chorus.

　　Cond. Giuseppe Sinopoli. Warner, 1996. CD.

For a song, put the title in quotation marks. If you include the name of the album or CD, italicize it.

Blige, Mary J. "Be without You." *The Breakthrough*. Geffen, 2005. CD.

■ **60. Film**   Begin with the title, italicized. Then give the director ("Dir.") and the lead actors ("Perf.") or narrator ("Narr."); the distributor; the year of the film's release; and the medium ("Film," "Videocassette"). If your paper emphasizes a person or category of people involved with the film, you may begin with those names and titles (see item 61).

　　movie title　　　　director　　　　　　　major performers

Frozen River. Dir. Courtney Hunt. Perf. Melissa Leo, Charlie McDermott, and

　　　　　　　　　　　release
　　　　　distributor　date　medium

　　Misty Upham. Sony, 2008. Film.

■ **61. DVD** For a film on DVD or a similar medium, such as Blu-ray Disc (BD), cite as you would a film (see item 60), giving "DVD" (or "BD") as the medium.

Forster, Marc, dir. *Finding Neverland*. Perf. Johnny Depp, Kate Winslet,

Julie Christie, Radha Mitchell, and Dustin Hoffman. Miramax,

2004. DVD.

For any other work on DVD, such as an educational work or a game, cite as you would a film, giving whatever information is available about the author, director, distributor, and so on.

Across the Drafts: Students and Teachers Talk about Feedback. Harvard

Expository Writing Program, 2005. DVD.

■ **62. Special feature on a DVD** Begin with the title of the feature, in quotation marks, and the names of any important contributors, as for films or DVDs (item 60 or 61). End with information about the DVD, as in item 61, including the disc number, if any.

"Sweeney's London." Prod. Eric Young. *Sweeney Todd: The Demon Barber of*

Fleet Street. Dir. Tim Burton. DreamWorks, 2007. DVD. Disc 2.

■ **63. CD-ROM** Treat a CD-ROM as you would any other source, but add the medium ("CD-ROM").

"Pimpernel." *The American Heritage Dictionary of the English Language*.

4th ed. Boston: Houghton, 2000. CD-ROM.

■ **64. Computer software or video game** List the developer or author of the software (if any); the title, italicized; the distributor and date of publication; and the platform or medium.

Firaxis Games. *Sid Meier's Civilization Revolution*. Take-Two Interactive,

2008. Xbox 360.

■ **65. Radio or television program** Begin with the title of the radio segment or television episode (if there is one), in quotation marks. Then give the title of the program or series, italicized; relevant information about the program, such as the writer ("By"), director ("Dir."), performers ("Perf."), or narrator ("Narr."); the network; the local station (if any) and location; the date of broadcast; and the medium ("Television," "Radio"). For a program you accessed online, after the information about the program give the network, the original broadcast date, the title of the Web site, the medium ("Web"), and your date of access.

"Machines of the Gods." *Ancient Discoveries*. History Channel. 14 Oct.

2008. Television.

"Elif Shafak: Writing under a Watchful Eye." *Fresh Air*. Narr. Terry Gross.

Natl. Public Radio, 6 Feb. 2007. *NPR.org*. Web. 22 Feb. 2009.

⬤ **66. Radio or television interview** Begin with the name of the person who was interviewed, followed by the word "Interview" and the interviewer's name, if relevant. End with information about the program as in item 65.

De Niro, Robert, Barry Levinson, and Art Linson. Interview by Charlie

Rose. *Charlie Rose*. PBS. WGBH, Boston, 13 Oct. 2008. Television.

⬤ **67. Live performance** For a live performance of a concert, a play, a ballet, or an opera, begin with the title of the work performed, italicized. Then give the author or composer of the work ("By"); relevant information such as the director ("Dir."), the choreographer ("Chor."), the conductor ("Cond."), or the major performers ("Perf."); the orchestra or the theater, ballet, or opera company, if any; the theater and location; the date of the performance; and the label "Performance."

The Brothers Size. By Tarell Alvin McCraney. Dir. Bijan Sheibani. Young Vic

Theatre, London. 15 Oct. 2008. Performance.

Symphony no. 4 in G. By Gustav Mahler. Cond. Mark Wigglesworth. Perf.

Juliane Banse and Boston Symphony Orch. Symphony Hall, Boston.

17 Apr. 2009. Performance.

⬤ **68. Lecture or public address** Begin with the speaker's name, followed by the title of the lecture (if any), in quotation marks; the organization sponsoring the lecture; the location; the date; and a label such as "Lecture" or "Address."

Wellbery, David E. "On a Sentence of Franz Kafka." Franke Inst. for the

Humanities. Gleacher Center, Chicago. 1 Feb. 2006. Lecture.

■ **69. Work of art** Cite the artist's name; the title of the art-work, italicized; the date of composition; the medium of composition (for instance, "Lithograph on paper," "Photograph," "Charcoal on paper"); and the institution and city in which the artwork is located. For artworks found online, omit the medium of composition and include the title of the Web site, the medium ("Web"), and your date of access.

Constable, John. *Dedham Vale*. 1802. Oil on canvas. Victoria and Albert

Museum, London.

Hessing, Valjean. *Caddo Myth*. 1976. Joslyn Art Museum, Omaha. *Joslyn*

Art Museum. Web. 19 Apr. 2009.

■ **70. Cartoon** Give the cartoonist's name; the title of the car-toon, if it has one, in quotation marks; the label "Cartoon" or "Comic strip"; publication information; and the medium. To cite an online cartoon, instead of publication information give the title of the Web site, the sponsor or publisher, the date of publica-tion, the medium, and your date of access.

Keefe, Mike. "Veterans Affairs Overruns." Cartoon. *Denverpost.com*. Denver

Post, 11 Oct. 2009. Web. 12 Dec. 2009.

■ **71. Advertisement** Name the product or company being ad-vertised, followed by the word "Advertisement." Give publication information for the source in which the advertisement appears.

Truth by Calvin Klein. Advertisement. *Vogue* Dec. 2000: 95-98. Print.

Arbella Insurance. Advertisement. *Boston.com*. NY Times, n.d. Web.

3 Sept. 2009.

■ **72. Map or chart** Cite a map or a chart as you would a book or a short work within a longer work. Use the word "Map" or "Chart" following the title. Add the medium and, for an online source, the sponsor or publisher and the date of access.

Joseph, Lori, and Bob Laird. "Driving While Phoning Is Dangerous." Chart.

USA Today 16 Feb. 2001: 1A. Print.

"Serbia." Map. *Syrena Maps*. Syrena, 2 Feb. 2001. Web. 17 Mar. 2009.

Other sources (including online versions)

This section includes a variety of sources not covered elsewhere. For online sources, consult the appropriate model in this section and also see items 34–55.

73. Government document   Treat the government agency as the author, giving the name of the government followed by the name of the department and the agency, if any. For print sources, add the medium at the end of the entry. For online sources, follow the model for an entire Web site (item 34) or a short work from a Web site (item 35).

> government — department — agency
>
> United States. Dept. of the Interior. Office of Inspector General. "Excessive
>
> document title
> Indulgences: Personal Use of the Internet at the Department of the
>
> Web site title — publisher/sponsor
> Interior." *Office of Inspector General.* Dept. of the Interior,
>
> publication date — medium — date of access: day + month + year
> Sept. 1999. Web. 20 May 2010.

Canada. Minister of Indian Affairs and Northern Dev. *Gathering Strength: Canada's Aboriginal Action Plan.* Ottawa: Minister of Public Works and Govt. Services Can., 2000. Print.

74. Historical document   To cite a historical document, such as the US Constitution or the Canadian Charter of Rights and Freedoms, begin with the document author, if it has one, and then give the document title, neither italicized nor in quotation marks, and the document date. For a print version, continue as for a selection in an anthology (see item 24) or for a book (with the title not italicized). For an online version, cite as a short work from a Web site (see item 35).

Jefferson, Thomas. First Inaugural Address. 1801. *The American Reader.* Ed. Diane Ravitch. New York: Harper, 1990. 42-44. Print.

The Virginia Declaration of Rights. 1776. *A Chronology of US Historical Documents.* U of Oklahoma Coll. of Law, 2008. Web. 23 Feb. 2009.

75. Legal source

Legislative act (law)

Begin with the name of the act, neither italicized nor in quotation marks. Then provide the act's Public Law number; its Statutes at Large volume and page numbers; its date of enactment; and the medium of publication.

Electronic Freedom of Information Act Amendments of 1996. Pub. L.

    104-231. 110 Stat. 3048. 2 Oct. 1996. Print.

Court case

Name the first plaintiff and the first defendant. Then give the volume, name, and page numbers of the law report; the court name; the year of the decision; and publication information. Do not italicize the name of the case. (In the text of the paper, the name of the case is italicized; see item 19 on p. 487.)

Utah v. Evans. 536 US 452. Supreme Court of the US. 2002. *Supreme Court*

    Collection. Legal Information Inst., Cornell U Law School, n.d. Web.

    30 Apr. 2008.

76. Pamphlet or brochure Cite as you would a book (see items 16–33).

Commonwealth of Massachusetts. Dept. of Jury Commissioner. *A Few Facts*

    about Jury Duty. Boston: Commonwealth of Massachusetts, 2004.

    Print.

77. Unpublished dissertation Begin with the author's name, followed by the dissertation title in quotation marks; the abbreviation "Diss."; the name of the institution; the year the dissertation was accepted; and the medium of the dissertation.

Jackson, Shelley. "Writing Whiteness: Contemporary Southern Literature

    in Black and White." Diss. U of Maryland, 2000. Print.

78. Published dissertation For dissertations that have been published in book form, italicize the title. After the title and before the book's publication information, give the abbreviation

"Diss.," the name of the institution, and the year the dissertation
was accepted. Add the medium of publication at the end.

Damberg, Cheryl L. *Healthcare Reform: Distributional Consequences of an*
    Employer Mandate for Workers in Small Firms. Diss. Rand Graduate
    School, 1995. Santa Monica: Rand, 1996. Print.

■ **79. Abstract of a dissertation**   Cite an abstract as you would
an unpublished dissertation. After the dissertation date, give the abbreviation *DA* or *DAI* (for *Dissertation Abstracts* or *Dissertation Abstracts International*), followed by the volume and issue numbers; the
year of publication; inclusive page numbers or, if the abstract is not
numbered, the item number; and the medium of publication. For an
abstract accessed in an online database, give the item number in place
of the page number, followed by the name of the database, the medium, and your date of access.

Chen, Shu-Ling. "Mothers and Daughters in Morrison, Tan, Marshall,
    and Kincaid." Diss. U of Washington, 2000. *DAI* 61.6 (2000):
    AAT9975963. *ProQuest Dissertations and Theses.* Web. 22 Feb. 2009.

■ **80. Published proceedings of a conference**   Cite as you would
a book, adding the name, date, and location of the conference after
the title.

Urgo, Joseph R., and Ann J. Abadie, eds. *Faulkner and Material Culture.*
    Proc. of Faulkner and Yoknapatawpha Conf., 25-29 July 2004, U of
    Mississippi. Jackson: UP of Mississippi, 2007. Print.

■ **81. Paper in conference proceedings**   Cite as you would a selection in an anthology (see item 24), giving information about
the conference after the title and editors of the conference proceedings (see item 80).

Henninger, Katherine R. "Faulkner, Photography, and a Regional Ethics
    of Form." *Faulkner and Material Culture.* Ed. Joseph R. Urgo and Ann
    J. Abadie. Proc. of Faulkner and Yoknapatawpha Conf., 25-29 July
    2004, U of Mississippi. Jackson: UP of Mississippi, 2007. 121-38.
    Print.

■ **82. Published interview**   Name the person interviewed, followed by the title of the interview (if there is one). If the interview does not have a title, include the word "Interview" after the interviewee's name. Give publication information for the work in which the interview was published.

Simon, David. "Beyond the Choir: An Interview with David Simon." *Film*

   Quarterly 62.2 (2008/2009): 44-49. Print.

If you wish to include the name of the interviewer, put it after the title of the interview (or after the name of the interviewee if there is no title).

Florida, Richard. "The Great Reset." Interview by Conor Clarke. *Atlantic.*

   Atlantic Monthly Group, Feb. 2009. Web. 28 Feb. 2010.

■ **83. Personal interview**   To cite an interview that you conducted, begin with the name of the person interviewed. Then write "Personal interview" or "Telephone interview," followed by the date of the interview.

Akufo, Dautey. Personal interview. 11 Apr. 2010.

■ **84. Personal letter**   To cite a letter that you received, begin with the writer's name and add the phrase "Letter to the author," followed by the date. Add the medium ("MS" for "manuscript," or a handwritten letter; "TS" for "typescript," or a typed letter).

Primak, Shoshana. Letter to the author. 6 May 2010. TS.

■ **85. Published letter**   Begin with the writer of the letter, the words "Letter to" and the recipient, and the date of the letter (use "N.d." if the letter is undated). Then add the title of the collection and proceed as for a selection in an anthology (see item 24).

Wharton, Edith. Letter to Henry James. 28 Feb. 1915. *Henry James and*

   Edith Wharton: Letters, 1900-1915. Ed. Lyall H. Powers. New York:

   Scribner's, 1990. 323-26. Print.

■ **86. Manuscript**   Give the author, a title or a description of the manuscript, and the date of composition, followed by the abbreviation "MS" for "manuscript" (handwritten) or "TS" for "typescript." Add the name and location of the institution housing the material. For a manuscript found online, give the preceding information but omit "MS" or "TS." Then list the title of the Web site, the medium ("Web"), and your date of access.

Arendt, Hannah. *Between Past and Present*. N.d. 1st draft. Hannah

Arendt Papers. MS Div., Lib. of Cong. *Manuscript Division, Library of*

Congress. Web. 24 Apr. 2009.

59c MLA information notes (optional)

Researchers who use the MLA system of parenthetical documentation may also use information notes for one of two purposes:

1. to provide additional material that is important but might interrupt the flow of the paper
2. to refer to several sources that support a single point or to provide comments on sources

Information notes may be either footnotes or endnotes. Footnotes appear at the foot of the page; endnotes appear on a separate page at the end of the paper, just before the list of works cited. For either style, the notes are numbered consecutively throughout the paper. The text of the paper contains a raised arabic numeral that corresponds to the number of the note.

TEXT

In the past several years, employees have filed a number of lawsuits

against employers because of online monitoring practices.[1]

NOTE

1. For a discussion of federal law applicable to electronic

surveillance in the workplace, see Kesan 293.

60 MLA manuscript format; sample paper

The following guidelines are consistent with advice given in the *MLA Handbook for Writers of Research Papers*, 7th ed. (New York: MLA, 2009), and with typical requirements for student papers. For a sample MLA paper, see pages 527–32.

60a MLA manuscript format

Formatting the paper

Papers written in MLA style should be formatted as follows.

Materials and font   Use good-quality 8½″ × 11″ white paper. If your instructor does not require a specific font, choose one that is standard and easy to read (such as Times New Roman).

Title and identification   MLA does not require a title page. On the first page of your paper, place your name, your instructor's name, the course title, and the date on separate lines against the left margin. Then center your title. (See p. 527 for a sample first page.)

If your instructor requires a title page, ask for formatting guidelines.

Pagination   Put the page number preceded by your last name in the upper right corner of each page, one-half inch below the top edge. Use arabic numerals (1, 2, 3, and so on).

Margins, line spacing, and paragraph indents   Leave margins of one inch on all sides of the page. Left-align the text.

Double-space throughout the paper. Do not add extra space above or below the title of the paper or between paragraphs.

Indent the first line of each paragraph one-half inch from the left margin.

Capitalization and italics   In titles of works, capitalize all words except articles (*a, an, the*), prepositions (*to, from, between,* and so on), coordinating conjunctions (*and, but, or, nor, for, so, yet*), and the *to* in infinitives — unless they are the first or last word of the title or subtitle. Follow these guidelines in your paper even if the title appears in all capital or all lowercase letters in the source.

In the text of an MLA paper, when a complete sentence follows a colon, lowercase the first word following the colon unless the sentence is a direct quotation or a well-known expression or principle. (See the examples in item 1 on p. 481.)

Italicize the titles of books, periodicals, and other long works, such as Web sites. Use quotation marks around the titles of periodical articles, short stories, poems, and other short works. (If your instructor prefers underlining, use it consistently in place of italics.)

Long quotations   When a quotation is longer than four typed lines of prose or three lines of verse, set it off from the text by indenting the entire quotation one inch from the left margin. Double-space the indented quotation, and do not add extra space above or below it.

Do not use quotation marks when a quotation has been set off from the text by indenting. See page 528 for an example.

URLs (Web addresses)   When you need to break a URL at the end of a line in the text of your paper, break it only after a double slash or a slash and do not insert a hyphen. For MLA rules on dividing URLs in your list of works cited, see page 526.

Headings   MLA neither encourages nor discourages the use of headings and provides no guidelines for their use. If you would like to insert headings in a long essay or research paper, check first with your instructor.

Visuals   MLA classifies visuals as tables and figures (figures include graphs, charts, maps, photographs, and drawings). Label each table with an arabic numeral ("Table 1," "Table 2," and so on) and provide a clear caption that identifies the subject. Capitalize the caption as you would a title (see 45c); do not italicize the label and caption or place them in quotation marks. The label and caption should appear on separate lines above the table, flush with the left margin.

For a table that you have borrowed or adapted, give the source below the table in a note like the following:

Source: David N. Greenfield and Richard A. Davis; "Lost in Cyberspace:

The Web @ Work"; *CyberPsychology and Behavior* 5.4 (2002): 349; print.

For each figure, place the figure number (using the abbreviation "Fig.") and a caption below the figure, flush left. Capitalize the caption as you would a sentence; include source information following the caption. (When referring to the figure in your paper, use the abbreviation "fig." in parenthetical citations; otherwise spell out the word.) See page 531 for an example of a figure in a paper.

Place visuals in the text, as close as possible to the sentences that relate to them, unless your instructor prefers that visuals appear in an appendix.

Preparing the list of works cited

Begin the list of works cited on a new page at the end of the paper. Center the title "Works Cited" about one inch from the top of the page. Double-space throughout. See page 532 for a sample list of works cited.

Alphabetizing the list   Alphabetize the list by the last names of the authors (or editors); if a work has no author or editor, alphabetize by the first word of the title other than *A*, *An*, or *The*.

If your list includes two or more works by the same author, use the author's name for the first entry only. For subsequent entries, use three hyphens followed by a period. List the titles in alphabetical order. (See item 6 on p. 493.)

Indenting   Do not indent the first line of each works cited entry, but indent any additional lines one-half inch. This technique highlights the beginning of each entry, making it easy for readers to scan the alphabetized list. See page 532.

URLs (Web addresses)   If you need to include a URL in a works cited entry and it must be divided across lines, break the URL only after a double slash or a slash. Do not insert a hyphen at the end of the line. Insert angle brackets around the URL. (See the note following item 34 on p. 506.) If your word processing program automatically turns URLs into links (by underlining them and changing the color), turn off this feature.

60b Sample research paper: MLA style

On the following pages is a research paper on the topic of electronic surveillance in the workplace, written by Anna Orlov, a student in a composition class. Orlov's paper is documented with in-text citations and a list of works cited in MLA style. Annotations in the margins of the paper draw your attention to Orlov's use of MLA style and her effective writing.

MODELS   hackerhandbooks.com/rules

> Model papers > MLA research papers: Orlov; Daly; Levi

> MLA annotated bibliography: Orlov

Orlov 1

Anna Orlov

Professor Willis

English 101

17 March 2009

Online Monitoring:

A Threat to Employee Privacy in the Wired Workplace

As the Internet has become an integral tool of businesses, company policies on Internet usage have become as common as policies regarding vacation days or sexual harassment. A 2005 study by the American Management Association and ePolicy Institute found that 76% of companies monitor employees' use of the Web, and the number of companies that block employees' access to certain Web sites has increased 27% since 2001 (1). Unlike other company rules, however, Internet usage policies often include language authorizing companies to secretly monitor their employees, a practice that raises questions about rights in the workplace. Although companies often have legitimate concerns that lead them to monitor employees' Internet usage— from expensive security breaches to reduced productivity—the benefits of electronic surveillance are outweighed by its costs to employees' privacy and autonomy.

While surveillance of employees is not a new phenomenon, electronic surveillance allows employers to monitor workers with unprecedented efficiency. In his book *The Naked Employee*, Frederick Lane describes offline ways in which employers have been permitted to intrude on employees' privacy for decades, such as drug testing, background checks, psychological exams, lie detector tests, and in-store video surveillance. The difference, Lane argues, between these old methods of data gathering and electronic surveillance involves quantity:

Title is centered.

Opening sentences provide background for the thesis.

Thesis asserts Orlov's main point.

Summary and long quotation are each introduced with a signal phrase naming the author.

Marginal annotations indicate MLA-style formatting and effective writing.

Long quotation is set off from the text; quotation marks are omitted.

> Technology makes it possible for employers to gather enormous amounts of data about employees, often far beyond what is necessary to satisfy safety or productivity concerns. And the trends that drive technology—faster, smaller, cheaper—make it possible for larger and larger numbers of employers to gather ever-greater amounts of personal data. (3-4)

Page number is given in parentheses after the final period.

In an age when employers can collect data whenever employees use their computers—when they send e-mail, surf the Web, or even arrive at or depart from their workstations—the challenge for both employers and employees is to determine how much is too much.

Clear topic sentences, like this one, are used throughout the paper.

Another key difference between traditional surveillance and electronic surveillance is that employers can monitor workers' computer use secretly. One popular monitoring method is keystroke logging, which is done by means of an undetectable program on employees' computers. The Web site of a vendor for Spector Pro, a popular keystroke logging program, explains that the software can be installed to operate in "Stealth" mode so that it "does not show up as an icon, does not appear in the Windows system tray, . . . [and] cannot be uninstalled without

Source with an unknown author is cited by a shortened title.

the Spector Pro password which YOU specify" ("Automatically"). As Lane explains, these programs record every key entered into the computer in hidden directories that can later be accessed or uploaded by supervisors; the programs can even scan for keywords tailored to individual companies (128-29).

Orlov anticipates objections and provides sources for opposing views.

Some experts have argued that a range of legitimate concerns justifies employer monitoring of employee Internet usage. As *PC World* columnist Daniel Tynan points out, companies that don't monitor network traffic can be penalized for their ignorance: "Employees could accidentally (or deliberately) spill

Orlov 3

confidential information . . . or allow worms to spread throughout a corporate network." The ePolicy Institute, an organization that advises companies about reducing risks from technology, reported that breaches in computer security cost institutions $100 million in 1999 alone (Flynn). Companies also are held legally accountable for many of the transactions conducted on their networks and with their technology. Legal scholar Jay Kesan points out that the law holds employers liable for employees' actions such as violations of copyright laws, the distribution of offensive or graphic sexual material, and illegal disclosure of confidential information (312).

These kinds of concerns should give employers, in certain instances, the right to monitor employee behavior. But employers rushing to adopt surveillance programs might not be adequately weighing the effect such programs can have on employee morale. Employers must consider the possibility that employees will perceive surveillance as a breach of trust that can make them feel like disobedient children, not responsible adults who wish to perform their jobs professionally and autonomously.

Transition helps readers move from one paragraph to the next.

Yet determining how much autonomy workers should be given is complicated by the ambiguous nature of productivity in the wired workplace. On the one hand, computers and Internet access give employees powerful tools to carry out their jobs; on the other hand, the same technology offers constant temptations to avoid work. As a 2005 study by *Salary.com* and *America Online* indicates, the Internet ranked as the top choice among employees for ways of wasting time on the job; it beat talking with co-workers—the second most popular method—by a margin of nearly two to one (Frauenheim). Chris Gonsalves, an editor for *eWeek.com*, argues that the technology has changed the terms between employers and employees: "While bosses can

Orlov treats both sides fairly; she provides a transition to her own argument.

Orlov 4

easily detect and interrupt water-cooler chatter," he writes, "the
employee who is shopping at Lands' End or IMing with fellow
fantasy baseball managers may actually appear to be working."
The gap between behaviors that are observable to managers and
the employee's actual activities when sitting behind a computer
has created additional motivations for employers to invest in
surveillance programs. "Dilbert," a popular cartoon that spoofs
office culture, aptly captures how rampant recreational Internet
use has become in the workplace (see fig. 1).

But monitoring online activities can have the unintended
effect of making employees resentful. As many workers would be
quick to point out, Web surfing and other personal uses of the
Internet can provide needed outlets in the stressful work
environment; many scholars have argued that limiting and
policing these outlets can exacerbate tensions between employees
and managers. Kesan warns that "prohibiting personal use can
seem extremely arbitrary and can seriously harm morale. . . .
Imagine a concerned parent who is prohibited from checking on
a sick child by a draconian company policy" (315-16). As this
analysis indicates, employees can become disgruntled when
Internet usage policies are enforced to their full extent.

Additionally, many experts disagree with employers'
assumption that online monitoring can increase productivity.
Employment law attorney Joseph Schmitt argues that, particularly
for employees who are paid a salary rather than an hourly wage,
"a company shouldn't care whether employees spend one or
10 hours on the Internet as long as they are getting their jobs
done—and provided that they are not accessing inappropriate
sites" (qtd. in Verespej). Other experts even argue that time
spent on personal Internet browsing can actually be productive
for companies. According to Bill Coleman, an executive at

No page number is available for this Web source.

Orlov counters opposing views and provides support for her argument.

Orlov uses a brief signal phrase to move from her argument to the words of a source.

Orlov cites an indirect source: words quoted in another source.

Orlov 5

Fig. 1. This "Dilbert" comic strip suggests that personal Internet usage is widespread in the workplace (Adams 106).

Illustration has figure number, caption, and source information.

Salary.com, "Personal Internet use and casual office conversations often turn into new business ideas or suggestions for gaining operating efficiencies" (qtd. in Frauenheim). Employers, in other words, may benefit from showing more faith in their employees' ability to exercise their autonomy.

Employees' right to privacy and autonomy in the workplace, however, remains a murky area of the law. Although evaluating where to draw the line between employee rights and employer powers is often a duty that falls to the judicial system, the courts have shown little willingness to intrude on employers' exercise of control over their computer networks. Federal law provides few guidelines related to online monitoring of employees, and only Connecticut and Delaware require companies to disclose this type of surveillance to employees (Tam et al.). "It is unlikely that we will see a legally guaranteed zone of privacy in the American workplace," predicts Kesan (293). This reality leaves employees and employers to sort the potential risks and benefits of technology in contract agreements and terms of employment. With continuing advances in technology, protecting both employers and employees will require greater awareness of these programs, better disclosure to employees, and a more public discussion about what types of protections are necessary to guard individual freedoms in the wired workplace.

Orlov sums up her argument and suggests a course of action.

Orlov 6

Works Cited

Adams, Scott. *Dilbert and the Way of the Weasel.* New York:
Harper, 2002. Print.

American Management Association and ePolicy Institute.
"2005 Electronic Monitoring and Surveillance Survey."
American Management Association. Amer. Management
Assn., 2005. Web. 15 Feb. 2009.

"Automatically Record Everything They Do Online! Spector Pro 5.0
FAQ's." *Netbus.org.* Netbus.Org, n.d. Web. 17 Feb. 2009.

Flynn, Nancy. "Internet Policies." *ePolicy Institute.* ePolicy
Inst., n.d. Web. 15 Feb. 2009.

Frauenheim, Ed. "Stop Reading This Headline and Get Back
to Work." *CNET News.com.* CNET Networks, 11 July
2005. Web. 17 Feb. 2009.

Gonsalves, Chris. "Wasting Away on the Web." *eWeek.com.*
Ziff Davis Enterprise Holdings, 8 Aug. 2005. Web.
16 Feb. 2009.

Kesan, Jay P. "Cyber-Working or Cyber-Shirking? A First Principles
Examination of Electronic Privacy in the Workplace."
Florida Law Review 54.2 (2002): 289-332. Print.

Lane, Frederick S., III. *The Naked Employee: How Technology
Is Compromising Workplace Privacy.* New York: Amer.
Management Assn., 2003. Print.

Tam, Pui-Wing, et al. "Snooping E-Mail by Software Is Now
a Workplace Norm." *Wall Street Journal* 9 Mar. 2005:
B1+. Print.

Tynan, Daniel. "Your Boss Is Watching." *PC World.* PC World
Communications, 6 Oct. 2004. Web. 17 Sept. 2009.

Verespej, Michael A. "Inappropriate Internet Surfing."
Industry Week. Penton Media, 7 Feb. 2000. Web.
16 Feb. 2009.

Heading is centered.

List is alphabetized by authors' last names (or by title when a work has no author).

Abbreviation "n.d." indicates that the online source has no update date.

First line of each entry is at the left margin; extra lines are indented ½".

Double-spacing is used throughout.

A work with four authors is listed by the first author's name and the abbreviation "et al." (for "and others").

Writing
Papers in
APA Style

Most social science instructors will ask you to document your sources with the American Psychological Association (APA) system of in-text citations and references described in 64. You face three main challenges when writing a social science paper that draws on sources: (1) supporting a thesis, (2) citing your sources and avoiding plagiarism, and (3) integrating quotations and other source material.

Examples in this section are drawn from one student's research for a review of the literature on treatments for childhood obesity. Luisa Mirano's paper appears on pages 583–94.

61 Supporting a thesis

Most assignments ask you to form a thesis, or main idea, and to support that thesis with well-organized evidence. (See also 1c.) In a paper reviewing the literature on a topic, the thesis analyzes the often competing conclusions drawn by a variety of researchers.

61a Form a working thesis.

Once you have read a variety of sources and considered your issue from different perspectives, you are ready to form a working thesis: a one-sentence (or occasionally a two-sentence) statement of your central idea. (See also 1c.) Because it is a working, or tentative, thesis, you can remain flexible and revise it as your ideas develop. Ultimately, your thesis will express not just your opinion but your informed, reasoned answer to your research question (see 53a). Here, for example, is a research question posed by Luisa Mirano, a student in a psychology class, followed by her thesis in answer to that question.

RESEARCH QUESTION

Is medication the right treatment for the escalating problem of childhood obesity?

WORKING THESIS

Treating cases of childhood obesity with medication alone is too narrow an approach for this growing problem.

Notice that the thesis expresses a view on a debatable issue — an issue about which intelligent, well-meaning people might disagree. The writer's job is to persuade such readers that this view is worth taking seriously.

61b Organize your ideas.

The American Psychological Association encourages the use of headings to help readers follow the organization of a paper. For an original research report, the major headings often follow a standard model: Method, Results, Discussion. The introduction is not given a heading; it consists of the material between the title of the paper and the first heading.

For a literature review, headings will vary. The student who wrote about treatments for childhood obesity used four questions to focus her research; the questions then became headings in her paper (see pp. 583–94).

> **Making the most of your handbook**
> A working thesis and rough outline can help writers get started.
> ▶ Drafting a working thesis: 1c
> ▶ Sketching a plan: 1d

61c Use sources to inform and support your argument.

Used thoughtfully, your source materials will make your argument more complex and convincing for readers. Sources can play several different roles as you develop your points.

Providing background information or context

You can use facts and statistics to support generalizations or to establish the importance of your topic, as student writer Luisa Mirano does in her introduction.

In March 2004, U.S. Surgeon General Richard Carmona called attention to a health problem in the United States that, until recently, has been overlooked: childhood obesity. Carmona said that

the "astounding" 15% child obesity rate constitutes an "epidemic."
Since the early 1980s, that rate has "doubled in children and tripled
in adolescents." Now more than 9 million children are classified
as obese.

Explaining terms or concepts

If readers are unlikely to be familiar with a word, a phrase, or an
idea important to your topic, you must explain it for them. Quoting or paraphrasing a source can help you define terms and concepts in accessible language. Luisa Mirano uses a scholarly source
to explain how one of the major obesity drugs functions.

> Sibutramine suppresses appetite by blocking the reuptake of the
> neurotransmitters serotonin and norepinephrine in the brain
> (Yanovski & Yanovski, 2002, p. 594).

Supporting your claims

As you draft your argument, make sure to back up your assertions
with facts, examples, and other evidence from your research (see
also 6e). Luisa Mirano, for example, uses one source's findings to
support her central idea that the medical treatment of childhood
obesity has limitations.

> As journalist Greg Critser (2003) noted in his book *Fat Land*, use of
> weight-loss drugs is unlikely to have an effect without the proper
> "support system"—one that includes doctors, facilities, time, and
> money (p. 3).

Lending authority to your argument

Expert opinion can add credibility to your argument (see also 6e).
But don't rely on experts to make your argument for you. Construct
your argument in your own words and, when appropriate, cite the
judgment of an authority in the field for support.

> Both medical experts and policymakers recognize that solutions
> might come not only from a laboratory but also from policy,
> education, and advocacy. A handbook designed to educate

doctors on obesity called for "major changes in some aspects of western culture" (Hoppin & Taveras, 2004, Conclusion section, para. 1).

Anticipating and countering alternative interpretations

Do not ignore sources that seem contrary to your position or that offer interpretations different from your own. Instead, use them to give voice to opposing points of view and alternative interpretations before you counter them (see 6f). Readers often have objections in mind already, whether or not they agree with you. Mirano uses a source to acknowledge value in her opponents' position that medication alone can successfully treat childhood obesity.

> As researchers Yanovski and Yanovski (2002) have explained, obesity was once considered "either a moral failing or evidence of underlying psychopathology" (p. 592). But this view has shifted: Many medical professionals now consider obesity a biomedical rather than a moral condition, influenced by both genetic and environmental factors. Yanovski and Yanovski have further noted that the development of weight-loss medications in the early 1990s showed that "obesity should be treated in the same manner as any other chronic disease . . . through the long-term use of medication" (p. 592).

 62 **Citing sources; avoiding plagiarism**

Your research paper is a collaboration between you and your sources. To be fair and ethical, you must acknowledge your debt to the writers of those sources. When you acknowledge your sources, you avoid plagiarism, a form of academic dishonesty.

Three different acts are considered plagiarism: (1) failing to cite quotations and borrowed ideas, (2) failing to enclose borrowed language in quotation marks, and (3) failing to put summaries and paraphrases in your own words. It's a good idea to find out how your school defines and addresses academic dishonesty. (See also 55c.)

62a Cite quotations and borrowed ideas.

Sources are cited for two reasons:

- to tell readers where your information comes from — so that they can assess its reliability and, if interested, find and read the original source
- to give credit to the writers from whom you have borrowed words and ideas

You must cite anything you borrow from a source, including direct quotations; statistics and other specific facts; visuals such as tables, graphs, and diagrams; and any ideas you present in a summary or paraphrase.

The only exception is common knowledge — information that your readers may know or could easily locate in any number of reference sources. For example, most general encyclopedias will tell readers that Sigmund Freud wrote *The Interpretation of Dreams* and that chimpanzees can learn American Sign Language.

As a rule, when you have seen certain information repeatedly in your reading, you don't need to cite it. However, when information has appeared in only a few sources, when it is highly specific (as with statistics), or when it is controversial, you should cite the source.

The American Psychological Association recommends an author-date system of citations. The following is a brief description of how the author-date system often works.

1. The source is introduced by a signal phrase that includes the last name of the author followed by the date of publication in parentheses.
2. The material being cited is followed by a page number in parentheses.
3. At the end of the paper, an alphabetized list of references gives complete publication information for the source.

IN-TEXT CITATION

As researchers Yanovski and Yanovski (2002) have explained, obesity was once considered "either a moral failing or evidence of underlying psychopathology" (p. 592).

ENTRY IN THE LIST OF REFERENCES

Yanovski, S. Z., & Yanovski, J. A. (2002). Drug therapy: Obesity. *The New England Journal of Medicine, 346,* 591-602.

This basic APA format varies for different types of sources. For a detailed discussion and other models, see 64.

62b Enclose borrowed language in quotation marks.

To indicate that you are using a source's exact phrases or sentences, you must enclose them in quotation marks unless they have been set off from the text by indenting (see p. 545). To omit the quotation marks is to claim — falsely — that the language is your own. Such an omission is plagiarism even if you have cited the source.

ORIGINAL SOURCE

In an effort to seek the causes of this disturbing trend, experts have pointed to a range of important potential contributors to the rise in childhood obesity that are unrelated to media: a reduction in physical education classes and after-school athletic programs, an increase in the availability of sodas and snacks in public schools, the growth in the number of fast-food outlets across the country, the trend toward "super-sizing" food portions in restaurants, and the increasing number of highly processed high-calorie and high-fat grocery products.

— Henry J. Kaiser Family Foundation, "The Role of Media in Childhood Obesity" (2004), p. 1

PLAGIARISM

According to the Henry J. Kaiser Family Foundation (2004), experts have pointed to a range of important potential contributors to the rise in childhood obesity that are unrelated to media (p. 1).

BORROWED LANGUAGE IN QUOTATION MARKS

According to the Henry J. Kaiser Family Foundation (2004), "experts have pointed to a range of important potential contributors to the rise in childhood obesity that are unrelated to media" (p. 1).

NOTE: Quotation marks are not used when quoted sentences are set off from the text by indenting (see p. 545).

62c Put summaries and paraphrases in your own words.

Summaries and paraphrases are written in your own words. A summary condenses information; a paraphrase conveys the information using roughly the same number of words as in the original source. When you summarize or paraphrase, it is not enough to name the source; you must restate the source's meaning using your own language. (See also 55c.) You commit plagiarism if you half-copy the author's sentences — either by mixing the author's phrases with your own without using quotation marks or by plugging your own synonyms into the author's sentence structure. The following paraphrases are plagiarized — even though the source is cited — because their language and sentence structure are too close to those of the source.

ORIGINAL SOURCE

In an effort to seek the causes of this disturbing trend, experts have pointed to a range of important potential contributors to the rise in childhood obesity that are unrelated to media.

— Henry J. Kaiser Family Foundation, "The Role of Media in Childhood Obesity" (2004), p. 1

UNACCEPTABLE BORROWING OF PHRASES

According to the Henry J. Kaiser Family Foundation (2004), experts have indicated a range of significant potential contributors to the rise in childhood obesity that are not linked to media (p. 1).

UNACCEPTABLE BORROWING OF STRUCTURE

According to the Henry J. Kaiser Family Foundation (2004), experts have identified a variety of key factors causing a rise in childhood obesity, factors that are not tied to media (p. 1).

To avoid plagiarizing an author's language, resist the temptation to look at the source while you are summarizing or paraphrasing. After you have read the passage you want to paraphrase, set the source aside. Ask yourself, "What is the author's meaning?" In your own words, state your understanding of the author's basic point. Return to the source and check that you haven't used the author's language or sentence structure or misrepresented the author's ideas. When you fully understand another writer's meaning, you can more easily and accurately present those ideas in your own words.

ACCEPTABLE PARAPHRASE

A report by the Henry J. Kaiser Family Foundation (2004) described causes other than media for the childhood obesity crisis.

 Integrating sources

Quotations, summaries, paraphrases, and facts will help you develop your argument, but they cannot speak for you. You can use several strategies to integrate information from sources into your paper while maintaining your own voice.

63a Use quotations appropriately.

In your academic writing, keep the emphasis on your ideas; use your own words to summarize and to paraphrase your sources and to explain your points. Sometimes, however, quotations can be the most effective way to integrate a source.

Limiting your use of quotations

Although it is tempting to insert many quotations in your paper and to use your own words only for connecting passages, do not quote excessively. It is almost impossible to integrate numerous long quotations smoothly into your own text.

WHEN TO USE QUOTATIONS
- When language is especially vivid or expressive
- When exact wording is needed for technical accuracy
- When it is important to let the debaters of an issue explain their positions in their own words
- When the words of an authority lend weight to an argument
- When the language of a source is the topic of your discussion

It is not always necessary to quote full sentences from a source. To reduce your reliance on the words of others, you can often integrate language from a source into your own sentence structure.

> Carmona (2004) advised the subcommittee that the situation constitutes an "epidemic" and that the skyrocketing statistics are "astounding."

> As researchers continue to face a number of unknowns about obesity, it may be helpful to envision treating the disorder, as Yanovski and Yanovski (2002) suggested, "in the same manner as any other chronic disease" (p. 592).

Using the ellipsis mark

To condense a quoted passage, you can use the ellipsis mark (three periods, with spaces between) to indicate that you have omitted words. What remains must be grammatically complete.

> Roman (2003) reported that "social factors are nearly as significant as individual metabolism in the formation of . . . dietary habits of adolescents" (p. 345).

The writer has omitted the words *both healthy and unhealthy* from the source.

When you want to leave out one or more full sentences, use a period before the three ellipsis dots.

> According to Sothern and Gordon (2003), "Environmental factors may contribute as much as 80% to the causes of childhood obesity. . . . Research suggests that obese children demonstrate decreased levels of physical activity and increased psychosocial problems" (p. 104).

Ordinarily, do not use an ellipsis mark at the beginning or at the end of a quotation. Readers will understand that you have taken the quoted material from a longer passage, so such marks are not necessary. The only exception occurs when you have dropped words at the end of the final quoted sentence. In such cases, put three ellipsis dots before the closing quotation mark. Make sure that omissions and ellipsis marks do not distort the meaning of your source.

Using brackets

Brackets allow you to insert your own words into quoted material. You can insert words in brackets to clarify a confusing reference or to keep a sentence grammatical in your context.

> The cost of treating obesity currently totals $117 billion per year—a price, according to the surgeon general, "second only to the cost of [treating] tobacco use" (Carmona, 2004).

To indicate an error such as a misspelling in a quotation, insert [*sic*], italicized and with brackets around it, right after the error. (See 39c.)

Setting off long quotations

When you quote forty or more words from a source, set off the quotation by indenting it one-half inch from the left margin. Use the normal right margin and do not single-space the quotation.

Long quotations should be introduced by an informative sentence, usually followed by a colon. Quotation marks are unnecessary because the indented format tells readers that the passage is taken word-for-word from the source.

> Yanovski and Yanovski (2002) have described earlier treatments of obesity that focused on behavior modification:
>
>> With the advent of behavioral treatments for obesity in the 1960s, hope arose that modification of maladaptive eating and exercise habits would lead to sustained weight loss, and that time-limited programs would produce permanent changes in weight. Medications for the treatment of obesity were proposed as short-term adjuncts for patients, who would presumably then acquire the skills necessary to continue to lose weight, reach "ideal body weight," and maintain a reduced weight indefinitely. (p. 592)

Notice that at the end of an indented quotation the parenthetical citation goes outside the final mark of punctuation. (When a quotation is run into your text, the opposite is true. See the sample citations on p. 544.)

63b Use signal phrases to integrate sources.

Whenever you include a paraphrase, summary, or direct quotation of another writer's work in your paper, prepare your readers for it with a signal phrase. A signal phrase usually names the author of the source, gives the publication year in parentheses, and often provides some context. It commonly appears before the source material. To vary your sentence structure, you may decide to interrupt source material with a signal phrase or place the signal phrase after your paraphrase, summary, or direct quotation. It is generally acceptable in the social sciences to call authors by their last name only, even on a first mention. If your paper refers to two authors with the same last name, use initials as well.

Using signal phrases in APA papers

To avoid monotony, try to vary both the language and the placement of your signal phrases.

Model signal phrases

In the words of Carmona (2004), "..."

As Yanovski and Yanovski (2002) have noted, "..."

Hoppin and Taveras (2004), medical researchers, pointed out that "..."

"...," claimed Critser (2003).

"...," wrote Duenwald (2004), "..."

Researchers McDuffie et al. (2003) have offered a compelling argument for this view: "..."

Hilts (2002) answered objections with the following analysis: "..."

Verbs in signal phrases

admitted	contended	reasoned
agreed	declared	refuted
argued	denied	rejected
asserted	emphasized	reported
believed	insisted	responded
claimed	noted	suggested
compared	observed	thought
confirmed	pointed out	wrote

When you write a signal phrase, choose a verb that is appropriate for the way you are using the source (see 61c). Are you providing background, explaining a concept, supporting a claim, lending authority, or refuting an argument? See the chart on page 546 for a list of verbs commonly used in signal phrases. Note that APA requires using verbs in the past tense or present perfect tense (*explained* or *has explained*) to introduce source material. Use the present tense only for discussing the results of an experiment (*the results show*) or knowledge that has been clearly established (*researchers agree*).

Marking boundaries

Readers need to move from your words to the words of a source without feeling a jolt. Avoid dropping direct quotations into your text without warning. Instead, provide clear signal phrases, including at least the author's name and the year of publication. Signal phrases mark the boundaries between source material and your own words; they can also tell readers why a source is worth quoting. (The signal phrase is highlighted in the second example.)

DROPPED QUOTATION

Obesity was once considered in a very different light. "For many years, obesity was approached as it if were either a moral failing or evidence of underlying psychopathology" (Yanovski & Yanovski, 2002, p. 592).

QUOTATION WITH SIGNAL PHRASE

Obesity was once considered in a very different light. As researchers Yanovski and Yanovski (2002) have explained, obesity was widely thought of as "either a moral failing or evidence of underlying psychopathology" (p. 592).

Using signal phrases with summaries and paraphrases

As with quotations, you should introduce most summaries and paraphrases with a signal phrase that mentions the author and the year and places the material in the context of your argument. Readers will then understand where the summary or paraphrase begins.

Without the signal phrase (highlighted) in the example on page 548, readers might think that only the last sentence is being cited, when in fact the whole paragraph is based on the source.

> Carmona (2004) advised a Senate subcommittee that the problem
> of childhood obesity is dire and that the skyrocketing statistics—
> which put the child obesity rate at 15%—are cause for alarm. More
> than 9 million children, double the number in the early 1980s, are
> classified as obese. Carmona warned that obesity can cause myriad
> physical problems that only worsen as children grow older.

There are times, however, when a summary or a paraphrase does not require a signal phrase naming the author. When the context makes clear where the cited material begins, you may omit the signal phrase and include the author's name and the year in parentheses. Unless the work is short, also include the page number in the parentheses.

Integrating statistics and other facts

When you are citing a statistic or another specific fact, a signal phrase is often not necessary. In most cases, readers will understand that the citation refers to the statistic or fact (not the whole paragraph).

> In purely financial terms, the drugs cost more than $3 a day on
> average (Duenwald, 2004).

There is nothing wrong, however, with using a signal phrase to introduce a statistic or another fact.

> Duenwald (2004) reported that the drugs cost more than $3 a day
> on average.

Putting source material in context

Readers should not have to guess why source material appears in your paper. If you use another writer's words, you must explain how they relate to your point. In other words, you must put the source in context. It's a good idea to embed a quotation between sentences of your own, introducing it with a signal phrase and following it up with interpretive comments that link the quotation to your paper's argument. (See also 63c.)

> **QUOTATION WITH EFFECTIVE CONTEXT**
>
> A report by the Henry J. Kaiser Family Foundation (2004) outlined
> trends that may have contributed to the childhood obesity crisis,
> including food advertising for children as well as

> a reduction in physical education classes . . . , an increase
> in the availability of sodas and snacks in public schools, the
> growth in the number of fast-food outlets . . . , and the
> increasing number of highly processed high-calorie and
> high-fat grocery products. (p. 1)

Addressing each of these areas requires more than a doctor armed with
a prescription pad; it requires a broad mobilization not just of doctors
and concerned parents but of educators, food industry executives,
advertisers, and media representatives.

63c Synthesize sources.

When you synthesize multiple sources in a research paper, you
create a conversation about your research topic. You show readers how the ideas of one source relate to those of another by connecting and analyzing the ideas in the context of your argument.
Keep the emphasis on your own writing. The thread of your argument should be easy to identify and to understand, with or
without your sources.

SAMPLE SYNTHESIS (DRAFT)

Student writer Luisa Mirano begins with a claim that needs support.

Medical treatments have clear costs for
individual patients, including unpleasant side
effects, little information about long-term use,
and uncertainty that they will yield significant
weight loss. The financial burden is heavy as well;

Student writer

Signal phrases indicate how sources contribute to Mirano's paper and show that the ideas that follow are not her own.

the drugs cost more than $3 a day on average
(Duenwald, 2004). In each of the clinical trials,
use of medication was accompanied by expensive
behavioral therapies, including counseling,
nutrition education, fitness advising, and
monitoring. As Critser (2003) noted in his book

Source 1

Student writer

Mirano interprets and connects sources. Each paragraph ends with her own thoughts.

Fat Land, use of weight-loss drugs is unlikely
to have an effect without the proper "support
system"—one that includes doctors, facilities,
time, and money (p. 3). For many families, this
level of care is prohibitively expensive.

Source 2

Student writer

> Both medical experts and policymakers
> recognize that solutions might come not only from
> a laboratory but also from policy, education, and
> advocacy. A handbook designed to educate doctors
> on obesity called for "major changes in some
> aspects of western culture" (Hoppin & Taveras,
> 2004, Conclusion section, para. 1). Solving the
> childhood obesity problem will require broad
> mobilization of doctors and concerned parents
> and also of educators, food industry executives,
> advertisers, and media representatives.

(right margin annotations: Student writer; Source 3; Student writer)

In this draft, Mirano uses her own analyses to shape the conversation among her sources. She does not simply string quotations and statistics together or allow her sources to overwhelm her writing. The final sentence, written in her own voice, gives her an opportunity to explain to readers how her sources support and extend her argument.

When synthesizing sources, ask yourself these questions:

- Which sources inform, support, or extend your argument?
- Have you varied the functions of sources — to provide background, explain concepts, lend authority, and anticipate counterarguments? Do your signal phrases indicate these functions?
- Do you explain how your sources support your argument?
- Do you connect and analyze sources in your own voice?
- Is your own argument easy to identify and to understand, with or without your sources?

64 Documenting sources in APA style

In most social science classes, you will be asked to use the APA system for documenting sources, which is set forth in the *Publication Manual of the American Psychological Association*, 6th ed. (Washington: APA, 2010). APA recommends in-text citations that refer readers to a list of references.

An in-text citation usually gives the author of the source (often in a signal phrase), the year of publication, and at times a page number in parentheses. At the end of the paper, a list of references provides publication information about the source (see pp. 593–94 for a sample list). The direct link between the in-text citation and the entry in the reference list is highlighted in the following example.

IN-TEXT CITATION

Yanovski and Yanovski (2002) reported that "the current state of the treatment for obesity is similar to the state of the treatment of hypertension several decades ago" (p. 600).

ENTRY IN THE LIST OF REFERENCES

Yanovski, S. Z., & Yanovski, J. A. (2002). Drug therapy: Obesity. *The New England Journal of Medicine, 346,* 591-602.

For a reference list that includes this entry, see pages 593–94.

64a APA in-text citations

APA's in-text citations provide at least the author's last name and the year of publication. For direct quotations and some paraphrases, a page number is given as well.

NOTE: APA style requires the use of the past tense or the present perfect tense in signal phrases introducing cited material: *Smith (2005) reported . . . , Smith (2005) has argued. . . .*

⬛ **1. Basic format for a quotation** Ordinarily, introduce the quotation with a signal phrase that includes the author's last name followed by the year of publication in parentheses. Put the page number (preceded by "p.") in parentheses after the quotation.

Critser (2003) noted that despite growing numbers of overweight Americans, many health care providers still "remain either in ignorance or outright denial about the health danger to the poor and the young" (p. 5).

PRACTICE hackerhandbooks.com/rules
> APA > 64–1 to 64–3

If the author is not named in the signal phrase, place the author's name, the year, and the page number in parentheses after the quotation: (Critser, 2003, p. 5).

NOTE: APA style requires the year of publication in an in-text citation. Do not include a month, even if the entry in the reference list includes the month.

■ **2. Basic format for a summary or a paraphrase** Include the author's last name and the year either in a signal phrase introducing the material or in parentheses following it. A page number is not required for a summary or a paraphrase, but include one if it would help readers find the passage in a long work. (For the use of other locators, such as paragraph numbers or section names in online sources, see p. 555.)

> Yanovski and Yanovski (2002) explained that sibutramine suppresses appetite by blocking the reuptake of the neurotransmitters serotonin and norepinephrine in the brain (p. 594).

> Sibutramine suppresses appetite by blocking the reuptake of the neurotransmitters serotonin and norepinephrine in the brain (Yanovski & Yanovski, 2002, p. 594).

■ **3. Work with two authors** Give the names of both authors in the signal phrase or the parentheses each time you cite the work. In the parentheses, use "&" between the authors' names; in the signal phrase, use "and."

> According to Sothern and Gordon (2003), "Environmental factors may contribute as much as 80% to the causes of childhood obesity" (p. 104).

> Obese children often engage in limited physical activity (Sothern & Gordon, 2003, p. 104).

■ **4. Work with three to five authors** Identify all authors in the signal phrase or the parentheses the first time you cite the source.

> In 2003, Berkowitz, Wadden, Tershakovec, and Cronquist concluded, "Sibutramine . . . must be carefully monitored in adolescents, as in adults, to control increases in [blood pressure] and pulse rate" (p. 1811).

In subsequent citations, use the first author's name followed by "et al." in either the signal phrase or the parentheses.

> As Berkowitz et al. (2003) advised, "Until more extensive safety and efficacy data are available, . . . weight-loss medications should be used only on an experimental basis for adolescents" (p. 1811).

5. Work with six or more authors Use the first author's name followed by "et al." in the signal phrase or the parentheses.

> McDuffie et al. (2002) tested 20 adolescents, aged 12-16, over a three-month period and found that orlistat, combined with behavioral therapy, produced an average weight loss of 4.4 kg, or 9.7 pounds (p. 646).

6. Work with unknown author If the author is unknown, mention the work's title in the signal phrase or give the first word or two of the title in the parenthetical citation. Titles of short works such as articles and chapters are put in quotation marks; titles of long works such as books and reports are italicized. (For online sources with no author, see item 12 on pp. 554–55.)

> Children struggling to control their weight must also struggle with the pressures of television advertising that, on the one hand, encourages the consumption of junk food and, on the other, celebrates thin celebrities ("Television," 2002).

NOTE: In the rare case when "Anonymous" is specified as the author, treat it as if it were a real name: (Anonymous, 2001). In the list of references, also use the name Anonymous as author.

7. Organization as author If the author is a government agency or another organization, name the organization in the signal phrase or in the parenthetical citation the first time you cite the source.

> Obesity puts children at risk for a number of medical complications, including Type 2 diabetes, hypertension, sleep apnea, and orthopedic problems (Henry J. Kaiser Family Foundation, 2004, p. 1).

If the organization has a familiar abbreviation, you may include it in brackets the first time you cite the source and use the abbreviation alone in later citations (see p. 554).

FIRST CITATION (Centers for Disease Control and Prevention [CDC], 2009)

LATER CITATIONS (CDC, 2009)

■ **8. Authors with the same last name** To avoid confusion, use initials with the last names if your reference list includes two or more authors with the same last name.

Research by E. Smith (1989) revealed that. . . .

■ **9. Two or more works by the same author in the same year** When your list of references includes more than one work by the same author in the same year, use lowercase letters ("a," "b," and so on) with the year to order the entries in the reference list. (See item 6 on p. 558.) Use those same letters with the year in the in-text citation.

Research by Durgin (2003b) has yielded new findings about the role of counseling in treating childhood obesity.

■ **10. Two or more works in the same parentheses** When your parenthetical citation names two or more works, put them in the same order that they appear in the reference list, separated with semicolons.

Researchers have indicated that studies of pharmacological treatments for childhood obesity are inconclusive (Berkowitz et al., 2003; McDuffie et al., 2002).

■ **11. Personal communication** Personal interviews, memos, letters, e-mail, and similar unpublished communications should be cited in the text only, not in the reference list. (Use the first initial with the last name in parentheses.)

One of Atkinson's colleagues, who has studied the effect of the media on children's eating habits, has contended that advertisers for snack foods will need to design ads responsibly for their younger viewers (F. Johnson, personal communication, October 20, 2009).

■ **12. Electronic source** When possible, cite electronic sources, including online sources, as you would any other source, giving the author and the year.

Atkinson (2001) found that children who spent at least four hours
a day watching TV were less likely to engage in adequate physical
activity during the week.

Electronic sources sometimes lack authors' names, dates, or page
numbers.

Unknown author

If no author is named in the source, mention the title of the
source in the signal phrase or give the first word or two of the title
in the parentheses (see also item 6). (If an organization serves as
the author, see item 7.)

The body's basal metabolic rate, or BMR, is a measure of its at-rest
energy requirement ("Exercise," 2003).

Unknown date

When the date is unknown, use the abbreviation "n.d." (for "no date").

Attempts to establish a definitive link between television programming
and children's eating habits have been problematic (Magnus, n.d.).

No page numbers

APA ordinarily requires page numbers for quotations, and it
recommends them for summaries and paraphrases from long
sources. When an electronic source lacks stable numbered pages,
include whatever information is available to help readers locate
the particular passage you are citing.

If the source has numbered paragraphs, use the paragraph
number preceded by the abbreviation "para.": (Hall, 2008, para. 5).
If the source contains headings, cite the appropriate heading in parentheses; you may also indicate the paragraph under the heading
that you are referring to, even if the paragraphs are not numbered.

Hoppin and Taveras (2004) pointed out that several other medications
were classified by the Drug Enforcement Administration as having the
"potential for abuse" (Weight-Loss Drugs section, para. 6).

NOTE: Electronic files in portable document format (PDF) often
have stable page numbers. For such sources, give the page number in the parenthetical citation.

■ **13. Indirect source**   If you use a source that was cited in another source (a secondary source), name the original source in your
signal phrase. List the secondary source in your reference list and

include it in your parenthetical citation, preceded by the words "as cited in." In the following example, Satcher is the original source; Critser is the secondary source, given in the reference list.

> Former surgeon general Dr. David Satcher described "a nation of
> young people seriously at risk of starting out obese and dooming
> themselves to the difficult task of overcoming a tough illness" (as
> cited in Critser, 2003, p. 4).

■ **14. Sacred or classical text** Identify the text, the version or edition you used, and the relevant part (chapter, verse, line). It is not necessary to include the source in the reference list.

> Peace activists have long cited the biblical prophet's vision of a
> world without war: "And they shall beat their swords into plowshares,
> and their spears into pruning hooks; nation shall not lift up sword
> against nation, neither shall they learn war any more" (Isaiah 2:4,
> Revised Standard Version).

64b APA list of references

In APA style, the alphabetical list of works cited, which appears at the end of the paper, is titled "References." For advice on preparing the list, see pages 581–82. For a sample reference list, see pages 593–94.

Alphabetize entries in the reference list by authors' last names; if a work has no author, alphabetize it by its title. The first element of each entry is important because citations in the text of the paper refer to it and readers will be looking for it in the alphabetized list. The date of publication appears immediately after the first element of the citation.

In APA style, titles of books are italicized; titles of articles are neither italicized nor put in quotation marks. (For rules on capitalization of titles in the list of references, see p. 581.)

NOTE: Many sources, both print and online, include a unique, permanent number called a digital object identifier (DOI) that allows users to access a source in a variety of ways. For a reference list entry for a print source, give all the print publication information and add the DOI, if the source has one, at the end of the entry (see item 7). For an online source, give the DOI at the end of the entry in place of a URL (see item 30).

General guidelines for listing authors (print and online)

In APA style, all authors' names are inverted (the last name comes first), and initials are used for all first and middle names.

NAME AND DATE CITED IN TEXT

Duncan (2008) has reported that. . . .

BEGINNING OF ENTRY IN THE LIST OF REFERENCES

Duncan, B. (2008).

1. Single author

author: last name
+ initial(s)   year   title (book)

Egeland, J. (2008). *A billion lives: An eyewitness report from the frontlines*

place of
publication   publisher

of humanity. New York, NY: Simon & Schuster.

2. Multiple authors

List up to seven authors by last names followed by initials. Use an ampersand (&) before the name of the last author. If there are more than seven authors, list the first six followed by three ellipsis dots and the last author's name. (See items 3–5 on pp. 552–53 for citing works with multiple authors in the text of your paper.)

Two to seven authors

all authors:
last name + initial(s)   year   title (book)

Musick, M. A., & Wilson, J. (2007). *Volunteers: A social profile.*

place of
publication   publisher

Bloomington: Indiana University Press.

all authors:
last name + initial(s)

Diessner, R., Solom, R. C., Frost, N. K., Parsons, L., & Davidson, J.

year   title (article)

(2008). Engagement with beauty: Appreciating natural, artistic, and

journal title   volume   page(s)

moral beauty. *The Journal of Psychology, 142,* 303-329.

Eight or more authors

Mulvaney, S. A., Mudasiru, E., Schlundt, D. G., Baughman, C. L., Fleming, M.,

VanderWoude, A., . . . Rothman, R. (2008). Self-management in Type 2

diabetes: The adolescent perspective. *The Diabetes Educator, 34*, 118-127.

3. Organization as author

author:
organization name   year   title (book)

American Psychiatric Association. (1994). *Diagnostic and statistical*

edition   place   organization as author
number   of publication   and publisher

manual of mental disorders (4th ed.). Washington, DC: Author.

If the publisher is not the same as the author, give the publisher's
name at the end as you would for any other source.

4. Unknown author   Begin the entry with the work's title.

place of
title (book)   year   publication   publisher

New concise world atlas. (2007). New York, NY: Oxford University Press.

year + month + day   volume,
title (article)   (for weekly publication)   journal title   issue   page(s)

Order in the jungle. (2008, March 15). *The Economist, 386*(8571), 83-85.

5. Two or more works by the same author   Use the author's
name for all entries. List the entries by year, the earliest first.

Barry, P. (2007, December 8). Putting tumors on pause. *Science News,*

172, 365.

Barry, P. (2008, August 2). Finding the golden genes. *Science News, 174,*

16-21.

6. Two or more works by the same author in the same year
List the works alphabetically by title. In the parentheses, following
the year add "a," "b," and so on. Use these same letters when giving
the year in the in-text citation. (See also p. 581.)

Elkind, D. (2008a, Spring). Can we play? *Greater Good, 4*(4), 14-17.

Elkind, D. (2008b, June 27). The price of hurrying children [Web log

post]. Retrieved from http://blogs.psychologytoday.com/blog

/digital-children

Articles in periodicals (print)

Periodicals include journals, magazines, and newspapers. For a journal or a magazine, give only the volume number if the publication is paginated continuously throughout each volume; give the volume and issue numbers if each issue of the volume begins on page 1. Italicize the volume number and put the issue number, not italicized, in parentheses.

For all periodicals, when an article appears on consecutive pages, provide the range of pages. When an article does not appear on consecutive pages, give all page numbers: A1, A17. (See also "Online sources" beginning on p. 565 for online articles and articles accessed through a library's database.) For an illustrated citation of an article in a print journal or magazine, see page 560.

7. Article in a journal

author: last name
+ initial(s)   year   article title

Holtug, N. (2010). Immigration and the politics of social cohesion.

  journal title volume page(s)   DOI

  Ethnicities, 10, 435-451. doi:10.1177/1468796810378320

8. Article in a magazine   Cite as you would a journal article, but give the year and the month for monthly magazines; add the day for weekly magazines.

McKibben, B. (2007, October). Carbon's new math. *National Geographic,*

  212(4), 32-37.

9. Article in a newspaper

author: last name year + month + day
+ initial(s) (for daily publication)   article title

Svoboda, E. (2008, October 21). Deep in the rain forest, stalking the next

       newspaper title page(s)

  pandemic. *The New York Times,* p. D5.

Give the year, month, and day for daily and weekly newspapers. Use "p." or "pp." before page numbers.

10. Article with three to seven authors

Ungar, M., Brown, M., Liebenberg, L., Othman, R., Kwong, W. M.,

  Armstrong, M., & Gilgun, J. (2007). Unique pathways to resilience

  across cultures. *Adolescence, 42,* 287-310.

Citation at a glance: Article in a journal or magazine (APA)

To cite an article in a print journal or magazine in APA style, include the following elements:

1 Author
2 Year of publication for journal; complete date for magazine
3 Title of article
4 Name of journal or magazine
5 Volume number; issue number, if required (see p. 559)
6 Page number(s) of article
7 DOI (digital object identifier), if available

FIRST PAGE OF ARTICLE

feature

An Appeal to
3 **Authority**

The new paternalism in urban schools

By the time youngsters reach high school in the United States,

1 BY DAVID WHITMAN

2 4 6
FALL 2008 / EDUCATION NEXT 53

5 VOLUME 8, NUMBER 4

JOURNAL CONTENTS PAGE

EDUCATION 4
next

features

12 The 2008 *Education Next*–PEPG Survey of Public Opinion
Americans think less of their schools than of their police departments and post offices
BY WILLIAM G. HOWELL, MARTIN R. WEST, and PAUL E. PETERSON

28 The Early Education of Our Next President
Not much in public schools
BY PETER MEYER

36 Scrap the Sacrosanct Salary Schedule
How about more pay for new teachers, less for older ones?
BY JACOB VIGDOR

44 Out of Jail and Into Jobs
Maya Angelou Public Charter School offers hope and an education to kids in trouble
BY JAMES FORMAN JR.

52 An Appeal to Authority
The new paternalism in urban schools
BY DAVID WHITMAN

FALL 2008 / EDUCATION NEXT 3

REFERENCE LIST ENTRY FOR AN ARTICLE IN A PRINT JOURNAL OR MAGAZINE

1 2 3
Whitman, D. (2008). An appeal to authority: The new paternalism in
4 5 6
urban schools. *Education Next, 8*(4), 53-58.

For variations on citing articles in print journals or magazines in APA style, see pages 559–61.

11. Article with eight or more authors List the first six authors followed by three ellipsis dots and the last author.

Krippner, G., Granovetter, M., Block, F., Biggart, N., Beamish, T., Hsing, Y., . . . O'Riain, S. (2004). Polanyi Symposium: A conversation on embeddedness. *Socio-Economic Review, 2,* 109-135.

12. Abstract of a journal article

Lahm, K. (2008). Inmate-on-inmate assault: A multilevel examination of prison violence [Abstract]. *Criminal Justice and Behavior, 35*(1), 120-137.

13. Letter to the editor Follow the appropriate model for a journal, magazine, or newspaper (see items 7–9) and insert the words "Letter to the editor" in brackets after the title of the letter. If the letter has no title, use the bracketed words as the title.

Park, T. (2008, August). Defining the line [Letter to the editor]. *Scientific American, 299*(2), 10.

14. Editorial or other unsigned article

The global justice movement [Editorial]. (2005). *Multinational Monitor, 26*(7/8), 6.

15. Newsletter article

Setting the stage for remembering. (2006, September). *Mind, Mood, and Memory, 2*(9), 4-5.

16. Review Give the author and title of the review (if any) and, in brackets, the type of work, the title, and the author for a book or the year for a motion picture. If the review has no author or title, use the material in brackets as the title.

Applebaum, A. (2008, February 14). A movie that matters [Review of the motion picture *Katyn,* 2007]. *The New York Review of Books, 55*(2), 13-15.

Agents of change. (2008, February 2). [Review of the book *The power of unreasonable people: How social entrepreneurs create markets that change the world,* by J. Elkington & P. Hartigan]. *The Economist, 386*(8565), 94.

Books (print)

Items 17–29 apply to print books. For online books, see items 36 and 37. For an illustrated citation of a print book, see page 564.

Take the information about a book from its title page and copyright page. If more than one place of publication is listed, use only the first. Give the city and the state (abbreviated) for all US cities or the city and the country (not abbreviated) for all non-US cities; also include the province for Canadian cities. Do not give a state if the publisher's name includes it (as in many university presses, for example).

■ 17. Basic format for a book

author: last   year of
name + initial(s) publication   book title

McKenzie, F. R. (2008). *Theory and practice with adolescents: An applied approach.*

place of
publication   publisher

Chicago, IL: Lyceum Books.

■ 18. Book with an editor

all editors: year of
last name + initial(s) publication   book title

Aronson, J., & Aronson, E. (Eds.). (2008). *Readings about the social animal*

               place of
edition   publication publisher

(10th ed.). New York, NY: Worth.

The abbreviation "Eds." is for multiple editors. If the book has one editor, use "Ed."

■ 19. Book with an author and an editor

author: last name   year of
+ initial(s)   publication   book title

McLuhan, M. (2003). *Understanding me: Lectures and interviews*

        name(s) of editor(s):   place of publication
        in normal order   (city, province, country)

(S. McLuhan & D. Staine, Eds.). Toronto, Ontario, Canada:

        publisher

McClelland & Stewart.

The abbreviation "Eds." is for multiple editors. If the book has one editor, use "Ed."

book • basic format • editor • translator • edition (2nd, 3rd, etc.) • article, chapter • anthology • volumes • foreword

APA
64b 563

🔲 **20. Book with an author and a translator**   After the title, name the translator, followed by "Trans.," in parentheses. Add the original date of publication at the end of the entry.

Steinberg, M. D. (2003). *Voices of revolution, 1917* (M. Schwartz, Trans.).

New Haven, CT: Yale University Press. (Original work published 2001)

🔲 **21. Edition other than the first**

O'Brien, J. A. (Ed.). (2006). *The production of reality: Essays and readings on*

social interaction (4th ed.). Thousand Oaks, CA: Pine Forge Press.

If the entry also requires volume numbers (see item 23), put the volume numbers after the edition number: (3rd ed., Vols. 1-3).

🔲 **22. Article or chapter in an edited book or an anthology**

author of chapter: year of
last name + initial(s)   publication   title of chapter

Denton, N. A.   (2006).   Segregation and discrimination in housing.

                        book editor(s):
                        in normal order   book title

In R. G. Bratt, M. E. Stone, & C. Hartman (Eds.), *A right to housing:*

                     page(s)   place of
                     for chapter   publication

Foundation of a new social agenda (pp. 61-81). Philadelphia, PA:

     publisher

Temple University Press.

The abbreviation "Eds." is for multiple editors. If the book has one editor, use "Ed."

🔲 **23. Multivolume work**   Give the number of volumes after the title.

Luo, J. (Ed.). (2005). *China today: An encyclopedia of life in the People's*

Republic (Vols. 1-2). Westport, CT: Greenwood Press.

If the work is published in an edition other than the first (see item 21), put the edition number before the volume numbers: (3rd ed., Vols. 1-3).

🔲 **24. Introduction, preface, foreword, or afterword**

Gore, A. (2000). Foreword. In B. Katz (Ed.), *Reflections on regionalism*

(pp. ix-x). Washington, DC: Brookings Institution Press.

Citation at a glance: Book (APA)

To cite a print book in APA style, include the following elements:

1 Author
2 Year of publication
3 Title and subtitle
4 Place of publication
5 Publisher
6 DOI (digital object identifier), if available

2
Copyright © 2008 by Thomas L. Friedman

TITLE PAGE

1 THOMAS L. FRIEDMAN

3 *Hot, Flat, and Crowded*
WHY WE NEED A GREEN REVOLUTION—
AND HOW IT CAN RENEW AMERICA

5 FARRAR, STRAUS AND GIROUX
4 NEW YORK

FARRAR, STRAUS AND GIROUX
NEW YORK

COPYRIGHT PAGE

Farrar, Straus and Giroux
18 West 18th Street, New York 10011

Copyright © 2008 by Thomas L. Friedman
All rights reserved
Distributed in Canada by Douglas & McIntyre Ltd.
Printed in the United States of America
First edition, 2008

Grateful acknowledgment is made for permission to reprint the following material:
Excerpts from *Three Cups of Tea* by Greg Mortenson and David Oliver Relin,
copyright © 2006 by Greg Mortenson and David Oliver Relin. Used by permission of
Viking Penguin, a division of Penguin Group (USA) Inc.
Graphs reproduced with permission from *Foreign Policy*, www.ForeignPolicy.com,
#154, May/June 2006. Copyright © 2006 by the Carnegie Endowment for International
Peace.

Library of Congress Control Number: 2008930589
ISBN-13: 978-0-374-16685-4
ISBN-10: 0-374-16685-4

Designed by Jonathan D. Lippincott

www.fsgbooks.com

1 3 5 7 9 10 8 6 4 2

FSC
Mixed Sources

This book was printed on text paper containing
30 percent post-consumer recycled content.

REFERENCE LIST ENTRY FOR A PRINT BOOK

—1— —2— —————3—————
Friedman, T. L. (2008). *Hot, flat, and crowded: Why we need a green*

——————————————— ————4————
revolution—And how it can renew America. New York, NY:

——————5——————
Farrar, Straus and Giroux.

For more on citing print books in APA style, see pages 562–65.

25. Dictionary or other reference work

Leong, F. T. L. (Ed.). (2008). *Encyclopedia of counseling* (Vols. 1-4). Thousand
Oaks, CA: Sage.

26. Article in a reference work

Konijn, E. A. (2008). Affects and media exposure. In W. Donsbach (Ed.),
The international encyclopedia of communication (Vol. 1, pp. 123-129).
Malden, MA: Blackwell.

27. Republished book

Mailer, N. (2008). *Miami and the siege of Chicago: An informal history of
the Republican and Democratic conventions of 1968.* New York, NY:
New York Review Books. (Original work published 1968)

28. Book with a title in its title   If the book title contains an-
other book title or an article title, neither italicize the internal
title nor place it in quotation marks.

Marcus, L. (Ed.). (1999). *Sigmund Freud's* The interpretation of dreams*:
New interdisciplinary essays.* Manchester, England: Manchester
University Press.

29. Sacred or classical text   It is not necessary to list sacred
works such as the Bible or the Qur'an or classical Greek and Roman
works in your reference list. See item 14 on page 556 for how to cite
these sources in the text of your paper.

Online sources

When citing an online article, include publication information as
for a print periodical (see items 7–16) and add information about
the online version (see items 30–35).

Use a retrieval date for an online source only if the content
is likely to change. Most of the examples in this section do not
show a retrieval date because the content of the sources is stable;
if you are unsure about whether to use a retrieval date, consult
your instructor. If the source includes a DOI (digital object identifier), use the DOI in place of a URL at the end of the entry (see
the note on p. 556).

If you must break a DOI or a URL at the end of a line, break it after a double slash or before any other mark of punctuation; do not add a hyphen. Do not put a period at the end of the entry.

30. Article in an online journal

| author: last
name + initial(s) | year of
publication | article title | journal title |

Whitmeyer, J. M. (2000). Power through appointment. *Social Science Research,*

| volume | page(s) | DOI |

29, 535-555. doi:10.1006/ssre.2000.0680

If there is no DOI, include the URL for the journal's home page.

Ashe, D. D., & McCutcheon, L. E. (2001). Shyness, loneliness, and attitude

toward celebrities. *Current Research in Social Psychology, 6,* 124-133.

Retrieved from http://www.uiowa.edu/~grpproc/crisp/crisp.html

31. Article in an online magazine
Give the author, date, article title, and magazine title. Follow with the volume, issue, and page numbers, if they are available. End with the URL for the magazine's home page.

Shelburne, E. C. (2008, September). The great disruption. *The Atlantic,*

302(2). Retrieved from http://www.theatlantic.com/

Rupley, S. (2010, February 26). The myth of the benign monopoly. *Salon.*

Retrieved from http://www.salon.com/

32. Article in an online newspaper
Give the author, date, article title, and newspaper title. Follow with the page numbers, if they are available. End with the URL for the newspaper's home page.

Watson, P. (2008, October 19). Biofuel boom endangers orangutan habitat.

Los Angeles Times. Retrieved from http://www.latimes.com/

33. Supplemental material published only online
If a journal, magazine, or newspaper contains extra material (an article or a chart, for example) only in its online version, give whatever publication information is available in the source and add the description "Supplemental material" in brackets after the title.

Samuel, T. (2009, March 27). Mind the wage gap [Supplemental material].

The American Prospect. Retrieved from http://www.prospect.org/

34. Article from a database   Start with the publication information for the source (see items 7–16). If the database entry includes a DOI for the article, use the DOI number at the end. For an illustrated citation of an article from a database, see page 568.

all authors:
last name + initial(s)   year   article title

Eskritt, M., & McLeod, K. (2008). Children's note taking as a mnemonic tool.

journal title   volume page(s)   DOI

Journal of Experimental Child Psychology, 101, 52-74. doi:10.1016

/jecp.2008.05.007

If there is no DOI, include the URL for the home page of the journal. If the URL is not included in the database entry, you can search for it on the Web.

Howard, K. R. (2007). Childhood overweight: Parental perceptions and

readiness for change. *The Journal of School Nursing, 23,* 73-79.

Retrieved from http://jsn.sagepub.com/

35. Abstract for an online article

Brockerhoff, E. G., Jactel, H., Parrotta, J. A., Quine, C. P., & Sayer, J.

(2008). Plantation forests and biodiversity: Oxymoron or opportunity?

[Abstract]. *Biodiversity and Conservation, 17,* 925-951. doi:10.1007

/s10531-008-9380-x

36. Online book

Adams, B. (2004). *The theory of social revolutions.* Retrieved from http://

www.gutenberg.org/catalog/world/readfile?fk_files=44092 (Original

work published 1913)

37. Chapter in an online book

Clinton, S. J. (1999). What can be done to prevent childhood obesity? In

Understanding childhood obesity (pp. 81-98). Retrieved from http://

www.questia.com/

Citation at a glance: Article from a database (APA)

To cite an article from a database in APA style, include the following elements:

1. Author(s)
2. Date of publication
3. Title of article
4. Name of periodical
5. Volume number; issue number, if required (see p. 559)
6. Page number(s)
7. DOI (direct object identifier), if available
8. URL for journal's home page (if there is no DOI)

ON-SCREEN VIEW OF DATABASE RECORD

New Search | Publications | Company Profiles | Thesaurus | More ▾
Sign In to My EBSCOhost | 📁 Folder | New Features! | Help

Searching: **Business Source Premier**   Choose Databases »

☐ Suggest Subject Terms

AN 27711104   in Select a Field (optional) ▾
and ▾   in Select a Field (optional) ▾
and ▾   in Select a Field (optional) ▾

Search **Clear** ❓

Basic Search | Advanced Search | Visual Search | Search History/Alerts | Preferences »

◀ 1 of 1 ▶ Result List | Refine Search

▤ Citation   Cited References (38)   🖨 ✉ 💾 📄 ↪ 🗑

Times Cited in this Database (3)

Title: **3** International Human Rights and Consumer Quality of Life: An Ethical Perspective.

Authors: Hill, Ronald Paul[1]
          Felice, William F.[2]
          Ainscough, Thomas[3]

Source: **4** Journal of Macromarketing; Dec2007, Vol. 27 Issue 4, p370-379, 10p, 2 charts

Document Type: Article

Subject Terms: *PRIMARY commodities
               *MACROMARKETING

END OF DATABASE RECORD

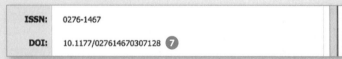

ISSN:	0276-1467
DOI:	10.1177/027614670307128 **7**

REFERENCE LIST ENTRY FOR AN ARTICLE FROM A DATABASE

Hill, R. P., Felice, W. F., & Ainscough, T. (2007). International human

rights and consumer quality of life: An ethical perspective. *Journal*

of Macromarketing, 27, 370-379. doi:10.1177/027614670307128

— 1 — 2 — 3 — 4 — 5 — 6 — 7

For more on citing articles from a database in APA style, see item 34.

38. Online reference work

Swain, C. M. (2004). Sociology of affirmative action. In N. J. Smelser

& P. B. Baltes (Eds.), *International encyclopedia of the social and*

behavioral sciences. Retrieved from http://www.sciencedirect.com

/science/referenceworks/9780080430768

Include a retrieval date only if the content of the work is likely
to change.

39. Report or long document from a Web site
List the author's
name, publication date (or "n.d." if there is no date), document title
(in italics), and URL for the document. Give a retrieval date only if
the content of the source is likely to change. If a source has no author, begin with the title and follow it with the date in parentheses
(see item 4 on p. 558).

Source with date

all authors:
last name + initial(s)   online publication date   document title

Cain, A., & Burris, M. (1999, April). *Investigation of the use of mobile*

URL

phones while driving. Retrieved from http://www.cutr.eng.usf.edu

/its/mobile_phone_text.htm

Source with no date

Archer, D. (n.d.). *Exploring nonverbal communication.* Retrieved from http://

nonverbal.ucsc.edu/

40. Section in a Web document

author (organization) year title of section
National Institute on Media and the Family. (2009). Mobile networking. In

title of Web document
Guide to social networking: Risks. Retrieved from http://www.mediafamily

URL
.org/network_pdf/MediaWise_Guide_to_Social_Networking_Risks_09.pdf

For an illustrated citation of a section in a Web document, see page 572.

41. Short work from a Web site

NATO statement endangers patients in Afghanistan. (2010, March 11).

Médecins sans frontières/Doctors without borders. Retrieved from

http://www.doctorswithoutborders.org/

42. Document from a university or government agency Web site

Cosmides, L., & Tooby, J. (1997). *Evolutionary psychology: A primer.*

Retrieved from University of California, Santa Barbara, Center for

Evolutionary Psychology website: http://www.psych.ucsb.edu

/research/cep/primer.html

43. Article in an online newsletter

Cite as an online article (see items 30–32), giving the title of the newsletter and whatever other information is available, including volume and issue numbers.

In the face of extinction. (2008, May). *NSF Current.* Retrieved from

http://www.nsf.gov/news/newsletter/may_08/index.jsp

44. Podcast

organization as producer date of posting
National Academies (Producer). (2007, June 6). Progress in preventing

podcast title descriptive label
childhood obesity: How do we measure up? [Audio podcast].

series title URL
The sounds of science podcast. Retrieved from http://media.nap.edu

/podcasts/

writer/
presenter   date of posting   podcast title

Chesney, M. (2007, September 13). Gender differences in the use of

podcast number   descriptive label

complementary and alternative medicine (No. 12827) [Audio podcast].

Web site hosting podcast

Retrieved from University of California Television website:

URL

http://www.uctv.tv/ondemand/

45. Blog (Weblog) post Give the writer's name, the date of the
post, the subject, the label "Web log post" in brackets, and the URL.
For a response to a post, use the label "Web log comment."

Kellermann, M. (2007, May 23). Disclosing clinical trials [Web log post].

Retrieved from http://www.iq.harvard.edu/blog/sss/archives/2007/05

46. Online audio or video file Give the medium or a description of the source file in brackets following the title.

writer/   no   descriptive
presenter   date   title   label

Chomsky, N. (n.d.). The new imperialism [Audio file]. Retrieved from

URL

http://www.rhapsody.com/noamchomsky

Zakaria, F. (Host), & McCullough, C. (Writer). (2007, March 6). In focus:

American teens, Rwandan truths [Video file]. Retrieved from http://

www.pulitzercenter.org/showproject.cfm?id=26

47. Entry in a wiki Begin with the title of the entry and the
date of posting, if there is one (use "n.d." for "no date" if there is
not). Then add your retrieval date and the URL for the wiki entry.
Include the date of retrieval because the content of a wiki can
change frequently. If an author or an editor is identified, include
that name at the beginning of the entry.

Ethnomethodology. (n.d.). Retrieved June 18, 2010, from http://stswiki

.org/index.php?title=Ethnomethodology

48. Data set or graphic representation Give information
about the type of source in brackets following the title. If there

Citation at a glance: Section in a Web document (APA)

To cite a section in a Web document in APA style, include the following elements:

1. Author
2. Date of publication or most recent update
3. Title of section
4. Title of document
5. URL of section

BROWSER PRINTOUT OF WEB SITE

2008 Minnesota Health Statistics Annual Summary – Minnesota Dept. of Health

 Minnesota Department of Health
Protecting, maintaining and improving the health of all Minnesotans   MDH

4 **2008 Minnesota Health Statistics Annual Summary**

The Minnesota "Annual Summary" or "Minnesota Health Statistics" is a report published yearly. The most recent version of this report is ***2008 Minnesota Health Statistics***, published January 2010. This report provides statistical data on the following subjects for the state of Minnesota.

published January 2010.

To view the PDF files, you will need Adobe Acrobat Re
site).

- Introduction, Technical Notes, Definitions (PDF: 42KB/7 pages)
- Overview of 2008 Annual Summary (PDF: 66KB/11 pages)
- Live Births (PDF: 196KB/21 pages)
- Fertility (PDF: 26KB/2 pages)
- Infant Mortality and Fetal Deaths (PDF: 188KB/15 pages)
- General Mortality (PDF: 333KB/40 pages)
- Marriage/Dissolution of Marriage Divorce (PDF: 25KB/2 pages)
- Population (PDF: 73KB/12 pages)

Note: Induced abortion statistics previously reported in this publication are now published separately.
See Report to the Legislature: Induced Abortions in Minnesota

See also Minnesota Health Statistics Annual Summary Main Page

For further information about the Annual Summary, please contact:

Center for Health Statistics
Minnesota Department of Health
Golden Rule Building, 3rd Floor
85 East Seventh Place

http://www.health.state.mn.us/divs/chs/annsum/08annsum/index.html   Page 1 of 2

5 MDB http://www.health.state.mn.us/divs/chs/annsum/08annsum/Fertility08.pdf

ON-SCREEN VIEW OF DOCUMENT

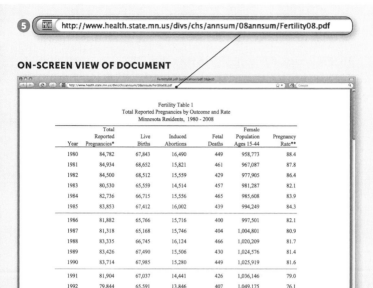

Fertility Table 1
Total Reported Pregnancies by Outcome and Rate
Minnesota Residents, 1980 - 2008

Year	Total Reported Pregnancies*	Live Births	Induced Abortions	Fetal Deaths	Female Population Ages 15-44	Pregnancy Rate**
1980	84,782	67,843	16,490	449	958,773	88.4
1981	84,934	68,652	15,821	461	967,087	87.8
1982	84,500	68,512	15,559	429	977,905	86.4
1983	80,530	65,559	14,514	457	981,287	82.1
1984	82,736	66,715	15,556	465	985,608	83.9
1985	83,853	67,412	16,002	439	994,249	84.3
1986	81,882	65,766	15,716	400	997,501	82.1
1987	81,318	65,168	15,746	404	1,004,801	80.9
1988	83,335	66,745	16,124	466	1,020,209	81.7
1989	83,426	67,490	15,506	430	1,024,576	81.4
1990	83,714	67,985	15,280	449	1,025,919	81.6
1991	81,904	67,037	14,441	426	1,036,146	79.0
1992	79,844	65,591	13,846	407	1,049,175	76.1
1993	77,939	64,646	12,955	338	1,060,396	73.5

REFERENCE LIST ENTRY FOR A SECTION IN A WEB DOCUMENT

┌——1——┐ ┌——2——┐ ┌—3—┐ ┌—4—┐
Minnesota Department of Health. (2010, January). Fertility. In *2008*

┌—5—┐
Minnesota health statistics annual summary. Retrieved from http://

www.health.state.mn.us/divs/chs/annsum/08annsum/Fertility08.pdf

For more on citing documents from Web sites in APA style, see pages
569–74.

is no title, give a brief description of the content of the source in brackets in place of the title.

U.S. Department of Agriculture, Economic Research Service. (2009). *Eating and health module (ATUS): 2007 data* [Data set]. Retrieved from http://www.ers.usda.gov/Data/ATUS/Data/2007/2007data.htm

Gallup. (2008, October 23). *No increase in proportion of first-time voters* [Graphs]. Retrieved from http://www.gallup.com/poll/111331 /No-Increase-Proportion-First-Time-Voters.aspx

49. Conference hearing

Carmona, R. H. (2004, March 2). *The growing epidemic of childhood obesity.* Testimony before the Subcommittee on Competition, Foreign Commerce, and Infrastructure of the U.S. Senate Committee on Commerce, Science, and Transportation. Retrieved from http://www.hhs.gov/asl/testify /t040302.html

50. E-mail
E-mail messages, letters, and other personal communications are not included in the list of references. (See item 11 on p. 554 for citing these sources in the text of your paper.)

51. Online posting
If an online posting is not archived, cite it as a personal communication in the text of your paper and do not include it in the list of references. If the posting is archived, give the URL and the name of the discussion list if it is not part of the URL.

McKinney, J. (2006, December 19). Adult education-healthcare partnerships [Electronic mailing list message]. Retrieved from http://www.nifl.gov /pipermail/healthliteracy/2006/000524.html

Other sources (including online versions)

52. Dissertation from a database

Hymel, K. M. (2009). *Essays in urban economics* (Doctoral dissertation). Available from ProQuest Dissertations and Theses database. (AAT 3355930)

53. Unpublished dissertation

Mitchell, R. D. (2007). *The Wesleyan Quadrilateral: Relocating the conversation* (Unpublished doctoral dissertation). Claremont School of Theology, Claremont, CA.

54. Government document

U.S. Census Bureau. (2006). *Statistical abstract of the United States.* Washington, DC: Government Printing Office.

U.S. Census Bureau, Bureau of Economic Analysis. (2008, August). *U.S. international trade in goods and services* (Report No. CB08-121, BEA08-37, FT-900). Retrieved from http://www.census.gov /foreign-trade/Press-Release/2008pr/06/ftdpress.pdf

55. Report from a private organization
If the publisher is also the author, begin with the publisher's name in the author position. For a print source, use "Author" in the publisher position at the end of the entry (see item 3); for an online source, give the URL. If the report has a number, put it in parentheses following the title.

Ford Foundation. (n.d.). *Helping citizens to understand and influence state budgets.* Retrieved from http://www.fordfound.org/pdfs/impact /evaluations/state_fiscal_initiative.pdf

56. Legal source

Sweatt v. Painter, 339 U.S. 629 (1950). Retrieved from Cornell University Law School, Legal Information Institute website: http://www.law .cornell.edu/supct/html/historics/USSC_CR_0339_0629_ZS.html

57. Conference proceedings

Stahl, G. (Ed.). (2002). *Proceedings of CSCL '02: Computer support for collaborative learning.* Hillsdale, NJ: Erlbaum.

58. Paper presented at a meeting or symposium (unpublished)

Anderson, D. N. (2008, May). *Cab-hailing and the micropolitics of gesture.* Paper presented at the Arizona Linguistics and Anthropology Symposium, Tucson, AZ.

59. Poster session at a conference

Wang, Z., & Keogh, T. (2008, June). *A click away: Student response to clickers.* Poster session presented at the annual conference of the American Library Association, Anaheim, CA.

60. Map, chart, or illustration

Ukraine [Map]. (2008). Retrieved from the University of Texas at Austin Perry-Castañeda Library Map Collection website: http://www.lib .utexas.edu/maps/cia08/ukraine_sm_2008.gif

61. Advertisement

Xbox 360 [Advertisement]. (2007, February). *Wired, 15*(2), 71.

62. Published interview

Murphy, C. (2007, June 22). As the Romans did [Interview by G. Hahn]. Retrieved from http://www.theatlantic.com/

63. Lecture, speech, or address

Fox, V. (2008, March 5). *Economic growth, poverty, and democracy in Latin America: A president's perspective.* Address at the Freeman Spogli Institute, Stanford University, Stanford, CA.

64. Work of art or photograph

Weber, J. (1992). *Toward freedom* [Outdoor mural]. Sherman Oaks, CA.

Newkirk, K. (2006). *Gainer (part II).* Museum of Contemporary Art, Chicago, IL.

65. Brochure, pamphlet, or fact sheet

National Council of State Boards of Nursing. (n.d.). *Professional boundaries* [Brochure]. Retrieved from https://www.ncsbn.org /Professional_Boundaries_2007_Web.pdf

World Health Organization. (2007, October). *Health of indigenous peoples* (No. 326) [Fact sheet]. Retrieved from http://www.who.int /mediacentre/factsheets/fs326/en/index.html

📷 66. Presentation slides

Boeninger, C. F. (2008, August). *Web 2.0 tools for reference and instructional*
   services [Presentation slides]. Retrieved from http://libraryvoice.com
   /archives/2008/08/04/opal-20-conference-presentation-slides/

📷 67. Film or video (motion picture)   Give the director, producer, and other relevant contributors, followed by the year of the film's release, the title, the description "Motion picture" in brackets, the country where the film was made, and the studio. If you viewed the film on videocassette or on DVD or Blu-ray Disc (BD), indicate that medium in brackets in place of "Motion picture." If the original release date and the date of the videocassette, DVD, or BD are different, add "Original release" and that date in parentheses at the end of the entry. If the motion picture would be difficult for your readers to find, include the name and address of its distributor instead of the country and studio.

Guggenheim, D. (Director), & Bender, L. (Producer). (2006). *An inconvenient*
   truth [DVD]. United States: Paramount Home Entertainment.

Spurlock, M. (Director). (2004). *Super size me* [Motion picture]. Available
   from IDP Films, 1133 Broadway, Suite 926, New York, NY 10010

📷 68. Television program   List the producer and the date of the program. Give the title, followed by "Television broadcast" in brackets, the city, and the television network or service.

Pratt, C. (Executive producer). (2008, October 5). *Face the nation*
   [Television broadcast]. Washington, DC: CBS News.

For a television series, use the year in which the series was produced, and follow the title with "Television series" in brackets. For an episode in a series, list the writer and director and the year. After the episode title, put "Television series episode" in brackets. Follow with information about the series.

Fanning, D. (Executive producer). (2008). *Frontline* [Television series].
   Boston, MA: WGBH.

Smith, M. (Writer/producer). (2008). Heat [Television series episode]. In
   D. Fanning (Executive producer), *Frontline*. Boston, MA: WGBH.

69. Sound recording

Thomas, G. (1996). Breath. On *Didgeridoo: Ancient sound of the future*

[CD]. Oxnard, CA: Aquarius International Music.

70. Computer software or video game Add the words "Computer software" in brackets after the title of the program.

Sims 2 [Computer software]. (2005). New York, NY: Maxis.

65 APA manuscript format; sample paper

The American Psychological Association makes a number of recommendations for formatting a paper and preparing a list of references. The following guidelines are consistent with advice given in the *Publication Manual of the American Psychological Association*, 6th ed. (Washington: APA, 2010).

65a APA manuscript format

The APA manual provides guidelines for papers prepared for publication in a scholarly journal; it does not provide separate guidelines for papers prepared for undergraduate classes. The formatting guidelines in this section and the sample paper on pages 583–94 can be used for either type of paper. (See p. 595 for alternative formatting.) If you are in doubt about the specific format preferred or required in your course, ask your instructor.

Formatting the paper

Many instructors in the social sciences require students to follow APA guidelines for formatting a paper.

Materials and font Use good-quality 8½″ × 11″ white paper. If your instructor does not require a specific font, choose one that is standard and easy to read (such as Times New Roman).

Title page Begin at the top left with the words "Running head," followed by a colon and the title of your paper (shortened to no more than fifty characters) in all capital letters. Put the page number 1 flush with the right margin.

About halfway down the page, center the full title of your paper (capitalizing all words of four letters or more), your name, and your school's name. At the bottom of the page, you may add the heading "Author Note," centered, followed by a brief paragraph that lists specific information about the course or department or provides acknowledgments or contact information. See page 583 for a sample title page.

Some instructors may instead require a title page like the one on page 595. If in doubt about the requirements in your course, check with your instructor.

Page numbers and running head   Number all pages with arabic numerals (1, 2, 3, and so on) in the upper right corner about one-half inch from the top of the page. The title page should be numbered 1.

On every page, in the upper left corner on the same line as the page number, place a running head. The running head consists of the title of the paper (shortened to no more than fifty characters) in all capital letters. (On the title page only, include the words "Running head" followed by a colon before the shortened title.) See pages 583–94. (See an alternative running head on p. 595.)

Margins, line spacing, and paragraph indents   Use margins of one inch on all sides of the page. Left-align the text.

Double-space throughout the paper. Indent the first line of each paragraph one-half inch.

Capitalization, italics, and quotation marks   Capitalize all words of four letters or more in titles of works and in headings that appear in the text of the paper. Capitalize the first word after a colon if the word begins a complete sentence.

Italicize the titles of books, periodicals, and other long works, such as Web sites. Use quotation marks around the titles of periodical articles, short stories, poems, and other short works.

NOTE: APA has different requirements for titles in the reference list. See page 581.

Long quotations and footnotes   When a quotation is longer than forty words, set it off from the text by indenting it one-half inch from the left margin. Double-space the quotation. Do not use quotation marks around it. See page 591 for an example.

If you insert a footnote number in the text of your paper, place the note at the bottom of the page on which the number appears. Insert an extra double-spaced line between the last line of text on the page and the footnote. Double-space the footnote and indent the first line one-half inch. Begin the note with the superscript arabic numeral that corresponds to the number in the text. See page 585 for an example.

Abstract If your instructor requires an abstract, include it immediately after the title page. Center the word "Abstract" one inch from the top of the page; double-space the abstract.

An abstract is a 100-to-150-word paragraph that provides readers with a quick overview of your essay. It should express your main idea and your key points; it might also briefly suggest any implications or applications of the research you discuss in the paper. See page 584 for an example.

Headings Although headings are not always necessary, their use is encouraged in the social sciences. For most undergraduate papers, one level of heading will usually be sufficient.

In APA style, major headings are centered and boldface. Capitalize the first word of the heading along with all words except articles, short prepositions, and coordinating conjunctions. See the sample paper on pages 583–94 for the use of headings.

Visuals APA classifies visuals as tables and figures (figures include graphs, charts, drawings, and photographs). Keep visuals as simple as possible.

Label each table with an arabic numeral (Table 1, Table 2, and so on) and provide a clear title. The label and title should appear on separate lines above the table, flush left and double-spaced.

Below the table, give its source in a note. If any data in the table require an explanatory footnote, use a superscript lowercase letter in the body of the table and in a footnote following the source note. Double-space source notes and footnotes and do not indent the first line of each note. See page 589 for an example of a table in a student paper.

For each figure, place a label and a caption below the figure, flush left and double-spaced. The label and caption need not appear on separate lines.

In the text of your paper, discuss significant features of each visual. Place the visual as close as possible to the sentences that relate to it unless your instructor prefers that visuals appear in an appendix.

Preparing the list of references

Begin your list of references on a new page at the end of the paper. Center the title "References" one inch from the top of the page, and double-space throughout. For a sample reference list, see pages 593–94.

Indenting entries   Use a hanging indent in the reference list: Type the first line of each entry flush left and indent any additional lines one-half inch, as shown on page 593.

Alphabetizing the list   Alphabetize the reference list by the last names of the authors (or editors); when a work has no author (or editor), alphabetize by the first word of the title other than *A*, *An*, or *The*.

If your list includes two or more works by the same author, arrange the entries by year, the earliest first. If your list includes two or more works by the same author in the same year, arrange the works alphabetically by title. Add the letters "a," "b," and so on within the parentheses after the year. Use only the year and the letter for articles in journals: (2002a). Use the full date and the letter for articles in magazines and newspapers in the reference list: (2005a, July 7). Use only the year and the letter in the in-text citation.

Authors' names   Invert all authors' names and use initials instead of first names. Separate the names with commas. With two to seven authors, use an ampersand (&) before the last author's name. If there are eight or more authors, give the first six authors, three ellipsis dots, and the last author (see p. 558).

Titles of books and articles   Italicize the titles and subtitles of books. Do not italicize or use quotation marks around the titles of articles. Capitalize only the first word of the title and subtitle (and all proper nouns) of books and articles. Capitalize names of periodicals as you would capitalize them normally (see 45c).

Abbreviations for page numbers   Abbreviations for "page" and "pages" ("p." and "pp.") are used before page numbers of newspaper articles and articles in edited books (see item 9 on p. 559 and item 22 on p. 563) but not before page numbers of articles in magazines and scholarly journals (see items 7 and 8 on p. 559).

Breaking a URL or DOI When a URL or a DOI (digital object identifier) must be divided, break it after a double slash or before any other mark of punctuation. Do not insert a hyphen, and do not add a period at the end.

For information about the exact format of each entry in your list, consult the models on pages 557–78.

65b Sample research paper: APA style

On pages 583–94 is a research paper on the effectiveness of treatments for childhood obesity, written by Luisa Mirano, a student in a psychology class. Mirano's assignment was to write a review of the literature and to document it with APA-style citations and references. (See p. 595 for a sample of alternative formatting.)

MODELS hackerhandbooks.com/rules
> Model papers > APA papers: Mirano; Charat; Gibson; Riss; Thompson
> APA annotated bibliography: Haddad

Running head: CAN MEDICATION CURE OBESITY IN CHILDREN?   1

The header consists of a shortened title in all capital letters at the left margin and the page number at the right margin; on the title page only, the shortened title is preceded by the words "Running head" and a colon.

Can Medication Cure Obesity in Children?

A Review of the Literature

Luisa Mirano

Northwest-Shoals Community College

Full title, writer's name, and school name are centered halfway down the page.

Author Note

This paper was prepared for Psychology 108, Section B, taught by Professor Kang.

An author's note lists specific information about the course or department and can provide acknowledgments and contact information.

Marginal annotations indicate APA-style formatting and effective writing.

CAN MEDICATION CURE OBESITY IN CHILDREN?   2

Abstract

In recent years, policymakers and medical experts have
expressed alarm about the growing problem of childhood
obesity in the United States. While most agree that the
issue deserves attention, consensus dissolves around how to
respond to the problem. This literature review examines one
approach to treating childhood obesity: medication. The
paper compares the effectiveness for adolescents of the only
two drugs approved by the Food and Drug Administration
(FDA) for long-term treatment of obesity, sibutramine and
orlistat. This examination of pharmacological treatments
for obesity points out the limitations of medication
and suggests the need for a comprehensive solution
that combines medical, social, behavioral, and political
approaches to this complex problem.

Abstract appears on
a separate page.

CAN MEDICATION CURE OBESITY IN CHILDREN?   3

Can Medication Cure Obesity in Children?

A Review of the Literature

In March 2004, U.S. Surgeon General Richard Carmona called attention to a health problem in the United States that, until recently, has been overlooked: childhood obesity. Carmona said that the "astounding" 15% child obesity rate constitutes an "epidemic." Since the early 1980s, that rate has "doubled in children and tripled in adolescents." Now more than 9 million children are classified as obese.[1] While the traditional response to a medical epidemic is to hunt for a vaccine or a cure-all pill, childhood obesity is more elusive. The lack of success of recent initiatives suggests that medication might not be the answer for the escalating problem. This literature review considers whether the use of medication is a promising approach for solving the childhood obesity problem by responding to the following questions:

    1. What are the implications of childhood obesity?

    2. Is medication effective at treating childhood obesity?

    3. Is medication safe for children?

    4. Is medication the best solution?

Understanding the limitations of medical treatments for children highlights the complexity of the childhood obesity problem in the United States and underscores the need for physicians, advocacy groups, and policymakers to search for other solutions.

What Are the Implications of Childhood Obesity?

Obesity can be a devastating problem from both an

[1]Obesity is measured in terms of body-mass index (BMI): weight in kilograms divided by square of height in meters. A child or an adolescent with a BMI in the 95th percentile for his or her age and gender is considered obese.

Full title, centered.

Mirano sets up her organization by posing four questions.

Mirano states her thesis.

Headings, centered, help readers follow the organization.

Mirano uses a footnote to define an essential term that would be cumbersome to define within the text.

CAN MEDICATION CURE OBESITY IN CHILDREN?   4

individual and a societal perspective. Obesity puts children
at risk for a number of medical complications, including
Type 2 diabetes, hypertension, sleep apnea, and orthopedic
problems (Henry J. Kaiser Family Foundation, 2004, p. 1).
Researchers Hoppin and Taveras (2004) have noted that
obesity is often associated with psychological issues such as
depression, anxiety, and binge eating (Table 4).

> In a signal phrase, the word "and" links the names of two authors; the date is given in parentheses.

Obesity also poses serious problems for a society
struggling to cope with rising health care costs. The cost
of treating obesity currently totals $117 billion per year—a
price, according to the surgeon general, "second only to the
cost of [treating] tobacco use" (Carmona, 2004). And as
the number of children who suffer from obesity grows, long-
term costs will only increase.

> Because the author (Carmona) is not named in the signal phrase, his name and the date appear in parentheses.

Is Medication Effective at Treating Childhood Obesity?

The widening scope of the obesity problem has
prompted medical professionals to rethink old conceptions
of the disorder and its causes. As researchers Yanovski
and Yanovski (2002) have explained, obesity was once
considered "either a moral failing or evidence of underlying
psychopathology" (p. 592). But this view has shifted: Many
medical professionals now consider obesity a biomedical
rather than a moral condition, influenced by both genetic and
environmental factors. Yanovski and Yanovski have further
noted that the development of weight-loss medications in the
early 1990s showed that "obesity should be treated in the
same manner as any other chronic disease . . . through the
long-term use of medication" (p. 592).

> Ellipsis mark indicates omitted words.

The search for the right long-term medication has been
complicated. Many of the drugs authorized by the Food and
Drug Administration (FDA) in the early 1990s proved to be a

APA

CAN MEDICATION CURE OBESITY IN CHILDREN?   5

disappointment. Two of the medications—fenfluramine and dexfenfluramine—were withdrawn from the market because of severe side effects (Yanovski & Yanovski, 2002, p. 592), and several others were classified by the Drug Enforcement Administration as having the "potential for abuse" (Hoppin & Taveras, 2004, Weight-Loss Drugs section, para. 6). Currently only two medications have been approved by the FDA for long-term treatment of obesity: sibutramine (marketed as Meridia) and orlistat (marketed as Xenical). This section compares studies on the effectiveness of each.

In a parenthetical citation, an ampersand links the names of two authors.

Sibutramine suppresses appetite by blocking the reuptake of the neurotransmitters serotonin and norepinephrine in the brain (Yanovski & Yanovski, 2002, p. 594). Though the drug won FDA approval in 1998, experiments to test its effectiveness for younger patients came considerably later. In 2003, University of Pennsylvania researchers Berkowitz, Wadden, Tershakovec, and Cronquist released the first double-blind placebo study testing the effect of sibutramine on adolescents, aged 13-17, over a 12-month period. Their findings are summarized in Table 1.

Mirano draws attention to an important article.

After 6 months, the group receiving medication had lost 4.6 kg (about 10 pounds) more than the control group. But during the second half of the study, when both groups received sibutramine, the results were more ambiguous. In months 6-12, the group that continued to take sibutramine gained an average of 0.8 kg, or roughly 2 pounds; the control group, which switched from placebo to sibutramine, lost 1.3 kg, or roughly 3 pounds (p. 1808). Both groups received behavioral therapy covering diet, exercise, and mental health.

These results paint a murky picture of the effectiveness

of the medication: While initial data seemed promising, the results after one year raised questions about whether medication-induced weight loss could be sustained over time. As Berkowitz et al. (2003) advised, "Until more extensive safety and efficacy data are available, . . . weight-loss medications should be used only on an experimental basis for adolescents" (p. 1811).

A study testing the effectiveness of orlistat in adolescents showed similarly ambiguous results. The FDA approved orlistat in 1999 but did not authorize it for adolescents until December 2003. Roche Laboratories (2003), maker of orlistat, released results of a one-year study testing the drug on 539 obese adolescents, aged 12-16. The drug, which promotes weight loss by blocking fat absorption in the large intestine, showed some effectiveness in adolescents: an average loss of 1.3 kg, or roughly 3 pounds, for subjects taking orlistat for one year, as opposed to an average gain of 0.67 kg, or 1.5 pounds, for the control group (pp. 8-9). See Table 1.

Short-term studies of orlistat have shown slightly more dramatic results. Researchers at the National Institute of Child Health and Human Development tested 20 adolescents, aged 12-16, over a three-month period and found that orlistat, combined with behavioral therapy, produced an average weight loss of 4.4 kg, or 9.7 pounds (McDuffie et al., 2002, p. 646). The study was not controlled against a placebo group; therefore, the relative effectiveness of orlistat in this case remains unclear.

Is Medication Safe for Children?

While modest weight loss has been documented for both medications, each carries risks of certain side effects. Sibutramine has been observed to increase blood pressure

For a source with six or more authors, the first author's surname followed by "et al." is used for the first and subsequent references.

CAN MEDICATION CURE OBESITY IN CHILDREN? 7

Table 1

Effectiveness of Sibutramine and Orlistat in Adolescents

Medication	Subjects	Treatment[a]	Side effects	Average weight loss/gain
Sibutramine	Control	0-6 mos.: placebo 6-12 mos.: sibutramine	Mos. 6-12: increased blood pressure; increased pulse rate	After 6 mos.: loss of 3.2 kg (7 lb) After 12 mos.: loss of 4.5 kg (9.9 lb)
	Medicated	0-12 mos.: sibutramine	Increased blood pressure; increased pulse rate	After 6 mos.: loss of 7.8 kg (17.2 lb) After 12 mos.: loss of 7.0 kg (15.4 lb)
Orlistat	Control	0-12 mos.: placebo	None	Gain of 0.67 kg (1.5 lb)
	Medicated	0-12 mos.: orlistat	Oily spotting; flatulence; abdominal discomfort	Loss of 1.3 kg (2.9 lb)

Note. The data on sibutramine are adapted from "Behavior Therapy and Sibutramine for the Treatment of Adolescent Obesity," by R. I. Berkowitz, T. A. Wadden, A. M. Tershakovec, & J. L. Cronquist, 2003, *Journal of the American Medical Association, 289*, pp. 1807-1809. The data on orlistat are adapted from *Xenical (Orlistat) Capsules: Complete Product Information*, by Roche Laboratories, December 2003, retrieved from http://www.rocheusa.com/products/xenical/pi.pdf
[a]The medication and/or placebo were combined with behavioral therapy in all groups over all time periods.

Mirano uses a table to summarize the findings presented in two sources.

A note gives the source of the data.

A content note explains data common to all subjects.

and pulse rate. In 2002, a consumer group claimed that the medication was related to the deaths of 19 people and filed a petition with the Department of Health and Human Services to ban the medication (Hilts, 2002). The sibutramine study by Berkowitz et al. (2003) noted elevated blood pressure as a side effect, and dosages had to be reduced or the medication discontinued in 19 of the 43 subjects in the first six months (p. 1809).

> When this article was first cited, all four authors were named. In subsequent citations of a work with three to five authors, "et al." is used after the first author's name.

The main side effects associated with orlistat were abdominal discomfort, oily spotting, fecal incontinence, and nausea (Roche Laboratories, 2003, p. 13). More serious for long-term health is the concern that orlistat, being a fat-blocker, would affect absorption of fat-soluble vitamins, such as vitamin D. However, the study found that this side effect can be minimized or eliminated if patients take vitamin supplements two hours before or after administration of orlistat (p. 10). With close monitoring of patients taking the medication, many of the risks can be reduced.

Is Medication the Best Solution?

The data on the safety and efficacy of pharmacological treatments of childhood obesity raise the question of whether medication is the best solution for the problem. The treatments have clear costs for individual patients, including unpleasant side effects, little information about long-term use, and uncertainty that they will yield significant weight loss.

In purely financial terms, the drugs cost more than $3 a day on average (Duenwald, 2004). In each of the clinical trials, use of medication was accompanied by an expensive regime of behavioral therapies, including counseling, nutritional education, fitness advising, and monitoring. As journalist Greg

CAN MEDICATION CURE OBESITY IN CHILDREN?   9

Critser (2003) noted in his book *Fat Land,* use of weight-loss
drugs is unlikely to have an effect without the proper "support
system"—one that includes doctors, facilities, time, and money
(p. 3). For some, this level of care is prohibitively expensive.

A third complication is that the studies focused on
adolescents aged 12-16, but obesity can begin at a much
younger age. Few data exist to establish the safety or efficacy
of medication for treating very young children.

While the scientific data on the concrete effects of these
medications in children remain somewhat unclear, medication
is not the only avenue for addressing the crisis. Both medical
experts and policymakers recognize that solutions might come
not only from a laboratory but also from policy, education,
and advocacy. A handbook designed to educate doctors on
obesity called for "major changes in some aspects of western
culture" (Hoppin & Taveras, 2004, Conclusion section,
para. 1). Cultural change may not be the typical realm of
medical professionals, but the handbook urged doctors to be
proactive and "focus [their] energy on public policies and
interventions" (Conclusion section, para. 1).

The solutions proposed by a number of advocacy groups
underscore this interest in political and cultural change.
A report by the Henry J. Kaiser Family Foundation (2004)
outlined trends that may have contributed to the childhood
obesity crisis, including food advertising for children as well as

> a reduction in physical education classes and after-
> school athletic programs, an increase in the availability
> of sodas and snacks in public schools, the growth in the
> number of fast-food outlets . . . , and the increasing
> number of highly processed high-calorie and high-fat
> grocery products. (p. 1)

Marginal notes:

Mirano develops the paper's thesis.

Brackets indicate a word not in the original source.

A quotation longer than forty words is indented without quotation marks.

CAN MEDICATION CURE OBESITY IN CHILDREN?   10

Mirano interprets the evidence; she doesn't just report it.

Addressing each of these areas requires more than a doctor armed with a prescription pad; it requires a broad mobilization not just of doctors and concerned parents but of educators, food industry executives, advertisers, and media representatives.

The tone of the conclusion is objective.

The barrage of possible approaches to combating childhood obesity—from scientific research to political lobbying—indicates both the severity and the complexity of the problem. While none of the medications currently available is a miracle drug for curing the nation's 9 million obese children, research has illuminated some of the underlying factors that affect obesity and has shown the need for a comprehensive approach to the problem that includes behavioral, medical, social, and political change.

References

Berkowitz, R. I., Wadden, T. A., Tershakovec, A. M., & Cronquist, J. L. (2003). Behavior therapy and sibutramine for the treatment of adolescent obesity. *Journal of the American Medical Association, 289,* 1805-1812.

Carmona, R. H. (2004, March 2). *The growing epidemic of childhood obesity.* Testimony before the Subcommittee on Competition, Foreign Commerce, and Infrastructure of the U.S. Senate Committee on Commerce, Science, and Transportation. Retrieved from http://www.hhs .gov/asl/testify/t040302.html

Critser, G. (2003). *Fat land.* Boston, MA: Houghton Mifflin.

Duenwald, M. (2004, January 6). Slim pickings: Looking beyond ephedra. *The New York Times,* p. F1. Retrieved from http://nytimes.com/

Henry J. Kaiser Family Foundation. (2004, February). *The role of media in childhood obesity.* Retrieved from http:// www.kff.org/entmedia/7030.cfm

Hilts, P. J. (2002, March 20). Petition asks for removal of diet drug from market. *The New York Times,* p. A26. Retrieved from http://nytimes.com/

Hoppin, A. G., & Taveras, E. M. (2004, June 25). Assessment and management of childhood and adolescent obesity. *Clinical Update.* Retrieved from http://www.medscape .com/viewarticle/481633

McDuffie, J. R., Calis, K. A., Uwaifo, G. I., Sebring, N. G., Fallon, E. M., Hubbard, V. S., & Yanovski, J. A. (2002). Three-month tolerability of orlistat in adolescents with obesity-related comorbid conditions. *Obesity Research, 10,* 642-650.

List of references begins on a new page. Heading is centered.

List is alphabetized by authors' last names. All authors' names are inverted (last name followed by initials).

The first line of an entry is at the left margin; subsequent lines indent ½".

Double-spacing is used throughout.

CAN MEDICATION CURE OBESITY IN CHILDREN?   12

Roche Laboratories. (2003, December). *Xenical (orlistat)*
     capsules: Complete product information. Retrieved from
     http://www.rocheusa.com/products/xenical/pi.pdf

Yanovski, S. Z., & Yanovski, J. A. (2002). Drug therapy:
     Obesity. *The New England Journal of Medicine, 346,*
     591-602.

ALTERNATIVE APA TITLE PAGE

Obesity in Children 1

Short title and page number in the upper right corner on all pages.

Can Medication Cure Obesity in Children?
A Review of the Literature

Full title, centered.

Luisa Mirano
Psychology 108, Sector B
Professor Kang
October 31, 2004

Writer's name, course, instructor's name, and date, all centered at the bottom of the page.

ALTERNATIVE APA RUNNING HEAD

Obesity in Children 5

were classified by the Drug Enforcement Administration as having the "potential for abuse" (Hoppin & Taveras, 2004, Weight-Loss Drugs section, para. 6). Currently only two medications have been approved by the FDA for long-term

Marginal annotations indicate APA-style formatting.

Glossary of Usage

This glossary includes words commonly confused (such as *accept* and *except*), words commonly misused (such as *aggravate*), and words that are nonstandard (such as *hisself*). It also lists colloquialisms and jargon. Colloquialisms are casual expressions that may be appropriate in informal speech but are inappropriate in formal writing. Jargon is needlessly technical or pretentious language that is inappropriate in most contexts. If an item is not listed here, consult the index. For irregular verbs (such as *sing, sang, sung*), see 27a. For idiomatic use of prepositions, see 18d.

a, an Use *an* before a vowel sound, *a* before a consonant sound: *an apple, a peach.* Problems sometimes arise with words beginning with *h* or *u*. If the *h* is silent, the word begins with a vowel sound, so use *an*: *an hour, an honorable deed.* If the *h* is pronounced, the word begins with a consonant sound, so use *a*: *a hospital, a historian, a hotel.* Words such as *university* and *union* begin with a consonant sound (a *y* sound), so use *a*: *a union.* Words such as *uncle* and *umbrella* begin with a vowel sound, so use *an*: *an underground well.* When an abbreviation or an acronym begins with a vowel sound, use *an*: *an EKG, an MRI, an AIDS prevention program.*

accept, except *Accept* is a verb meaning "to receive." *Except* is usually a preposition meaning "excluding." *I will accept all the packages except that one. Except* is also a verb meaning "to exclude." *Please except that item from the list.*

adapt, adopt *Adapt* means "to adjust or become accustomed"; it is usually followed by *to. Adopt* means "to take as one's own." *Our family adopted a Vietnamese child, who quickly adapted to his new life.*

adverse, averse *Adverse* means "unfavorable." *Averse* means "opposed" or "reluctant"; it is usually followed by *to. I am averse to your proposal because it could have an adverse impact on the economy.*

advice, advise *Advice* is a noun, *advise* a verb. *We advise you to follow John's advice.*

affect, effect *Affect* is usually a verb meaning "to influence." *Effect* is usually a noun meaning "result." *The drug did not affect the disease, and* *it had adverse side effects. Effect* can also be a verb meaning "to bring about." *Only the president can effect such a dramatic change.*

aggravate   *Aggravate* means "to make worse or more troublesome." *Overgrazing aggravated the soil erosion.* In formal writing, avoid the use of *aggravate* meaning "to annoy or irritate." *Her babbling annoyed* (not *aggravated*) *me.*

agree to, agree with   *Agree to* means "to give consent to." *Agree with* means "to be in accord with" or "to come to an understanding with." *He agrees with me about the need for change, but he won't agree to my plan.*

ain't   *Ain't* is nonstandard. Use *am not, are not* (*aren't*), or *is not* (*isn't*). *I am not* (not *ain't*) *going home for spring break.*

all ready, already   *All ready* means "completely prepared." *Already* means "previously." *Susan was all ready for the concert, but her friends had already left.*

all right   *All right*, written as two words, is correct. *Alright* is nonstandard.

all together, altogether   *All together* means "everyone or everything in one place." *Altogether* means "entirely." *We were not altogether certain that we could bring the family all together for the reunion.*

allude   To *allude* to something is to make an indirect reference to it. Do not use *allude* to mean "to refer directly." *In his lecture, the professor referred* (not *alluded*) *to several pre-Socratic philosophers.*

allusion, illusion   An *allusion* is an indirect reference. An *illusion* is a misconception or false impression. *Did you catch my allusion to Shakespeare? Mirrors give the room an illusion of depth.*

a lot   *A lot* is two words. Do not write *alot. Sam lost a lot of weight.* See also *lots, lots of.*

among, between   See *between, among.*

amongst   In American English, *among* is preferred.

amoral, immoral   *Amoral* means "neither moral nor immoral"; it also means "not caring about moral judgments." *Immoral* means "morally wrong." *Until recently, most business courses were taught from an amoral perspective. Murder is immoral.*

amount, number   Use *amount* with quantities that cannot be counted; use *number* with those that can. *This recipe calls for a large amount of sugar. We have a large number of toads in our garden.*

an   See *a, an.*

and etc.   *Et cetera* (*etc.*) means "and so forth"; *and etc.* is redundant. See also *etc.*

and/or   Avoid the awkward construction *and/or* except in technical or legal documents.

angry at, angry with   Use *angry with*, not *angry at*, when referring to a person. *The coach was angry with the referee.*

ante-, anti-   The prefix *ante-* means "earlier" or "in front of"; the prefix *anti-* means "against" or "opposed to." *William Lloyd Garrison was a leader of the antislavery movement during the antebellum period.* *Anti-* should be used with a hyphen when it is followed by a capital letter or a word beginning with *i*.

anxious   *Anxious* means "worried" or "apprehensive." In formal writing, avoid using *anxious* to mean "eager." *We are eager* (not *anxious*) *to see your new house.*

anybody, anyone   *Anybody* and *anyone* are singular. (See 21e and 22a.)

anymore   Use the adverb *anymore* in a negative context to mean "any longer" or "now." *The factory isn't producing shoes anymore.* Using *anymore* in a positive context is colloquial; in formal writing, use *now* instead. *We order all our food online now* (not *anymore*).

anyone   See *anybody, anyone.*

anyone, any one   *Anyone*, an indefinite pronoun, means "any person at all." *Any one*, the pronoun *one* preceded by the adjective *any*, refers to a particular person or thing in a group. *Anyone from the winning team may choose any one of the games on display.*

anyplace   In formal writing, use *anywhere.*

anyways, anywheres   *Anyways* and *anywheres* are nonstandard. Use *anyway* and *anywhere.*

as   Do not use *as* to mean "because" if there is any chance of ambiguity. *We canceled the picnic because* (not *as*) *it began raining. As* here could mean either "because" or "when."

as, like   See *like, as.*

as to   *As to* is jargon for *about*. *He inquired about* (not *as to*) *the job.*

averse   See *adverse, averse.*

awful   The adjective *awful* and the adverb *awfully* are not appropriate in formal writing.

awhile, a while   *Awhile* is an adverb; it can modify a verb, but it cannot be the object of a preposition such as *for*. The two-word form *a while* is a noun preceded by an article and therefore can be the object of a preposition. *Stay awhile. Stay for a while.*

back up, backup   *Back up* is a verb phrase. *Back up the car carefully. Be sure to back up your hard drive. Backup* is a noun meaning "a copy of electronically stored data." *Keep your backup in a safe place. Backup* can also be used as an adjective. *I regularly create backup disks.*

bad, badly   *Bad* is an adjective, *badly* an adverb. *They felt bad about ruining the surprise. Her arm hurt badly after she slid into second base.* (See 26a, 26b, and 26c.)

being as, being that   *Being as* and *being that* are nonstandard expressions. Write *because* instead. *Because* (not *Being as*) *I slept late, I had to skip breakfast.*

beside, besides   *Beside* is a preposition meaning "at the side of" or "next to." *Annie sleeps with a flashlight beside her bed. Besides* is a preposition meaning "except" or "in addition to." *No one besides Terrie can have that ice cream. Besides* is also an adverb meaning "in addition." *I'm not hungry; besides, I don't like ice cream.*

between, among   Ordinarily, use *among* with three or more entities, *between* with two. *The prize was divided among several contestants. You have a choice between carrots and beans.*

bring, take   Use *bring* when an object is being transported toward you, *take* when it is being moved away. *Please bring me a glass of water. Please take these forms to Mr. Scott.*

burst, bursted; bust, busted   *Burst* is an irregular verb meaning "to come open or fly apart suddenly or violently." Its past tense is *burst*. The past-tense form *bursted* is nonstandard. *Bust* and *busted* are slang for *burst* and, along with *bursted*, should not be used in formal writing.

can, may   The distinction between *can* and *may* is fading, but some writers still observe it in formal writing. *Can* is traditionally reserved for ability, *may* for permission. *Can you speak French? May I help you?*

capital, capitol   *Capital* refers to a city, *capitol* to a building where lawmakers meet. *Capital* also refers to wealth or resources. *The residents of the state capital protested plans to close the streets surrounding the capitol.*

censor, censure   *Censor* means "to remove or suppress material considered objectionable." *Censure* means "to criticize severely." *The administration's policy of censoring books has been censured by the media.*

cite, site   *Cite* means "to quote as an authority or example." *Site* is usually a noun meaning "a particular place." *He cited the zoning law in his argument against the proposed site of the gas station.* Locations on the Internet are usually referred to as *sites. The library's Web site improves every week.*

climactic, climatic   *Climactic* is derived from *climax*, the point of greatest intensity in a series or progression of events. *Climatic* is derived from *climate* and refers to meteorological conditions. *The climactic period in the dinosaurs' reign was reached just before severe climatic conditions brought on an ice age.*

coarse, course   *Coarse* means "crude" or "rough in texture." *The coarse weave of the wall hanging gave it a three-dimensional quality. Course* usually refers to a path, a playing field, or a unit of study; the expression *of course* means "certainly." *I plan to take a course in car repair this summer. Of course, you are welcome to join me.*

compare to, compare with   *Compare to* means "to represent as similar." *She compared him to a wild stallion. Compare with* means "to examine similarities and differences." *The study compared the language ability of apes with that of dolphins.*

complement, compliment   *Complement* is a verb meaning "to go with or complete" or a noun meaning "something that completes." As a verb, *compliment* means "to flatter"; as a noun, it means "flattering remark." *Her skill at rushing the net complements his skill at volleying. Martha's flower arrangements receive many compliments.*

conscience, conscious   *Conscience* is a noun meaning "moral principles." *Conscious* is an adjective meaning "aware or alert." *Let your conscience be your guide. Were you conscious of his love for you?*

continual, continuous   *Continual* means "repeated regularly and frequently." *She grew weary of the continual telephone calls. Continuous* means "extended or prolonged without interruption." *The broken siren made a continuous wail.*

could care less   *Could care less* is nonstandard. Write *couldn't care less* instead. *He couldn't* (not *could*) *care less about his psychology final.*

could of   *Could of* is nonstandard for *could have. We could have* (not *could of*) *taken the train.*

council, counsel   A *council* is a deliberative body, and a *councilor* is a member of such a body. *Counsel* usually means "advice" and can also mean "lawyer"; a *counselor* is one who gives advice or guidance. *The councilors met to draft the council's position paper. The pastor offered wise counsel to the troubled teenager.*

criteria   *Criteria* is the plural of *criterion*, which means "a standard or rule or test on which a judgment or decision can be based." *The only criterion for the scholarship is ability.*

data   *Data* is a plural noun technically meaning "facts or results." But *data* is increasingly being accepted as a singular noun. *The new data suggest* (or *suggests*) *that our theory is correct.* (The singular *datum* is rarely used.)

different from, different than   Ordinarily, write *different from. Your sense of style is different from Jim's.* However, *different than* is acceptable to avoid an awkward construction. *Please let me know if your plans are different than* (to avoid *from what*) *they were six weeks ago.*

differ from, differ with   *Differ from* means "to be unlike"; *differ with* means "to disagree with." *My approach to the problem differed from hers. She differed with me about the wording of the agreement.*

disinterested, uninterested *Disinterested* means "impartial, objective"; *uninterested* means "not interested." *We sought the advice of a disinterested counselor to help us solve our problem. Mark was uninterested in anyone's opinion but his own.*

don't *Don't* is the contraction for *do not. I don't want any. Don't* should not be used as the contraction for *does not*, which is *doesn't. He doesn't* (not *don't*) *want any.*

due to *Due to* is an adjective phrase and should not be used as a preposition meaning "because of." *The trip was canceled because of* (not *due to*) *lack of interest. Due to* is acceptable as a subject complement and usually follows a form of the verb *be. His success was due to hard work.*

each *Each* is singular. (See 21e and 22a.)

effect See *affect, effect.*

e.g. In formal writing, replace the Latin abbreviation *e.g.* with its English equivalent: *for example* or *for instance.*

either *Either* is singular. (See 21e and 22a.) For *either . . . or* constructions, see 21d and 22a.

elicit, illicit *Elicit* is a verb meaning "to bring out" or "to evoke." *Illicit* is an adjective meaning "unlawful." *The reporter was unable to elicit any information from the police about illicit drug traffic.*

emigrate from, immigrate to *Emigrate* means "to leave one country or region to settle in another." *In 1903, my great-grandfather emigrated from Russia to escape the religious pogroms. Immigrate* means "to enter another country and reside there." *More than fifty thousand Bosnians immigrated to the United States in the 1990s.*

eminent, imminent *Eminent* means "outstanding" or "distinguished." *We met an eminent professor of Greek history. Imminent* means "about to happen." *The snowstorm is imminent.*

enthused Many people object to the use of *enthused* as an adjective. Use *enthusiastic* instead. *The children were enthusiastic* (not *enthused*) *about going to the circus.*

etc. Avoid ending a list with *etc.* It is more emphatic to end with an example, and in most contexts readers will understand that the list is not exhaustive. When you don't wish to end with an example, *and so on* is more graceful than *etc.* (See also *and etc.*)

eventually, ultimately Often used interchangeably, *eventually* is the better choice to mean "at an unspecified time in the future," and *ultimately* is better to mean "the furthest possible extent or greatest extreme." *He knew that eventually he would complete his degree. The existentialists considered suicide the ultimately rational act.*

everybody, everyone *Everybody* and *everyone* are singular. (See 21e and 22a.)

everyone, every one *Everyone* is an indefinite pronoun. *Every one*, the pronoun *one* preceded by the adjective *every*, means "each individual or thing in a particular group." *Every one* is usually followed by *of. Everyone wanted to go. Every one of the missing books was found.*

except See *accept, except.*

expect Avoid the informal use of *expect* meaning "to believe, think, or suppose." *I think* (not *expect*) *it will rain tonight.*

explicit, implicit *Explicit* means "expressed directly" or "clearly defined"; *implicit* means "implied, unstated." *I gave him explicit instructions not to go swimming. My mother's silence indicated her implicit approval.*

farther, further *Farther* usually describes distances. *Further* usually suggests quantity or degree. *Chicago is farther from Miami than I thought. I would be grateful for further suggestions.*

fewer, less Use *fewer* for items that can be counted; use *less* for items that cannot be counted. *Fewer people are living in the city. Please put less sugar in my tea.*

finalize *Finalize* is jargon meaning "to make final or complete." Use ordinary English instead. *The architect prepared final drawings* (not *finalized the drawings*).

firstly *Firstly* sounds pretentious, and it leads to the ungainly series *firstly, secondly, thirdly,* and so on. Write *first, second, third* instead.

further See *farther, further.*

get *Get* has many colloquial uses. In writing, avoid using *get* to mean the following: "to evoke an emotional response" (*That music always gets to me*); "to annoy" (*After a while, his sulking got to me*); "to take revenge on" (*I got back at her by leaving the room*); "to become" (*He got sick*); "to start or begin" (*Let's get going*). Avoid using *have got to* in place of *must. I must* (not *have got to*) *finish this paper tonight.*

good, well *Good* is an adjective, *well* an adverb. (See 26a, 26b, and 26c.) *He hasn't felt good about his game since he sprained his wrist last season. She performed well on the uneven parallel bars.*

graduate Both of the following uses of *graduate* are standard: *My sister was graduated from UCLA last year. My sister graduated from UCLA last year.* It is nonstandard, however, to drop the word *from: My sister graduated UCLA last year.* Though this usage is common in informal English, many readers object to it.

grow Phrases such as *to grow the economy* and *to grow a business* are jargon. Usually the verb *grow* is intransitive (it does not take a direct object). *Our business has grown very quickly.* Use *grow* in a transitive sense, with a direct object, to mean "to cultivate" or "to allow to grow." *We plan to grow tomatoes this year. John is growing a beard.*

hanged, hung *Hanged* is the past-tense and past-participle form of the verb *hang* meaning "to execute." *The prisoner was hanged at dawn. Hung* is the past-tense and past-participle form of the verb *hang* meaning "to fasten or suspend." *The stockings were hung by the chimney with care.*

hardly Avoid expressions such as *can't hardly* and *not hardly*, which are considered double negatives. *I can* (not *can't*) *hardly describe my surprise at getting the job.* (See 26e.)

has got, have got *Got* is unnecessary and awkward in such constructions. It should be dropped. *We have* (not *have got*) *three days to prepare for the opening.*

he At one time *he* was commonly used to mean "he or she." Today such usage is inappropriate. (See 17e and 22a.)

he/she, his/her In formal writing, use *he or she* or *his or her*. For alternatives to these wordy constructions, see 17e and 22a.

hisself *Hisself* is nonstandard. Use *himself*.

hopefully *Hopefully* means "in a hopeful manner." *We looked hopefully to the future.* Some usage experts object to the use of *hopefully* as a sentence adverb, apparently on grounds of clarity. To be safe, avoid using *hopefully* in sentences such as the following: *Hopefully, your son will recover soon.* Instead, indicate who is doing the hoping: *I hope that your son will recover soon.*

however In the past, some writers objected to the conjunctive adverb *however* at the beginning of a sentence, but current experts allow placing the word according to the intended meaning and emphasis. All of the following sentences are correct. *Pam decided, however, to attend the lecture. However, Pam decided to attend the lecture.* (She had been considering other activities.) *Pam, however, decided to attend the lecture.* (Unlike someone else, Pam chose to attend the lecture.) (See 32f.)

hung See *hanged, hung*.

i.e. In formal writing, replace the Latin abbreviation *i.e.* with its English equivalent: *that is*.

if, whether Use *if* to express a condition and *whether* to express alternatives. *If you go on a trip, whether to Nebraska or Italy, remember to bring traveler's checks.*

illusion See *allusion, illusion*.

immigrate See *emigrate from, immigrate to*.

imminent See *eminent, imminent*.

immoral See *amoral, immoral*.

USAGE hackerhandbooks.com/rules
> Language Debates > Sexist language
> *however* at the beginning of a sentence

implement   *Implement* is a pretentious way of saying "do," "carry out," or "accomplish." Use ordinary language instead. *We carried out* (not *implemented*) *the director's orders.*

imply, infer   *Imply* means "to suggest or state indirectly"; *infer* means "to draw a conclusion." *John implied that he knew all about computers, but the interviewer inferred that John was inexperienced.*

in, into   *In* indicates location or condition; *into* indicates movement or a change in condition. *They found the lost letters in a box after moving into the house.*

in regards to   *In regards to* confuses two different phrases: *in regard to* and *as regards.* Use one or the other. *In regard to* (or *As regards*) *the contract, ignore the first clause.*

irregardless   *Irregardless* is nonstandard. Use *regardless.*

is when, is where   These mixed constructions are often incorrectly used in definitions. *A runoff election is a second election held to break a tie* (not *is when a second election is held to break a tie*). (See 11c.)

its, it's   *Its* is a possessive pronoun; *it's* is a contraction of *it is.* (See 36c and 36e.) *It's always fun to watch a dog chase its tail.*

kind(s)   *Kind* is singular and should be treated as such. Don't write *These kind of chairs are rare.* Write instead *This kind of chair is rare. Kinds* is plural and should be used only when you mean more than one kind. *These kinds of chairs are rare.*

kind of, sort of   Avoid using *kind of* or *sort of* to mean "somewhat." *The movie was somewhat* (not *sort of*) *boring.* Do not put *a* after either phrase. *That kind of* (not *kind of a*) *salesclerk annoys me.*

lay, lie   See *lie, lay.*

lead, led   *Lead* is a metallic element; it is a noun. *Led* is the past tense of the verb *lead. He led me to the treasure.*

learn, teach   *Learn* means "to gain knowledge"; *teach* means "to impart knowledge." *I must teach* (not *learn*) *my sister to read.*

leave, let   *Leave* means "to exit." Avoid using it with the nonstandard meaning "to permit." *Let* (not *Leave*) *me help you with the dishes.*

less   See *fewer, less.*

let, leave   See *leave, let.*

liable   *Liable* means "obligated" or "responsible." Do not use it to mean "likely." *You're likely* (not *liable*) *to trip if you don't tie your shoelaces.*

lie, lay   *Lie* is an intransitive verb meaning "to recline or rest on a surface." Its forms are *lie, lay, lain. Lay* is a transitive verb meaning "to put or place." Its forms are *lay, laid, laid.* (See 27b.)

like, as   *Like* is a preposition, not a subordinating conjunction. It can be followed only by a noun or a noun phrase. *As* is a subordinating conjunction that introduces a subordinate clause. In casual speech, you may say *She looks like she hasn't slept* or *You don't know her like I do.* But in formal writing, use *as. She looks as if she hasn't slept. You don't know her as I do.* (See also 46f and 46g.)

loose, lose   *Loose* is an adjective meaning "not securely fastened." *Lose* is a verb meaning "to misplace" or "to not win." *Did you lose your only loose pair of work pants?*

lots, lots of   *Lots* and *lots of* are informal substitutes for *many, much,* or *a lot.* Avoid using them in formal writing.

mankind   Avoid *mankind* whenever possible. It offends many readers because it excludes women. Use *humanity, humans, the human race,* or *humankind* instead. (See 17e.)

may   See *can, may.*

maybe, may be   *Maybe* is an adverb meaning "possibly." *Maybe the sun will shine tomorrow. May be* is a verb phrase. *Tomorrow may be brighter.*

may of, might of   *May of* and *might of* are nonstandard for *may have* and *might have. We might have* (not *might of*) *had too many cookies.*

media, medium   *Media* is the plural of *medium. Of all the media that cover the Olympics, television is the medium that best captures the spectacle of the events.*

most   *Most* is informal when used to mean "almost" and should be avoided. *Almost* (not *Most*) *everyone went to the parade.*

must of   See *may of, might of. Must of* is nonstandard for *must have.*

myself   *Myself* is a reflexive or intensive pronoun. Reflexive: *I cut myself.* Intensive: *I will drive you myself.* Do not use *myself* in place of *I* or *me. He gave the flowers to Melinda and me* (not *myself*). (See also 24a and 24b.)

neither   *Neither* is singular. (See 21e and 22a.) For *neither . . . nor* constructions, see 21d, 22a, and 22d.

none   *None* may be singular or plural. (See 21e.)

nowheres   *Nowheres* is nonstandard. Use *nowhere* instead.

number   See *amount, number.*

of   Use the verb *have,* not the preposition *of,* after the verbs *could, should, would, may, might,* and *must. They must have* (not *must of*) *left early.*

off of   *Off* is sufficient. Omit *of. The ball rolled off* (not *off of*) *the table.*

OK, O.K., okay   All three spellings are acceptable, but avoid these expressions in formal speech and writing.

parameters   *Parameter* is a mathematical term that has become jargon for "fixed limit," "boundary," or "guideline." Use ordinary English instead. *The task force worked within certain guidelines* (not *parameters*).

passed, past   *Passed* is the past tense of the verb *pass*. *Ann passed me another slice of cake. Past* usually means "belonging to a former time" or "beyond a time or place." *Our past president spoke until past midnight. The hotel is just past the next intersection.*

percent, per cent, percentage   *Percent* (also spelled *per cent*) is always used with a specific number. *Percentage* is used with a descriptive term such as *large* or *small*, not with a specific number. *The candidate won 80 percent of the primary vote. A large percentage of registered voters turned out for the election.*

phenomena   *Phenomena* is the plural of *phenomenon*, which means "an observable occurrence or fact." *Strange phenomena occur at all hours of the night in that house, but last night's phenomenon was the strangest of all.*

plus   *Plus* should not be used to join independent clauses. *This raincoat is dirty; moreover* (not *plus*), *it has a hole in it.*

precede, proceed   *Precede* means "to come before." *Proceed* means "to go forward." *As we proceeded up the mountain path, we noticed fresh tracks in the mud, evidence that a group of hikers had preceded us.*

principal, principle   *Principal* is a noun meaning "the head of a school or an organization" or "a sum of money." It is also an adjective meaning "most important." *Principle* is a noun meaning "a basic truth or law." *The principal expelled her for three principal reasons. We believe in the principle of equal justice for all.*

proceed, precede   See *precede, proceed.*

quote, quotation   *Quote* is a verb; *quotation* is a noun. Avoid using *quote* as a shortened form of *quotation*. *Her quotations* (not *quotes*) *from current movies intrigued us.*

raise, rise   *Raise* is a transitive verb meaning "to move or cause to move upward." It takes a direct object. *I raised the shades. Rise* is an intransitive verb meaning "to go up." *Heat rises.*

real, really   *Real* is an adjective; *really* is an adverb. *Real* is sometimes used informally as an adverb, but avoid this use in formal writing. *She was really* (not *real*) *angry.* (See 26a and 26b.)

reason . . . is because   Use *that* instead of *because*. *The reason she's cranky is that* (not *because*) *she didn't sleep last night.* (See 11c.)

reason why   The expression *reason why* is redundant. *The reason* (not *The reason why*) *Jones lost the election is clear.*

relation, relationship   *Relation* describes a connection between things. *Relationship* describes a connection between people. *There is a relation between poverty and infant mortality. Our business relationship has cooled over the years.*

respectfully, respectively   *Respectfully* means "showing or marked by respect." *Respectively* means "each in the order given." *He respectfully submitted his opinion to the judge. John, Tom, and Larry were a butcher, a baker, and a lawyer, respectively.*

sensual, sensuous   *Sensual* means "gratifying the physical senses," especially those associated with sexual pleasure. *Sensuous* means "pleasing to the senses," especially those involved in the experience of art, music, and nature. *The sensuous music and balmy air led the dancers to more sensual movements.*

set, sit   *Set* is a transitive verb meaning "to put" or "to place." Its past tense is *set*. *Sit* is an intransitive verb meaning "to be seated." Its past tense is *sat*. *She set the dough in a warm corner of the kitchen. The cat sat in the doorway.*

shall, will   *Shall* was once used in place of the helping verb *will* with *I* or *we*: *I shall, we shall*. Today, however, *will* is generally accepted even when the subject is *I* or *we*. The word *shall* occurs primarily in polite questions (*Shall I find you a pillow?*) and in legalistic sentences suggesting duty or obligation (*The applicant shall file form A by December 31*).

should of   *Should of* is nonstandard for *should have*. *They should have* (not *should of*) *been home an hour ago.*

since   Do not use *since* to mean "because" if there is any chance of ambiguity. *Because* (not *Since*) *we won the game, we have been celebrating with a pitcher of root beer. Since* here could mean "because" or "from the time that."

sit   See *set, sit*.

site   See *cite, site*.

somebody, someone   *Somebody* and *someone* are singular. (See 21e and 22a.)

something   *Something* is singular. (See 21e.)

sometime, some time, sometimes   *Sometime* is an adverb meaning "at an indefinite or unstated time." *Some time* is the adjective *some* modifying the noun *time* and means "a period of time." *Sometimes* is an adverb meaning "at times, now and then." *I'll see you sometime soon. I haven't lived there for some time. Sometimes I see him at the library.*

suppose to   Write *supposed to*.

sure and   Write *sure to*. *We were all taught to be sure to* (not *sure and*) *look both ways before crossing a street.*

take   See *bring, take*.

than, then   *Than* is a conjunction used in comparisons; *then* is an adverb denoting time. *That pizza is more than I can eat. Tom laughed, and then we recognized him.*

that   See *who, which, that.*

that, which   Many writers reserve *that* for restrictive clauses, *which* for nonrestrictive clauses. (See 32e.)

theirselves   *Theirselves* is nonstandard for *themselves. The crash victims pushed the car out of the way themselves* (not *theirselves*).

them   The use of *them* in place of *those* is nonstandard. *Please take those* (not *them*) *flowers to the patient in room 220.*

then, than   See *than, then.*

there, their, they're   *There* is an adverb specifying place; it is also an expletive (placeholder). Adverb: *Sylvia is sitting there patiently.* Expletive: *There are two plums left. Their* is a possessive pronoun. *Fred and Jane finally washed their car. They're* is a contraction of *they are. They're later than usual today.*

they   The use of *they* to indicate possession is nonstandard. Use *their* instead. *Cindy and Sam decided to sell their* (not *they*) *1975 Corvette.*

they, their   The use of the plural pronouns *they* and *their* to refer to singular nouns or pronouns is nonstandard. *No one handed in his or her* (not *their*) *draft on time.* (See 22a.)

this kind   See *kind(s).*

to, too, two   *To* is a preposition; *too* is an adverb; *two* is a number. *Too many of your shots slice to the left, but the last two were just right.*

toward, towards   *Toward* and *towards* are generally interchangeable, although *toward* is preferred in American English.

try and   *Try and* is nonstandard for *try to. The teacher asked us all to try to* (not *try and*) *write an original haiku.*

ultimately, eventually   See *eventually, ultimately.*

unique   Avoid expressions such as *most unique, more straight, less perfect, very round.* Either something is unique or it isn't. It is illogical to suggest degrees of uniqueness. (See 26d.)

usage   The noun *usage* should not be substituted for *use* when the meaning is "employment of." *The use* (not *usage*) *of insulated shades has cut fuel costs dramatically.*

use to   Write *used to.*

USAGE hackerhandbooks.com/rules
> Language Debates > *that* versus *which*
> Absolute concepts such as *unique*

utilize   *Utilize* means "to make use of." It often sounds pretentious; in most cases, *use* is sufficient. *I used* (not *utilized*) *the laser printer.*

wait for, wait on   *Wait for* means "to be in readiness for" or "to await." *Wait on* means "to serve." *We're waiting for* (not *waiting on*) *Ruth to take us to the museum.*

ways   *Ways* is colloquial when used to mean "distance." *The city is a long way* (not *ways*) *from here.*

weather, whether   The noun *weather* refers to the state of the atmosphere. *Whether* is a conjunction referring to a choice between alternatives. *We wondered whether the weather would clear.*

well, good   See *good, well.*

where   Do not use *where* in place of *that. I heard that* (not *where*) *the crime rate is increasing.*

which   See *that, which* and *who, which, that.*

while   Avoid using *while* to mean "although" or "whereas" if there is any chance of ambiguity. *Although* (not *While*) *Gloria lost money in the slot machine, Tom won it at roulette.* Here *While* could mean either "although" or "at the same time that."

who, which, that   Do not use *which* to refer to persons. Use *who* instead. *That*, though generally used to refer to things, may be used to refer to a group or class of people. *The player who* (not *that* or *which*) *made the basket at the buzzer was named MVP. The team that scores the most points in this game will win the tournament.*

who, whom   *Who* is used for subjects and subject complements; *whom* is used for objects. (See 25.)

who's, whose   *Who's* is a contraction of *who is; whose* is a possessive pronoun. *Who's ready for more popcorn? Whose coat is this?* (See 36c and 36e.)

will   See *shall, will.*

would of   *Would of* is nonstandard for *would have. She would have* (not *would of*) *had a chance to play if she had arrived on time.*

you   In formal writing, avoid *you* in an indefinite sense meaning "anyone." (See 23d.) *Any spectator* (not *You*) *could tell by the way John caught the ball that his throw would be too late.*

your, you're   *Your* is a possessive pronoun; *you're* is a contraction of *you are. Is that your new bike? You're in the finals.* (See 36c and 46b.)

USAGE hackerhandbooks.com/rules
> Language Debates > *who* versus *which* or *that*
> *who* versus *whom*
> *you*

Answers to Lettered Exercises

EXERCISE 7–1, page 110

a. hasty generalization; b. false analogy; c. *either . . . or* fallacy; d. faulty cause-and-effect reasoning; e. non sequitur

EXERCISE 8–1, page 115 *Possible revisions:*

  a. The Prussians defeated the Saxons in 1745.
  b. Ahmed, the producer, manages the entire operation.
  c. The tour guides expertly paddled the sea kayaks.
  d. Emphatic and active; no change
  e. Protesters were shouting on the courthouse steps.

EXERCISE 9–1, page 119 *Possible revisions:*

  a. Police dogs are used for finding lost children, tracking criminals, and detecting bombs and illegal drugs.
  b. Hannah told her rock-climbing partner that she bought a new harness and that she wanted to climb Otter Cliffs.
  c. It is more difficult to sustain an exercise program than to start one.
  d. During basic training, I was told not only what to do but also what to think.
  e. Jan wanted to drive to the wine country or at least to Sausalito.

EXERCISE 10–1, page 123 *Possible revisions:*

  a. A grapefruit or an orange is a good source of vitamin C.
  b. The women entering VMI can expect haircuts as short as those of the male cadets.
  c. Looking out the family room window, Sarah saw that her favorite tree, which she had climbed as a child, was gone.
  d. The graphic designers are interested in and knowledgeable about producing posters for the balloon race.
  e. The Great Barrier Reef is larger than any other coral reef in the sea.

EXERCISE 11–1, page 126 *Possible revisions:*

  a. Using surgical gloves is a precaution now taken by dentists to prevent contact with patients' blood and saliva.
  b. A career in medicine, which my brother is pursuing, requires at least ten years of challenging work.
  c. The pharaohs had bad teeth because tiny particles of sand found their way into Egyptian bread.
  d. Recurring bouts of flu caused the team to forfeit a record number of games.
  e. This box contains the key to your future.

EXERCISE 12–1, page 130 *Possible revisions:*

  a. More research is needed to evaluate effectively the risks posed by volcanoes in the Pacific Northwest.
  b. Many students graduate from college with debt totaling more than fifty thousand dollars.
  c. It is a myth that humans use only 10 percent of their brains.

610

d. A coolhunter is a person who can find the next wave of fashion in the unnoticed corners of modern society.
e. Not all geese fly beyond Narragansett for the winter.

EXERCISE 12–2, page 134   *Possible revisions:*

a. Though Martha was only sixteen, UCLA accepted her application.
b. To replace the gear mechanism, you can use the attached form to order the part by mail.
c. As I settled in the cockpit, the pounding of the engine was muffled only slightly by my helmet.
d. After studying polymer chemistry, Phuong found computer games less complex.
e. When I was a young man, my mother enrolled me in tap dance classes.

EXERCISE 13–3, page 139   *Possible revisions:*

a. An incredibly talented musician, Ray Charles mastered R&B, soul, and gospel styles. He even performed country music well.
b. Environmentalists point out that shrimp farming in Southeast Asia is polluting water and making farmlands useless. They warn that governments must act before it is too late.
c. We observed the samples for five days before we detected any growth. *Or* The samples were observed for five days before any growth was detected.
d. In his famous soliloquy, Hamlet contemplates whether death would be preferable to his difficult life and, if so, whether he is capable of committing suicide.
e. The lawyer told the judge that Miranda Hale was innocent and asked that she be allowed to prove the allegations false. *Or* The lawyer told the judge, "Miranda Hale is innocent. Please allow her to prove the allegations false."

EXERCISE 13–4, page 140   *Possible revisions:*

a. Courtroom lawyers have more than a touch of theater in their blood.
b. The interviewer asked if we had brought our proof of citizenship and our passports.
c. Reconnaissance scouts often have to make fast decisions and use sophisticated equipment to keep their teams from being detected.
d. After the animators finish their scenes, the production designer arranges the clips according to the storyboard and makes synchronization notes for the sound editor and the composer.
e. Madame Defarge is a sinister figure in Dickens's *A Tale of Two Cities*. On a symbolic level, she represents fate; like the Greek Fates, she knits the fabric of individual destiny.

EXERCISE 14–1, page 144   *Possible revisions:*

a. Williams played for the Boston Red Sox from 1939 to 1960, and he managed the Washington Senators and the Texas Rangers for several years after retiring as a player.
b. In 1941, Williams finished the season with a batting average of .406; no player has hit over .400 for a season since then.
c. Although he acknowledged that Joe DiMaggio was a better all-around player, Williams felt that he was a better hitter than DiMaggio.
d. Williams was a stubborn man; for example, he always refused to tip his cap to the crowd after a home run because he claimed that fans were fickle.
e. Williams's relationship with the media was unfriendly at best; he sarcastically called baseball writers the "knights of the keyboard" in his memoir.

EXERCISE 14–2, page 147 *Possible revisions:*

a. The X-Men comic books and Japanese woodcuts of kabuki dancers, all part of Marlena's research project on popular culture, covered the table-top and the chairs.
b. Our waitress, costumed in a kimono, had painted her face white and arranged her hair in a lacquered beehive.
c. Students can apply for a spot in the leadership program, which teaches thinking and communication skills.
d. Shore houses were flooded up to the first floor, beaches were washed away, and Brant's Lighthouse was swallowed by the sea.
e. Laura Thackray, an engineer at Volvo Car Corporation, addressed women's safety needs by designing a pregnant crash-test dummy.

EXERCISE 14–3, page 148 *Possible revisions:*

a. These particles, known as "stealth liposomes," can hide in the body for a long time without detection.
b. Jan, a competitive gymnast majoring in biology, intends to apply her athletic experience and her science degree to a career in sports medicine.
c. Because students, textile workers, and labor unions have loudly protested sweatshop abuses, apparel makers have been forced to examine their labor practices.
d. Developed in a European university, IRC (Internet relay chat) was created as a way for a group of graduate students to talk about projects from their dorm rooms.
e. The cafeteria's new menu, which has an international flavor, includes everything from enchiladas and pizza to pad thai and sauerbraten.

EXERCISE 14–4, page 150 *Possible revisions:*

a. Working as an aide for the relief agency, Gina distributed food and medical supplies.
b. Janbir, who spent every Saturday learning tabla drumming, noticed with each hour of practice that his memory for complex patterns was improving.
c. When the rotor hit, it gouged a hole about an eighth of an inch deep in my helmet.
d. My grandfather, who was born eighty years ago in Puerto Rico, raised his daughters the old-fashioned way.
e. By reversing the depressive effect of the drug, the Narcan saved the patient's life.

EXERCISE 15–1, page 155 *Possible revisions:*

a. Across the hall from the fossils exhibit are the exhibits for insects and spiders.
b. After growing up desperately poor in Japan, Sayuri becomes a successful geisha.
c. Researchers believe that a series of nearby earthquakes contributed to the 1980 eruption of Mount St. Helens, the deadliest, most destructive volcanic eruption in US history.
d. Ice cream typically contains 10 percent milk fat, but premium ice cream may contain up to 16 percent milk fat and has considerably less air in the product.
e. If home values climb, the economy may recover more quickly than expected.

EXERCISE 16–1, page 160 *Possible revisions:*

a. Martin Luther King Jr. set a high standard for future leaders.
b. Alice has loved cooking since she could first peek over a kitchen tabletop.

c. Bloom's race for the governorship is futile.
d. A successful graphic designer must have technical knowledge and an eye for color and balance.
e. You will deliver mail to all employees.

EXERCISE 17–1, page 163   *Possible revisions:*

a. When I was young, my family was poor.
b. This conference will help me serve my clients better.
c. The meteorologist warned the public about the possible dangers of the coming storm.
d. Government studies show a need for after-school programs.
e. Passengers should try to complete the customs declaration form before leaving the plane.

EXERCISE 17–4, page 169   *Possible revisions:*

a. Dr. Geralyn Farmer is the chief surgeon at University Hospital. Dr. Paul Green is her assistant.
b. All applicants want to know how much they will earn.
c. Elementary school teachers should understand the concept of nurturing if they intend to be effective.
d. Obstetricians need to be available to their patients at all hours.
e. If we do not stop polluting our environment, we will perish.

EXERCISE 18–2, page 173   *Possible revisions:*

a. We regret this delay; thank you for your patience.
b. Ada's plan is to acquire education and experience to prepare herself for a position as property manager.
c. Peyton Manning, the ultimate competitor, has earned millions of dollars just in endorsements.
d. Many people take for granted that public libraries have up-to-date computer systems.
e. The effect of Gao Xinjian's novels on Chinese exiles is hard to gauge.

EXERCISE 18–3, page 175   *Possible revisions:*

a. Queen Anne was so angry with Sarah Churchill that she refused to see her again.
b. Correct
c. The parade moved off the street and onto the beach.
d. The frightened refugees intend to make the dangerous trek across the mountains.
e. What type of wedding are you planning?

EXERCISE 18–4, page 177   *Possible revisions:*

a. John stormed into the room like a hurricane.
b. Some people insist that they'll always be available to help, even when they haven't been before.
c. The Cubs easily beat the Mets, who were in trouble early in the game today at Wrigley Field.
d. We worked out the problems in our relationship.
e. My mother accused me of evading her questions when in fact I was just saying the first thing that came to mind.

EXERCISE 19–1, page 187 *Possible revisions:*

a. Listening to the CD her sister had sent, Mia was overcome with a mix of emotions: happiness, homesickness, and nostalgia.
b. Cortés and his soldiers were astonished when they looked down from the mountains and saw Tenochtitlán, the magnificent capital of the Aztecs.
c. Although my spoken Spanish is not very good, I can read the language with ease.
d. There are several reasons for not eating meat. One reason is that dangerous chemicals are used throughout the various stages of meat production.
e. To learn how to sculpt beauty from everyday life is my intention in studying art and archaeology.

EXERCISE 20–1, page 193 *Possible revisions:*

a. The city had one public swimming pool that stayed packed with children all summer long.
b. The building is being renovated, so at times we have no heat, water, or electricity.
c. The view was not what the travel agent had described. Where were the rolling hills and the shimmering rivers?
d. All those gnarled equations looked like toxic insects; maybe I was going to have to rethink my major.
e. City officials had good reason to fear a major earthquake: Most [*or* most] of the business district was built on landfill.

EXERCISE 20–2, page 194 *Possible revisions:*

a. Wind power for the home is a supplementary source of energy that can be combined with electricity, gas, or solar energy.
b. Correct
c. In the Middle Ages, when the streets of London were dangerous places, it was safer to travel by boat along the Thames.
d. "He's not drunk," I said. "He's in a state of diabetic shock."
e. Are you able to endure extreme angle turns, high speeds, frequent jumps, and occasional crashes? Then supermoto racing may be a sport for you.

EXERCISE 21–2, page 206

a. One of the main reasons for elephant poaching is the profits received from selling the ivory tusks.
b. Correct
c. A number of students in the seminar were aware of the importance of joining the discussion.
d. Batik cloth from Bali, blue and white ceramics from Delft, and a bocce ball from Turin have made Angelie's room the talk of the dorm.
e. Correct

EXERCISE 22–1, page 211 *Possible revisions:*

a. Every presidential candidate must appeal to a wide variety of ethnic and social groups to win the election.
b. David lent his motorcycle to someone who allowed a friend to use it.
c. The aerobics teacher motioned for all the students to move their arms in wide, slow circles.
d. Correct
e. Applicants should be bilingual if they want to qualify for this position.

EXERCISE 23–1, page 216   *Possible revisions:*

a. Some professors say that engineering students should have hands-on experience with dismantling and reassembling machines.
b. Because she had decorated her living room with posters from chamber music festivals, her date thought that she was interested in classical music. Actually she preferred rock.
c. In my high school, students didn't need to get all A's to be considered a success; they just needed to work to their ability.
d. Marianne told Jenny, "I am worried about your mother's illness." [*or* ". . . about my mother's illness."]
e. Though Lewis cried for several minutes after scraping his knee, eventually his crying subsided.

EXERCISE 24–1, page 221

a. Correct [But the writer could change the end of the sentence: . . . *than he is.*]
b. Correct [But the writer could change the end of the sentence: . . . *that she was the coach.*]
c. She appreciated his telling the truth in such a difficult situation.
d. The director has asked you and me to draft a proposal for a new recycling plan.
e. Five close friends and I rented a station wagon, packed it with food, and drove two hundred miles to Mardi Gras.

EXERCISE 25–1, page 225

a. The roundtable featured scholars whom I had never heard of. [*or* . . . scholars I had never heard of.]
b. Correct
c. Correct
d. Daniel always gives a holiday donation to whoever needs it.
e. So many singers came to the audition that Natalia had trouble deciding whom to select for the choir.

EXERCISE 26–1, page 231   *Possible revisions:*

a. Did you do well on last week's chemistry exam?
b. With the budget deadline approaching, our office has hardly had time to handle routine correspondence.
c. Correct
d. The customer complained that he hadn't been treated nicely.
e. Of all my relatives, Uncle Roberto is the cleverest.

EXERCISE 27–1, page 237

a. When I get the urge to exercise, I lie down until it passes.
b. Grandmother had driven our new hybrid to the sunrise church service on Savage Mountain, so we were left with the station wagon.
c. A pile of dirty rags was lying at the bottom of the stairs.
d. How did the game know that the player had gone from the room with the blue ogre to the hall where the gold was heaped?
e. Abraham Lincoln took good care of his legal clients; the contracts he drew for the Illinois Central Railroad could never be broken.

EXERCISE 27–2, page 242

a. The glass sculptures of the Swan Boats were prominent in the brightly lit lobby.
b. Visitors to the glass museum were not supposed to touch the exhibits.
c. Our church has all the latest technology, even a closed-circuit television.
d. Christos didn't know about Marlo's promotion because he never listens. He is [*or* He's] always talking.
e. Correct

EXERCISE 27–3, page 250 *Possible revisions:*

a. Correct
b. Watson and Crick discovered the mechanism that controls inheritance in all life: the workings of the DNA molecule.
c. When city planners proposed rezoning the waterfront, did they know that the mayor had promised to curb development in that neighborhood?
d. Correct
e. Correct

EXERCISE 28–1, page 257

a. In the past, tobacco companies denied any connection between smoking and health problems.
b. There is nothing in the world that TV has not touched on.
c. I want to register for a summer tutoring session.
d. By the end of the year, the state will have tested 139 birds for avian flu.
e. The benefits of eating fruits and vegetables have been promoted by health care providers.

EXERCISE 28–2, page 258

a. A major league pitcher can throw a baseball more than ninety-five miles per hour.
b. The writing center tutor will help you revise your essay.
c. A reptile must adjust its body temperature to its environment.
d. Correct
e. My uncle, a cartoonist, could sketch a face in less than two minutes.

EXERCISE 28–3, page 264 *Possible revisions:*

a. The electrician might have discovered the broken circuit if she had gone through the modules one at a time.
b. If Verena wins a scholarship, she will go to graduate school.
c. Whenever there is a fire in our neighborhood, everybody comes out to watch.
d. Sarah did not understand the terms of her internship.
e. If I lived in Budapest with my cousin Szusza, she would teach me Hungarian cooking.

EXERCISE 28–4, page 267 *Possible answers:*

a. I enjoy riding my motorcycle.
b. The tutor told Samantha to come to the writing center.
c. The team hopes to work hard and win the championship.
d. Ricardo and his brothers miss surfing during the winter.
e. The babysitter let Roger stay up until midnight.

EXERCISE 29–1, page 275

a. Doing volunteer work often brings satisfaction.
b. As I looked out the window of the plane, I could see Cape Cod.
c. Melina likes to drink her coffee with lots of cream.
d. Correct
e. I completed my homework assignment quickly. *Or* I completed the homework assignment quickly.

EXERCISE 30–1, page 280

a. There are some cartons of ice cream in the freezer.
b. I don't use the subway because I am afraid.
c. The prime minister is the most popular leader in my country.
d. We tried to get in touch with the same manager whom we spoke to earlier.
e. Recently there have been a number of earthquakes in Turkey.

EXERCISE 30–2, page 282 *Possible revisions:*

a. Although freshwater freezes at 32° Fahrenheit, ocean water freezes at 28° Fahrenheit.
b. Because we switched cable packages, our channel lineup has changed.
c. The competitor confidently mounted his skateboard.
d. My sister performs the *legong*, a Balinese dance, well.
e. Correct

EXERCISE 30–3, page 284

a. Listening to everyone's complaints all day was irritating.
b. The long flight to Singapore was exhausting.
c. Correct
d. After a great deal of research, the scientist made a fascinating discovery.
e. Surviving that tornado was one of the most frightening experiences I've ever had.

EXERCISE 30–4, page 285

a. an intelligent young Vietnamese woman; b. a dedicated Catholic priest;
c. her old blue wool sweater; d. Joe's delicious Scandinavian bread; e. many beautiful antique jewelry boxes

EXERCISE 31–1, page 287

a. Whenever we eat at the Centerville Café, we sit at a small table in the corner of the room.
b. Correct
c. On Thursday, Nancy will attend her first home repair class at the community center.
d. Correct
e. We decided to go to a restaurant because there was no fresh food in the refrigerator.

EXERCISE 32–1, page 294

a. Alisa brought the injured bird home and fashioned a splint out of Popsicle sticks for its wing.
b. Considered a classic of early animation, *The Adventures of Prince Achmed* used hand-cut silhouettes against colored backgrounds.

c. If you complete the evaluation form and return it within two weeks, you will receive a free breakfast during your next stay.

d. Correct

e. Roger had always wanted a handmade violin, but he couldn't afford one.

EXERCISE 32–2, page 294

a. J. R. R. Tolkien finished writing his draft of *The Lord of the Rings* trilogy in 1949, but the first book in the series wasn't published until 1954.

b. In the first two minutes of its ascent, the space shuttle had broken the sound barrier and reached a height of over twenty-five miles.

c. German shepherds can be gentle guide dogs, or they can be fierce attack dogs.

d. Some former professional cyclists claim that the use of performance-enhancing drugs is widespread in cycling, and they argue that no rider can be competitive without doping.

e. As an intern, I learned most aspects of the broadcasting industry, but I never learned about fundraising.

EXERCISE 32–3, page 297

a. The cold, impersonal atmosphere of the university was unbearable.

b. An ambulance threaded its way through police cars, fire trucks, and irate citizens.

c. Correct

d. After two broken arms, three cracked ribs, and one concussion, Ken quit the varsity football team.

e. Correct

EXERCISE 32–4, page 297

a. NASA's rovers on Mars are equipped with special cameras that can take close-up, high-resolution pictures of the terrain.

b. Correct

c. Correct

d. Love, vengeance, greed, and betrayal are common themes in Western literature.

e. Many experts believe that shark attacks on surfers are a result of the sharks' mistaking surfboards for small injured seals.

EXERCISE 32–5, page 302

a. Choreographer Alvin Ailey's best-known work, *Revelations*, is more than just a crowd-pleaser.

b. Correct

c. Correct

d. A member of an organization that provides job training for teens was also appointed to the education commission.

e. Brian Eno, who began his career as a rock musician, turned to meditative compositions in the late seventies.

EXERCISE 32–6, page 307

a. Cricket, which originated in England, is also popular in Australia, South Africa, and India.

b. At the sound of the starting pistol, the horses surged forward toward the first obstacle, a sharp incline three feet high.

c. After seeing an exhibition of Western art, Gerhard Richter escaped from East Berlin and smuggled out many of his notebooks.

d. Corrie's new wet suit has an intricate blue pattern.
e. The cookies will keep for two weeks in sturdy, airtight containers.

EXERCISE 32–7, page 307

a. On January 15, 2008, our office moved to 29 Commonwealth Avenue, Mechanicsville, VA 23111.
b. Correct
c. Ms. Carlson, you are a valued customer whose satisfaction is very important to us.
d. Mr. Mundy was born on July 22, 1939, in Arkansas, where his family had lived for four generations.
e. Correct

EXERCISE 33–1, page 313

a. Correct
b. Tricia's first artwork was a bright blue clay dolphin.
c. Some modern musicians (trumpeter John Hassell is an example) blend several cultural traditions into a unique sound.
d. Myra liked hot, spicy foods such as chili, kung pao chicken, and buffalo wings.
e. On the display screen was a soothing pattern of light and shadow.

EXERCISE 34–1, page 317

a. Do not ask me to be kind; just ask me to act as though I were.
b. When men talk about defense, they always claim to be protecting women and children, but they never ask the women and children what they think.
c. When I get a little money, I buy books; if any is left, I buy food and clothes.
d. Correct
e. Wit has truth in it; wisecracking is simply calisthenics with words.

EXERCISE 34–2, page 318

a. Strong black coffee will not sober you up; the truth is that time is the only way to get alcohol out of your system.
b. Margaret was not surprised to see hail and vivid lightning; conditions had been right for violent weather all day.
c. There is often a fine line between right and wrong, good and bad, truth and deception.
d. Correct
e. Severe, unremitting pain is a ravaging force, especially when the patient tries to hide it from others.

EXERCISE 35–1, page 320

a. Correct [Either *It* or *it* is correct.]
b. If we have come to fight, we are far too few; if we have come to die, we are far too many.
c. The travel package includes a round-trip ticket to Athens, a cruise through the Cyclades, and all hotel accommodations.
d. The news article portrays the land use proposal as reckless, although 62 percent of the town's residents support it.

e. Psychologists Kindlon and Thompson (2000) offer parents a simple start-ing point for raising male children: "Teach boys that there are many ways to be a man" (p. 256).

EXERCISE 36–1, page 325

a. Correct
b. The innovative shoe fastener was inspired by the designer's young son.
c. Each day's menu features a different European country's dish.
d. Sue worked overtime to increase her family's earnings.
e. Ms. Jacobs is unwilling to listen to students' complaints about computer failures.

EXERCISE 37–1, page 331

a. As for the advertisement "Sailors have more fun," if you consider chip-ping paint and swabbing decks fun, then you will have plenty of it.
b. Correct
c. After winning the lottery, Juanita said that she would give half the money to charity.
d. After the movie, Vicki said, "The reviewer called this flick 'trash of the first order.' I guess you can't believe everything you read."
e. Correct

EXERCISE 39–1, page 339

a. A client left his or her [*or* a] cell phone in our conference room after the meeting.
b. The films we made of Kilauea on our trip to Hawaii Volcanoes National Park illustrate a typical spatter cone eruption.
c. Correct
d. Correct
e. Of three engineering fields — chemical, mechanical, and materials — Keegan chose materials engineering for its application to toy manufacturing.

EXERCISE 40–1, page 344

a. Correct
b. Some combat soldiers are trained by government diplomats to be sensi-tive to issues of culture, history, and religion.
c. Correct
d. How many pounds have you lost since you began running four miles a day?
e. Denzil spent all night studying for his psychology exam.

EXERCISE 41–1, page 346

a. The carpenters located three maple timbers, twenty-one sheets of cherry, and ten oblongs of polished ebony for the theater set.
b. Correct
c. Correct
d. Eight students in the class had been labeled "learning disabled."
e. The Vietnam Veterans Memorial in Washington, DC, had 58,132 names inscribed on it when it was dedicated in 1982.

EXERCISE 42–1, page 349

a. Howard Hughes commissioned the *Spruce Goose*, a beautifully built but thoroughly impractical wooden aircraft.

b. The old man screamed his anger, shouting to all of us, "I will not leave my money to you worthless layabouts!"

c. I learned the Latin term *ad infinitum* from an old nursery rhyme about fleas: "Great fleas have little fleas upon their back to bite 'em, / Little fleas have lesser fleas and so on *ad infinitum*."

d. Correct

e. Neve Campbell's lifelong interest in ballet inspired her involvement in the film *The Company*, which portrays a season with the Joffrey Ballet.

EXERCISE 44–1, page 361

a. Correct

b. The swiftly moving tugboat pulled alongside the barge and directed it away from the oil spill in the harbor.

c. Correct

d. Your dog is well known in our neighborhood.

e. Roadblocks were set up along all the major highways leading out of the city.

EXERCISE 45–1, page 365

a. Assistant Dean Shirin Ahmadi recommended offering more world language courses.

b. Correct

c. Kalindi has an ambitious semester, studying differential calculus, classical Hebrew, brochure design, and Greek literature.

d. Lydia's aunt and uncle make modular houses as beautiful as modernist works of art.

e. We amused ourselves on the long flight by discussing how spring in Kyoto stacks up against summer in London.

EXERCISE 46–1, page 368

a. stage, confrontation, proportions; b. courage, mountain (noun/adjective), climber, inspiration, rescuers; c. need, guest, honor, fog; d. defense (noun/adjective), attorney, appeal, jury; e. museum, women (noun/adjective), artists, 1987

EXERCISE 46–2, page 371

a. his; b. that, our (pronoun/adjective); c. that, he, himself, some, his (pronoun/adjective); d. I, my (pronoun/adjective), you, one; e. no one, her

EXERCISE 46–3, page 373

a. told; b. were, killed; c. brought down; d. Stay, 'll [will] arrive; e. struggled, was trapped

EXERCISE 46–4, page 375

a. Adjectives: weak, unfocused; b. Adjectives: The (article), Spanish, flexible; adverb: wonderfully; c. Adjectives: The (article), fragrant, the (article), steady; adverb: especially; d. Adjectives: hot, cold; adverbs: rather, slightly, bitterly; e. Adjectives: The (article), its (pronoun/adjective), wicker (noun/adjective); adverb: soundly

EXERCISE 47–1, page 383

a. Complete subjects: The hills and mountains, the snow atop them; simple subjects: hills, mountains, snow; b. Complete subject: points; simple subject:

points; c. Complete subject: (You); d. Complete subject: hundreds of fire-flies; simple subject: hundreds; e. Complete subject: The evidence against the defendant; simple subject: evidence

EXERCISE 47–2, page 387

a. Subject complement: expensive; b. Direct object: death; c. Direct object: their players' efforts; d. Subject complement: the capital of the Russian Empire; e. Subject complement: bitter

EXERCISE 47–3, page 387

a. Direct objects: adults and children; object complement: weary; b. Direct object: community service; object complement: her priority; c. Direct object: the work; object complement: finished; d. Indirect objects: the agent, us; direct objects: our tickets, boarding passes; e. Indirect object: students; direct object: healthy meal choices

EXERCISE 48–1, page 391

a. In northern Italy, as their first language (adverb phrases modifying *speak*); b. through the thick forest (adjective phrase modifying *hike*); with ease (adverb phrase modifying *completed*); c. To my boss's dismay (adverb phrase modifying *was*); for work (adverb phrase modifying *late*); d. of Mayan artifacts (adjective phrase modifying *exhibit*); into pre-Columbian culture (adjective phrase modifying *insight*); e. In 2002, in twelve European countries (adverb phrases modifying *became*)

EXERCISE 48–2, page 394

a. Updating your software (gerund phrase used as subject); b. decreasing the town budget (gerund phrase used as object of the preposition *in*); identifying nonessential services (gerund phrase used as subject complement); c. to help her mother by raking the lawn (infinitive phrase used as direct object); raking the lawn (gerund phrase used as object of the preposition *by*); d. Understanding little (participial phrase modifying *I*); passing my biology final (gerund phrase used as object of the preposition *of*); e. Working with animals (gerund phrase used as subject)

EXERCISE 48–3, page 397

a. so that every vote would count (adverb clause modifying *adjusted*); b. that targets baby boomers (adjective clause modifying *campaign*); c. After the Tambora volcano erupted in the southern Pacific in 1815 (adverb clause modifying *realized*); that it would contribute to the "year without a summer" in Europe and North America (noun clause used as direct object of *realized*); d. that at a certain point there will be no more oil to extract from the earth (noun clause used as direct object of *implies*); e. when you are rushing (adverb clause modifying *are overlooked*)

EXERCISE 49–1, page 400

a. Complex; that are ignited in dry areas (adjective clause); b. Compound; c. Simple; d. Complex; Before we leave for the station (adverb clause); e. Compound-complex; when you want to leave (noun clause)

Acknowledgments

Scott Adams, "Dilbert and the Way of the Weasel." Copyright © 2000 by United Feature Syndicate. Reprinted with permission of United Media.

Jonathan Adler, excerpt from "Little Green Lies." Copyright © 1992 *Policy Review*. Reprinted by permission.

Nelson W. Aldrich, Jr., excerpt from "Old Money."

American Heritage Dictionary, definition for "regard" from *The American Heritage Dictionary of the English Language, Fourth Edition*. Copyright © 2010 by Houghton Mifflin Harcourt Publishing Company. Reproduced by permission from The American Heritage Dictionary of the English Language, Fourth Edition.

Eugene Boe, excerpt from "Pioneers to Eternity: Norwegians on the Prairie" from *The Immigrant Experience*, edited by Thomas C. Wheeler. Copyright © 1971 by Doubleday, a division of Random House, Inc. Used by permission of Doubleday, a division of Random House, Inc.

Carl Botan and Mihaela Vorvoreanu, excerpt from "What Do Employees Think about Electronic Surveillance at Work?" p. 126.

Jane Brody, excerpt from *Jane Brody's Nutrition Book*. Copyright © 1981 W. W. Norton & Company.

Bruce Catton, excerpt from "Grant and Lee: A Study in Contrasts."

Napolean A. Chagnon, excerpt from *Yanomamo: The Fierce People*. Copyright © 1992 Harcourt Brace College Publishers.

Barnaby Conrad III, excerpt from "Train of Kings."

Earl Conrad, excerpt from *Harriet Tubman*. Copyright © 1943 Associated Publishers.

James Crocket et al., excerpt from *Wildflower Gardening*. Copyright © 1977 Time-Life Education.

EBSCO Information Services, various screen shots. Reprinted with permission of EBSCO Information Services.

Equal Exchange, Inc., coffee advertisement. Copyright © Equal Exchange, Inc. Reprinted by permission.

Thomas L. Friedman, screen shots of the copyright page and title page from *Hot, Flat, and Crowded: Why We Need a Green Revolution — And How It Can Renew America*. Copyright © 2008 by Thomas Friedman. Reprinted by permission of Farrar, Straus & Giroux, LLC.

Gale, screen shot from Academic OneFile. Reprinted with permission from Cengage Learning.

Jane Goodall, excerpt from *In the Shadow of Man*. Copyright © 2010 Mariner Books, 50th Anniversary of Gombe Edition.

Stephen Jay Gould, excerpt from "Were Dinosaurs Dumb?" *Natural History* 87.5: 9–16. Reprinted by permission of Rhonda R. Shearer.

Dan Gutman, excerpt from "The Way Baseball Works."

Hillary Hauser, excerpt from "Exploring a Sunken Realm in Australia."

Richart Hofstadter, excerpt from "America at 1750."

Lynn Hunt et al., map, "Castile and Portugal" from *The Making of the West, Volume II*. Copyright © 2005 by Bedford/St. Martin's. Reprinted by permission of Bedford/St. Martin's.

International Monetary Fund, graph "Wishing-well," GDP forecasts, percentage increase on previous year. Source: International Monetary Fund.

Henry J. Kaiser Family Foundation, excerpt from "The Role of Media in Childhood Obesity" (2004), p. 1 (#7030). Copyright © 2004 by The Henry J. Kaiser Family Foundation. This information was reprinted with permission from the Henry J. Kaiser Family Foundation. The Kaiser Family Foundation is a non-profit private operating foundation, based in Menlo Park, California, dedicated to producing and communicating the best possible analysis and information on health issues.

Dorling Kindersley, excerpt from *Encyclopedia of Fishing*. Copyright © 1994 by DK Publishing.

Frederic Lane, excerpt from *The Naked Employee: How Technology Is Compromising Workplace Privacy*, p. 142. Copyright © AMACOM.

Shirley Geok-lin Lim (book), Mitsuye Tamada (selection), screen shots of the title page and first page of selection, "Guilty on Both Counts" from *Asian American Literature, An Anthology*. Copyright © 2000 NTC/Contemporary Publishing Company; Teachers Edition.

Robert MacNeil and William Cran, excerpt from *Do You Speak American?* Copyright © 2004 by Neely Productions, Inc. and William Cran. Used by permission of Doubleday, a division of Random House, Inc.

Margaret Mead, excerpt from "New Superstitions for Old."

Chris Meleksi, excerpt from student essay.

Merriam-Webster Online, screen shot of dictionary entry for "regard." Reprinted by permission from *Merriam-Webster's Collegiate Dictionary, 11th Edition*. Copyright © 2011 by Merriam-Webster, Incorporated (www.Merriam-Webster.com).

Minnesota Department of Health, browser printout of Web site and on-screen view of document from Minnesota Department of Health.

The New Bedford Whaling Museum & Old Dartmouth Historical Society, screen shot from "Overview of American Whaling" with internal page and footer. Reprinted with permission from The New Bedford Whaling Museum & Old Dartmouth Historical Society.

The New York Times, link to embedded online article "Window into Fed Debate over a Crucial Program" www.newyorktimes.com 10/14/09. (A version of this article appeared in print on October 15, 2009 on page 83 of the New York edition.)

Chet Raymo, excerpt from "Curious Stuff, Water and Ice."

Anne and Jack Rudloe, excerpt from "Electric Warfare: The Fish That Kill with Thunderbolts" from *Smithsonian* 24.5: 95–105.

Constance M. Ruzich, screen shots of the title page and first page of "For the Love of Joe: The Language of Starbucks" from *The Journal of Popular Culture* 41.3 (2008).

Ray Rychnovsky, excerpt from "Clawing into Controversy" from *Outdoor Life* (Jan. 1995): 40. Copyright © 1995 by Bonnier Corporation. Reproduced with permission of Bonnier Corporation in the format Textbook and Other book via Copyright Clearance Center.

Michael J. Sandel, excerpt from "The Case against Perfection." *The Atlantic Monthly* 293.3 (April 2004).

Index

J

O

S

Multilingual/ESL Menu

Writing *Chicago* Papers

From *The Bedford Handbook,*
Eighth Edition

Diana Hacker

Nancy Sommers
Harvard University

Writing *Chicago* Papers

57 *Chicago* papers

Most history instructors and some humanities instructors require you to document sources with footnotes or endnotes based on *The Chicago Manual of Style*, 16th ed. (Chicago: U of Chicago P, 2010). (See 57f.)

When you write a paper using sources, you face three main challenges: (1) supporting a thesis, (2) citing your sources and avoiding plagiarism, and (3) integrating quotations and other source material.

57a Supporting a thesis

Most research assignments ask you to form a thesis, or main idea, and to support that thesis with well-organized evidence. Remain flexible as you draft because you may need to revise your approach later. Writing about a subject is a way of learning about it; as you write, your understanding of your subject will almost certainly deepen.

Forming a working thesis

Once you have read a variety of sources and considered your issue from different perspectives, you are ready to form a working thesis: a one-sentence (or occasionally a two-sentence) statement of your central idea. Because it is a working, or tentative, thesis, it is flexible enough to change as your ideas develop. Ultimately, the thesis expresses not just your opinion but your informed, reasoned judgment.

In a research paper, your thesis will answer the central research question that you posed earlier. Here, for example, are student writer Ned Bishop's research question and working thesis statement.

RESEARCH QUESTION

To what extent was Confederate Major General Nathan Bedford Forrest responsible for the massacre of Union troops at Fort Pillow?

WORKING THESIS

By encouraging racism among his troops, Nathan Bedford Forrest was directly responsible for the massacre of Union troops at Fort Pillow.

Notice that the thesis expresses a view on a debatable issue—an issue about which intelligent, well-meaning people might disagree. The writer's job is to convince such readers that this view is worth taking seriously.

The thesis usually appears at the end of the introductory paragraph. To read Ned Bishop's thesis in the context of his introduction, see page 719.

Organizing your ideas

The body of your paper will consist of evidence in support of your thesis. Instead of getting tangled up in a complex, formal outline, sketch an informal plan that organizes your evidence in bold strokes. Ned Bishop, for example, used a simple outline to structure his ideas. In the paper itself, these points became headings that helped readers follow his line of argument.

What happened at Fort Pillow?

Did Forrest order the massacre?

Can Forrest be held responsible for the massacre?

hackerhandbooks.com/bedhandbook > Research exercises
> *Chicago* > E-ex 57–1 and 57–2

Using sources to inform and support your argument

Used thoughtfully, the source materials you have gathered will make your argument more complex and convincing for readers. Sources can play several different roles as you develop your points.

Providing background information or context   You can use facts and statistics to support generalizations or to establish the importance of your topic, as student writer Ned Bishop does early in his paper.

> Fort Pillow, Tennessee, which sat on a bluff overlooking the Mississippi River, had been held by the Union for two years. It was garrisoned by 580 men, 292 of them from United States Colored Heavy and Light Artillery regiments, 285 from the white Thirteenth Tennessee Cavalry. Nathan Bedford Forrest commanded about 1,500 troops.[1]

Explaining terms or concepts   If readers are unlikely to be familiar with a word or an idea important to your topic, you must explain it for them. Quoting or paraphrasing a source can help you define terms and concepts clearly and concisely.

> The Civil War practice of giving no quarter to an enemy—in other words, "denying [an enemy] the right of survival"—defied Lincoln's mandate for humane and merciful treatment of prisoners.[9]

Supporting your claims As you draft your argument, make sure to back up your assertions with facts, examples, and other evidence from your research. Ned Bishop, for example, uses an eyewitness report of the racially motivated violence perpetrated by Nathan Bedford Forrest's troops.

> The slaughter at Fort Pillow was no doubt driven in large part by racial hatred. . . . A Southern reporter traveling with Forrest makes clear that the discrimination was deliberate: "Our troops maddened by the excitement, shot down the ret[r]eating Yankees, and not until they had attained t[h]e water's edge and turned to beg for mercy, did any prisoners fall in [t]o our hands— Thus the whites received quarter, but the negroes were shown no mercy."[19]

Lending authority to your argument Expert opinion can give weight to your argument. But don't rely on experts to make your argument for you. Construct your argument in your own words and, when appropriate, cite the judgment of an authority in the field to support your position.

> Fort Pillow is not the only instance of a massacre or threatened massacre of black soldiers by troops under Forrest's command. Biographer Brian Steel Wills points out that at Brice's Cross Roads in June 1864, "black soldiers suffered inordinately" as Forrest looked the other way and Confederate soldiers deliberately sought out those they termed "the damned negroes."[21]

Anticipating and countering objections Do not ignore sources that seem contrary to your position or that offer arguments different from your own. Instead, use them to give voice to opposing points of view and to state potential objections to your arguments before you counter them. Readers often have opposing points of view in mind already, whether or not they agree with you. Ned Bishop, for example, presents conflicting evidence to acknowledge that some readers may credit Nathan

Bedford Forrest with stopping the massacre. In doing so, Bishop creates an opportunity to counter that objection and persuade those readers that Forrest can be held accountable.

> Hurst suggests that the temperamental Forrest "may have ragingly ordered a massacre and even intended to carry it out— until he rode inside the fort and viewed the horrifying result" and ordered it stopped.[15] While this is an intriguing interpretation of events, even Hurst would probably admit that it is merely speculation.

57b Citing sources; avoiding plagiarism

In a research paper, you will draw on the work of other writers, and you must document their contributions by citing your sources. Sources are cited for two reasons:

- to tell readers where your information comes from—so that they can assess its reliability and, if interested, find and read the original source
- to give credit to the writers from whom you have borrowed words and ideas

Borrowing another writer's language, sentence structures, or ideas without proper acknowledgment is a form of dishonesty known as *plagiarism.*

Using the Chicago *system for citing sources*

You must include a citation when you quote from a source, when you summarize or paraphrase a source, and when you borrow facts that are not common knowledge. (See also "Avoiding plagiarism" on p. 690.)

Chicago citations consist of superscript numbers in the text of the paper that refer readers to notes with corresponding numbers either at the foot of the page (footnotes) or at the end of the paper (endnotes).

TEXT

Governor John Andrew was not allowed to recruit black soldiers from out of state. "Ostensibly," writes Peter Burchard, "no recruiting was done outside Massachusetts, but it was an open secret that Andrew's agents were working far and wide."[1]

NOTE

    1. Peter Burchard, *One Gallant Rush: Robert Gould Shaw and His Brave Black Regiment* (New York: St. Martin's, 1965), 85.

For detailed advice on using *Chicago*-style notes, see 57d. When you use footnotes or endnotes, you will usually need to provide a bibliography as well (see p. 716).

Avoiding plagiarism

Your research paper is a collaboration between you and your sources. To be fair and ethical, you must acknowledge your debt to the writers of those sources. If you don't, you commit plagiarism, a serious academic offense.

In general, these three acts are considered plagiarism: (1) failing to cite quotations and borrowed ideas, (2) failing to enclose borrowed language in quotation marks, and (3) failing to put summaries and paraphrases in your own words. Definitions of plagiarism may vary; it's a good idea to find out how your school defines academic dishonesty.

Citing quotations and borrowed ideas You must cite all direct quotations. You must also cite any ideas you borrow from a source: summaries and paraphrases; statistics and other specific facts; and visuals such as cartoons, graphs, and diagrams.

The only exception is common knowledge—information your readers could easily find in any number of general sources. For example, most encyclopedias will tell readers that the Korean War ended in 1953 and that President Theodore Roosevelt was the first American to receive the Nobel Prize.

As a rule, when you have seen certain general information repeatedly in your reading, you don't need to cite it. However, when information has appeared in only a few sources, when it is highly specific (as with statistics), or when it is controversial, you should cite the source. If a topic is new to you and you are not sure what is considered common knowledge or what is controversial, ask your instructor or someone else with expertise. When in doubt, cite the source. (See 57d for details.)

Enclosing borrowed language in quotation marks   To indicate that you are using a source's exact phrases or sentences, you must enclose them in quotation marks unless they have been set off from the text by indenting (see p. 695). To omit the quotation marks is to claim—falsely—that the language is your own. Such an omission is plagiarism even if you have cited the source.

ORIGINAL SOURCE

For many Southerners it was psychologically impossible to see a black man bearing arms as anything but an incipient slave uprising complete with arson, murder, pillage, and rapine.
—Dudley Taylor Cornish, *The Sable Arm*, p. 158

PLAGIARISM

According to Civil War historian Dudley Taylor Cornish, for many Southerners it was psychologically impossible to see a black man bearing arms as anything but an incipient slave uprising complete with arson, murder, pillage, and rapine.[2]

BORROWED LANGUAGE IN QUOTATION MARKS

According to Civil War historian Dudley Taylor Cornish, "For many Southerners it was psychologically impossible to see a black man bearing arms as anything but an incipient slave uprising complete with arson, murder, pillage, and rapine."[2]

Putting summaries and paraphrases in your own words   Summaries and paraphrases are written in your own words. A summary condenses information; a paraphrase uses roughly the same number of words as the original source to convey the information. When you summarize or paraphrase, it is not enough to name the source; you must restate the source's meaning using your own language. You commit plagiarism if you half-copy the author's sentences—either by mixing the author's phrases with your own without using quotation marks or by plugging your own synonyms into the author's sentence structure.

The first paraphrase of the following source is plagiarized—even though the source is cited—because too much of its language is borrowed from the original. The underlined strings of words have been copied exactly (without quotation marks). In addition, the writer has closely followed the sentence structure of the original source, merely making a few substitutions (such as *Fifty percent* for *Half* and *angered and perhaps frightened* for *enraged and perhaps terrified*).

ORIGINAL SOURCE

Half of the force holding Fort Pillow were Negroes, former slaves now enrolled in the Union Army. Toward them Forrest's troops had the fierce, bitter animosity of men who had been educated to regard the colored race as inferior and who for the first time had encountered that race armed and fighting against white men. The sight enraged and perhaps terrified many of the Confederates and aroused in them the ugly spirit of a lynching mob.

—Albert Castel, "The Fort Pillow Massacre," pp. 46–47

PLAGIARISM: UNACCEPTABLE BORROWING

Albert Castel suggests that much of the brutality at Fort Pillow can be traced to racial attitudes. Fifty percent of the troops <u>holding Fort Pillow were Negroes, former slaves</u> who had joined the Union Army. <u>Toward them Forrest's</u> soldiers displayed the savage hatred of men who had been taught the inferiority of blacks and <u>who for the first time had</u> confronted them <u>armed and fighting against white men.</u> The vision angered and perhaps frightened the Confederates and <u>aroused in them the ugly spirit of a lynching mob.</u>[3]

To avoid plagiarizing an author's language, resist the temptation to look at the source while you are summarizing or paraphrasing. After you have read the passage you want to paraphrase, set the source aside. Ask yourself, "What is the author's meaning?" In your own words, state your understanding of the author's basic point. Return to the source and check that you haven't used the author's language or sentence structure or misrepresented the author's ideas. Following these steps will help you avoid plagiarizing the source. When you fully understand another writer's meaning, you can more easily and accurately represent those ideas in your own words.

ACCEPTABLE PARAPHRASE

Albert Castel suggests that much of the brutality at Fort Pillow can be traced to racial attitudes. Fifty percent of the Union troops were blacks, men whom the Confederates had been raised to consider their inferiors. The shock and perhaps fear of facing armed ex-slaves in battle may well have unleashed the fury that led to the massacre.[3]

hackerhandbooks.com/bedhandbook > Research exercises
> *Chicago* > E-ex 57–3 to 57–7

57c Integrating sources

Quotations, summaries, paraphrases, and facts will support your argument, but they cannot speak for you. You can use several strategies to integrate information from research sources into your paper while maintaining your own voice.

Using quotations appropriately

In your academic writing, keep the emphasis on your ideas and your language; use your own words to summarize and to paraphrase your sources and to explain your points. Sometimes, however, quotations can be the most effective way to integrate a source.

WHEN TO USE QUOTATIONS

- When language is especially vivid or expressive
- When exact wording is needed for technical accuracy

- When it is important to let the debaters of an issue explain their positions in their own words
- When the words of an authority lend weight to an argument
- When the language of a source is the topic of your discussion (as in an analysis or interpretation)

Limiting your use of quotations   Although it is tempting to insert many quotations in your paper and to use your own words only for connecting passages, do not quote excessively. It is almost impossible to integrate numerous quotations smoothly into your own text.

It is not always necessary to quote full sentences from a source. To reduce your reliance on the words of others, you can often integrate language from a source into your own sentence structure.

> As Hurst has pointed out, until "an outcry erupted in the Northern press," even the Confederates did not deny that there had been a massacre at Fort Pillow.[4]

> Union surgeon Dr. Charles Fitch testified that after he was in custody he "saw" Confederate soldiers "kill every negro that made his appearance dressed in Federal uniform."[20]

Using the ellipsis mark   To condense a quoted passage, you can use the ellipsis mark (three periods, with spaces between) to indicate that you have left words out. What remains must be grammatically complete.

> Union surgeon Fitch's testimony that all women and children had been evacuated from Fort Pillow before the attack conflicts with Forrest's report: "We captured . . . about 40 negro women and children."[6]

The writer has omitted several words not relevant to the issue at hand: *164 Federals, 75 negro troops, and.*

When you want to leave out one or more full sentences, use a period before the three ellipsis dots. For an example, see the long quotation at the bottom of page 695.

Ordinarily, do not use the ellipsis mark at the beginning or at the end of a quotation. Readers will understand that the quoted material is taken from a longer passage, so such marks are not necessary. The only exception occurs when you have dropped words at the end of the final quoted sentence. In such cases, put three ellipsis dots before the closing quotation mark.

Make sure omissions and ellipsis marks do not distort the meaning of your source.

Using brackets Brackets allow you to insert words of your own into quoted material to clarify a confusing reference or to keep a sentence grammatical in your context.

> According to Albert Castel, "It can be reasonably argued that he [Forrest] was justified in believing that the approaching steamships intended to aid the garrison [at Fort Pillow]."[7]

NOTE: Use the word *sic* in brackets to indicate that an error in a quoted sentence appears in the original source. (An example appears on p. 696.) Do not overuse *sic* to call attention to errors in a source. Sometimes paraphrasing is a better option.

Setting off long quotations *Chicago* style allows you some leeway in deciding whether to set off a long quotation or run it into your text. For emphasis, you may want to set off a quotation of more than four or five typed lines of text; almost certainly you should set off quotations of ten or more lines. To set off a quotation, indent it one-half inch from the left margin and use the normal right margin. Double-space the indented quotation.

Long quotations should be introduced by an informative sentence, usually followed by a colon. Quotation marks are unnecessary because the indented format tells readers that the passage is taken word-for-word from the source.

> In a letter home, Confederate officer Achilles V. Clark recounted what happened at Fort Pillow:
>
> > Words cannot describe the scene. The poor deluded negroes would run up to our men fall upon their knees and with uplifted hands

scream for mercy but they were ordered to their feet and then shot down. The whitte [*sic*] men fared but little better. . . . I with several others tried to stop the butchery and at one time had partially succeeded[,] but Gen. Forrest ordered them shot down like dogs[,] and the carnage continued.[8]

Using signal phrases to integrate sources

Whenever you include a paraphrase, summary, or direct quotation of another writer in your paper, prepare your readers for it with introductory words called a *signal phrase*. A signal phrase names the author of the source and often provides some context for the source material.

When you write a signal phrase, choose a verb that is appropriate for the way you are using the source (see p. 687). Are you providing background, explaining a concept, supporting a claim, lending authority, or refuting a belief? By choosing an appropriate verb, you can make your source's role clear. See the chart on page 697 for a list of verbs commonly used in signal phrases.

Note that *Chicago* style calls for verbs in the present or present perfect tense (*points out, has pointed out*) to introduce source material unless you include a date that specifies the time of the original author's writing.

The first time you mention an author, use the full name: *Shelby Foote argues*. . . . When you refer to the author again, you may use the last name only: *Foote raises an important question.*

Marking boundaries   Readers should be able to move from your own words to the words you quote from a source without feeling a jolt. Avoid dropping quotations into the text without warning. Instead, provide clear signal phrases, usually including the author's name, to indicate the boundary between your words and the source's words. (The signal phrase is underlined in the second example.)

Using signal phrases in *Chicago* papers

To avoid monotony, try to vary both the language and the placement of your signal phrases.

Model signal phrases

In the words of historian James M. McPherson, ". . ."[1]

As Dudley Taylor Cornish has argued, ". . ."[2]

In a letter to his wife, a Confederate soldier who witnessed the massacre wrote that ". . ."[3]

". . . ," claims Benjamin Quarles.[4]

". . . ," writes Albert Castel, ". . ."[5]

Shelby Foote offers an intriguing interpretation: ". . ."[6]

Verbs in signal phrases

admits	compares	insists	rejects
agrees	confirms	notes	reports
argues	contends	observes	responds
asserts	declares	points out	suggests
believes	denies	reasons	thinks
claims	emphasizes	refutes	writes

DROPPED QUOTATION

Not surprisingly, those testifying on the Union and Confederate sides recalled events at Fort Pillow quite differently. Unionists claimed that their troops had abandoned their arms and were in full retreat. "The Confederates, however, all agreed that the Union troops retreated to the river with arms in their hands."[9]

QUOTATION WITH SIGNAL PHRASE

Not surprisingly, those testifying on the Union and Confederate sides recalled events at Fort Pillow quite differently. Unionists claimed that their troops had abandoned their arms and were in full retreat. "The Confederates, however," writes historian Albert Castel, "all agreed that the Union troops retreated to the river with arms in their hands."[9]

Using signal phrases with summaries and paraphrases   Introduce most summaries and paraphrases with a signal phrase that mentions the author and places the material in the context of your argument. Readers will then understand where the summary or paraphrase begins.

Without the signal phrase (underlined) in the following example, readers might think that only the last sentence is being cited, when in fact the whole paragraph is based on the source.

> <u>According to Jack Hurst</u>, official Confederate policy was that black soldiers were to be treated as runaway slaves; in addition, the Confederate Congress decreed that white Union officers commanding black troops be killed. Confederate Lieutenant General Kirby Smith went one step further, declaring that he would kill all captured black troops. Smith's policy never met with strong opposition from the Richmond government.[10]

Integrating statistics and other facts   When you are citing a statistic or another specific fact, a signal phrase is often not necessary. In most cases, readers will understand that the citation refers to the statistic or fact (not the whole paragraph).

> Of the 295 white troops garrisoned at Fort Pillow, 168 were taken prisoner. Black troops fared worse, with only 58 of 262 captured and most of the rest presumably killed or wounded.[12]

There is nothing wrong, however, with using a signal phrase to introduce a statistic or another fact.

Putting source material in context   Readers should not have to guess why source material appears in your paper. A signal phrase can help you make the connection between your own ideas and those of another writer by setting up how a source will contribute to your paper.

If you use another writer's words, you must explain how they relate to your point. It's a good idea to embed a quotation between sentences of your own. In addition to introducing it with a signal phrase, follow it with interpretive comments that link the source material to your paper's argument.

QUOTATION WITH EFFECTIVE CONTEXT

In a respected biography of Nathan Bedford Forrest, Hurst suggests that the temperamental Forrest "may have ragingly ordered a massacre and even intended to carry it out—until he rode inside the fort and viewed the horrifying result" and ordered it stopped.[15] While this is an intriguing interpretation of events, even Hurst would probably admit that it is merely speculation.

NOTE: When you bring other sources into a conversation about your research topic, you are synthesizing.

hackerhandbooks.com/bedhandbook > Research exercises
> *Chicago* > E-ex 57–8 to 57–11

57d *Chicago* documentation style

In history and some humanities courses, you may be asked to use the documentation system set forth in *The Chicago Manual of Style*, 16th ed. (Chicago: U of Chicago P, 2010). In *Chicago* style, superscript numbers in the text of the paper refer readers to notes with corresponding numbers either at the foot of the page (footnotes) or at the end of the paper (endnotes). A bibliography is often required as well; it appears at the end of the paper and gives publication information for all the works cited in the notes.

TEXT

A Union soldier, Jacob Thompson, claimed to have seen Forrest order the killing, but when asked to describe the six-foot-two general, he called him "a little bit of a man."[12]

FOOTNOTE OR ENDNOTE

12. Brian Steel Wills, *A Battle from the Start: The Life of Nathan Bedford Forrest* (New York: HarperCollins, 1992), 187.

BIBLIOGRAPHY ENTRY

Wills, Brian Steel. *A Battle from the Start: The Life of Nathan Bedford Forrest*. New York: HarperCollins, 1992.

First and subsequent notes for a source

The first time you cite a source, the note should include publication information for that work as well as the page number on which the passage being cited may be found.

1. Peter Burchard, *One Gallant Rush: Robert Gould Shaw and His Brave Black Regiment* (New York: St. Martin's, 1965), 85.

For subsequent references to a source you have already cited, you may simply give the author's last name, a short form of the title, and the page or pages cited. A short form of the title of a book is italicized; a short form of the title of an article is put in quotation marks.

4. Burchard, *One Gallant Rush*, 31.

When you have two consecutive notes from the same source, you may use "Ibid." (meaning "in the same place") and the page number for the second note. Use "Ibid." alone if the page number is the same.

5. Jack Hurst, *Nathan Bedford Forrest: A Biography* (New York: Knopf, 1993), 8.

6. Ibid., 174.

Chicago-*style bibliography*

A bibliography, which appears at the end of your paper, lists every work you have cited in your notes; in addition, it may include works that you consulted but did not cite. For advice on constructing the list, see page 716. A sample bibliography appears on page 726.

NOTE: If you include a bibliography, *The Chicago Manual of Style* suggests that you shorten all notes, including the first reference to a source, as described on page 700. Check with your instructor, however, to see whether using an abbreviated note for a first reference to a source is acceptable.

Model notes and bibliography entries

The following models are consistent with guidelines set forth in *The Chicago Manual of Style*, 16th ed. For each type of source, a model note appears first, followed by a model bibliography entry. The note shows the format you should use when citing a source for the first time. For subsequent citations of a source, use shortened notes (see p. 700).

Some online sources, typically periodical articles, use a permanent locator called a digital object identifier (DOI). Use the DOI, when it is available, in place of a URL in your citations of online sources.

When a Web address (URL) or a DOI must break across lines, do not insert a hyphen or break at a hyphen if the URL or DOI contains one. Instead, break after a colon or a double slash or before any other mark of punctuation.

Books (print and online)

1. Basic format for a print book

1. Mary N. Woods, *Beyond the Architect's Eye: Photographs and the American Built Environment* (Philadelphia: University of Pennsylvania Press, 2009), 45.

Woods, Mary N. *Beyond the Architect's Eye: Photographs and the American Built Environment*. Philadelphia: University of Pennsylvania Press, 2009.

2. Basic format for an online book

2. John Dewey, *Democracy and Education* (1916; ILT Digital Classics, 1994), chap. 4, http://www.ilt.columbia.edu/publications/dewey.html.

Dewey, John. *Democracy and Education*. 1916. ILT Digital Classics, 1994. http://www.ilt.columbia.edu/publications/dewey.html.

3. Basic format for an e-book (electronic book)

3. Leo Tolstoy, *War and Peace*, trans. Richard Pevear and Larissa Volokhonsky (New York: Knopf, 2007), Kindle edition, vol. 1, pt. 1, chap. 3.

Tolstoy, Leo. *War and Peace*. Translated by Richard Pevear and Larissa Volokhonsky. New York: Knopf, 2007. Kindle edition.

4. Two or more authors   For a work with two or three authors, give all authors' names in both the note and the bibliography entry. For a work with four or more authors, in the note give the first author's name followed by "et al." (for "and others"); in the bibliography entry, list all authors' names.

4. Chris Stringer and Peter Andrews, *The Complete World of Human Evolution* (London: Thames and Hudson, 2005), 45.

Stringer, Chris, and Peter Andrews. *The Complete World of Human Evolution*. London: Thames and Hudson, 2005.

4. Lynn Hunt et al., *The Making of the West: Peoples and Cultures*, 3rd ed. (Boston: Bedford/St. Martin's, 2009), 541.

Hunt, Lynn, Thomas R. Martin, Barbara H. Rosenwein, R. Po-chia Hsia, and Bonnie G. Smith. *The Making of the West: Peoples and Cultures*. 3rd ed. Boston: Bedford/St. Martin's, 2009.

5. Organization as author

5. Dormont Historical Society, *Images of America: Dormont* (Charleston, SC: Arcadia Publishing, 2008), 24.

Dormont Historical Society. *Images of America: Dormont*. Charleston, SC: Arcadia Publishing, 2008.

6. Unknown author

6. *The Men's League Handbook on Women's Suffrage* (London, 1912), 23.

The Men's League Handbook on Women's Suffrage. London, 1912.

7. Multiple works by the same author   In the bibliography, use three hyphens in place of the author's name in the second and subsequent entries. Arrange the entries alphabetically by title.

Harper, Raymond L. *A History of Chesapeake, Virginia*. Charleston, SC: History Press, 2008.

---. *South Norfolk, Virginia, 1661-2005*. Charleston, SC: History Press, 2005.

Directory to *Chicago*-style notes and bibliography entries

8. Edited work without an author

8. Jack Beatty, ed., *Colossus: How the Corporation Changed America* (New York: Broadway Books, 2001), 127.

Beatty, Jack, ed. *Colossus: How the Corporation Changed America*. New York: Broadway Books, 2001.

9. Edited work with an author

9. Ted Poston, *A First Draft of History,* ed. Kathleen A. Hauke (Athens: University of Georgia Press, 2000), 46.

Poston, Ted. *A First Draft of History*. Edited by Kathleen A. Hauke. Athens: University of Georgia Press, 2000.

10. Translated work

10. Tonino Guerra, *Abandoned Places,* trans. Adria Bernardi (Barcelona: Guernica, 1999), 71.

Guerra, Tonino. *Abandoned Places*. Translated by Adria Bernardi. Barcelona: Guernica, 1999.

11. Edition other than the first

11. Arnoldo DeLeon, *Mexican Americans in Texas: A Brief History*, 3rd ed. (Wheeling, IL: Harlan Davidson, 2009), 34.

DeLeon, Arnoldo. *Mexican Americans in Texas: A Brief History*. 3rd ed. Wheeling, IL: Harlan Davidson, 2009.

12. Volume in a multivolume work

12. Charles Reagan Wilson, ed., *Myth, Manner, and Memory,* vol. 4 of *The New Encyclopedia of Southern Culture* (Chapel Hill: University of North Carolina Press, 2006), 198.

Wilson, Charles Reagan, ed. *Myth, Manner, and Memory*. Vol. 4 of *The New Encyclopedia of Southern Culture*. Chapel Hill: University of North Carolina Press, 2006.

13. Work in an anthology

13. Zora Neale Hurston, "From *Dust Tracks on a Road,*" in *The Norton Book of American Autobiography*, ed. Jay Parini (New York: Norton, 1999), 336.

Hurston, Zora Neale. "From *Dust Tracks on a Road*." In *The Norton Book of American Autobiography*, edited by Jay Parini, 333-43. New York: Norton, 1999.

14. Introduction, preface, foreword, or afterword

14. Nelson DeMille, foreword to *Flag: An American Biography*, by Marc Leepson (New York: Thomas Dunne, 2005), xii.

DeMille, Nelson. Foreword to *Flag: An American Biography*, by Marc Leepson, xi-xiv. New York: Thomas Dunne, 2005.

15. Republished book

15. Garry Wills, *Inventing America: Jefferson's Declaration of Independence* (1978; repr., Boston: Houghton Mifflin, 2002), 86.

Wills, Garry. *Inventing America: Jefferson's Declaration of Independence*. 1978. Reprint, Boston: Houghton Mifflin, 2002.

16. Work with a title in its title   Use quotation marks around any title within an italicized title.

16. Gary Schmidgall, ed., *Conserving Walt Whitman's Fame: Selections from Horace Traubel's "Conservator," 1890-1919* (Iowa City: University of Iowa Press, 2006), 165.

Schmidgall, Gary, ed. *Conserving Walt Whitman's Fame: Selections from Horace Traubel's "Conservator," 1890-1919*. Iowa City: University of Iowa Press, 2006.

17. Letter in a published collection   Use the day-month-year form for the date of the letter. If the letter writer's name is part of the book title, begin the note with only the last name but begin the bibliography entry with the full name.

17. Mitford to Esmond Romilly, 29 July 1940, in *Decca: The Letters of Jessica Mitford*, ed. Peter Y. Sussman (New York: Knopf, 2006), 55-56.

Mitford, Jessica. *Decca: The Letters of Jessica Mitford*. Edited by Peter Y. Sussman. New York: Knopf, 2006.

18. Work in a series

18. R. Keith Schoppa, *The Columbia Guide to Modern Chinese History*, Columbia Guides to Asian History (New York: Columbia University Press, 2000), 256-58.

Schoppa, R. Keith. *The Columbia Guide to Modern Chinese History*. Columbia Guides to Asian History. New York: Columbia University Press, 2000.

19. Encyclopedia or dictionary entry

19. *Encyclopaedia Britannica*, 15th ed., s.v. "Monroe Doctrine."

19. Bryan A. Garner, *Garner's Modern American Usage* (Oxford: Oxford University Press, 2003), s.v. "brideprice."

Garner, Bryan A. *Garner's Modern American Usage.* Oxford: Oxford University Press, 2003.

The abbreviation "s.v." is for the Latin *sub verbo* ("under the word").

Well-known reference works such as encyclopedias do not require publication information and are usually not included in the bibliography.

20. Sacred text

20. Matt. 20:4-9 (Revised Standard Version).

20. Qur'an 18:1-3.

Sacred texts are usually not included in the bibliography.

21. Source quoted in another source

21. Ron Grossman and Charles Leroux, "A Local Outpost of Democracy," *Chicago Tribune*, March 5, 1996, quoted in William Julius Wilson and Richard P. Taub, *There Goes the Neighborhood: Racial, Ethnic, and Class Tensions in Four Chicago Neighborhoods and Their Meaning for America* (New York: Knopf, 2006), 18.

Grossman, Ron, and Charles Leroux. "A Local Outpost of Democracy." *Chicago Tribune*, March 5, 1996. Quoted in William Julius Wilson and Richard P. Taub, *There Goes the Neighborhood: Racial, Ethnic, and Class Tensions in Four Chicago Neighborhoods and Their Meaning for America* (New York: Knopf, 2006), 18.

Articles in periodicals (print and online)

22. Article in a print journal   Include the volume and issue numbers and the date; end the bibliography entry with the page range of the article.

22. T. H. Breen, "Will American Consumers Buy a Second American Revolution?," *Journal of American History* 93, no. 2 (2006): 405.

Breen, T. H. "Will American Consumers Buy a Second American Revolution?" *Journal of American History* 93, no. 2 (2006): 404-8.

23. Article in an online journal　Give the DOI if the article has one; if there is no DOI, give the URL for the article. For unpaginated online articles, you may include in your note a locator, such as a numbered paragraph or a heading from the article.

23. Brian Lennon, "New Media Critical Homologies," *Postmodern Culture* 19, no. 2 (2009), http://pmc.iath.virginia.edu/text-only/issue.109/19.2lennon.txt.

Lennon, Brian. "New Media Critical Homologies." *Postmodern Culture* 19, no. 2 (2009). http://pmc.iath.virginia.edu/text-only/issue.109/19.2lennon.txt.

24. Journal article from a database　Give whatever identifying information is available in the database listing: a DOI for the article; or the name of the database and the number assigned by the database; or a "stable" or "persistent" URL for the article.

24. Constant Leung, "Language and Content in Bilingual Education," *Linguistics and Education* 16, no. 2 (2005): 239, doi:10.1016/j.linged.2006.01.004.

Leung, Constant. "Language and Content in Bilingual Education." *Linguistics and Education* 16, no. 2 (2005): 238-52. doi:10.1016/j.linged.2006.01.004.

25. Article in a print magazine

25. Tom Bissell, "Improvised, Explosive, and Divisive," *Harper's*, January 2006, 42.

Bissell, Tom. "Improvised, Explosive, and Divisive." *Harper's*, January 2006, 41-54.

26. Article in an online magazine　Include the URL for the article.

26. Katharine Mieszkowski, "A Deluge Waiting to Happen," *Salon*, July 3, 2008, http://www.salon.com/news/feature/2008/07/03/floods/index.html.

Mieszkowski, Katharine. "A Deluge Waiting to Happen." *Salon*, July 3, 2008. http://www.salon.com/news/feature/2008/07/03/floods/index.html.

27. Magazine article from a database Give whatever identifying information is available in the database listing: a DOI for the article; or the name of the database and the number assigned by the database; or a "stable" or "persistent" URL for the article.

27. "Facing Facts in Afghanistan," *National Review*, November 2, 2009, 14, Expanded Academic ASAP (A209905060).

"Facing Facts in Afghanistan." *National Review*, November 2, 2009, 14. Expanded Academic ASAP (A209905060).

28. Article in a print newspaper Page numbers are not necessary; a section letter or number, if available, is sufficient.

28. Randal C. Archibold, "These Neighbors Are Good Ones without a New Fence," *New York Times*, October 22, 2008, sec. A.

Archibold, Randal C. "These Neighbors Are Good Ones without a New Fence." *New York Times*, October 22, 2008, sec. A.

29. Article in an online newspaper Include the URL for the article; if the URL is very long, use the URL for the newspaper's home page. Omit page numbers, even if the source provides them.

29. Doyle McManus, "The Candor War," *Chicago Tribune*, July 29, 2010, http://www.chicagotribune.com/.

McManus, Doyle. "The Candor War." *Chicago Tribune*, July 29, 2010. http://www.chicagotribune.com/.

30. Newspaper article from a database Give whatever identifying information is available in the database listing: a DOI for the article; or the name of the database and the number assigned by the database; or a "stable" or "persistent" URL for the article.

30. Clifford J. Levy, "In Kyrgyzstan, Failure to Act Adds to Crisis," *New York Times*, June 18, 2010, General OneFile (A229196045).

Levy, Clifford J. "In Kyrgyzstan, Failure to Act Adds to Crisis." *New York Times*, June 18, 2010. General OneFile (A229196045).

31. Unsigned newspaper article

31. "Renewable Energy Rules," *Boston Globe*, August 11, 2003, sec. A.

Boston Globe. "Renewable Energy Rules." August 11, 2003, sec. A.

32. Book review

32. Benjamin Wittes, "Remember the Titan," review of *Louis D. Brandeis: A Life*, by Melvin T. Urofsky, *Wilson Quarterly* 33, no. 4 (2009): 100.

Wittes, Benjamin. "Remember the Titan." Review of *Louis D. Brandeis: A Life,* by Melvin T. Urofsky. *Wilson Quarterly* 33, no. 4 (2009): 100-101.

33. Letter to the editor   Do not use the letter's title, even if the publication gives one.

33. David Harlan, letter to the editor, *New York Review of Books*, October 9, 2008.

Harlan, David. Letter to the editor. *New York Review of Books*, October 9, 2008.

Online sources

For most Web sites, include an author if a site has one, the title of the site, the sponsor, the date of publication or modified (update) date, and the site's URL. Do not italicize a Web site title unless the site is an online book or periodical. Use quotation marks for the titles of sections or pages in a Web site. If a site does not have a date of publication or modified date, give the date you accessed the site ("accessed January 3, 2010").

34. Web site

34. Chesapeake and Ohio Canal National Historical Park, National Park Service, last modified April 9, 2010, http://www.nps.gov/choh/index.htm.

Chesapeake and Ohio Canal National Historical Park. National Park Service. Last modified April 9, 2010. http://www.nps.gov/choh/index.htm.

35. Short work from a Web site   Place the title of the short work in quotation marks.

35. George P. Landow, "Victorian and Victorianism," Victorian Web, last modified August 2, 2009, http://victorianweb.org/vn/victor4.html.

Landow, George P. "Victorian and Victorianism." Victorian Web. Last modified August 2, 2009. http://victorianweb.org/vn/victor4.html.

36. Online posting or e-mail   If an online posting has been archived, include a URL. E-mails that are not part of an online discussion are treated as personal communications (see item 42). Online postings and e-mails are not included in the bibliography.

36. Susanna J. Sturgis to Copyediting-L discussion list, July 17, 2010, http://listserv.indiana.edu/archives/copyediting-l.html.

37. Blog (Weblog) post   Treat as a short document from a Web site (see item 35). Put the title of the posting in quotation marks, and italicize the name of the blog. Insert "blog" in parentheses after the name if the word *blog* is not part of the name.

37. Miland Brown, "The Flawed Montevideo Convention of 1933," World History Blog, May 31, 2008, http://www.worldhistoryblog.com/2008 /05/flawed-montevideo-convention-of-1933.html.

Brown, Miland. "The Flawed Montevideo Convention of 1933." *World History Blog.* May 31, 2008. http://www.worldhistoryblog.com/2008 /05/flawed-montevideo-convention-of-1933.html.

38. Podcast   Treat as a short work from a Web site (see item 35), including the following, if available: the author's (or speaker's) name; the title of the podcast, in quotation marks; an identifying number, if any; the title of the site on which it appears; the sponsor of the site; and the URL. Identify the type of podcast or file format and the date of posting or your date of access before the URL.

38. Paul Tiyambe Zeleza, "Africa's Global Past," Episode 40, Africa Past and Present, African Online Digital Library, podcast audio, April 29, 2010, http://afripod.aodl.org/.

Zeleza, Paul Tiyambe. "Africa's Global Past." Episode 40. Africa Past and Present. African Online Digital Library. Podcast audio. April 29, 2010. http://afripod.aodl.org/.

39. Online audio or video   Cite as a short work from a Web site (see item 35). If the source is a downloadable file, identify the file format or medium before the URL.

39. Richard B. Freeman, "Global Capitalism, Labor Markets, and Inequality," Institute of International Studies, University of California at Berkeley, October 31, 2007, http://www.youtube.com/watch?v=cgNCFsXGUa0.

Freeman, Richard B. "Global Capitalism, Labor Markets, and Inequality." Institute of International Studies, University of California at Berkeley. October 31, 2007. http://www.youtube.com/watch?v=cgNCFsXGUa0.

Other sources (including online versions)

40. Government document

40. U.S. Department of State, *Foreign Relations of the United States: Diplomatic Papers, 1943* (Washington, DC: GPO, 1965), 562.

U.S. Department of State. *Foreign Relations of the United States: Diplomatic Papers, 1943*. Washington, DC: GPO, 1965.

41. Unpublished dissertation

41. Stephanie Lynn Budin, "The Origins of Aphrodite" (PhD diss., University of Pennsylvania, 2000), 301-2, ProQuest (AAT 9976404).

Budin, Stephanie Lynn. "The Origins of Aphrodite." PhD diss., University of Pennsylvania, 2000. ProQuest (AAT 9976404).

42. Personal communication

42. Sara Lehman, e-mail message to author, August 13, 2009.

Personal communications are not included in the bibliography.

43. Published or broadcast interview

43. Robert Downey Jr., interview by Graham Norton, *The Graham Norton Show*, BBC America, December 14, 2009.

Downey, Robert, Jr. Interview by Graham Norton. *Graham Norton Show*. BBC America, December 14, 2009.

44. Published proceedings of a conference

44. Julie Kimber, Peter Love, and Phillip Deery, eds., *Labour Traditions: Proceedings of the Tenth National Labour History Conference*, University of Melbourne, Carlton, Victoria, Australia, July 4-6, 2007 (Melbourne: Australian Society for the Study of Labour History, 2007), 5.

Kimber, Julie, Peter Love, and Phillip Deery, eds. *Labour Traditions: Proceedings of the Tenth National Labour History Conference*. University of Melbourne, Carlton, Victoria, Australia, July 4-6, 2007. Melbourne: Australian Society for the Study of Labour History, 2007.

45. Video or DVD

45. *The Secret of Roan Inish*, directed by John Sayles (1993; Culver City, CA: Columbia TriStar Home Video, 2000), DVD.

The Secret of Roan Inish. Directed by John Sayles. 1993; Culver City, CA: Columbia TriStar Home Video, 2000. DVD.

46. Sound recording

46. Gustav Holst, *The Planets*, Royal Philharmonic Orchestra, conducted by André Previn, Telarc 80133, compact disc.

Holst, Gustav. *The Planets*. Royal Philharmonic Orchestra. Conducted by André Previn. Telarc 80133, compact disc.

47. Musical score or composition

47. Antonio Vivaldi, *L'Estro armonico*, op. 3, ed. Eleanor Selfridge-Field (Mineola, NY: Dover, 1999).

Vivaldi, Antonio. *L'Estro armonico*, op. 3. Edited by Eleanor Selfridge-Field. Mineola, NY: Dover, 1999.

48. Work of art

48. Aaron Siskind, *Untitled (The Most Crowded Block)*, gelatin silver print, 1939, Kemper Museum of Contemporary Art, Kansas City, MO.

Siskind, Aaron. *Untitled (The Most Crowded Block)*. Gelatin silver print, 1939. Kemper Museum of Contemporary Art, Kansas City, MO.

49. Performance

49. Robert Schenkkan, *The Kentucky Cycle*, directed by Richard Elliott, Willows Theatre, Concord, CA, August 31, 2007.

Schenkkan, Robert. *The Kentucky Cycle*. Directed by Richard Elliott. Willows Theatre, Concord, CA, August 31, 2007.

hackerhandbooks.com/bedhandbook > Research exercises
> *Chicago* > E-ex 57–12 to 57–19

57e *Chicago* manuscript format

The following guidelines for formatting a *Chicago*-style paper and preparing its endnotes and bibliography are based on *The Chicago Manual of Style*, 16th ed. (Chicago: U of Chicago P, 2010). For a sample paper, see 57f.

Formatting the paper

Chicago manuscript guidelines are fairly generic because they were not created with a specific type of writing in mind.

Materials and font   Use good-quality 8½" × 11" white paper. Avoid a font that is unusual or hard to read.

Title page   Include the full title of your paper, your name, the course title, the instructor's name, and the date. See page 718 for a sample title page.

Pagination   Using arabic numerals, number the pages in the upper right corner. Do not number the title page but count it in the manuscript numbering; that is, the first page of the text will be numbered 2. Depending on your instructor's preference, you may also use a short title or your last name before the page numbers to help identify pages.

Margins and line spacing   Leave margins of at least one inch at the top, bottom, and sides of the page. Double-space the body of the paper, including long quotations that have been set off from the text. (For line spacing in notes and the bibliography, see p. 716.) Left-align the text.

Capitalization and italics   In titles of works, capitalize all words except articles (*a, an, the*), prepositions (*at, from, between*, and so on), coordinating conjunctions (*and, but, or, nor, for, so, yet*), and *to* and *as*—unless one of these words is first or last in the title or subtitle. Follow these guidelines in your paper even if the title is styled differently in the source.

Lowercase the first word following a colon even if the word begins a complete sentence. When the colon introduces a series of sentences or questions, capitalize all sentences in the series, including the first.

Italicize the titles of books and other long works. Use quotation marks around the titles of periodical articles, short stories, poems, and other short works.

Long quotations   You can choose to set off a long quotation of five to ten typed lines by indenting the entire quotation one-half inch from the left margin. (You should always set off quotations of ten or more lines.) Double-space the quotation; do not use quotation marks. (See pp. 720 and 722 for long quotations in the text of a paper; also see p. 695.)

Visuals   *Chicago* classifies visuals as tables and illustrations (illustrations, or figures, include drawings, photographs, maps, and charts). Keep visuals as simple as possible.

Label each table with an arabic numeral (Table 1, Table 2, and so on) and provide a clear title that identifies the table's subject. The label and the title should appear on separate lines above the table, flush left. Below the table, give its source in a note like this one:

Source: Edna Bonacich and Richard P. Appelbaum, *Behind the Label* (Berkeley: University of California Press, 2000), 145.

For each figure, place a label and a caption below the figure, flush left. The label and caption need not appear on separate lines. The word "Figure" may be abbreviated to "Fig."

In the text of your paper, discuss the most significant features of each visual. Place visuals as close as possible to the sentences that relate to them unless your instructor prefers that visuals appear in an appendix.

Web addresses (URLs)   When a URL must break across lines, do not insert a hyphen or break at a hyphen if the URL contains one. Instead, break the URL after a colon or a double slash or before any other mark of punctuation. If your word processing program automatically turns URLs into links (by underlining them and changing the color), turn off this feature.

Headings   *Chicago* does not provide guidelines for the use of headings in student papers. If you would like to insert headings in a long essay or research paper, check first with your instructor. See the sample *Chicago*-style paper on pages 718–26 for typical placement and formatting of headings.

Preparing the endnotes

Begin the endnotes on a new page at the end of the paper. Center the title Notes about one inch from the top of the page, and number the pages consecutively with the rest of the manuscript. See page 724 for an example.

Indenting and numbering   Indent the first line of each note one-half inch from the left margin; do not indent additional lines in the note. Begin the note with the arabic numeral that corresponds to the number in the text. Put a period after the number.

Line spacing   Single-space each note and double-space between notes (unless your instructor prefers double-spacing throughout).

Preparing the bibliography

Typically, the notes in *Chicago*-style papers are followed by a bibliography, an alphabetically arranged list of all the works cited or consulted. Center the title Bibliography about one inch from the top of the page. Number bibliography pages consecutively with the rest of the paper. See page 726 for a sample bibliography.

Alphabetizing the list   Alphabetize the bibliography by the last names of the authors (or editors); when a work has no author or editor, alphabetize it by the first word of the title other than *A*, *An*, or *The*.

If your list includes two or more works by the same author, use three hyphens instead of the author's name in all entries after the first. Arrange the entries alphabetically by title.

Indenting and line spacing   Begin each entry at the left margin, and indent any additional lines one-half inch. Single-space each entry and double-space between entries (unless your instructor prefers double-spacing throughout).

57f Sample *Chicago* research paper

Following is a research paper by Ned Bishop, a student in a history class. Bishop was asked to document his paper using *Chicago*-style endnotes and bibliography. In preparing his manuscript, Bishop also followed *Chicago* guidelines.

hackerhandbooks.com/bedhandbook > Model papers > *Chicago* paper: Bishop

Title of paper.

The Massacre at Fort Pillow:

Holding Nathan Bedford Forrest Accountable

Writer's name.

Ned Bishop

Title of course,
instructor's name,
and date.

History 214

Professor Citro

March 22, 2001

Marginal annotations indicate *Chicago*-style formatting and effective writing.

Bishop 2

Although Northern newspapers of the time no doubt exaggerated some of the Confederate atrocities at Fort Pillow, most modern sources agree that a massacre of Union troops took place there on April 12, 1864. It seems clear that Union soldiers, particularly black soldiers, were killed after they had stopped fighting or had surrendered or were being held prisoner. Less clear is the role played by Major General Nathan Bedford Forrest in leading his troops. Although we will never know whether Forrest directly ordered the massacre, evidence suggests that he was responsible for it.

Thesis asserts Bishop's main point.

What happened at Fort Pillow?

Headings, centered, help readers follow the organization.

Fort Pillow, Tennessee, which sat on a bluff overlooking the Mississippi River, had been held by the Union for two years. It was garrisoned by 580 men, 292 of them from United States Colored Heavy and Light Artillery regiments, 285 from the white Thirteenth Tennessee Cavalry. Nathan Bedford Forrest commanded about 1,500 troops.[1]

Statistics are cited with an endnote.

The Confederates attacked Fort Pillow on April 12, 1864, and had virtually surrounded the fort by the time Forrest arrived on the battlefield. At 3:30 p.m., Forrest demanded the surrender of the Union forces, sending in a message of the sort he had used before: "The conduct of the officers and men garrisoning Fort Pillow has been such as to entitle them to being treated as prisoners of war. . . . Should my demand be refused, I cannot be responsible for the fate of your command."[2] Union Major William Bradford, who had replaced Major Booth, killed earlier by sharpshooters, asked for an hour to consider the demand. Forrest, worried that vessels in the river were bringing in more troops, "shortened the time to twenty minutes."[3] Bradford refused to surrender, and Forrest quickly ordered the attack.

Quotation is cited with an endnote.

The Confederates charged to the fort, scaled the parapet, and fired on the forces within. Victory came quickly, with the Union forces

Bishop 3

running toward the river or surrendering. Shelby Foote describes the scene like this:

> Some kept going, right on into the river, where a number drowned and the swimmers became targets for marksmen on the bluff. Others, dropping their guns in terror, ran back toward the Confederates with their hands up, and of these some were spared as prisoners, while others were shot down in the act of surrender.[4]

In his own official report, Forrest makes no mention of the massacre. He does make much of the fact that the Union flag was not lowered by the Union forces, saying that if his own men had not taken down the flag, "few, if any, would have survived unhurt another volley."[5] However, as Jack Hurst points out and Forrest must have known, in this twenty-minute battle, "Federals running for their lives had little time to concern themselves with a flag."[6]

The federal congressional report on Fort Pillow, which charged the Confederates with appalling atrocities, was strongly criticized by Southerners. Respected writer Shelby Foote, while agreeing that the report was "largely" fabrication, points out that the "casualty figures . . . indicated strongly that unnecessary killing had occurred."[7] In an important article, John Cimprich and Robert C. Mainfort Jr. argue that the most trustworthy evidence is that written within about ten days of the battle, before word of the congressional hearings circulated and Southerners realized the extent of Northern outrage. The article reprints a group of letters and newspaper sources written before April 22 and thus "untainted by the political overtones the controversy later assumed."[8] Cimprich and Mainfort conclude that these sources "support the case for the occurrence of a massacre" but that Forrest's role remains "clouded" because of inconsistencies in testimony.[9]

Margin annotations:

Long quotation is set off from text by indenting. Quotation marks are omitted.

Bishop uses a primary source as well as secondary sources.

Quotation is introduced with a signal phrase.

Bishop draws attention to an article that reprints primary sources.

Bishop 4

Did Forrest order the massacre?

We will never really know whether Forrest directly ordered the massacre, but it seems unlikely. True, Confederate soldier Achilles Clark, who had no reason to lie, wrote to his sisters that "I with several others tried to stop the butchery . . . but Gen. Forrest ordered them [Negro and white Union troops] shot down like dogs[,] and the carnage continued."[10] But it is not clear whether Clark heard Forrest giving the orders or was just reporting hearsay. Many Confederates had been shouting "No quarter! No quarter!" and, as Shelby Foote points out, these shouts were "thought by some to be at Forrest's command."[11] A Union soldier, Jacob Thompson, claimed to have seen Forrest order the killing, but when asked to describe the six-foot-two general, he called him "a little bit of a man."[12]

Perhaps the most convincing evidence that Forrest did not order the massacre is that he tried to stop it once it had begun. Historian Albert Castel quotes several eyewitnesses on both the Union and Confederate sides as saying that Forrest ordered his men to stop firing.[13] In a letter to his wife three days after the battle, Confederate soldier Samuel Caldwell wrote that "if General Forrest had not run between our men & the Yanks with his pistol and sabre drawn not a man would have been spared."[14]

In a respected biography of Nathan Bedford Forrest, Hurst suggests that the temperamental Forrest "may have ragingly ordered a massacre and even intended to carry it out—until he rode inside the fort and viewed the horrifying result" and ordered it stopped.[15] While this is an intriguing interpretation of events, even Hurst would probably admit that it is merely speculation.

Can Forrest be held responsible for the massacre?

Even assuming that Forrest did not order the massacre, he can still be held accountable for it. That is because he created an

Topic sentence states the main idea for this section.

Writer presents a balanced view of the evidence.

Topic sentence for this section reinforces the thesis.

atmosphere ripe for the possibility of atrocities and did nothing to ensure that it wouldn't happen. Throughout his career Forrest repeatedly threatened "no quarter," particularly with respect to black soldiers, so Confederate troops had good reason to think that in massacring the enemy they were carrying out his orders. As Hurst writes, "About all he had to do to produce a massacre was issue no order against one."[16] Dudley Taylor Cornish agrees:

> It has been asserted again and again that Forrest did not order a massacre. He did not need to. He had sought to terrify the Fort Pillow garrison by a threat of no quarter, as he had done at Union City and at Paducah in the days just before he turned on Pillow. If his men did enter the fort shouting "Give them no quarter; kill them; kill them; it is General Forrest's orders," he should not have been surprised.[17]

The slaughter at Fort Pillow was no doubt driven in large part by racial hatred. Numbers alone suggest this: of 295 white troops, 168 were taken prisoner, but of 262 black troops, only 58 were taken into custody, with the rest either dead or too badly wounded to walk.[18] A Southern reporter traveling with Forrest makes clear that the discrimination was deliberate: "Our troops maddened by the excitement, shot down the ret[r]eating Yankees, and not until they had attained t[h]e water's edge and turned to beg for mercy, did any prisoners fall in [t]o our hands—Thus the whites received quarter, but the negroes were shown no mercy."[19] Union surgeon Dr. Charles Fitch, who was taken prisoner by Forrest, testified that after he was in custody he "saw" Confederate soldiers "kill every negro that made his appearance dressed in Federal uniform."[20]

Transition sentence links new material to old.

Fort Pillow is not the only instance of a massacre or threatened massacre of black soldiers by troops under Forrest's command.

Bishop 6

Biographer Brian Steel Wills points out that at Brice's Cross Roads in June 1864, "black soldiers suffered inordinately" as Forrest looked the other way and Confederate soldiers deliberately sought out those they termed "the damned negroes."[21] Just a day after Fort Pillow, on April 13, 1864, one of Forrest's generals, Abraham Buford, after consulting with Forrest, demanded that the federal garrison in Columbus, Kentucky, surrender. The demand stated that if an attack became necessary, "no quarter will be shown to the negro troops whatever; the white troops will be treated as prisoners of war."[22]

Nathan Bedford Forrest, a crude man who had made his fortune as a slave trader, was noted for both his violence and his hatred of blacks. In the words of historian James M. McPherson, "Forrest possessed a killer instinct toward . . . blacks in any capacity other than slave."[23] Forrest's battle successes were largely due to his brazen tactics—tactics that Hurst says would not have occurred to the "aristocratic, well-educated Confederate military hierarchy."[24] Some Southerners, in fact, found Forrest's leadership style distasteful. As one Mississippi aristocrat put it, "Forrest may be, and no doubt is, the best cavalry officer in the West, but I object to a tyrannical [sic], hot-headed vulgarian's commanding me."[25]

> Ellipsis mark indicates that words have been omitted.

Because he was so crudely racist, Forrest surely understood the rage that his troops felt toward the very idea of blacks as soldiers. Further, he must have known that his standard threats of "No quarter" would fuel the Confederate soldiers' rage. Although Forrest may have tried to prevent the massacre once it was under way, he can still be held accountable for it. That is because he created the conditions that led to the massacre (especially of black troops) and with full knowledge of those conditions took no steps to prevent what was a nearly inevitable bloodbath.

> Conclusion supports the writer's central argument.

Notes begin on a new page.

Notes

First line of each note is indented ½".

    1. John Cimprich and Robert C. Mainfort Jr., eds., "Fort Pillow Revisited: New Evidence about an Old Controversy," *Civil War History* 28, no. 4 (1982): 293-94.

Note number is not raised and is followed by a period.

    2. Quoted in Brian Steel Wills, *A Battle from the Start: The Life of Nathan Bedford Forrest* (New York: HarperCollins, 1992), 182.

    3. Ibid., 183.

    4. Shelby Foote, *The Civil War, a Narrative: Red River to Appomattox* (New York: Vintage, 1986), 110.

Authors' names are not inverted.

    5. Nathan Bedford Forrest, "Report of Maj. Gen. Nathan B. Forrest, C. S. Army, Commanding Cavalry, of the Capture of Fort Pillow," *Shotgun's Home of the American Civil War*, accessed March 6, 2001, http://www.civilwarhome.com/forrest.htm.

    6. Jack Hurst, *Nathan Bedford Forrest: A Biography* (New York: Knopf, 1993), 174.

Last name and title refer to an earlier note by the same author.

    7. Foote, *Civil War*, 111.

    8. Cimprich and Mainfort, "Fort Pillow," 295.

    9. Ibid., 305.

    10. Ibid., 299.

    11. Foote, *Civil War*, 110.

    12. Quoted in Wills, *Battle from the Start*, 187.

Notes are single-spaced, with double-spacing between notes. (Some instructors may prefer double-spacing throughout.)

    13. Albert Castel, "The Fort Pillow Massacre: A Fresh Examination of the Evidence," *Civil War History* 4, no. 1 (1958): 44-45.

    14. Cimprich and Mainfort, "Fort Pillow," 300.

    15. Hurst, *Nathan Bedford Forrest*, 177.

    16. Ibid.

Bishop 8

17. Dudley Taylor Cornish, *The Sable Arm: Black Troops in the Union Army, 1861-1865* (Lawrence: University Press of Kansas, 1987), 175.

18. Foote, *Civil War*, 111.

19. Cimprich and Mainfort, "Fort Pillow," 304.

20. Quoted in Wills, *Battle from the Start*, 189.

21. Ibid., 215.

22. Quoted in Hurst, *Nathan Bedford Forrest*, 177.

23. Quoted in James M. McPherson, *Battle Cry of Freedom: The Civil War Era* (New York: Oxford University Press, 1988), 402.

24. Hurst, *Nathan Bedford Forrest*, 74.

25. Quoted in Foote, *Civil War*, 106.

Bibliography begins on a new page.

Bibliography

Entries are alphabetized by authors' last names.

Castel, Albert. "The Fort Pillow Massacre: A Fresh Examination of the Evidence." *Civil War History* 4, no. 1 (1958): 37-50.

Cimprich, John, and Robert C. Mainfort Jr., eds. "Fort Pillow Revisited: New Evidence about an Old Controversy." *Civil War History* 28, no. 4 (1982): 293-306.

First line of entry is at left margin; additional lines are indented ½".

Cornish, Dudley Taylor. *The Sable Arm: Black Troops in the Union Army, 1861-1865*. Lawrence: University Press of Kansas, 1987.

Foote, Shelby. *The Civil War, a Narrative: Red River to Appomattox*. New York: Vintage, 1986.

Forrest, Nathan Bedford. "Report of Maj. Gen. Nathan B. Forrest, C. S. Army, Commanding Cavalry, of the Capture of Fort Pillow." Shotgun's Home of the American Civil War. Accessed March 6, 2001. http://www.civilwarhome.com/forrest.htm.

Entries are single-spaced, with double-spacing between entries. (Some instructors may prefer double-spacing throughout.)

Hurst, Jack. *Nathan Bedford Forrest: A Biography*. New York: Knopf, 1993.

McPherson, James M. *Battle Cry of Freedom: The Civil War Era*. New York: Oxford University Press, 1988.

Wills, Brian Steel. *A Battle from the Start: The Life of Nathan Bedford Forrest*. New York: HarperCollins, 1992.

D

Writing in the Disciplines

Advice and Models

A Hacker Handbooks Supplement

Jonathan S. Cullick
Northern Kentucky University

Terry Myers Zawacki
George Mason University

BEDFORD / ST. MARTIN'S   BOSTON ◆ NEW YORK

DISCIPLINE SPECIALISTS

For their assistance and advice as discipline specialists, we thank the followir
Diana Belland, Northern Kentucky University (music); Jules Benjamin, Itha
College (history); Dorinda J. Carter, Michigan State University (educatio
Jennifer DeForest, University of Virginia (education); Susan Durham, Geor
Mason University (nursing); C. Dale Elifrits, Northern Kentucky Univers
(geology/engineering); Aimee Frame, University of Cincinnati (engineerin
Devon Johnson, George Mason University (criminal justice); Victoria McMilla
Colgate University (biology); James Morris, Harvard University (biology); Kirst
Olson, Wheaton College (education); Shannon Portillo, George Mason Univers
(criminal justice); Sherry Robertson, Arizona State University (business); and Be
Schneider, George Mason University (business).

Manufactured in the United States of America.

6   5   4   3   2   1
f   e   d   c   b   a

For information, write: Bedford/St. Martin's, 75 Arlington Street, Boston,
MA 02116   (617-399-4000)

ISBN-10: 0-312-65683-1
ISBN-13: 978-0-312-65683-6

ACKNOWLEDGMENTS

Jules Benjamin, "Wage Slavery or True Independence? Women Workers in the
   Lowell, Massachusetts, Textile Mills, 1820–1850," excerpt from *A Student's
   Guide to History*, Eleventh Edition. Copyright © 2010 by Bedford/St. Martin's
   Reprinted with permission. "Regulations for the Boarding Houses of the
   Middlesex Company." Reprinted by permission of the American Textile Histo
   Museum, Lowell, MA.
Valerie Charat, "Always Out of Their Seats (and Fighting): Why Are Boys
   Diagnosed with ADHD More Often Than Girls?" (December 15, 2006).
   Reprinted with permission.
Onnalee L. Gibson, "A Reflection on Service Learning: Working with Eric" (April
   25, 2006). Reprinted with permission.
Tom Houston, "Concert Review" (February 27, 2008). Reprinted with permission
Marin Johnson and Laura Arnold, "Distribution Pattern of Dandelion (*Taraxacu
   officinale*) on an Abandoned Golf Course" (September 13, 2005). Reprinted wi
   permission.
Victoria McMillan, excerpt from *Writing Papers in the Biological Sciences*, Fourt
   Edition. Copyright © 2006 by Bedford/St. Martin's. Reprinted with permissio
Alice O'Bryan, "Site Stabilization Plan for Erosion Control" (May 5, 2008).
   Reprinted with permission.
Kelly Ratajczak, "Proposal to Add a Wellness Program" (April 21, 2006). Reprint
   with permission.
Julie Riss, "Acute Lymphoblastic Leukemia and Hypertension in One Client: A
   Nursing Practice Paper" (May 18, 2006). Reprinted with permission.
Brian Spencer, "Positively Affecting Employee Motivation" (March 9, 2006).
   Reprinted with permission.
Chris Thompson, "Crime in Leesburg, Virginia." Reprinted with permission.

D

Writing in the Disciplines

Advice and Models

D Writing in the Disciplines

D1 Introduction: Writing in different disciplines

Succeeding in college requires performing well in different kinds of courses and on various kinds of assignments. As you probably know, you will be assigned writing in your college writing courses. It may surprise you to know, however, that other college courses require writing—courses you might not expect, like nursing and psychology. The strategies you develop in your first-year composition course will help you write well in other academic courses.

The academic community is divided into broad subject areas called *disciplines*. The disciplines are generally grouped into five major fields of study, which are further broken down into more specific subjects. The five disciplines and a few representative subjects are social sciences (psychology, sociology, criminology); natural sciences (biology and chemistry); mathematics and engineering; humanities and the arts (history, literature, music); and professions and applied sciences (business, education, nursing).

Each discipline has its own set of expectations and conventions for both reading and writing. Some of the expectations and conventions—writing with a clear main idea, for instance—are common across disciplines; those are covered in your handbook. Other expectations and conventions are unique to each discipline. These include the following:

- purpose for writing
- audience
- questions asked by scholars and practitioners
- types of evidence used
- language and writing conventions
- citation style

When you are asked to write in a specific discipline, start by becoming familiar with the distinctive features of writing in that discipline. For example, if you are asked to write a lab report for a biology class, your purpose might be to present results of an experiment. Your evidence would be the data you collected while conducting your experiment, and you would use scientific terms in your report. You would also use the CSE (Council of Science Editors) guidelines for citation of your sources. If you are asked to write a case study for an education class, your purpose might be to analyze student-teacher interactions in a single classroom. Your evidence might be data on a

combination of personal observations and interviews. You would us
terms from the field in your case study and cite your sources usin,
the guidelines of the American Psychological Association (APA).

The following sections provide guidelines for writing in nine dis
ciplines: biology, business, criminal justice/criminology, education
engineering, history, music, nursing, and psychology. Each section
begins with advice about the expectations for writing in that disci
pline and closes with a model or two of student writing.

D2 Writing in the biological sciences

Biologists use writing in many ways. They write reports analyzin,
the data they collect from their experiments as well as reviews o
other scientists' research or proposed research. They write proposal
to convince funding agencies to award grants for their research. I
they teach, biologists also write lectures. Some biologists may com
municate with a general audience by writing newspaper and mag
azine articles. In addition, they may lend their expertise to public
policy decision making by government officials, weighing in on, sa'
the issue of global warming or stem cell research.

When you write in biology courses, your goal will generally b
to convince readers of the validity of the conclusions you draw from
observations, from experimental data, or from your evaluations o
previously published or proposed research. For most assignments
you will need to use a scientific style of writing, conveying your infor
mation to readers as succinctly and accurately as possible.

D2-a Determine your audience and their needs in the biological sciences.

When you write in biology, your audience may consist of research
ers, professors, other students, and sometimes members of the gov
ernment or business communities and the general public. Research
ers or teachers may read to find out the results of an experiment, a
analysis of new data, or information supporting or critiquing a theor
They may need this information to guide their own research project
or improve their assignments and classroom materials. Students rea
to learn about major concepts and discoveries as well as methods fo
conducting laboratory experiments. Researchers, teachers, and stu
dents expect detailed, specific presentation of data and findings i
words and in graphic form, such as diagrams and graphs. Member

f the general public want to understand how concepts affect per-
onal decisions they must make about issues such as medical care or
nutritional choices. People working in government or business may
ave to make decisions about funding for research proposals. For
nore general audiences, you may not need to provide the same level
f detail. For example, the public or businesspeople may not need spe-
ies names to be written in Latin. In all cases, however, your readers
xpect you to be completely objective and to present information as
learly as possible.

D2-b Recognize the forms of writing in the biological sciences.

When you take courses in biology, you may be asked to write any of
he following:

- laboratory notebooks
- research papers
- laboratory reports
- literature reviews
- research proposals
- poster presentations

Laboratory notebooks

f you are required to complete laboratory exercises, you will need to
arefully record your experiments in a notebook. A laboratory note-
ook should be detailed and accurate so that anyone who wishes to
epeat your experiment can do so. The laboratory notebook also pro-
ides crucial material for any report or article you may write later
bout your experiment. Researchers take notebooks seriously, never
emoving a page or erasing entries. That practice keeps them from
nisrepresenting results.

Your notebook will typically have the following components:

- table of contents
- date of each experiment
- title
- purpose (the objective of the experiment)
- materials (a list of equipment, specimens, and chemicals you
  used in the experiment)

- procedures (the method you planned to follow as well as any alterations you made to that procedure while conducting the experiment)
- results (the data gathered from the experiment)
- data analysis (calculations based on your data)
- discussion (your assessment of whether the experiment was successful, your interpretation of your results, your accounting for any surprising results, and your conclusions about what you learned from the experiment)
- acknowledgments (those who helped you with the experiment)

Research papers and laboratory reports

When instructors refer to *research papers*, they may have different assignments in mind. One assignment might ask you to present your synthesis of many sources of information about, for instance, a genetic syndrome to demonstrate your understanding of the characteristics of the disorder and other researchers' investigations of the causes of the syndrome.

Another assignment might require you to report on the results of an experiment you conducted and to interpret your results; this document is typically called a *laboratory report*. Unlike the laboratory notebook, a lab report may relate your interpretations to what others in the field have concluded from their own experiments. Biologists publish research papers and reports in journals after the papers have undergone rigorous and impartial review by other biologists, called a *peer review*, to make sure that the scientific process used by the researchers is sound.

Whether published in a journal or written for a college course, research papers and reports based on original experiments follow a standard format and include the following sections:

- abstract (a 100-to-125-word summary of your report)
- introduction (the context for your experiment, such as what has been published on the topic in the field, as well as the purpose of the experiment)
- materials and methods (details of how you conducted the experiment so that other researchers can repeat the experiment to try to reproduce your results; your description of the methodology you used so that readers can determine if your interpretations are supported by the data)
- results (a presentation of what you observed in the experiment)
- figures and tables

- discussion (your interpretation of the results as well as a comparison of your interpretation and that of other researchers in the field)
- references (a list of the sources cited in your paper)

Literature reviews

Literature reviews can have different objectives, such as comparing or contrasting approaches to a problem or examining the literature in the field to propose an alternative theory. Another purpose is to inform biologists about the latest advances in the field. In a review, you will consider the findings of a number of research papers and evaluate those papers' conclusions and perhaps suggest a direction for future research. A critical review analyzes the methods and interpretations of data from one or more journal articles. You may be asked to write a literature review as an introduction to a larger piece of writing, such as a report of a study you conducted. In that case, the review will survey previously published findings relevant to the question that your study investigates.

A literature review assignment is an opportunity to learn about an area in the field and to see what old or new questions may benefit from research.

While the format of reviews varies with their purpose, reviews typically have an abstract, an introduction, a discussion of the research being reviewed, a conclusion, and a references section.

Research proposals

In a research proposal, the biologist poses a significant question and a hypothesis (or hypotheses) and suggests one or more experiments to test the hypothesis. The project can have specific practical applications; for example, one Arctic biologist submitted to the United States Geological Survey a proposal for an ecological monitoring program at a national park. Research proposals that seek funding for an experiment must include detailed budgets.

Whether written by scholars requesting support from an agency or by students in a course, research proposals are evaluated for how well they justify their project with a carefully conceived experiment design.

Poster presentations

At professional gatherings such as annual conventions in the field, biologists have the opportunity to present their work in the form of a poster rather than as a formal talk. Conference attendees approach presenters in an exhibit area to talk about their research, which the posters concisely summarize. A poster features a brief introduction to the presenter's research project, a description of the method, information about the experiment's subjects, the experiment's results, and the presenter's conclusions. Poster presentations also feature graphs and tables since it is important to convey information to attendees quickly and concisely as they walk through the exhibit area. An effective poster presentation will encourage the audience to ask questions and carry on an informal conversation with the presenter.

Your instructor may ask you to create a poster presentation about an experiment you or other researchers have conducted both to help you understand complex concepts and to practice your communication skills.

NOTE: Some presenters use presentation software to create a slide show that they can click through for a small audience or project on a screen for a larger group. Presenters generally include the same kind of information in slide presentations as they do in poster presentations.

D2-c Know the questions biologists ask.

Biologists, like other scientists, ask questions about the natural world. Their questions are either *why* questions or *how* questions such as the following:

- Why don't newborns see well?
- Why does body size of species skew to the right on a distribution curve? That is, why are there so many small animals?
- How does cellular senescence prevent cancer?
- How do island plants self-pollinate?

As they attempt to answer such questions, biologists first offer a tentative explanation, or hypothesis, for something they have observed. They perform an experiment to test their hypothesis. If the results from the experiment match the original predictions, then they consider the hypothesis supported, but not proved, since biologists cannot account for all conditions. Other biologists will continue to formulate new hypotheses and offer new findings.

D2-d Understand the kinds of evidence biologists use.

Biologists use many kinds of evidence:

- data from site studies or site surveys
- observations of specimens with the aid of special equipment, such as a microscope

- observations and measurements made in experimental settings
- data taken from reports that other biologists have published

Data in biology, which are either quantitative (that which can be counted) or qualitative (that which can be described without numbers), can take various forms, depending on the nature of the site, the type of experiment, or the specialized field in which the research is performed. Following are some examples:

- For a study of the mating choices of female swordfish, biologists might record and analyze responses from females placed in tanks with males.
- In forensic biology, researchers might interpret the data they collect from tests on criminal suspects' DNA samples.
- Plant biologists might analyze the rates of survival of native tree seedlings affected by chemicals released by invasive plant species.

Because evidence can have more than one plausible interpretation, biologists offer alternative explanations for the results obtained in experiments. For example, the authors of one article suggested that differences in the type and availability of prey could account for why Atlantic blue marlin larvae grew faster in one body of water than in another, but they also recognized that other possible causes related to differences in spawning populations.

D2-e Become familiar with writing conventions in the biological sciences.

Biologists agree on several conventions when they write:

- Scientific writing often uses the passive voice to describe how a researcher has performed an experiment (*Blue marlin larvae were collected*). The passive voice can be useful for drawing attention to the action itself, not to who has performed the action. But biologists use the active voice whenever possible to convey information clearly and efficiently (*Researchers collected blue marlin larvae*). With the use of the active voice, the first-person pronouns *I* and *we* are acceptable, even preferred, if the passive voice creates awkward-sounding sentences and adds unnecessary words.
- Direct quotation of sources is rare; instead, biologists paraphrase to demonstrate their understanding of the source material and to convey information economically.

- Biologists use the past tense to describe the materials and methods and the results of their own experiments.
- Biologists use the present tense to describe the published findings of other studies.
- Biologists often include specific scientific names for species (*Canis latrans* for the coyote, for instance).

D2-f Use the CSE system for citing sources.

Biologists typically use the style recommended by the Council of Science Editors (CSE) to format their paper, to cite sources in the text of the paper, and to list the sources at the end. The CSE describes three citation systems in *Scientific Style and Format: The CSE Manual for Authors, Editors, and Publishers*, 7th ed. (Reston: CSE, 2006). In the *name-year* system, the author's last name and the date of publication are cited in the text. In the *citation-sequence* system, each source is assigned a number the first time it is used in the text, and the same number identifies the source each time it appears. In the *citation-name* system, each source is assigned a number in the order in which it appears in the alphabetical list at the end of the paper. That number is used each time the source is cited in the text.

With all three systems, biologists place bibliographic information for each source at the end of the paper in a section called References or Cited References.

D2-g Sample student paper: Laboratory report

Conducting an experiment gives you practice in collecting and interpreting data. Writing a laboratory report allows you to describe an experiment and its results. The following laboratory report was written for a botany course. The writers used the style guidelines of the Council of Science Editors (CSE) for formatting their paper and citing and listing sources in the citation-sequence system.

Distribution Pattern of Dandelion

(*Taraxacum officinale*)

on an Abandoned Golf Course

Title page consists
of a descriptive title
and the writers'
names in the center
of the page and the
course, instructor,
and date centered at
the bottom of the
page.

Marin Johnson

Laura Arnold

Lab 4

Botany 100A

Professor Ketchum

September 13, 2005

Distribution Pattern of Dandelion 2

ABSTRACT

This paper reports our study of the distribution pattern of the common dandelion (*Taraxacum officinale*) at an abandoned golf course in Hilton, NY, on 10 July 2005. An area of 6 ha was sampled with 111 randomly placed 1×1 m^2 quadrats. The dandelion count from each quadrat was used to test observed frequencies against expected frequencies based on a hypothesized random distribution. We concluded that the distribution of dandelions was not random. We next calculated the coefficient of dispersion to test whether the distribution was aggregated (clumped) or uniform. The calculated value of this coefficient was greater than 1.0, suggesting that the distribution was aggregated. Such aggregated distributions are the most commonly observed types in natural populations.

INTRODUCTION

Theoretically, plants of a particular species may be aggregated (clumped), random, or uniformly distributed in space [1]. The distribution type may be determined by many factors, such as availability of nutrients, competition, distance of seed dispersal, and mode of reproduction [2].

The purpose of this study was to determine if the distribution pattern of the common dandelion (*Taraxacum officinale*) on an abandoned golf course was aggregated, random, or uniform.

METHODS

The study site was an abandoned golf course in Hilton, NY. The vegetation was predominantly grasses, along with dandelions, broad-leaf plantain (*Plantago major*), and bird's-eye speedwell (*Veronica chamaedrys*). We sampled an area of approximately 6 ha on 10 July 2005, approximately two weeks after the golf course had been mowed.

To ensure random sampling, we threw a tennis ball high in the air over the study area. At the spot where the tennis ball came to rest, we placed one corner of a 1×1 m^2 metal frame (quadrat). We then counted the number of dandelion plants within this quadrat. We repeated this procedure for a total of 111 randomly placed quadrats.

We used a two-step procedure [2]. We first tested whether the distribution of dandelion was random or nonrandom. From the counts of the number of dandelions in our 111 quadrats, we used a log-likelihood ratio

---

An abstract summarizes the report in about 100–125 words. You may or may not be required to include an abstract with a brief lab report.

Introduction states the purpose of the experiment.

Citations are numbered in the order in which they appear in the text (citation-sequence system).

The writers use scientific names for plant species.

Detailed description of researchers' methods.

Header contains a short title and the page number.

(G) test to examine the goodness of fit between our observed frequencies and those expected based on the Poisson series $e^{-\mu}$, $\mu e^{-\mu}$, $\mu^2/2!e^{-\mu}$, $\mu^3/3!e^{-\mu}$, . . . , where μ is the mean density of plants per quadrat. In carrying out this test, we grouped observed and expected frequencies so that no group had an expected frequency less than 1.0 [3]. We then determined whether the distribution was aggregated or uniform by calculating the coefficient of dispersion (ratio of the variance to the mean). A coefficient > 1 indicates an aggregated distribution whereas a coefficient < 1 indicates a more uniform distribution. Finally, we tested the significance of any departure of the ratio from a value of 1 by means of a t-test.

Specialized language of the field.

RESULTS

Table 1 shows the number of quadrats containing 0, 1, 2, . . . , 17 dandelion plants. More than two-thirds (67.6%) of the 111 quadrats contained no dandelion plants; almost 90% (89.2%) of the quadrats contained fewer than 3 dandelion plants. We observed a highly significant lack of fit between our observed frequencies and expected frequencies based on the Poisson distribution ($G = 78.4$, df $= 3$, $P < 0.001$). Thus, our data indicated that the distribution pattern of dandelion plants on the abandoned golf course was not random. The mean number of dandelion plants per quadrat was 1.05 (SD $= 2.50$), and the coefficient of dispersion was 5.95. A t-test showed that this value is significantly greater than 1.0 ($t = 36.7$, df $= 110$, $P < 0.001$), which strongly supports an aggregated distribution of the dandelion plants.

Headings organize the report into major sections.

DISCUSSION

An aggregated (clumped) distribution is the most commonly observed distribution type in natural populations [4]. Among plants, aggregated distributions often arise in species that have poorly dispersed seeds or vegetative reproduction [2]. In the dandelion, the seeds are contained in light, parachute-bearing fruits that are widely dispersed by the wind. This method of seed dispersal would tend to produce a random distribution. However, dandelion plants also reproduce vegetatively by producing new shoots from existing taproots, and what we considered as groups of closely spaced separate individuals probably represented

Writers interpret their results and compare them with results of other researchers.

Distribution Pattern of Dandelion 4

Table presents the data collected by the researchers in an accessible format.

Table 1 Frequency distribution of dandelion (*Taraxacum officinale*) plants in 1×1 m^2 quadrats positioned randomly over 6 ha on an abandoned golf course

Nr per quadrat	Observed frequency (f_i)	Expected frequency (f_i)[a]
0	75	38.68594
1	12	40.77707
2	12	21.49062
3	2	7.550757
4	3	1.989727
5	2	0.419456
6	0	0.073688
7	2	0.011096
8	0	0.001462
9	1	0.000171
10	0	1.8×10^{-5}
11	0	1.73×10^{-6}
12	0	1.52×10^{-7}
13	1	1.23×10^{-8}
14	0	9.27×10^{-10}
15	0	6.52×10^{-11}
16	0	4.29×10^{-12}
17	1	2.66×10^{-13}
	Total 111	

[a] Expected frequencies were calculated from the successive terms of the Poisson distribution (see Methods).

shoots originating from the same plant. Thus, vegetative reproduction probably accounted for the observed aggregated distribution in this species.

REFERENCES

Sources are listed and numbered in the order in which they appear in the text.

1. Ketchum J. Lab manual for Botany 100; 2005.

2. Kershaw KA, Looney JHH. Quantitative and dynamic plant ecology. 3rd ed. London: Edward Arnold; 1985.

3. Zar JH. Biostatistical analysis. 5th ed. Englewood Cliffs (NJ): Prentice Hall; 2005.

4. Begon M, Harper JL, Townsend CR. Ecology: individuals, populations and communities. Oxford: Blackwell Science Limited; 1996.

D3 Writing in business

Communication, especially writing, is central to the business world. Because business writers generally aim to persuade or inform their audiences, they place a premium on clarity, brevity, and focus. When you write in business courses, your goal will be to communicate in a straightforward manner and with a clear purpose.

D3-a Determine your audience and their needs in business.

When you write in business, your audience may be varied. One type of audience might be executives, managers, and employees in various departments of a company—accounting, research and development, sales, and clerical support. Another audience might consist of stockholders, clients, and potential customers. Audiences within a business organization read to consider proposals for revising existing products, services, projects, policies, or procedures or for creating new ones. Business owners and executives may read to gather information to help them evaluate projects in progress, to assess sales, and to make decisions about changing product designs or adopting new marketing strategies. They read to understand whether a course of action would be feasible and profitable for the business. Managers, salespeople, and other employees read memos, e-mail, and other documents to help them conduct the daily transactions and activities of the organization, solve daily problems, and respond to customers. Customers read the publications of a business to learn about products and services and to determine whether it would benefit them to do business with a particular company.

For all of your readers, present empirical data such as sales figures or cost structures in easily readable formats such as tables, charts, and graphs. It might also be appropriate to give your readers opinions from questionnaires or surveys. A business owner deciding whether to adopt a marketing strategy might want to read feedback from potential customers, and a potential customer might want to read testimonials from satisfied customers. Respect your readers' time. Make sure your writing is clear, straightforward, focused, attractively presented on paper or a Web site, and as brief as possible. Because trust is essential in business transactions, maintain a respectful tone and project a credible image. Business writing should make personal connections and use inclusive language.

D3-b Recognize the forms of writing in business.

In business courses, you will be asked to create documents that mirror the ones written in professional settings. The different forms of business writing covered in this section are used for varied purposes such as informing and persuading. Assignments in business courses may include the following:

- reports
- proposals
- executive summaries
- memos and correspondence
- presentations
- brochures, newsletters, and Web sites

Reports

Reports present factual information for a variety of purposes. If your company is considering the development of a new product, you may be asked to write a feasibility report that lays out the pros and cons. If you are asked to determine how your sales compare with those of a competitor, you will need to write an investigative report. A progress report updates a client or supervisor about the status of a project. A formal report details a major project and generally requires research.

Proposals

Proposals are written with the goal of convincing a specific audience to adopt a plan. A solicited proposal is directed to an audience that has requested it. An unsolicited proposal is written for an audience that has not indicated interest. An internal proposal is directed at others within an organization. An external proposal is directed at clients or potential clients. The length of a proposal will vary depending on your goals and your intended audience.

Executive summaries

An executive summary provides a concise summary of the key points in a longer document, such as a proposal or a report, with the goal of drawing the reader's attention to the longer document.

Memos and correspondence

In business, communication often takes place via letter, memo, or e-mail. Letters and e-mail are written to clients, customers, and

olleagues. Memos convey information to others in the same organiza-
ion for a variety of purposes. A memo might summarize the results
f a study or project, describe policies or standards, put forth a plan,
r assign tasks.

Presentations

Presentations are usually done orally, in front of a group, to instruct,
ersuade, or inform. Presenters often use presentation software or
ools such as whiteboards to prepare and display visuals—graphs,
ables, charts, transparencies, and so on.

Brochures, newsletters, and Web sites

Brochures generally convey information about products or services to
lients, donors, or consumers. Newsletters generally provide informa-
ion about an organization to clients, members, or subscribers. Web
ites may either advertise products or provide information about an
rganization.

D3-c Know the questions business writers ask.

n business, your purpose and your understanding of your audience
ill determine the questions you ask.

- If you are writing a proposal to persuade a client to adopt a
  product, you will ask, "How will this product benefit my client?"
  and "What does my client need?"
- If you are asked to write a report informing your supervisor of
  your progress on a project, you will ask, "What does my supervisor need to know to authorize me to proceed?" You will also want
  to ask, "What does my supervisor already know?" and "How can I
  target this report to address my supervisor's specific concerns?"
- If you are applying for a job, you will ask, "What qualifications
  do I have for this job?"

D3-d Understand the kinds of evidence business writers use.

n business, your purpose for writing, your audience, and the ques-
ions you ask will determine the type of evidence you use. The follow-
ng are some examples of the way you might use evidence in business
riting:

- If you are writing a report or a proposal, you may need to gather data through interviews, direct observation, surveys, or questionnaires. The sources of data you choose will be determined by your audience. For example, if you are studying the patterns of customer traffic at a supermarket to recommend a new layout, you might go to the supermarket and observe customers or you might ask them to fill out surveys as they leave the store. If your audience is the store manager, you might focus on surveys at one store. If your audience is the owner of a large grocery chain, you would probably need to use data from several stores.

- If you are writing an investigative report in which you consider how to entice users to a health club, your evidence might include facts and statistics about the health benefits of exercise that you have drawn from published materials such as books, articles, and reports. You might also conduct research about the facilities of a competitor. In a long proposal or report, your evidence will probably come from a variety of sources rather than just one source.

- If you are applying for a job, your evidence will be your past experience and qualifications. For example, you might explain that you have worked in the industry for six years and held three management positions. You might also discuss how the skills you learned in those jobs will be transferable to the new position.

- If you are writing a brochure to promote a service, your evidence might be testimonials from satisfied users of the service. For example, a brochure advertising nanny services might quote a customer who says, "We found a full-time nanny who is both experienced and energetic—a perfect fit for our family."

D3-e Become familiar with writing conventions in business.

In business, writing should be straightforward and professional, but not too formal.

- Buzzwords (*value-added*, *win-win*, *no-brainer*) and clichés (*The early bird catches the worm*) should be used sparingly. This kind of vocabulary is imprecise and can sound phony or insincere.

- Use personal pronouns such as *you* and *I*. Where appropriate (in letters, e-mail, proposals), you can use the pronoun *you* to emphasize the interests of your readers. When you are addressing multiple readers, you might want to avoid using *you* unless it is clear that you are referring to all readers. When you are

expressing your opinion, you should use the pronoun *I*. When
you are speaking on behalf of your company, you should use the
pronoun *we*.

- It is important to avoid language that could offend someone on
the grounds of race, gender, sexual orientation, or disability. Use
terms like *chair* or *chairperson* instead of *chairman* or *chair-
woman*. Unless it is relevant to your point, avoid describing
people by race or ethnicity. If you are describing someone with a
disability, use phrases like *client with a disability* rather than
disabled client to show that you recognize the disability as one
trait rather than as a defining characteristic of the person. (Also
see "appropriate language" in your handbook.)

- Business writing should always be concise. Avoid using words
that are not essential to your point. Instead of writing *at this
point in time*, just write *now*. Also avoid words that make a simple idea unnecessarily complicated. Using the passive voice often
creates such complications. Instead of writing *This report was
prepared to inform our customers*, write *We prepared this report
to inform our customers*.

D3-f Use the APA or CMS (*Chicago*) system in business writing.

Business students typically use the style guidelines of the American Psychological Association (APA) or *The Chicago Manual of Style*
(CMS) for formatting their paper, for citing sources in the text of their
paper, and for listing sources at the end. The APA system is set forth
in the *Publication Manual of the American Psychological Association*,
6th ed. (Washington, DC: APA, 2010). CMS style is found in *The Chicago Manual of Style*, 16th ed. (Chicago: University of Chicago Press,
2010). (For more details, see the documentation sections in your handbook.) In business courses, instructors will usually indicate which
style they prefer.

D3-g Sample student papers: An investigative report and a proposal

Sample report

Different business situations require different types of reports. Formal reports are comprehensive discussions of a topic from multiple
angles, while investigative reports often focus on a specific issue. If

you are asked to write a report, you should always be sure that y
understand the expectations of your audience.

The investigative report beginning on page D-21 was written for
introductory course in business writing. The student, Brian Spenc
was asked to research the problem of employee motivation at a sm
company. He used the style guidelines of the American Psychologic
Association (APA) to format the paper and to cite and list sources.

Sample proposal

Proposals are written to convince a specific audience to adopt a pl
If you are asked to write a proposal, you might start by identifying t
purpose and the audience for the document.

The internal proposal beginning on page D-28 was written fo
course in business writing. The student, Kelly Ratajczak, wrote h
proposal in the form of a memorandum to the senior vice president
human resources at the medium-size company at which she was
intern. Her goal was to convince the vice president to adopt a we
ness program for employees.

.MPLE REPORT

The title page of a business report is counted in the numbering, although a header and page number do not appear.

Positively Affecting Employee Motivation

Title, writer's name, and date, centered on page; company name, centered at bottom.

Prepared by Brian Spencer

Report Distributed March 9, 2006

Prepared for OAISYS

ginal annotations indicate business-style formatting **and** effective writing.

In a typical business report, the page header contains an abbreviated title and the page number.

Abstract

Corporate goals, such as sales quotas or increases in market share, do not always take into account employee motivation. Motivating employees is thus a challenge and an opportunity for firms that want to outperform their competitors. For a firm to achieve its goals, its employees must be motivated to perform effectively.

Abstract, on a separate page, provides a brief summary of the report.

Empirical research conducted with employees of a subject firm, OAISYS, echoed theories published by leading authorities in journals, books, and online reports. These theories argue that monetary incentives are not the primary drivers for employee motivation. Clear expectations, communication of progress toward goals, accountability, and public appreciation are common primary drivers. A firm aiming to achieve superior performance should focus on these activities.

While not strictly APA style, the formatting of the business report is consistent with the style typically used in businesses. Headings are flush with the left margin and boldface. Paragraphs are separated by an extra line of space, and the first line of each paragraph is not indented.

Employee Motivation 3

Introduction

All firms strive to maximize performance. Such performance is typically
defined by one or more tangible measurements such as total sales, earnings
per share, return on assets, and so on. The performance of a firm is created
and delivered by its employees. Employees, however, are not necessarily
motivated to do their part to maximize a firm's performance. Factors that
motivate employees can be much more complex than corporate goals. This
report will define the problem of employee motivation in one company and
examine potential solutions.

OAISYS is a small business based in Tempe, Arizona, that manufactures
business call recording products. Currently OAISYS employs 27 people. The
business has been notably successful, generating annual compound sales
growth of over 20% during the last three years. The company's management
and board of directors expect revenue growth to accelerate over the coming
three years to an annual compound rate of over 35%. This ambitious
corporate goal will require maximum productivity and effectiveness from all
employees, both current and prospective. OAISYS's management requested
an analysis of its current personnel structure focused on the alignment of
individual employee motivation with its corporate goal.

Background on Current Human Resources Program

OAISYS is currently structured departmentally by function. It has teams
for research and development, sales, marketing, operations, and
administration. Every employee has access to the same employment
benefits, consisting of medical insurance, a 401(k) plan, flexible spending
accounts, short- and long-term disability insurance, and the like.

Members of the sales team receive a yearly salary, quarterly commissions
tied to sales quotas, and quarterly bonuses tied to the performance of
specific tasks. These tasks can change quarterly to maintain alignment with
strategic initiatives.

All employees not in the sales department receive a yearly salary and profit
sharing at the end of the year. The formula for profit sharing is not

Introduction clearly
presents the problem
to be discussed and
sets forth the scope
of the report.

Heading announces
the purpose of each
section.

known by the employees, and specific information about profits is
infrequently communicated. When profitability is discussed, it is only in
general terms. Key employees, as determined by the management, are
given stock option grants periodically. This process is informal and very
confidential.

Disconnect Between Company and Employees

One common assumption is that a human resources program such as
OAISYS's should be the platform for motivation. But monetary
compensation is not the only driver of employee motivation (Dickson,
1973). In fact, studies have found that other factors are actually the
primary drivers of employee motivation. Security, career advancement, the
type of work, and pride in one's company are actually the highest-rated
factors in employee satisfaction (Accel TEAM, 2005).

These conclusions drawn from the empirical research of others are
supported by interviews conducted with current OAISYS employees. Justin
Crandall, a current design engineer, stated that his primary motivation is
the opportunity to work with leading-edge development tools to pursue
results of the highest quality (personal communication, March 1, 2006).
Crandall's strongest sense of frustration comes from a cluttered
organizational structure because it restricts his ability to pursue
innovative, high-quality results.

Todd Lindburg, the most senior design engineer on staff, had similar
sentiments. His greatest motivator is the opportunity to create something
lasting and important to the long-term success of the business (personal
communication, March 2, 2006). Jack Wikselaar, vice president of sales,
said he receives his strongest motivation from providing fulfilling job
opportunities for others (personal communication, March 3, 2006).

These findings of what motivates employees tell only half the story.
Other research (*Motivating*, 2006) suggests that businesses can actually
demotivate employees through certain behaviors, such as the
following:

Spencer presents
evidence from
research studies.

Spencer provides
evidence from
interviews with
current employees.

Interviews are
considered personal
communication in
APA style; they are
cited in the text of
the paper but not
given in the
reference list.

Employee Motivation 5

- company politics
- unclear expectations
- unnecessary rules and procedures
- unproductive meetings
- poor communication
- toleration of poor performance

A list draws readers' attention to important information.

Doug Ames, manager of operations for OAISYS, noted that some of these issues keep the company from outperforming expectations: "Communication is not timely or uniform, expectations are not clear and consistent, and some employees do not contribute significantly yet nothing is done" (personal communication, February 28, 2006).

Recommendations

It appears that a combination of steps can be used to unlock greater performance for OAISYS. Most important, steps can be taken to strengthen the corporate culture in key areas such as communication, accountability, and appreciation. Employee feedback indicates that these are areas of weakness or motivators that can be improved. This feedback is summarized in Figure 1.

The author lays out recommendations for action. Some reports also include a Conclusions section.

A plan to use communication effectively to set expectations, share results in a timely fashion, and publicly offer appreciation to specific contributors will likely go a long way toward aligning individual motivation with corporate goals. Additionally, holding individuals accountable for results will bring parity to the workplace.

Figure 1. Areas of greatest need for improvements in motivation.

Graphic illustrates support for the report's key recommendation.

One technique that might be effective is basing compensation on specific responsibilities. Rather than tying compensation to corporate profit, tying it to individual performance will result in direct correlation between results and reward. Those who do what is necessary to achieve expected results will be rewarded. Those who miss the mark will be required to address the reasons behind their performance and either improve or take a different role. Professor of organizational behavior Jesper Sorenson (2002) has noted that "quantitative analyses have shown that firms with strong cultures outperform firms with weak cultures" (p. 70). Taking steps to strengthen the corporate culture is critical to the company's success.

References

Accel TEAM. (2005). *Employee motivation in the workplace*. Retrieved from http://www.accel-team.com/motivation

Dickson, W. J. (1973). Hawthorne experiments. In C. Heyel (Ed.), *The encyclopedia of management* (2nd ed., pp. 298-302). New York, NY: Van Nostrand Reinhold.

Motivating employees without money. (2006). Retrieved from http://www .employer-employee.com/howtomot.htm

Sorenson, J. B. (2002). The strength of corporate culture and the reliability of firm performance. *Administrative Science Quarterly, 47*(1), 70-71.

Spencer provides a list of sources using APA style.

SAMPLE PROPOSAL

MEMORANDUM

Internal proposal is structured in memo format; subject is identified in the header.

To: Jay Crosson, Senior Vice President, Human Resources

From: Kelly Ratajczak, Intern, Purchasing Department

Subject: Proposal to Add a Wellness Program

Date: April 24, 2006

Ratajczak opens with a clear, concise statement of her main point.

Health care costs are rising. In the long run, implementing a wellness program in our corporate culture will decrease the company's health care costs.

Introductory section provides supporting background information.

Research indicates that nearly 70% of health care costs are from common illnesses related to high blood pressure, overweight, lack of exercise, high cholesterol, stress, poor nutrition, and other preventable health issues (Hall, 2006). Health care costs are a major expense for most businesses, and they do not reflect costs due to the loss of productivity or absenteeism. A wellness program would address most, if not all, of these health care issues and related costs.

Headings clearly define the sections of the proposal.

Benefits of Healthier Employees

While not strictly APA style, the memo format for a proposal is consistent with the style typically used in businesses. A header at the top of each page contains an abbreviated title and an arabic page number (the first page is counted in the numbering, although a number does not appear). Headings are flush with the left margin and boldface. Paragraphs are separated by an extra line of space, and the first line of each paragraph is not indented.

A wellness program would substantially reduce costs associated with employee health care, and in addition our company would prosper through many other benefits. Businesses that have wellness programs show a lower cost in production, fewer sick days, and healthier employees ("Workplace Health," 2006). Our healthier employees will help to cut not only our production and absenteeism costs but also potential costs such as higher turnover because of low employee morale.

Implementing the Program

Implementing a good wellness program means making small changes to the work environment, starting with a series of information sessions. Simple changes to our work environment should include healthier food selections in vending machines and in the employee cafeteria. A smoke-free environment, inside and outside the building, could be a new company policy. An important step is to educate our employees through information seminars and provide health care guides and pamphlets for work and home. In addition, the human resources department could expand the current

---

Marginal annotations indicate business-style formatting and effective writing.

employee assistance program by developing online materials that help employees and their families to assess their individual health goals.

Each health program is different in its own way, and there are a number of programs that can be designed to meet the needs of our individual employees. Some programs that are becoming increasingly popular in the workplace are the following ("Workplace Health," 2006):

- health promotion programs
- subsidized health club membership
- return-to-work programs
- health-risk appraisals and screenings

Obstacles: Individual and Financial

The largest barrier in a wellness program is changing the habits and behaviors of our employees. Various incentives such as monetary bonuses, vacation days, merchandise rewards, recognition, and appreciation help to instill new habits and attitudes. Providing a healthy environment and including family in certain programs also help to encourage healthier choices and behaviors (Hall, 2006).

In the long run, the costs of incorporating a wellness program will be far less than rising costs associated with health care. An employee's sense of recognition, appreciation, or accomplishment is an incentive that has relatively low or no costs. The owner of Natural Ovens Bakery, Paul Sitt, has stated that his company gained financially after providing programs including free healthy lunches for employees (Springer, 2005). Sitt said he believes that higher morale and keeping valuable employees have helped his business tremendously.

It is important that our company be healthy in every way possible. Research shows that 41% of businesses already have some type of wellness program in progress and that 32% will incorporate programs within the next year ("Workplace Health," 2006). Our company should always be ahead of our competitors. I want to thank you for your time, and I look forward to discussing this proposal with you further next week.

> Ratajczak identifies and responds to potential concerns.

> The concluding paragraph summarizes the main point, provides support for being competitive, and indicates a willingness to discuss the proposal.

Ratajczak provides a list of the sources she used in her proposal. The reference list is formatted in APA style.

Wellness Program Proposal 3

References

Hall, B. (2006). Good health pays off! Fundamentals of health promotion
incentives. *Journal of Deferred Compensation 11*(2), 16-26. Retrieved
from http://www.aspenpublishers.com/

Springer, D. (2005, October 28). Key to business success? *La Crosse
Tribune*. Retrieved from http://lacrossetribune.com/

Workplace health and productivity programs lower absenteeism,
costs. (2006). *Managing Benefit Plans 6*(2), 1-4. Retrieved
from http://www.ioma.com/

D4 Writing in criminal justice and criminology

Criminal justice and criminology are part of the same broad field. Criminal justice refers to the application of policing practices and policies, and criminology is chiefly concerned with the theories that explain those practices and policies. The field of criminal justice and criminology draws from a diverse range of disciplines, including sociology, political science, public administration, psychology, history, and the law. Holding this multidisciplinary field together is its fundamental focus on justice. Whatever your specialization as a student—policing, law enforcement management, juvenile justice, corrections, law and the courts, or homeland security—you may be asked to write papers on topics such as policing practices and policies, the administration of justice, legal decision making, and the theories criminologists use to explain and analyze crime. Your instructors may also ask you to imagine different audiences and purposes for this writing to prepare you for the complexity of writing tasks and the readers you'll encounter in the workplaces you enter.

D4-a Determine your audience and their needs in criminal justice and criminology.

Criminal justice professionals write for diverse audiences, including peers and supervisors in an organization or members of other, related organizations, readers of professional and academic publications, and the general public. When you write in a criminal justice course, you might be asked to imagine that you are writing a memo to a new police chief explaining local crime trends and demographics. Or you might write a memo to the head of a law enforcement organization describing a policing practice or policy and making recommendations for change. You might write about the same practice or policy for an audience of public defenders or for public resources officers who must make sure that citizens understand what the policy means to them. You might be asked to write an article about the practice or policy for a magazine such as *Police Chief*, whose audience consists of many different kinds of practitioners in the field. Given these multiple and often overlapping audiences, you must analyze your readers' needs carefully.

D4-b Recognize the forms of writing in criminal justice and criminology.

When you take courses in criminal justice and criminology, you ma be asked to write in a variety of forms for diverse audiences and pu poses. These forms include the following:

- research papers
- analytical papers
- argument or position papers
- investigative and administrative reports
- policy memos
- case briefs and legal briefs
- case plans (or case notes)

Research papers

A research paper in a criminal justice course requires you to ide tify an issue or a topic and then to research what has been writt about the topic or to explore the data that have been compiled abo the topic (called *secondary sources*). You might also be expected to u *primary sources*—interviews or surveys that you conduct. In mo cases, you'll be expected to find your own angle on the topic and make an argument about it. You might also be required to apply theory you've studied to your research findings. In a policing cours you might investigate whether police officers from different racial an ethnic backgrounds make decisions differently. To obtain informatio you might conduct interviews and read published studies. In a soci inequality and justice class, you might investigate whether the focu of racial profiling shifted from African Americans to Muslims aft September 11, 2001, and what scholars are saying about possib trends. In a course on corrections, you might examine the puniti practice of solitary confinement and consider what this prison pra tice indicates about US law and society.

Analytical papers

Often you'll be given assignments that ask you to apply the the ries you've studied to a situation, a legal case, or a personal accou written by someone in the criminal justice system. For assignmen like these, you will generally be expected to describe the theory an its main components and to use the theory to explain specific situ tions and people's behaviors and life choices. For example, you mig e asked to analyze how discretionary theory applies to street-level policing or to critique a theory by comparing it with other theories that attempt to explain the same behaviors and choices. Sometimes analytical papers conclude with program or policy recommendations based on the usefulness or persuasiveness of the theory.

rgument or position papers

n argument or position papers, you are expected to present both sides f an issue in a balanced way and then to take a position. Your position will be based on your analysis of the course readings and lectures or n research you've conducted, not on your personal opinion. You might also be asked to compare or contrast relevant theories and cases to upport your position. For example, an assignment might ask you to rgue for more or less discretionary power for street-level policing, using as evidence cases in which that power has been used or abused. Or, after investigating trends in racial profiling, you might take a position supporting or opposing changes in the current policies. Or you might argue that the practice of long-term solitary confinement is or is not justified as a crime control approach in US penal policy.

nvestigative and administrative reports

Law enforcement professionals and criminologists write both investigative and administrative reports. Some common investigative reports are crime and arrest reports, incident and accident reports, and pre-sentencing reports. A typical crime or arrest report includes a clear timeline of events, for both the crime and the investigation, such as when the defendant was taken into custody, read his or her Miranda rights, and interviewed. The report should also include other details about the criminal investigation—for example, where the interview with the defendant took place, who else was present, and whether any other witnesses were interviewed. Administrative reports typically include a description of a problem, supported by research and statistical data, and recommendations based on an analysis of the data. A consultant's administrative report to a new police chief, for example, may include a briefing about the demographics and crime problems in the local area, an analysis of official crime statistics using the FBI's Uniform Crime Reports, a summary of the findings, and recommendations based on the findings.

Both investigative and administrative reports may be formatted as memos and written to specific audiences who need the information to make decisions, formulate policy, and implement recommendations. In all cases, accuracy, completeness, and objectivity are key to an effective report.

Policy memos

Policy memos are written for many purposes—to inform, to explain, to document, to persuade, or to make a request. The format and style will vary from organization to organization, so you must be aware of the audience's expectations and the conventions set by the organization you're writing for. Typically, the purpose of a policy memo is to help the audience understand the issue and interpret the policy to make practical judgments. You might be asked to write a policy memo to the head of a criminal justice organization, such as the Transportation Security Administration, about the effects of racial profiling on a particular group. Your memo might include a description of the policies being used to address the problem; an argument, based on research, for changing the policies; and recommendations for policies or programs that would benefit the group about which you're concerned.

Case briefs and legal briefs

A brief is a document presented to interested members of a court of law. Briefs are addressed to a specific audience and typically include a short description of a legal case, highlighting key issues, relevant facts, and, if applicable, a history of related court decisions; an analysis and interpretation of how the case applies to a particular organization; and the legal principles and jurisdictional issues related to the desired outcome. For a case brief assignment, you might be asked to write to a public defender or a future judge on how to interpret issues involved in a specific case. A legal brief assignment might ask you to analyze documents submitted for a moot court exercise and to argue for one side.

Your instructor may ask you to follow the IRAC model when you write case and legal briefs. IRAC is an organizational approach used in legal writing as a method for problem solving and structuring an analysis. The acronym IRAC stands for the following steps:

Issue: State the legal issue of relevance.

Rules: List all the statutes and case law relevant to your brief.

Analysis or Application: Provide arguments in favor of and against the decision in this case.

Conclusion: Provide an answer to the legal issue raised.

Another organizational approach is based on the acronym PEAR:

Position: State a position.

Explanation: Explain the position.

Alternatives: Examine the alternative positions.

Response: Respond to potential objections.

NOTE: The explanations of the IRAC and PEAR models are adapted from the *Criminology, Law, and Society Writing Guide* from George Mason University at http://classweb.gmu.edu/WAC/adjguide/legal briefs/case_briefs.html.

Case plans (or case notes)

Case plans, or case notes, may be written as memos or as part of pre-sentencing and postsentencing reports. They might be addressed to courtroom work groups, such as public defenders, prosecutors, judges, and probation officers. Case notes may be addressed to social workers and treatment providers in problem-solving courts such as drug and mental health courts. As the number of work groups expands, audience analysis becomes more complicated because each group may have different goals for its clients and constituencies. For example, a social worker might be interested in resources and treatment; lawyers, in justice; and judges, in the legal aspects of the case. Given the complexity of this writing task, there is no template to guide you. You will typically learn on the job or from models your instructor provides. In general, case notes and plans must be straightforward, clear, and well organized, with the goals and purpose carefully laid out in the introduction along with a preview of the main topics that you will cover. Be sure to include subheadings so that the various audiences can skim through the notes to identify information related to their concerns.

D4-c Know the questions criminal justice professionals and criminologists ask.

Generally, the questions that criminal justice professionals and criminologists ask can be divided into two broad areas of inquiry, one focused on legal systems, the other focused on justice organizations. Within these two broad areas are big-issue questions about crime, law enforcement, society, ethics, and social justice:

- What is deviance, and what is crime?
- What are the causes of crime?
- What is the difference between the law on the books and the law in action?
- What is effective policing?
- What are the theories and laws related to discretionary decision making for practitioners in the field?
- What policing, corrections, and court system policies and practices work to reduce crime and its social effects?

While most of your courses will take up these broad questions in one way or another, each course will have its own focusing questions. A course on policing in the United States, for example, will focus on the role of police in protecting the public against crime and disorder, influences on the decisions police make, the moral and ethical issues they confront, what good policing looks like, and the trends, innovations, and reforms that affect the policing profession. In a corrections course, the focus will be on postsentencing and postrelease issues, with questions about jail and prison management, probation and parole, and compliance with supervision and treatment follow-up requirements.

D4-d Understand the kinds of evidence criminal justice professionals and criminologists use.

Criminal justice professionals and criminologists use many different kinds of evidence — quantitative, qualitative, historical, and legal — to answer the questions they pose. Most practitioners rely on methods derived from the social sciences to gather evidence: interviews, direct observation, surveys, narrative analysis, natural setting experiments, and analysis of demographic, statistical, legal, geographic, and historical data. Criminologists also use theory-based evidence or the history of a theory or law enforcement policy.

As a student, you will probably be required to use both primary and secondary sources as evidence and to gather and analyze both quantitative and qualitative data. Quantitative data may include crime statistics, incarceration rates, racial profiling data from police stops, ticketing rates, and data on crime statistics linked to geographic areas. Qualitative data may include your own observations, others' responses to interviews and surveys, and the stories people tell about their encounters with crime and the criminal justice system.

Your instructors will also expect you to consult relevant secondary sources, including articles in scholarly and popular periodicals (such as *Police Chief*), news media, government and legal documents, statistical reports, and organizational Web sites, reports, and studies.

D4-e Become familiar with writing conventions in criminal justice and criminology.

Scholars and practitioners in the criminal justice field value independent thought; the ability to gather, synthesize, and analyze evidence from diverse sources; and the ability to interpret theory and to apply evidence • primary sources • secondary sources • qualitative • quantitative • conventions • objectivity • APA • CMS • citing sources

D4-f

D-37

heory to practice and practice to theory. Beyond these broad goals, practitioners agree that writing in the field must be clear, concise, accurate, objective, and well organized, with a clear statement of the writer's purpose and main points. Writers must convey knowledge of the topic in a voice, tone, and format appropriate to the purpose and audience. They must present facts and evidence in an objective, balanced way to allow readers to draw their own conclusions.

To be objective, writers must strive for factual description. For example, in a crime report they should note the date, time, and location of a crime or suspected criminal behavior; they should also describe people and their actions as factually as possible, including identifying characteristics such as gender, race or ethnicity, age, height, weight, and distinctive features like facial hair, tattoos, scars, or physical mannerisms. Subjective descriptions such as "the perpetrator looked suspicious" are meaningless and unfair if not backed up with factual details. It is also important to avoid language that could be construed as offensive or that reveals biases toward gender, race, ethnicity, disabilities, and socioeconomic class.

In the criminal justice field, accuracy is crucial, whether in an arrest report, a briefing memo, a case plan, a researched report, or the application of a theory to an issue, practice, or policy. Errors and inaccuracies can cause readers to misinterpret a report, disregard a memo, or throw a case out of court.

First-person pronouns are rarely used in research papers, reports, policy memos, briefings, or analytical papers, in part because writers must present their views objectively, logically, and factually. While the writer of a memo or briefing report may use *I* on occasion, the content of the memo or report itself and the recommendations being made must be based on the writer's analysis of the evidence, not on personal opinions or biases. The diverse audiences for these documents also expect clear, concise writing, so writers typically use active voice and paraphrases rather than extensive quotations from their research. In some circumstances, however, it is important to include direct quotations as this information might be critical to an accurate interpretation of the problem, issue, or policy.

D4-f Use the APA or CMS (*Chicago*) system in writing in criminal justice and criminology.

While professionals in the field generally use the documentation style prescribed by the organization or academic journal for which they are writing, instructors typically ask students to use the style guidelines of the American Psychological Association (APA) or the name-year system of *The Chicago Manual of Style* (CMS) to format their paper, to document sources in the text of their paper, and to list sources at the end. Both systems call for in-text, parenthetical citations rather than footnotes or endnotes. The APA system is set forth in the *Publication Manual of the American Psychological Association*, 6th ed. (Washington, DC: APA, 2010). CMS style is found in *The Chicago Manual of Style*, 16th ed. (Chicago: University of Chicago Press, 2010). (For more details, see the documentation sections in your handbook.)

Sometimes students are asked to use *Bluebook* style (or, as it's sometimes called, modified Bluebooking) when they cite sources in case briefs and legal briefs. *Bluebook* format is used by courts, attorneys, and law schools; however, most instructors do not require students to learn this specialized style.

D4-g Sample student paper: Administrative report

Administrative reports are written for specific audiences, typically supervisors, to provide information about an issue or a problem of concern to an organization. When you are asked to write a report, you will be expected to identify the issue or problem, find and analyze relevant statistics and other research, and make recommendations for future actions.

The following administrative report was written for an introductory course on crime and crime policy. Students were asked to imagine that they had been hired as a consultant by the new police chief in their hometown. They were asked to brief the chief about crime in the area, to explain how crime statistics for their town compare with the national average using the FBI's Uniform Crime Reports, and to interpret the statistics so that the chief could decide how best to use the department's resources. The student writer, Chris Thompson, analyzed crime statistics for his hometown of Leesburg, Virginia. He used APA guidelines to format his paper and to cite and list his sources.

Running head: CRIME IN LEESBURG, VIRGINIA

1 The header consists of a shortened title in all capital letters at the left margin and the page number at the right margin; on the title page only, the shortened title is preceded by the words "Running head" and a colon.

Crime in Leesburg, Virginia

Chris Thompson

George Mason University

Full title, writer's name, and school, halfway down the page.

An author's note lists specific information about the course or department and can provide acknowledgments and contact information.

Author Note

This paper was prepared for Administration of Justice 305: Crime Policy, taught by Professor Devon Johnson.

Crime in Leesburg, Virginia

This report reviews crime statistics in Leesburg, Virginia, to familiarize the new police chief with the town and offer some suggestions about where to focus law enforcement resources. It analyzes local and national statistics from the FBI's Uniform Crime Reports (UCR) for the United States and for Leesburg and offers a basic assessment of the town's needs to provide a useful snapshot for the chief of police.

Description of Leesburg, Virginia

Leesburg, Virginia, is a suburb of Washington, DC, 40 miles to the northwest. In 2008, its population was 39,899 (U.S. Department of Justice, 2009, Table 8). Like many northern Virginia and southern Maryland communities, it serves as a suburban bedroom community to those employed in the nation's capital. The town has grown significantly in the last three decades.

Leesburg's population is predominantly middle and upper middle class, with a median household income 75% higher than the national average (Town of Leesburg, Virginia, 2009a). Leesburg is populated by young (median age 32.3), well educated (about 50% with a bachelor's degree, about 17% with an advanced degree) citizens; half are white-collar professionals (Town of Leesburg, Virginia, 2009a).

The Leesburg Police Department has 77 sworn officers, operates 24 hours a day, and uses numerous special teams and modern law enforcement techniques. The department has divided the city into three patrol areas to address the specific needs of each zone (Town of Leesburg, Virginia, 2009b).

Nature and Extent of Crime in Leesburg, Virginia

Tables 1 and 2 show the FBI's UCR statistics for 2008. Table 1 contains statistics for Leesburg and the United States, and Table 2 presents the crime rate in Leesburg as a percentage of the national average. A discussion of the accuracy of the UCR is on page 5.

Crime Rates in Leesburg Compared With the National Average

The following list of index crimes compares their rates in Leesburg, Virginia (first value), with the national average (second value). In general, the crime rate in Leesburg is lower than it is across the country. This may be due in part to the demographics of the town's residents and the commuter-oriented suburban nature of the community.

Full title, repeated.

Introduction establishes the purpose of the report and acknowledges the audience.

Centered headings define the major sections of the report.

Thompson provides demographic information relevant to the crime statistics he will analyze.

In-text citation from a Web site is in APA style.

Thompson points to the data tables, explaining their purpose and sources.

Thompson uses a major section of the report to analyze details from the tables.

CRIME IN LEESBURG, VIRGINIA   3

Table 1

Crime Rates, by Crime, in Leesburg, Virginia, and in the United States, 2008

	Leesburg		United States	
Offense type	No. reported offenses	Rate per 100,000 inhabitants	No. reported offenses	Rate per 100,000 inhabitants
Violent crime				
Forcible rape	7	17.5	89,000	29.3
Murder and nonnegligent manslaughter	1	2.5	16,272	5.4
Robbery	22	55.1	441,855	145.3
Aggravated assault	29	72.7	834,885	274.6
Total violent crime	59	147.8	1,382,012	454.5
Property crime				
Larceny theft	715	1,792	6,588,873	2,167
Burglary	62	155.4	2,222,196	730.8
Vehicle theft	25	62.7	956,846	314.7
Total property crime	802	2,010	9,767,915	3,212.5

Note. The data for Leesburg, Virginia, are from U.S. Department of Justice (2009), Table 8. The data for the United States are from U.S. Department of Justice (2009), Table 1.

Larceny Theft: 1,792 vs. 2,167 per 100,000

Larceny theft is one of the few index crimes found close to the same level in Leesburg as in the entire nation and thus represents an area of interest for the Leesburg police.

Forcible Rape: 17.5 vs. 29.3 per 100,000

The incidence of forcible rape is slightly more than half the national average. Rape crimes may be an area of concern in Leesburg.

Murder and Nonnegligent Manslaughter: 2.5 vs. 5.4 per 100,000

The most serious crimes, those involving the loss of a human life, are approximately half as prevalent in Leesburg as in the United States as a whole. Murder is typically not a crime that can be countered through patrol.

Robbery: 55.1 vs. 145.3 per 100,000

Robbery (a direct, personal theft from an individual) in Leesburg is approximately one-third the national average. Leesburg is not prone

The data tables are presented in APA style. The columns are clearly labeled, and the data categories reinforce the writer's purpose.

Thompson organizes his discussion of the crimes in Leesburg by most to least concerning.

Subheadings are flush left and boldface.

Table 2

Crime Rates in Leesburg, Virginia, Compared With the National Average, 2008

Offense type	Crime rate in Leesburg per 100,000 inhabitants	Crime rate in the United States per 100,000 inhabitants	Crime rate in Leesburg compared with national average (%)
Violent crime			
Forcible rape	17.5	29.3	59.7
Murder and nonnegligent manslaughter	2.5	5.4	46.2
Robbery	55.1	145.3	37.9
Aggravated assault	72.7	274.6	26.4
Total violent crime	147.8	454.5	32.5
Property crime			
Larceny theft	1,792	2,167	82.6
Burglary	155.4	730.8	21.2
Vehicle theft	62.7	314.7	19.9
Total property crime	2,010	3,212.5	62.5

Note. The data for Leesburg, Virginia, are from U.S. Department of Justice (2009), Table 8. The data for the United States are from U.S. Department of Justice (2009), Table 1.

to the frequency of robberies found in urban areas, perhaps because most robberies are committed by residents of the same community, and the community of Leesburg is fairly homogeneous in terms of income levels.

Aggravated Assault: 72.7 vs. 274.6 per 100,000

The rate of felony assaults (attempts to commit or acts resulting in serious bodily harm) in Leesburg is roughly one-quarter that in the nation as a whole.

Burglary: 155.4 vs. 730.8 per 100,000

The incidence of burglary (breaking into the home of another person with the intent to commit a felony) in Leesburg is one-fifth the national average. The suburban nature of Leesburg may contribute to this low level.

CRIME IN LEESBURG, VIRGINIA   5

Vehicle Theft: 62.7 vs. 314.7 per 100,000

Motor vehicle theft is uncommon in Leesburg, about one-fifth as likely as in the nation as a whole.

Areas of Interest for a New Police Chief

Overall, forcible rape and larceny theft are the two crimes of most interest to the Leesburg police because their frequency is closer to the national average than the frequency of other crimes. While overall crime is low in Leesburg, these two crimes stand out based solely on the FBI UCR statistics. The police may want to pay particular attention to these crimes for reasons not apparent in the UCR.

Forcible rape is typically an underreported crime because of victim-related factors such as shame and distrust of the system. This crime is of particular concern because even the UCR statistics may not reflect an accurate crime rate (Mosher, Miethe, & Phillips, 2002). The actual instances of rape may be significantly higher than those reported in the UCR. Policy implications may include an increased community policing focus on rape prevention as well as targeted police patrolling of areas where reported rapes occur.

The desire to file an insurance claim for larceny theft (which often requires a police report) may cause more citizens to come forward when they are victims of this particular crime. For this reason, the actual instances of larceny theft are likely closer to those captured in the UCR. Increased patrolling of residential neighborhoods during work hours may reduce burglary rates because most burglaries occur during the day when the occupants are at work.

Accuracy of UCR Statistics

The FBI's UCR, while useful in showing crime trends, is not without its faults. The UCR contains only crimes reported to or observed by law enforcement officers; therefore, it does not provide a complete portrait of crime. The National Crime Victimization Survey (NCVS) revealed that, in many cases, roughly half of the total crimes committed in the United States go unreported (Mosher et al., 2002). The reasons vary but include distrust or lack of faith in the police and the judicial system, shame about or apathy toward the crime, fear of reprisals, inability to recognize the perpetrator, and victim participation in illegal activities at the time of

> Thompson interprets the crime statistics and makes recommendations for allocating department resources.

> Thompson discusses issues related to the reporting of crime and the accuracy of the UCR. To analyze the strengths and weaknesses of the UCR, he draws on secondary sources.

In APA style for a work with three to five authors, all authors are given the first time the source is cited; in subsequent citations, the first author is followed by "et al."

victimization (Mosher et al., 2002). The new police chief should keep these limitations in mind when evaluating UCR statistics.

In addition, classifying crimes is often subjective. Mosher et al. (2002) pointed out that "political manipulation and fabrication of these data by police departments" can easily distort statistics related to an individual incident or a whole reporting agency (p. 84). Some of these distortions are a product of police officer discretion stemming from the "legal seriousness of the crime," "the complainant's preferences," any relationship between the police officer and the offender, the level of respect shown by the complainant, and the financial or social status of the complainant (p. 85).

Conclusion

Thompson summarizes the findings in the report and provides a recommendation. He ends by explaining the importance of crime data analysis for policymaking and assessment.

The town of Leesburg, Virginia, is, in general, a safe place to live. Overall, it experiences a rate of crime considerably lower than the national average. The incidence of property crime is 62.5% of the national average, and the incidence of violent crime is 32.5% of the national average. Leesburg does, however, have two potential problem areas: forcible rape and larceny theft.

This report's initial examination of the data from the UCR is of limited value because of the UCR's lack of depth and breadth in exploring local crime. To obtain a better picture of crime in Leesburg, the new police chief should request a report that compares local, regional, and national crime statistics over several years using the FBI's UCR combined with NCVS data to develop an accurate picture of overall crime. Carefully weighing that information and evaluating it to reveal the big picture are both a means and an end in the law enforcement world: They allow policymakers to make decisions that may reduce the crime rate.

CRIME IN LEESBURG, VIRGINIA   7

References

U.S. Department of Justice, Federal Bureau of Investigation. (2009). *Crime
    in the United States 2008*. Retrieved from http://www2.fbi.gov/ucr
    /cius2008/index.html

Mosher, C. J., Miethe, T. D., & Phillips, D. M. (2002). *The mismeasure of
    crime*. Thousand Oaks, CA: Sage.

Town of Leesburg, Virginia. (2009a). *Demographics*. Retrieved from http://
    www.leesburgva.gov/index.aspx?page=210

Town of Leesburg, Virginia. (2009b). *Field operations division*. Retrieved
    from http://www.leesburgva.gov/index.aspx?page=955

List of references is
in APA style.

List of references
begins on a new
page. The first line
of each entry is at
the left margin;
subsequent lines
indent ½".

≣ **D5** Writing in education

The field of education draws on the knowledge and the methods of a variety of disciplines. As you study to become a teacher, you will take courses that focus on such diverse topics as the history of education, the psychology of teaching and learning, the development of curriculum, and instructional methods. You will also learn how to navigate classrooms and schools through both course work and field placements. Depending on what you plan to teach, you may also take courses in a specific content area (such as history or mathematics) or courses that focus on children with special needs. The writing you do in education courses will be designed to help you become a successful teacher.

D5-a **Determine your audience and their needs in education.**

Audiences in the field of education may be school administrators, teachers, students, parents, or policymakers. Administrators read documents to evaluate faculty and assess programs, to revise or develop new programs and curricula, to create policy, to solve problems, to resolve student issues, and to communicate with parents. Teachers read scholarship in their fields to learn about new theoretical findings and methods. Because assessment is a major topic in academic institutions, teachers read reports on student and program assessment as well as informational documents that help them participate in making school policy for testing and placement. Students and parents read publications from their schools and school district to learn about student performance and school policy. Policymakers such as school board members and state legislators expect information, assessment reports, and proposals about schools, curricula, and programs to be presented with numerical data in the form of graphs and tables.

When you write in education courses, be sure to give your readers empirical data, such as test scores, presented in an easily understandable format. You may need to provide direct observations of student performance as well. Always maintain student confidentiality. Because student groups are so diverse and because positive community relations are essential to every school, be sensitive to student backgrounds and respectful toward students and parents.

D5-b Recognize the forms of writing in education.

Although there are many paths you can take as you train to become a teacher, you will encounter similar writing assignments in different courses. These may include the following:

- reflective essays, journals, and field notes
- curriculum designs and lesson plans
- reviews of instructional materials
- case studies
- research papers
- self-evaluations
- portfolios

Reflective essays, journals, and field notes

Much of the writing you do in education courses will encourage you to reflect on your own attitudes, beliefs, and experiences and how they inform your thoughts about teaching and learning. In an introductory course, for example, you may be asked to write an essay in which you discuss your own education in the context of a theory that you are studying. As a field observer or student teacher, you may be asked to keep a journal or notes in which you reflect on your interaction with students, teacher-student interactions, student-student interactions, diversity issues, and student progress. These reflections might then serve as the basis for an essay in which you connect your experiences to course content.

Curriculum designs and lesson plans

In some courses, especially those focused on teaching methods, you will be asked to design individual lessons or units in a particular content area. In an early childhood education course, for example, you might be asked to read one or more children's books and write a plan for a class activity that is related to the reading. In a science methods course, you might be asked to design a unit about plant biology. In a methods course for special education, you might be asked to design an individualized education plan for a specific student. For any of these courses, you might also be asked to integrate technology into your curriculum design.

Reviews of instructional materials

In a review of materials, you assess the value of a set of instructional materials for classroom use. For example, you might be asked to look at several textbooks or software applications and explain which would be most useful in a particular classroom setting.

Case studies

Some education courses require students to conduct and write case studies. Case studies may involve observation and analysis of an individual student, a teacher, or classroom interactions. The goal of a case study may be to determine how the process of teaching or learning takes place or how an event can illuminate something about learning or classroom dynamics.

Research papers

In some education courses, you might be assigned papers that focus on broader educational issues or problems and that require you to conduct research and then formulate your own ideas about the topic. In a course about the history of education, you might be asked to research the evolution of literacy in the United States. In a developmental psychology course, you might be asked to research how students learn mathematics.

Self-evaluations

As a teacher candidate, you will be asked to evaluate your own teaching and learning. The format of the self-evaluation will vary depending on whether you are evaluating yourself as a learner or as a teacher. Sample questions of self-evaluation as a teacher may include the following:

- What were the strengths and weaknesses of your lesson or unit plan?
- How did your lesson further student learning?
- What have you learned about yourself and your students from teaching this class?
- How can you improve your teaching?

Portfolios

Most teacher education programs require you to assemble a teaching portfolio before you graduate. The purpose of the portfolio is to provide information about your teaching experience and your teaching philosophy. The contents of portfolios vary, but common documents include

. statement of teaching philosophy, a statement of professional goals, a résumé, evaluations, and sample course materials. Education departments at some institutions will require you to assemble an electronic portfolio as well as a print version.

D5-c Know the questions educators ask.

Educators ask questions that are practical, theoretical, and self-reflective. Practical questions tend to focus on classroom and curriculum issues such as student progress and implementation of new approaches. Theoretical questions focus on how students should be educated and on the intellectual, political, and social contexts of learning. Self-reflective questions allow for discussion of the teacher's own role in the educational process. Any of the following questions could form the basis for a paper in an education course:

- How does this school's language arts curriculum prepare students to be information-literate?
- What are the effects of the use of standardized tests in economically disadvantaged districts in comparison with more affluent districts?
- How do my perceptions of my own education influence the way I approach teaching?

D5-d Understand the kinds of evidence educators use.

Educators and education students rely on evidence that is both quantitative (statistics, survey results, test scores) and qualitative (case studies, observation, personal experience). The following are some examples of evidence used in different situations:

- If you are writing a research paper that compares different approaches to social studies education, you might rely on quantitative evidence such as the results of standardized tests from different school districts.
- For a paper on child development, you might use a combination of personal observation and evidence from published case studies.
- If you are keeping a journal of your student teaching experiences, your evidence would come from your experiences in the classroom and from the changes in your attitudes over time.
- If you are creating a lesson plan, you will focus on your teaching objectives and explain how your plan will achieve those objectives.

D5-e Become familiar with writing conventions in education.

Educators agree on several conventions when they write:

- The personal pronoun *I* is commonly used in reflective writing. It is sometimes used to communicate observations and recommendations.

- Research papers and case studies are generally written in the third person (*he*, *she*, *it*, *they*) and in a formal, objective tone.

- Educators have a specialized vocabulary that includes terms such as *pedagogy* (teaching principles and methods), *practice* (actual teaching), *curriculum* (the written lesson plans followed by a class or school), *assessment* (the determination of whether students or teachers are successful), *achievement tests* (tests that measure what students have learned), and *NCLB* (the No Child Left Behind Act). You will likely use such terms in your writing.

Because the field of education draws on various disciplines, including psychology, history, and sociology, it is important to be aware of writing conventions in those disciplines as well. (See D7 and D10.)

D5-f Use the APA or CMS (*Chicago*) system in writing in education.

Writers in education typically use the style guidelines of the American Psychological Association (APA) or *The Chicago Manual of Style* (CMS) for formatting their paper, for citing sources in the text of their paper, and for listing sources at the end. The APA system is set forth in the *Publication Manual of the American Psychological Association*, 6th ed. (Washington, DC: APA, 2010). CMS style is found in *The Chicago Manual of Style*, 16th ed. (Chicago: University of Chicago Press, 2010). (For more details, see the documentation sections in your handbook.) In education courses, instructors will usually indicate which style they prefer.

D5-g Sample student paper: Reflective essay

In some education courses, you may be asked to write reflective essays in which you describe and analyze your own attitudes, beliefs, and experiences. Some reflective essays focus solely on personal observations while others integrate ideas from other sources as well.

The following reflective essay was written for a service learning course in which students explored issues of diversity, power, and opportunity in school settings. The writer, Onnalee Gibson, used a variety of professional sources to inform her own ideas about her experiences working with an eleventh-grade student. She formatted her paper and cited and listed her sources following the guidelines of the American Psychological Association (APA).

The header consists of a shortened title in all capital letters at the left margin and the page number at the right margin; on the title page only, the shortened title is preceded by the words "Running head" and a colon.

Full title, writer's name, and school halfway down the page.

A Reflection on Service Learning:

Working with Eric

Onnalee L. Gibson

Michigan State University

An author's note lists specific information about the course or department and can provide acknowledgments and contact information.

Author Note

This paper was prepared for Teacher Education 250, taught by

Professor Carter. The author wishes to thank the guidance staff of Waverly

High School for advice and assistance.

Marginal annotations indicate APA-style formatting and effective writing.

A Reflection on Service Learning:

Working with Eric

The first time I saw the beautiful yet simple architecture of Waverly High School, I was enchanted. I remember driving by while exploring my new surroundings as a transfer student to Michigan State University and marveling at the long front wall of reflective windows, the shapely bushes, and the general cleanliness of the school grounds. When I was assigned to do a service learning project in a local school district, I hoped for the opportunity to find out what it would be like to work at a school like Waverly—a school where the attention to its students' needs was evident from the outside in.

> Reflective essays may include descriptive passages.

Waverly High School, which currently enrolls about 1,100 students in grades 9 through 12 and has a teaching staff of 63, is extremely diverse in several ways. Economically, students range from poverty level to affluent. Numerous ethnic and racial groups are represented. And in terms of achievement, the student body boasts an assortment of talents and abilities.

> Background information about the school sets the scene for Gibson's personal experiences.

The school provides a curriculum that strives to meet the needs of each student and uses a unique grade reporting system that itemizes each aspect of a student's grade. The system allows both teachers and parents to see where academic achievement and academic problems surface. Unlike most schools, which evaluate students on subjects in one number or letter grade, Waverly has a report card that lists individual grades for tests, homework, exams, papers, projects, participation, community service, and attendance. Thus, if a student is doing every homework assignment and is still failing tests, this breakdown of the grades may effectively highlight how the student can be helped.

It was this unique way of evaluating students that led to my first meeting with Eric Johnson, an 11th grader to whom I was assigned as a tutor. Eric is an African American male who grew up in a nuclear middle-class family in a Lansing suburb. Teachers noticed over time that Eric's grades were dropping, yet his attendance, participation, and motivation were above average. Surprisingly, Eric himself was the one who asked for a tutor to help him raise his grades. What initially struck me about Eric was the level of responsibility he seemed to take for his own academic

> Transition leads from background information about the school to Gibson's personal experiences.

SERVICE LEARNING: ERIC   3

Journal entries are considered personal communication and are cited in the text but not included in the reference list.

Personal observations lead to broader insights.

Gibson analyzes her evidence to draw a broader conclusion.

This section bridges academic theory and personal experience.

achievement. At the time I wrote in my journal (January 31, 2006), "He appears to be a good student. He is trying his best to succeed in school. *He* came to *me* for help and realizes the need for a tutor."

While tutoring Eric, I paid attention to the way he talked about his classes and to the types of assignments he was being asked to complete. My impression was that Waverly High School was fostering student success by doing more than just placing posters in the hallways. Waverly's curriculum encourages analytical thinking, requires group and individual projects that depend on creativity and research, and includes open-ended writing assignments designed to give students opportunities to form their own conclusions. I found this reality both difficult and inspiring; I had not expected an 11th grader's homework to be so challenging. I once said so to Eric, and he responded with a smile: "Yeah. My teachers say it's going to help us when we get to college to already know how to do some of these things."

What was surprising to me was the faculty's collective assumption that high school was not the end of a student's career. The fact that teachers talk with students about what will be expected *when* (not *if*) they go to college is significant. That kind of positive language, which I heard many times at Waverly, most certainly affects students' sense of themselves as achievers. In this case, Eric was not preoccupied with worrying about whether he wanted to go to college or would be accepted; rather, he mentally prepared himself for the time when he would actually enroll.

According to education researcher Jean Anyon (1981), "Students from higher social class backgrounds may be exposed to legal, medical, or managerial knowledge . . . while those of the working classes may be offered a more 'practical' curriculum" (p. 5). I do not see this gravitation toward social reproduction holding true for most students at Waverly High School. Waverly's student body is a mix of social classes, yet the school's philosophy is to push each of its students to consider college. Through its curriculum, its guidance department literature, and its opportunities for career field trips, Waverly is opening doors for all of its students. In Eric's case, I also observed the beginnings of a break in social reproduction. From the start of our tutoring sessions, Eric frequently mentioned that neither of his parents went to college (O. Gibson, journal entry, March 14, 2006). This made me wonder how his parents talk to him about college. Is the desire to go to college something they have instilled in him? Have they given him the message that if he works hard and goes to college he will be successful? If that is the case, then Eric's parents are attempting to break the cycle with their children—and they have the good fortune to live in a school district that supports their desires. In contrast to the idea that most people have nothing more than social reproduction to thank for their socioeconomic status (Bowles & Gintis, 1976), Eric seems to believe that hard work and a college education are keys to his success.

> Source is cited in APA in-text citation style.

    Another key to Eric's success will be the resources he enjoys as a student at Waverly. Abundance of or lack of resources can play an important part in students' opportunities to learn and succeed. Because nearly half of all school funding comes from local property taxes (D. Carter, class lecture, April 4, 2006), areas with smaller populations or low property values do not have the tax base to fund schools well. As a result, one education finance expert has argued, some children receive substandard education (Parrish, 2002). Waverly does not appear to have serious financial or funding issues. Each student has access to current textbooks, up-to-date computer labs, a well-stocked library, a full art and music curriculum, and numerous extracurricular activities. While countless schools are in desperate need of a better-equipped library, Waverly's library has a rich collection of books, magazines and journals, computer stations, and spaces in which to use all of these materials. It is a very user-friendly library. This has shown me what the power of funding can do for a school. Part of Waverly's (and its students') success results from the ample resources spent on staff and curriculum materials. Adequate school funding is one of the factors that drive school and student success.

> Class lecture (personal communication) is cited in the text only, not in the reference list.

> Gibson considers the larger implications of her personal observations.

    Aside from funding, placement policies determine school and student success. A major concern of both educators and critics of education policies is that schools will place students into special education programs unnecessarily. Too often students who do not need special education are coded for special ed—even when they have a learning issue that can be handled with a good teacher in a mainstream class (D. Carter, class lecture, April 6, 2006). At Waverly High School, teachers and counselors are not so quick to shuffle Eric into special ed. I agree with several of Eric's teachers

SERVICE LEARNING: ERIC   5

who feel that he may have a mild learning disability. I began to feel this way when Eric and I moved from working in a private tutoring space to working in the library. It was clear to me that he had difficulty paying attention in a public setting. On February 9, I wrote in my journal:

A quotation longer than forty words is indented without quotation marks.

> Eric was extremely distracted. He couldn't pay attention to what I was asking, and he couldn't keep his eyes on his work. There were other students in the library today, and he kept eavesdropping on their conversations and shaking his head when they said things he did not agree with. This is how he must behave in the classroom; he is easily distracted but he wants to work hard. I see that it is not so much that he needs a tutor because he can't understand what his teachers are telling him; it is more that he needs the one-on-one attention in a confined room free of distractions.

Even though Eric showed signs of distraction, I never felt as if he should be coded for special education. I am pleased that the administration and learning specialists did not decide to place Eric in a special education track. Eric is exceedingly intelligent and shows promise in every academic area. He seems to be able to succeed by identifying problems on his own and seeking resources to help him solve those problems. He is a motivated and talented student who simply seems like a typical adolescent.

I came away from my service learning project with an even stronger conviction about the importance of quality education for a student's success. Unlike the high school I attended, Waverly pays close attention to each child and thinks about how to get all its students to succeed at their own level. Jean Patrice, an administrator, told me, "You have to be able to reach a student where *they* are instead of making them come to you. If you don't, you'll lose them" (personal communication, April 10, 2006), expressing her desire to see all students get something out of their educational experience. This feeling is common among members of Waverly's faculty. With such a positive view of student potential, it is no wonder that 97% of Waverly High School graduates go on to a four-year university (Patrice, 2006). I have no doubt that Eric Johnson will attend college and that he will succeed there.

As I look toward my teaching future, I know there is plenty that I

SERVICE LEARNING: ERIC   6

have left to learn. Teaching is so much more than getting up in front of a
class, reiterating facts, and requiring students to learn a certain amount of
material by the end of the year. Teaching is about getting students—one
by one—to realize and act on their potential. This course and this service
learning experience have made me realize that we should never have a
trial-and-error attitude about any student's opportunities and educational
quality.

Conclusion raises
questions for further
reflection.

List of references, in APA style, begins on a new page.

List is alphabetized by authors' last names.

Double-spacing is used throughout.

References

Anyon, J. (1981). Social class and school knowledge. *Curriculum Inquiry,
11*(1), 5.

Bowles, S., & Gintis, H. (1976). *Schooling in capitalist America: Educational
reform and contradictions of economic life.* New York, NY: Basic
Books.

Parrish, T. (2002). Racial disparities in identification, funding, and
provision of special education. In D. Losen & G. Orfield (Eds.), *Racial
inequity in special education.* Cambridge, MA: Civil Rights Project and
Harvard Education Press.

D6 Writing in engineering

ngineers use the language of mathematics and the methods of science along with the experiences of society to design machines, tools, ocesses, and systems that will solve problems and accomplish tasks fely and efficiently. There are many different types of engineers: echanical, chemical, electrical, civil, geological, environmental, and erospace, to name a few. Each type of engineer addresses problems nd tasks in a particular part of the physical world.

Writing plays a major role in the work of engineers, who write ports and recommendations based on their research and their esign ideas. Engineers write technical reports addressed to manu- cturers or the companies or agencies that hire them. Engineers also mmunicate their solutions to clients in their own organizations.

As a student of engineering, you will be challenged to devise lutions to real-world problems. Most of your assignments will be en-ended questions that will involve finding or proposing solutions design challenges; you will be required to compose rationales for ur solutions in writing. In laboratory experiments, you will main- in a lab notebook and write reports about your hands-on research. ecause engineers usually work in teams, some writing assignments ill involve working with other students to give you practice with llaboration.

6-a Determine your audience and their needs in ngineering.

ngineers usually write for readers who have a definite interest in hat they have to say. Research and design in engineering never take ace in isolation; these activities occur in universities, private indus- y, and government.

Sometimes your readers will be other engineers and decision akers working in your team or in other groups in your organiza- on; they will expect you to provide a high level of technical detail d to use specialized vocabulary. They need to be able to replicate ur work and confirm the results. Sometimes your audience will be corporate client outside your organization in industry or govern- ent. Or your audience might be public-policy decision makers or the neral public. Some of these audiences might not have your level technical expertise, so your writing must be accessible and clear, ith a minimum of technical language and jargon. For example, if u are writing a proposal to win a contract for your company or

to receive funding for a project, your proposal will have to be written appropriately for an audience consisting of both specialists and
nonspecialists.

When you write in engineering courses, keep in mind that you
are learning to write for readers who probably have not done the
study, research, or design work that you have done. When writing a
report, for example, you will write for a reader who was not present
in the laboratory or in the field. Even though your professor is in the
laboratory with you, always describe your research and experimentation process carefully and thoroughly as if he or she is not familiar
with your process. Add spreadsheets, drawings, plates, or illustrations to help your readers visualize your findings.

D6-b Recognize the forms of writing in engineering.

When you take courses in engineering, you may be asked to write any
of the following:

- project notebooks
- laboratory reports
- technical reports
- proposals
- progress reports

Project notebooks

A project notebook is like a personal journal in which you record your
work in progress. It is a log in which you can write your observations
and data from the experimentation and design processes or brainstorm and explore explanations or interpretations of the data. You
might describe the materials you use and the procedures you follow
or draw sketches of your design and, later, its construction. A project
notebook can be useful as you work through mathematical analysis of
your data and your designs and as you pose questions and plan solutions to problems. It can also provide the space in which you make
note of tests that work and those that do not. You can write reflections
on articles you read, notes from meetings you attend, and logistics for
projects you are working on. You might also record your instructor's
and peers' comments and critiques.

Make your project notebook as complete and as neat as possible;
sign and date entries daily. Remember that your notebook will be useful in your later research, design, and writing. If your notebook is part
of an ongoing project that someone else will continue after you, the

rmality, thoroughness, and neatness will be critical. Notebooks are aditionally kept on paper, but you may keep one electronically to ake it easier to record, update, and read. As you move into profesonal practice, these notebooks will become part of any project's foral records.

aboratory reports

ngineers present the procedures, materials, and results of their periments in laboratory reports. These reports are essential to the velopment of the discipline, as it is through these reports that new nowledge is recorded and communicated to researchers, teachers, d students. Laboratory reports for some assignments may have rticular requirements. Generally, the laboratory reports you are signed will follow the organization used in laboratory reports writn by engineers working in industry and government.

Your report will need to accomplish the following:

- establish the main question or problem under investigation and provide some background

- state the objective of the laboratory work (to measure, to verify, to compare, and so on) and the exact methods and procedures step-by-step

- describe and comment on your results, explain what they mean, put any unexpected results in context, and compare your results with established knowledge in the discipline

- place your results in the context of your stated purpose; note patterns apparent in the results, implications for future consideration, and any questions that remain unanswered

- tell your reader if you achieved the predicted or anticipated results; account for any differences if possible

The structure of your laboratory report will function as "instrucns" for anyone who wants to replicate your experiment, verify your sults, or use your work as a foundation for his or her own research.

You can use the same method and structure to record and report engineering design projects.

chnical reports

technical report describes the structure and functions of a design. the report's purpose is to investigate the failure of a design, tool, machine, then it is a *forensic report*. The audience for a technical design report is usually other engineers or a similar audience of perts; it can also be decision makers, regulators, and the courts.

A technical report usually has the following structure:

- executive summary, a one-page concise statement of the most important points in the report
- introduction
- purpose and goals
- methods
- data and findings
- recommendations and action items
- conclusion
- appendices if necessary

Use tables, charts, spreadsheets, maps, figures, and illustration in the body of your report to present your data and findings or appendices to support your conclusions. Your recommendations an conclusion should interpret your data, discuss any limitations boundaries of your work, and suggest action items for this project other, related projects. Document your work by citing your referenc in the style recommended by your instructor or the organization f which you are writing.

Proposals

Engineers write project proposals to seek funding from academic an government sources or to describe a project to potential clients. "Sellin a customer on a project is thus an important function of an enginee: job. Many proposals are written with cross-disciplinary teams includin sales, marketing, production, and legal departments. A proposal for client may include a price quote or estimate, also called a "bid."

For your classes, you may write proposals for laboratory projec or to suggest solutions for a hypothetical client (usually your professc who has given you a technical problem or design problem. Prepa your proposals with sufficient research, appropriate graphics, caref organization, and neat presentation to assist your readers and sho them that you are credible.

To make it easy for your readers to say yes to your proposal, gi them clear, sufficient information about the project. Begin with a introduction that includes a brief project description and lays out t cost, completion date, and rate of return on investment. In the body the proposal, provide the following:

- background and rationale for the project, describing the need t be met or the problem to be solved
- how the project will be accomplished

- expected outcomes
- materials and methods
- method of evaluation that will be used to determine that the objectives have been achieved
- timeline (sometimes presented in a Gantt chart, a graphical representation of the overlapping deadlines and milestones for all aspects of the project)
- budget, including deadlines and a list of items that must be funded

You can assume that your readers are receiving other proposals, so you might also provide a résumé or a section describing your skills and experiences that qualify you for the project.

Progress reports

Once a proposal is accepted and a project is under way, an engineer must write progress reports regularly to inform the client of the work accomplished. A progress report can be in the form of a business letter or a memo. It describes any milestones that have been achieved or tasks that have been completed. In engineering classes, your progress reports will be written to your professor to document your accomplishments and to describe the work still to be completed.

In your progress report, you might provide the following:

- a brief project description as a reminder of the scope of the project
- a summary of progress with a list of the tasks that have been completed
- a list of any problems that have arisen and solutions implemented or suggested
- any necessary alterations in deadlines or the budget
- a description of work remaining before the next progress report

Engineers frequently use spreadsheets to present data and provide a "snapshot" of the project at various stages. Spreadsheets can be converted into slides for PowerPoint presentations along with images of the work. Complete project reports will assure your readers that you are reliable, punctual, and in control of progress.

D6-c Know the questions engineers ask.

Engineers explore questions related to designing, repairing, and improving aspects of the physical world. Wherever people require a safer, faster, more effective, more efficient, more comfortable, or less expensive way to accomplish a task, engineers investigate and suggest solutions. The tasks might be related to transportation, to the construction of buildings and bridges, to the design of electrical grid and other city infrastructure, or to the invention of appliances and tools in the home or in the workplace.

Engineers explore questions such as these:

- An aging bridge in an area with heavy traffic must be replaced as soon as possible. What is the best design for a new bridge that can support a heavy payload but can also be built in a short period of time?

- Can a liquid laundry detergent be invented that will dissolve more quickly in water and flow more efficiently through the hoses of a new high-efficiency washing machine?

- What material would be best for resurfacing a parking lot in an area that often floods when it rains? What are the properties of different materials that might be used for this construction project?

- Two aerospace companies have proposed different configurations for the wings of a new fighter plane. Which of the two wing designs will allow the aircraft to achieve the highest possible speed with the lowest possible vibration at the most affordable cost?

- Is it possible to invent electronic devices that can be powered wirelessly rather than with batteries or electrical power?

- Because customers want more environmentally friendly equipment for the home, a manufacturer of lawn mowers asks whether it is possible to construct a new kind of engine, similar to the engines in hybrid cars, that would burn fuel more efficiently and more cleanly than current engines.

D6-d Understand the kinds of evidence engineers use.

Engineers use particular kinds of evidence:

- data from laboratory reports published by other engineers
- observations and measurements of apparatus and processes inside the laboratory
- observations and measurements from building models of proposed projects
- observations and measurements from computer simulations and models
- observations and measurements made in real-world settings

Engineers often begin the design process with computer simulations and analysis. Then they verify the simulated results with models
and laboratory experiments. This process saves money for engineering firms and their clients. For example, car companies use multiple
computer simulations of car crashes before they crash-test a real car.
In your classes, your projects may be "pen and paper" designs: You
design and test the project on the computer or with manual calculations but do not actually build the project.

Data in engineering are quantitative; they can be counted.
Depending on the nature of the problem or experiment, some data
can be qualitative, described without numbers. When a structure fails
or displays flaws, forensic engineers perform physical tests and sometimes collect and analyze witness testimony as they seek the causes
of the problem.

For example, after a passenger airplane exploded in midair in
1996, engineers spent months reconstructing the aircraft to locate the
cause. They discovered that structural problems had resulted in small
vibrations. Over a long period of time, the vibrations had caused two
electrical wires located near a fuel tank to rub against each other.
Eventually the insulation of one of the wires had rubbed away, and
the electrical current in the wire caused a spark that ignited vapors
from the fuel tank. The engineers arrived at this conclusion only after
painstakingly examining numerous components, sometimes in micro-
scopic detail, ruling out many of them, focusing on the relevant ones,
and ultimately performing tests in the laboratory to replicate the
effects of vibrations on the wires.

6-e Become familiar with writing conventions in engineering.

Engineers agree on several conventions when they write:

- Engineers often work in teams on research and laboratory
  projects. In your classes, you will often collaborate with other
  students. Collaboration requires that team members delegate
  and accept responsibility, report to one another, share ideas,
  listen to one another, negotiate differences, and compromise on
  solutions. Usually one person on the team will be in charge of
  combining the individually written sections of a report into a
  single document. Some team members may not be engineers or
  engineering students. Developing relationships with nonengi-
  neering and nonscience students and professionals is essential
  to effective work and communication in engineering.

- Each type of writing should include standard sections. For example, a laboratory report is not complete if it does not include a section that interprets results.

- Engineers must be brief and clear. When describing a process or an apparatus you used, you will need to write exactly what you did and what resulted. You must present the order of the steps you followed in logical sequence.

- Engineers try to avoid ambiguous pronoun use so that readers will know exactly what a pronoun refers to. Instead of writing *This confirms the original results*, an engineer should write *This new set of data confirms the original results*.

- Engineers use headings and subheadings in their reports and proposals. Engineering reports can be long and detailed, and headings mark the important categories of information and help readers follow the organization. Engineers also divide their reports into clear parts with combinations of numbers and letters denoting major sections and their subsections.

- Engineering is a visual field. Readers expect writers to provide diagrams, illustrations, charts, tables, and graphs. Graphics should support the data and other information in a report; they should be easy to understand, with clear labels and captions.

- Engineers use verb tenses deliberately. They use past tense for laboratory reports (*These results demonstrated*). They use future tense in proposals (*This design will require*). They use both present tense and past tense in progress reports (*The design phase is on schedule* or *The foundation was poured during week 3*).

- Engineers usually use third-person pronouns (*he*, *she*, *it*, *they* rather than *I*, *me*, *we*). They use active voice where possible because it is more direct and concise. For instance, instead of writing *The viability of the instrument was demonstrated by the results*, they write *The results demonstrated the viability of the instrument*.

D6-f Use the CMS (*Chicago*), IEEE, or USGS system in writing in engineering.

Writers in different fields of engineering use different styles to cite sources in their papers and to list sources at the ends of their papers. Civil engineers, chemical engineers, industrial engineers, and mechanical engineers usually use the name-year system of *The Chicago Manual of Style*, 16th ed. (2010).

Electrical engineers, computer engineers, and mechanical engineers use the *IEEE Editorial Style Manual*, published by the Institute of Electrical and Electronics Engineers.

Engineers and scientists in geology usually use *Suggestions to Authors of the Reports of the United States Geological Survey*, 7th ed. 1991).

When you begin a project in an engineering class, check with your instructor about which style is required for your assignment.

D6-g Sample student paper: Proposal

A proposal recommends a solution to a design or technical problem posed by a client. A typical proposal includes details about how the project will be completed, the required materials and methods of construction, and the expected costs. It often includes alternatives for comparison. The following proposal was written in a junior-level geology engineering course. The student, Alice O'Bryan, explores the options that a fictional company called Ajax might consider for providing proper drainage for a planned park. O'Bryan presents descriptions of several alternatives, including costs, benefits, and overall effectiveness. She used the United States Geological Survey (USGS) guidelines to format her paper and to cite and list her sources.

O'Bryan 1

Full title, writer's
name, course, and
date, centered
halfway down the
page.

Site Stabilization Plan for Erosion Control

Alice O'Bryan

GLY 341

May 5, 2008

Marginal annotations indicate USGS-style formatting and effective writing.

CONTENTS

The contents page lists all the major headings and subheadings; it can also list minor subheadings, as here. The indentation of headings in the contents indicates the hierarchy and organization of the paper.

A USGS proposal often begins with an executive summary that briefly provides background, findings, and recommendations.

EXECUTIVE SUMMARY

Ajax is seeking to develop a 44-acre parcel of land into a recreational park and has requested proposals for erosion control. This proposal recommends a system of terraces and a grassed waterway culminating in a 1-acre constructed lake. While this is not the least expensive method of erosion control, it will be effective at preventing erosion and also will meet Ajax's goals for an aesthetically pleasing park that can attract human visitors as well as aquatic life and wildlife. Two less desirable plans are a system of terraces with a riprapped waterway and a buried pipeline. Both plans are less expensive, but both have drawbacks and do not meet all of Ajax's goals.

The recommended proposal (proposal A) will create a series of 13 vegetative terraces that flow into a grassed waterway approximately 1,200 feet long. The waterway will culminate in a 1-acre lake that will collect the drainage and provide a recreational fishing hole. This proposal has the advantage of not disrupting the open land and in fact enhancing it with planted vegetation along the terraces and waterway and with a lake that can attract wildlife and that can be used for recreational purposes. The cost of this proposal is as follows:

- Terraces: $15,034
- Grassed waterway: $4,000
- 1-acre lake: $18,000-60,000
- Total: $37,034-79,034

Additional costs will be incurred for recovery of the soil if more surface is disturbed than just the terrace and waterway construction areas. (See the summary of costs at the end of the proposal.)

The proposal for terraces and a riprapped waterway (proposal B) includes a riprapped channel that would disrupt the parklike atmosphere and that may not prevent off-site erosion. Its costs are as follows:

- Terraces: $15,034
- Riprapped waterway: $6,000
- Total: $21,034

The buried pipeline (proposal C) is the least desirable option because it is hard to maintain, requires an unattractive retaining wall, and is not suited for the soil type in this area. Its costs are as follows:

O'Bryan 4

- Buried pipeline: $6,000
- Gabion retaining wall: $25,000-50,000
- Total: $31,000-56,000

ANALYSIS OF PROPOSALS

PROPOSAL A: TERRACES AND GRASSED WATERWAY

Nonstructural and preventive erosion control provided by proposal A is the best choice for Ajax because the land is to be developed into a park. It is not the least expensive method, but it is likely to be most effective at meeting all the goals of the project. This proposal recommends a system of 7 terraces, each pair spaced 120 feet apart in the clayey silt soil, and 6 terraces, each pair spaced 150 feet apart in the silty clay soil. These terraces would have a 0.60% channel gradient, which would direct the water into a grassed waterway culminating in a 1-acre lake. A lake of this size is reasonable on a site of 44 acres and is more cost-effective than a smaller lake or a pond, which requires more specialized equipment to construct. The site is well suited for a lake because of its gently sloping topography. While a well-built lake can be expensive, Ajax can save money by using the excavated soil to build the terraces.

PROPOSAL B: TERRACES AND RIPRAPPED WATERWAY

Proposal B includes the same terraces as in proposal A, but the terraces flow into a riprapped channel going through the site and leading water beyond the boundaries of the property. A filter material must underlay the entire area that the riprap will cover (Minnesota Department of Transportation, 2005). Geotextile is the best material for this purpose. On top of this will be a 6-inch layer of granular filter material of uniform thickness over the prepared foundation. With geotextile, the foundation surface must be smooth and free of stones or other debris, and the fabric must not be torn during application. The riprap rocks should be placed from the bottom of the waterway to the top to achieve a uniform size distribution, with the smallest percent of void space possible. When completed, the riprap should not be less than 95% of the specified thickness.

PROPOSAL C: BURIED PIPELINE

A buried pipeline is the least optimal choice for the site. Methods

O'Bryan provides an analysis of three proposals, giving an overview of how each proposal would be implemented and recommending one.

First- and second-level headings are centered in all capital letters.

O'Bryan uses USGS style for citing sources in the text.

of erosion control that are constructed aboveground are preferred because it is much easier to perform maintenance on them. There is no room for error in the design and construction of a buried pipeline. Also, in the site area, clay makes up a large percentage of the soil; the shrink-swell potential of the soil could later damage the pipes. Pipelines are also just as expensive as riprap. For this method, a retaining wall would be constructed of gabion baskets, which are more flexible than concrete and allow for the possibility of establishing vegetation in the spaces. As with the riprap plan, an erosion control blanket is required under the gabion to prevent scouring. There are several drawbacks to the use of gabions. As Lynn Merill (2004) writes, quoting engineer Mark North, "'Gabions may not be appropriate for use in high-traffic areas' where people coming in contact with them run the risk of 'snagging their clothes on the wire.'" In addition, gabions can be very expensive.

GUIDELINES FOR CONSTRUCTION[1]

Geotextile material.—Geotextile material should be "woven, nonwoven, or knit fabric of polymeric filaments or yarns such as polypropylene, polyethylene, polyester, or polyamide formed into a stable network such that the filaments/yarns retain their relative position to each other" (Minnesota Department of Transportation, 2005, p. 907). If the geotextile is being used as an earth reinforcement or under riprap, all sewn seams on the fabric must meet strength requirements.

Erosion control blankets.—Erosion control blankets are designed to be used until vegetation can be established. There are nine different categories of blankets based on use longevity and flow velocity; use longevity ranges from 6-8 weeks through permanent. The category chosen should be specific to the method of construction and to the site. For example, if gabions are built and the flow velocity is calculated to be less than 6.5 ft/s, a category 6 erosion control blanket should be used. The blanket should be laid out parallel to the direction of flow, and adjacent blanket edges should overlap by at least 4 inches and should be stapled.

---

[1]All guidelines are based on Minnesota Department of Transportation, 2005, and Beasley and others, 1984, unless stated otherwise.

O'Bryan provides guidelines that should be followed for any of the three proposals. She uses a footnote to give the sources of her guidelines.

In USGS style, minor subheadings are indented and italicized, followed by a period and a dash.

O'Bryan uses a footnote for a general point related to the entire section.

At the top of the slope, the blanket should be buried in a check slot, which should be backfilled and compacted. Within the channel, the blanket should be stapled every foot.

Silt fences.—No silt should be washed off-site, and the soil must be seeded if it is to be bare for more than 45 days. It is expected that silt fences will be required at some point during construction of any of the proposed plans. It is acceptable to use the standard machine-sliced silt fencing during site grading to keep sediment from moving. Each post of the silt fence should be secured by a minimum of five gun staples 1 inch long.

Excavation.—During excavation, a well-drained condition must be maintained through planned drainage facilities. Topsoil should be stockpiled and covered. If blasting is required, it must be conducted so that materials will not be thrown out of the area and will be easily recoverable. Excavations must have a secure uniformity in grade; if excavations fall below final grade, they must be done with the provision that they are subject to change.

Pipe installation.—Pipes should be installed to collect and discharge water infiltrating into the soil or accumulated in a subcut or to cut off or intercept groundwater flow. The pipes should be constructed of nonperforated threadless copper (TP) pipe. Minimum trench width should be the diameter of the pipe plus two times the diameter. All rocks within the trench should be removed. A fine filter aggregate layer of one pipe diameter should be laid in the bottom of the trench. If perforated pipe is used, it must be wrapped in geotextile. Pipes that will discharge at a constructed gabion wall should be installed so that small movements in the wall will not cause the pipes to separate.

Reseeding.—The purpose of reseeding the area is not just to beautify the landscape. Reseeding is also an effective erosion control method. The application of seed must be conducted with as much rigor and attention to detail as any construction project on the site will be carried out. The establishment of permanent vegetation requires soil tilling, liming, fertilizing, seeding, sodding, mulching, and any other work required to ensure that the plants survive to maturity. Proper planting times must be observed; until the time for seeding has arrived, previously

O'Bryan 7

mentioned methods of erosion control must be used. The recommended
temporary seeding mixture is mixture number 130; its seeding date varies
because this seed has 40% of both winter wheat and oats. The optimal
time for planting winter wheat is Aug. 1-Oct. 1, and for oats it is May
1-Aug. 1. Other seed mixture numbers have different planting seasons, as
shown in table 1.

If rills or gullies have formed anywhere on the site, they should
be filled in prior to seeding and compacted so that they are approximately
the same density as the surrounding soil. The seed should be applied
according to the seed application rate for its mixture number (see
table 2). Hydroseeding is prohibited when wind speeds exceed 15 mph.
The traditional seed mixes (numbers 100-280) should be applied through
hydroseeding; native mixes, because of the shape of the seed, require a
native seed drill. In hydroseeding, seed must be uniformly distributed;
otherwise the area must be reseeded. The permanent seed mixture can be
applied to an area that is covered with a temporary seed mixture without
additional tillage or site preparation. The water-to-straw-bale ratio with
tackifier for mulch is 100 gallons to every 50-pound bale.

PROPOSAL A: DETAILS AND GENERAL SPECIFICATIONS

Seeded terraces and waterway.—On this site, there will be 7 sets of
terraces 120 feet apart in the clayey silt soil and 6 sets of terraces 150 feet
apart in the silty clay soil. The terraces will have a 0.60% gradient. They
will begin at elevation 560 feet and will be 600 feet long, increasing by

Tables are referred to in the text and are placed as close as possible to their text reference.

O'Bryan gives specific details about her recommended proposal.

Table number and title appear above the table. A headnote, in brackets, gives source information; it also can explain abbreviations or symbols.

Table 1. Planting seasons for seed
[From Minnesota Department of Transportation, 2005, table 2575-1, p. 712]

Seed mixture number	Spring	Fall
100	—	Aug. 1-Oct. 1
110	May 1-Aug. 1	—
150, 190	Apr. 1-July 20	July 20-Oct. 20
240, 250, 260, 270	Apr. 1-June 1	July 20-Sept. 20
280	Apr. 1-Sept. 1	—
310, 325, 328, 330, 340, 350	Apr. 15-July 20	Sept. 20-Oct. 20

O'Bryan 8

Table 2. Seed application rates

[From Minnesota Department of Transportation, 2005, table 2575-2, p. 716]

Seed mixture number	Application rate (lb/acre)
100, 110	100
159	40
190	60
240	75
250	70
260	100
270	120
280	50
310	82
325	84
328	88
330, 340, 350	84.5

28.5 feet at each terrace until they reach 1,000 feet in length at elevation 480 feet. Work should start at the base of the area and proceed upward. The terraces will flow into a larger grassed waterway approximately 1,200 feet long that intersects the site.

In USGS style, most numbers are expressed as numerals.

The terraces will be grassed with a native harvest. The waterway will be lined with something comparable to C350 riprap replacement and will also be seeded with a native harvest. The native harvest should consist of seed harvests from stands within 25 miles of the area. Approximately 70% of the mixture should consist of big bluestem and/or Indian grass, though 50% would be acceptable. There should be at least five species of native grasses and 3% (by mass) of native forbs. Since this is to be a recreational area, it will be best not to use a variety of grass that needs seasonal burning unless the park can be closed without financial repercussions and without the fire damaging any infrastructure erected at a later time. The application of herbicides seasonally (spring or summer) is acceptable though not encouraged, as runoff could harm fish and wildlife.

Erosion barrier.—The developer may not disturb more than 14,400 ft^2 at a time in the clayey silt soil or more than 22,500 ft^2 at a time in the silty clay soil without erecting an erosion barrier such as a silt fence on the downslope side. The bare soil above the work area should be stabilized by rocks and mulch at the end of each workday. The developer should create and maintain a covered stockpile of topsoil. If soil is going to be left bare for more than 45 days, it must be seeded. Idle areas should be seeded as soon as possible after grading or within 7 days. The seed should be mixture number 130, consisting of 40% oats, 40% winter wheat, 10% rye grass, and 10% alfalfa, annual. Compacted soils in the area should be deep-tilled to a depth of 18-24 inches to allow for deep root penetration. Six or more inches of organic compost should be laid on top of this and tilled into the top 10 inches of soil.

Lake.—Although a collection system for the runoff water was not a requirement for this proposal, a lake has several advantages and is not prohibitively expensive. It will collect drainage from the constructed waterway, it will attract wildlife to the area and enhance the appeal to visitors, and it can serve as a recreational fishing hole.

Other vegetation.—Revegetation should occur at the end of the major construction phase and should focus not only on establishing grasses in the area but also on planting other forms of vegetation. Some of the options for native plants that are readily available from nurseries are outlined in the "Shoreline Stabilization Handbook" (Northwest Regional Planning Commission, 2004). They include trees, shrubs, herbaceous plants, ferns, and vines. It is preferred that these be native to the area, such as Kentucky bluegrass, and not European or Asian in origin. While the European and Asian grasses have traditionally been used in American landscaping, they tend to have much smaller rooting zones and are not suitable for effective erosion control; they also require more effort to grow in this site soil. Native grasses would not have these problems and would be less expensive to maintain. Shrubs such as sumac, gray dogwood, wild rose, fragrant sumac, and hazelnut are also preferable because they have a dense, low-spreading growth pattern and are attractive.

Proposals usually provide itemized costs for the client.

Cost estimates.—The basic construction of Proposal A will cost Ajax $37,034-79,034. Additional costs of approximately $608,000 would provide

O'Bryan 10

for recovery of the runoff water and enhance the overall appearance and
appeal of the area.

DIMENSIONS

Disturbed area	216,283.5 yd^2
Total area	333,330 yd^2
Undisturbed area	117,046.5 yd^2

BASIC COSTS

Terraces	$	15,034.00
Grassed waterway		4,000.00
1-acre lake		18,000.00-60,000.00
TOTAL BASIC COSTS............................		$37,034.00-79,034.00

ADDITIONAL COSTS (OPTIONAL)

Hydroseeding, tackifier not required	$175,570.00
Hydroseeding, tackifier required	432,567.00
TOTAL ADDITIONAL COSTS................................	$608,137.00

CONCLUSION

While not the lowest-cost method of erosion control, proposal A
meets all the goals of the project and creates an aesthetically pleasing and
natural park atmosphere. The constructed appearance of the heavier erosion
control options such as riprap and gabions would not mesh well with
natural foliage. Such constructions also would not allow for aquatic life,
one of the stated goals of the project. Heavy vegetation with the more
aesthetic option of terraces is the correct choice in this situation. Native
grasses not only will facilitate slope stabilization because of their deep
rooting zones but also will attract birds and other wildlife, which would in
turn draw wildlife enthusiasts into the park.

A good model for the proposed park is the Rachel Carson National
Wildlife Refuge in Maine. While the type of land that is being protected in
Maine is different from the land found on the Kentucky site, the Maine park
combines the elements Ajax is seeking in its new park: a wildlife refuge,
full of native plants, and a recreational area. The Maine park has trails
throughout so that visitors have many different views of the beauty of the
site. It also offers fishing and hunting and appeals to many different
demographics. Ajax should consider this park as an ideal model.

In her conclusion,
O'Bryan states
again why she
recommends
proposal A. She ends
with a paragraph
that speaks plainly
to connect with her
readers.

O'Bryan 11

REFERENCES

Beasley, R.P., Gregory, J.M., and McCarty, T.R., 1984, Erosion and sediment
pollution control (2d ed.): Ames, Iowa, Iowa State University Press,
354 p.

Merill, L., 2004, Multitalented and versatile—gabions in stormwater
management and erosion control: Erosion Control, v. 11, no. 3,
http://www.erosioncontrol.com/may-june-2004/gabions-cages
-erosion.aspx.

Metropolitan Council, July 2001, Soil erosion control—vegetative
methods, *in* Minnesota urban small sites BMP manual: St. Paul,
Minn., Metropolitan Council Environmental Services, http://www
.metrocouncil.org/environment/Watershed/BMP/CH3_RPPSoilVeget
.pdf.

Minnesota Department of Transportation, 2005, Standard specifications
for construction: St. Paul, Minn., Minnesota Department of
Transportation, http://www.dot.state.mn.us/pre-letting/spec/2005
/2557-2582.pdf.

Northwest Regional Planning Commission, 2004, The shoreline stabilization
handbook for Lake Champlain and other inland lakes: St. Albans, Vt.,
Northwest Regional Planning Commission, http://nsgd.gso.uri.edu
/lcsg/lcsgh04001.pdf.

U.S. Fish and Wildlife Service, 2008, Rachel Carson National Wildlife
Refuge: Wells, Maine, U.S. Fish and Wildlife Service, http://www.fws
.gov/northeast/rachelcarson.

The writer uses USGS style to list the sources she consulted in preparing her proposal.

D7 Writing in history

Historians analyze the information available to them to develop theories about past events, experiences, ideas, and movements. Depending on their interests, historians may consider a variety of issues and sources related to economics, politics, social issues, science, the military, gender, the family, or popular culture.

Historians do not simply record what happened at a particular time; rather, they attempt to explain *why* or *how* events occurred as they did and to place those events in a larger context. For example, a historian writing about women in the British military during World War II would not simply describe the positions women held in the armed forces; through an analysis of the available information, the historian might develop a theory about why women were authorized to hold certain jobs and not others and how changes to women's roles affected the evolution of the women's rights movement in the decades that followed.

D7-a Determine your audience and their needs in history.

Historians write for diverse audiences. History scholars research and write books, articles, textbooks, Web sites, and film scripts for peers, teachers, and students. They also write for the general public, nonspecialists who are interested in history and may subscribe to history magazines or make frequent trips to museums. Amateur historians, often called "local historians," do genealogical or community research for a specific audience.

When you write in history, keep in mind that your audience appreciates an author who is knowledgeable and has done thorough research. Use multiple sources and cite your sources fully to assure your readers that your sources are credible. Because primary sources offer important evidence, include photos, maps, letters, or facsimiles. For example, if you are writing a newsletter article about a slave auction that occurred during the 1850s, you might add a picture of the poster that was used to advertise that auction.

D7-b Recognize the forms of writing in history.

Writing in history combines narrative (a description of what happened) and interpretation (an analysis of why events occurred). Historians ask questions that do not have obvious answers and analyze a variety of sources to draw conclusions.

When you take courses in history, you may be asked to write any of the following kinds of documents:

- critical essays
- book reviews
- research papers
- historiographic essays

Critical essays

For some assignments, you will be asked to write a short, critical essay in which you look at a document or group of documents—or perhaps a historical argument written by a scholar. For example, if you were studying the US decision to send troops to Vietnam, you might be asked to analyze one or more of John F. Kennedy's speeches and put forth a theory about why Kennedy chose to authorize the initial troop deployments. In the same course, you might be asked to read a journal article by a scholar analyzing Kennedy's decision and assess the way that scholar uses evidence to support his or her conclusion.

Book reviews

Because historians view their own work as part of an ongoing scholarly conversation, they value the serious discussion of the work of other scholars in the field. In some courses, you may be asked to write a book review analyzing the logic and accuracy of a scholarly work or of several works on the same topic. When you write a book review, you will have to make judgments about how much background information to provide about the book so that your readers will be able to understand and appreciate your critique.

Research papers

When you write a research paper in any course, you are expected to pose a question and examine the available evidence to find an answer to that question. In history courses, a research paper will generally focus on *why* and *how* questions that can be answered using a combination of sources. If you were studying the Vietnam War, you might ask how the rhetoric of the cold war shaped John F. Kennedy's early Vietnam policy. To answer this question, you might look at government documents from the Kennedy administration, press coverage of Kennedy's foreign policy, Kennedy's own writings, and interviews with those who were involved in policymaking. If you were interested in the role of women in the military during World War II, you might

critical essay • book review • research paper • analysis of
historians' methods • evidence • primary and secondary sources

D7-d   D-81

sk why the British government supported the expansion of women's
oles in ways that the US government did not.

Historiographic essays

Historiography is the study by historians of how history is written.
When you write a historiographic essay, you think about the meth-
ds by which other historians have drawn their conclusions. If you
vere writing a historiographic essay about how the cold war affected
ohn F. Kennedy's policies, you would analyze how other historians
ave answered this question. What assumptions or biases influenced
heir choice and interpretation of sources? What methods shaped
heir work?

D7-c Know the questions historians ask.

Historians generally ask *how* and *why* questions. Other, more basic
questions such as *What happened?* and *Who was involved?* will con-
ribute answers to inform the broader, more controversial questions.
Historians choose their questions by considering their own inter-
sts, the relevance to the ongoing discussions among scholars, and
he availability of sources on the topic. The answer to any one of
he following questions could form the basis of a thesis for a history
aper:

- What role did nationalism play in the breakup of Yugoslavia in
  the early 1990s?
- Why did the US Congress decide to grant women the vote?
- How did the Salem witch trials (1692–93) differ from the
  Salzburg witch trials (1675–90)?
- Why did the Roman Empire collapse?

D7-d Understand the kinds of evidence historians use.

As investigators of the past, historians rely on both primary sources
nd secondary sources. Primary sources are materials from the his-
orical period being studied—government documents, numerical
ata, speeches, diaries, letters, and maps. Secondary sources are
materials produced after the historical period that interpret or syn-
hesize historical events. The same source can function as either a
rimary or a secondary source depending on what you are writing
bout. For example, a newspaper article about Slobodan Milosevic's

decision to defend himself during his war crimes trial would be a secondary source in an essay about why Milosevic made this decision. The same article, however, would be a primary source in an essay about newspaper coverage of Milosevic's war crimes trial.

Following are some of the ways historians use evidence:

- For a research paper about the role of women in the British military during World War II, you might find evidence in women's diaries and letters. If you were interested in how the government decided to create women's military services, you could consult records of parliamentary debates or correspondence between military and government leaders. You could also find numerous books by other scholars with information on the topic.

- For a research paper about attitudes toward Prohibition in different parts of the United States, you might consult regional newspapers or correspondence between politicians and their constituents. You might also find numerical data on liquor sales and Prohibition violations to support a hypothesis about regional attitudes.

- For a review of several books about the causes of the Tiananmen Square massacre, your evidence would come from the books themselves as well as other respected sources on the topic.

D7-e Become familiar with writing conventions in history.

No matter what topic they are writing about, historians agree on some general conventions:

- Historians value counterargument. To draw a conclusion about why or how something happened, historians must weigh conflicting theories and interpretations carefully and judiciously. In an essay answering the question of why the US Congress passed the Nineteenth Amendment, you might conclude that politicians truly believed that women should have the right to vote. But you would also need to account for the failure of the same legislation several years earlier. Did politicians change their minds? Or were other factors at work?

- Historians conduct research. Historians, like detectives or forensic specialists, look for explanations by assessing the available evidence rather than relying on assumptions or personal opinions. They look for multiple sources of evidence to confirm their theories, and they avoid value judgments.

- Historians write in the past tense when they are focusing on past events, ideas, and movements. They use the present tense

(*Goodman's book reveals new evidence*) or present perfect tense
(*Olson has vividly depicted the political scene*) when talking
about the contents of another writer's work.

- Historians credit the scholarship of others. Historians are aware
that they are joining an existing scholarly conversation, and
they place great importance on citing the ideas of other scholars.

7-f Use the CMS (*Chicago*) system in writing in history.

 riters in history typically use the style guidelines of *The Chicago
 anual of Style* (CMS) for formatting their papers, for citing sources
 the text of their paper and in endnotes, and for listing sources in a
 bliography at the end. CMS style is set forth in *The Chicago Manual
 Style*, 16th ed. (Chicago: University of Chicago Press, 2010). (For
 ore details, see the CMS documentation sections in your handbook.)

7-g Sample student paper: Research essay

 history research paper generally focuses on a *how* or a *why* ques-
 on, and it answers this question with an analysis of available
 urces. The student paper beginning on the next page was written
 r a course on the history of the industrial revolution in the United
 ates. The student, Jenna Benjamin, used the style guidelines of
 e Chicago Manual of Style (CMS) to format her paper and to cite
 d list her sources.

Title page consists of a descriptive title and the writer's name in the center of the page and the course number, instructor, and date at the bottom of the page.

Wage Slavery or True Independence?
Women Workers in the Lowell, Massachusetts,
Textile Mills, 1820-1850

Jenna Benjamin

American History 200, Section 4
Professor Jones
May 22, 2010

Marginal annotations indicate CMS-style formatting **and** effective writing.

In 1813, New England merchant Francis Lowell introduced a new type of textile mill to Massachusetts that would have a permanent impact on family and village life. Over the next three decades, the transformation of home production to factory production of textiles would require a substantial labor force and would lead to the unprecedented hiring of thousands of women. The entrance of young women into the workforce sparked a passionate debate about whether factory work exploited young women and adversely affected society. The young women who worked in the mills received low pay for hard work and had little free time.[1] Were these women victims of the factory system? What was the long-term impact of their experiences? An analysis of the evidence reveals that rather than being exploited, these women workers shaped their experience for their own purposes and actively expanded the opportunities for women.

In the late eighteenth century, great changes in the production of textiles were taking place in England, with a transition from home production to factories using machines and employing children to do most of the work. Conditions in the factories were very bad, and stories of dark and dangerous mills reinforced Americans' prejudices against industrialization.[2] Meanwhile, New Englanders still spun yarn at home and some also wove their own cloth, mostly for their own families. Much of this work was done by women. A spinning wheel was a possession of almost every household.[3] But in the first two decades of the nineteenth century, a slow shift took place in New England from home to factory production.

Some American merchants, like Samuel Slater and Francis Cabot Lowell, began to envision an American textile industry. The first mills they built in the United States were in rural villages and employed whole families, not just children. Since the textile mills hired whole families who already lived in the villages, family and village life was not greatly altered.[4]

A dramatic change in textile production, however, came from a new machine, the power loom, and a new mechanized mill, built first in Waltham, Massachusetts, in 1813 by Francis Lowell and a small group of wealthy Boston merchants.[5] Waltham was not a village with a textile mill in it; it became a "mill town" in which the factory dominated the economic

---

Page header contains the writer's name followed by the page number. Since the title page is counted in the numbering, the first text page is numbered 2.

Introduction frames a debatable issue.

Research questions focus the essay.

Statement of thesis.

Section provides background about the historical period.

Historians write in the past tense when describing past events.

Benjamin 3

life of a rapidly growing city. Most significantly, the workers in Lowell's mill were not local families but individuals who came from great distances to live and work in the new mill town. When Lowell died in 1817, his business partners spread the new factory system to other places, notably a town on the Merrimack and Concord Rivers twenty-seven miles from Boston; in honor of their friend, they named the town Lowell. It soon became the biggest mill town in the nation, with more than a dozen large integrated mills using mechanical looms.[6]

Note numbers in text refer to endnotes at the end of the paper.

The growth of Lowell between 1821 and 1840 was unprecedented.[7] A rapidly developing textile industry like the one at Lowell needed more and more people to work the machines in the factories. The mill owners, aware of the negative view of English mill towns, decided to create a community where workers would live in solid, clean housing rather than slums. For their workers, they looked to a large group of people whose labor was not absolutely necessary to the New England farm economy— hundreds (later thousands) of young women who lived on the farms but who could be persuaded to come to Lowell and work in the mills.[8]

Topic sentence signals a transition to a specific discussion of the women workers.

Several factors in the social and economic history of New England made this group of workers available. Population growth and scarcity of land to pass down to younger generations of sons caused many New England farmers to send their sons to work on neighboring farms or as apprentices to craftsmen in towns or villages.[9] In addition, the position of women (wives and, especially, daughters) in the family was an inferior one. Adult, property-holding males were citizens with full civil rights, but the same was not true for women *of any age*. Wives had no legal rights, and daughters had no independence. Daughters were bound by social conventions to obey their fathers and rarely were able to earn money of their own. Even travel away from home was unusual. Although the family could not have functioned without the labor of wives and daughters at field work, food preparation, cleaning, washing, and so on, women gained no independent income or freedom as a result. For some young women, their subordinate position in family and society gave them an incentive to embrace the opportunities offered by mill work. Unlike the limited occupation of teaching, which was poorly paid and lasted for only a few months a year, the new mill work was steady, and it paid well.[10]

Benjamin 4

Hiring young women, of course, met strong resistance from fathers who saw their role as protecting their daughters and preparing them for marriage.[11] To confront this resistance, the mill owners created boardinghouses around the mills where groups of girls—ranging in age from fifteen to mid-twenties—lived and took their meals under the care of a housekeeper, usually an older woman. Strict boardinghouse rules were laid down by each company (see fig. 1). Moreover, the girls would never grow into a permanent working class, as it was expected that they

A primary source (a document) provides concrete evidence and adds historical interest.

REGULATIONS

FOR THE

BOARDING HOUSES

OF THE

MIDDLESEX COMPANY.

The tenants of the Boarding Houses are not to board, or permit any part of their houses to be occupied by any person except those in the employ of the Company.

They will be considered answerable for any improper conduct in their houses, and are not to permit their boarders to have company at unseasonable hours.

The doors must be closed at ten o'clock in the evening, and no one admitted after that time without some reasonable excuse.

The keepers of the Boarding Houses must give an account of the number, names, and employment of their boarders, when required; and report the names of such as are guilty of any improper conduct, or are not in the regular habit of attending public worship.

The buildings and yards about them must be kept clean and in good order, and if they are injured otherwise than from ordinary use, all necessary repairs will be made, and charged to the occupant.

It is indispensable that all persons in the employ of the Middlesex Company should be vaccinated who have not been, as also the families with whom they board; which will be done at the expense of the Company.

SAMUEL LAWRENCE, Agent.

JOEL TAYLOR, PRINTER, Daily Courier Office.

Fig. 1. Each mill company established strict rules for the boardinghouses where its women workers lived. (American Textile History Museum, Lowell, Massachusetts.)

would return to their homes for visits and after a year or two would go back to their villages permanently.[12] The mill owners did not advertise for help. They sent recruiters into the countryside to assure parents that their daughters would live under strict supervision in the boardinghouses and at work and that their behavior would be monitored. The owners' efforts were successful: over the years, thousands of young women took the long trip by stagecoach or wagon from their rural homes to mill towns like Lowell.[13]

Benjamin introduces evidence that appears to contradict her thesis (counterargument).

Besides having to adjust to living in a city in a strange house with a dozen or more other girls, the young women had to get used to the rigorous rules and long hours at the mills.[14] Mill work was an opportunity, but it also was hard work. The girls worked an average of twelve hours a day. The mills operated six days a week, so the only day off was Sunday, part of which was usually spent at church. Thus free time was confined to two or three hours in the evening and to Sunday afternoon.[15] For many, however, this was still more leisure (and more freedom) than they would have had at home.

Despite a workday that took up fourteen hours, including time spent traveling to and from their houses for meals, most of the young women did not find the work very strenuous or particularly dangerous. As the mill owners had promised, Lowell did not resemble the grimy, packed mill towns of England.[16] Still, the work was tedious and confining, with the girls doing the same operation over and over again under the watchful eye of the overseer.[17]

Benjamin develops a response to the counterargument, with strong evidence for her thesis.

The young women earned an average of three to four dollars a week, from which their board of $1.25 a week was deducted. At that time, no other jobs open to women paid as well.[18] Three or four dollars a week was enough to pay board, send badly needed money home, and still have enough left over for new clothes once in a while. Many women mill workers even established savings accounts, and some eventually left Lowell with several hundred dollars, something they never could have done at home.[19]

Details about the beneficial effects on the young mill workers come from primary and secondary sources.

Even though their free time was very limited, the young women engaged in a variety of activities. In the evenings, they wrote letters home, entertained visitors (though there was little privacy), repaired their

Benjamin 6

clothing, and talked about friends and relatives and also about conditions
in the mills. They could go out to the shops, especially clothing shops. The
mill girls at Lowell prided themselves on a wardrobe that, at least on
Sunday, was not inferior to that of the wives of prosperous citizens.[20] In
addition, they attended evening courses that enabled them to extend their
education beyond their few years of schooling. They also attended lectures
and read novels and essays. So strong was the girls' interest in reading that
many mills put up signs warning "No reading in the mills."[21] Some young
women even began writing. Determined to challenge the idea that mill girls
were mindless drones of the factory and lacked the refinement to ultimately
be good wives, about seventy-five mill girls and women contributed in the
1840s to publications featuring stories and essays by the workers
themselves.[22]

> Benjamin paraphrases information from a secondary source, a late-nineteenth-century book.

The best known of these publications was the *Lowell Offering*. The
Offering avoided sensitive issues about working conditions, but the women
controlled the content of the publication and wrote on subjects (family,
courtship, fashion, morality, nature) that interested them.[23] A few of the
Offering writers even went on to literary careers, not the kind of future
that most people expected of factory workers. Charles Dickens toured the
mills in 1842 and later said of the girls' writing: "Of the merits of the
Lowell Offering, as a literary production, I will only observe . . . that it will
compare advantageously with a great many English annuals."[24]

> Direct quotation provides evidence from the period.

Though the *Offering* was a sign that something unusual was
happening in this factory town, the women still worked in an industry that
caused them hardship. By the 1830s, tensions in the mills had begun to rise
as the companies became more interested in profits and less concerned
about their role as protectors of their young workers. Factory owners,
observing a decline in the price of their cloth and an increase in unsold
inventories, decided to lower their workers' wages.[25] When the reduction was
announced in February 1834, the women workers circulated petitions among
themselves pledging to stop work (or "turn out") if wages were lowered.[26]
When the leader of the petition drive at one mill was fired, many of the
women left work and marched to the other mills to call out their workers.
It is estimated that one-sixth of all women mill workers walked out as a
result. The strikers wrote another petition stating that "we will not go back

into the mills to work until our wages are continued . . . as they have been."[27]

Although the "turn out" was brief and did not achieve its purpose, it demonstrated that the women workers did not accept the owners' view that they were minors under the owners' benevolent care. The sense of independence gained by factory work and cash wages led them to reject the idea that they were mere factory hands. Petitions referred to their "unquestionable rights" and to "the spirit of our patriotic ancestors, who preferred privation to bondage." One petition ended, "We are free, we would remain in possession of what kind providence has bestowed upon us, and remain *daughters of free men still*."[28] This language indicates that the women did not think of themselves as laborers complaining about low wages. They were free citizens of a republic and deserved respect as such. Many young women left the mills and went home when mill work came to seem more like "slavery" than independence (a comparison that appeared in the petitions). In 1836, another effort to lower wages led to an even larger "turn out."[29] The willingness of these young women to challenge the authority of the mill owners is a sign that their new lives had given them a feeling of personal strength and solidarity with one another.[30]

Economic recession in the late 1830s and early 1840s led to the layoff of hundreds more women workers. In the 1840s and 1850s, the mill owners tried to maintain profits by increasing the workload and abandoning paternalism toward their workers. To save money, the companies stopped building boardinghouses.[31] The look of Lowell changed as well. Mill buildings took up more of the green space that had been part of the original town plan. By 1850, Lowell did indeed look something like an English mill town.

As conditions in the mills and in the city declined, young New England women were replaced by young Irish immigrants escaping the famine and the poor living conditions in Ireland. Slowly, Lowell became just another industrial city. It was dirty and overcrowded, and its mills were beginning to look run-down.[32]

By 1850, an era had passed. But from the 1820s to the 1840s, the majority of the textile workers were young women who helped make possible the industrialization of New England at the same time as they expanded

---

Margin annotations:

Benjamin analyzes the quotation to show how it supports the paragraph's main point.

Strong evidence supports the paper's thesis.

Concluding paragraph opens with a brief restatement of part of the thesis.

Benjamin 8

their own opportunities. These early mill workers became models for later women reformers and radicals who raised the banner for equal rights for women in more and more areas of life. The independent mill girls of the 1830s and 1840s resisted pressures from their employers, gained both freedom and maturity by living and working on their own, and showed an intense desire for independence and learning.[33] Great fortunes were made from the textile mills of that era, but within those mills a generation of young women gained something even more precious: a sense of self-respect.

Conclusion considers the broader implications of the thesis.

Notes

Endnotes begin on a new page. Sources are cited in CMS (Chicago) style. Complete source information is also listed in the bibliography.

1. Caroline F. Ware, *The Early New England Cotton Manufacture* (Boston: Houghton Mifflin, 1931), 4-8; Barbara M. Tucker, *Samuel Slater and the Origins of the American Textile Industry: 1790-1860* (Ithaca, NY: Cornell University Press, 1984), 38-41.

2. Tucker, *Samuel Slater*, 33-40.

3. Thomas Dublin, *Women at Work: The Transformation of Work and Community in Lowell, Massachusetts, 1826-1860* (New York: Columbia University Press, 1979), 14; Adrienne D. Hood, "The Gender Division of Labor in the Production of Textiles in Eighteenth-Century Rural Pennsylvania," *Journal of Social History* 27, no. 3 (1994), "Spinning as Women's Work" section, Academic OneFile (A15324645).

Citation of a journal article from a database. Section locator is used for unpaginated source.

4. Tucker, *Samuel Slater*, 79, 85, 99-100, 111; Barbara M. Tucker, "The Family and Industrial Discipline in Ante-Bellum New England," *Labor History* 21, no. 1 (1979): 56-60.

5. Robert F. Dalzell, *Enterprising Elite: The Boston Associates and the World They Made* (Cambridge, MA: Harvard University Press, 1987), 26-30; Tucker, *Samuel Slater*, 111-16.

Second reference to a source includes the author's name, a shortened title, and the page numbers.

6. Tucker, *Samuel Slater*, 116-17.

7. Dublin, *Women at Work*, 19-21, 133-35.

8. Ibid., 26, 76; Benita Eisler, ed., *The "Lowell Offering": Writings by New England Mill Women, 1840-1845* (Philadelphia: Lippincott, 1977), 15-16.

First line of each note is indented ½". All notes are single-spaced, with double-spacing between them. (Some instructors may prefer double-spacing throughout.)

9. Christopher Clark, "The Household Economy: Market Exchange and the Rise of Capitalism in the Connecticut Valley, 1800-1860," *Journal of Social History* 13, no. 2 (1979): 175-76, http://www.jstor.org/stable /3787339; Gail Fowler Mohanty, "Handloom Outwork and Outwork Weaving in Rural Rhode Island, 1810-1821," *American Studies* 30, no. 2 (1989): 42-43, 48-49.

10. Eisler, *"Lowell Offering,"* 16, 193; Clark, "Household Economy," 178-79; Dalzell, *Enterprising Elite*, 33.

11. On the influence of patriarchy, see Tucker, *Samuel Slater*, 25-26; Harriet H. Robinson, *Loom and Spindle; Or, Life among the Early Mill Girls* (1898), reprinted in *Women of Lowell* (New York: Arno Press, 1974), 194; Barbara Welter, "The Cult of True Womanhood," *American Quarterly* 18, no. 2, pt. 1 (1966): 151, 170-71.

Primary source (Robinson) reprinted in a secondary source.

Benjamin 12

Bibliography

Bartlett, Elisha. *A Vindication of the Character and Condition of the Females Employed in the Lowell Mills*. 1841. Reprinted in *Women of Lowell*. New York: Arno Press, 1974.

A Citizen of Lowell. *Corporations and Operatives: Being an Exposition of the Condition [of] Factory Operatives and a Review of the "Vindication," by Elisha Bartlett, MD*. 1843. Reprinted in *Women of Lowell*. New York: Arno Press, 1974.

Clark, Christopher. "The Household Economy: Market Exchange and the Rise of Capitalism in the Connecticut Valley, 1800-1860." *Journal of Social History* 13, no. 2 (1979): 169-89. http://www.jstor.org /stable/3787339.

Dalzell, Robert F. *Enterprising Elite: The Boston Associates and the World They Made*. Cambridge, MA: Harvard University Press, 1987.

Dublin, Thomas. *Women at Work: The Transformation of Work and Community in Lowell, Massachusetts, 1826-1860*. New York: Columbia University Press, 1979.

Eisler, Benita, ed. *The "Lowell Offering": Writings by New England Mill Women, 1840-1845*. Philadelphia: Lippincott, 1977.

"Factory Rules from the Handbook to Lowell, 1848." Illinois Labor History Society. Center for Law and Computers, Chicago-Kent School of Law. Accessed May 12, 2006. http://www.kentlaw.edu/ilhs/lowell.html.

Hood, Adrienne D. "The Gender Division of Labor in the Production of Textiles in Eighteenth-Century Rural Pennsylvania." *Journal of Social History* 27, no. 3 (1994). Academic OneFile (A15324645).

Larcom, Lucy. "Among Lowell Mill-Girls: A Reminiscence." 1881. Reprinted in *Women of Lowell*. New York: Arno Press, 1974.

Mohanty, Gail Fowler. "Handloom Outwork and Outwork Weaving in Rural Rhode Island, 1810-1821." *American Studies* 30, no. 2 (1989): 41-68.

Robinson, Harriet H. *Loom and Spindle; Or, Life among the Early Mill Girls*. 1898. Reprinted in *Women of Lowell*. New York: Arno Press, 1974.

Sins of Our Mothers. Boston: PBS Video, 1988. Videocassette.

Stearns, Bertha Monica. "Early Factory Magazines in New England: The *Lowell Offering* and Its Contemporaries." *Journal of Economic and Business History* (1930): 685-705.

Bibliography begins on a new page and includes all the sources cited in the paper.

Online article with a stable URL.

Entries are listed alphabetically by authors' last names or by title for works with no author.

First line of each entry is at the left margin; subsequent lines are indented ½".

Entries are single-spaced, with double-spacing between entries. (Some instructors may prefer double-spacing throughout.)

≡ **D8** Writing in music

Musicians and musicologists—those who study, analyze, and inter pret music—write about music for themselves or for larger audiences Your instructor might ask you to keep a journal to record your impres sions and ideas about concerts you attend. If you are a music student you might write personal reflections about works that you are prepar ing for performance. Other kinds of writing are intended to inform or educate general audiences. They include reviews of performances and press releases that are published in newspapers, blogs, or other publications. More specialized publications are scholarly journals and concert program notes.

If you are a student learning how to write about music, you will need to train yourself to listen actively rather than passively. Pas sive listening means just enjoying a performance or recording. This kind of listening is certainly a valid way to hear music, but to write about music you must become more aware of what you are hearing. You must intentionally listen for certain qualities in the music. Active listening also involves learning about the background of a composer or musician to deepen your understanding of the music. As an active listener, you can observe how the audience responds during a perfor mance, and you can analyze and critique the performance as you lis ten. To help you become a more active listener, your instructor might take your class on field trips to concerts so you can experience a vari ety of performances. You might attend a classical symphony concert a chamber music performance, a recital showcasing the talents of single performer, or a concert by a rock band or a jazz ensemble.

D8-a Determine your audience and their needs in music

Audiences for music writers include professional musicians, music historians, and researchers, teachers, and students. They read scholarly or teaching journals to learn about new analyses or inter pretations of musical compositions and about methods that other musicians, researchers, or teachers are using. Other audiences may include members of the general public, who read reviews of perfor mances in newspapers or on Web sites to help them decide whether attend concerts. Serious concertgoers read reviews after they attend a performance as a way of helping them think more about their expe rience at the concert. Audiences attending performances read the printed programs to learn about the biographies of composers and the histories of pieces they will hear. Some readers are in businesses

overnment agencies, or nonprofit organizations that fund musicians
nd arts groups. They read grant proposals written by researchers,
usicians, teachers, and even students who are seeking funds to sup-
ort their study or practice of music.

Readers in the field of music want to know the writer's opinion,
ut they expect the writing to contain more than just statements
f personal taste. If the piece of writing is a music review, readers
ant the writer to evaluate the performance with specific details
nd examples to justify the writer's opinion. Because the discipline
f music is a diverse field with a very long history, understanding one
omposer or work or performer requires making connections to others
n the field. All readers expect writers about music to make references
o other composers, styles, or musicians.

8-b Recognize the forms of writing in music.

'hen you take courses in music, you may be asked to write any of the
llowing:

- response papers
- program notes
- press releases
- concert reviews
- journal articles
- grant proposals

esponse papers

response paper is your personal reflection on a piece of music, a
omposer, a performance, or your own progress as a musician. Your
nstructor may ask you to write the paper as a brief assignment or
s part of a journal that you keep during the course. The purpose of
ersonal response is to brainstorm some initial ideas or to reflect on a
ork you are studying or a concert you attended. These writing activ-
ies will help you generate topics for larger, more formal projects. To
elp you focus your attention on particular elements of a performance,
ur instructor may provide questions you can use in forming your
esponse. Your instructor might assign a response paper after you
tend a concert and then later require a concert review using your
esponse paper as a starting point. Thus a response paper can help
u move from your immediate reactions to a more objective piece
f writing. To be sure that your responses are useful for later assign-
ents, make them detailed and thorough. Avoid simply writing that

you like or dislike a particular work or performer. Instead, provide details that illustrate exactly why you have that particular reaction.

Program notes

When people attend a concert, they are usually given a program that lists the pieces they will hear and describes those pieces so they can understand and appreciate the music they will hear. Those descriptions are called *program notes*. A program note usually includes a biographical profile of the composer, background information about the composer's historical period, some mention of the first performance of the piece with a list or survey of major performances, and a description of the piece. The description will guide audience members through the performance, describing what they can expect to hear in each section of the piece. One kind of program note is a profile of each performer, describing the performer's major accomplishments and listing schools attended and major past performances. It may also give a brief discography, a listing of recordings that the performer has made professionally. Writing program notes will require you to do some research so you can provide the information readers expect to enhance their enjoyment and understanding of the performance. Think of program notes as small research papers that teach your readers about the music they are going to listen to.

Press releases

A press release is a brief document of no more than 250 words announcing an upcoming musical event to the general public. It is written by the event's organizers and distributed locally for publication in newspapers, in magazines, and on Web sites and as announcements on radio and television. Begin a press release with a one- or two-sentence statement giving the most important information about the event: what it is, who the main performers will be, and the time, date, and location of the event. Your press release can continue with a description of the composers and performers who will be featured. The press release should conclude with any other relevant information such as cost, parking, and a Web site or phone number where readers can get more information.

Concert reviews

Concert reviews might be the most popular kind of writing about music. The reviewer attends a concert, listens actively and intently, and tells readers about the experience. When you write a concert review, begin by engaging your audience with one or more sentences

at capture the quality and mood of the entire performance. Tell
readers what composers and works were featured and who the performers were. Then write about each part of the concert. Briefly
describe what was played and how it was played, stating your opinions about the music and the performers, with examples to illustrate
your opinions. You might also integrate historical information about
the composer, the piece of music, or the performers. Vivid words and
active sentences will give readers a sense of how it felt to attend the
performance.

Journal articles

Musicologists research and write about the history and literature of
music, and they analyze works of music. They publish their interpretations in scholarly journals and present their work at professional
conferences. You may be assigned a paper that involves research and
musical analysis. A typical assignment might ask you to explain how
a composition reflects its historical period or to trace trends in music
in a time period or region. You might explore larger issues such as
music in mass media or how technology has changed music. Your
assignment might ask you to focus on a less-known composer, performer, or work. If you are writing a journal article about the teaching
of music, you might write a how-to paper that proposes an improved
way to do something — how to rehearse a high school band more effectively, how to teach jazz improvisation, or how to start a school chamber music festival, for example. A paper of that type would involve
reading articles, interviewing teachers and administrators, and using
personal observations and experiences.

Grant proposals

Musicians and music teachers often apply for funding to support their
projects. They might request money to purchase new equipment for
their schools, to organize a summer workshop or camp, to travel to a
library for research, or to attend a summer academy or workshop for
intense study with well-known teachers. Whether you write a grant
proposal on a form provided by the funding agency or draft your own,
it typically includes several sections:

- an introduction that briefly describes the project and covers
  basic details about when, where, and how you expect the project
  to be achieved

- an outcomes section describing all the objectives you expect to
  attain with your project

- an itemized list of anticipated expenses

- a timeline section providing a schedule for completion, including deadlines for specific tasks
- a list of qualifications — the personal skills and experience that will enable you to complete the project
- a résumé

D8-c Know the questions musicians and musicologists ask.

Writers about music ask questions that guide them toward analysis and interpretation. The following are some questions that would lead to topics for research papers in music:

- In what ways do the symphonies of Brahms show the influence of earlier classical composers as well as the qualities of the Romantic period?
- How did rock and roll develop from earlier forms of music?
- How did changes in US society and mass media in the 1950s and 1960s influence the development of country music?
- What techniques of music composition and instrumentation has Alison Krauss used to create her unique bluegrass sound?
- What elements of blues and rock and roll does Green Day use most effectively in its hit single "September Song"?
- What challenges do symphony orchestras in the United States encounter, what are the causes of those challenges, and what are some effective strategies that cities have developed or could develop to build and sustain orchestras?

D8-d Understand the kinds of evidence musicians and musicologists use.

Musicians and musicologists use primary and secondary sources for evidence. A primary source is a music composition that the writer is analyzing or a concert or recording that the writer is reviewing. Secondary sources are books, articles, and Web sites about composers, musicians, or music.

The following are examples of the ways you might use evidence when you write about music:

- For program notes, you would use secondary sources for biographical material about the performer and historical information about the work of music to be performed. You might interview some of the performers (primary sources); for an original work, you might interview the composer, if possible.

- For a research paper tracing the development of Creole music in southern Louisiana, your primary sources could be songs representing different styles of Creole music and stages in the evolution of the music. Secondary sources would be books and other materials about the history of southern society and culture.

- For a review of a performance of Handel's *Messiah*, you would use specific moments from the concert itself as evidence to illustrate your opinions. You might mention how the conductor and the soloists interpreted particular parts of the piece and describe how sections of the orchestra and chorus performed. You might also note performers or moments from the performance that stood out because of their strengths or weaknesses.

D8-e Become familiar with writing conventions in music.

Musicians and musicologists agree on several conventions when they write:

- Musical compositions are known and categorized by detailed or specialized titles. For example, Beethoven's fifth symphony is Symphony no. 5 in C Minor, op. 67 (*op.* is the abbreviation for *opus*, or "work").

- Musicians and musicologists use a specialized vocabulary from music theory and history. Often that vocabulary includes words in Italian, German, or French. For example, movements of a symphony are known by their technical terms, such as the *adagio* section or the *allegro* movement.

- In reflective writing, the first-person pronoun *I* is acceptable. In a music review, it should be used sparingly so the review remains fair and analytical and does not seem to be merely a statement of personal taste. The first person can be used in grant proposals but not in press releases, program notes, or research papers in music.

- Writers use past tense to describe past events such as a composer's life or a performance. They use present tense when reviewing a recording or analyzing a work of music (for example, *In Nickel Creek's new song, the mandolin plays variations on an old folk tune*).

• Music writers use active voice and active verbs to keep their writing lively and engaging.

D8-f Use the MLA system in writing in music.

Writers in music typically use the style guidelines of the Modern Language Association (MLA), to format a paper, to document sources within the paper, and to cite sources at the end of the paper. Those guidelines are set forth in the *MLA Handbook for Writers of Research Papers*, 7th ed. (2009). (For more details, see the MLA documentation sections in your handbook.)

In addition, specific information about writing in music can be found in D. Kern Holoman, *Writing about Music: A Style Sheet*, 2nd ed. (2008), and Jonathan Bellman, *A Short Guide to Writing about Music*, 2nd ed. (2006).

D8-g Sample student paper: Concert review

A typical assignment in music courses is a review of a performance or a recording. Reviews appear in newspapers, in magazines, and on Web sites. The following student paper was written in a writing course for music majors and other students interested in music. The student, Tom Houston, attended a local concert for this assignment. He used the style guidelines in the *MLA Handbook* to format his paper and to cite and list his sources.

Writer's name and
page number, flush
right on every page.

Tom Houston

Dr. Belland

MUS 291 W

27 February 2008

Concert Review: Cincinnati Symphony Orchestra

The Cincinnati Symphony Orchestra performed a stunning concert
Saturday evening, February 23, 2008. Those who came, filling Music Hall
to almost two-thirds capacity, were immersed in what became a soul-
searching musical experience provided by Maestro John Adams. The
program selections and the exquisite performances offered the audience
an opportunity to expand their appreciation for contemporary music.

> Houston begins with
> the time and place
> of the concert and
> then gives his overall
> evaluation of the
> performance.

Opening this energetic program was *Tod und Verklärung* ("Death and
Transfiguration"), a tone poem by Richard Strauss. Following the Strauss,
Adams led the orchestra in *On the Transmigration of Souls* and, after the
intermission, *The Dharma at Big Sur*, both composed by Adams.

> Houston provides
> context by listing
> the pieces on the
> program.

Strauss wrote *Tod und Verklärung*, a lively musical stampede, when he
was just twenty-five years old. This seems to be a relatively young age to
tackle such a profoundly heavy subject. In his preconcert talk, Adams
observed that at the time Strauss was "a bit overwhelmed at his own
orchestral virtuosity." Very effective in the introduction of this tone poem
is the motif played by the timpani suggesting the faltering heartbeat of a
dying elderly man. Then the music grows to a galloping romp—a very
young Strauss's concept of the old man's entrance into Glory Land. At least
this is the generally accepted interpretation. Listening carefully, one can
hear partway through the Glory Land section the faltering heart still
beating. Strauss might be giving us pre-death hallucinations followed by a
slightly subdued entrance into heaven.

> This section vividly
> describes the history
> and sound of the
> Strauss composition.

The orchestra under Adams gave an intense interpretation of this
Strauss masterpiece. The gentle, soft voice usually brought to this orchestra
by music director Paavo Järvi would have added a welcome intensified
dramatic contrast to what was a rendition with merely adequate drama
under Adams's baton.

> Houston evaluates
> how the orchestra
> performed the piece,
> giving supporting
> details from the
> performance.

It is strange to think of the Strauss piece as whimsical. It is a
heavyweight probe into heavyweight matter. However, in his preconcert
talk to the early concertgoers, Adams said that he added it to the program

Marginal annotations indicate MLA-style formatting and effective writing.

Houston 2

as "whimsy" but that it might not have been the most effective selection because it added more weight to an already heavy program. The truth of this comment became apparent during Adams's own *On the Transmigration of Souls*.

As the program notes by Richard E. Rodda indicate, *Transmigration* was originally written for and performed by the New York Philharmonic Orchestra in honor of the victims of the September 11, 2001, terrorist attacks. Adding to the orchestra the voices of the May Festival Chorus, the Cincinnati Children's Choir, and a prerecorded soundtrack, Adams transformed Music Hall into a cathedral. Adams's music avoids evoking the terrible scenes seen so many times, using as the text the simple, heartrending statements of both victims and their loved ones. Each poignant word was sung exquisitely, every phrase clearly understood through the appropriate musical dissonance of the orchestra.

The depth of the significance of this work cannot be overstated. Adams captured this event not only through the souls of the victims but also through the souls of the surviving loved ones and the souls of all whose lives were forever changed that morning. The performance began with Adams standing motionless in a silent hall, and it ended with him standing motionless in a silent hall. It seemed almost a sacrilege to clap, but that is all an audience can do. It was like clapping after Communion. Soon Robert Porco, director of the May Festival Chorus, and Robyn Lana, director of the Cincinnati Children's Choir, appeared with Adams to accept a well-deserved tribute from the audience. This seemed to make the extended applause more appropriate and a welcome emotional release.

Following the intermission, violinist Leila Josefowicz appeared with the orchestra to perform Adams's *The Dharma at Big Sur*. This is quintessential Adams at his compositional best. The entire work sounds improvisational, especially the solo violin. The instrument, made especially for Josefowicz, is a six-string electric violin with a very wide range, so different from a traditional violin that the performer is required to learn new technique to play it. The music, moving beyond traditional Western tones, employs quarter, or in-between, tones, which slide up or down, giving a sound that is strange to Western, classically trained ears.

Transition contrasts the first work on the program with the next work to be discussed.

Houston provides background, description, and an opinion about the performance of the second piece.

Houston uses vivid description to give readers a sense of what it was like to attend the concert.

Houston provides background about an instrument and music that might be unfamiliar to readers.

Josefowicz's enduring energy and technique, the controlled orchestral dissonance and extraordinarily equipped percussion section, and the leprechaunesque gyrations of Adams gave the audience an exciting listening and viewing experience.

Houston supports his opinion about the final piece with vivid details.

We Cincinnatians are traditionally a conservative people, preferring an orchestra to have a traditionally "full" or lush sound, but Adams composes on the leading crest of the wave of minimalism, a contemporary, spare sound that can make an audience uncomfortable. The concert Saturday night moved the Cincinnati audience a step or two forward.

The conclusion summarizes the general impact of the performance on the audience.

Houston 4

Works cited list
begins on a new
page and is
formatted in MLA
style.

Works Cited

Adams, John. Preconcert talk. Cincinnati Symphony Orchestra. Music Hall,
    Cincinnati. 23 Feb. 2008. Address.

Cincinnati Symphony Orchestra, perf. Concert. Cond. John Adams. Music
    Hall, Cincinnati. 23 Feb. 2008. Performance.

Rodda, Richard E. "John Adams: *On the Transmigration of Souls*." Program
    notes. Cincinnati Symphony Orchestra. 23 Feb. 2008. Print.

≡ **D9** Writing in nursing

Writing is an important tool in the education of nursing students as well as in the everyday workplaces of the profession. For students learning to become nurses, writing about specific nursing theories and practices, medical cases, and client experiences helps them better understand concepts and skills through research and analytical thinking.

For professional nurses, writing is a crucial means of communication with colleagues in the health care profession, communication that can improve the quality of care for patients, or *clients*, as they are increasingly called. Nurses write charts about their clients (a practice called *charting*), staff memos, patient education booklets, and policies for health care facilities. They may also contribute research articles to journals in the field or craft arguments to attempt to persuade decision makers to change or adopt a particular health care policy.

To write effectively in nursing, you need to support your claims with accurate client observations and current, researched evidence.

D9-a Determine your audience and their needs in nursing.

Nurses write for health care providers such as other nurses, patients or clients, and the staff and administrators of institutions such as clinics and hospitals. Health care providers read documents that inform them about a client's history and needs and a nurse's recommended interventions. Patients or clients read documents to learn about their health care options, home care needs, and nutrition and lifestyle choices. Administrators and staff read instructions, procedures, guidelines, reports, proposals, and policy recommendations that will enable them to make decisions and perform their functions effectively.

Your readers will expect your writing to be grounded in data, with a client's chart information and lab results clearly presented in an objective tone. You should describe your observations of a client's physical and emotional condition directly and thoroughly. You may present those observations using the first-person pronoun *I* or *we*, but be as objective as possible. Confidentiality and sensitivity to a client's background and diversity are essential.

Clients often feel anxious about their medical conditions, and many clients may not be familiar with medical terminology. When you write for clients, respect their right to understand their own medical documents. Write in plain language that is direct and easy to understand, using a minimum of technical terminology and defining such terms when it is necessary to use them. When you write for health care professionals, be precise and use relevant specialized medical terminology.

D9-b Recognize the forms of writing in nursing.

Students in nursing school are asked to write many different kinds of papers. You might be required to write some of the following types of documents:

- statements of philosophy
- nursing practice papers
- case studies
- research papers
- literature reviews
- experiential or reflective narratives
- position papers

Statements of philosophy

To help you articulate why you want to become a nurse, your instructor may ask you to write your personal philosophy of nursing at the beginning of your professional schooling. This assignment is an opportunity to explain what principles you value, what experiences have shaped your career path, how you plan to put your principles into practice, and perhaps what specialization you are interested in pursuing.

Nursing practice papers

Assignments that ask you to apply your growing knowledge about medicine and care practices can take different forms: a nursing care plan, a concept map, or a nursing process paper. For these practice papers, you provide

- a detailed client history and a nursing diagnosis of the client's health problems
- the interventions you recommend for the client
- your rationales for the interventions
- expected outcomes for the client
- actual, observed outcomes

A concept map is an important technique that students can use to understand how to approach client care or how to sort through possible solutions to a problem. Students create a diagram that shows the connections between the possible diagnoses, the client and medical research data that could support each diagnosis, and the plans for client care that follow from each diagnosis.

Case studies

When you are asked to do a case study, you are given detailed information about a hypothetical client's health issue and are instructed to analyze the data. Case studies help you develop a global view of the many elements that make up a client's health problems and shape the health care decisions you make for the client. In a case study, you might

- interpret laboratory results
- evaluate data from a chart that a nurse on the previous shift has completed
- prioritize the client's medical needs
- determine the necessary guidelines for carrying out any required procedures (such as wound care)
- consider, with sensitivity, how the client's personal history, including language and cultural background, might inform how you interact with the client, answer questions, and respond to his or her needs

Research papers

A research paper assignment calls on you to research and report on a topic relevant to the nursing field—perhaps a particular disease, such as Alzheimer's, or an issue that challenges medical professionals, such as maintaining quality care when the downsizing of nursing staffs leads to longer, more fatiguing shifts. Typically, you are required to use as sources as many as twenty-five scholarly articles published in peer-reviewed journals in medical fields. (Peer-reviewed journals publish manuscripts only after they have been carefully reviewed anonymously by experts in the field.)

In some cases, you will be asked to formulate a research question (such as *Is the use of animal-assisted therapy effective in managing behavioral problems of clients with Alzheimer's?*) and come to a conclusion based on a review of recently published research. In other cases, you may be expected to synthesize information from a number of published articles to answer questions about a nursing practice, such as medication administration, or about a disorder, such as muscular dystrophy.

Literature reviews

Review assignments ask you to read and synthesize published work on a nursing topic. Since as a nursing student you must read many scholarly articles about medical conditions and nursing practices, it is important to understand and stay current with the latest advances in the field. In a literature review, you summarize the arguments or findings of one or more journal articles or of a larger body of recent scholarship on a topic. In some cases, you may be asked more specifically to analyze the works critically, evaluating whether the findings seem justified by the data. Such an assignment may be called a *critical review*.

Experiential or reflective narratives

Some of the writing you do as a nursing student will be reflective. To begin to understand what clients are experiencing because of an illness, you might write a personal narrative about what happened to you while caring for a client or what happened to your client as he or she coped with an illness. For example, one student wrote about the increasing sense of isolation and hopelessness that an elderly woman suffered because of her late-stage glaucoma.

Position papers

In a position paper, you take a stance on a controversial issue in the field, such as whether the government should prohibit junk food commercials during children's television programming. You must support your argument with evidence from published research and show the evidence and reasoning that may support an opposing position. A good position paper makes clear why the issue is controversial and important to debate.

D9-c Know the questions nurses ask.

Nursing students ask questions in their writing that help them effectively care for clients. You might ask questions such as the following to understand the needs of clients:

- What information should you collect each day from a client with a particular condition?

literature review • narrative • position paper • asking questions • evidence • lab results • vital signs • observations • conventions

D9-e   D-109

- Do the data in the client's chart indicate a normal or an abnormal status of his or her condition?
- What interventions should you take based on the diagnosis of the client's condition? Why are those interventions necessary?
- How do you care for a surgical patient with chronic pain?

D9-d Understand the kinds of evidence nurses use.

When you are writing a paper in nursing, sometimes your evidence will be quantitative (such as lab results or a client's vital signs), and sometimes it will be qualitative (such as your observations and descriptions of a client's appearance or state of mind). The following are examples of the kinds of evidence you might use:

- a client's lab test results
- data from a nurse's client chart
- research findings in a journal article
- direct observation of a client's physical or mental state

Because clients can have multiple medical problems that need to be prioritized for treatment, nurses use evidence to support more than one nursing diagnosis.

D9-e Become familiar with writing conventions in nursing.

Nurses agree on some conventions when they write:

- Nurses increasingly refer to the people in their care as "clients," not "patients."
- Evaluations and conclusions must be based on accurate and detailed information (*At the time of his diagnosis, the client had experienced a 20-lb weight loss in the previous 6 months. His CBC showed a WBC count of 32, an H & H of 13/38, and a platelet count of 34,000*).
- The first-person pronoun *I* is acceptable in reflective papers about your own experience, but you should use an objective voice in the third person for research papers, reviews, case studies, position papers, and papers describing nursing practices (*Postoperative findings: External fixation devices extend from the proximal tibia and fibular shafts of the left foot*).
- Nurses often use passive voice in describing procedures or recording their observations (*Inflammation was observed at the site of the incision*).

- The identity of clients whose cases are discussed in writing must remain confidential (nurses often make up initials to denote a client's name).

- Direct quotation of sources is rare; instead, nurses paraphrase to demonstrate their understanding of the source material and to convey information economically.

- The APA (American Psychological Association) system of headings and subheadings helps readers see the hierarchy of sections in a paper.

D9-f Use the APA system in writing in nursing.

Writers in nursing typically use the style guidelines of the American Psychological Association (APA) for formatting their paper, for citing sources in the text of their paper, and for listing sources at the end. The APA system is set forth in the *Publication Manual of the American Psychological Association*, 6th ed. (Washington, DC: APA, 2010). (For more details, see the APA documentation sections in your handbook.)

D9-g Sample student paper: Nursing practice paper

If you are asked to write a nursing practice paper, you will need to provide a detailed client history, a nursing diagnosis of the client's health problems, the interventions you recommend to care for the client and your rationales for those interventions, and the expected and actual outcomes for your client. The following student paper was written for a nursing course that focused on clinical experience. The writer, Julie Riss, used the style guidelines of the American Psychological Association (APA) to format her paper and to cite and list her sources.

1 The header consists of a shortened title in all capital letters at the left margin and the page number at the right margin; on the title page only, the shortened title is preceded by the words "Running head" and a colon.

Acute Lymphoblastic Leukemia and Hypertension in One Client:

A Nursing Practice Paper

Julie Riss

George Mason University

Full title, writer's name, and school halfway down the page.

An author's note lists specific information about the course or department and can provide acknowledgments and contact information.

Author Note

This paper was prepared for Nursing 451, taught by Professor Durham. The author wishes to thank the nursing staff of Milltown General Hospital for help in understanding client care and diagnosis.

Marginal annotations indicate APA-style formatting and effective writing.

Acute Lymphoblastic Leukemia and Hypertension in One Client:

A Nursing Practice Paper

Historical and Physical Assessment

Physical History

E.B. is a 16-year-old white male 5'10" tall weighing 190 lb.
He was admitted to the hospital on April 14, 2006, due to decreased
platelets and a need for a PRBC transfusion. He was diagnosed in October
2005 with T-cell acute lymphoblastic leukemia (ALL), after a 2-week period
of decreased energy, decreased oral intake, easy bruising, and petechia.
The client had experienced a 20-lb weight loss in the previous 6 months.
At the time of diagnosis, his CBC showed a WBC count of 32, an H & H of
13/38, and a platelet count of 34,000. His initial chest X-ray showed an
anterior mediastinal mass. Echocardiogram showed a structurally normal
heart. He began induction chemotherapy on October 12, 2005, receiving
vincristine, 6-mercaptopurine, doxorubicin, intrathecal methotrexate, and
then high-dose methotrexate per protocol. He was diagnosed with
hypertension (HTN) due to systolic blood pressure readings consistently
ranging between 130s and 150s and was started on nifedipine. E.B. has
a history of mild ADHD, migraines, and deep vein thrombosis (DVT). He
has tolerated the induction and consolidation phases of chemotherapy
well and is now in the maintenance phase, in which he receives a daily
dose of mercaptopurine, weekly doses of methotrexate, and intermittent
doses of steroids.

Psychosocial History

There is a possibility of a depressive episode a year previously when
he would not attend school. He got into serious trouble and was sent to a
shelter for 1 month. He currently lives with his mother, father, and 14-year-
old sister.

Family History

Paternal: prostate cancer and hypertension in grandfather

Maternal: breast cancer and heart disease

Current Assessment

Client's physical exam reveals him to be alert and oriented to person,
place, and time. He communicates, though not readily. His speech and
vision are intact. He has an equal grip bilaterally and can move all

Full title, repeated.

Headings and
subheadings, in
APA style, mark the
sections of the
report and help
readers follow the
organization.

Riss begins by
summarizing the
client's history using
information from his
chart and her
interview.

Riss respects the
client's privacy by
using only his initials
in her paper.

Riss describes her
detailed assessment
of the client, using
appropriate medical
terminology.

extremities, though he is generally weak. Capillary refill is less than
2 s. His peripheral pulses are strong and equal, and he is positive for
posterior tibial and dorsalis pedis bilaterally. His lungs are clear to
auscultation, his respiratory rate is 16, and his oxygen saturation is 99%
on room air. He has positive bowel sounds in all quadrants, and his
abdomen is soft, round, and nontender. He is on a regular diet, but his
appetite has been poor. Client is voiding appropriately and his urine is
clear and yellow. He appears pale and is unkempt. His skin is warm, dry,
and intact. He has alopecia as a result of chemotherapy. His mediport site
has no redness or inflammation. He appears somber and is slow to comply
with nursing instructions.

> Assessment uses a neutral tone.

Medical Diagnosis #1: Acute Lymphoblastic Leukemia

> APA allows extra space above headings when it improves readability.

Leukemia is a neoplastic disease that involves the blood-forming
tissues of the bone marrow, spleen, and lymph nodes. In leukemia the
ratio of red to white blood cells is reversed. There are approximately
2,500 cases of acute lymphoblastic leukemia (ALL) per year in the United
States, and it is the most common type of leukemia in children—it
accounts for 75%-80% of childhood leukemias. The peak age of onset
is 4 years, and it affects whites more often than blacks and males more
often than females. Risk factors include Down syndrome or genetic
disorders; exposures to ionizing radiation and certain chemicals such as
benzene; human T-cell leukemia/lymphoma virus-1; and treatment for
certain cancers.

ALL causes an abnormal proliferation of lymphoblasts in
the bone marrow, lymph nodes, and spleen. As the lymphoblasts
proliferate, they suppress the other hematopoietic elements in the
marrow. The leukemic cells do not function as mature cells and so do not
work as they should in the immune and inflammatory processes. Because
the growth of red blood cells and platelets is suppressed, the signs and
symptoms of the disease are infections, bleeding, pallor, bone pain,
weight loss, sore throat, fatigue, night sweats, and weakness. Treatment
involves chemotherapy, bone marrow transplant, or stem cell transplant
(Lemone & Burke, 2004).

> Riss paraphrases the source and uses an APA-style in-text citation.

D9-g Writing in nursing

Medical Diagnosis #2: Hypertension

Primary hypertension in adolescence is a condition in which the blood pressure is persistently elevated to the 95th to 99th percentile for age, sex, and weight (Hockenberry, 2003). It must be elevated on three separate occasions for diagnosis to be made. Approximately 50 million people in the United States suffer from hypertension. It most often affects middle-aged and older adults and is more prevalent in black adults than in whites and Hispanics. In blacks the prevalence between males and females is equal, but in whites and Hispanics more males than females are affected. Risk factors include family history, age, race, mineral intake, obesity, insulin resistance, excess alcohol consumption, smoking, and stress. Hypertension results from sustained increases in blood volume and peripheral resistance. The increased blood volume causes an increase in cardiac output, which causes systemic arteries to vasoconstrict. This increased vascular resistance causes hypertension. Hypertension accelerates the rate of atherosclerosis, increasing the risk factor for heart disease and stroke. The workload of the heart is increased, causing ventricular hypertrophy, which increases risk for heart disease, dysrhythmias, and heart failure. Early hypertension usually exhibits no symptoms. The elevations in blood pressure are temporary at first but then progress to being permanent. A headache in the back of the head when awakening may be the only symptom. Other symptoms include blurred vision, nausea and vomiting, and nocturia. Treatment involves medications such as ACE inhibitors, diuretics, beta-adrenergic blockers, calcium channel blockers, and vasodilators as well as changes in diet, such as decreased sodium intake. An increase in physical activity is essential to aid in weight loss and to reduce stress (Lemone & Burke, 2004).

Chart Review

Active Orders

Vital signs q4h

Fall precautions

OOB as tolerated

Oximetry monitoring—continuous

Riss demonstrates her understanding of the medical condition.

ALL AND HTN IN ONE CLIENT   5

CBC with manual differential daily in am

Regular diet

Weight—daily

Strict intake and output monitoring

Type and cross match

PRBCs—2 units

Platelets—1 unit

Discharge after CBC results posttransfusion shown to MD

Rationale for Orders

Vital signs are monitored every four hours per unit standard. In
addition, the client's hypertension is an indication for close monitoring
of blood pressure. He has generalized weakness, so fall precautions should
be implemented. Though he is weak, ambulation is important, especially
considering the client's history of DVT. A regular diet is ordered—I'm not
sure why the client is not on a low-sodium diet, given his hypertension.
Intake and output monitoring is standard on the unit. His hematological
status needs to be carefully monitored due to his anemia and
thrombocytopenia; therefore he has a CBC with manual differential done
each morning. In addition, his hematological status is checked
posttransfusion to see if the blood and platelets he receives increase
his RBC and platelet counts. Transfused platelets survive in the body
approximately 1-3 days, and the peak effect is achieved about 2 hr
posttransfusion. Though platelets normally do not have to be
cross-matched for blood group or type, children who receive multiple
transfusions may become sensitized to a platelet group other than
their own. Therefore, platelets are cross-matched with the donor's
blood components. Blood and platelet transfusions may result in
hemolytic, febrile, or allergic reactions, so the client is carefully
monitored during the transfusion. Hospital protocol requires a set of
baseline vital signs prior to transfusion vital signs. After the blood and
platelets have been given, the physician is apprised of CBC results to
be sure that the client's thrombocytopenia has resolved before he is
discharged.

Riss uses specialized
medical terminology.

Riss shows how
physiology,
prescribed
treatments, and
nursing practices
are related.

Pharmacological Interventions and Goals

Medications and Effects

ondansetron hydrochloride (Zofran) 8 mg PO PRN	serotonin receptor antagonist, antiemetic—prevention of nausea and vomiting associated with chemotherapy
famotidine (Pepcid) 10 mg PO ac	H2 receptor antagonist, antiulcer agent—prevention of heartburn
nifedipine (Procardia) 30 mg PO bid	calcium channel blocker, antihypertensive—prevention of hypertension
enoxaparin sodium (Lovenox) 60 mg SQ bid	low-molecular-weight heparin derivative, anticoagulant—prevention of DVT
mercaptopurine (Purinethol) 100 mg PO qhs	antimetabolite, antineoplastic—treatment of ALL
PRBCs—2 units leukoreduced, irradiated[a]	to increase RBC count
platelets—1 unit[a]	to treat thrombocytopenia

[a]Because these products are dispensed by pharmacy, they are considered a pharmacological intervention, even though technically not medications.

Laboratory Tests and Significance

Complete Blood Count (CBC)[a]

Result name	Result	Abnormal	Normal range
WBC	3.0	*	4.5-13.0
RBC	3.73	*	4.20-5.40
Hgb	11.5		11.1-15.7
Hct	32.4	*	34.0-46.0
MCV	86.8		78.0-95.0
MCH	30.7		26.0-32.0
MCHC	35.4		32.0-36.0
RDW	14.6		11.5-15.5
Platelet	98	*	140-400
MPV	8.3		7.4-10.4

[a]*Rationale:* Client's ALL diagnosis and treatment necessitate frequent monitoring of his hematological status. WBC count, RBC, and hematocrit are decreased due to chemotherapy. The platelet count is low.

Short tables, like those in this paper, are placed within the text. A longer table can be placed on a separate page.

Riss presents data in several tables for easy reference.

ALL AND HTN IN ONE CLIENT 7

Type and Cross-Match[a]

Result name	Result
ABORH	APOS
ANTIBODY SCR INTERP	NEGATIVE

[a]*Rationale:* To determine client's blood type and to screen for antibodies.

Vital Signs Before, During, and After Blood Transfusion[a]

Vital signs	Time	BP	Pulse	Resp	Temp (oral)
Pre	1705	113/74	92	18	98.7
15 min	1720	118/74	104	12	98.3
30 min	1735	121/74	96	16	99.3
45 min	1750	129/76	101	16	99.3
Post	1805	108/59	99	15	98.9

[a]*Rationale:* To monitor for reaction.

Nursing Diagnosis #1:
Injury, Risk for, Related to Decreased Platelet Count and Administration of Lovenox

Desired Outcome: Client will remain free of injury.

Interventions

Monitor vital signs q4h

Assess for manifestations of bleeding such as

- Skin and mucous membranes for petechiae, ecchymoses, and hematoma formation
- Gums and nasal membranes for bleeding
- Overt or occult blood in stool or urine
- Neurologic changes

Provide sponge to clean gums and teeth

Apply pressure to puncture sites for 3-5 min

Avoid invasive procedures when possible

Administer stool softeners as prescribed

Implement fall precautions

Monitor lab values for platelets

Administer platelets as prescribed

Measurable Outcomes

Mediport site will remain intact with no signs of bleeding.

Riss prioritizes her diagnoses and recommended interventions and gives a detailed description and rationales for each.

Urine and stool will remain free of blood.

Lab values for anticoagulant therapy will remain in desired range.

Platelet count will remain in normal range.

Client Teaching

Riss uses specific examples.

Instruct client to avoid forcefully blowing nose, straining to have a bowel movement, and forceful coughing or sneezing, all of which increase the risk for external and internal bleeding

Discharge Planning

Instruct client to monitor for signs of decreased platelet count such as easy bruising, petechiae, or inappropriate bleeding

Nursing Diagnosis #2:

Infection, Risk for, Related to Depressed Body Defenses

Desired Outcome: Client will remain free of infection.

Interventions

Screen all visitors and staff for signs of infection to minimize exposure to infectious agents

Use aseptic technique for all procedures

Monitor temperature to detect possible infection

Evaluate client for potential sites of infection: needle punctures, mucosal ulcerations

Provide nutritionally complete meals to support the body's natural defenses

Monitor lab values for CBC

Administer G-CSF if prescribed

Measurable Outcomes

Mediport site will remain free of erythema, purulent drainage, odor, and edema.

Client will remain afebrile.

Client Teaching

Instruct client and caregivers in correct hand-washing technique

Discharge Planning

Instruct client and caregivers to avoid live attenuated virus vaccines

Instruct client to avoid large crowds

Nursing Diagnosis #3:
Noncompliance, Related to HTN, as Evidenced by Lack of
Consistent Medication Regimen and Adherence to Dietary Plan

Desired Outcome: Client will follow treatment plan.

Interventions

Inquire about reasons for noncompliance

Listen openly and without judgment

Evaluate knowledge of HTN, its long-term effects, and treatment

Arrange for nutritional consult with dietitian

Measurable Outcomes

Client will take medication as prescribed.

Client's systolic blood pressure will remain in normal range.

Client Teaching

Instruct on medication regimen: appropriate administration and potential
   adverse effects

Provide information on hypertension and its treatment

Discharge Planning

Provide prescriptions

Nursing Diagnosis #4:
Health Maintenance, Ineffective, Related to
Unhealthy Lifestyle and Behaviors

Desired Outcome: Client will make changes in lifestyle.

Interventions

Assist in identifying behaviors that contribute to hypertension

Assist in developing a realistic health maintenance plan including
   modifying risk factors such as exercise, diet, and stress

Help client and family identify strengths and weaknesses in maintaining
   health

Measurable Outcomes

Client will verbalize ways to control his hypertension.

Client will identify methods to relieve stress.

Discharge Planning

Provide information on possible exercise programs

D9-g   Writing in nursing

Analysis

Riss summarizes the client's conditions, treatments, and consequences for nursing and discusses client education in psychological and social contexts.

In the case of E.B., there are two separate disease processes at work—ALL and HTN. The ALL is the most immediately pressing of the two and is indirectly responsible for the client's current hospitalization. The chemotherapy treatment for his leukemia has caused thrombocytopenia. This condition places him at high risk for hemorrhage. The anticoagulant therapy for DVT increases this risk even further, not only because it may cause bleeding complications, but because in itself it may cause thrombocytopenia. Therefore, it is imperative to raise his platelet count as quickly as possible. Surprisingly, there were no lab tests ordered to determine his PT and INR, both of which are monitored when a client is on anticoagulant therapy. As his CBC demonstrates, not only is his platelet count low, but his red blood cells are decreased. That is why his physician ordered a transfusion of both PRBCs and platelets.

In terms of E.B.'s diagnosis of HTN, he has a positive family history, which is a major risk factor for developing the disease. Excess weight is also a risk factor, and the client has a history of obesity as well. Because exercise is an important factor in managing the excess weight and stress associated with the disease, his leukemia and the chemotherapy treatments aimed at curing E.B.'s leukemia actually negatively affect his ability to manage the hypertension: He is often too weak and fatigued to participate in much physical activity. Additionally, the steroids have resulted in added weight gain, increasing instead of decreasing the problem. To date, the client has failed to maintain a favorable diet regimen.

E.B.'s family circumstances must be taken into consideration when managing his treatment. Though he resides with both parents, there is some question as to the support and consistency of care he receives. He often appears very unkempt and is at times noncompliant with his hypertension medication. Due to his parents' inability to care for a central venous line (CVL) at home, he has a mediport that can be accessed as needed but requires care. On a positive note, the father is aware of their limitations and tries to work with the staff to make sure that E.B.'s ALL is managed appropriately.

ALL AND HTN IN ONE CLIENT   11

References

Hockenberry, M. (2003). *Wong's nursing care of infants and children.*
    St. Louis, MO: Mosby.

Lemone, P., & Burke, K. (2004). *Medical surgical nursing: Critical thinking in*
    client care. Upper Saddle River, NJ: Pearson Education.

Riss provides a reference list for sources she cited in her paper. The list is formatted in APA style.

≡ **D10** Writing in psychology

Psychologists write with various purposes in mind. They frequently publish articles about their research or present their work at professional conferences. They write proposals to convince funding agencies to award grants for their research. Sometimes psychologists write to influence the opinions held by the public or by decision makers in government, lending their expertise to discussions on issues such as the effects of racism, the challenges of aging, or children's mental health. Psychologists may write analyses for newspaper and magazine opinion pages as well as policy recommendations and advocacy statements.

D10-a Determine your audience and their needs in psychology.

Psychologists write for researchers, psychotherapists, teachers, students, clients, and sometimes members of the government or business community and the general public. Researchers or clinical psychologists may read to find out the results of an experiment, the analysis of new data, or information supporting or critiquing a theory. The information may be useful to readers in developing new research projects or providing services to their clients. Students read to learn about major concepts in the field. Researchers, teachers, and students expect data and findings to be communicated thoroughly in words and in graphics such as diagrams, tables, charts, and graphs. People working in government or academic settings may need information and support for decisions about funding proposed research projects.

In all cases, your readers will expect your writing to be completely objective and to present information as clearly as possible. When you are writing in psychology, you should make thorough use of others' research in the field to demonstrate your credibility. Readers are interested more in empirical data that can be presented quantitatively than in statements from experts. Qualitative information in the form of direct observations and statements from research subjects can help readers understand your conclusions or recommendations.

Your readers will appreciate your precise use of words and a scientific stance with an objective tone. When writing for clients of psychiatric or psychotherapy services, use straightforward language that respects the clients and their right to understand their condition and needs. Such clients will also expect confidentiality and respect for diversity.

10-b Recognize the forms of writing in psychology.

When you take courses in psychology, you may be asked to write any of the following:

- literature reviews
- research papers
- theoretical papers
- poster presentations

Literature reviews

You will likely write review papers early in your course work. In a review paper, you report on and evaluate the research that has been published in the field about a particular topic. A literature review does not merely summarize researchers' findings but argues a position with evidence that you assemble from the empirical (that is, experiment-based) studies that you review.

Sometimes a literature review stands alone as a paper, such as a survey of findings from research performed in the past century on what causes loss of memory in old age. In some cases, you will be asked to write a critical review, in which you will analyze the methods and interpretations of data in one or more journal articles. More often you will write a literature review as an introduction to a larger piece of writing, such as a report of your own empirical study. In that case, the literature review surveys previously published findings relevant to the question that your study investigates.

Research papers

When instructors refer to *research papers*, they may have different assignments in mind. A research paper might present your synthesis of many sources of information about, say, emotional responses to music. Your purpose would be to demonstrate your understanding of research findings and the ongoing debates emerging from researchers' investigations.

A research paper might also be a report on the results of an experiment you've conducted and on your interpretation of those results; in this case, your research paper would be an empirical study. A research paper might also relate your interpretations to what others in the field have concluded from their own experiments. Like other scientists, psychologists publish research papers in journals after the papers have undergone rigorous and impartial review by other psychologists (called *peer review*) to make sure that the scientific process used by the researchers is sound.

Whether published in a journal or written for a college course, research papers based on original experiments have the following standard elements:

- the question you set out to research and why your question is important
- a review of research relevant to your question
- your hypotheses (tentative, plausible answers to the research question that your experiment will test) and your predictions that follow from the hypotheses
- the method you used to conduct your experiment
- the results from the experiment
- your analysis of those results

Writers of research reports also use tables and figures to present experimental data in easy-to-grasp visual form.

Theoretical papers

Psychologists often write theoretical papers in which they propose their own theories or extend existing theories about a research problem in the field. For example, in one journal article, a psychologist argues that the field needs to combine attachment theory and social network theory to understand child and adolescent development.

If you are asked to write a theoretical paper for a course, you will be expected to support the theory you propose by pointing to evidence and counterevidence from the literature in the field, to compare your theory with other theories, and possibly to suggest experiments that could test your theory.

Poster presentations

At professional gatherings such as annual conventions, psychologists have the opportunity to present their work in the form of a poster rather than as a formal talk. Conference attendees approach presenters in an exhibit area to talk about the presenters' research, which the posters concisely summarize. A poster typically features an introduction to the project, the method, information about the research or the subjects of an experiment, the results, and the presenter's conclusions.

Poster presentations also feature graphs and tables since it is important to convey information to conference attendees quickly and

ncisely as they walk through the exhibit area. An effective poster
resentation will encourage the audience to ask questions and carry
n an informal conversation with the presenter.

Your instructor may ask you to create a poster presentation
bout an experiment you or other researchers have conducted both to
elp you understand complex concepts and to practice your communi-
ation skills.

OTE: Some presenters use presentation software to create a slide
how that they can click through for a small audience or project on
screen for a larger group. Presenters generally include the same
inds of information in slide presentations as they do in poster
resentations.

10-c Know the questions psychologists ask.

sychologists generally investigate human behavior and perceptions.
heir questions range widely across the different specializations that
ake up the field, such as animal cognition, personality, social inter-
ctions, and infant development, to name a few. The following are
uestions that specialists in psychology might ask:

- What personality characteristics might affect employees'
  personal use of work computers?

- When adult learners return to school, what is the impact on
  their families and working lives?

- Do variations in cerebral blood flow in different areas of the
  brain predict variations in performance of different imagery
  tasks?

10-d Understand the kinds of evidence psychologists se.

o back up their conclusions, psychologists look for evidence in case
udies and the results of experiments. They do not use expert opin-
n as evidence; direct quotations of what other psychologists have
ritten are rare in psychology papers. Instead, papers focus on data
he results of experiments) and on the analysis of the results that
e writer has collected.

Depending on their specialization, psychologists may ask ques-
ons that require quantitative or qualitative evidence. Quantita-
ve evidence involves numerical measurement; qualitative evidence
volves examples and illustrations.

- Quantitative evidence might be facts and statistics: *Regional cerebral blood flow in a total of 26 areas predicted performance, and 20 of these areas predicted performance only in a single task. In a study on what motivates adolescents to quit smoking, 44.7% of the participants reported that they wanted to quit because their parents wanted them to.* Or it might be results of original experiments: *Fraudulent excuse scores were correlated with cheating scores* ($r = .37$, $n = 211$, $p < .0001$).

- Qualitative evidence might be descriptions of interviews or statements of the researcher's observations: *Many of the respondents believed that girls' tendency either to address indirectly or to avoid conflict was supported by adults, who expected them to be* ladylike; *when asked to define this term, they used such descriptors as "mature" and "calm."*

D10-e Become familiar with writing conventions in psychology.

Psychologists use straightforward and concise language and depend on special terms to explain their findings.

- Specialized vocabulary may include terms such as *methods, results, double-blind study, social identity perspective,* and *nonverbal emotions.*

- Often researchers use specific, technical definitions of terms that nonspecialists use differently. For example, if a psychologist asks whether adults with eating disorders are "depressed," the term refers to a specific mental disorder, not to a general mood of sadness.

- When reporting conclusions, writers in psychology use the past tense (*Berkowitz found*) or the present perfect tense (*Berkowitz has found*). When discussing results, they use the present tense (*The results confirm*). They avoid using subjective expressions like *I think* and *I feel*.

D10-f Use the APA system in writing in psychology.

Writers in psychology typically use the style guidelines of the American Psychological Association (APA) for formatting their papers, for citing sources in the text of their papers, and for listing sources at the end. The APA system is set forth in the *Publication Manual of the American Psychological Association*, 6th ed. (Washington, DC: APA,

)10). (For more details, see the APA documentation sections in your
andbook.)

10-g Sample student paper: Literature review (excerpt)

psychology literature review assignment usually asks you both to
irvey published research on a topic in the field and to argue your
wn position with evidence that you assemble from your survey. The
udent paper excerpted beginning on the next page was written for
second-year developmental psychology course. The student, Valerie
harat, used the style guidelines of the American Psychological Asso-
ation (APA) to format her paper and to cite and list her sources.

The header consists of a shortened title in all capital letters at the left margin and the page number at the right margin; on the title page only, the shortened title is preceded by the words "Running head" and a colon.

Running head: ADHD IN BOYS VS. GIRLS   1

Full title, writer's name, and school halfway down the page.

Always out of Their Seats (and Fighting):

Why Are Boys Diagnosed with ADHD More Often Than Girls?

Valerie Charat

Harvard University

An author's note lists specific information about the course or department and can provide acknowledgments and contact information.

Author Note

This paper was prepared for Psychology 1806, taught by Professor Korfine.

Marginal annotations indicate APA-style formatting **and** effective writing.

Abstract

Until the early 1990s, most research on attention deficit hyperactivity disorder (ADHD) focused on boys and did not explore possible gender differences. Recent studies have suggested that gender differences do exist and are caused by personality differences between boys and girls, by gender bias in referring teachers and clinicians, or by the diagnostic procedures themselves. But the most likely reason is that ADHD is often comorbid—that is, it coexists with other behavior disorders that are not diagnosed properly and that do exhibit gender differences. This paper first considers studies of gender differences only in ADHD and then looks at studies of gender differences when ADHD occurs with comorbid disorders. Future research must focus more specifically on how gender differences are influenced by factors such as referrals, family history, and comorbid conditions.

Abstract, a 100-to-150-word overview of the paper, appears on a separate page.

D10-g   Writing in psychology

Full title, repeated.

Charat gives abbreviations in parentheses the first time she uses common psychology terms.

Introduction provides background to the topic and establishes why a literature review on ADHD is necessary.

Thesis states what Charat will argue by describing and analyzing the sources she has reviewed.

Charat uses APA style to cite her sources. Two sources in one parenthetical citation are separated with a semicolon.

Headings, centered, divide the paper into two main sections.

Always out of Their Seats (and Fighting):

Why Are Boys Diagnosed with ADHD More Often Than Girls?

Attention deficit hyperactivity disorder (ADHD) is a commonly diagnosed disorder in children that affects social, academic, or occupational functioning. As the name suggests, its hallmark characteristics are hyperactivity and lack of attention as well as impulsive behavior. For decades, studies have focused on the causes, expression, prevalence, and outcome of the disorder, but until recently very little research investigated gender differences. In fact, until the early 1990s most research focused exclusively on boys (Brown, Madan-Swain, & Baldwin, 1991), perhaps because many more boys than girls are diagnosed with ADHD. Researchers have speculated on the possible explanations for the disparity, citing reasons such as true sex differences in the manifestation of the disorder's symptoms, gender biases in those who refer children to clinicians, and possibly even the diagnostic procedures themselves (Gaub & Carlson, 1997). But the most persuasive reason is that ADHD is often a comorbid condition—that is, it coexists with other behavior disorders that are not diagnosed properly and that do exhibit gender differences.

It has been suggested that in the United States children are often misdiagnosed as having ADHD when they actually suffer from a behavior disorder such as conduct disorder (CD) or a combination of ADHD and another behavior disorder (Disney, Elkins, McGue, & Iancono, 1999; Lilienfeld & Waldman, 1990). Conduct disorder is characterized by negative and criminal behavior in children and is highly correlated with adult diagnoses of antisocial personality disorder (ASPD). This paper first considers research that has dealt only with gender difference in the occurrence of ADHD and then looks at research that has studied the condition along with other behavior disorders.

Gender Differences in Studies of ADHD

Most of the research on ADHD has lacked a comparative component. Throughout the 1970s and 1980s, most research focused only on boys. If girls were included, it was often in such low numbers that gender-based comparisons were unwarranted (Gaub & Carlson, 1997). One of the least debated differences is the dissimilarity in male and female prevalence

ADHD IN BOYS VS. GIRLS   4

rates. Some studies have claimed a 3:1 ratio of boys with ADHD to girls with ADHD (American Psychiatric Association, 1987), while others have cited ratios as high as 9:1 (Brown et al., 1991). The differences in prevalence have been attributed to a variety of causes, one of which is that girls may have more internalized symptoms and may be overlooked in ADHD diagnoses (Brown et al., 1991).

> Charat summarizes key research findings about the paper's central question.

A study conducted by Breen (1989) sought to test the differences in cognition, behavior, and academic functioning for boys and girls. Past research had indicated that boys with ADHD showed more aggressive behavior while girls showed more learning problems, but the results were often conflicting. To clarify the existing information, Breen conducted a study on 39 children aged 6 to 11, from a group of children referred to a pediatric psychology clinic. All subjects were white, with varying socioeconomic status. He broke the subjects into three groups: boys with ADHD, girls with ADHD, and a control group of girls without any psychiatric or family history of behavioral or emotional problems. Each group was given a battery of tests to assess cognitive functioning. All children were also observed in a playroom while they worked math problems, and all were coded for a variety of behaviors including fidgeting, vocalizing, being out of their seats, and so on.

> A signal phrase names the author and gives the date of the source in parentheses.

> Charat examines an important study in detail. She summarizes experimental methods used by researchers.

The results showed that while both groups with ADHD performed nearly equally across most measures, ADHD boys were generally viewed as more deviant than normal girls. Girls with ADHD were closer behaviorally to girls in the control group than to ADHD boys. This finding indicates that it may be difficult to distinguish girls with ADHD from girls without the disorder based solely on behavior. This conclusion was corroborated by the later finding (Brown et al., 1991) that girls with ADHD are often not clinically referred unless they demonstrate a more severe form of the disorder than boys do. A contradictory finding (Breen, 1989) was that ADHD boys and girls displayed rates of disruptive behavior that were not significantly different from each other, although Breen did not indicate what forms the disruptive behavior took and whether the girls were less aggressive than the boys. But as Brown et al. (1991) later pointed out, it was easier to differentiate ADHD in externalized behaviors—aggression, inattention, and overactivity—than in internalized behaviors—depression,

> Charat uses the specialized language of the field.

> Source first mentioned on page 3. In subsequent citations, for a source with three to five authors "et al." is used after the first author's name in the text and in parentheses.

anxiety, and withdrawal. It is striking, however, that the distinction in Breen's study was clearer not between boys and girls but between girls with and girls without ADHD. Breen concluded that differences between boys and girls with the disorder do not seem significant.

A few drawbacks to Breen's study include a lack of screening for comorbid conduct disorders, which were no doubt present in some of the subjects. The small sample size could have hindered the results, with only 13 subjects in each group. Another limitation is the small cross section: All subjects were white and clinically referred. Therefore, the findings cannot be generalized to a nonclinical, racially diverse population. Finally, the lack of male controls is surprising, given the usual trend to overrepresent boys when studying ADHD. A reasonable comparison would have been between girls with ADHD and boys in a control group to see if the girls' range of antisocial behavior was beyond that of control boys.

Another study (Maughan, Pickles, Hagell, Rutter, & Yule, 1996) investigated the association between reading problems and antisocial behavior. The researchers cited a connection that had previously been made (Hinshaw, 1992, as cited in Maughan et al., 1996) between antisocial behavior and underachievement in early childhood, while aggression and antisocial behavior became salient in later years. Maughan et al. looked specifically at reading because research has shown that children who develop reading problems have higher rates of behavioral problems even before they learn to read (Jorm, Share, Matthews, & Mclean, 1986). It had also been shown that reading problems can affect behavioral development (Pianta & Caldwell, 1992, as cited in Maughan et al., 1996). However, since most studies had been done with boys, the researchers also compared gender differences.

Subjects were selected from a previously conducted study in a population of children who were 10 years old in 1970. The majority were British-born Caucasians of low socioeconomic status. The analysis used two subsamples, one with poor reading scores, the other a randomly sampled control group with average IQ and no reading difficulties. Poor readers were rated as either "backward" or "retarded." The subjects in the backward group were 28 months below average in reading level for their age and IQ. At age 10, children had received psychometric testing, and the study

---

Margin notes:

Charat analyzes the study's shortcomings.

Topic sentence states paragraph's main point.

An indirect source (work quoted in another source) is indicated with the words "as cited in."

An ampersand separates the authors' names in parentheses.

Charat describes the study's methods in detail.

accounted for parental occupation, the child's government benefits status, and the ranking of the child's state school in terms of economic adversity. There were follow-ups at ages 14, 17, and early 20s.

Poor readers demonstrated high rates of behavior problems by age 10. About 40% of the girls and almost 50% of the boys in the retarded reading group exhibited antisocial behavior at age 10. Interestingly, reading-retarded girls showed high rates of conduct problems, while the boys did not. Also, among girls there were much higher rates of antisocial behavior in the lowest socioeconomic category than in slightly higher socioeconomic categories. In boys, the differences were not as pronounced. For boys, poor performance in school was the only predictor of antisocial behavior, while for girls poor school performance and reading level were predictors. This finding suggests that for boys, learning difficulties do not increase the risk of behavior problems, while for girls they do. Inattentiveness and overactivity were also related to reading problems and were highly related to antisocial behavior. When inattentiveness and overactivity were factored in, there were no direct links between reading difficulties and antisocial behavior. This absent connection means that reading problems do not cause antisocial behavior. It is when they cannot pay attention or sit long enough to read that both boys and girls exhibit elevated rates of antisocial behavior.

By age 14, girls still showed a significant correlation between reading problems and antisocial behavior, while boys showed no association. In early adulthood (ages 17 and early 20s), criminality, alcohol problems, aggression, and personality disorders were found in low rates in girls. In the sample of girls interviewed in their 20s, 1.9% had juvenile offense records and 5.4% had records of adult crime. In boys, poor readers did not show any significant rates of antisocial personality disorders.

The study had several drawbacks. Subject responses at follow-up periods were not uniformly gathered, and the lack of analysis of female juvenile offenders made it harder to understand the results in terms of gender differences and antisocial behavior. The sample consisted only of inner-city children of low socioeconomic status because they had higher rates of reading difficulty than other children. But because economic adversity was found to be a predictor for poor conduct in girls, this group

In APA style, the numbers 10 and above are expressed in numerals; percentages are expressed in numbers with a percent symbol.

After presenting the study's findings, Charat analyzes the study's weaknesses.

of subjects may have contained a disproportionate number of female subjects with more severe antisocial behavior.

Charat speculates on possible explanations for the results of the study.

Of particular interest was that for girls but not for boys, reading level and low socioeconomic status predicted antisocial behavior. However, when the children were followed into adulthood, the females who had originally displayed antisocial behavior did not show elevated rates of juvenile offenses or adult crime. Perhaps the results indicate that girls with antisocial and hyperactive behavior in childhood are different from boys in that they are responding to passing learning impairments rather than permanent personality problems. Or girls may have continued to have ADHD, but with internalized rather than externalized symptoms. Another possibility is that the girls had more severe forms of ADHD because of sampling bias for socioeconomic status but that they eventually grew out of the disorder in adolescence while the boys did not.

Another study (Brown et al., 1991) looked specifically at the cognitive and academic performance of children with ADHD and compared internalizing versus externalizing features of the disorder across genders. As in Breen (1989), Brown et al. (1991) found there were few gender differences on measures of attention, concentration, and distractibility. However, some significant differences were found. Parent and teacher ratings of internalizing and externalizing characteristics described boys as more aggressive and girls as more unpopular. Girls were also more commonly held back one or two grades, a finding the researchers interpreted as evidence of female academic difficulties and possible neurological disorders or impairments. This would correlate with the findings of Maughan et al. (1996) of an association between reading impairment and antisocial behaviors in ADHD girls. However, the data must

If a source is cited in the text of the paragraph, only the authors' names are given when the source is cited later in the text of the same paragraph. (The date is required in all parenthetical citations.)

also be regarded cautiously. Brown et al. did not use a control group and thus did not have a standard by which to measure the differences. Any implication of a neurological impairment in females with ADHD should be viewed skeptically. The historical perception of women as the weaker or more defective sex should make any researcher reluctant to postulate . . .

[Charat continues to describe and analyze researchers' studies and findings.]

Conclusion

Although the studies presented here are filled with flaws and contradictory findings, they have a unifying thread. Through direct findings or indirect lack of information, all suggest that the higher rate of male diagnoses of ADHD does not necessarily mean that the disorder actually occurs in boys more often than in girls. Although boys are more commonly diagnosed, this phenomenon could reflect a long-standing history of misperceptions. Since hyperactive and inattentive boys are also often aggressive and disruptive, girls who do not demonstrate similar behaviors may be overlooked.

It is important to reevaluate the way boys and girls are observed and understood when attention and hyperactivity are being assessed. Males and females may display different behaviors, and parents and teachers may interpret their behaviors differently. But when rated by trained researchers, boys and girls identified as having ADHD are rated similarly. However, it is easier to identify externalizing, aggressive behavior than it is to identify internalizing behavior, and this difference may be one of the main factors at the root of the perceived gender differences in the prevalence of ADHD. There is not enough concrete evidence to rule out the possibility that a gender difference does exist, regardless of the fact that boys and girls seem to show equal rates and degrees of symptoms. Until more studies look at population samples, exclude conduct disorders, and take into account possible differences in the ways the symptoms are manifested, it is impossible to conclude that gender differences are the result of social and clinical biases and stereotypes. Further research on genetics and familial rates of the disorder are also necessary to help clarify the relationship between adult antisocial personality disorder and ADHD. Also, until a clear distinction is made between conduct disorder and ADHD, not only in the text of the *DSM-IV* but also in the minds of laypeople and clinicians, it will be difficult to separate children with comorbid disorder and those without it and to assess gender differences as well.

Conclusion presents a synthesis of the paper's points.

Charat raises questions about the research she reviews but adopts a balanced tone in summarizing the sources.

Charat suggests areas for future research.

Conclusion affirms the necessity of continuing investigation.

References

American Psychiatric Association. (1987). *Diagnostic and statistical manual of mental disorders* (3rd ed., rev.). Washington, DC: Author.

American Psychiatric Association. (1994). *Diagnostic and statistical manual of mental disorders* (4th ed.). Washington, DC: Author.

Breen, M. J. (1989). Cognitive and behavioral differences in AdHD boys and girls. *Journal of Child Psychology and Psychiatry, 30,* 711-716. doi:10.1111/j.1469-7610.1989.tb00783.x

Breen, M. J., & Altepeter, T. S. (1990). Situational variability in boys and girls identified as ADHD. *Journal of Clinical Psychology, 46,* 486-490.

Brown, R. T., Madan-Swain, A., & Baldwin, K. (1991). Gender differences in a clinic-referred sample of attention-deficit-disordered children. *Child Psychiatry and Human Development, 22,* 111-127.

Disney, E. R., Elkins, J. J., McGue, M., & Iancono, W. G. (1999). Effects of ADHD, conduct disorder, and gender on substance use and abuse in adolescence. *American Journal of Psychiatry, 156,* 1515-1521.

Faraone, S. V., Biederman, J., Chen, W. J., Milberger, S., Warburton, R., & Tsuang, M. T. (1995). Genetic heterogeneity in attention-deficit hyperactivity disorder (ADHD): Gender, psychiatric comorbidity, and maternal ADHD. *Journal of Abnormal Psychology, 104,* 334-345.

Gaub, M., & Carlson, C. L. (1997). Gender differences in ADHD: A meta-analysis and critical review. *Journal of the American Academy of Child and Adolescent Psychiatry, 36,* 1036-1045.

Jorm, A. F., Share, D. L., Matthews, R., & Mclean, R. (1986). Behaviour problems in specific reading retarded and general reading backward children: A longitudinal study. *Journal of Child Psychology and Psychiatry, 27,* 33-43. doi:10.1111/j.1469-7610.1986.tb00619.x

Lahey, B. B., Piacentini, J. C., McBurnett, K., Stone, P., Hartdagen, S., & Hynd, G. (1988). Psychopathology in the parents of children with conduct disorder and hyperactivity. *Journal of the American Academy of Child and Adolescent Psychiatry, 27,* 163-170.

Lilienfeld, S. O., & Waldman, I. D. (1990). The relation between childhood attention-deficit hyperactivity disorder and adult antisocial behavior reexamined: The problem of heterogeneity. *Clinical Psychology Review, 10,* 699-725.

List of references begins on a new page. The first line of an entry is at the left margin; subsequent lines indent ½".

If an online source has a DOI (digital object identifier), no URL is given.

A work with up to seven authors lists all authors' names. A work with more than seven authors lists the first six followed by three ellipsis dots and the last author's name.

List is alphabetized by authors' last names. All authors' names are inverted; an ampersand separates the last two authors.

Maughan, B., Pickles, A., Hagell, A., Rutter, M., & Yule, W. (1996). Reading
        problems and antisocial behavior: Developmental trends in
        comorbidity. *Journal of Child Psychology and Psychiatry, 37,* 405-418.
        doi:10.1111/j.1469-7610.1996.tb01421.x

Oltmanns, T. F., & Emery, R. E. (1998). Psychological disorders of
        childhood. In *Abnormal psychology* (2nd ed., pp. 572-607). Upper
        Saddle River, NJ: Prentice Hall.

Sprock, J., Blashfield, R. K., & Smith, B. (1990). Gender weighting of
        DSM-III-R personality disorder criteria. *American Journal of
        Psychiatry, 147,* 586-590.

Index

Revision Symbols

Boldface numbers refer to sections of the handbook.

abbr	faulty abbreviation **40**		*p*	error in punctuation
adj/adv	misuse of adjective or adverb **26**		$\stackrel{\wedge}{,}$	comma **32**
add	add needed word **10**		*no ,*	no comma **33**
agr	faulty agreement **21, 22**		*;*	semicolon **34**
appr	inappropriate language **17**		*:*	colon **35**
art	article (*a, an, the*) **29**		$\stackrel{?}{v}$	apostrophe **36**
awk	awkward		" "	quotation marks **37**
cap	capital letter **45**		. ?	period, question mark,
case	error in case **24, 25**		!	exclamation point **38**
cliché	cliché **18e**		— ( )	dash, parentheses,
coh	coherence **4d**		[ ] ...	brackets, ellipsis mark,
coord	faulty coordination **14a**		/	slash **39**
cs	comma splice **20**		¶	new paragraph **4e**
dev	inadequate development **4b, 6e**		*pass*	ineffective passive **8**
dm	dangling modifier **12e**		*pn agr*	pronoun agreement **22**
-ed	error in *-ed* ending **27d**		*proof*	proofreading problem **3c**
emph	emphasis **14**		*ref*	error in pronoun reference **23**
ESL	English as a second language **28–31**		*run-on*	run-on sentence **20**
exact	inexact language **18**		*-s*	error in *-s* ending **21, 27c**
frag	sentence fragment **19**		*sexist*	sexist language **17e, 22a**
fs	fused sentence **20**		*shift*	distracting shift **13**
gl/us	see Glossary of Usage		*sl*	slang **17c**
hyph	error in use of hyphen **44**		*sp*	misspelled word **43**
idiom	idioms **18d**		*sub*	faulty subordination **14a**
inc	incomplete construction **10**		*sv agr*	subject-verb agreement **21, 27c**
irreg	error in irregular verb **27a**		*t*	error in verb tense **27f**
ital	italics **42**		*trans*	transition needed **4d**
jarg	jargon **17a**		*usage*	see Glossary of Usage
lc	lowercase letter **45**		*v*	voice **8a**
mix	mixed construction **11**		*var*	lack of variety in sentence structure **14, 15**
mm	misplaced modifier **12a–d**		*vb*	verb problem **27, 28**
mood	error in mood **27g**		*w*	wordy **16**
nonst	nonstandard usage **17c, 27**		*//*	faulty parallelism **9**
num	error in use of numbers **41**		$\wedge$	insert
om	omitted word **10, 30b**		*x*	obvious error
			#	insert space
			$\smile$	close up space

Detailed Menu